LOWE'S
Home Plans
MW01048504

Residential Creations

HOMES FROM 864 - 2,806 SQ. FT.

Home Plans - Residential Creations - This book is a collection of best-selling residential style plans from some of the nation's leading designers and architects. Only quality plans with sound design, functional layout, energy efficiency and affordability have been selected.

These plans cover a wide range of architectural styles in a popular range of sizes. A broad assortment is presented to match a wide variety of lifestyles and budgets. Each design page features floor plans, a front view of the house, and a list of special features. All floor plans show room dimensions, exterior dimensions and the interior square footage of the home.

Technical Specifications - At the time the construction drawings were prepared, every effort was made to ensure that these plans and specifications meet nationally recognized building codes (BOCA, Southern Building Code Congress and others). Because national building codes change or vary from area to area some drawing modifications and/ or the assistance of a professional designer or architect may be necessary to comply with your local codes or to accommodate specific building site conditions. We advise you to consult with your local building official for information regarding codes governing your area.

Blueprint Ordering - Fast and Easy - Your ordering is made simple by following the instructions on page 290. See page 289 for more information on which types of blueprint packages are available and how many plan sets to order.

Your Home, Your Way - The blueprints you receive are a master plan for building your new home. They start you on your way to what may well be the most rewarding experience of your life.

House shown on front cover is Plan #527-0209 and is featured on page 68.

Lowe's Residential Creations Home Plans is published by Home Design Alternatives, Inc. (HDA, Inc.) 4390 Green Ash Drive, St. Louis, MO 63045.

CONTENTS

Extras Available With The Lowe's Signature Series Home Plans 4-5

Lowe's Signature Series Home Plans 6-130

Designer Series Home Plans ... 131-285

Our Blueprint Packages Offer... 286

Other Helpful Building Aids 287

Home Plans Index 288-289

What Kind Of Plan Package Do You Need? 289

To Order Home Plans 290

Current Printing 5 4 3 2

LOWE'S

Signature SERIES

Home Design Alternatives is proud to bring you this unprecedented offer of our Lowe's Signature Series featuring our most popular residential plans. Never before has there been a compilation of home plans offering such unique services as you will find in this publication.

Home Plans included in the Lowe's Signature Series are indicated by the Lowe's Signature Series logo shown above, and are found on pages 6 through 130.

One of the main reasons for purchasing home plans from a publication such as this is to save you time and money. And, you will discover the extra benefits of the unique services offered through our Lowe's Signature Series of Home Plans.

Besides providing the expected beauty and functional efficiency of all our home plans, the Lowe's Signature Series offers you detailed Material Lists, Customizing Kits, free Estimated Material Pricing and a free Fax-a-Plan Service. This combination of services are not to be found in any other home plan book or magazine on the market today.

ESTIMATED MATERIAL PRICES FROM HOME DESIGN ALTERNATIVES (HDA)

Plan Number 0108
Dry-In Price $28,800
Total Price $47,500

Free Estimated Material Pricing

When selecting the home plan that's right for you, the cost of materials can play a major roll. Staying within your budget is easier when choosing a plan from the Lowe's Signature Series. We provide free estimated material pricing on home plans you've selected. Call us at 1-314-770-2228. This unique service is provided "around-the-clock" to enable us to better serve you.

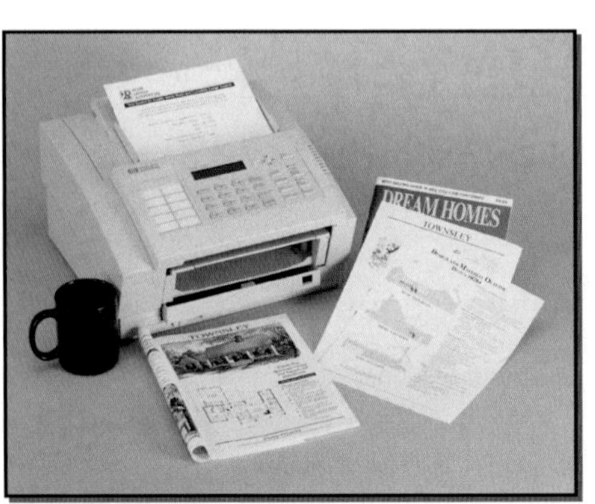
DREAM HOMES

Fax-a-Plan™ Service

Our free Fax-a-Plan service offers the ideal option for those who have interest in several home designs and want more information to help narrow down the selection. Rear and side views for designs in the Signature Series are available via fax, along with a list of key construction features (i.e. roof slopes, ceiling heights, insulation values, type of roof and wall construction) and more. Just call our automated FAX-A-PLAN service at 1-314-770-2228 available 24 hours a day - 7 days a week and the cost is FREE.

Material Lists

To enhance the quality of our blueprint packages, we offer one of the most precise and thorough material lists in the industry. An accurate and detailed material list can save you a considerable amount of time and money. Our material lists give you the quantity, dimensions, and descriptions of the major building materials necessary to construct your home. You'll get faster and more accurate bids from your contractors and material suppliers and you'll save money by paying for only the materials you need.

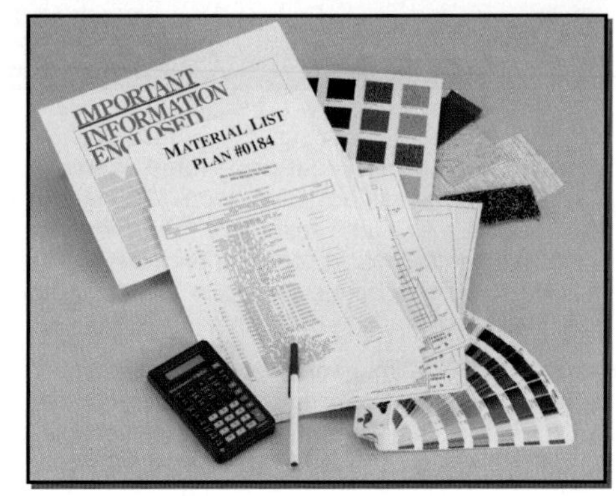
IMPORTANT INFORMATION ENCLOSED
MATERIAL LIST
PLAN #0184

How *You* Can Customize Our Plans Into *Your* Dream Home

Get exactly what you want with the help of our exclusive Customizer Kit™ and discover unlimited design possibilities available to you when building a new home. The Customizer Kit, available with any of the Lowe's Signature Series Plans, allows you to alter virtually any architectural element you wish, both on the exterior and interior of the home. The Kit comes complete with simplified drawings of your selected home plan so that you can sketch out any and all of your changes. To help you through this process, the Kit also includes a workbook called "The Customizer," a special correction pen, a red marking pencil, an architect's scale and furniture layout guides. These tools, along with the simplified customizer drawings, allow you to experiment with various design changes prior to having a design professional modify the actual working drawings.

Before placing your order for blueprints consider the type and number of changes you plan to make to your selected design. If you wish to make only minor design changes such as moving interior walls, changing window styles, or altering foundation types, we strongly recommend that you purchase reproducible masters along with the Customizer Kit. These master drawings, which contain the same information as the blueprints, are easy to modify because they are printed on erasable, reproducible paper. Also, by starting with complete detailed drawings, and planning out your changes with the Customizer Kit, the cost of having a design professional or your builder make the required drawing changes will be considerably less. After the master drawings are altered, multiple blueprint copies can be made from them.

If you anticipate making a lot of changes, such as moving exterior walls and changing the overall appearance of the house, we suggest you purchase only one set of blueprints as a reference set and the Customizer Kit to document your desired changes. When making major design changes, it is always advisable to seek out the assistance of an architect or design professional to review and redraw that portion of the blueprints affected by your changes.

Typically, having a set of reproducible masters altered by a local designer can cost as little as a couple hundred dollars, whereas redrawing a portion or all of the blueprints can cost considerably more depending on the extent of the changes. Like most projects, the more planning and preparation you can do on your own, the greater the savings to you.

Finally, you'll have the satisfaction of knowing that your custom home is uniquely and exclusively yours.

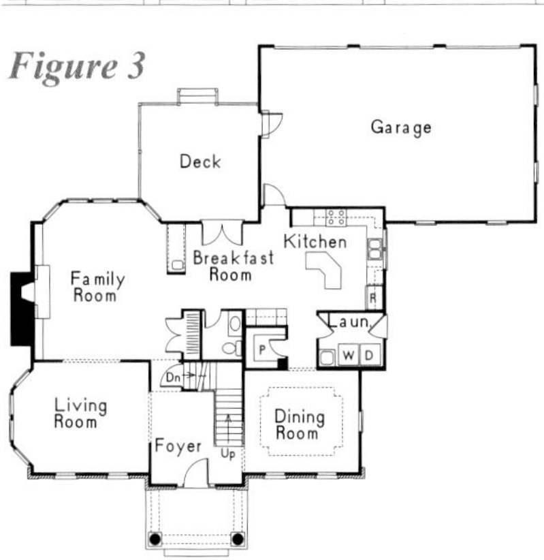
Garage
Deck
Kitchen
Breakfast Room
Family Room
Laun
W D
Living Room
Foyer
Dining Room

Figure 3

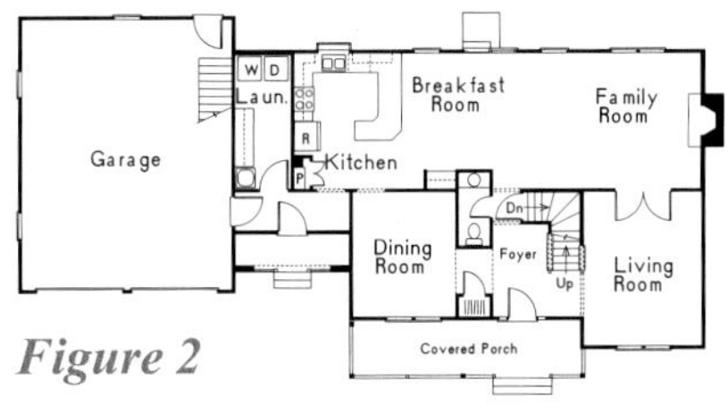
Garage
W D
Laun.
Kitchen
Breakfast Room
Family Room
Dining Room
Foyer
Living Room
Covered Porch

Figure 2

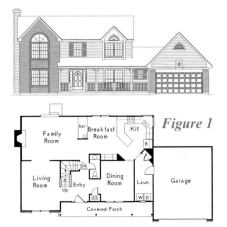

Figure 1

Examples of Customizing

Thousands of builders and home buyers have used the HDA Customizer Kit to help them modify their home plans, some involving minor changes, many with dramatic alterations. Examples of actual projects are shown here.

Figure 1 shows the front elevation and first floor plan for one of HDA's best-selling designs.

Figure 2 shows how one plan customer made few but important design changes such as completely reversing the plan to better accommodate his building site; adding a second entrance for ease of access to the front yard from the kitchen; making provisions for a future room over the garage by allowing for a stairway and specifying windows in place of louvers, plus other modifications.

Figure 3 shows another example of an actual project where the design shown in Figure 1 was dramatically changed to achieve all of the desired features requested by the customer. This customized design proved to be so successful that HDA obtained permission to offer it as a standard plan.

LOWE'S

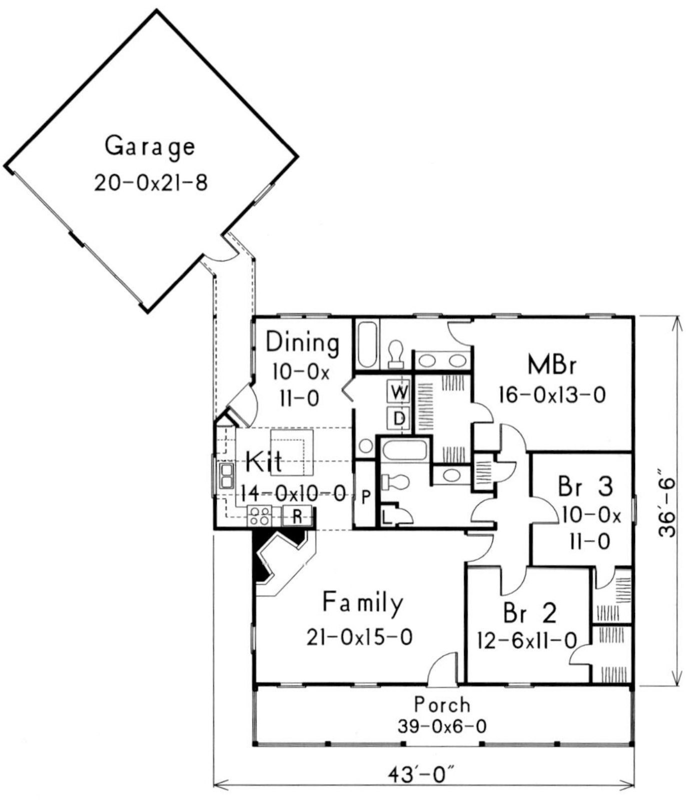
Garage
20-0x21-8
Dining
10-0x
11-0
MBr
16-0x13-0
W
D
Kit
14-0x10-0
P
L
R
Br 3
10-0x
11-0
Family
21-0x15-0
Br 2
12-6x11-0
Porch
39-0x6-0
36'-6"
43'-0"

Plan #527-0203

Price Code B

Total Living Area: 1,475 Sq. Ft.

Home has 3 bedrooms, 2 baths, 2-car detached garage and slab foundation, drawings also include crawl space foundation.

Special features

- Family room features a high ceiling and prominent corner fireplace
- Kitchen with island counter and garden window makes a convenient connection between the family and dining rooms
- Hallway leads to three bedrooms all with large walk-in closets
- Covered breezeway joins main house and garage
- Full-width entry covered porch lends a country touch

Summer Home Or Year Round

LOWE'S

Signature SERIES

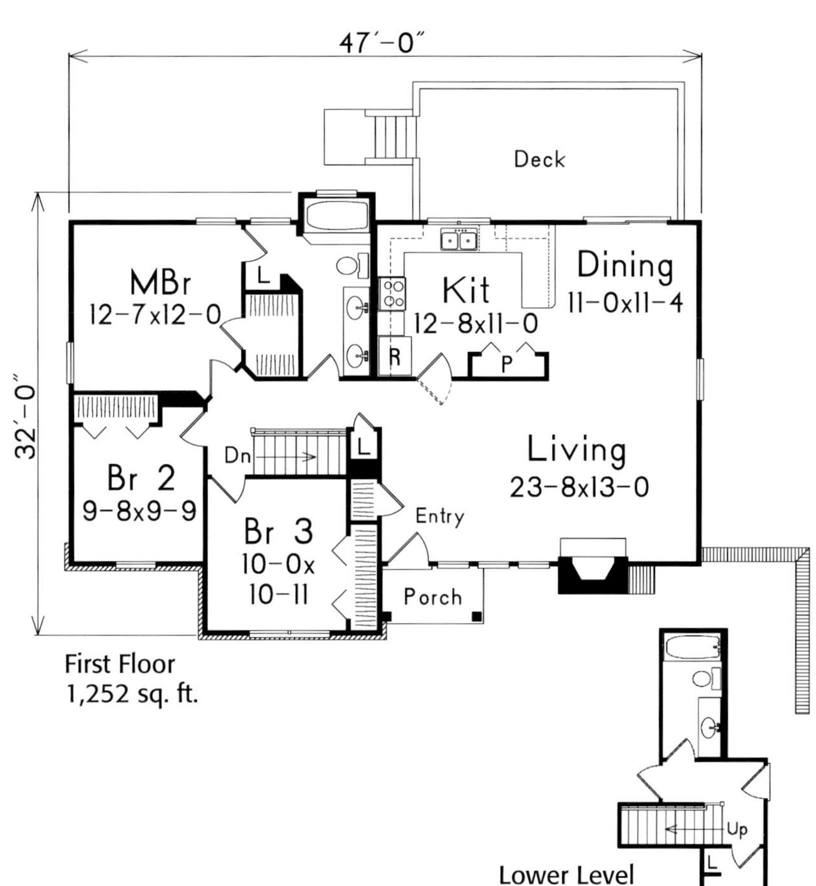
47'-0"
32'-0"
Deck
MBr
12-7x12-0
L
Kit
12-8x11-0
R
P
Dining
11-0x11-4
Br 2
9-8x9-9
Dn
L
Living
23-8x13-0
Br 3
10-0x
10-11
Entry
Porch
First Floor
1,252 sq. ft.
Up
L
Lower Level
151 sq. ft.

Plan #527-0484

Price Code A

Total Living Area: 1,403 Sq. Ft.

Home has 3 bedrooms, 2 baths, 2-car drive under garage, second bath on lower level and basement foundation.

Special features

- Impressive living areas for modest-sized home
- Special master/hall bath linen storage, step-up tub and lots of window light
- Spacious closets everywhere you look

Vaulted Ceilings Enhance Spacious Home

Plan #527-0230

Price Code D

Total Living Area: 2,073 Sq. Ft.

Home has 4 bedrooms, 2 1/2 baths, 2-car side entry garage and basement foundation.

Special features

- Family room provides ideal gathering area with a fireplace, large windows and vaulted ceiling
- Private first floor master bedroom suite with a vaulted ceiling and luxury bath
- Kitchen features angled bar connecting kitchen and breakfast area

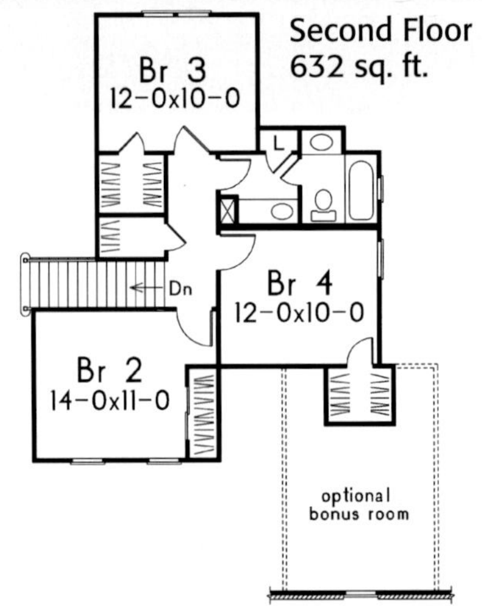
Second Floor
632 sq. ft.
Br 3
12-0x10-0
L
Dn
Br 4
12-0x10-0
Br 2
14-0x11-0
optional
bonus room

First Floor
1,441 sq. ft.

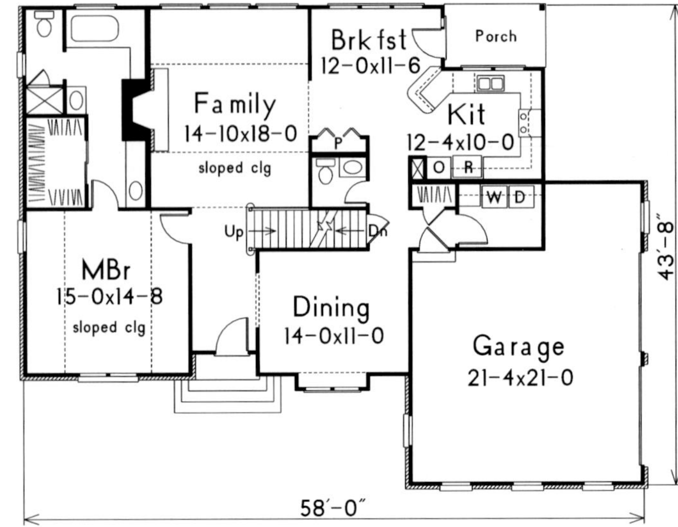
Brk fst
12-0x11-6
Porch
Family
14-10x18-0
sloped clg
P
Kit
12-4x10-0
O
R
W
D
Up
Dn
MBr
15-0x14-8
sloped clg
Dining
14-0x11-0
Garage
21-4x21-0
43'-8"
58'-0"

Bay Window Graces Luxury Master Bedroom

LOWE'S

Signature
SERIES

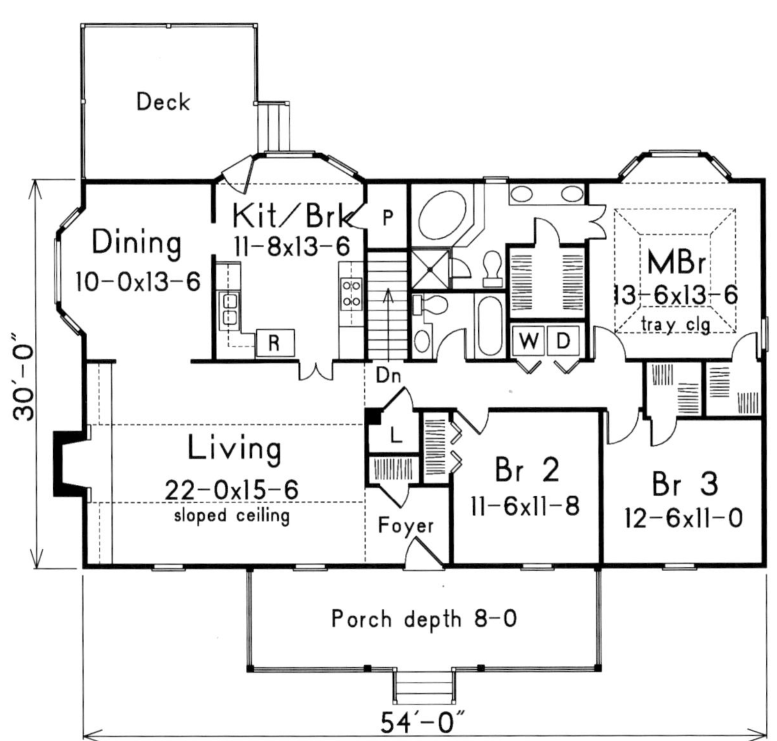
Deck
Dining
10-0x13-6
Kit/Brk
11-8x13-6
P
R
MBr
13-6x13-6
tray clg
W
D
Dn
L
Living
22-0x15-6
sloped ceiling
Foyer
Br 2
11-6x11-8
Br 3
12-6x11-0
Porch depth 8-0
30'-0"
54'-0"

Plan #527-0112

Price Code C

Total Living Area:	1,668 Sq. Ft.

Home has 3 bedrooms, 2 baths, 2-car drive under garage and basement foundation.

Special features

- Large bay windows in breakfast area, master bedroom and dining room
- Extensive walk-in closets and storage spaces throughout the home
- Handy entry covered porch
- Large living room has fireplace, built-in bookshelves and sloped ceiling

Quaint Exterior, Full Front Porch

Plan #527-0174

Price Code B

Total Living Area: 1,657 Sq. Ft.

Home has 3 bedrooms, 2 1/2 baths, 2-car drive under garage and basement foundation.

Special features

- Stylish pass-through between living and dining areas
- Master bedroom is secluded from living area for privacy
- Large windows in breakfast and dining areas

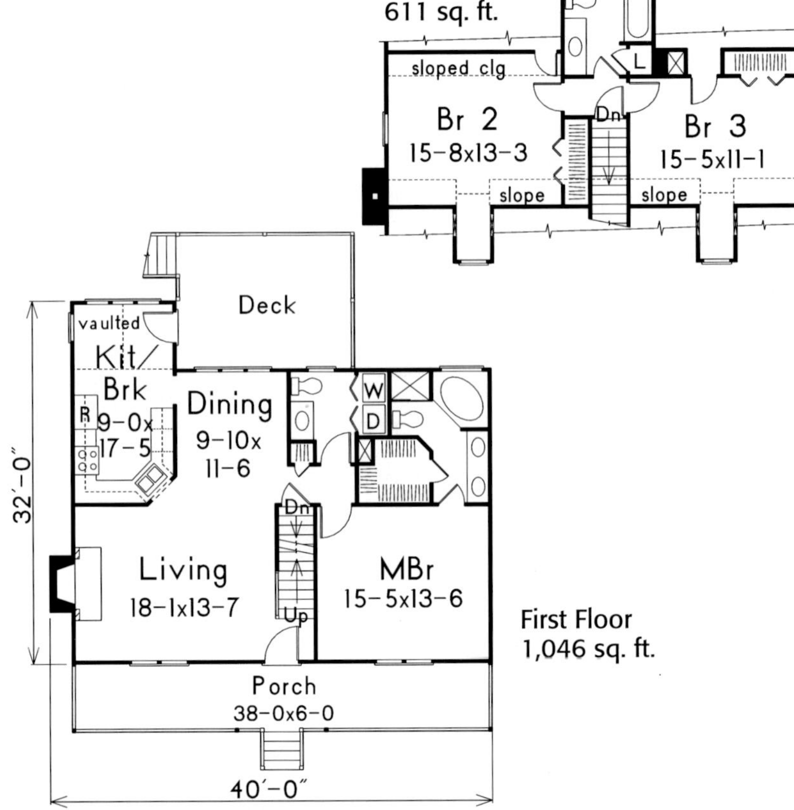

Second Floor
611 sq. ft.
sloped clg
L
Dn
Br 2
15-8x13-3
Br 3
15-5x11-1
slope
slope
Deck
vaulted
Kit/
Brk
9-0x
17-5
R
Dining
9-10x
11-6
W
D
Dn
Living
18-1x13-7
MBr
15-5x13-6
Up
32'-0"
First Floor
1,046 sq. ft.
Porch
38-0x6-0
40'-0"

TO ORDER BLUEPRINTS USE THE FORM ON PAGE 290 OR CALL TOLL-FREE **1-800-DREAM HOME** (373-2646)

Private Breakfast Room Provides Casual Dining

LOWE'S

Signature SERIES

Plan #527-0450

Price Code B

Total Living Area: 1,708 Sq. Ft.

Home has 3 bedrooms, 2 baths, 2-car garage and basement foundation, drawings also include crawl space foundation.

Special features

- Massive family room enhanced with several windows, fireplace and access to porch
- Deluxe master bath accented by step-up corner tub flanked by double vanities
- Closets throughout maintain organized living
- Bedrooms isolated from living areas

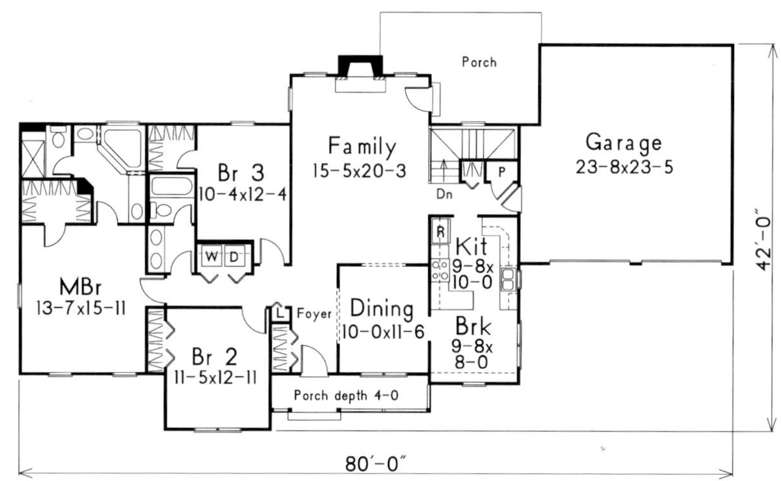
Porch
Family
15-5x20-3
Garage
23-8x23-5
Br 3
10-4x12-4
Dn
P
R
Kit
9-8x
10-0
W D
MBr
13-7x15-11
L
Foyer
Dining
10-0x11-6
Brk
9-8x
8-0
Br 2
11-5x12-11
Porch depth 4-0
42'-0"
80'-0"

LOWE'S

Signature
SERIES

Plan #527-0419

Price Code C

Total Living Area: 1,882 Sq. Ft.

Home has 4 bedrooms, 2 baths, 2-car side entry garage and basement foundation.

Special features

- Handsome brick facade
- Spacious great room and dining room combination brightened by unique corner windows and patio access
- Well-designed kitchen incorporates breakfast bar peninsula, sweeping casement window above sink and walk-in pantry island
- Master suite features large walk-in closet and private bath with bay window

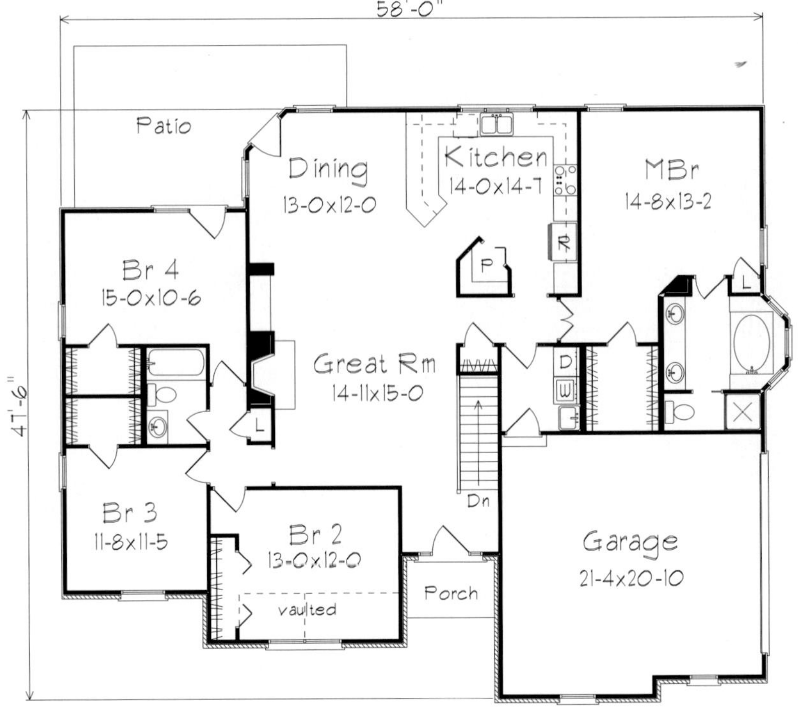
58'-0"
47'-6"
Patio
Dining
13-0x12-0
Kitchen
14-0x14-7
MBr
14-8x13-2
Br 4
15-0x10-6
P
Great Rm
14-11x15-0
L
D
W
Br 3
11-8x11-5
Br 2
13-0x12-0
vaulted
Dn
Porch
Garage
21-4x20-10

 TO ORDER BLUEPRINTS USE THE FORM ON PAGE 290 OR CALL TOLL-FREE **1-800-DREAM HOME** (373-2646)

Comfortable Family Living In This Ranch

LOWE'S

Signature SERIES

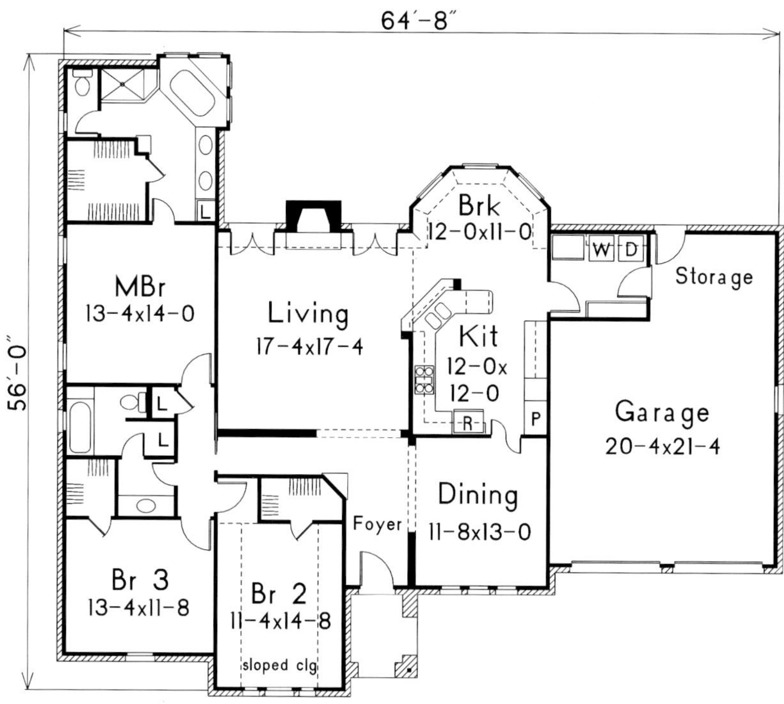
64'-8"
56'-0"
MBr
13-4x14-0
Living
17-4x17-4
Brk
12-0x11-0
Kit
12-0x
12-0
W
D
Storage
Garage
20-4x21-4
Dining
11-8x13-0
Foyer
Br 3
13-4x11-8
Br 2
11-4x14-8
sloped clg
L
P
R

Plan #527-0244

Price Code D

Total Living Area: 1,994 Sq. Ft.

Home has 3 bedrooms, 2 baths, 2-car garage and slab foundation.

Special features

- Convenient entrance from the garage into the main living area through the utility room
- Standard 9' ceilings, bedroom #2 features a 12' vaulted ceiling and a 10' ceiling in the dining room
- Master bedroom offers a full bath with oversized tub, separate shower and walk-in closet
- Entry leads to formal dining room and attractive living room with double French doors and fireplace

Transom Windows Create Impressive Front Entry

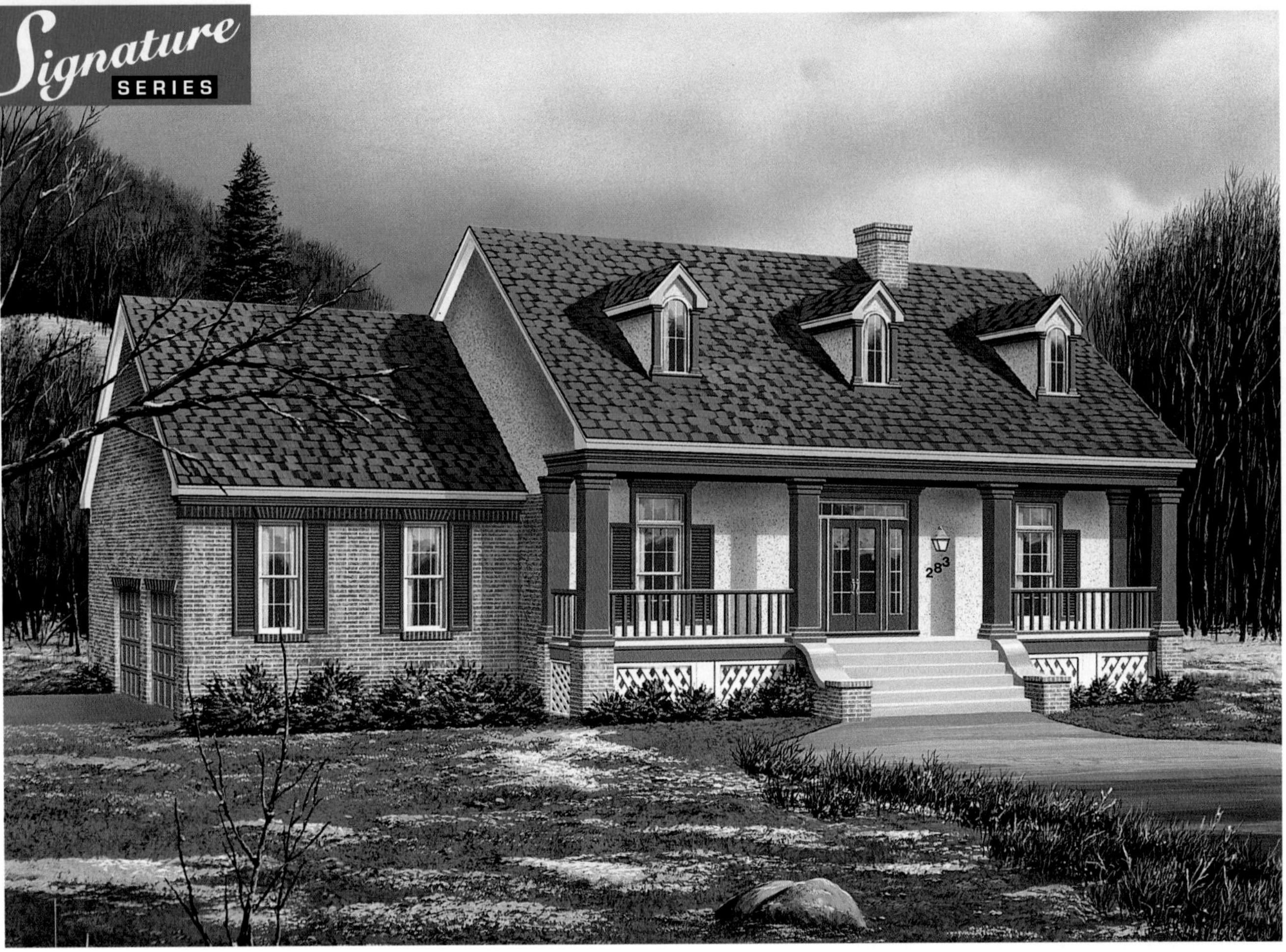

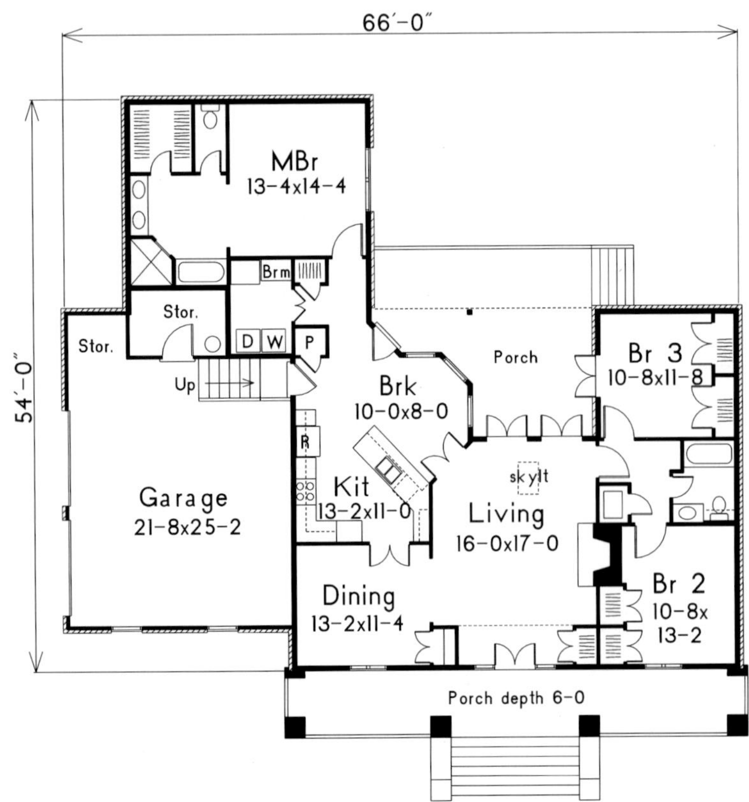
66'-0"
54'-0"
MBr
13-4x14-4
Brm
Stor.
Stor.
D
W
P
Up
Garage
21-8x25-2
Brk
10-0x8-0
Porch
Br 3
10-8x11-8
R
skylt
Kit
13-2x11-0
Living
16-0x17-0
Dining
13-2x11-4
Br 2
10-8x
13-2
Porch depth 6-0

Plan #527-0283

Price Code D

Total Living Area: 1,800 Sq. Ft.

Home has 3 bedrooms, 2 baths, 2-car side entry garage and crawl space foundation, drawings also include slab foundation.

Special features

- Energy efficient home with 2" x 6" exterior walls
- Covered front and rear porches add outdoor living area
- 12' ceilings in kitchen, eating area, dining and living rooms
- Private master suite features expansive bath
- Side entry garage with two storage areas
- Pillared styling with brick and stucco exterior finish

Country Home With Front Orientation

LOWE'S

Signature
SERIES

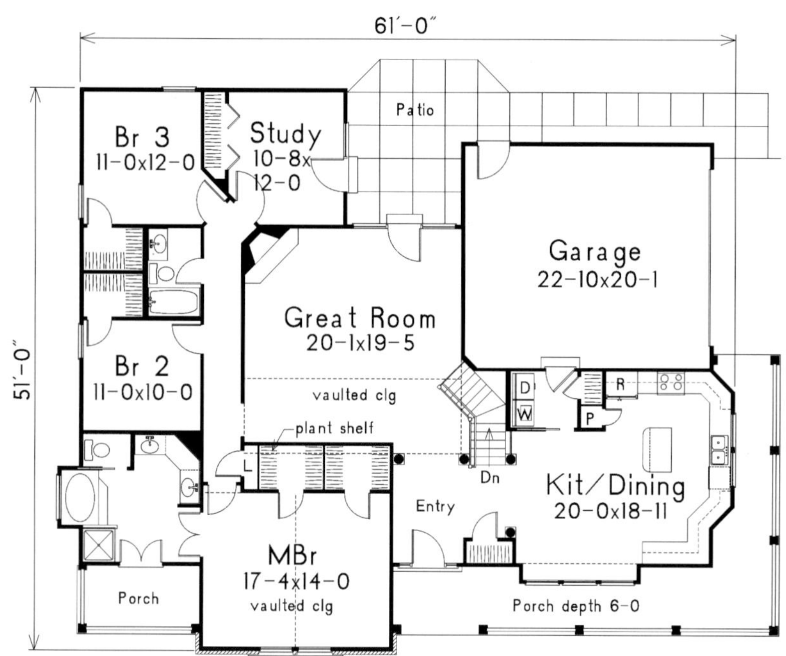
61′-0″
51′-0″
Patio
Br 3
11-0x12-0
Study
10-8x
12-0
Garage
22-10x20-1
Great Room
20-1x19-5
vaulted clg
Br 2
11-0x10-0
plant shelf
D
W
R
P
L
Dn
Kit/Dining
20-0x18-11
Entry
MBr
17-4x14-0
vaulted clg
Porch
Porch depth 6-0

Plan #527-0712

Price Code C

Total Living Area: 2,029 Sq. Ft.

Home has 4 bedrooms, 2 baths, 2-car side entry garage and basement foundation.

Special features

- Stonework, gables, roof dormer and double porches create a country flavor
- Kitchen enjoys extravagant cabinetry and counterspace in a bay, island snack bar, built-in pantry and cheery dining area with multiple tall windows
- Angled stair descends from large entry with wood columns and is open to vaulted great room with corner fireplace
- Master bedroom boasts his and hers walk-in closets, double doors leading to an opulent master bath and private porch

LOWE'S

Signature
SERIES

Charming Country Styling In This Ranch

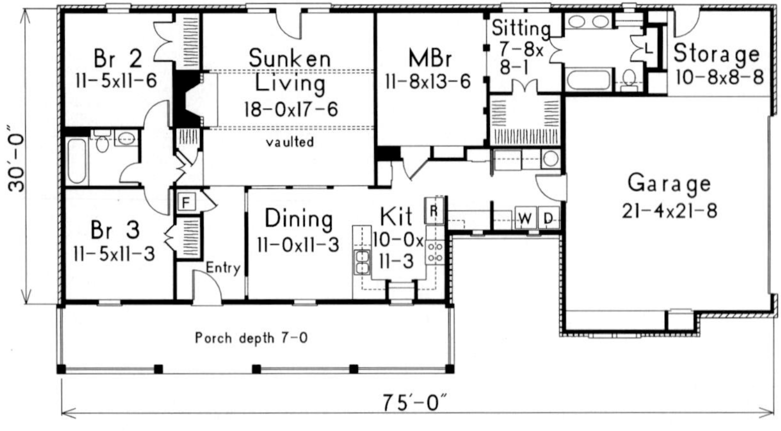
Br 2
11-5x11-6
Sunken
Living
18-0x17-6
vaulted
MBr
11-8x13-6
Sitting
7-8x
8-1
L
Storage
10-8x8-8
Garage
21-4x21-8
F
Br 3
11-5x11-3
Entry
Dining
11-0x11-3
Kit
10-0x
11-3
R
W
D
Porch depth 7-0
30'-0"
75'-0"

Plan #527-0190

Price Code C

Total Living Area: 1,600 Sq. Ft.

Home has 3 bedrooms, 2 baths, 2-car side entry garage and slab foundation, drawings also include crawl space and basement foundations.

Special features

- Impressive sunken living room with massive stone fireplace and 16' vaulted ceilings
- Dining room conveniently located next to kitchen and divided for privacy
- Energy efficient home with 2" x 6" exterior walls
- Special amenities include sewing room, glass shelves in kitchen and master bath and a large utility area
- Sunken master bedroom features a distinctive sitting room

 TO ORDER BLUEPRINTS USE THE FORM ON PAGE 290 OR CALL TOLL-FREE **1-800-DREAM HOME** (373-2646)

Smaller Home Offers Stylish Exterior

LOWE'S

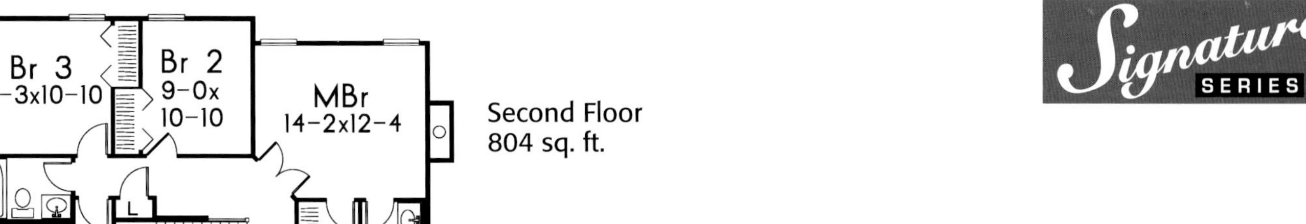
Signature
SERIES

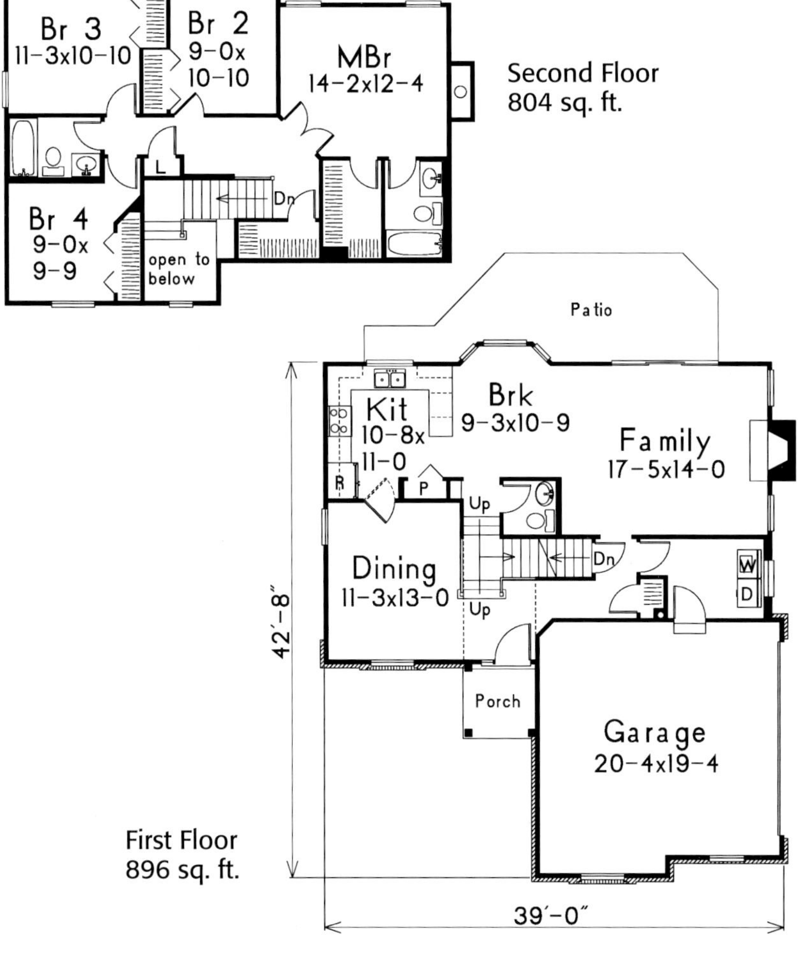
Br 3
11-3x10-10
Br 2
9-0x
10-10
MBr
14-2x12-4
Br 4
9-0x
9-9
open to below
L
Dn
Second Floor
804 sq. ft.
Patio
Kit
10-8x
11-0
Brk
9-3x10-9
Family
17-5x14-0
R
P
Up
Dn
W
D
Dining
11-3x13-0
Porch
Garage
20-4x19-4
42'-8"
39'-0"
First Floor
896 sq. ft.

Plan #527-0656

Price Code B

Total Living Area: 1,700 Sq. Ft.

Home has 4 bedrooms, 2 1/2 baths, 2-car side entry garage and basement foundation.

Special features

- Two-story entry with T-stair is illuminated with decorative oval window
- Skillfully designed U-shaped kitchen with built-in pantry
- All bedrooms have generous closet storage and are common to spacious hall with walk-in cedar closet

LOWE'S

Signature SERIES

Enchanting Country Cottage

Plan #527-0477

Price Code AA

Total Living Area: 1,140 Sq. Ft.

Home has 3 bedrooms, 2 baths, 2-car drive under garage and basement foundation.

Special features

- Open and spacious living and dining areas for family gatherings
- Well-organized kitchen with an abundance of cabinetry and built-in pantry
- Roomy master bath features double-bowl vanity

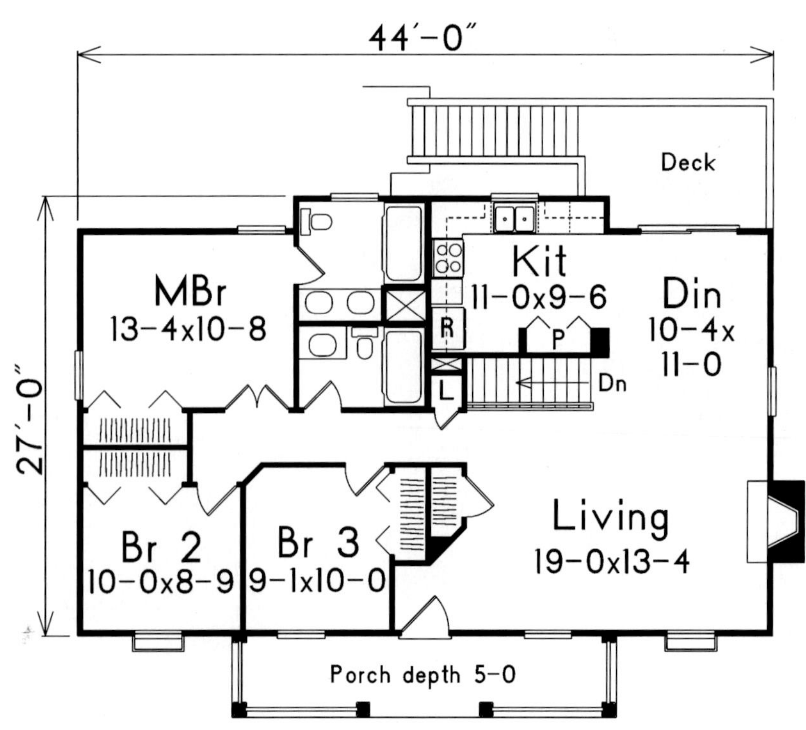
44'-0"
Deck
Kit
11-0x9-6
Din
10-4x
11-0
MBr
13-4x10-8
R
P
L
Dn
27'-0"
Living
19-0x13-4
Br 2
10-0x8-9
Br 3
9-1x10-0
Porch depth 5-0

LOWE'S

Signature SERIES

Plan #527-0587

Price Code AA

Total Living Area: 1,120 Sq. Ft.

Home has 3 bedrooms, 1 1/2 baths and crawl space foundation, drawings also include basement and slab foundations.

Special features

- Master bedroom includes a half bath with laundry area, linen closet and kitchen access
- Kitchen has charming double-door entry, breakfast bar and a convenient walk-in pantry
- Welcoming front porch opens to large living room with coat closet

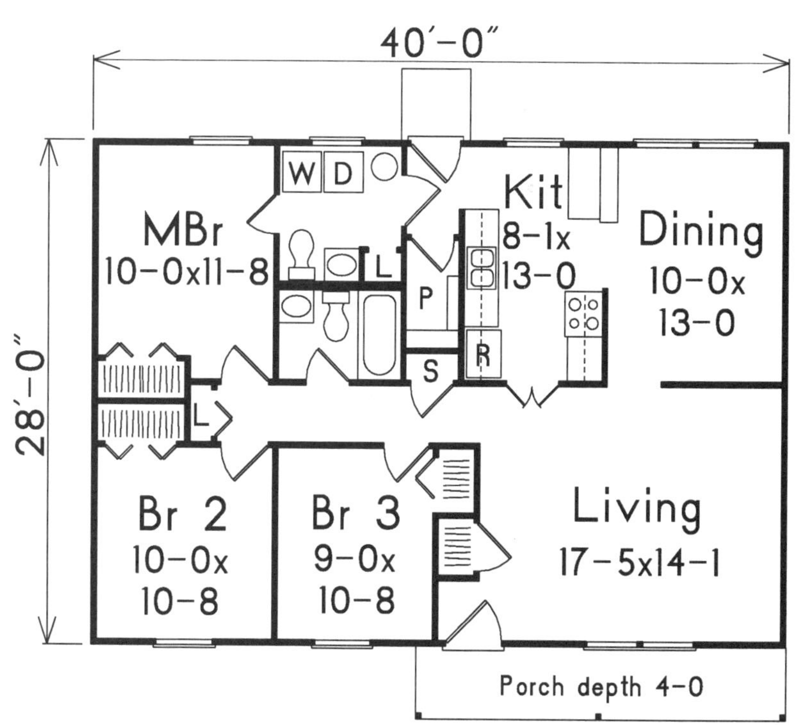
40′-0″
28′-0″
W D
MBr
10-0x11-8
L
Kit
8-1x
13-0
P
S
R
Dining
10-0x
13-0
L
Br 2
10-0x
10-8
Br 3
9-0x
10-8
Living
17-5x14-1
Porch depth 4-0

LOWE'S

Signature SERIES

Dining With A View

Plan #527-0652

Price Code B

Total Living Area: 1,524 Sq. Ft.

Home has 3 bedrooms, 2 1/2 baths, 2-car garage and basement foundation.

Special features

- Delightful balcony overlooks two-story entry illuminated by oval window
- Roomy first floor master suite offers quiet privacy
- All bedrooms feature one or more walk-in closets

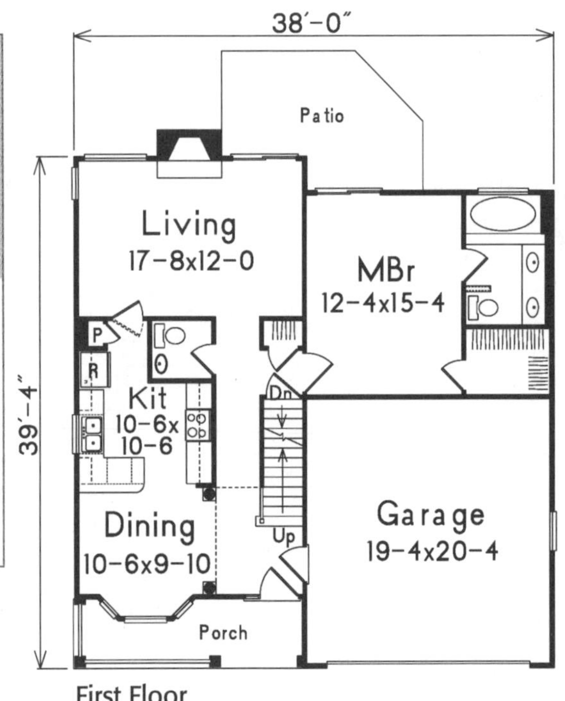
38'-0"
Patio
Living
17-8x12-0
MBr
12-4x15-4
P
R
Kit
10-6x
10-6
Dn
Dining
10-6x9-10
Up
Garage
19-4x20-4
Porch
39'-4"

First Floor
951 sq. ft.

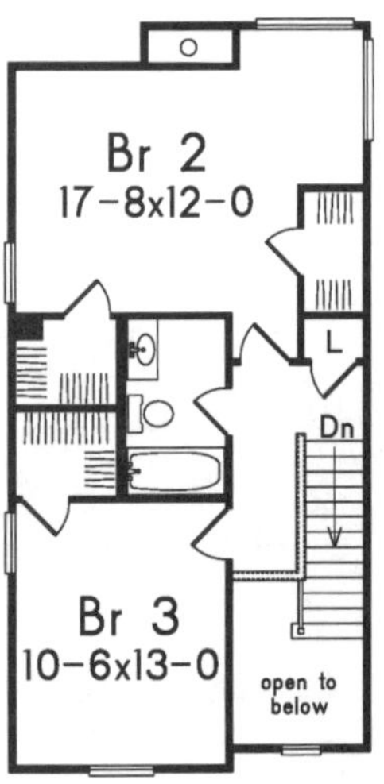
Br 2
17-8x12-0
L
Dn
Br 3
10-6x13-0
open to below

Second Floor
573 sq. ft.

LOWE'S

Signature
SERIES

Plan #527-0510

Price Code A

Total Living Area: 1,400 Sq. Ft.

Home has 3 bedrooms, 2 baths, 2-car garage and crawl space foundation, drawings also include basement and slab foundations.

Special features

- Front porch offers warmth and welcome
- Large great room opens into dining room creating open living atmosphere
- Kitchen features convenient laundry area, pantry and breakfast bar

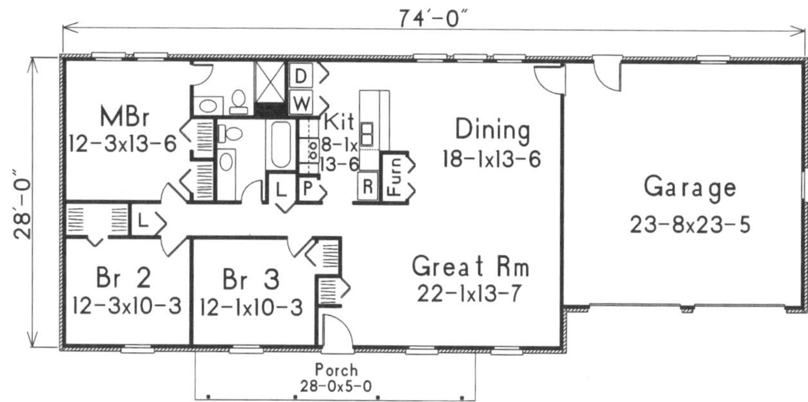
74'-0"
28'-0"
MBr
12-3x13-6
D
W
Kit
8-1x
13-6
Dining
18-1x13-6
L
P
R
Furn
Garage
23-8x23-5
L
Br 2
12-3x10-3
Br 3
12-1x10-3
Great Rm
22-1x13-7
Porch
28-0x5-0

LOWE'S

Signature SERIES

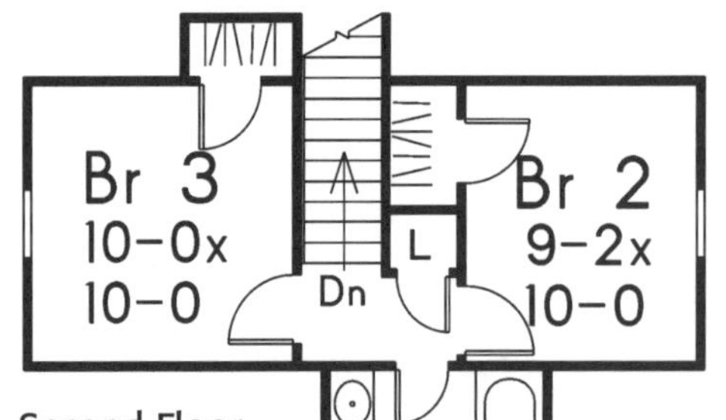
Br 3
10-0x
10-0
Dn
L
Br 2
9-2x
10-0

Second Floor
336 sq. ft.

First Floor
618 sq. ft.

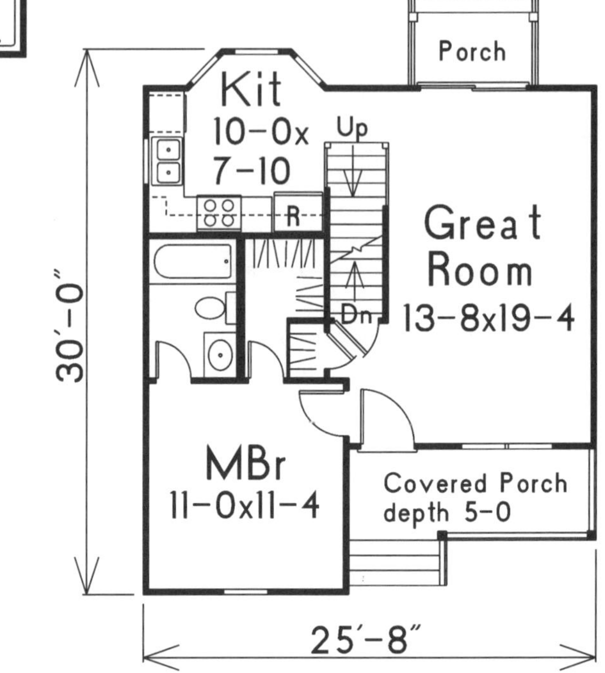
Porch
Kit
10-0x
7-10
Up
R
Great
Room
13-8x19-4
Dn
MBr
11-0x11-4
Covered Porch
depth 5-0
30'-0"
25'-8"

Plan #527-0498

Price Code AA

Total Living Area: 954 Sq. Ft.

Home has 3 bedrooms, 2 baths and basement foundation.

Special features

- Kitchen has cozy bayed eating area
- Master bedroom has a walk-in closet and private bath
- Large great room has access to the back porch
- Convenient coat closet near front entry

LOWE'S

Signature SERIES

Plan #527-0252

Price Code A

Total Living Area: 1,364 Sq. Ft.

Home has 3 bedrooms, 2 baths, 2-car drive under garage and basement foundation.

Special features

- Master bedroom includes full bath
- Pass-through kitchen opens into breakfast room with laundry closet and access to deck
- Adjoining dining and living rooms with vaulted ceilings and a fireplace creates an open living area
- Dining room features large bay window

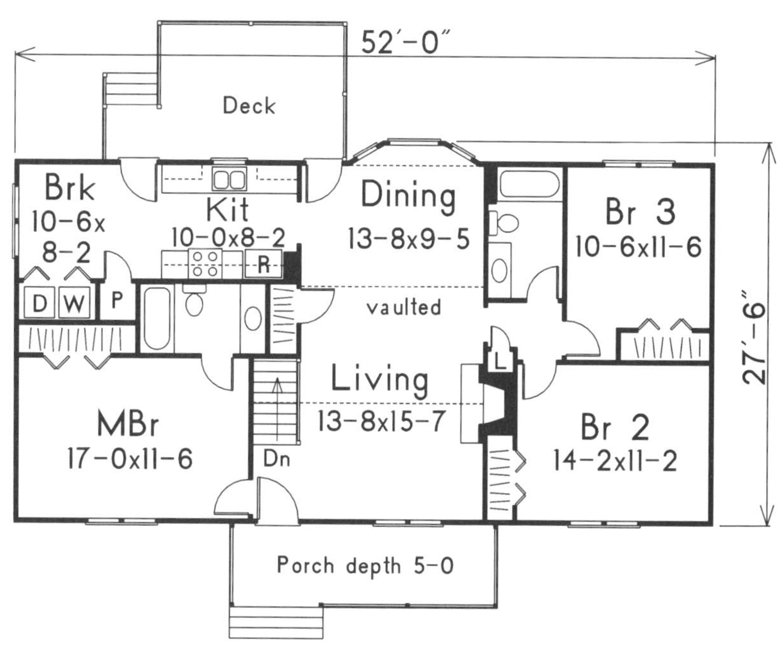
52′-0″
Deck
Brk
10-6x
8-2
Kit
10-0x8-2
R
Dining
13-8x9-5
Br 3
10-6x11-6
D
W
P
vaulted
27′-6″
L
Living
13-8x15-7
MBr
17-0x11-6
Br 2
14-2x11-2
Dn
Porch depth 5-0

SPARR

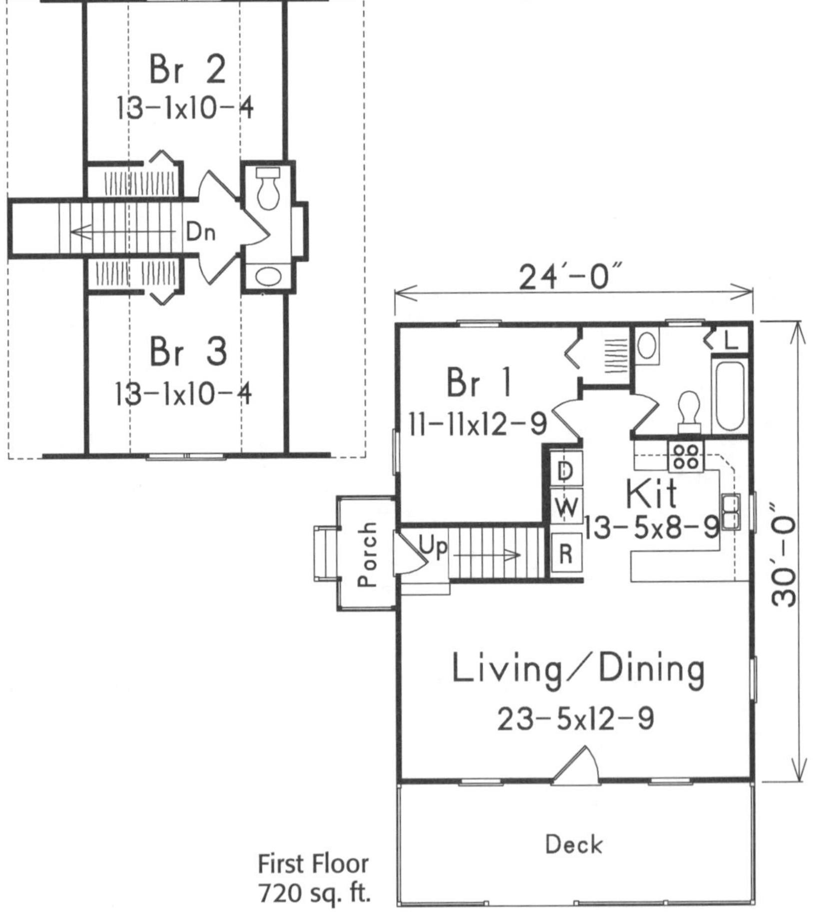
Second Floor
434 sq. ft.
Br 2
13-1x10-4
Dn
Br 3
13-1x10-4
24'-0"
Br 1
11-11x12-9
L
D
W
R
Kit
13-5x8-9
Porch
Up
30'-0"
Living/Dining
23-5x12-9
Deck
First Floor
720 sq. ft.

Plan #527-0548

Price Code AA

Total Living Area: 1,154 Sq. Ft.

Home has 3 bedrooms, 1 1/2 baths and crawl space foundation, drawings also include slab foundation.

Special features

- U-shaped kitchen with large breakfast bar and handy laundry area
- Private second floor bedrooms share half bath
- Large living/dining area opens to deck

Atrium's Dramatic Ambiance

LOWE'S

Signature
SERIES

Plan #527-0370

Price Code C

Total Living Area: 1,721 Sq. Ft.

Home has 3 bedrooms, 2 baths, 3-car garage and walk-out basement foundation, drawings also include crawl space and slab foundations.

Special features

- Roof dormers add great curb appeal
- Vaulted great room and dining room immersed in light from atrium window wall
- Breakfast room opens onto covered porch
- Functionally designed kitchen

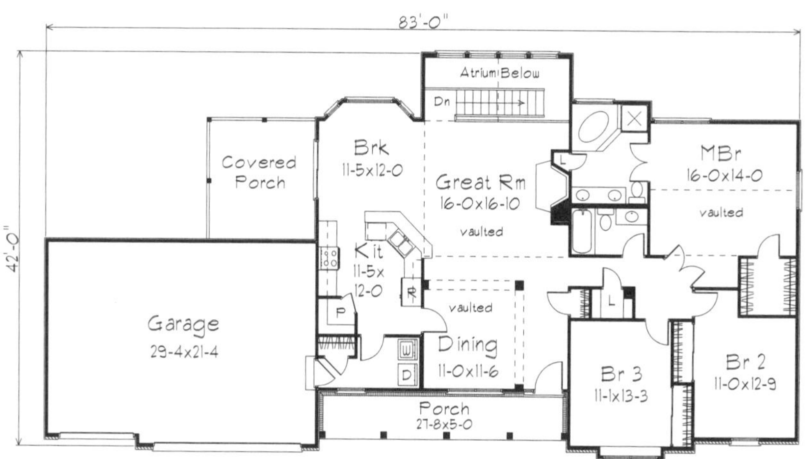
83'-0"
42'-0"
Atrium Below
Dn
Covered Porch
Brk 11-5x12-0
Great Rm 16-0x16-10
vaulted
MBr 16-0x14-0
vaulted
Kit 11-5x 12-0
P
vaulted
Dining 11-0x11-6
Garage 29-4x21-4
Porch 27-8x5-0
Br 3 11-1x13-3
Br 2 11-0x12-9

Rear View

Atrium Living For Views On A Narrow Lot

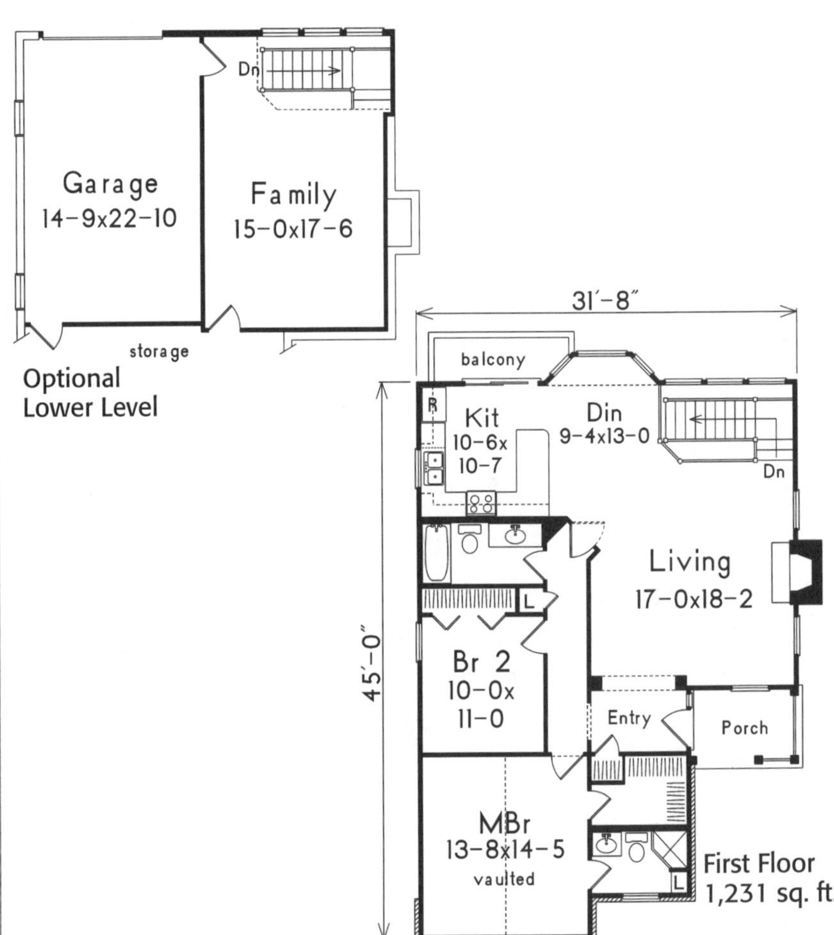
Dn
Garage
14-9x22-10
Family
15-0x17-6
storage
Optional
Lower Level
31'-8"
balcony
R
Kit
10-6x
10-7
Din
9-4x13-0
Dn
Living
17-0x18-2
L
45'-0"
Br 2
10-0x
11-0
Entry
Porch
MBr
13-8x14-5
vaulted
L
First Floor
1,231 sq. ft.

Plan #527-0807

Price Code A

Total Living Area: 1,231 Sq. Ft.

Home has 2 bedrooms, 2 baths, 1-car drive under garage and walk-out basement foundation.

Special features

- Dutch gables and stone accents provide an enchanting appearance for a small cottage
- The spacious living room offers a masonry fireplace, atrium with window wall and is open to a dining area with bay window
- A breakfast counter, lots of cabinet space and glass sliding doors to a walk-out balcony create a sensational kitchen
- 380 square feet of optional living area on the lower level

TO ORDER BLUEPRINTS USE THE FORM ON PAGE 290 OR CALL TOLL-FREE **1-800-DREAM HOME** (373-2646)

LOWE'S

Signature
SERIES

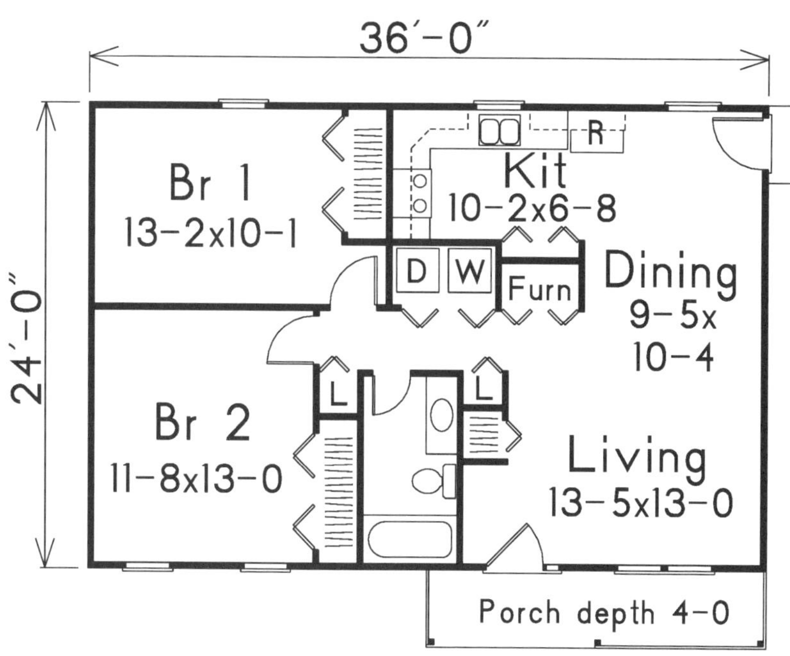
36′-0″
24′-0″
Br 1
13-2x10-1
R
Kit
10-2x6-8
D
W
Furn
Dining
9-5x
10-4
L
L
Br 2
11-8x13-0
Living
13-5x13-0
Porch depth 4-0

Plan #527-0502

Price Code AAA

Total Living Area: 864 Sq. Ft.

Home has 2 bedrooms, 1 bath and crawl space foundation, drawings also include basement and slab foundations.

Special features

- L-shaped kitchen with convenient pantry is adjacent to dining area
- Easy access to laundry area, linen closet and storage closet
- Both bedrooms include ample closet space

Plan #527-0102

Price Code A

Total Living Area: 1,246 Sq. Ft.

Home has 3 bedrooms, 2 baths, 2-car garage and basement foundation.

Special features

- Corner living room window adds openness and light
- Out-of-the-way kitchen with dining area accesses the outdoors
- Private first floor master bedroom with corner window
- Large walk-in closet is located in bedroom #3
- Easily built perimeter allows economical construction

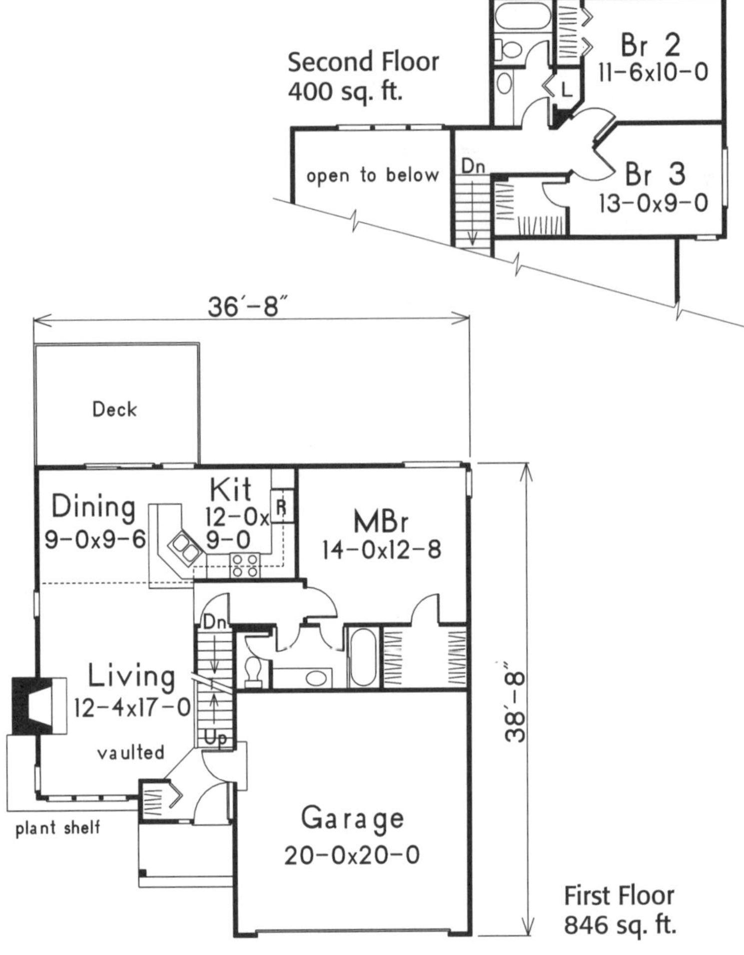
Second Floor
400 sq. ft.
Br 2
11-6x10-0
L
open to below
Dn
Br 3
13-0x9-0
36'-8"
Deck
Dining
9-0x9-6
Kit
12-0x
9-0
R
MBr
14-0x12-8
Dn
Living
12-4x17-0
vaulted
Up
38'-8"
plant shelf
Garage
20-0x20-0
First Floor
846 sq. ft.

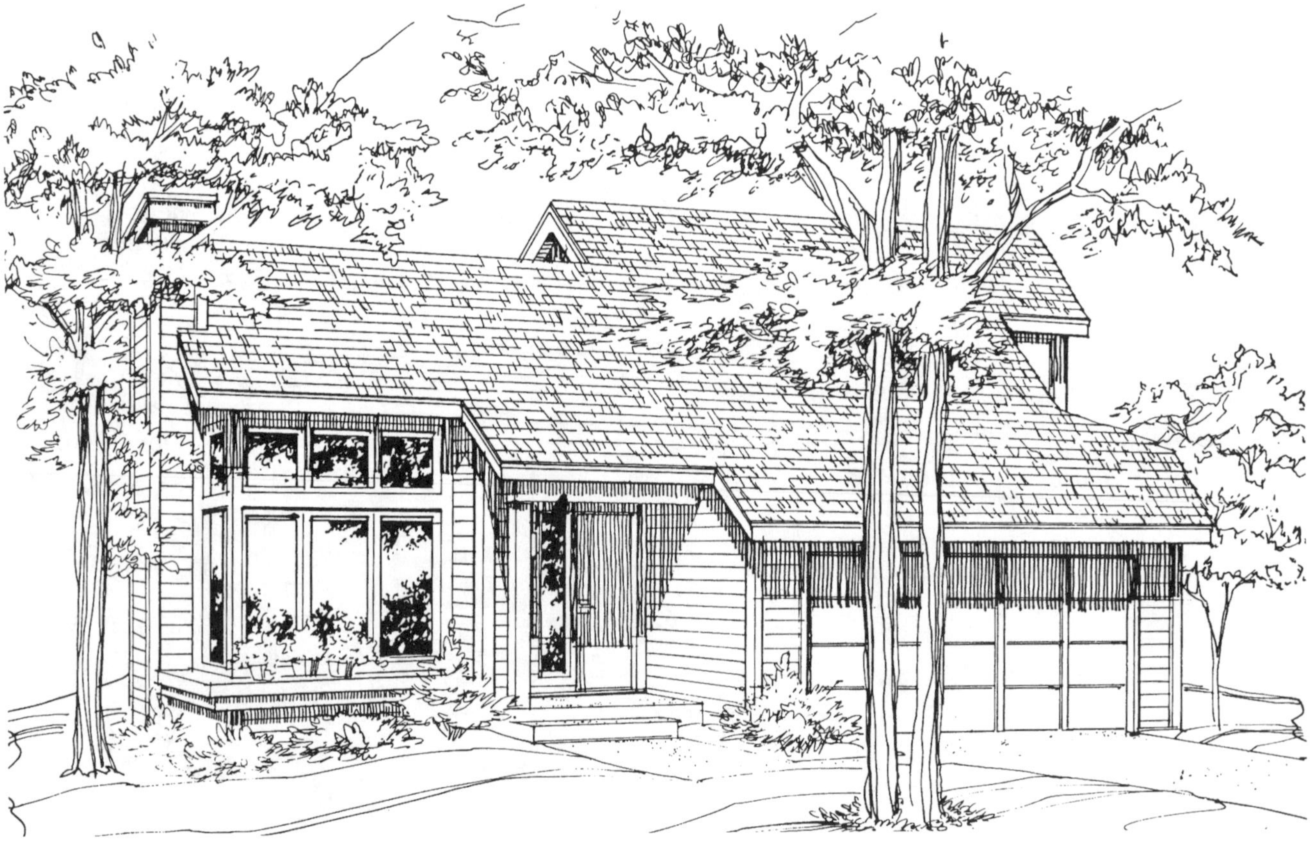

TO ORDER BLUEPRINTS USE THE FORM ON PAGE 290 OR CALL TOLL-FREE **1-800-DREAM HOME** (373-2646)

Inviting Gabled And Arched Brick Entry

LOWE'S

Signature
SERIES

Plan #527-0412

Price Code C

Total Living Area: 2,109 Sq. Ft.

Home has 3 bedrooms, 2 baths, 2-car side entry garage and slab foundation, drawings also include crawl space foundation.

Special features

- 12' ceilings in living and dining rooms
- Kitchen designed as an integral part of the family and breakfast rooms
- Secluded and generous-sized master bedroom includes a plant shelf, walk-in closet and private bath with separate tub and shower
- Stately columns and circle-top window frame dining room

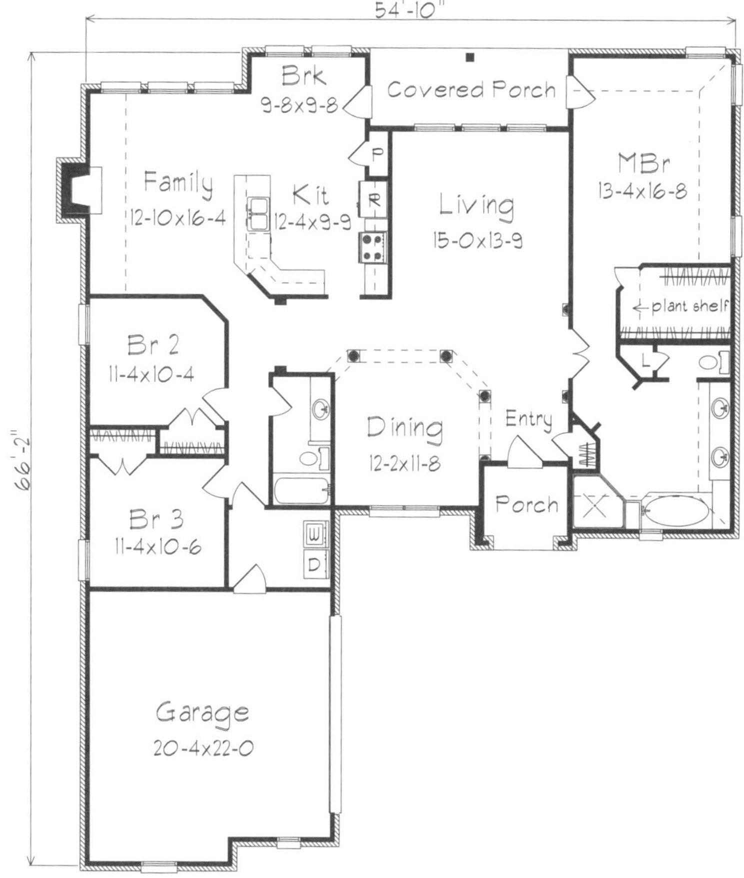
54'-10"
66'-2"
Brk
9-8x9-8
Covered Porch
Family
12-10x16-4
Kit
12-4x9-9
P
R
Living
15-0x13-9
MBr
13-4x16-8
plant shelf
L
Br 2
11-4x10-4
Dining
12-2x11-8
Entry
Porch
Br 3
11-4x10-6
W
D
Garage
20-4x22-0

LOWE'S

Signature SERIES

Two-Story Offers Attractive Exterior

Plan #527-0526

Price Code D

Total Living Area: 2,262 Sq. Ft.

Home has 3 bedrooms, 2 1/2 baths, 2-car rear entry garage and crawl space foundation, drawings also include basement and slab foundations.

Special features

- Charming exterior features include large front porch, two patios, front balcony and double bay windows
- Den/office area provides impressive entry to sunken family room
- Conveniently located first floor laundry
- Large master bedroom with walk-in closet, dressing area and bath

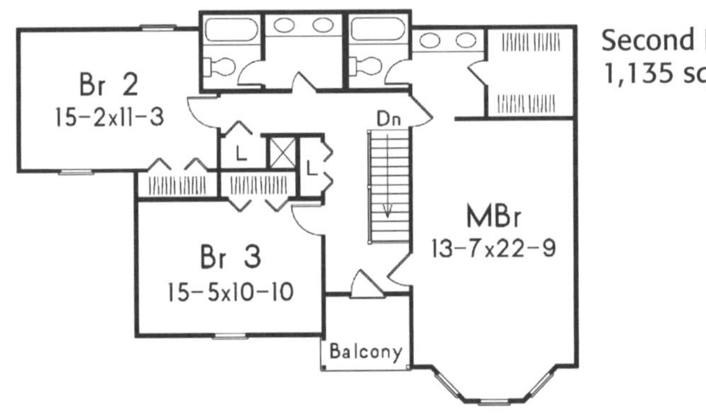
Br 2
15-2x11-3
L
L
Dn
MBr
13-7x22-9
Br 3
15-5x10-10
Balcony

Second Floor
1,135 sq. ft.

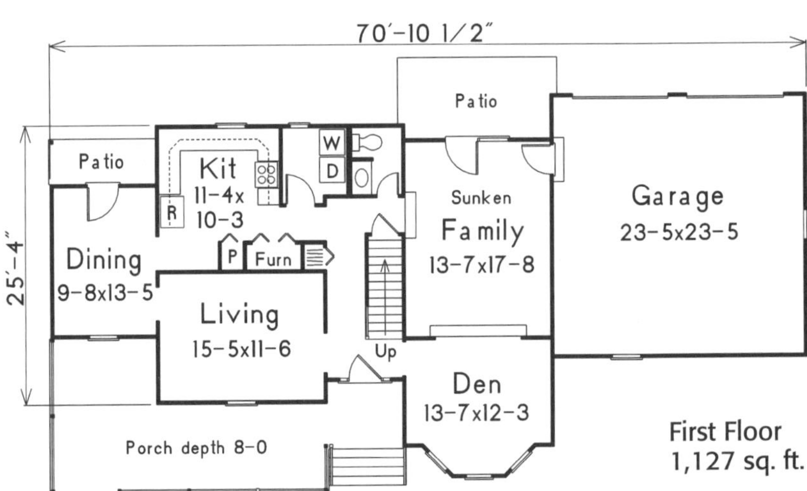
70'-10 1/2"
Patio
Patio
Kit
11-4x
10-3
R
W
D
Sunken
Family
13-7x17-8
Garage
23-5x23-5
25'-4"
Dining
9-8x13-5
P
Furn
Living
15-5x11-6
Up
Den
13-7x12-3
Porch depth 8-0

First Floor
1,127 sq. ft.

Vaulted Ceilings Add Dimension

LOWE'S

Signature SERIES

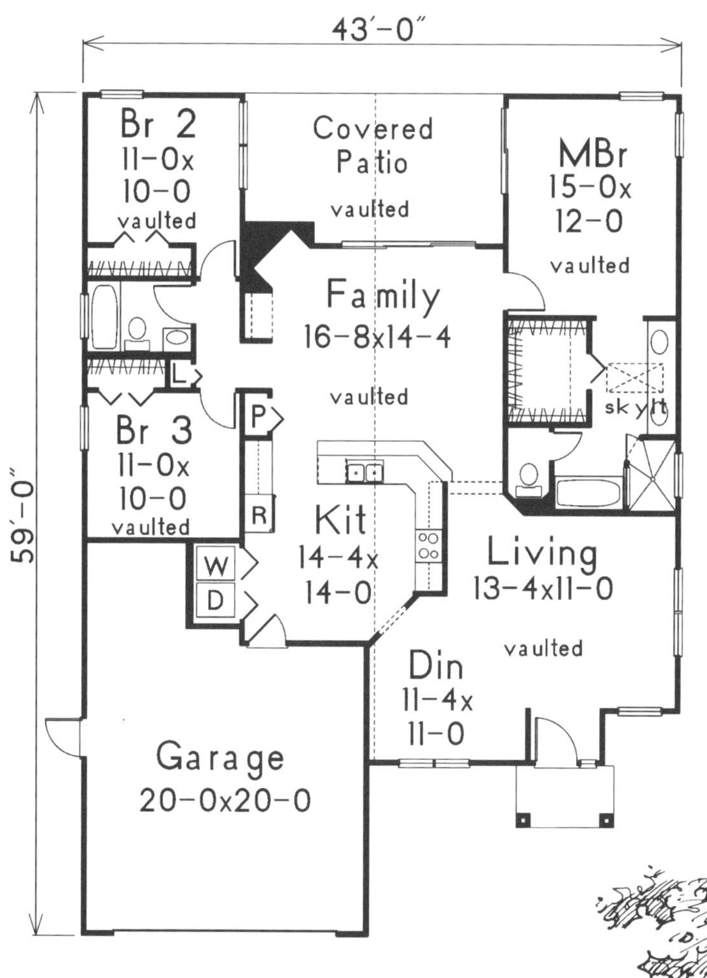
43'-0"
59'-0"
Br 2
11-0x
10-0
vaulted
Covered
Patio
vaulted
MBr
15-0x
12-0
vaulted
Family
16-8x14-4
vaulted
skylt
L
P
Br 3
11-0x
10-0
vaulted
R
Kit
14-4x
14-0
W
D
Living
13-4x11-0
vaulted
Din
11-4x
11-0
Garage
20-0x20-0

Plan #527-0357

Price Code B

Total Living Area: 1,550 Sq. Ft.

Home has 3 bedrooms, 2 baths, 2-car garage and slab foundation.

Special features

- Cozy corner fireplace provides focal point in family room
- Master bedroom features large walk-in closet, skylight and separate tub and shower
- Convenient laundry closet
- Kitchen with pantry and breakfast bar connects to family room
- Family room and master bedroom access covered patio

LOWE'S
Signature
SERIES

Two-Story Foyer Adds Spacious Feeling

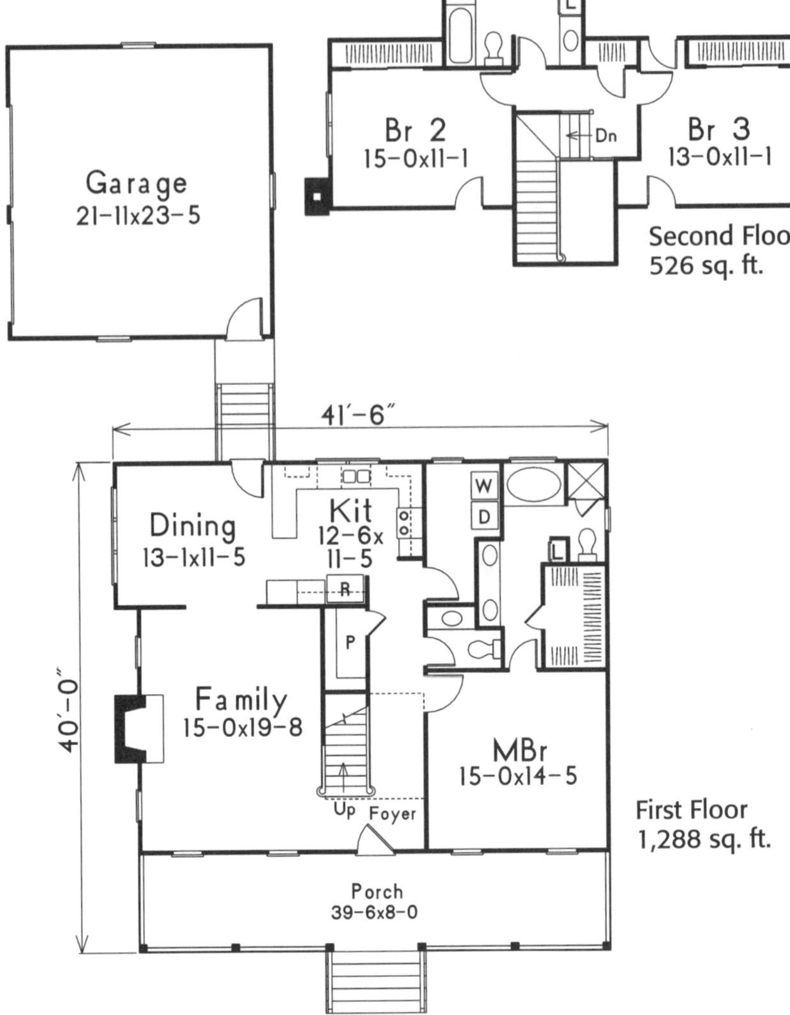
Garage
21-11x23-5
Br 2
15-0x11-1
Dn
Br 3
13-0x11-1
Second Floor
526 sq. ft.
41'-6"
40'-0"
Dining
13-1x11-5
Kit
12-6x
11-5
W
D
P
R
Family
15-0x19-8
MBr
15-0x14-5
Up
Foyer
Porch
39-6x8-0
First Floor
1,288 sq. ft.

Plan #527-0201

Price Code D

Total Living Area: 1,814 Sq. Ft.

Home has 3 bedrooms, 2 1/2 baths, 2-car detached garage and crawl space foundation, drawings also include slab foundation.

Special features

- Large master suite includes a spacious bath with garden tub, separate shower and large walk-in closet
- Spacious kitchen and dining area brightened by large windows and patio access
- Detached two-car garage with walkway leading to house adds to the charm of this country home
- Large front porch

TO ORDER BLUEPRINTS USE THE FORM ON PAGE 290 OR CALL TOLL-FREE **1-800-DREAM HOME** (373-2646)

Peaceful Shaded Front Porch

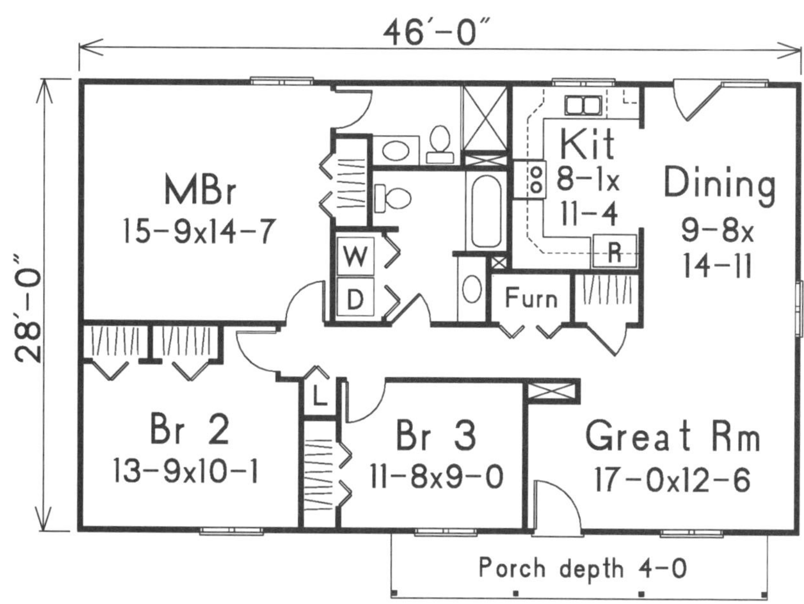
46'-0"
28'-0"
MBr
15-9x14-7
Kit
8-1x
11-4
Dining
9-8x
14-11
W
D
R
Furn
L
Br 2
13-9x10-1
Br 3
11-8x9-0
Great Rm
17-0x12-6
Porch depth 4-0

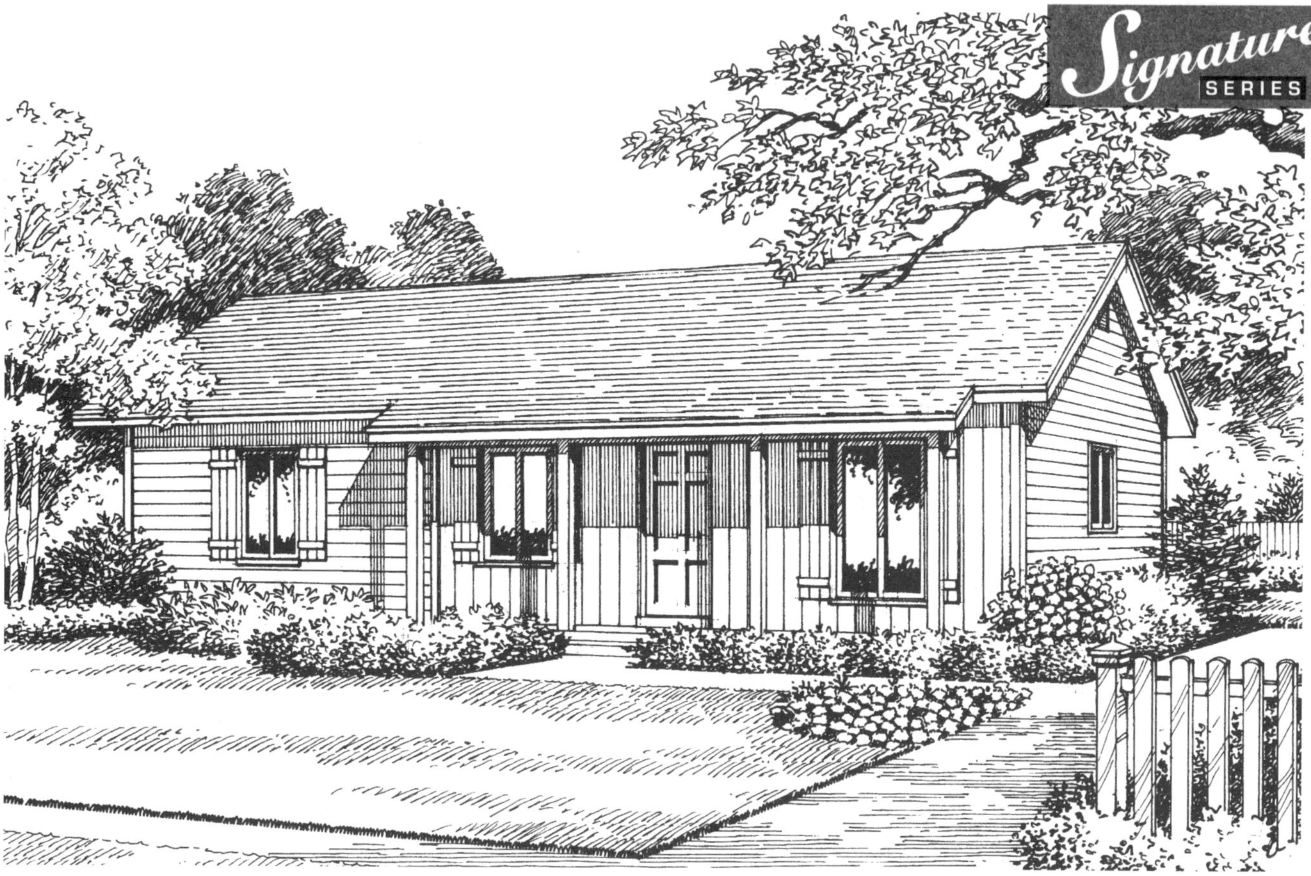

Plan #527-0534

Price Code A

Total Living Area: 1,288 Sq. Ft.

Home has 3 bedrooms, 2 baths and crawl space foundation, drawings also include basement and slab foundations.

Special features

- Kitchen, dining and great rooms join to create an open living space
- Master bedroom includes private bath
- Secondary bedrooms include ample closet space
- Hall bath features convenient laundry closet
- Dining room accesses outdoors

Stylish Ranch With Rustic Charm

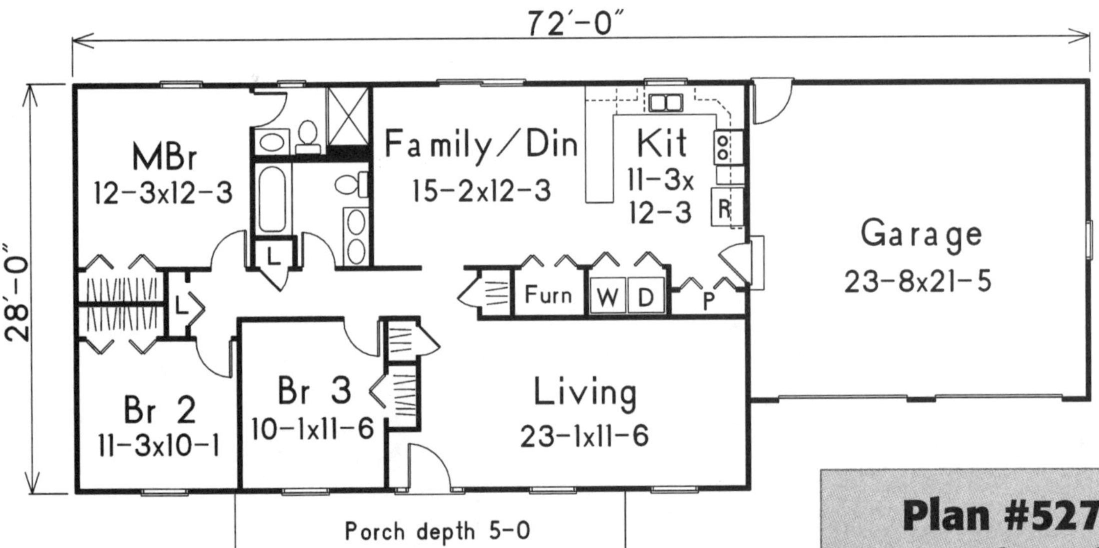
72'-0"
28'-0"
MBr
12-3x12-3
Family/Din
15-2x12-3
Kit
11-3x
12-3
R
L
L
Furn
W
D
P
Garage
23-8x21-5
Br 2
11-3x10-1
Br 3
10-1x11-6
Living
23-1x11-6
Porch depth 5-0

Plan #527-0515

Price Code A

Total Living Area: 1,344 Sq. Ft.

Home has 3 bedrooms, 2 baths, 2-car garage and crawl space foundation, drawings also include basement and slab foundations.

Special features

- Family/dining room has sliding door
- Master bedroom has private bath
- Hall bath includes double vanity for added convenience
- U-shaped kitchen feature large pantry and laundry area

Wrap-Around Country Porch

LOWE'S

Signature
SERIES

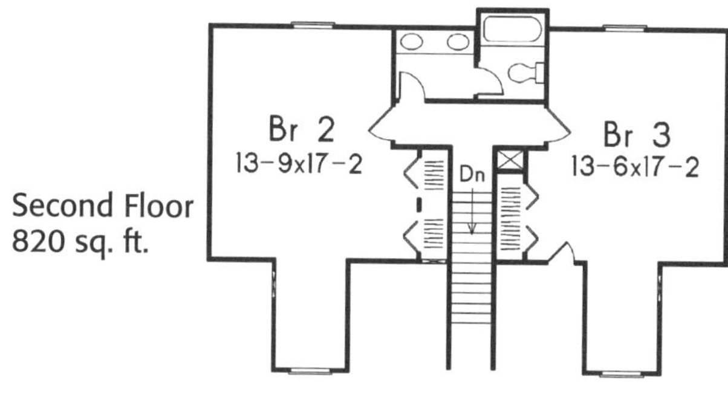
Br 2
13-9x17-2
Br 3
13-6x17-2
Dn
Second Floor
820 sq. ft.

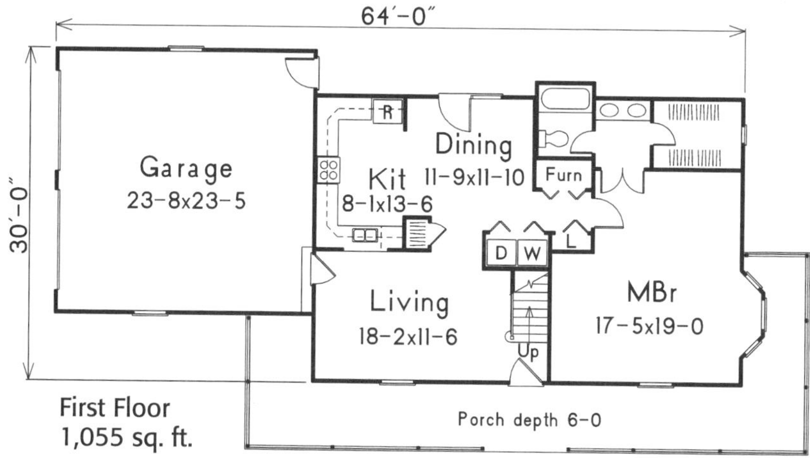
64'-0"
30'-0"
Garage
23-8x23-5
R
Dining
11-9x11-10
Kit
8-1x13-6
Furn
D W
L
Living
18-2x11-6
MBr
17-5x19-0
Up
Porch depth 6-0
First Floor
1,055 sq. ft.

Plan #527-0523

Price Code C

Total Living Area: 1,875 Sq. Ft.

Home has 3 bedrooms, 2 baths, 2-car side entry garage and crawl space foundation, drawings also include basement and slab foundations.

Special features

- Country-style exterior with wrap-around porch and dormers
- Large second floor bedrooms share a dressing area and bath
- Master bedroom suite includes bay window, walk-in closet, dressing area and bath

Plan #527-0512

Price Code C

Total Living Area: 1,827 Sq. Ft.

Home has 4 bedrooms, 2 baths, 2-car garage and crawl space foundation, drawings also include basement and slab foundations.

Special features

- Two large bedrooms located on second floor for extra privacy, plus two bedrooms on first floor
- L-shaped kitchen adjacent to family room
- Ample closet space in all bedrooms

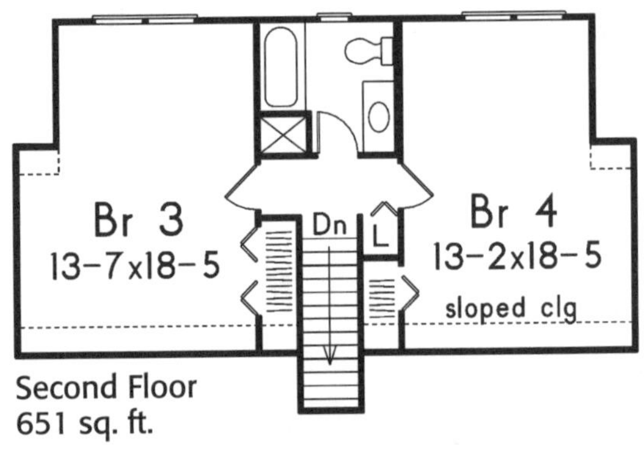
Br 3
13-7x18-5
Dn
L
Br 4
13-2x18-5
sloped clg

Second Floor
651 sq. ft.

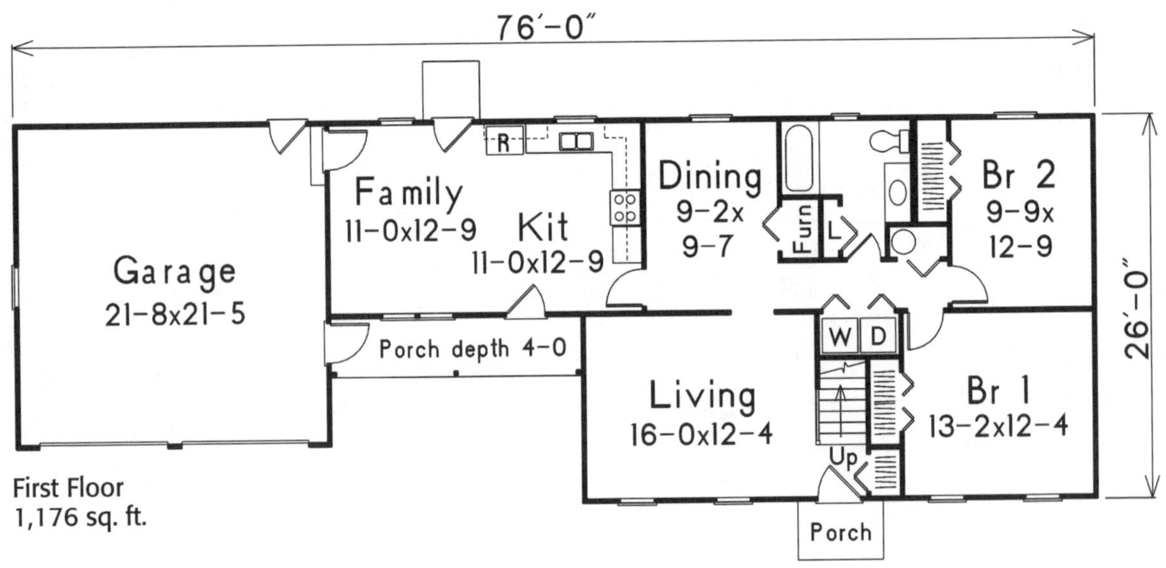
76'-0"
R
Family
11-0x12-9
Kit
11-0x12-9
Dining
9-2x
9-7
Furn
L
Br 2
9-9x
12-9
Garage
21-8x21-5
Porch depth 4-0
W
D
Living
16-0x12-4
Up
Br 1
13-2x12-4
26'-0"
Porch

First Floor
1,176 sq. ft.

TO ORDER BLUEPRINTS USE THE FORM ON PAGE 290 OR CALL TOLL-FREE **1-800-DREAM HOME** (373-2646)

Vaulted Ceilings And Light Add Dimension

LOWE'S

Signature
SERIES

Plan #527-0229

Price Code B

Total Living Area: 1,676 Sq. Ft.

Home has 3 bedrooms, 2 baths, 2-car garage and basement foundation, drawings also include crawl space and slab foundations.

Special features

- The living area skylights and large breakfast room with bay window provide plenty of sunlight
- The master bedroom has a walk-in closet and both the secondary bedrooms have large closets
- Vaulted ceilings, plant shelving and a fireplace provide a quality living area

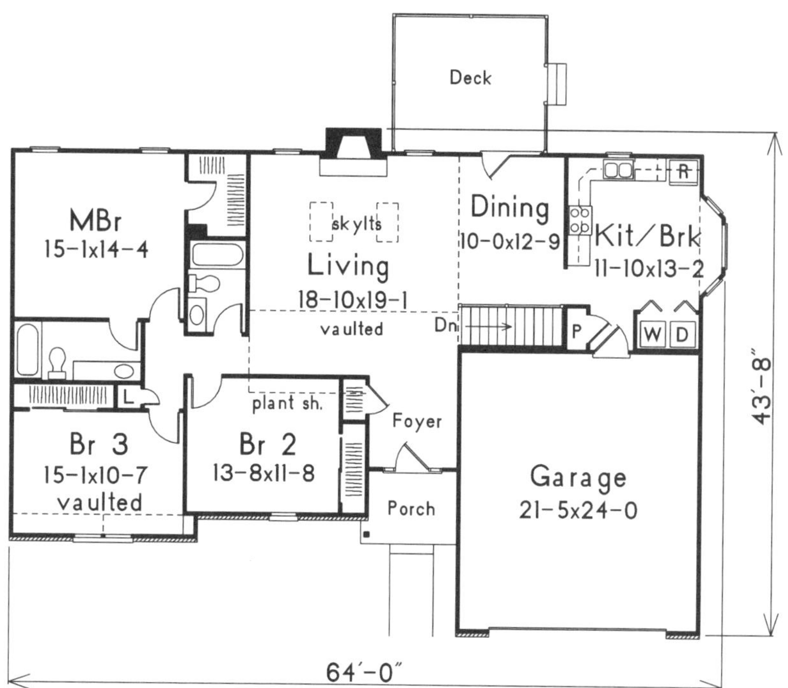
Deck
MBr
15-1x14-4
skylts
Living
18-10x19-1
vaulted
Dining
10-0x12-9
Kit/Brk
11-10x13-2
R
Dn
P
W
D
L
plant sh.
Foyer
Br 3
15-1x10-7
vaulted
Br 2
13-8x11-8
Porch
Garage
21-5x24-0
43'-8"
64'-0"

Interesting Plan For Narrow Lot

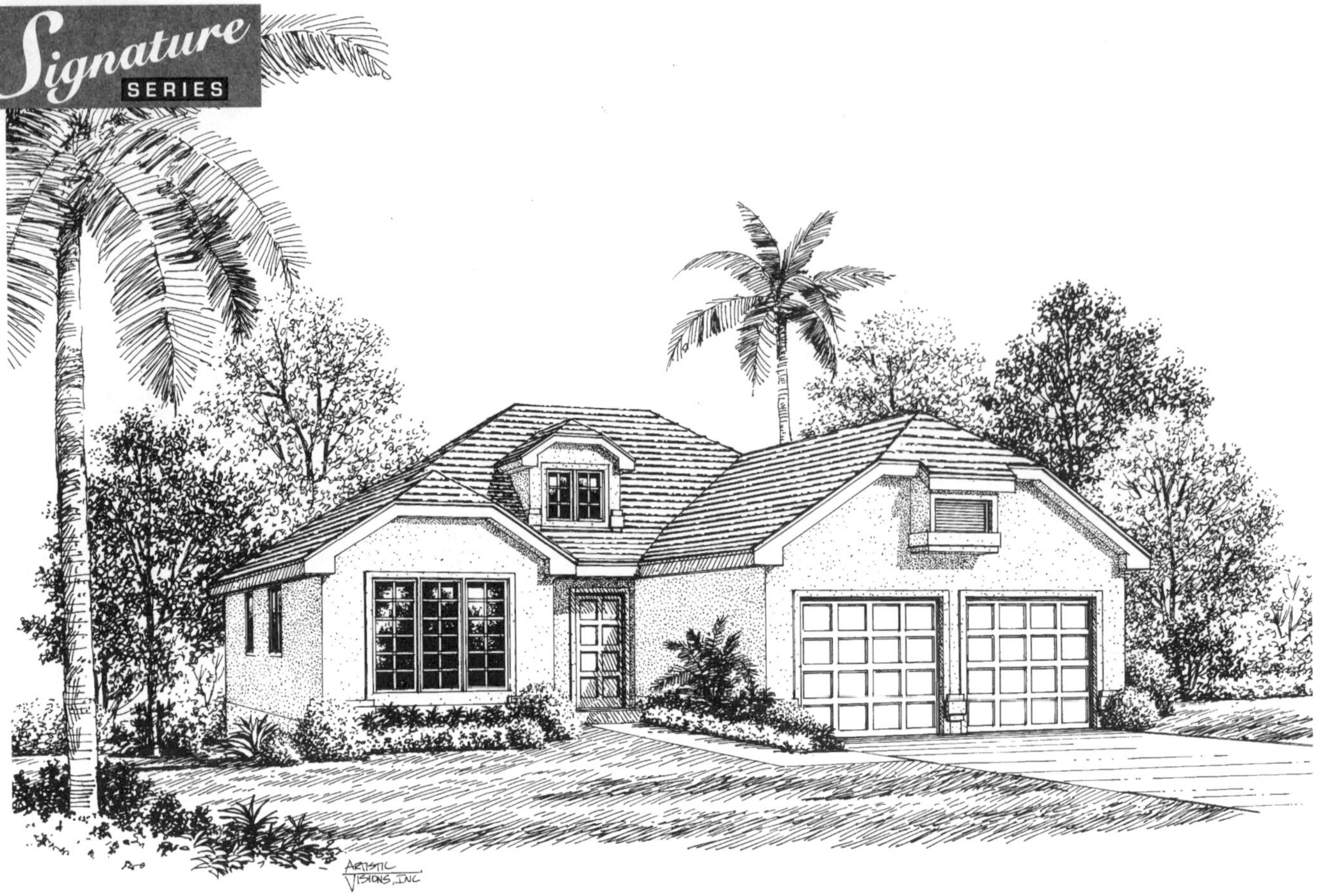

Plan #527-0659

Price Code B

Total Living Area: 1,516 Sq. Ft.

Home has 3 bedrooms, 2 baths, 2-car garage and basement foundation.

Special features

- Spacious great room is open to dining with a bay and unique stair location
- Attractive and well-planned kitchen offers breakfast bar and built-in pantry
- Smartly designed master suite enjoys patio views

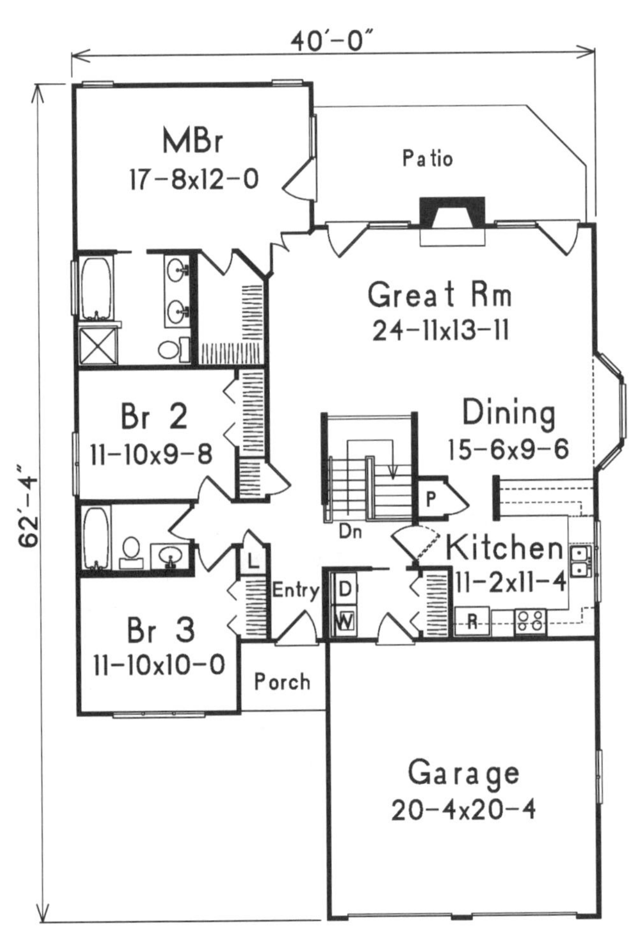
40'-0"
62'-4"
MBr
17-8x12-0
Patio
Great Rm
24-11x13-11
Dining
15-6x9-6
Br 2
11-10x9-8
Dn
P
Kitchen
11-2x11-4
L
Entry
D
W
R
Br 3
11-10x10-0
Porch
Garage
20-4x20-4

LOWE'S

Signature
SERIES

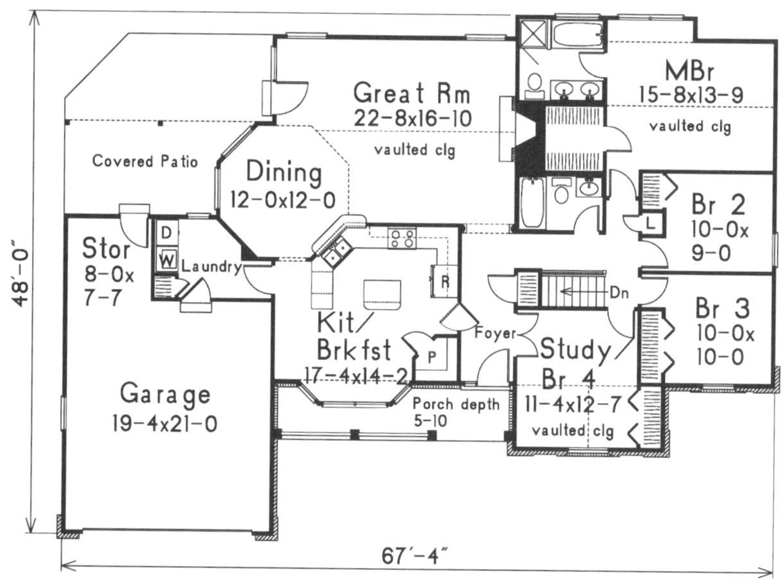
Great Rm
22-8x16-10
vaulted clg
MBr
15-8x13-9
vaulted clg
Covered Patio
Dining
12-0x12-0
Br 2
10-0x
9-0
Stor
8-0x
7-7
D
W
Laundry
R
Dn
Br 3
10-0x
10-0
Kit/
Brkfst
17-4x14-2
P
Foyer
Study/
Br 4
11-4x12-7
vaulted clg
Garage
19-4x21-0
Porch depth
5-10
48'-0"
67'-4"

Plan #527-0706

Price Code B

Total Living Area: 1,791 Sq. Ft.

Home has 4 bedrooms, 2 baths, 2-car garage and basement foundation.

Special features

- Vaulted great room and octagon-shaped dining area enjoy views of covered patio
- Kitchen features a pass-through to dining area, center island, large walk-in pantry and breakfast room with large bay window
- Master bedroom is vaulted with sitting area
- Extra storage in garage

LOWE'S

Signature SERIES

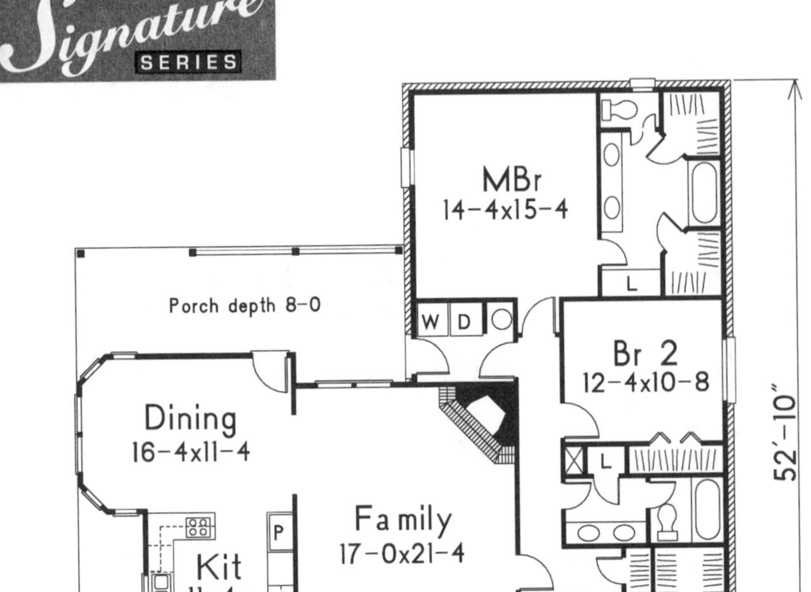
MBr
14-4x15-4
Porch depth 8-0
W
D
L
Br 2
12-4x10-8
Dining
16-4x11-4
L
Family
17-0x21-4
Kit
11-4x
12-4
P
R
Foyer
Br 3
11-4x13-8
Porch depth 5-0
52'-10"
51'-2"

Plan #527-0163

Price Code C

Total Living Area: 1,772 Sq. Ft.

Home has 3 bedrooms, 2 baths, 2-car detached garage and slab foundation, drawings also include crawl space foundation.

Special features

- Extended porches in front and rear provide a charming touch
- Large bay windows lend distinction to dining room and bedroom #3
- Efficient U-shaped kitchen
- Master bedroom includes two walk-in closets
- Full corner fireplace in family room

TO ORDER BLUEPRINTS USE THE FORM ON PAGE 290 OR CALL TOLL-FREE **1-800-DREAM HOME** (373-2646)

Stylish Living For A Narrow Lot

LOWE'S
Signature SERIES
36'-0"
46'-8"
Brk fst
10-0x11-0
Kit
9-0x11-7
Dining
12-0x11-0
Dn
R
D W
P
Living
15-7x14-4
Up
Garage
19-4x20-4
MBr
12-0x14-8
vaulted clg
Dn
Br 2
12-0x11-0
L
Br 3
12-0x11-3
vaulted clg
plant shelf

First Floor
802 sq. ft.

Second Floor
773 sq. ft.

Plan #527-0711

Price Code B

Total Living Area: 1,575 Sq. Ft.

Home has 3 bedrooms, 2 1/2 baths, 2-car garage and basement foundation.

Special features

- Inviting porch leads to spacious living and dining rooms
- Kitchen with corner windows features an island snack bar, attractive breakfast room bay, convenient laundry and built-in pantry
- A luxury bath and walk-in closet adorn master bedroom

Central Living Area Keeps Bedrooms Private

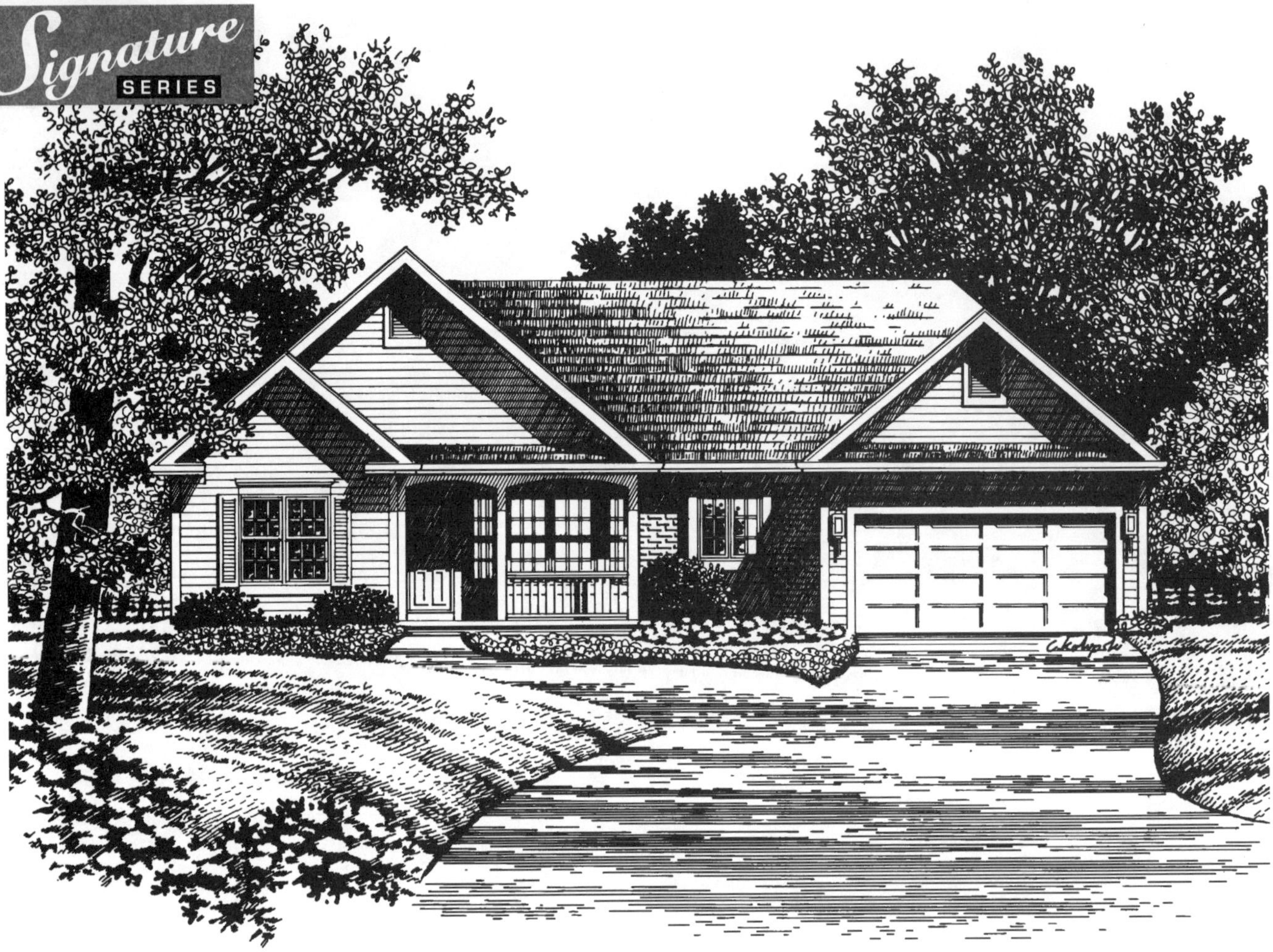

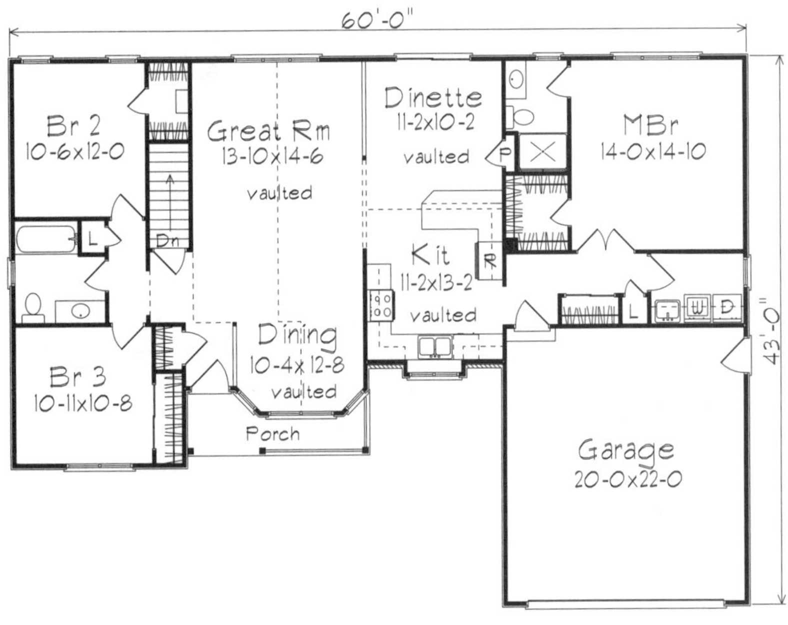
60'-0"
43'-0"
Br 2
10-6x12-0
Great Rm
13-10x14-6
vaulted
Dinette
11-2x10-2
vaulted
MBr
14-0x14-10
Kit
11-2x13-2
vaulted
Dn
Dining
10-4x12-8
vaulted
Br 3
10-11x10-8
Porch
Garage
20-0x22-0

Plan #527-0382

Price Code B

Total Living Area: 1,546 Sq. Ft.

Home has 3 bedrooms, 2 baths, 2-car garage and basement foundation.

Special features

- Spacious open rooms create casual atmosphere
- Master suite secluded for privacy
- Dining room features large bay window
- Kitchen/dinette combination offers access to the outdoors
- Large laundry room includes convenient sink

LOWE'S

Signature
SERIES

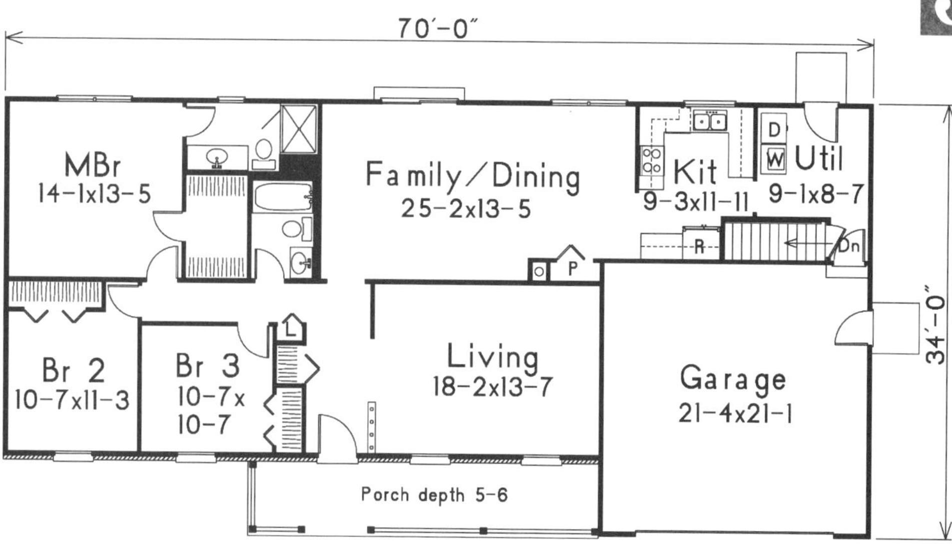
70'-0"
MBr
14-1x13-5
Family/Dining
25-2x13-5
Kit
9-3x11-11
Util
9-1x8-7
D
W
R
Dn
P
Br 2
10-7x11-3
Br 3
10-7x
10-7
L
Living
18-2x13-7
Garage
21-4x21-1
Porch depth 5-6
34'-0"

Plan #527-1101

Price Code B

Total Living Area: 1,643 Sq. Ft.

Home has 3 bedrooms, 2 baths, 2-car garage and basement foundation, drawings also include crawl space and slab foundations.

Special features

- Master suite has view to the rear of the home and a generous walk-in closet
- Formal living room provides area for quiet and privacy
- Kitchen and utility room are conveniently located near gathering areas
- Spacious family room is the focal point of this design
- Attractive front entry porch gives this ranch a country accent

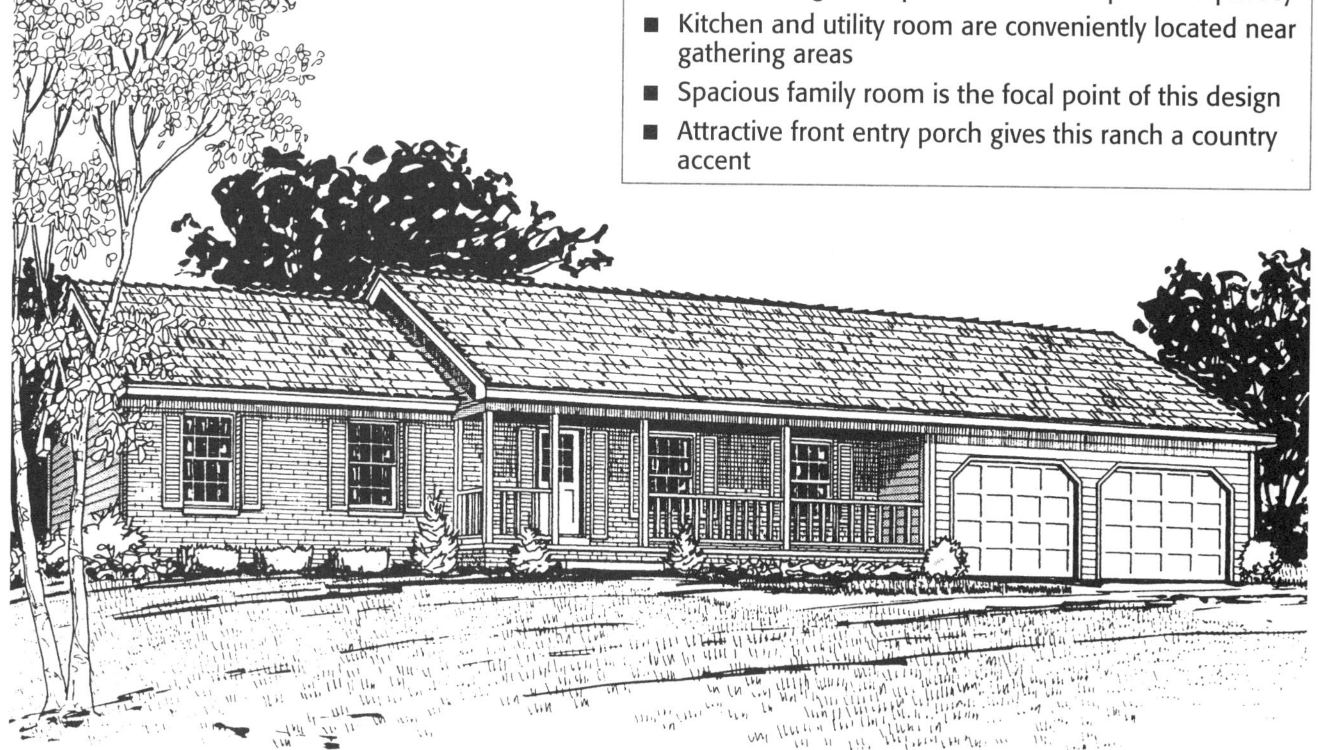

Victorian-Style Home Features Double Bays

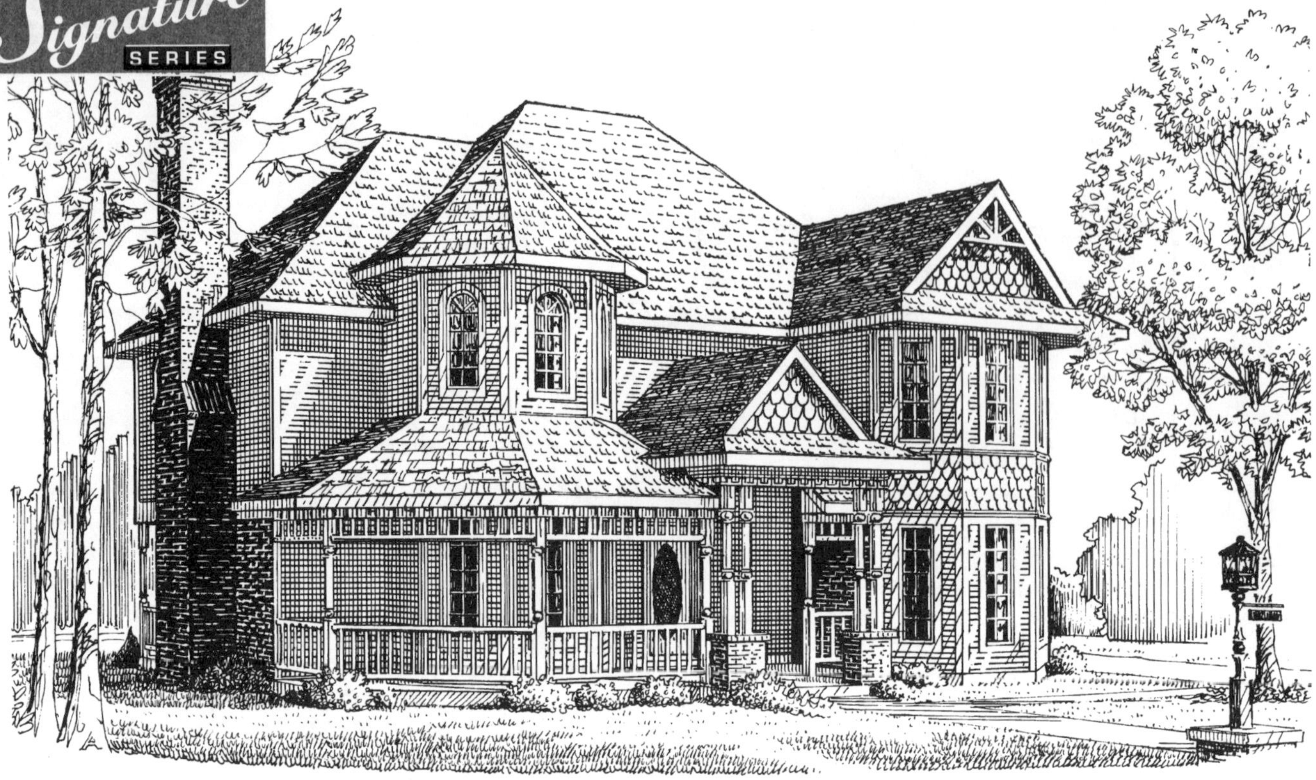

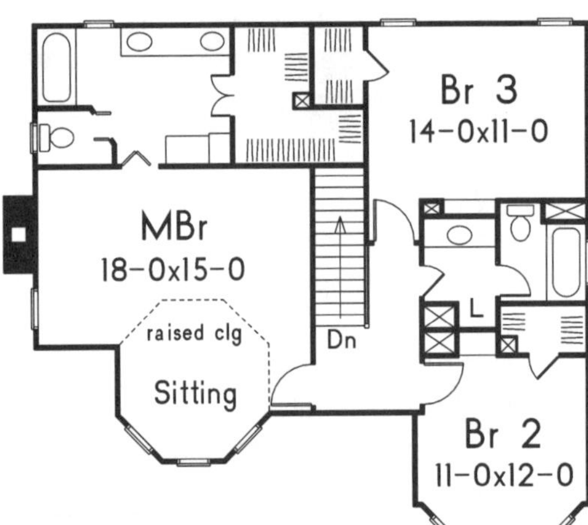
Br 3
14-0x11-0
MBr
18-0x15-0
raised clg
Sitting
Dn
L
Br 2
11-0x12-0

Second Floor
1,069 sq. ft.

First Floor
997 sq. ft.

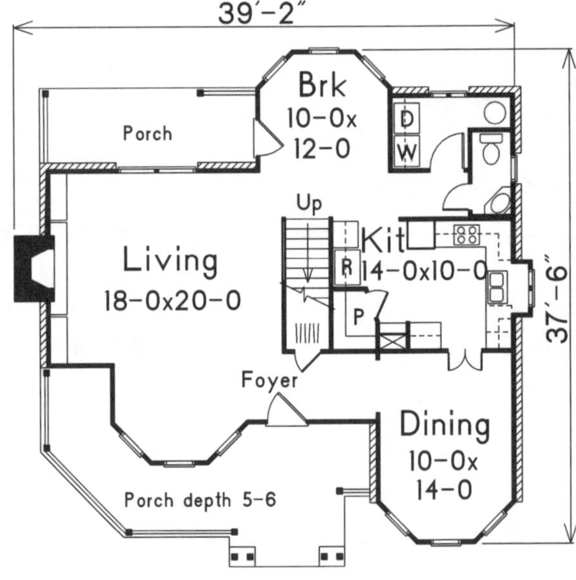
39'-2"
37'-6"
Porch
Brk
10-0x
12-0
D
W
Up
Kit
14-0x10-0
R
P
Living
18-0x20-0
Foyer
Dining
10-0x
14-0
Porch depth 5-6

Plan #527-0234

Price Code C

Total Living Area: 2,066 Sq. Ft.

Home has 3 bedrooms, 2 1/2 baths and slab foundation.

Special features

- Large master bedroom includes sitting area and private bath
- Open living room features a fireplace with built-in bookshelves
- Spacious kitchen accesses formal dining area and breakfast room

Home For Narrow Lot Offers Wide Open Spaces

LOWE'S

Signature
SERIES

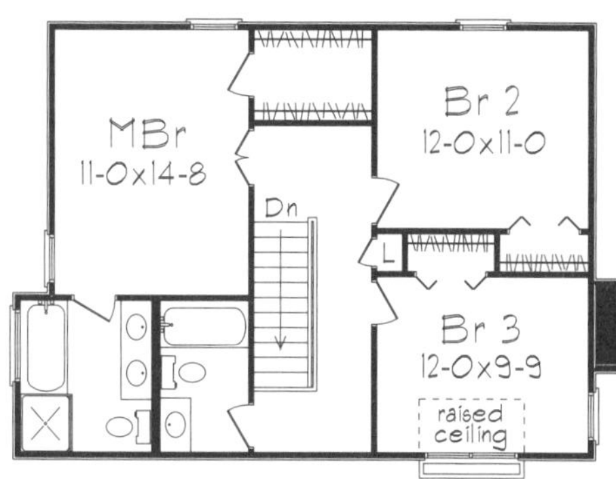
MBr
11-0x14-8
Br 2
12-0x11-0
Dn
L
Br 3
12-0x9-9
raised ceiling

Second Floor
732 sq. ft.

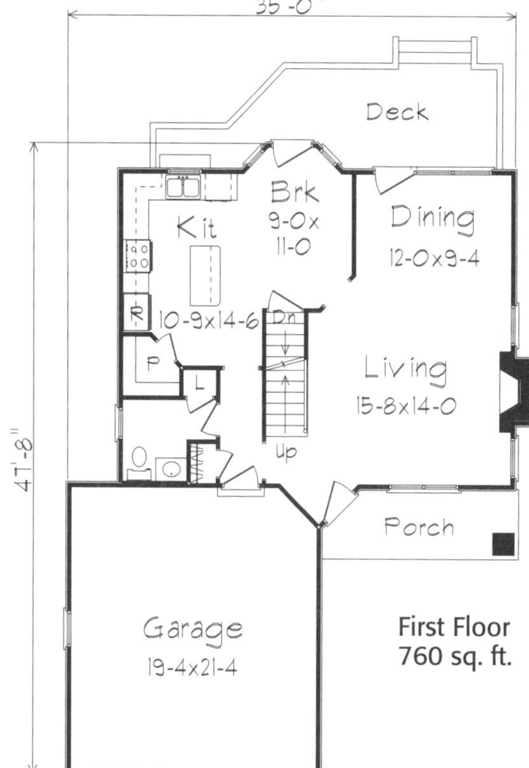
35'-0"
47'-8"
Deck
Brk
9-0x
11-0
Kit
10-9x14-6
Dining
12-0x9-4
Dn
R
P
L
Living
15-8x14-0
Up
Porch
Garage
19-4x21-4

First Floor
760 sq. ft.

Plan #527-0415

Price Code A

Total Living Area: 1,492 Sq. Ft.

Home has 3 bedrooms, 2 1/2 baths, 2-car garage and basement foundation.

Special features

- Cleverly angled entry spills into living and dining rooms which share warmth of fireplace flanked by arched windows
- Master suite includes double-door entry, huge walk-in closet, shower and bath with picture window
- Stucco and dutch hipped roofs add warmth and charm to facade

J.N. HANSEN S.D.G.

TO ORDER BLUEPRINTS USE THE FORM ON PAGE 290 OR CALL TOLL-FREE **1-800-DREAM HOME** (373-2646)

Signature SERIES

Spacious Vaulted Great Room

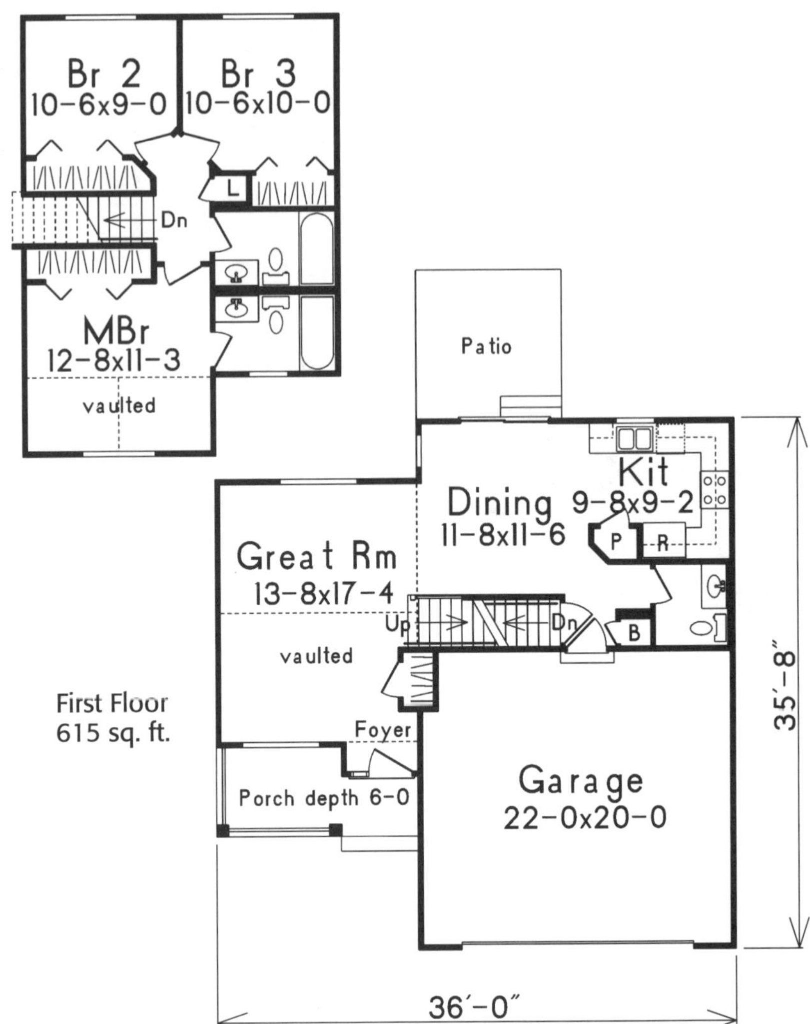
Br 2
10-6x9-0
Br 3
10-6x10-0
L
Dn
MBr
12-8x11-3
vaulted
Second Floor
574 sq. ft.
Patio
Kit
9-8x9-2
Dining
11-8x11-6
P
R
Great Rm
13-8x17-4
Up
Dn
B
vaulted
Foyer
First Floor
615 sq. ft.
Porch depth 6-0
Garage
22-0x20-0
35′-8″
36′-0″

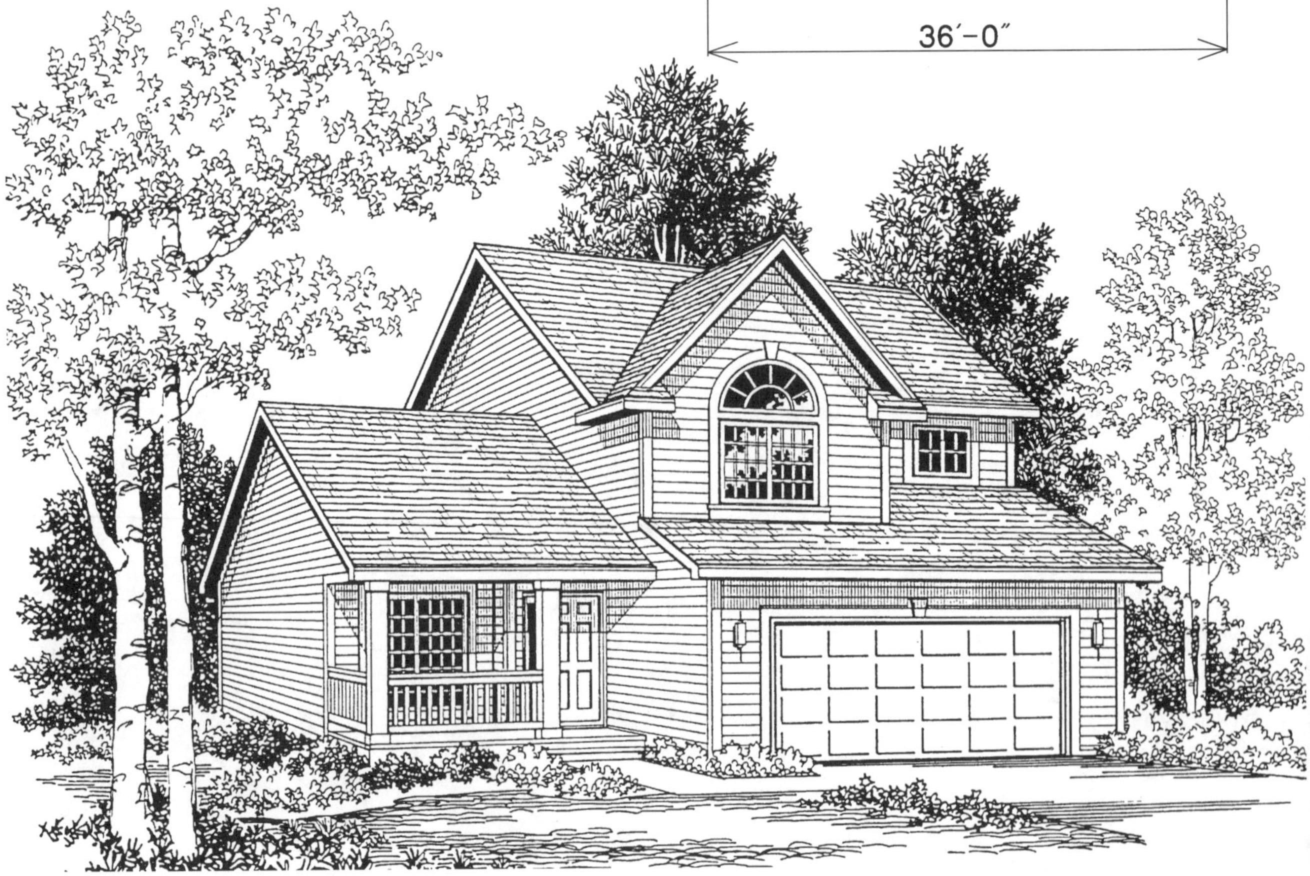

Plan #527-0487

Price Code AA

Total Living Area: 1,189 Sq. Ft.

Home has 3 bedrooms, 2 1/2 baths, 2-car garage and basement foundation.

Special features

- All bedrooms are located on the second floor
- Dining room and kitchen both have views of the patio
- Convenient half bath located near the kitchen
- Master bedroom has private bath

LOWE'S

Signature
SERIES

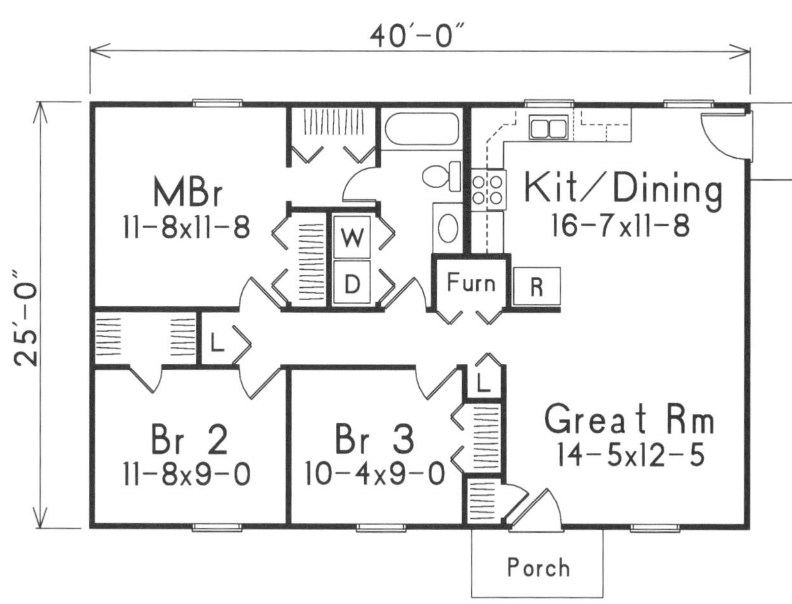
40'-0"
25'-0"
MBr
11-8x11-8
W
D
Kit/Dining
16-7x11-8
Furn
R
L
L
Br 2
11-8x9-0
Br 3
10-4x9-0
Great Rm
14-5x12-5
Porch

Plan #527-0503

Price Code AA

Total Living Area: 1,000 Sq. Ft.

Home has 3 bedrooms, 1 bath and crawl space foundation, drawings also include basement and slab foundations.

Special features

- Bath includes convenient closeted laundry area
- Master bedroom includes double closets and private access to bath
- Foyer features handy coat closet
- L-shaped kitchen provides easy access outdoors

LOWE'S

Signature
SERIES

Functional Layout For Comfortable Living

Plan #527-0217

Price Code A

Total Living Area: 1,360 Sq. Ft.

Home has 3 bedrooms, 2 baths, 2-car side entry garage and basement foundation, drawings also include crawl space and slab foundations.

Special features

- Kitchen/dining room features island work space and plenty of dining area
- Master bedroom with large walk-in closet and private bath
- Laundry room adjacent to the kitchen for easy access
- Convenient workshop in garage
- Large closets in secondary bedrooms

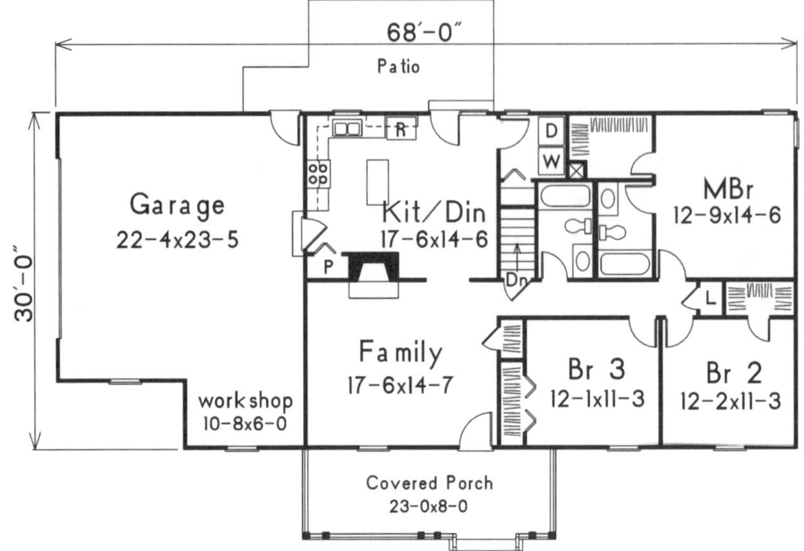
68'-0"
Patio
30'-0"
Garage
22-4x23-5
R
Kit/Din
17-6x14-6
P
Dn
D
W
MBr
12-9x14-6
L
Family
17-6x14-7
Br 3
12-1x11-3
Br 2
12-2x11-3
workshop
10-8x6-0
Covered Porch
23-0x8-0

L-Shaped Ranch With Many Amenities

LOWE'S

Signature
SERIES

Plan #527-0533

Price Code A

Total Living Area: 1,440 Sq. Ft.

Home has 3 bedrooms, 2 baths, 2-car side entry garage and crawl space foundation, drawings also include basement and slab foundations.

Special features

- Vaulted ceiling creates an impressive dining/living area
- Entry foyer features coat closet and half wall leading into living area
- Walk-in pantry adds convenience to U-shaped kitchen
- Spacious utility room adjacent to garage

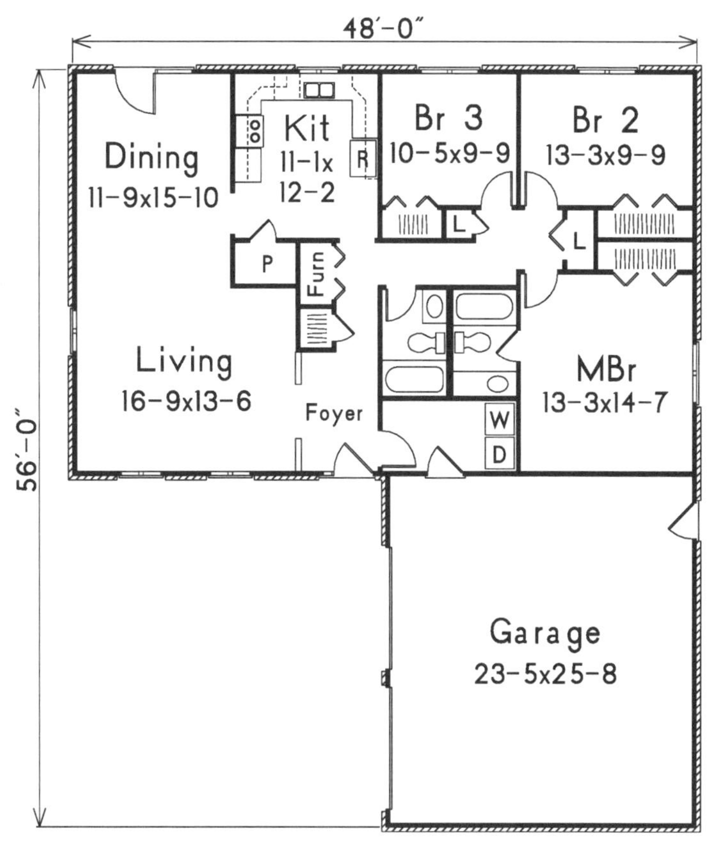
48'-0"
56'-0"
Dining
11-9x15-10
Kit
11-1x
12-2
R
P
Furn
Br 3
10-5x9-9
L
Br 2
13-3x9-9
L
Living
16-9x13-6
Foyer
W
D
MBr
13-3x14-7
Garage
23-5x25-8

LOWE'S

Four Bedroom Living For A Narrow Lot

Signature
SERIES

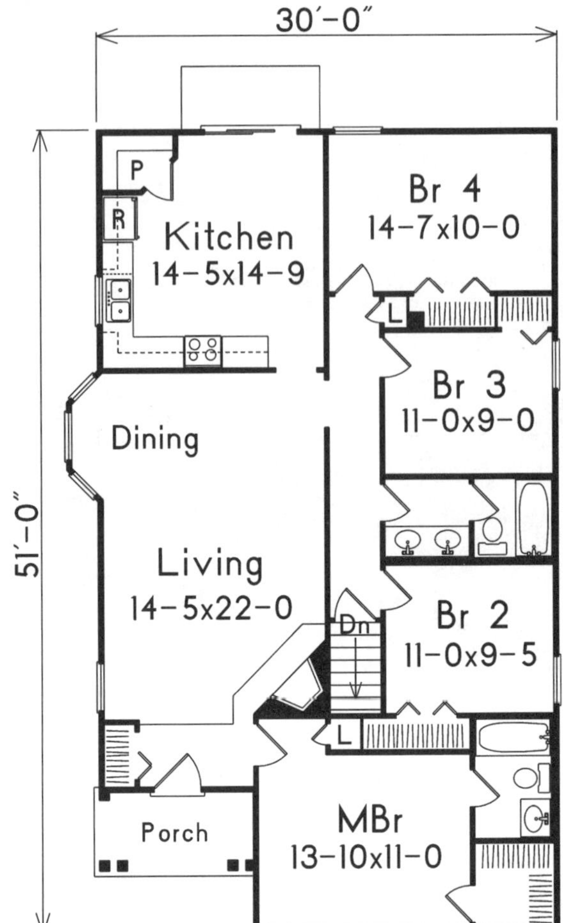
30'-0"
51'-0"
P
R
Kitchen
14-5x14-9
Br 4
14-7x10-0
L
Br 3
11-0x9-0
Dining
Living
14-5x22-0
Dn
Br 2
11-0x9-5
L
Porch
MBr
13-10x11-0

Plan #527-0806

Price Code A

Total Living Area: 1,452 Sq. Ft.

Home has 4 bedrooms, 2 baths, and basement foundation.

Special features

- Large living room features cozy corner fireplace, bayed dining area and access from entry with guest closet
- Forward master bedroom suite enjoys having its own bath and linen closet
- Three additional bedrooms share a bath with double-bowl vanity

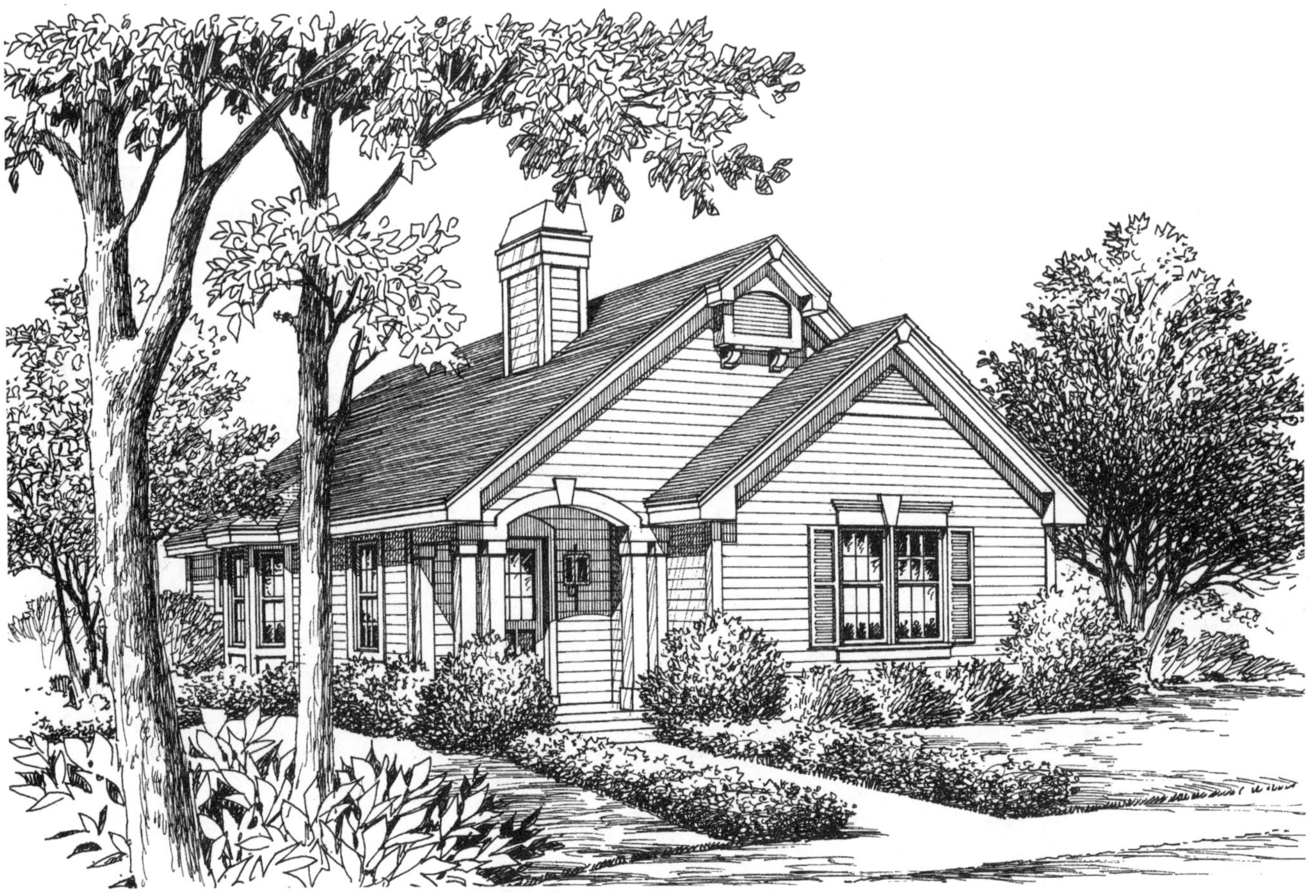

Spacious Dining And Living Areas

LOWE'S

Signature
SERIES

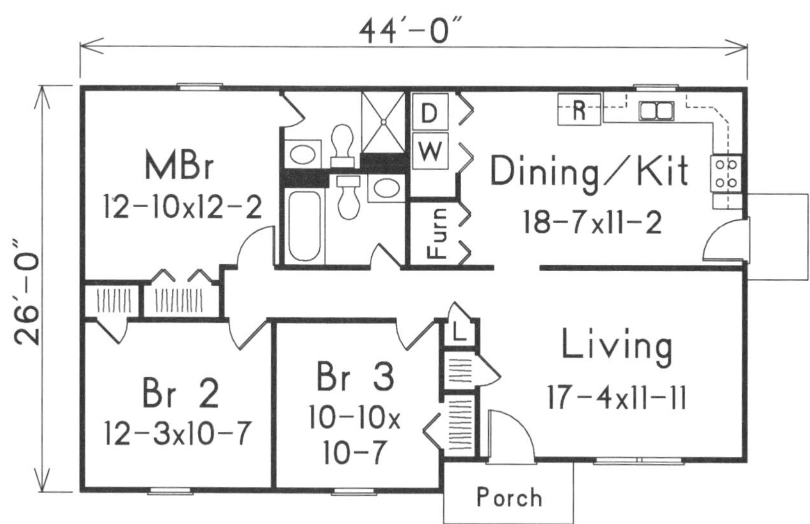
44'-0"
26'-0"
MBr
12-10x12-2
D
W
R
Dining/Kit
18-7x11-2
Furn
Living
17-4x11-11
Br 2
12-3x10-7
Br 3
10-10x
10-7
L
Porch

Plan #527-0505

Price Code AA

Total Living Area: 1,104 Sq. Ft.

Home has 3 bedrooms, 2 baths and crawl space foundation, drawings also include basement and slab foundations.

Special features

- Master bedroom includes private bath
- Convenient side entrance to kitchen/dining area
- Laundry area located near kitchen
- Large living area creates comfortable atmosphere

LOWE'S

Classic Ranch Has Grand Appeal

Plan #527-0690

Price Code A

Total Living Area: 1,400 Sq. Ft.

Home has 3 bedrooms, 2 baths, 2-car garage and basement foundation, drawings also include crawl space foundation.

Special features

- Master bedroom is secluded for privacy
- Large utility room with additional cabinet space
- Covered porch provides an outdoor seating area
- Roof dormers add great curb appeal
- Vaulted ceilings in living room and master bedroom
- Oversized two-car garage with storage

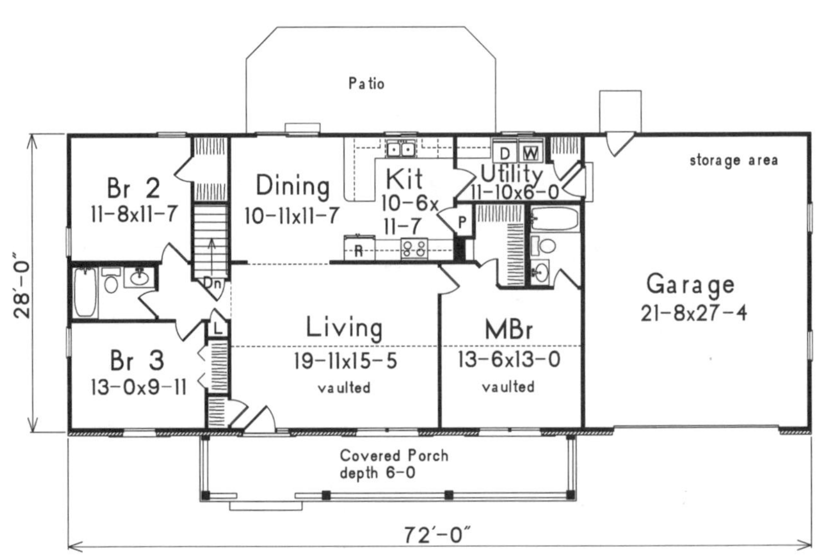
Patio
Br 2
11-8x11-7
Dining
10-11x11-7
Kit
10-6x
11-7
Utility
11-10x6-0
storage area
Garage
21-8x27-4
Living
19-11x15-5
vaulted
MBr
13-6x13-0
vaulted
Br 3
13-0x9-11
Covered Porch
depth 6-0
28'-0"
72'-0"

Country Charm For A Small Lot

LOWE'S

Signature
SERIES

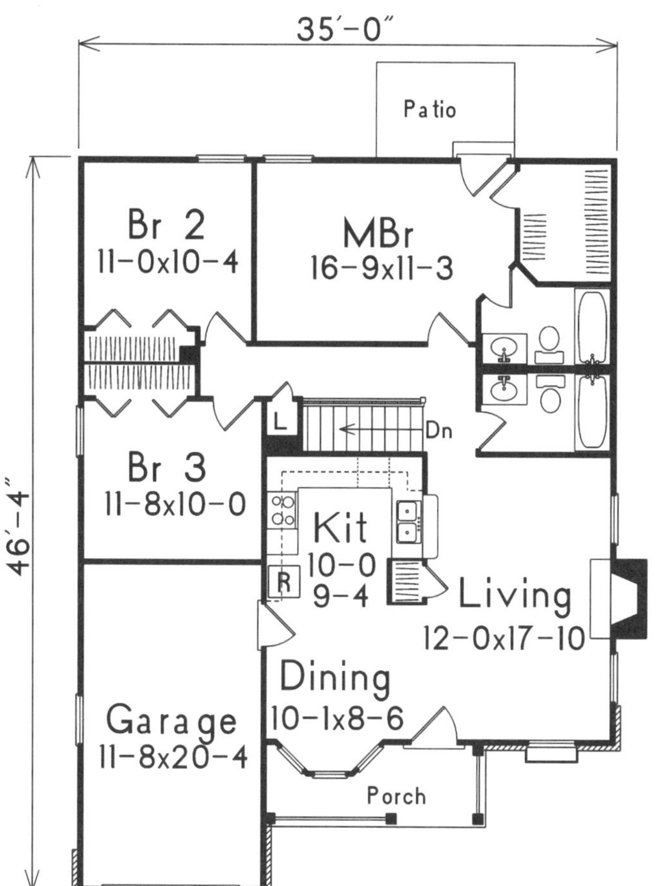
35'-0"
46'-4"
Patio
Br 2
11-0x10-4
MBr
16-9x11-3
L
Dn
Br 3
11-8x10-0
Kit
10-0
9-4
R
Living
12-0x17-10
Dining
10-1x8-6
Garage
11-8x20-4
Porch

Plan #527-0814

Price Code AA

Total Living Area: 1,169 Sq. Ft.

Home has 3 bedrooms, 2 baths, 1-car garage and basement foundation.

Special features

- Front facade features a distinctive country appeal
- Living room enjoys a wood-burning fireplace and pass-through to kitchen
- A stylish U-shaped kitchen offers an abundance of cabinet and counterspace with view to living room
- A large walk-in closet, access to rear patio and private bath are many features of the master bedroom

LOWE'S

Prestige Abounds In A Classic Ranch

J.N. HANSEN S.D.G.

Plan #527-0707

Price Code E

Total Living Area: 2,723 Sq. Ft.

Home has 3 bedrooms, 2 1/2 baths, 3-car side entry garage and basement foundation.

Special features

- Large porch invites you into an elegant foyer which accesses a vaulted study with private hall and coat closet
- Great room is second to none, comprised of fireplace, built-in shelves, vaulted ceiling and a 1 1/2 story window wall
- A spectacular hearth room with vaulted ceiling and masonry fireplace opens to an elaborate kitchen featuring two snack bars, cooking island and walk-in pantry

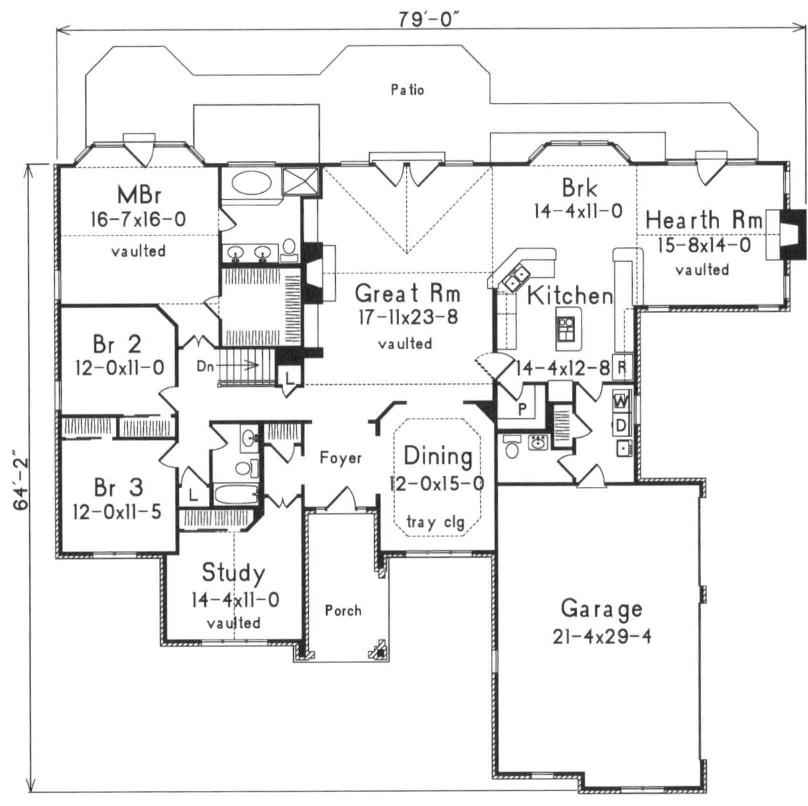
79'-0"
64'-2"
Patio
MBr
16-7x16-0
vaulted
Brk
14-4x11-0
Hearth Rm
15-8x14-0
vaulted
Great Rm
17-11x23-8
vaulted
Kitchen
14-4x12-8
R
Br 2
12-0x11-0
Dn
L
P
W
D
Br 3
12-0x11-5
L
Foyer
Dining
12-0x15-0
tray clg
Study
14-4x11-0
vaulted
Porch
Garage
21-4x29-4

TO ORDER BLUEPRINTS USE THE FORM ON PAGE 290 OR CALL TOLL-FREE **1-800-DREAM HOME** (373-2646)

Sculptured Roof Line And Facade Add Charm

LOWE'S

Signature SERIES

Plan #527-0227

Price Code B

Total Living Area: 1,674 Sq. Ft.

Home has 3 bedrooms, 2 baths, 2-car garage and basement foundation, drawings also include crawl space and slab foundations.

Special features

- Great room, dining area and kitchen, surrounded with vaulted ceiling, central fireplace and log bin
- Convenient laundry/mud room located between garage and family area with handy stairs to basement
- Easily expandable screened porch and adjacent patio with access from dining area
- Master bedroom features full bath with tub, separate shower and walk-in closet

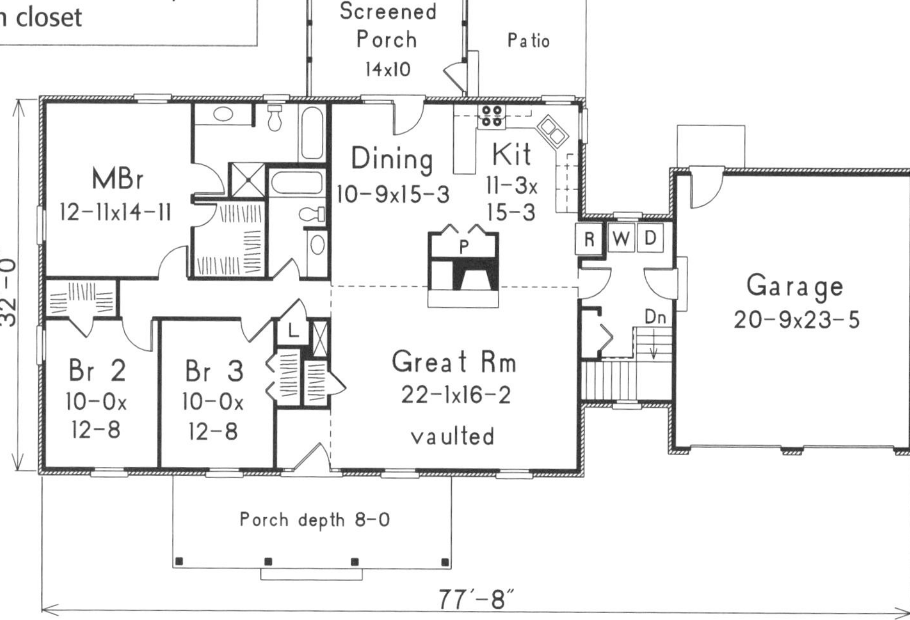
Screened Porch 14x10
Patio
MBr 12-11x14-11
Dining 10-9x15-3
Kit 11-3x 15-3
P
R W D
Garage 20-9x23-5
Dn
L
Br 2 10-0x 12-8
Br 3 10-0x 12-8
Great Rm 22-1x16-2 vaulted
32'-0"
Porch depth 8-0
77'-8"

Distinctive Turret Surrounds The Dining Bay

Plan #527-0410

Price Code B

Total Living Area: 1,742 Sq. Ft.

Home has 3 bedrooms, 2 baths, 2-car garage and slab foundation, drawings also include crawl space foundation.

Special features

- Efficient kitchen combines with breakfast area and great room creating spacious living area
- Master bedroom includes private bath with huge walk-in closet, shower and corner tub
- Great room boasts a fireplace and outdoor access
- Laundry room conveniently located near kitchen and garage

77'-2"
40'-0"
Brk
10-6x8-6
Great Rm
17-0x13-6
MBr
15-6x12-6
Garage
22-0x20-0
Kit
10-6x
16-6
Dining
10-6x13-0
Br 3
11-6x11-6
raised ceiling
Br 2
12-6x13-0

LOWE'S

Signature
SERIES

Plan #527-0682

Price Code C

Total Living Area: 1,941 Sq. Ft.

Home has 3 bedrooms, 2 1/2 baths, 2-car garage and crawl space foundation.

Special features

- Kitchen incorporates a cooktop island, a handy pantry, and adjoins the dining and family rooms
- Formal living room, to the left of the foyer, lends a touch of privacy
- Raised ceiling in foyer, kitchen, living and dining areas
- Laundry room, half bath and closet all located near the garage
- Both the dining and family rooms have access outdoors through sliding doors

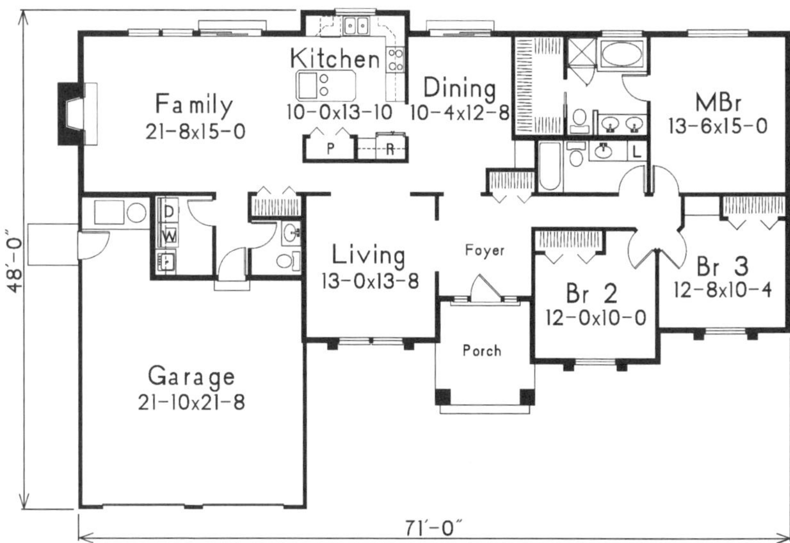
Kitchen
10-0x13-10
Family
21-8x15-0
Dining
10-4x12-8
MBr
13-6x15-0
P
R
D
W
Living
13-0x13-8
Foyer
Br 2
12-0x10-0
Br 3
12-8x10-4
Porch
Garage
21-10x21-8
48'-0"
71'-0"

LOWE'S

Roomy Two-Story Has Screened-In Rear Porch

Signature SERIES

Plan #527-0291

Price Code B

Total Living Area: 1,600 Sq. Ft.

Home has 3 bedrooms, 2 baths, 2-car side entry garage and crawl space foundation, drawings also include slab foundation.

Special features

- Energy efficient home with 2" x 6" exterior walls
- First floor master suite accessible from two points of entry
- Master suite dressing area includes separate vanities and mirrored make-up counter
- Second floor bedrooms with generous storage share a full bath

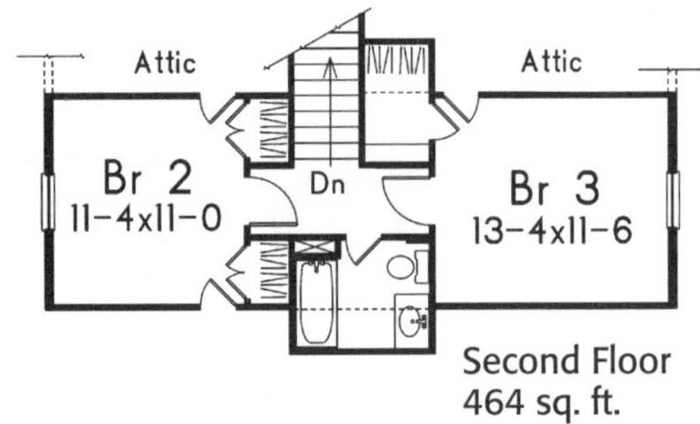
Attic
Attic
Br 2
11-4x11-0
Dn
Br 3
13-4x11-6

Second Floor
464 sq. ft.

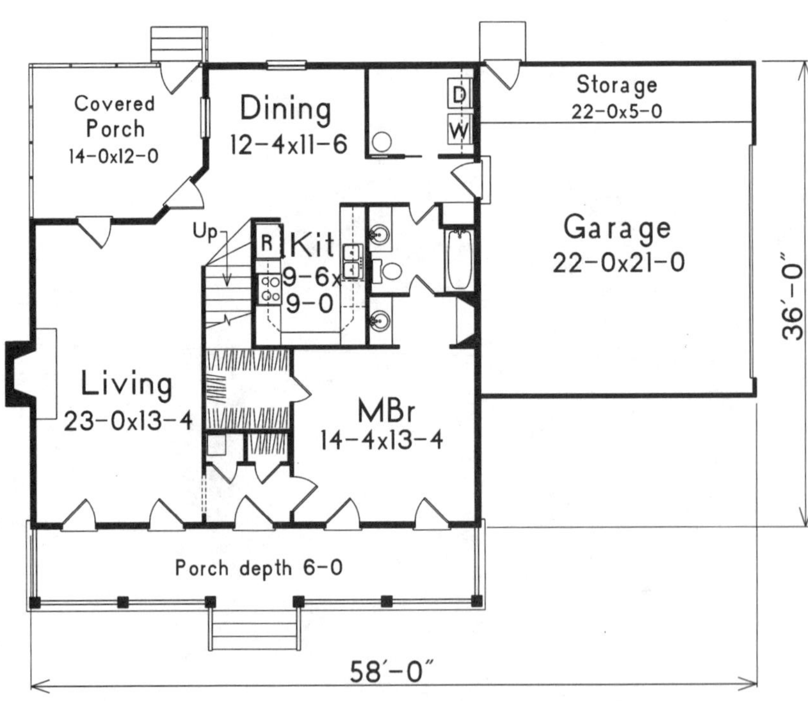
Covered Porch
14-0x12-0
Dining
12-4x11-6
D
W
Storage
22-0x5-0
Up
R
Kit
9-6x
9-0
Garage
22-0x21-0
36'-0"
Living
23-0x13-4
MBr
14-4x13-4
Porch depth 6-0
58'-0"

First Floor
1,136 sq. ft.

TO ORDER BLUEPRINTS USE THE FORM ON PAGE 290 OR CALL TOLL-FREE **1-800-DREAM HOME** (373-2646)

Old-Fashioned Porch Gives Welcoming Appeal

LOWE'S

Signature
SERIES

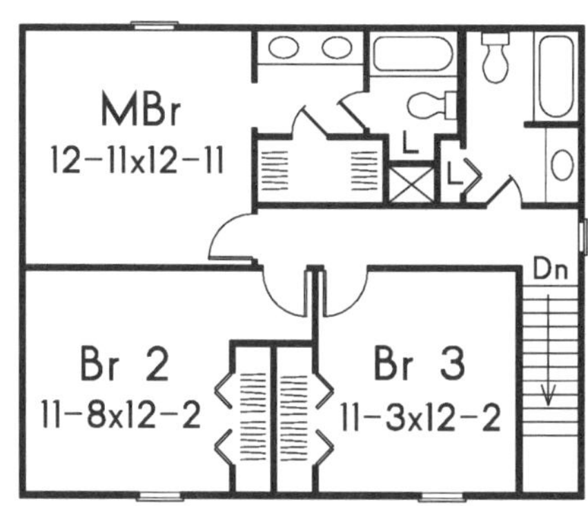
MBr
12-11x12-11
L
L
Dn
Br 2
11-8x12-2
Br 3
11-3x12-2

Second Floor
832 sq. ft.

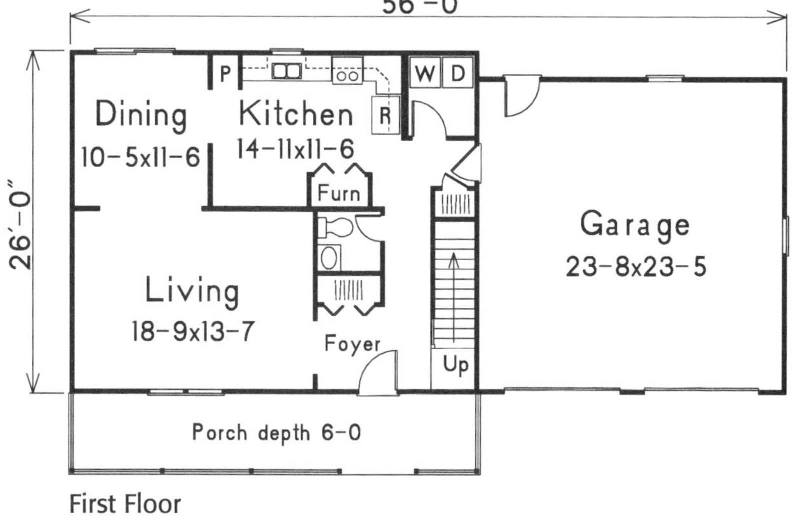
56'-0"
26'-0"
P
W D
Dining
10-5x11-6
Kitchen
14-11x11-6
R
Furn
Garage
23-8x23-5
Living
18-9x13-7
Foyer
Up
Porch depth 6-0

First Floor
832 sq. ft.

Plan #527-0536

Price Code B

Total Living Area: 1,664 Sq. Ft.

Home has 3 bedrooms, 2 1/2 baths, 2-car garage and crawl space foundation, drawings also include basement and slab foundations.

Special features

- L-shaped country kitchen includes pantry and cozy breakfast area
- Bedrooms located on second floor for privacy
- Master bedroom includes walk-in closet, dressing area and bath

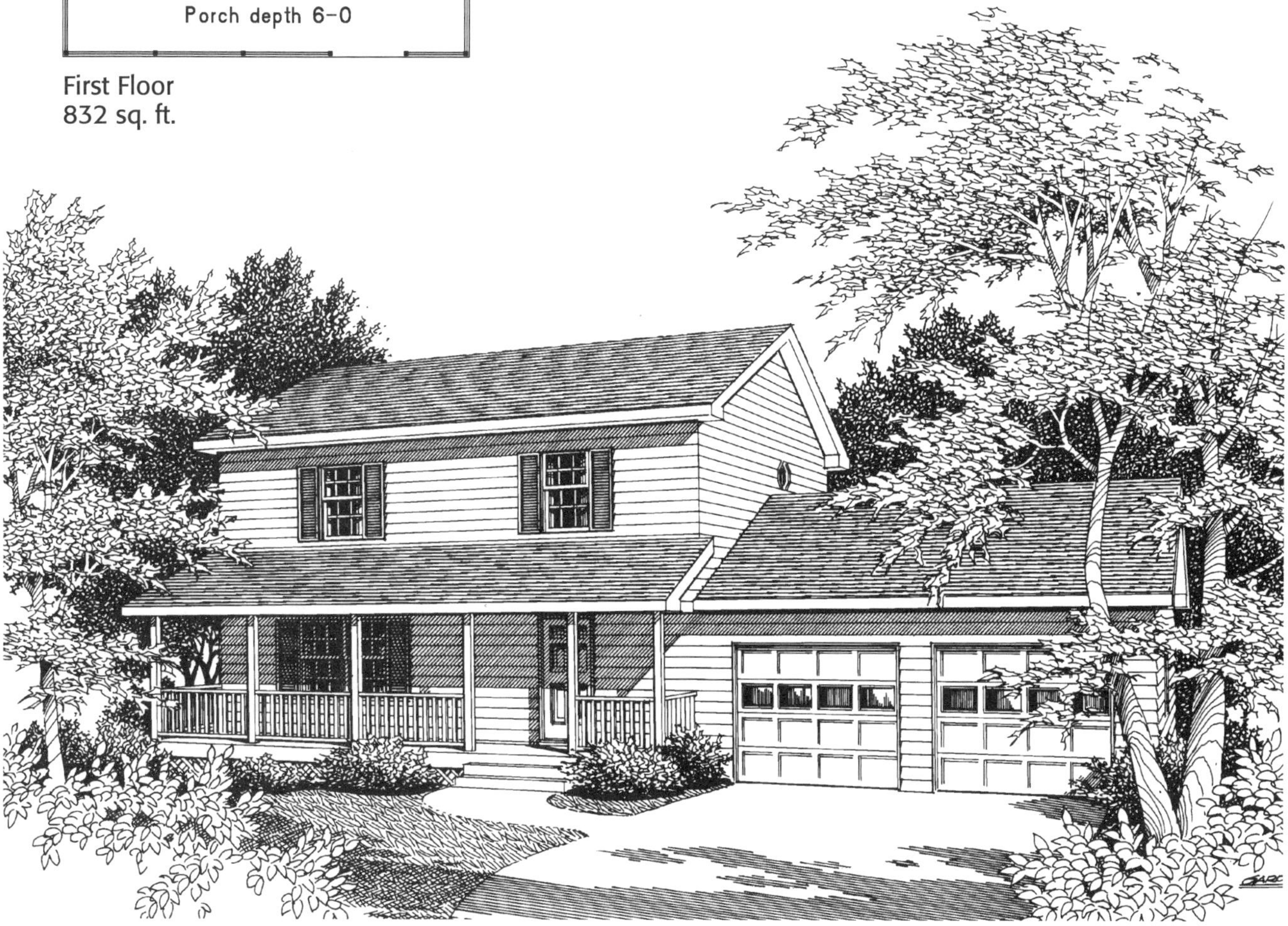

Open Living Centers On Windowed Dining Room

Plan #527-0348

Price Code D

Total Living Area: 2,003 Sq. Ft.

Home has 3 bedrooms, 2 baths, 2-car garage and basement foundation.

Special features

- Octagon-shaped dining room with tray ceiling and deck overlook
- L-shaped island kitchen serves living and dining rooms
- Master bedroom boasts luxury bath and walk-in closet
- Living room features columns, elegant fireplace and 10' ceiling

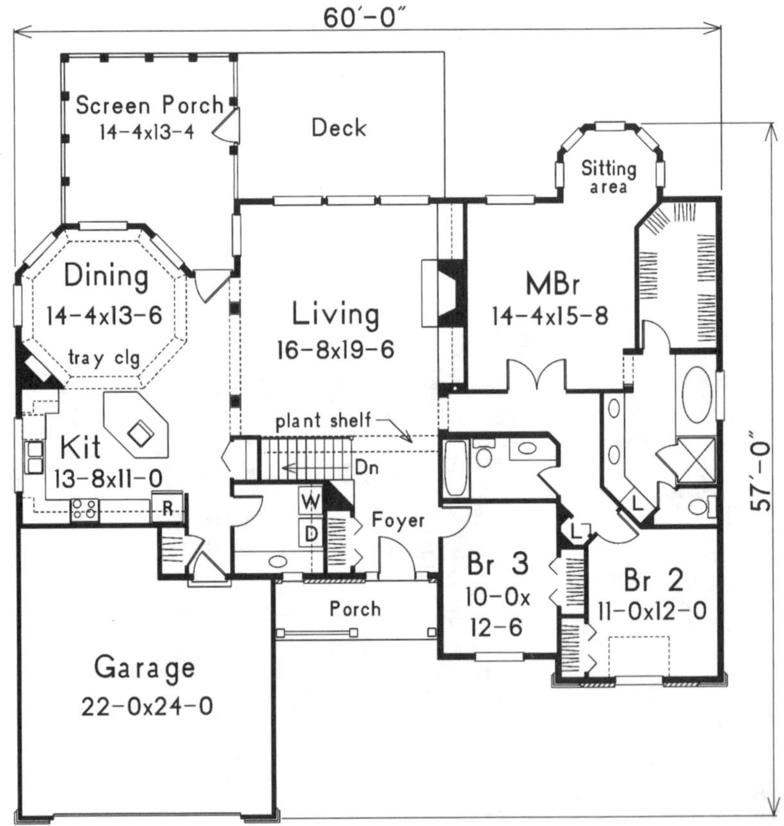
60'-0"
Screen Porch
14-4x13-4
Deck
Sitting area
Dining
14-4x13-6
tray clg
Living
16-8x19-6
MBr
14-4x15-8
plant shelf
Kit
13-8x11-0
R
Dn
W
D
Foyer
Br 3
10-0x
12-6
Br 2
11-0x12-0
Porch
Garage
22-0x24-0
57'-0"

Country-Style With Spacious Rooms

LOWE'S

Signature
SERIES

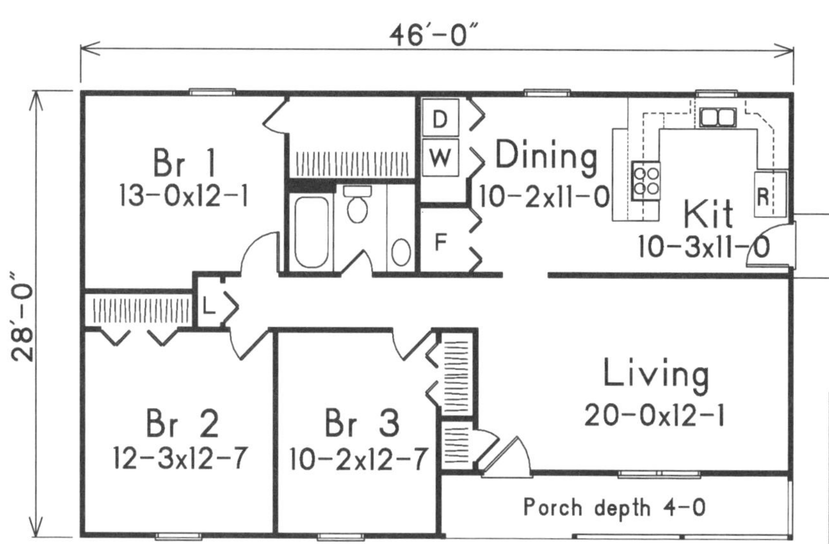
46'-0"
28'-0"
Br 1
13-0x12-1
D
W
Dining
10-2x11-0
R
Kit
10-3x11-0
F
L
Living
20-0x12-1
Br 2
12-3x12-7
Br 3
10-2x12-7
Porch depth 4-0

Plan #527-0507

Price Code AA

Total Living Area: 1,197 Sq. Ft.

Home has 3 bedrooms, 1 bath and crawl space foundation, drawings also include basement and slab foundations.

Special features

- U-shaped kitchen includes ample work space, breakfast bar, laundry area and direct access to the outdoors
- Large living room with convenient coat closet
- Master bedroom features large walk-in closet

LOWE'S

Signature SERIES

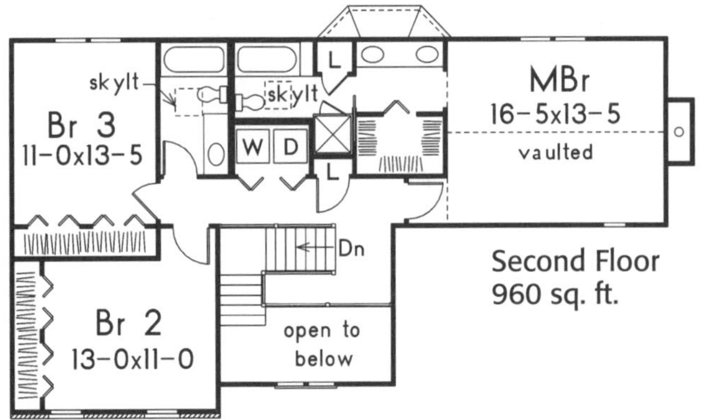
skylt
Br 3
11-0x13-5
W D
L
skylt
MBr
16-5x13-5
vaulted
L
Dn
Br 2
13-0x11-0
open to below
Second Floor
960 sq. ft.

Plan #527-0171

Price Code C

Total Living Area: 2,058 Sq. Ft.

Home has 3 bedrooms, 2 1/2 baths, 2-car garage and basement foundation, drawings also include slab and crawl space foundations.

Special features

- Handsome two-story foyer with balcony creates a spacious entrance area
- Vaulted ceiling in the master bedroom with private dressing area and large walk-in closet
- Skylights furnish natural lighting in the hall and master bathroom
- Conveniently located second floor laundry near bedrooms

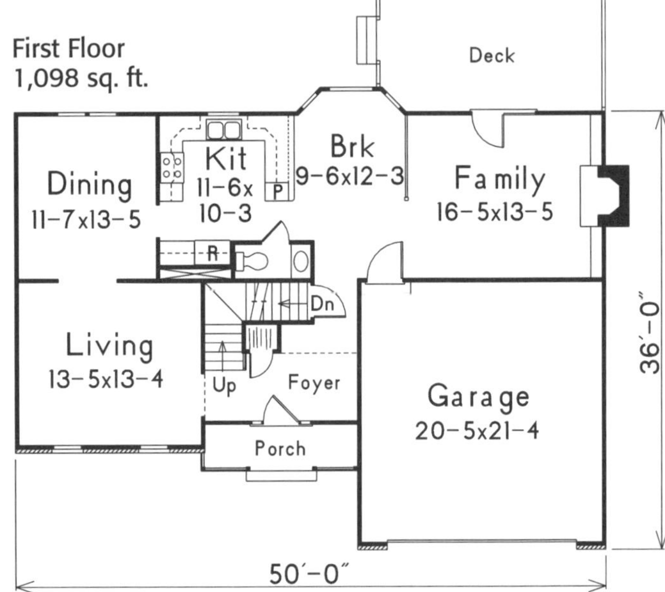
First Floor
1,098 sq. ft.
Deck
Dining
11-7x13-5
Kit
11-6x
10-3
P
Brk
9-6x12-3
Family
16-5x13-5
R
Dn
Living
13-5x13-4
Up
Foyer
Garage
20-5x21-4
Porch
36'-0"
50'-0"

TO ORDER BLUEPRINTS USE THE FORM ON PAGE 290 OR CALL TOLL-FREE **1-800-DREAM HOME** (373-2646)

Layout Creates Large Open Living Area

LOWE'S

Signature SERIES

Plan #527-0529

Price Code B

Total Living Area: 1,285 Sq. Ft.

Home has 3 bedrooms, 2 baths and crawl space foundation, drawings also include basement and slab foundations.

Special features

- Accommodating home with ranch-style porch
- Large storage area on back of home
- Master bedroom includes dressing area, private bath and built-in bookcase
- Kitchen features pantry, breakfast bar and complete view to dining room

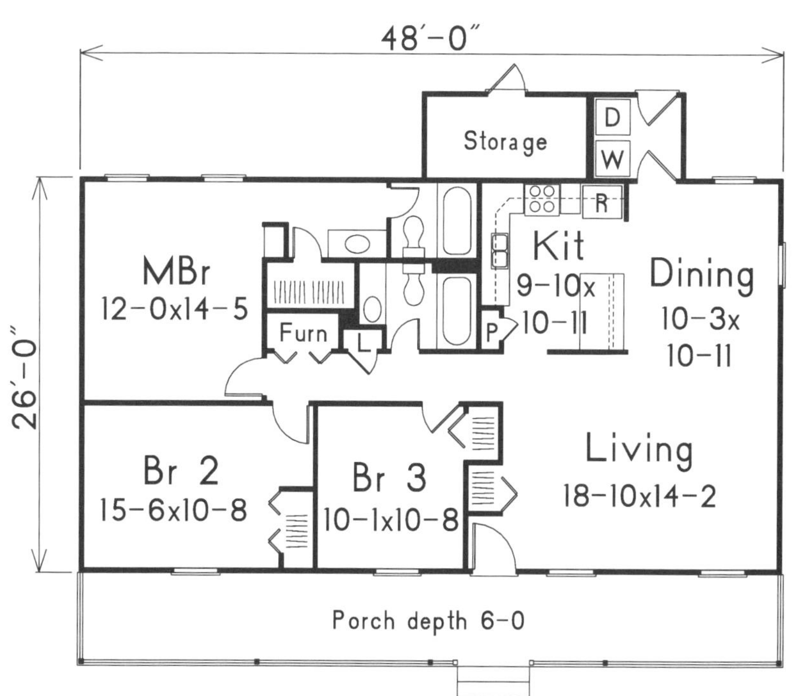
48′–0″
26′–0″
Storage
D
W
R
MBr
12–0x14–5
Kit
9–10x
10–11
Dining
10–3x
10–11
Furn
L
P
Br 2
15–6x10–8
Br 3
10–1x10–8
Living
18–10x14–2
Porch depth 6–0

LOWE'S

Signature SERIES

Stylish Retreat For A Narrow Lot

Plan #527-0809

Price Code AA

Total Living Area: 1,084 Sq. Ft.

Home has 2 bedrooms, 2 baths, and basement foundation.

Special features

- Delightful country porch for quiet evenings
- The living room offers a front feature window which invites the sun and includes a fireplace and dining area with private patio
- The U-shaped kitchen features lots of cabinets and bayed breakfast room with built-in pantry
- Both bedrooms have walk-in closets and access to their own bath

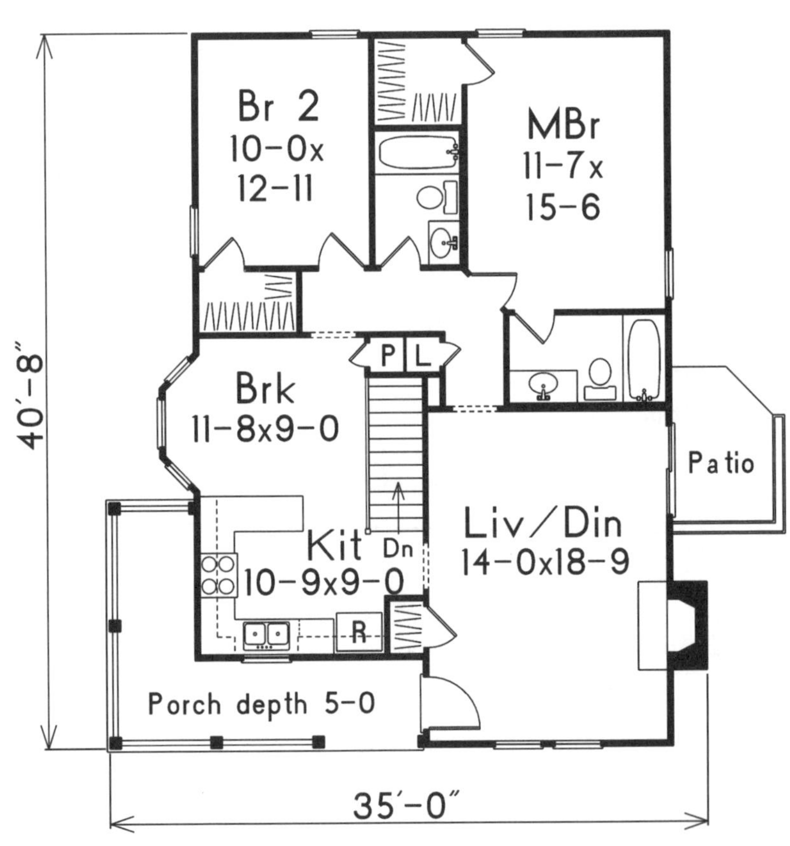
Br 2
10-0x
12-11
MBr
11-7x
15-6
P
L
Brk
11-8x9-0
Patio
Kit
Dn
10-9x9-0
R
Liv/Din
14-0x18-9
Porch depth 5-0
40'-8"
35'-0"

Great Room's Symmetry Steals The Show

Plan #527-0416

Price Code C

Total Living Area: 1,985 Sq. Ft.

Home has 4 bedrooms, 3 1/2 baths, 2-car garage and basement foundation.

Special features

- Charming design for narrow lot
- Dramatic sunken great room features vaulted ceiling, large double-hung windows and transomed patio doors
- Grand master suite includes double entry doors, large closet, elegant bath and patio access

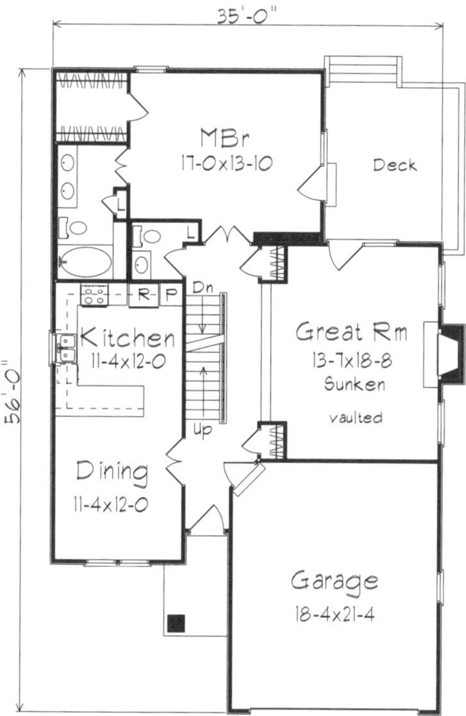
35'-0"
56'-0"
MBr
17-0x13-10
Deck
Kitchen
11-4x12-0
Dining
11-4x12-0
Great Rm
13-7x18-8
Sunken
vaulted
Garage
18-4x21-4
Dn
Up

First Floor
1,114 sq. ft.

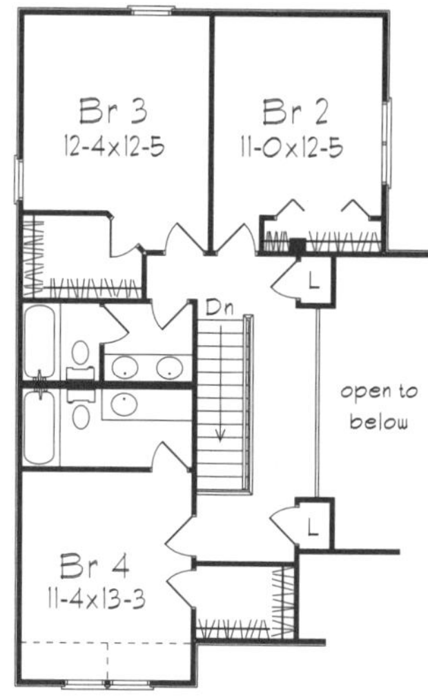
Br 3
12-4x12-5
Br 2
11-0x12-5
Dn
open to below
Br 4
11-4x13-3

Second Floor
871 sq. ft.

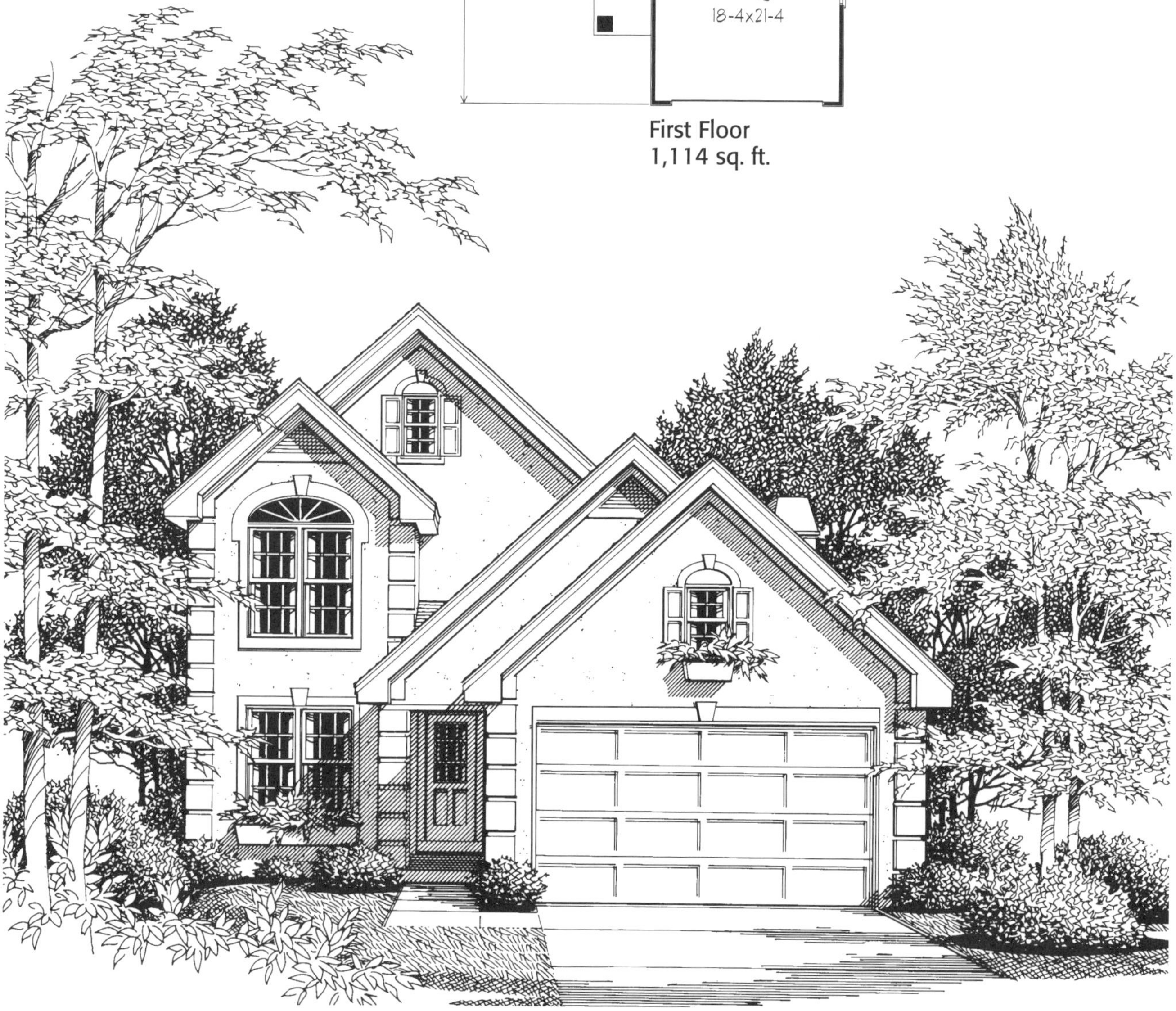

LOWE'S

Surrounding Porch For Country Views

Plan #527-0726

Price Code A

Total Living Area: 1,428 Sq. Ft.

Home has 3 bedrooms, 2 baths and basement foundation.

Special features

- A spacious loft/bedroom overlooking family room and an additional bedroom and bath conclude the second floor
- First floor master suite offers large bath, walk-in closet and nearby laundry facilities
- Large vaulted family room opens to dining and kitchen area with breakfast bar and access to surrounding porch

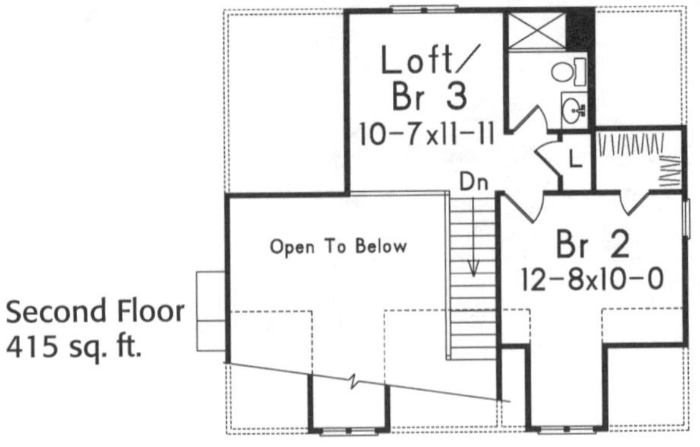
Loft/
Br 3
10-7x11-11
Dn
L
Open To Below
Br 2
12-8x10-0

Second Floor
415 sq. ft.

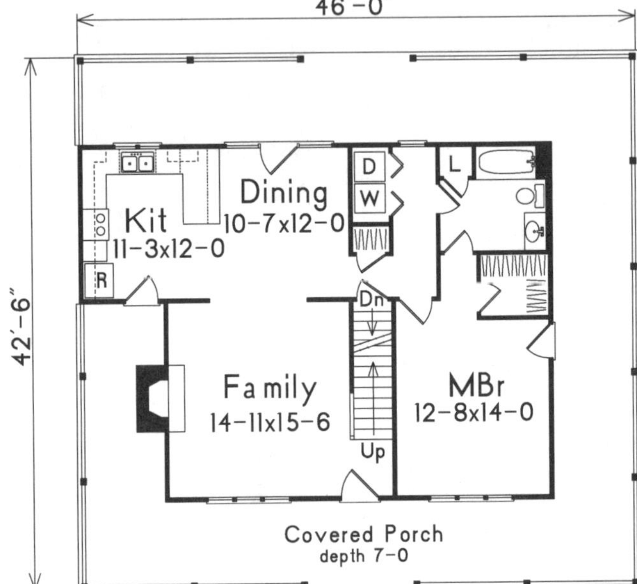
46'-0"
42'-6"
Kit
11-3x12-0
R
Dining
10-7x12-0
D
W
L
Dn
Family
14-11x15-6
Up
MBr
12-8x14-0
Covered Porch
depth 7-0

First Floor
1,013 sq. ft.

Dormers Accent Country Home

LOWE'S

Signature SERIES

Plan #527-0598

Price Code C

Total Living Area: 1,818 Sq. Ft.

Home has 4 bedrooms, 2 1/2 baths, 2-car drive under garage and basement foundation.

Special features

- Breakfast room is tucked behind the kitchen and has laundry closet and deck access
- Living and dining areas share vaulted ceiling and fireplace
- Master bedroom has two closets, large double-bowl vanity and separate tub and shower
- Large front porch wraps around home

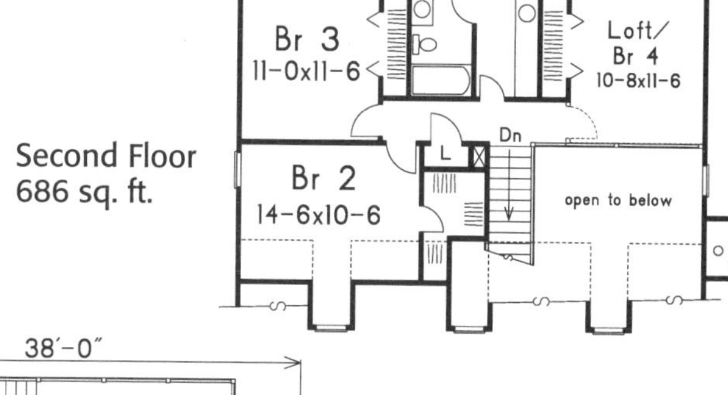

Br 3
11-0x11-6
Loft/
Br 4
10-8x11-6
Dn
L
Br 2
14-6x10-6
open to below

Second Floor
686 sq. ft.

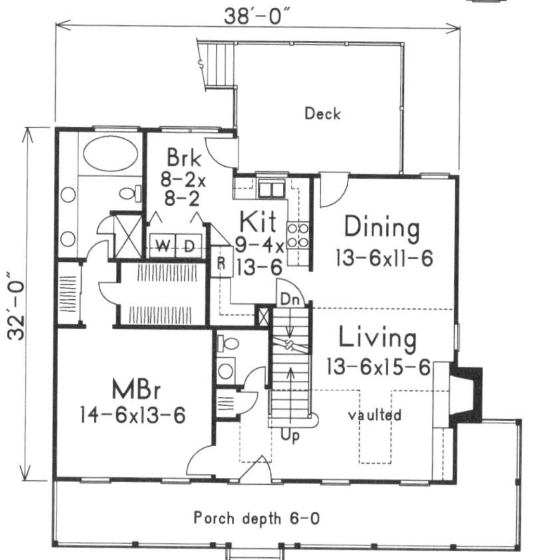

38'-0"
32'-0"
Deck
Brk
8-2x
8-2
W D
Kit
9-4x
13-6
R
Dining
13-6x11-6
Dn
Living
13-6x15-6
vaulted
Up
MBr
14-6x13-6
Porch depth 6-0

First Floor
1,132 sq. ft.

Country Kitchen Center Of Living Activities

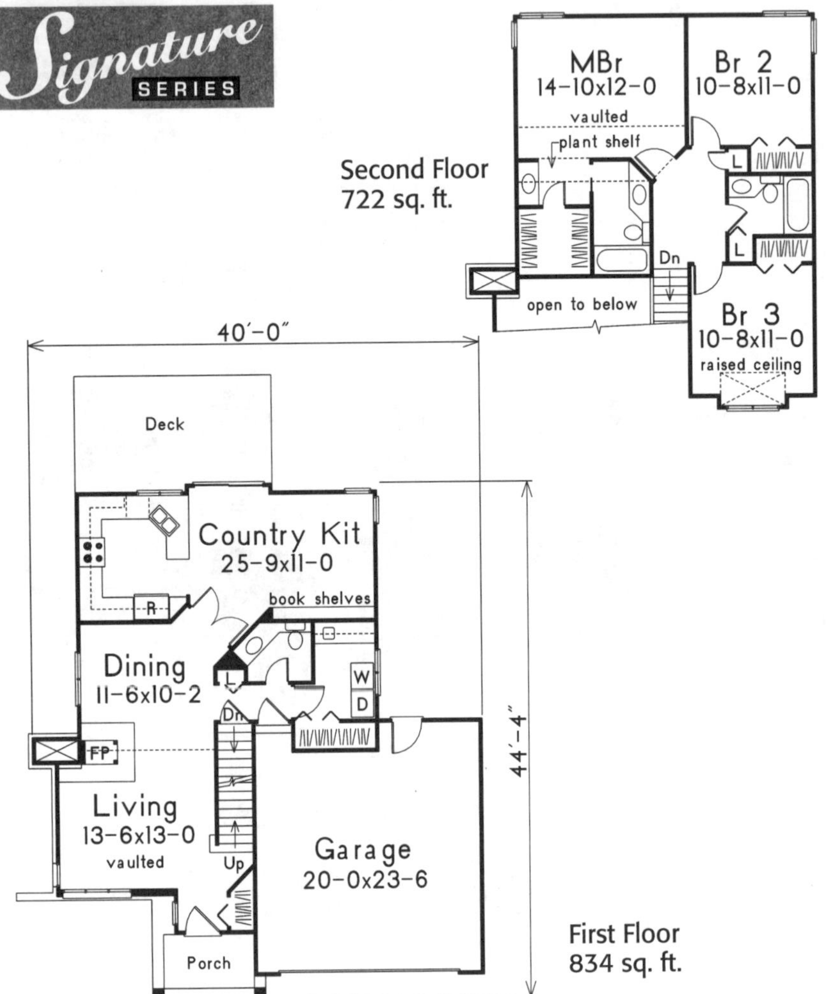

LOWE'S
Signature
SERIES
MBr
14-10x12-0
vaulted
plant shelf
Br 2
10-8x11-0
L
Dn
open to below
Br 3
10-8x11-0
raised ceiling
Second Floor
722 sq. ft.
40'-0"
Deck
Country Kit
25-9x11-0
R
book shelves
Dining
11-6x10-2
W
D
Dn
FP
Living
13-6x13-0
vaulted
Up
Garage
20-0x23-6
Porch
44'-4"
First Floor
834 sq. ft.

Plan #527-0209

Price Code B

Total Living Area: 1,556 Sq. Ft.

Home has 3 bedrooms, 2 1/2 baths, 2-car garage and basement foundation.

Special features

- A compact home with all the amenities
- Country kitchen combines practicality with access to other areas for eating and entertaining
- Two-way fireplace joins the dining and living areas
- Plant shelf and vaulted ceiling highlight the master bedroom

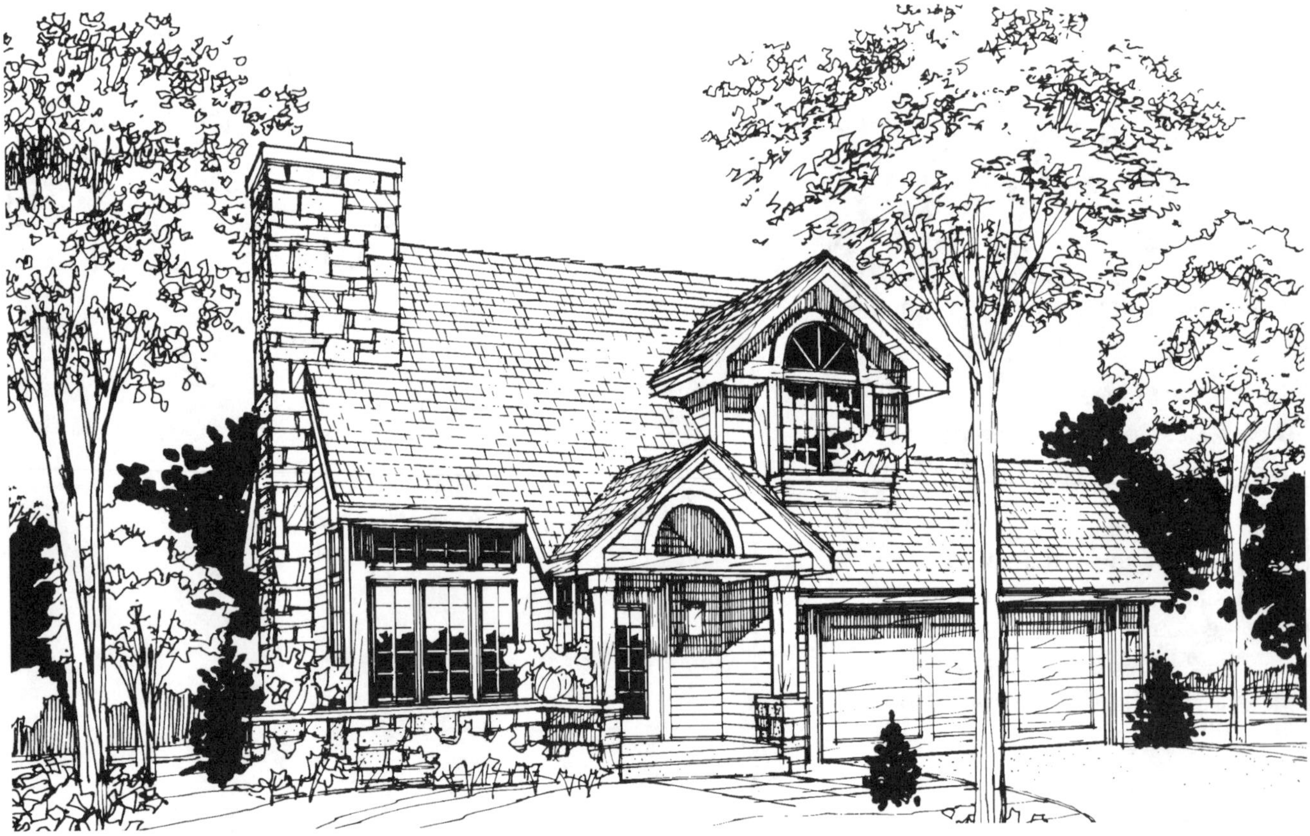

Large Living And Dining Area

LOWE'S Signature SERIES

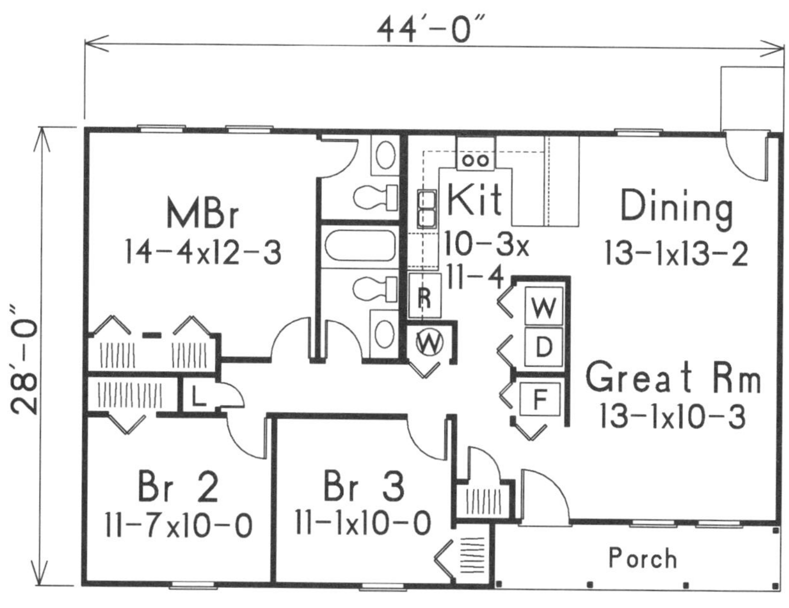

44'-0"
28'-0"
MBr
14-4x12-3
Kit
10-3x
11-4
Dining
13-1x13-2
R
W
W
D
F
Great Rm
13-1x10-3
L
Br 2
11-7x10-0
Br 3
11-1x10-0
Porch

Plan #527-0543

Price Code AA

Total Living Area: 1,160 Sq. Ft.

Home has 3 bedrooms, 1 1/2 baths and crawl space foundation, drawings also include basement and slab foundations.

Special features

- U-shaped kitchen includes breakfast bar and convenient laundry area
- Master bedroom features private half bath and large closet
- Dining room with handy outdoor access
- Dining and great rooms combine to create open living atmosphere

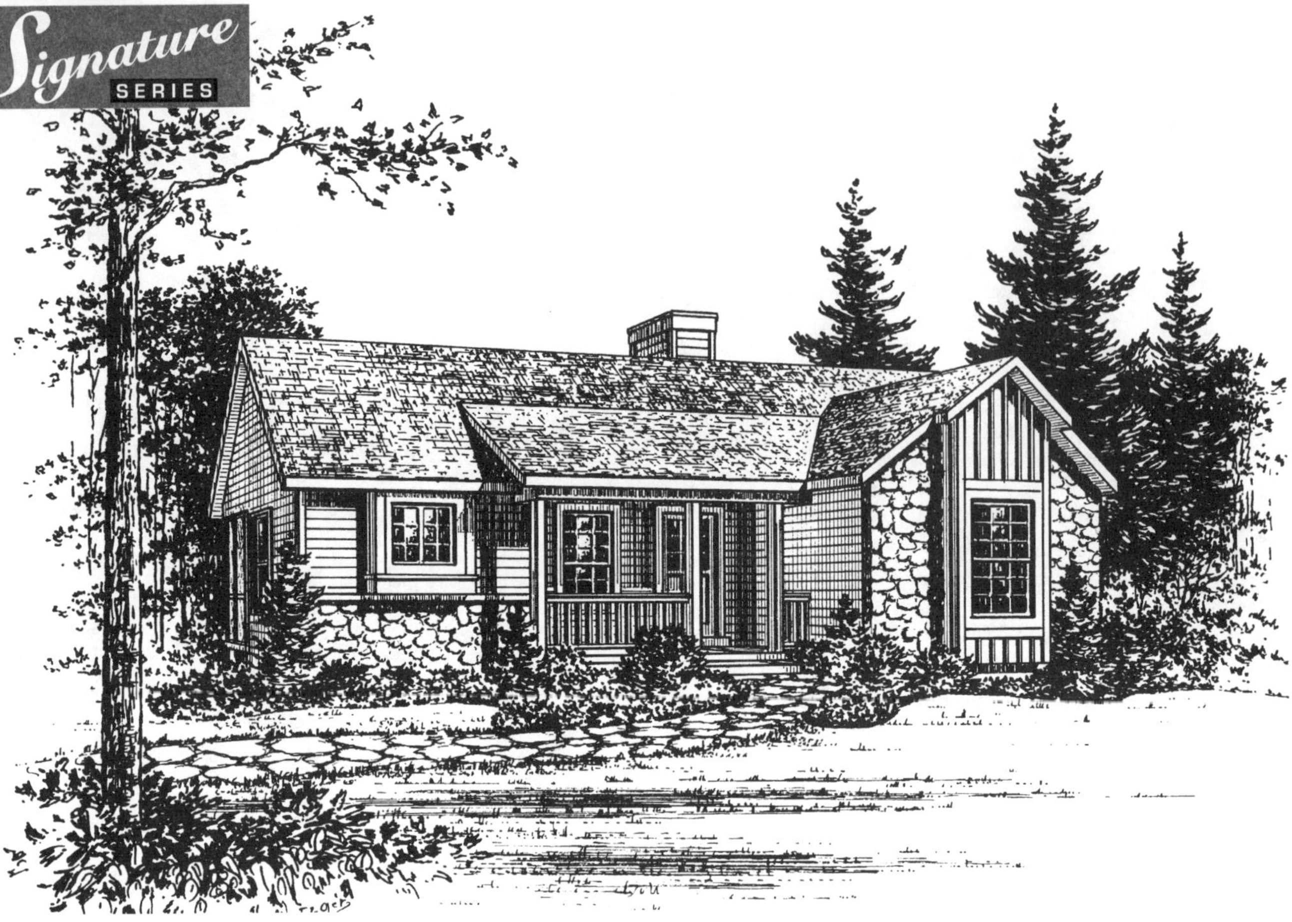

Plan #527-0699

Price Code AA

Total Living Area: 1,073 Sq. Ft.

Home has 2 bedrooms, 1 bath and crawl space foundation.

Special features

- Home includes lovely covered front porch and a screened porch off dining area
- Attractive box window brightens kitchen
- Space for efficiency washer and dryer located conveniently between bedrooms
- Family room spotlighted by fireplace with flanking bookshelves and spacious vaulted ceiling

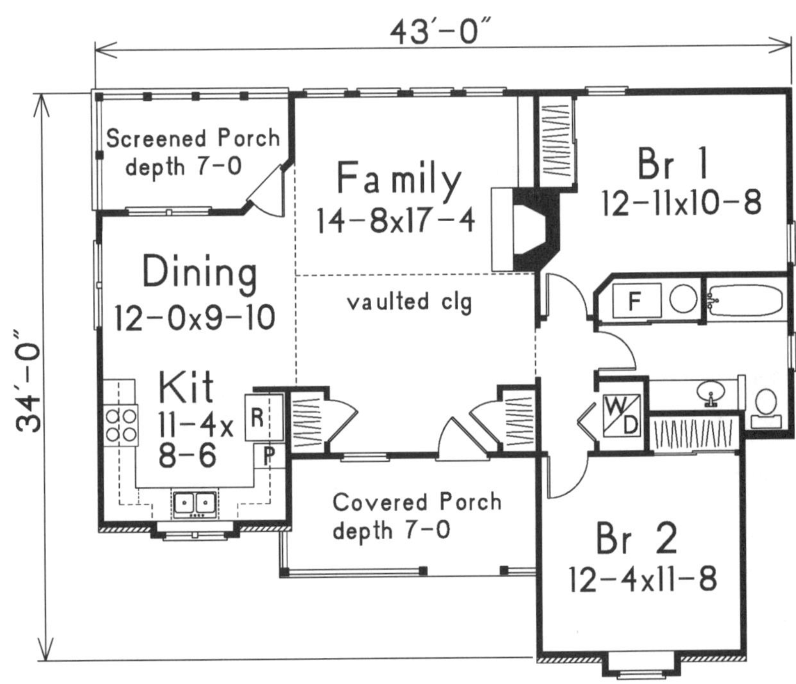
43'-0"
34'-0"
Screened Porch depth 7-0
Family 14-8x17-4
Br 1 12-11x10-8
Dining 12-0x9-10
vaulted clg
F
Kit 11-4x 8-6
R
P
W D
Covered Porch depth 7-0
Br 2 12-4x11-8

Vaulted Ceiling Frames Circle-Top Window

LOWE'S

Signature
SERIES

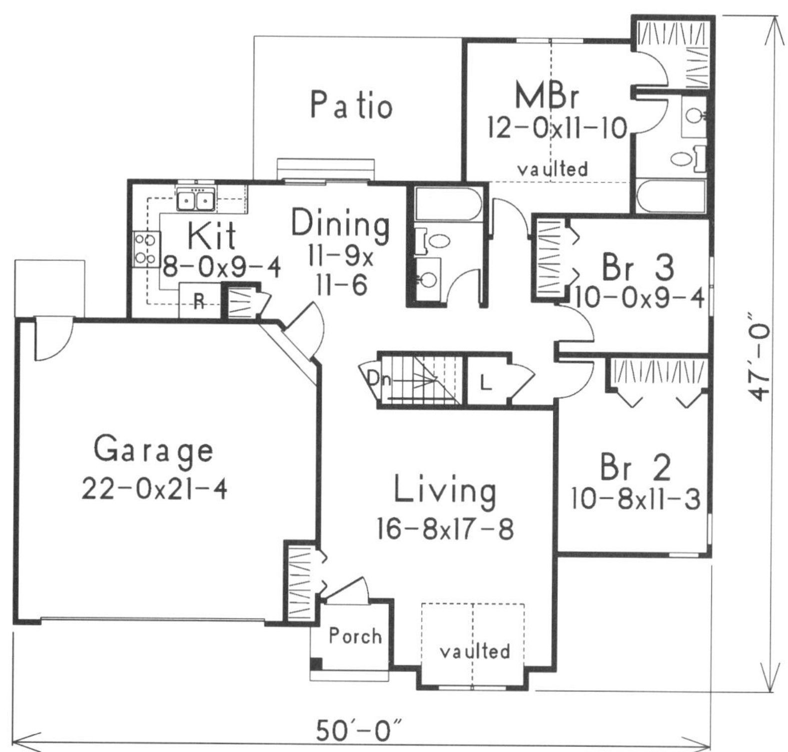
Patio
MBr
12-0x11-10
vaulted
Kit
8-0x9-4
R
Dining
11-9x
11-6
Br 3
10-0x9-4
Dn
L
Garage
22-0x21-4
Living
16-8x17-8
Br 2
10-8x11-3
Porch
vaulted
47'-0"
50'-0"

Plan #527-0485

Price Code AA

Total Living Area: 1,195 Sq. Ft.

Home has 3 bedrooms, 2 baths, 2-car garage and basement foundation.

Special features

- Kitchen/dining room opens onto the patio
- Master bedroom features vaulted ceiling, private bath and walk-in closet
- Coat closets located by both the entrances
- Convenient secondary entrance at the back of the garage

Charming Home Arranged For Open Living

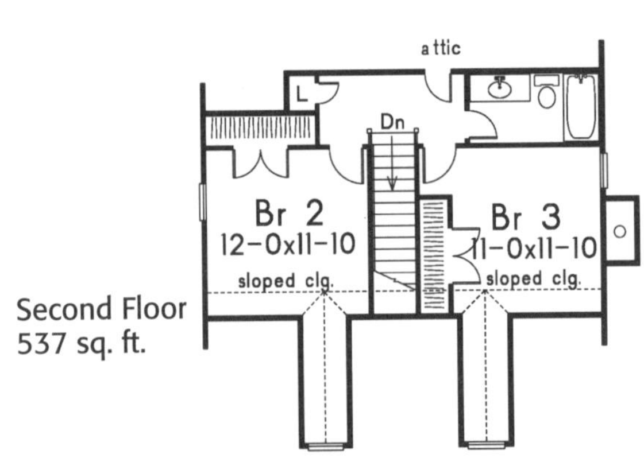
attic
L
Dn
Br 2
12-0x11-10
sloped clg.
Br 3
11-0x11-10
sloped clg.

Second Floor
537 sq. ft.

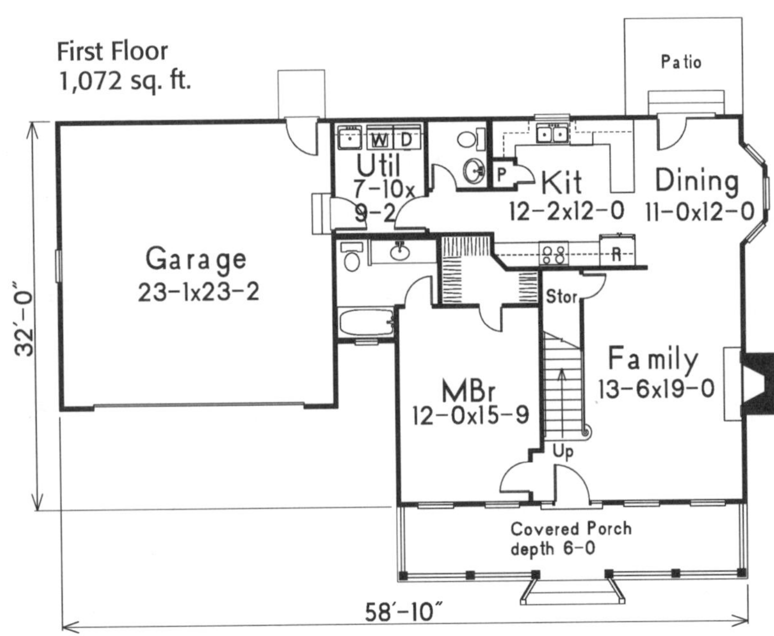
Patio
W D
Util
7-10x
9-2
P
Kit
12-2x12-0
Dining
11-0x12-0
Garage
23-1x23-2
R
Stor
Family
13-6x19-0
MBr
12-0x15-9
Up
Covered Porch
depth 6-0
32'-0"
58'-10"

First Floor
1,072 sq. ft.

Plan #527-0686

Price Code B

Total Living Area: 1,609 Sq. Ft.

Home has 3 bedrooms, 2 1/2 baths, 2-car garage and slab foundation.

Special features

- Kitchen captures full use of space with pantry, ample cabinets and workspace
- Master bedroom well-secluded with walk-in closet and private bath
- Large utility room includes sink and extra storage
- Attractive bay window in dining area provides light

Country Charm Wrapped In A Veranda

LOWE'S

Signature
SERIES

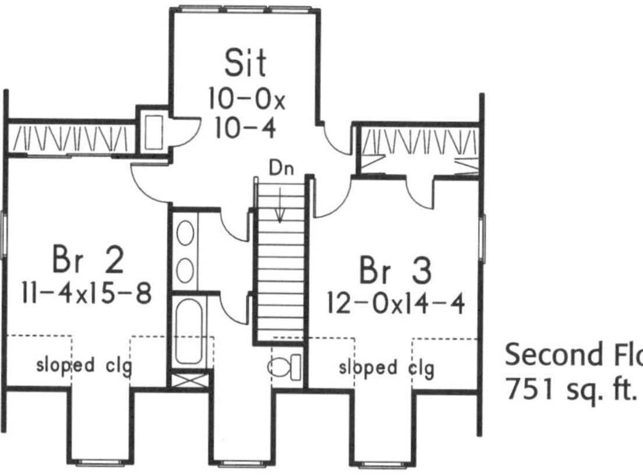
Sit
10-0x
10-4
Dn
Br 2
11-4x15-8
Br 3
12-0x14-4
sloped clg
sloped clg

Second Floor
751 sq. ft.

Plan #527-0213

Price Code C

Total Living Area: 2,059 Sq. Ft.

Home has 3 bedrooms, 2 1/2 baths, 2-car detached garage and slab foundation, drawings also include basement and crawl space foundations.

Special features

- Octagon-shaped breakfast room offers plenty of windows and creates a view to the veranda
- First floor master bedroom has large walk-in closet and deluxe bath
- 9' ceilings throughout the home
- Secondary bedrooms and bath feature dormers and are adjacent to cozy sitting area

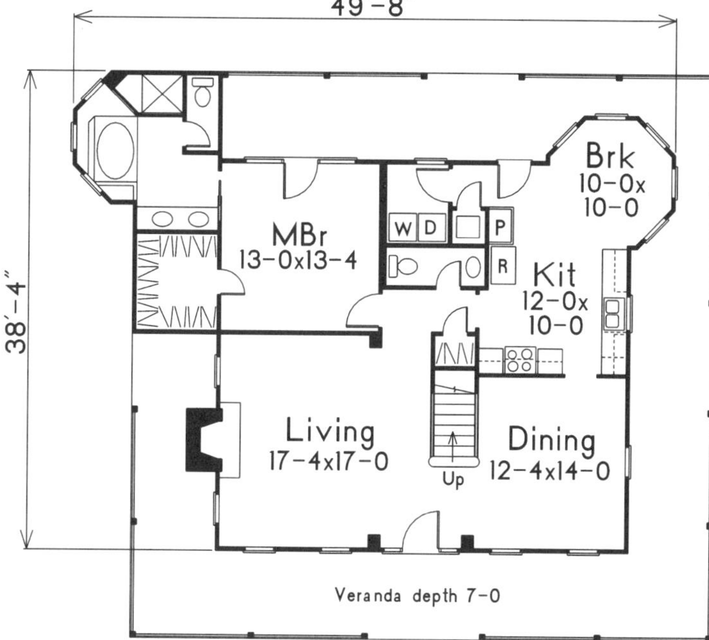
49'-8"
38'-4"
Brk
10-0x
10-0
W
D
P
R
MBr
13-0x13-4
Kit
12-0x
10-0
Living
17-4x17-0
Up
Dining
12-4x14-0
Veranda depth 7-0

First Floor
1,308 sq. ft.

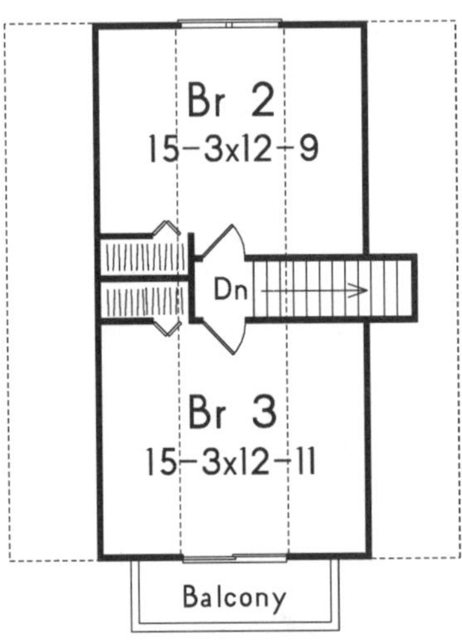
Br 2
15-3x12-9
Dn
Br 3
15-3x12-11
Balcony

Second Floor
450 sq. ft.

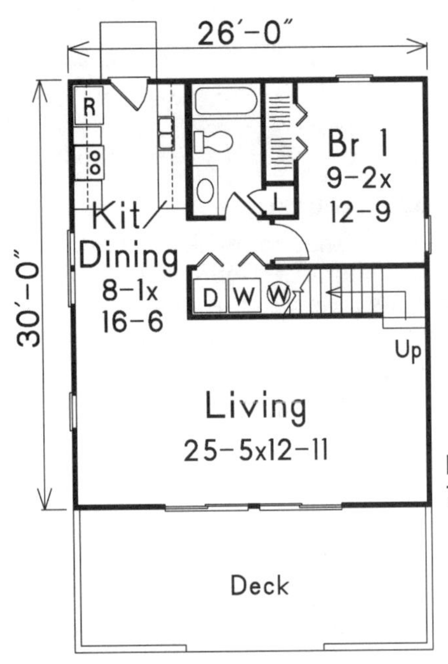
26′-0″
30′-0″
R
Kit/
Dining
8-1x
16-6
Br 1
9-2x
12-9
L
D
W
W
Up
Living
25-5x12-11
Deck

First Floor
780 sq. ft.

Plan #527-0549

Price Code A

Total Living Area: 1,230 Sq. Ft.

Home has 3 bedrooms, 1 bath and crawl space foundation, drawings also include slab foundation.

Special features

- Spacious living room accesses huge sun deck
- One of the second floor bedrooms features balcony overlooking deck
- Kitchen with dining area accesses outdoors
- Washer and dryer tucked under stairs

TO ORDER BLUEPRINTS USE THE FORM ON PAGE 290 OR CALL TOLL-FREE **1-800-DREAM HOME** (373-2646)

Compact Home Yet Charming And Functional

LOWE'S

Signature SERIES

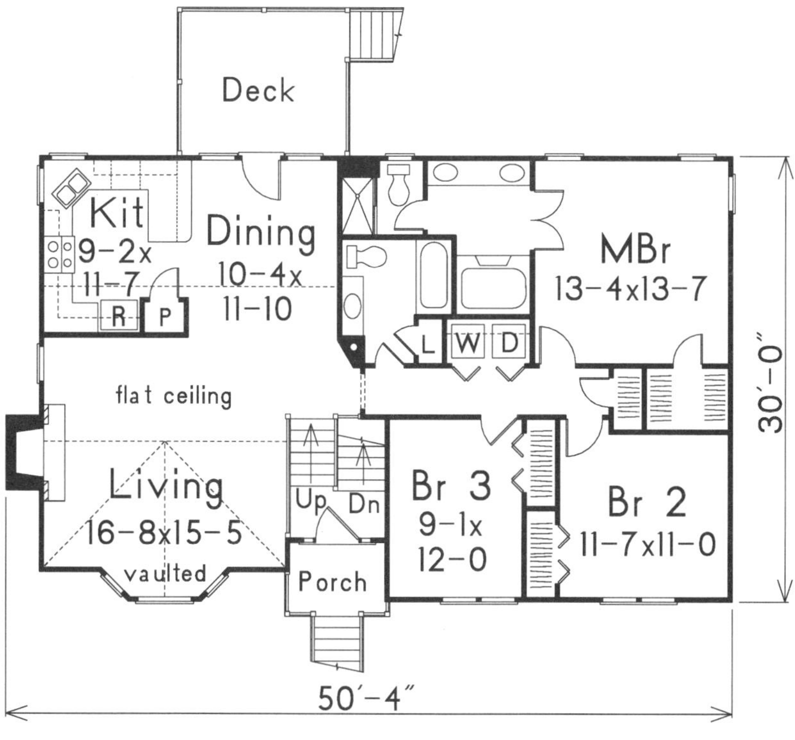
Deck
Kit
9-2x
11-7
Dining
10-4x
11-10
R
P
MBr
13-4x13-7
L
W
D
flat ceiling
Living
16-8x15-5
vaulted
Up
Dn
Porch
Br 3
9-1x
12-0
Br 2
11-7x11-0
30'-0"
50'-4"

Plan #527-0176

Price Code A

Total Living Area: 1,404 Sq. Ft.

Home has 3 bedrooms, 2 baths, 2-car drive under garage and basement foundation, drawings also include partial crawl space foundation.

Special features

- Split foyer entrance
- Bayed living area features unique vaulted ceiling and fireplace
- Wrap-around kitchen has corner windows for added sunlight and a bar that overlooks dining area
- Master suite features a garden tub with separate shower
- Back deck provides handy access to dining room and kitchen

LOWE'S

Signature
SERIES

Angled Porch Greets Guests

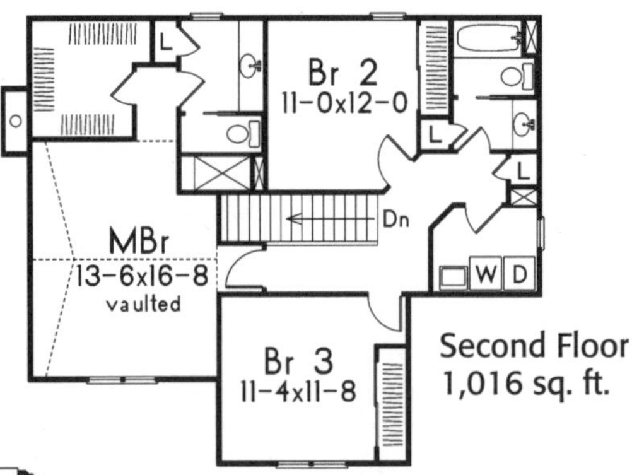
L
Br 2
11-0x12-0
L
L
Dn
MBr
13-6x16-8
vaulted
W
D
Br 3
11-4x11-8
Second Floor
1,016 sq. ft.

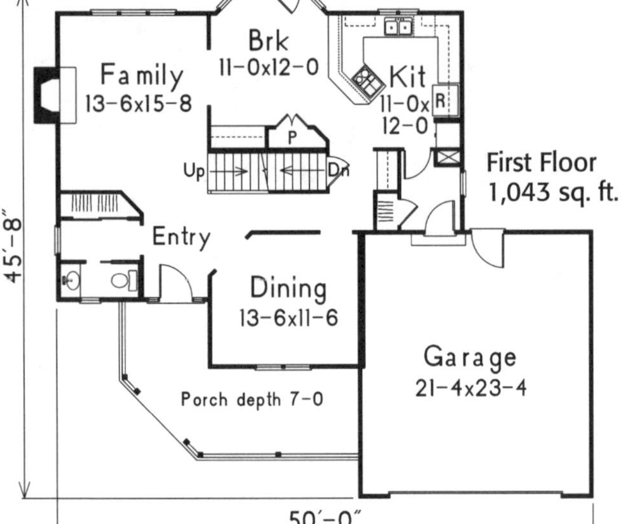
Brk
11-0x12-0
Family
13-6x15-8
Kit
11-0x
12-0
R
P
Up
Dn
First Floor
1,043 sq. ft.
45'-8"
Entry
Dining
13-6x11-6
Garage
21-4x23-4
Porch depth 7-0
50'-0"

Plan #527-0488

Price Code C

Total Living Area: 2,059 Sq. Ft.

Home has 3 bedrooms, 2 1/2 baths, 2-car garage and basement foundation.

Special features

- Large desk and pantry add to the breakfast room
- Laundry is located on second floor near bedrooms
- Vaulted ceiling in master suite
- Mud room is conveniently located near garage

Comfortable One-Story Country Home

LOWE'S

Signature SERIES

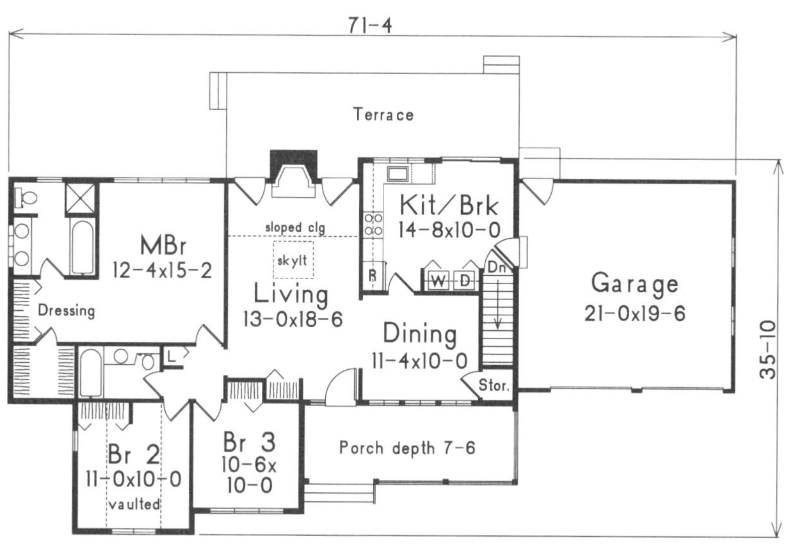
71-4
Terrace
Kit/Brk
14-8x10-0
MBr
12-4x15-2
sloped clg
skylt
Living
13-0x18-6
Dressing
Dining
11-4x10-0
Garage
21-0x19-6
35-10
Stor.
Dn
W
D
R
L
Br 2
11-0x10-0
vaulted
Br 3
10-6x
10-0
Porch depth 7-6

Plan #527-0676

Price Code A

Total Living Area: 1,367 Sq. Ft.

Home has 3 bedrooms, 2 baths, 2-car garage and basement foundation, drawings also include slab foundation.

Special features

- Neat front porch shelters the entrance
- Dining room has full wall of windows and convenient storage area
- Breakfast area leads to the rear terrace through sliding doors
- Large living room with high ceiling, skylight and fireplace

LOWE'S
Signature
SERIES

Brick And Siding Enhance This Traditional Home

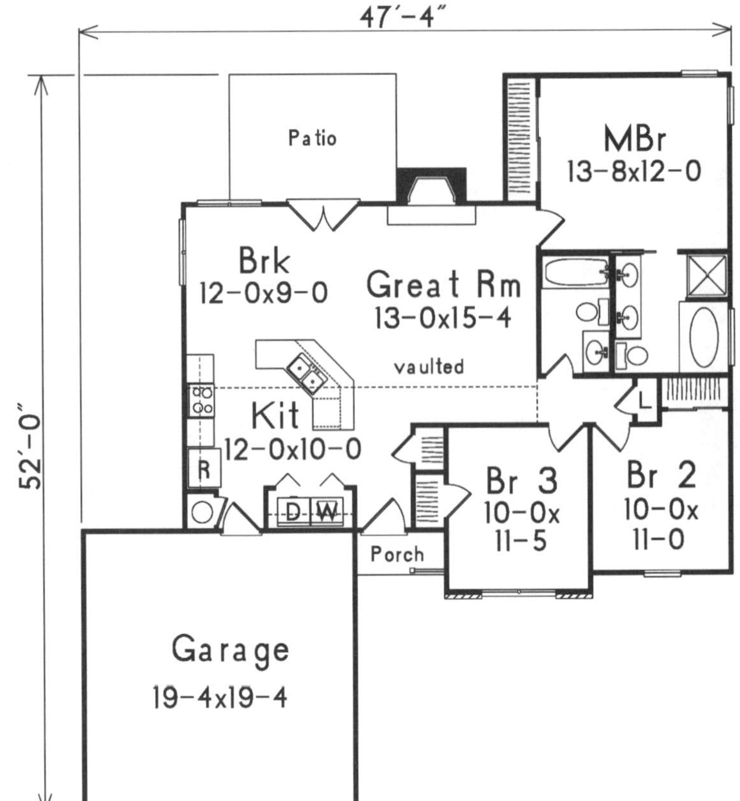
47'-4"
52'-0"
Patio
MBr
13-8x12-0
Brk
12-0x9-0
Great Rm
13-0x15-4
vaulted
Kit
12-0x10-0
R
DW
L
Br 3
10-0x
11-5
Br 2
10-0x
11-0
Porch
Garage
19-4x19-4

Plan #527-0670

Price Code AA

Total Living Area: 1,170 Sq. Ft.

Home has 3 bedrooms, 2 baths, 2-car garage and slab foundation.

Special features

- Master bedroom enjoys privacy at the rear of this home
- Kitchen has angled bar that overlooks great room and breakfast area
- Living areas combine to create a greater sense of spaciousness
- Great room has a cozy fireplace

Country-Style Home With Large Front Porch

LOWE'S

Signature SERIES

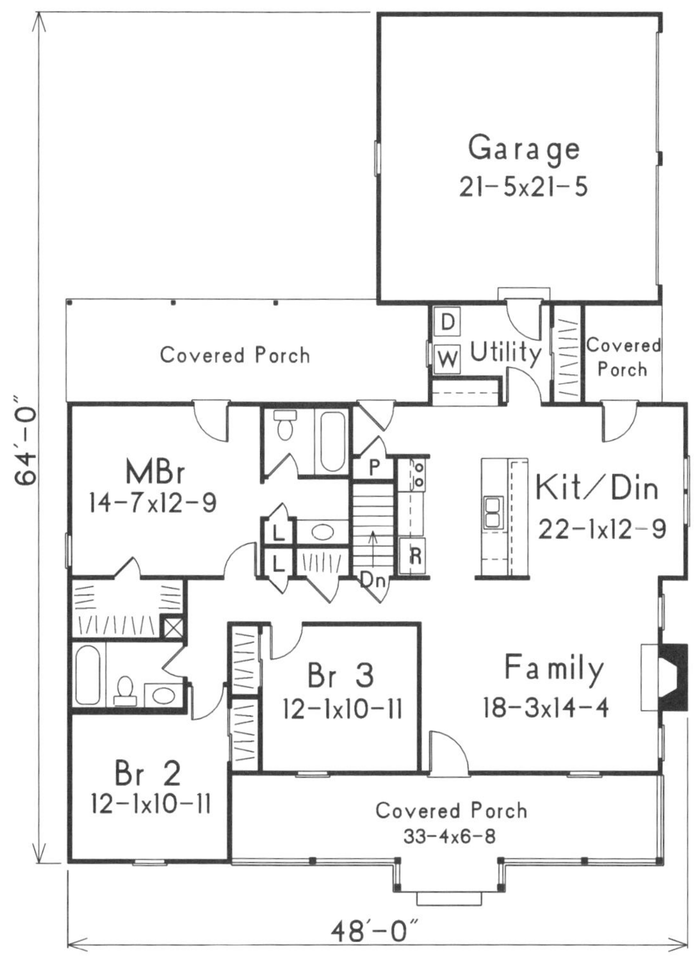
Garage
21-5x21-5
Covered Porch
D
W
Utility
Covered Porch
MBr
14-7x12-9
P
Kit/Din
22-1x12-9
L
L
R
Dn
Br 3
12-1x10-11
Family
18-3x14-4
Br 2
12-1x10-11
Covered Porch
33-4x6-8
64'-0"
48'-0"

Plan #527-0249

Price Code B

Total Living Area: 1,501 Sq. Ft.

Home has 3 bedrooms, 2 baths, 2-car side entry garage and basement foundation, drawings also include crawl space and slab foundations.

Special features

- Spacious kitchen with dining area open to outside
- Convenient utility room adjacent to garage
- Master suite with private bath, dressing area and access to large covered porch
- Large family room creates openness

Distinguished Styling For A Small Lot

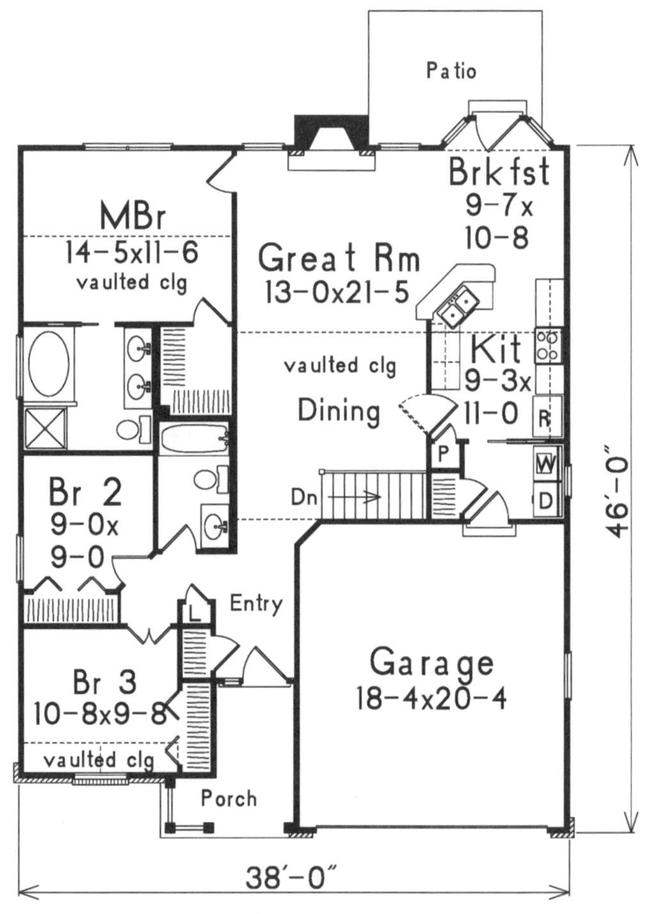
Patio
Brkfst
9-7x
10-8
MBr
14-5x11-6
vaulted clg
Great Rm
13-0x21-5
vaulted clg
Dining
Kit
9-3x
11-0
R
P
W
D
Dn
Br 2
9-0x
9-0
L
Entry
Br 3
10-8x9-8
vaulted clg
Porch
Garage
18-4x20-4
46'-0"
38'-0"

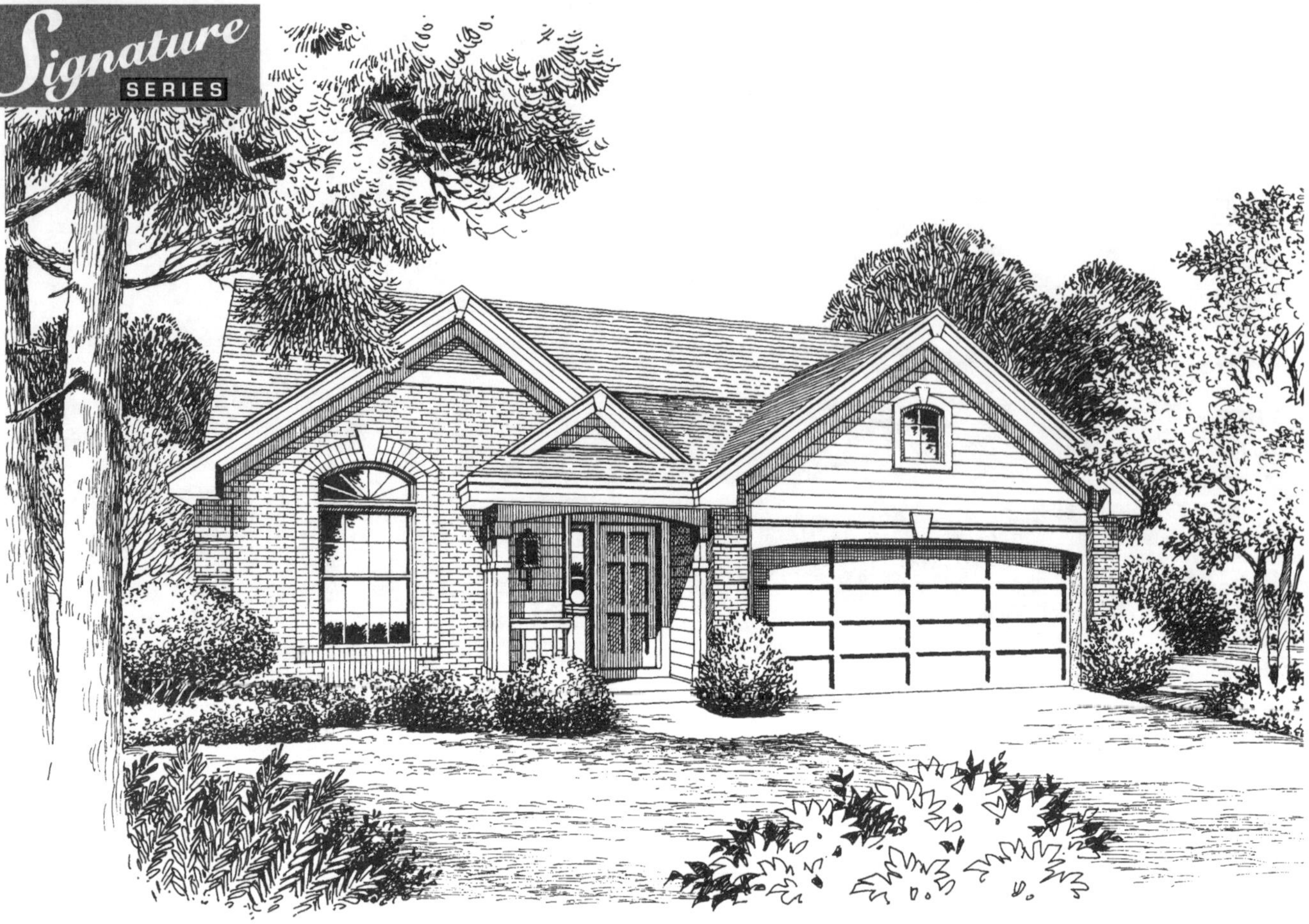

Plan #527-0717

Price Code A

Total Living Area: 1,268 Sq. Ft.

Home has 3 bedrooms, 2 baths, 2-car garage and basement foundation.

Special features

- Multiple gables, large porch and arched windows create classy exterior
- Innovative design provides openness in great room, kitchen and breakfast room
- Secondary bedrooms have private hall with bath

Pillared Front Porch Has Charm And Warmth

LOWE'S

Signature SERIES

Plan #527-0678

Price Code B

Total Living Area: 1,567 Sq. Ft.

Home has 3 bedrooms, 2 baths, 2-car side entry garage and basement foundation, drawings also include slab foundation.

Special features

- Living room flows into dining room shaped by an angled pass-through into the kitchen
- Cheerful, windowed dinette
- Bedrooms flank both sides of the living room, with the master suite located away from the other bedrooms for privacy and the two secondary bedrooms share a bath
- 338 square feet of optional living area on second floor

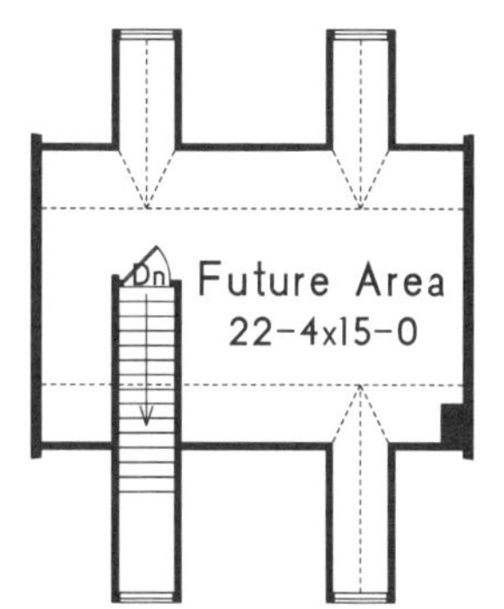
Dn
Future Area
22-4x15-0

Optional Second Floor

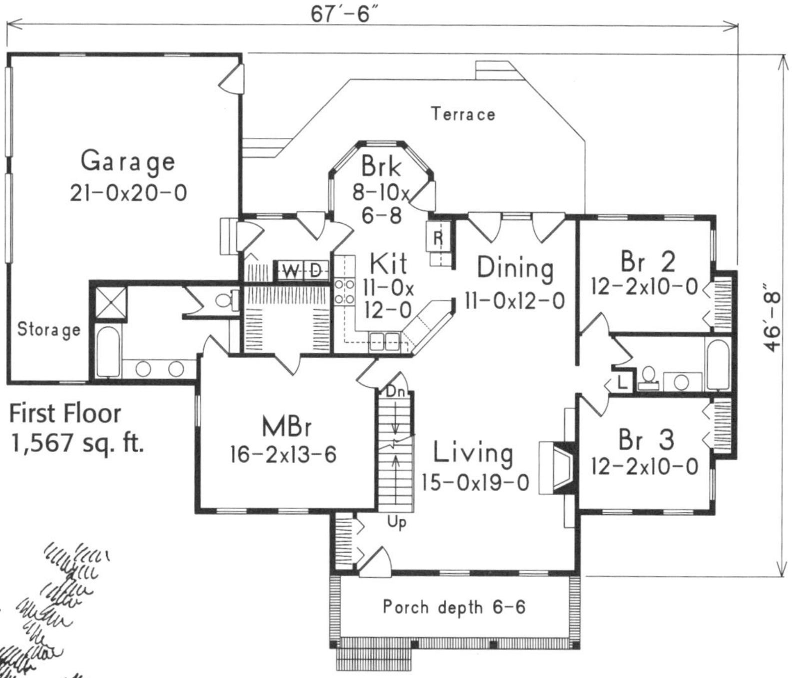

First Floor
1,567 sq. ft.

Traditional Exterior, Handsome Accents

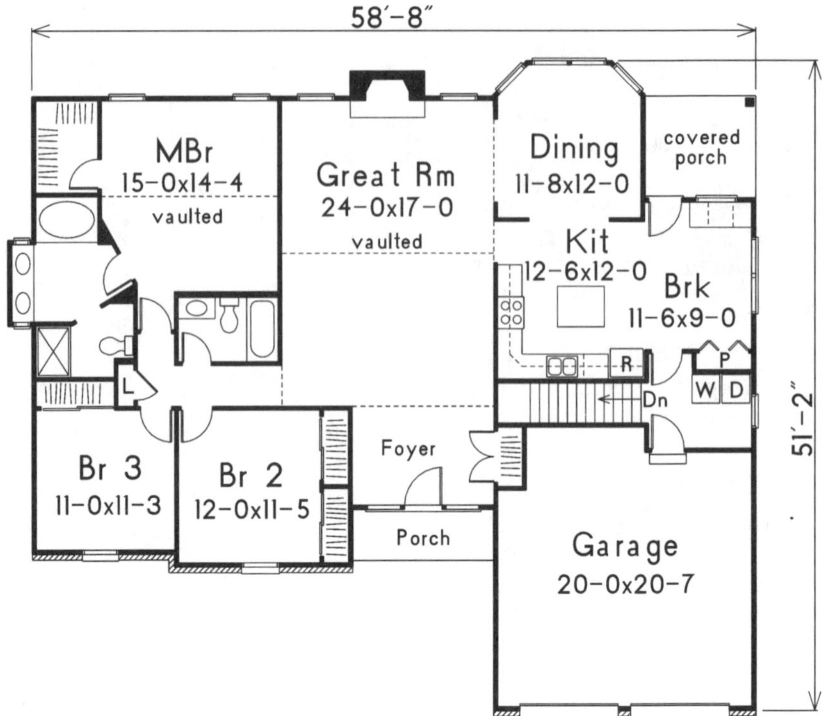
58'-8"
51'-2"
MBr
15-0x14-4
vaulted
Great Rm
24-0x17-0
vaulted
Dining
11-8x12-0
covered porch
Kit
12-6x12-0
Brk
11-6x9-0
R
P
W
D
Dn
L
Foyer
Br 3
11-0x11-3
Br 2
12-0x11-5
Porch
Garage
20-0x20-7

Plan #527-0162

Price Code D

Total Living Area: 1,882 Sq. Ft.

Home has 3 bedrooms, 2 baths, 2-car garage and basement foundation.

Special features

- Wide, handsome entrance opens to the vaulted great room with fireplace
- Living and dining areas are conveniently joined but still allow privacy
- Private covered porch extends breakfast area
- Practical passageway runs through laundry and mud room from garage to kitchen
- Vaulted ceiling in master bedroom

FOURNIER INC.

TO ORDER BLUEPRINTS USE THE FORM ON PAGE 290 OR CALL TOLL-FREE **1-800-DREAM HOME** (373-2646)

Compact Home With Functional Design

LOWE'S

Signature
SERIES

Plan #527-0296

Price Code A

Total Living Area: 1,396 Sq. Ft.

Home has 3 bedrooms, 2 baths, 1-car carport and basement foundation, drawings also include crawl space foundation.

Special features

- Gabled front adds interest to facade
- Living and dining rooms share a vaulted ceiling
- Master bedroom features a walk-in closet and private bath
- Functional kitchen with a center work island and convenient pantry

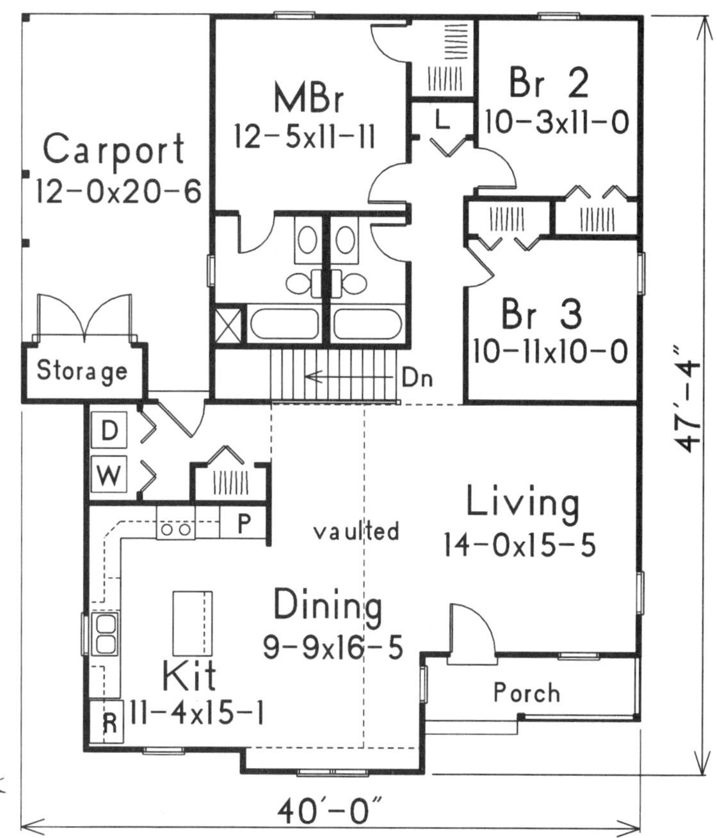
Carport
12-0x20-6
MBr
12-5x11-11
L
Br 2
10-3x11-0
Br 3
10-11x10-0
Storage
Dn
D
W
P
vaulted
Living
14-0x15-5
Dining
9-9x16-5
Kit
11-4x15-1
R
Porch
47'-4"
40'-0"

LOWE'S

Signature
SERIES

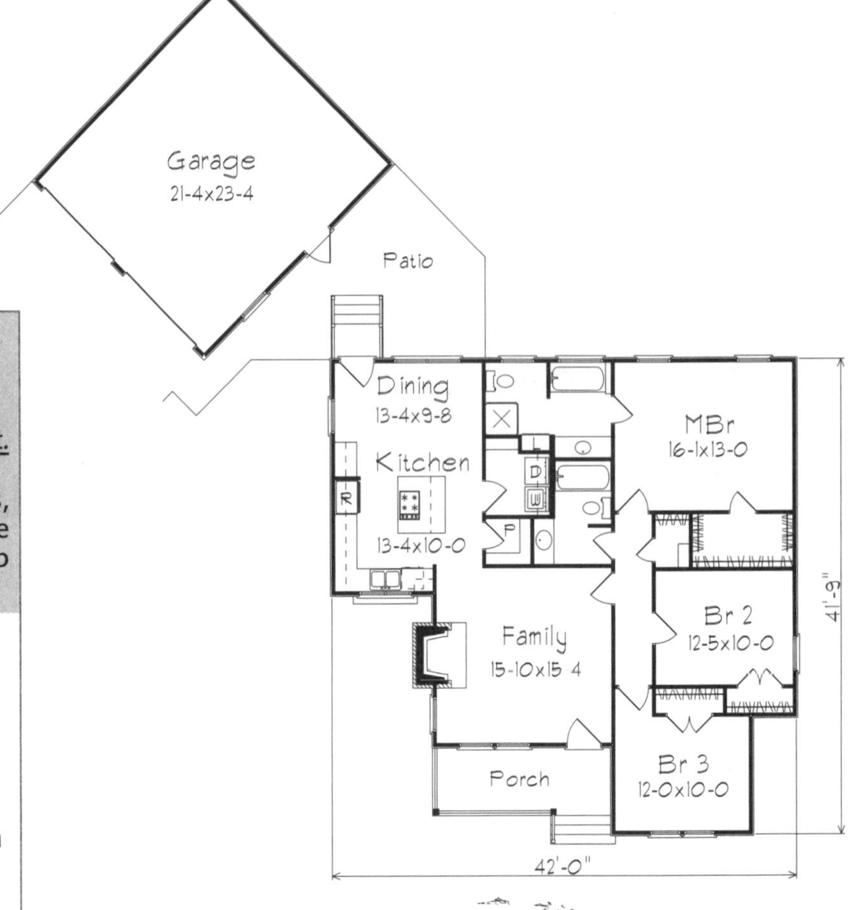
Garage
21-4x23-4
Patio
Dining
13-4x9-8
Kitchen
13-4x10-0
MBr
16-1x13-0
Br 2
12-5x10-0
Family
15-10x15 4
Porch
Br 3
12-0x10-0
42'-0"
41'-9"

Plan #527-0447

Price Code B

Total Living Area: 1,393 Sq. Ft.

Home has 3 bedrooms, 2 baths, 2-car detached garage and crawl space foundation, drawings also include slab foundation.

Special features

- L-shaped kitchen features walk-in pantry, island cooktop and is convenient to laundry room and dining area
- Master bedroom features large walk-in closet and private bath with separate tub and shower
- Convenient storage/coat closet in hall
- View to the patio from dining area

TO ORDER BLUEPRINTS USE THE FORM ON PAGE 290 OR CALL TOLL-FREE **1-800-DREAM HOME** (373-2646)

Well-Designed Plan Perfect For Entertaining

LOWE'S

Signature SERIES

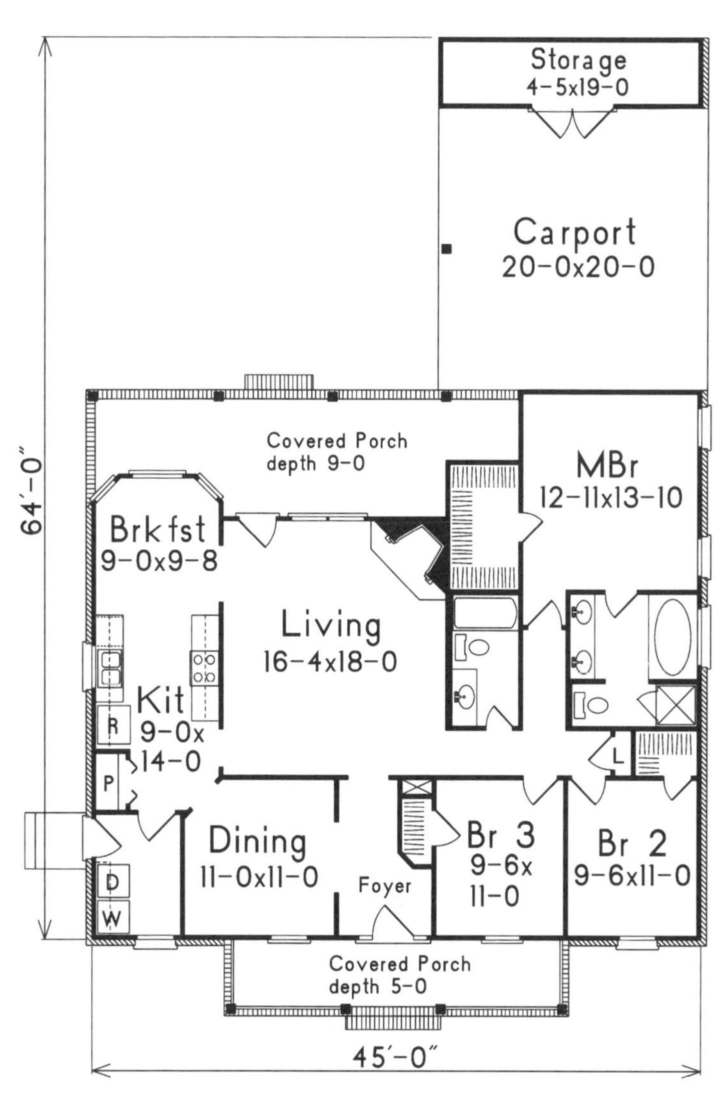
Storage
4-5x19-0
Carport
20-0x20-0
Covered Porch
depth 9-0
MBr
12-11x13-10
Brkfst
9-0x9-8
Living
16-4x18-0
Kit
9-0x
14-0
R
P
L
Dining
11-0x11-0
Foyer
Br 3
9-6x
11-0
Br 2
9-6x11-0
D
W
Covered Porch
depth 5-0
64'-0"
45'-0"

Plan #527-0688

Price Code B

Total Living Area: 1,556 Sq. Ft.

Home has 3 bedrooms, 2 baths, 2-car attached carport and slab foundation.

Special features

- Corner fireplace in living area warms surroundings
- Spacious master suite includes walk-in closet and private bath with double-bowl vanity
- Compact kitchen designed for efficiency
- Covered porches in both front and back of home add coziness

LOWE'S

Signature SERIES

Two-Story Country Style Home

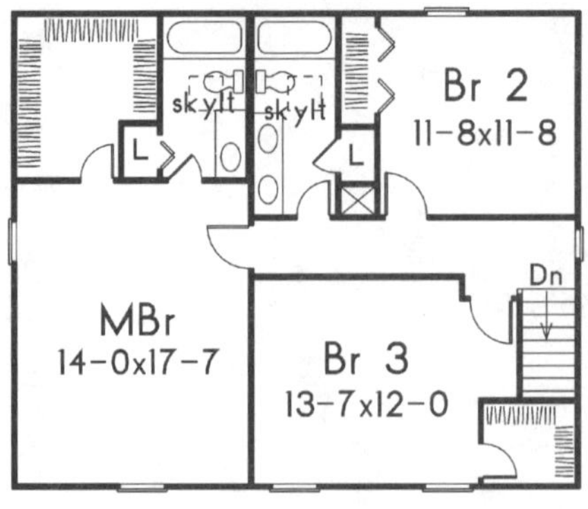
skylt
skylt
L
L
Br 2
11-8x11-8
Dn
MBr
14-0x17-7
Br 3
13-7x12-0

Second Floor
938 sq. ft.

Plan #527-0218

Price Code D

Total Living Area: 1,998 Sq. Ft.

Home has 3 bedrooms, 2 1/2 baths, 2-car side entry garage and basement foundation, drawings also include crawl space and slab foundations.

Special features

- Large family room features fireplace and access to kitchen and dining area
- Skylights add daylight to second floor baths
- Utility room conveniently located near garage and kitchen
- Kitchen/breakfast area includes pantry, island work space, and easy access to the patio

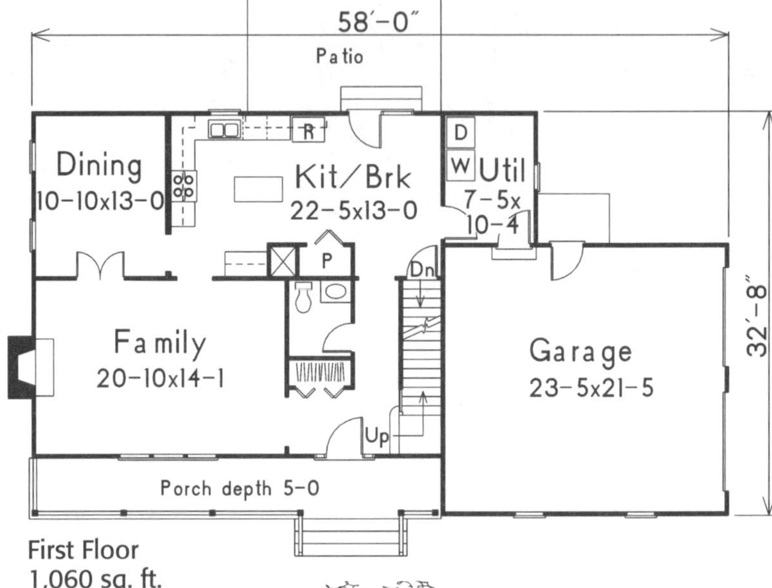
58′-0″
Patio
R
D
W
Util
7-5x
10-4
Dining
10-10x13-0
Kit/Brk
22-5x13-0
P
Dn
Family
20-10x14-1
Garage
23-5x21-5
32′-8″
Up
Porch depth 5-0

First Floor
1,060 sq. ft.

Prestigious Appeal For A Modest Home

Signature SERIES

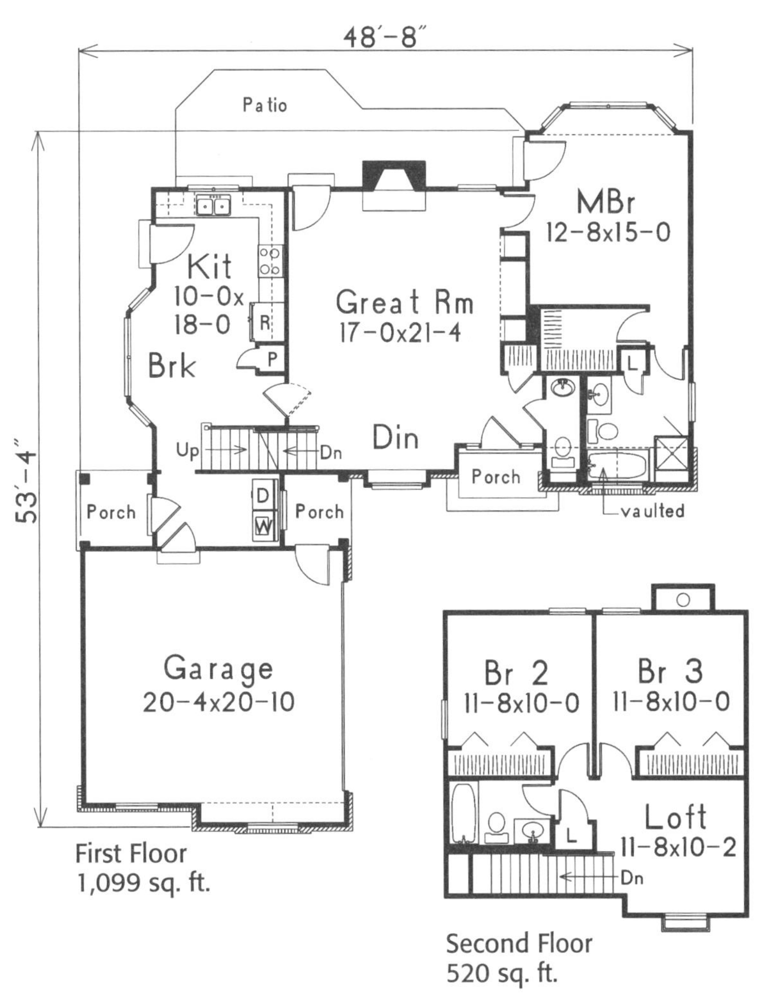

48'-8"
Patio
MBr
12-8x15-0
Kit
10-0x
18-0
Great Rm
17-0x21-4
Brk
Up
Dn
Din
Porch
vaulted
53'-4"
Porch
Porch
Garage
20-4x20-10
Br 2
11-8x10-0
Br 3
11-8x10-0
Loft
11-8x10-2
Dn

First Floor
1,099 sq. ft.

Second Floor
520 sq. ft.

Plan #527-0482

Price Code B

Total Living Area: 1,619 Sq. Ft.

Home has 3 bedrooms, 2 1/2 baths, 2-car side entry garage and basement foundation.

Special features

- Elegant home features three quaint porches and a large rear patio
- Grandscale great room offers dining area, fireplace and built-in alcove and shelves, a natural entertainment center
- First floor master bedroom suite has walk-in closet, luxury bath, bay window and access to rear patio
- Breakfast room with bay window contains stairs that lead to second floor bedrooms and loft

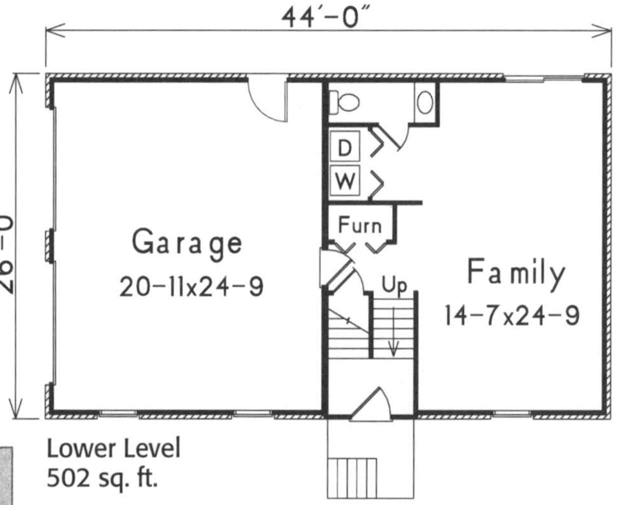

Unique Split Foyer Design

SPARR

44'-0"

26'-0"

Garage
20-11x24-9

D
W
Furn
Up

Family
14-7x24-9

Lower Level
502 sq. ft.

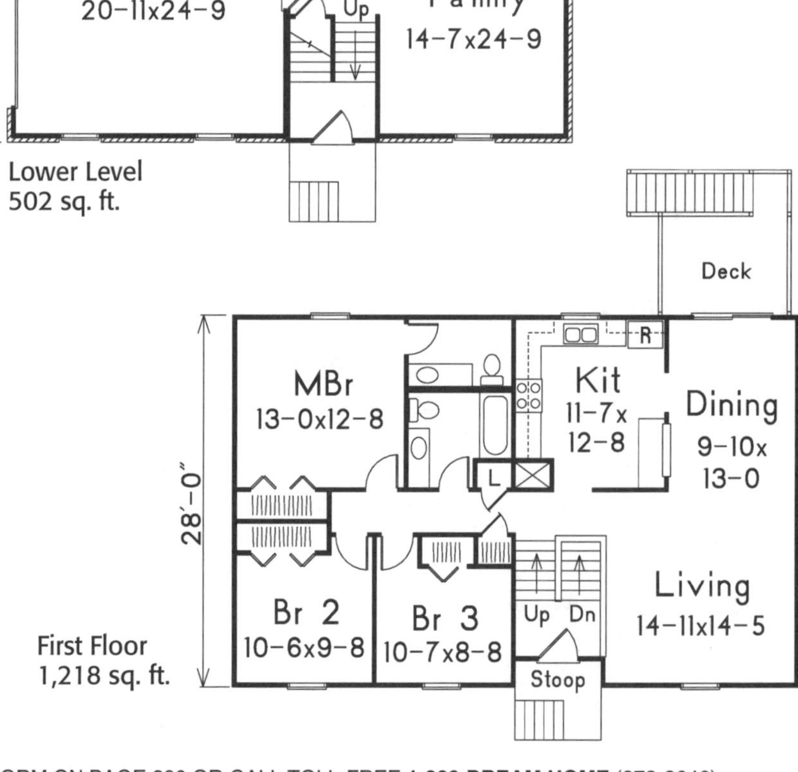
Deck
R
MBr
13-0x12-8
Kit
11-7x
12-8
Dining
9-10x
13-0
28'-0"
L
Br 2
10-6x9-8
Br 3
10-7x8-8
Up
Dn
Living
14-11x14-5
Stoop

First Floor
1,218 sq. ft.

Plan #527-0520

Price Code B

Total Living Area: 1,720 Sq. Ft.

Home has 3 bedrooms, 1 full bath, 2 half baths, 2-car drive under garage and basement foundation.

Special features

- Lower level includes large family room with laundry area and half bath
- L-shaped kitchen with convenient serving bar and pass-through to dining area
- Private half bath in master bedroom

TO ORDER BLUEPRINTS USE THE FORM ON PAGE 290 OR CALL TOLL-FREE **1-800-DREAM HOME** (373-2646)

Lovely, Spacious Floor Plan

LOWE'S

Signature
SERIES

Plan #527-0702

Price Code B

Total Living Area: 1,558 Sq. Ft.

Home has 3 bedrooms, 2 baths, 2-car garage and basement foundation.

Special features

- Spacious utility room located conveniently between garage and kitchen/dining area
- Private bedrooms separated off main living areas by hallway
- Enormous living area with fireplace and vaulted ceiling opens to kitchen and dining area
- Master suite enhanced with large bay window, walk-in closet and private bath

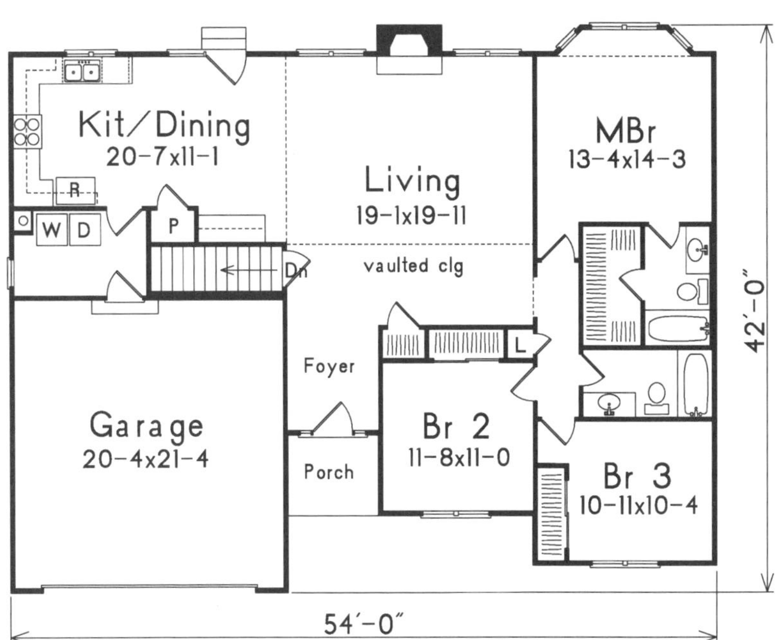
Kit/Dining
20-7x11-1
R
W D
P
Dn
Living
19-1x19-11
vaulted clg
MBr
13-4x14-3
L
Foyer
Garage
20-4x21-4
Br 2
11-8x11-0
Porch
Br 3
10-11x10-4
42'-0"
54'-0"

Covered Porch Adds Charm To Entrance

Plan #527-0294

Price Code B

Total Living Area: 1,655 Sq. Ft.

Home has 3 bedrooms, 2 baths, 2-car garage and crawl space foundation.

Special features

- Master bedroom features 9' ceiling, walk-in closet and bath with dressing area
- Oversized family room includes 10' ceiling and masonry see-through fireplace
- Island kitchen with convenient access to laundry room
- Handy covered walkway from garage to dining/kitchen area

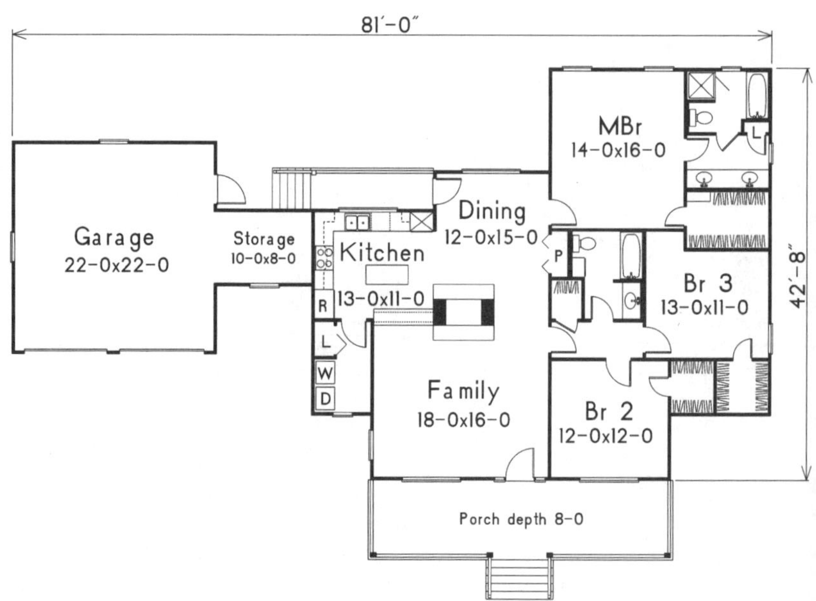
81'-0"
42'-8"
MBr
14-0x16-0
Dining
12-0x15-0
Garage
22-0x22-0
Storage
10-0x8-0
Kitchen
13-0x11-0
Br 3
13-0x11-0
Family
18-0x16-0
Br 2
12-0x12-0
Porch depth 8-0

 TO ORDER BLUEPRINTS USE THE FORM ON PAGE 290 OR CALL TOLL-FREE **1-800-DREAM HOME** (373-2646)

Distinctive Home For Sloping Terrain

LOWE'S

Signature
SERIES

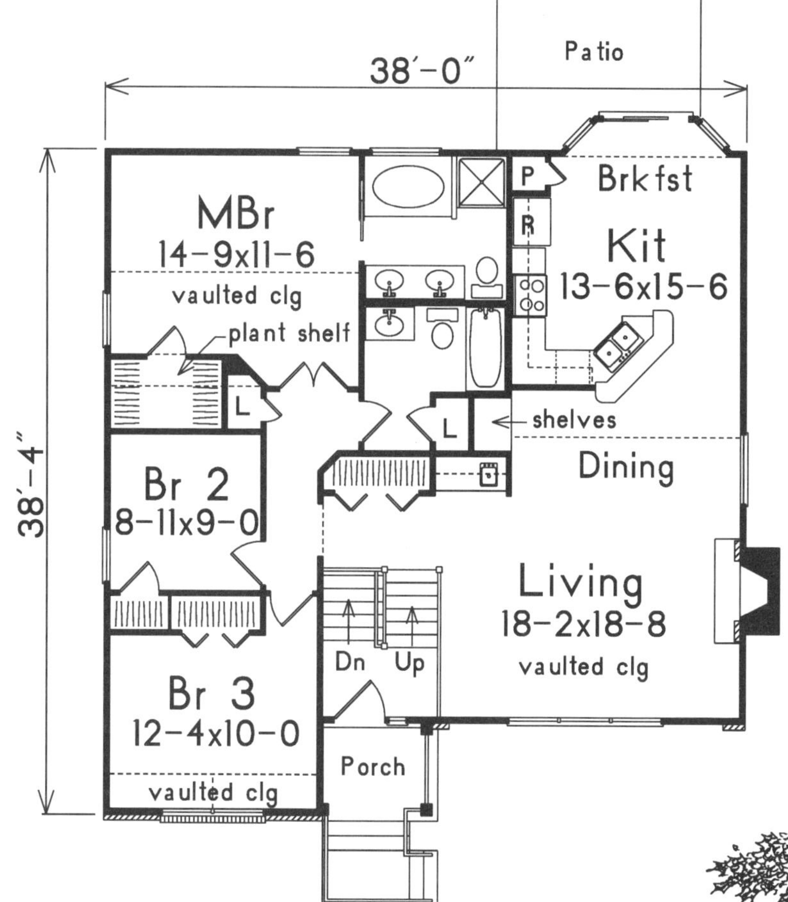
Patio
38'-0"
38'-4"
MBr
14-9x11-6
vaulted clg
plant shelf
P
R
Brkfst
Kit
13-6x15-6
L
L
shelves
Br 2
8-11x9-0
Dining
Living
18-2x18-8
vaulted clg
Dn
Up
Br 3
12-4x10-0
vaulted clg
Porch

Plan #527-0718

Price Code A

Total Living Area: 1,340 Sq. Ft.

Home has 3 bedrooms, 2 baths, 2-car drive under garage and basement foundation.

Special features

- Grand-sized vaulted living and dining rooms offer fireplace, wet bar and breakfast counter open to spacious kitchen
- Vaulted master suite features double entry doors, walk-in closet and elegant bath
- Basement includes a huge two-car garage and space for a bedroom/ bath expansion
- Extra storage in garage

TO ORDER BLUEPRINTS USE THE FORM ON PAGE 290 OR CALL TOLL-FREE **1-800-DREAM HOME** (373-2646)

LOWE'S Signature SERIES

Front Dormers Add Light, Space And Appeal

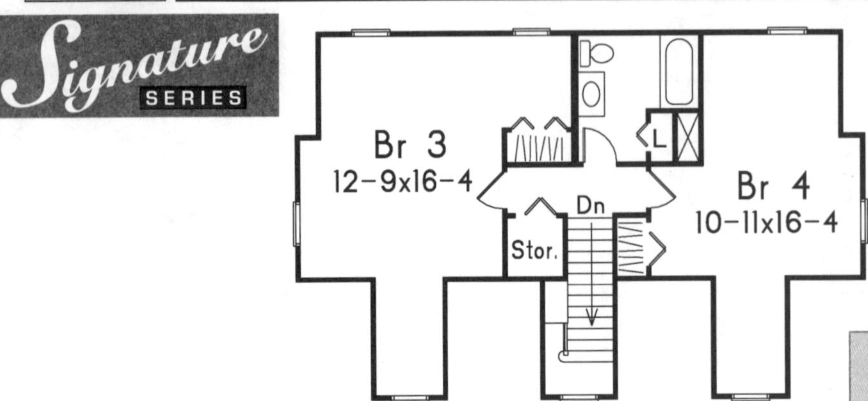
Br 3
12-9x16-4
Br 4
10-11x16-4
Dn
Stor.
L

Second Floor
665 sq. ft.

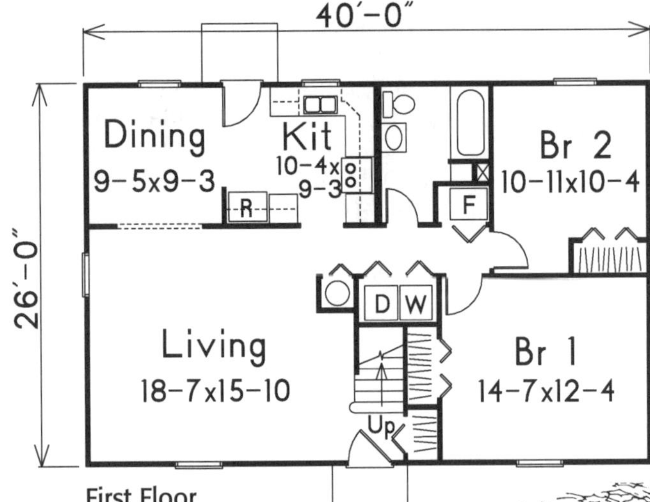
40'-0"
26'-0"
Dining
9-5x9-3
Kit
10-4x9-3
R
F
Br 2
10-11x10-4
D
W
Living
18-7x15-10
Br 1
14-7x12-4
Up

First Floor
1,040 sq. ft.

Plan #527-0518

Price Code B

Total Living Area: 1,705 Sq. Ft.

Home has 4 bedrooms, 2 baths and crawl space foundation, drawings also include basement and slab foundations.

Special features

- Cozy design includes two bedrooms on first floor and two bedrooms on second floor with added privacy
- L-shaped kitchen provides easy access to dining room and outdoors
- Convenient first floor laundry area

Wrap-Around Porch Adds Country Charm

LOWE'S

Signature SERIES

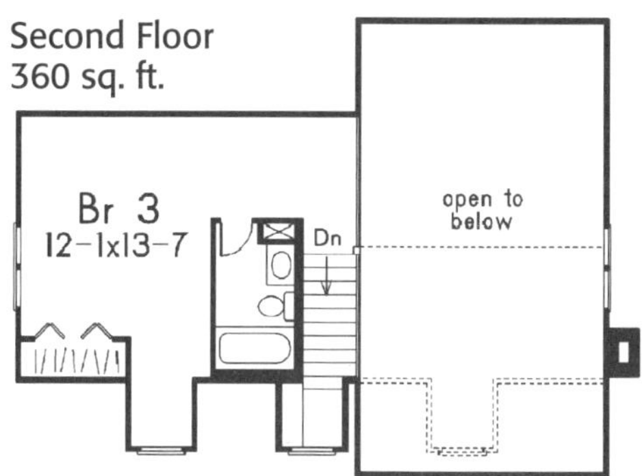

Br 3
12-1x13-7
Dn
open to below

Second Floor
360 sq. ft.

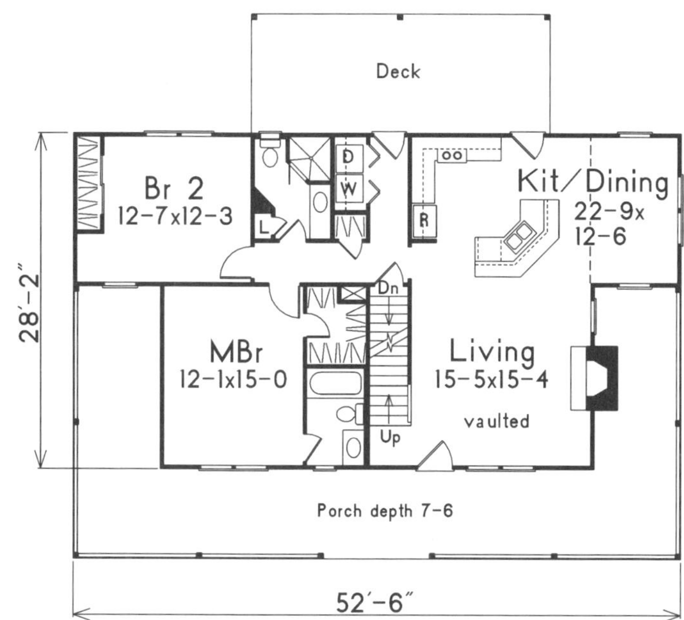

Deck
Br 2
12-7x12-3
D
W
R
L
Kit/Dining
22-9x
12-6
Dn
MBr
12-1x15-0
Living
15-5x15-4
vaulted
Up
28'-2"
Porch depth 7-6
52'-6"

First Floor
1,259 sq. ft.

Plan #527-0221

Price Code B

Total Living Area: 1,619 Sq. Ft.

Home has 3 bedrooms, 3 baths and basement foundation, drawings also include crawl space and slab foundations.

Special features

- Private second floor bedroom and bath
- Kitchen features a snack bar and adjacent dining area
- Master bedroom has private bath
- Centrally located washer and dryer

LOWE'S

Signature SERIES

Plan #527-0698

Price Code AA

Total Living Area: 1,143 Sq. Ft.

Home has 2 bedrooms, 1 bath and crawl space foundation.

Special features

- Enormous stone fireplace in family room adds warmth and character
- Spacious kitchen with breakfast bar overlooks family room
- Separate dining area great for entertaining
- Vaulted family and kitchen create open atmosphere

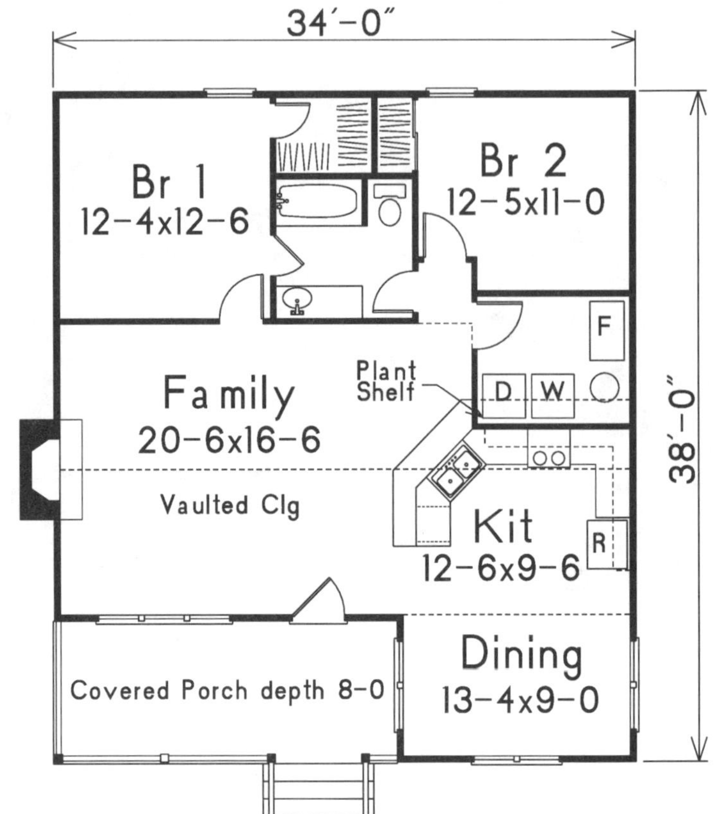
34'-0"
38'-0"
Br 1
12-4x12-6
Br 2
12-5x11-0
F
Plant Shelf
D
W
Family
20-6x16-6
Vaulted Clg
Kit
12-6x9-6
R
Covered Porch depth 8-0
Dining
13-4x9-0

TO ORDER BLUEPRINTS USE THE FORM ON PAGE 290 OR CALL TOLL-FREE **1-800-DREAM HOME** (373-2646)

Compact Home For Functional Living

LOWE'S

Signature SERIES

Plan #527-0173

Price Code A

Total Living Area: 1,220 Sq. Ft.

Home has 3 bedrooms, 2 baths, 2-car drive under garage and basement foundation.

Special features

- Vaulted ceilings add luxury to living room and master suite
- Spacious living room accented with a large fireplace and hearth
- Gracious dining area is adjacent to the convenient wrap-around kitchen
- Washer and dryer handy to the bedrooms
- Covered porch entry adds appeal

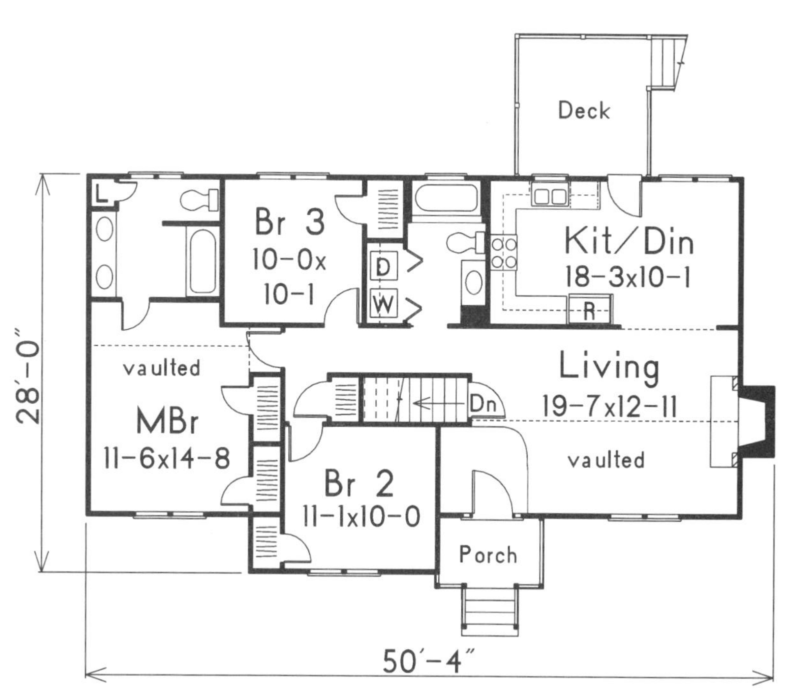

Deck
Br 3
10-0x
10-1
D
W
Kit/Din
18-3x10-1
R
L
vaulted
MBr
11-6x14-8
Dn
Living
19-7x12-11
vaulted
Br 2
11-1x10-0
Porch
28'-0"
50'-4"

LOWE'S

Signature
SERIES

Upscale Ranch With Formal And Informal Areas

Plan #527-0724

Price Code C

Total Living Area: 1,969 Sq. Ft.

Home has 3 bedrooms, 2 baths, 2-car garage and crawl space foundation, drawings also include slab foundation.

Special features

- Master suite boasts luxurious bath with double sinks, two walk-in closets and an oversized tub
- Corner fireplace warms a conveniently located family area
- Formal living and dining areas in the front of the home lend a touch of privacy when entertaining
- Spacious utility room has counter space and a sink

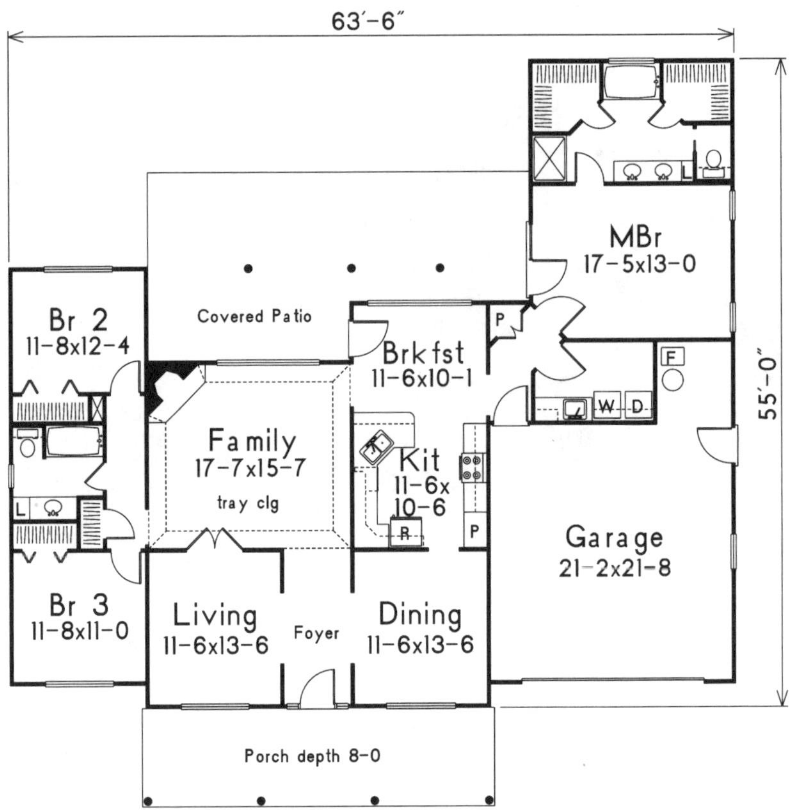
63'-6"
55'-0"
MBr
17-5x13-0
Covered Patio
Br 2
11-8x12-4
Brkfst
11-6x10-1
Family
17-7x15-7
tray clg
Kit
11-6x
10-6
Garage
21-2x21-8
Br 3
11-8x11-0
Living
11-6x13-6
Foyer
Dining
11-6x13-6
Porch depth 8-0

English Cottage With Modern Amenities

LOWE'S

Signature SERIES

Plan #527-0118

Price Code C

Total Living Area: 1,816 Sq. Ft.

Home has 3 bedrooms, 2 1/2 baths, 2-car detached garage and slab foundation, drawings also include crawl space foundation.

Special features

- Two-way living room fireplace with large nearby window seat
- Wrap-around dining room windows create sunroom appearance
- Master bedroom has abundant closet and storage space
- Rear dormers, closets and desk areas create interesting and functional second floor

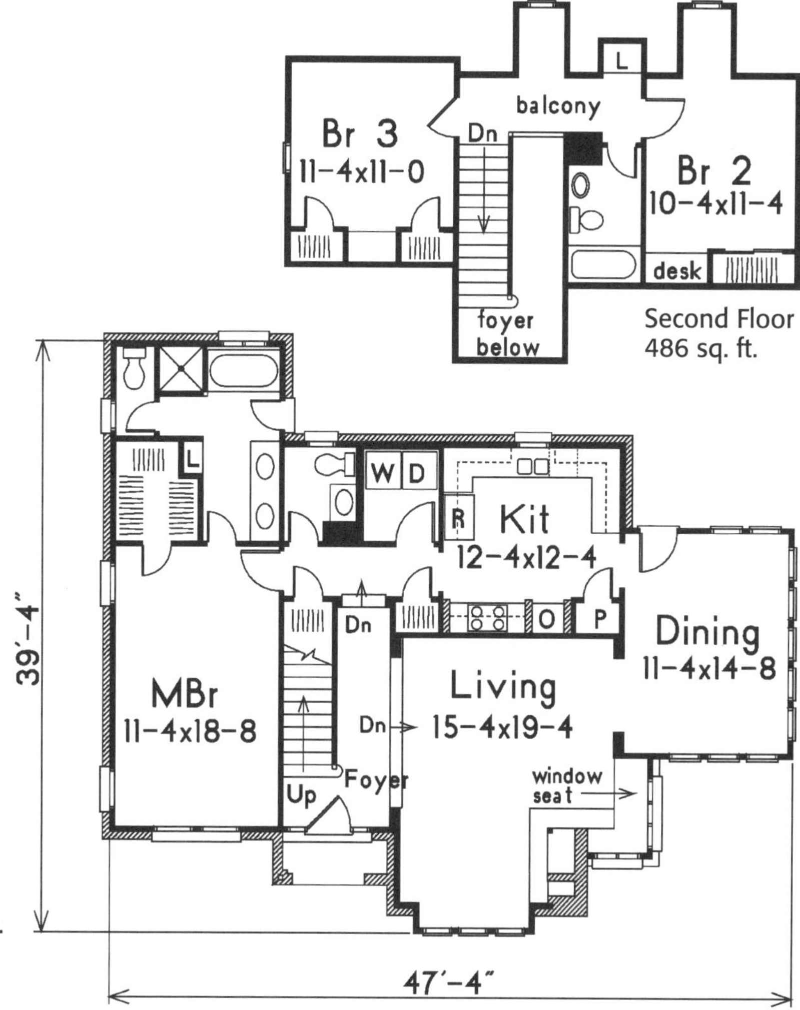
balcony
Br 3
11-4x11-0
Dn
L
Br 2
10-4x11-4
desk
foyer below
W
D
Kit
12-4x12-4
R
O
P
Dining
11-4x14-8
Dn
MBr
11-4x18-8
Living
15-4x19-4
Dn
Foyer
Up
window seat
39'-4"
47'-4"

Second Floor
486 sq. ft.

First Floor
1,330 sq. ft.

Lighted Charm

Plan #527-1220

Price Code B

Total Living Area: 1,540 Sq. Ft.

Home has 3 bedrooms, 2 baths, 2-car garage and basement foundation, drawings also include crawl space and slab foundations.

Special features

- Porch entrance into foyer leads to an impressive dining area with full window and half-circle window above
- Kitchen/breakfast room features a center island and cathedral ceiling
- Great room with cathedral ceiling and exposed beams accessible from foyer
- Master bedroom includes full bath and walk-in closet
- Two additional bedrooms share a full bath

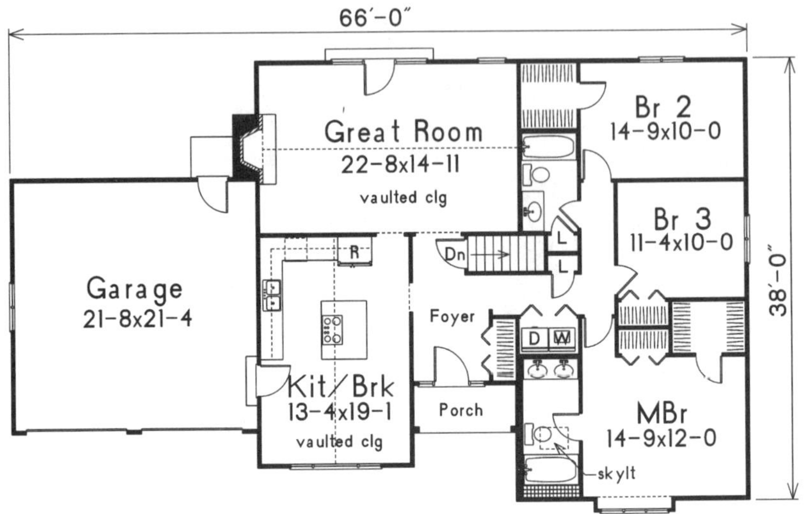

66'-0"
38'-0"
Great Room
22-8x14-11
vaulted clg
Br 2
14-9x10-0
Br 3
11-4x10-0
Garage
21-8x21-4
Dn
Foyer
D
W
Kit/Brk
13-4x19-1
vaulted clg
Porch
MBr
14-9x12-0
skylt

TO ORDER BLUEPRINTS USE THE FORM ON PAGE 290 OR CALL TOLL-FREE **1-800-DREAM HOME** (373-2646)

Year-Round Or Weekend Getaway Home

LOWE'S

Signature SERIES

Plan #527-0692

Price Code A

Total Living Area: 1,339 Sq. Ft.

Home has 3 bedrooms, 2 1/2 baths and crawl space foundation.

Special features

- Full-length covered porch enhances front facade
- Vaulted ceiling and stone fireplace add drama to family room
- Walk-in closets in bedrooms provide ample storage space
- Combined kitchen/dining area adjoins family room for perfect entertaining space

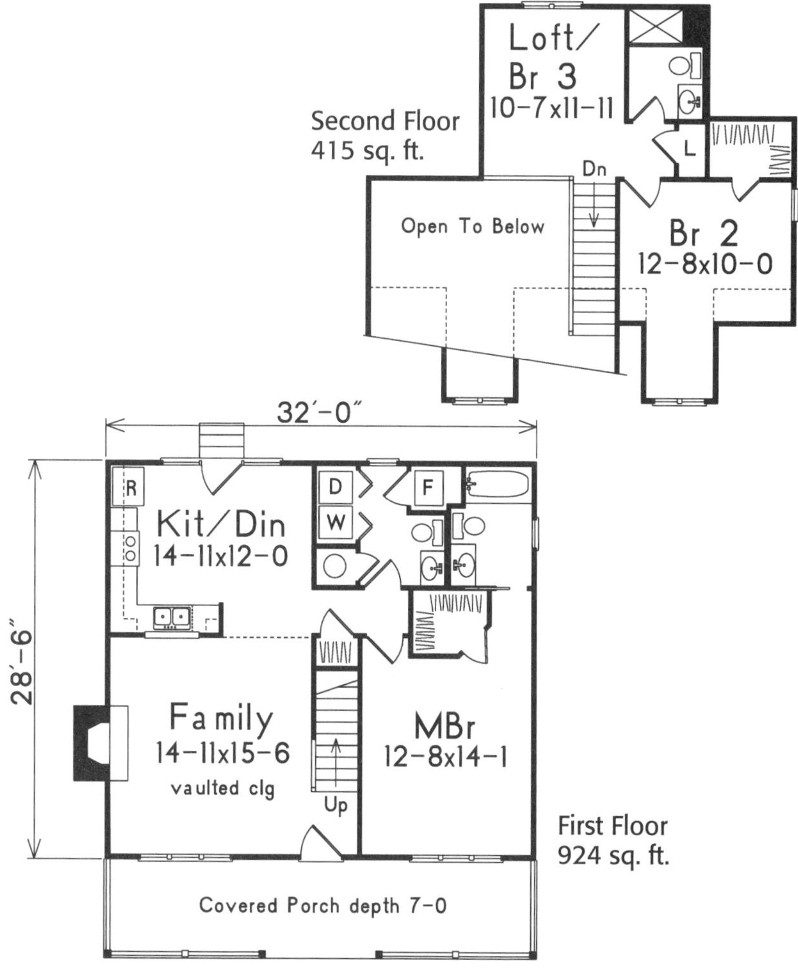
Loft/
Br 3
10-7x11-11
Second Floor
415 sq. ft.
L
Dn
Open To Below
Br 2
12-8x10-0
32'-0"
28'-6"
R
Kit/Din
14-11x12-0
D
W
F
Family
14-11x15-6
vaulted clg
Up
MBr
12-8x14-1
First Floor
924 sq. ft.
Covered Porch depth 7-0

LOWE'S

Signature
SERIES

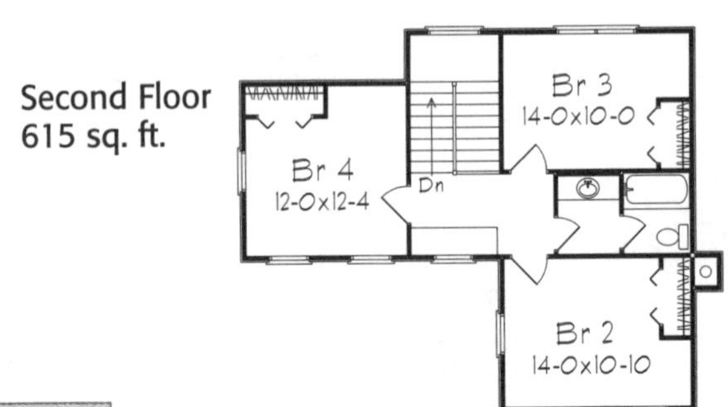
Second Floor
615 sq. ft.
Br 3
14-0x10-0
Br 4
12-0x12-4
Dn
Br 2
14-0x10-10

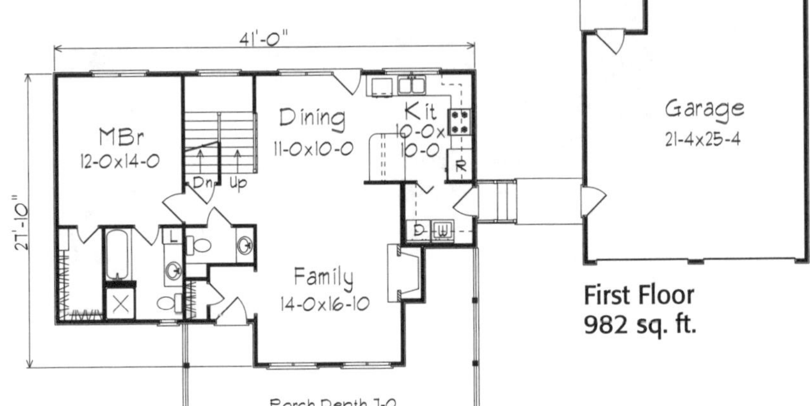
41'-0"
27'-10"
MBr
12-0x14-0
Dn
Up
Dining
11-0x10-0
Kit
10-0x
10-0
R
D
W
Family
14-0x16-10
Porch Depth 7-0
Garage
21-4x25-4
First Floor
982 sq. ft.

Plan #527-0448

Price Code C

Total Living Area: 1,597 Sq. Ft.

Home has 4 bedrooms, 2 1/2 baths, 2-car detached garage and basement foundation.

Special features

- Spacious family room includes fireplace and coat closet
- Open kitchen/dining room provides breakfast bar and access to outdoors
- Convenient laundry area located near kitchen
- Secluded master suite with walk-in closet and private bath

TO ORDER BLUEPRINTS USE THE FORM ON PAGE 290 OR CALL TOLL-FREE **1-800-DREAM HOME** (373-2646)

Circle-Top Windows Grace The Facade

LOWE'S

Signature SERIES

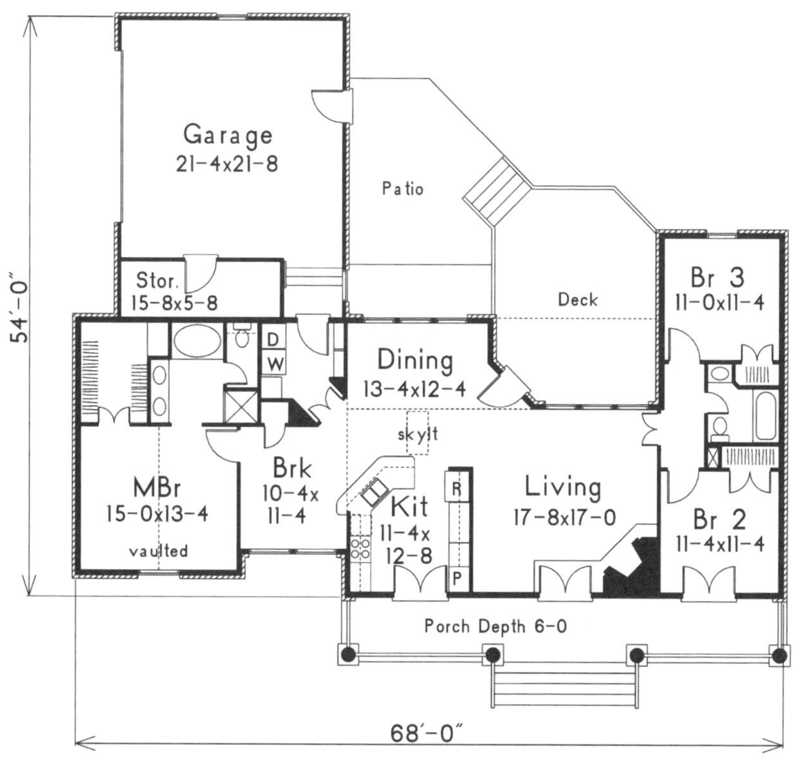
Garage
21-4x21-8
Patio
Stor.
15-8x5-8
Deck
Br 3
11-0x11-4
D
W
Dining
13-4x12-4
skylt
MBr
15-0x13-4
vaulted
Brk
10-4x
11-4
Kit
11-4x
12-8
R
P
Living
17-8x17-0
Br 2
11-4x11-4
Porch Depth 6-0
54'-0"
68'-0"

Plan #527-0284

Price Code C

Total Living Area: 1,672 Sq. Ft.

Home has 3 bedrooms, 2 baths, 2-car side entry garage and crawl space foundation, drawings also include basement and slab foundations.

Special features

- Vaulted master suite features walk-in closet and adjoining bath with separate tub and shower
- Energy efficient home with 2" x 6" exterior walls
- Covered front and rear porches
- 12' ceilings in living room, kitchen and front secondary bedroom
- Kitchen complete with pantry, angled bar and adjacent eating area
- Sloped ceiling in dining room

LOWE'S

Signature
SERIES

Plan #527-0727

Price Code A

Total Living Area: 1,477 Sq. Ft.

Home has 3 bedrooms, 2 baths, 2-car side entry garage and basement foundation.

Special features

- Oversized porch provides protection from the elements
- Innovative kitchen employs step-saving design
- Breakfast room offers bay window and snack bar open to kitchen with convenient laundry nearby
- Extra storage in garage

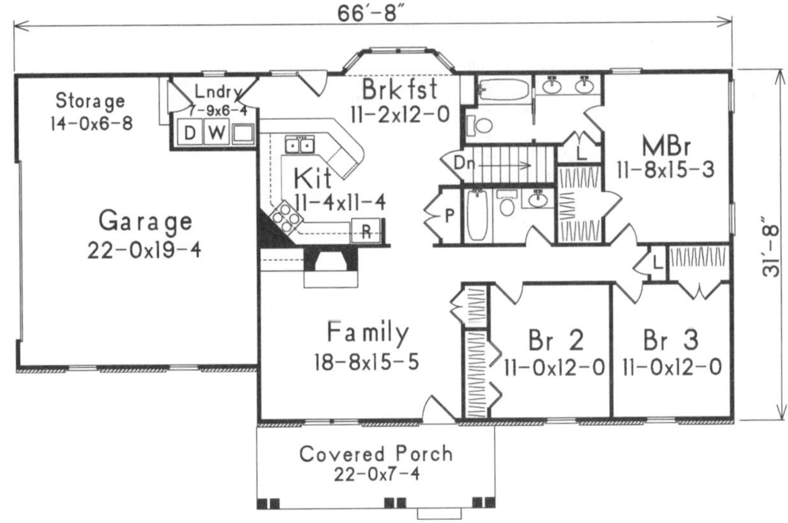
66'-8"
31'-8"
Storage
14-0x6-8
Lndry
7-9x6-4
D
W
Brkfst
11-2x12-0
Kit
11-4x11-4
R
Dn
P
L
MBr
11-8x15-3
Garage
22-0x19-4
Family
18-8x15-5
Br 2
11-0x12-0
Br 3
11-0x12-0
Covered Porch
22-0x7-4

 TO ORDER BLUEPRINTS USE THE FORM ON PAGE 290 OR CALL TOLL-FREE **1-800-DREAM HOME** (373-2646)

LOWE'S

Signature
SERIES

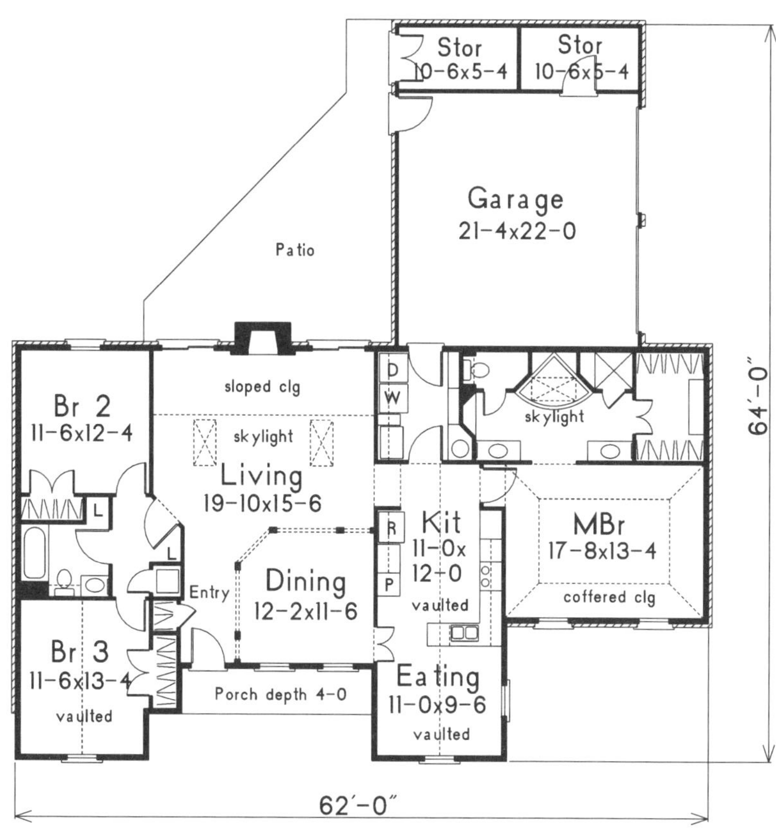
Stor
10-6x5-4
Stor
10-6x5-4
Garage
21-4x22-0
Patio
Br 2
11-6x12-4
sloped clg
skylight
Living
19-10x15-6
D
W
skylight
64'-0"
Kit
11-0x
12-0
vaulted
MBr
17-8x13-4
coffered clg
R
P
L
L
Entry
Dining
12-2x11-6
Br 3
11-6x13-4
vaulted
Porch depth 4-0
Eating
11-0x9-6
vaulted
62'-0"

Plan #527-0191

Price Code D

Total Living Area: 1,868 Sq. Ft.

Home has 3 bedrooms, 2 baths, 2-car side entry garage and slab foundation, drawings also include crawl space foundation.

Special features

- Luxurious master bath is impressive with its angled, quarter-circle tub, separate vanities and large walk-in closet
- Energy efficient home with 2" x 6" exterior walls
- Dining room is surrounded by series of arched openings which complement the open feeling of this design
- Living room has a 12' ceiling accented by skylights and a large fireplace flanked by sliding doors
- Large storage areas

Affordable Home Features Five Bedrooms

Plan #527-0481

Price Code C

Total Living Area: 2,012 Sq. Ft.

Home has 5 bedrooms, 2 1/2 baths, 2-car garage and basement foundation.

Special features

- Gables, cantilevers, angled and box bay windows all contribute to an elegant exterior
- Two-story entry leads to an efficient kitchen and bayed breakfast area with morning room
- Garage contains bonus area for a shop, bicycles and miscellaneous storage

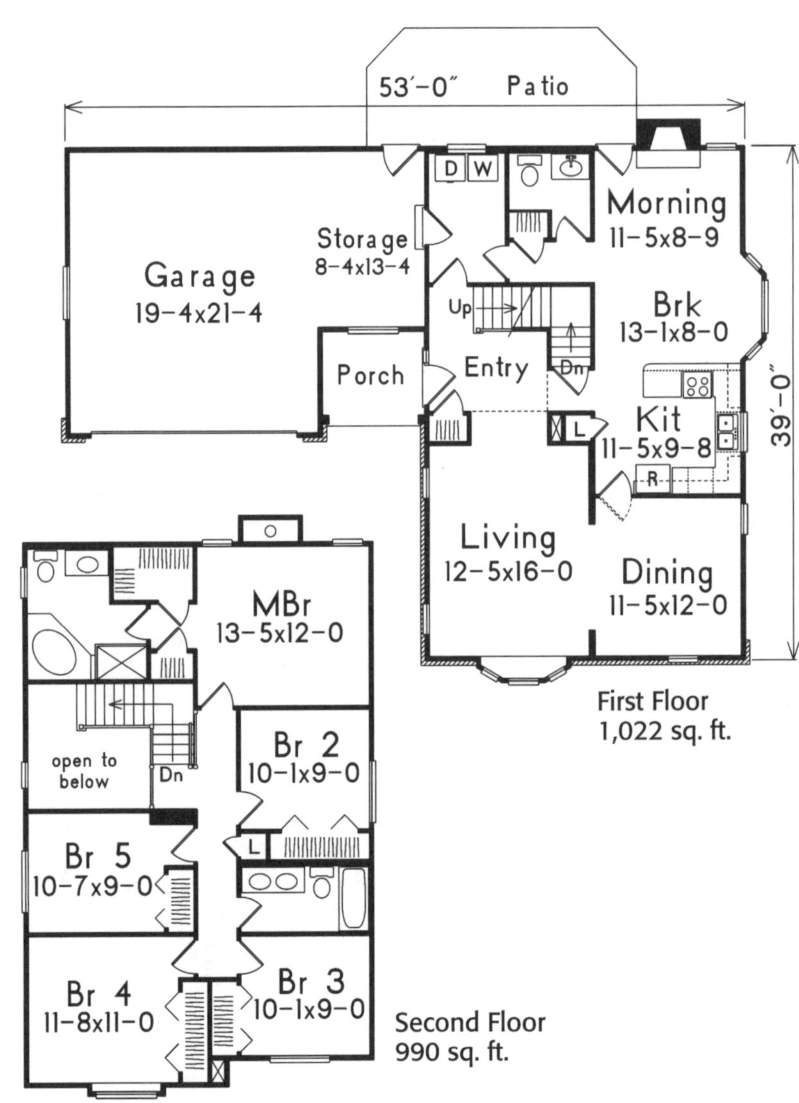
53′-0″
Patio
39′-0″
Garage 19-4x21-4
Storage 8-4x13-4
Porch
Entry
Up
Dn
D W
Morning 11-5x8-9
Brk 13-1x8-0
Kit 11-5x9-8
L
R
Living 12-5x16-0
Dining 11-5x12-0
MBr 13-5x12-0
open to below
Dn
Br 2 10-1x9-0
L
Br 5 10-7x9-0
Br 4 11-8x11-0
Br 3 10-1x9-0

First Floor
1,022 sq. ft.

Second Floor
990 sq. ft.

Contemporary Elegance With Efficiency

LOWE'S

Signature
SERIES

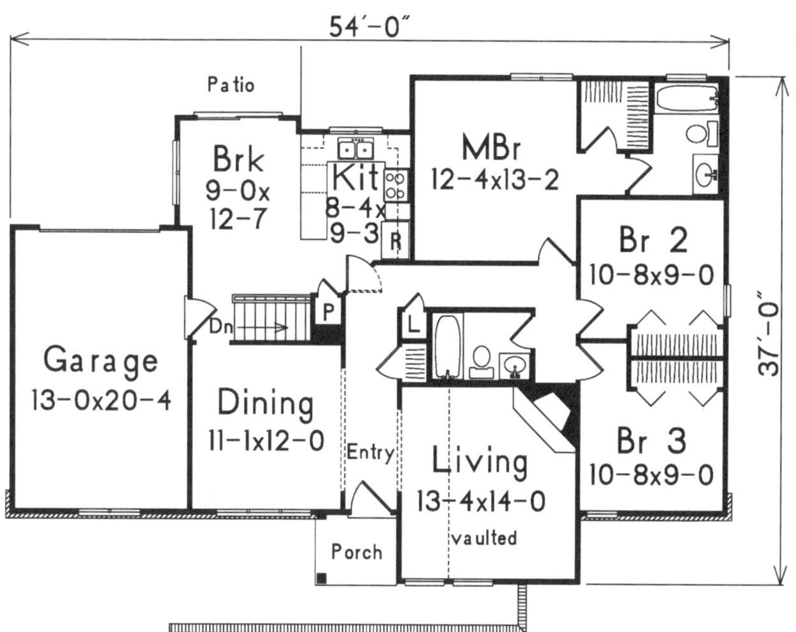
54'-0"
37'-0"
Patio
Brk
9-0x
12-7
Kit
8-4x
9-3
R
MBr
12-4x13-2
Br 2
10-8x9-0
Garage
13-0x20-4
Dn
P
L
Dining
11-1x12-0
Entry
Living
13-4x14-0
vaulted
Br 3
10-8x9-0
Porch

Plan #527-0660

Price Code A

Total Living Area: 1,321 Sq. Ft.

Home has 3 bedrooms, 2 baths, 1-car rear entry garage and basement foundation.

Special features

- Rear garage and elongated brick wall adds to appealing facade
- Dramatic vaulted living room includes corner fireplace and towering feature windows
- Kitchen/breakfast room is immersed in light from two large windows and glass sliding doors

Dramatic Layout Created By Victorian Turret

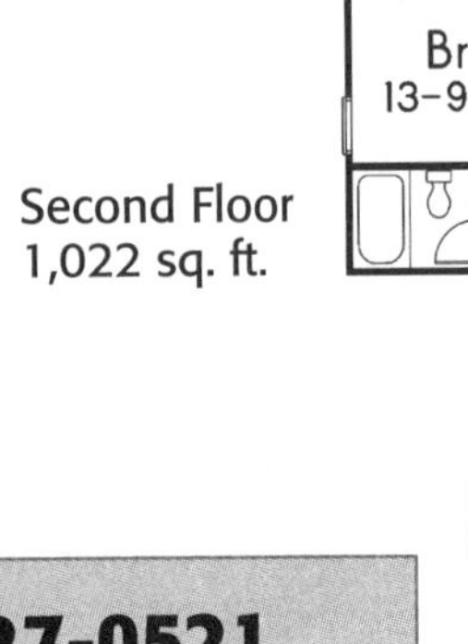
Br 2
13-9x10-5
skylts
W D
Br 3
9-4x
13-5
L
skylt
Dn
MBr
11-8x19-0

Second Floor
1,022 sq. ft.

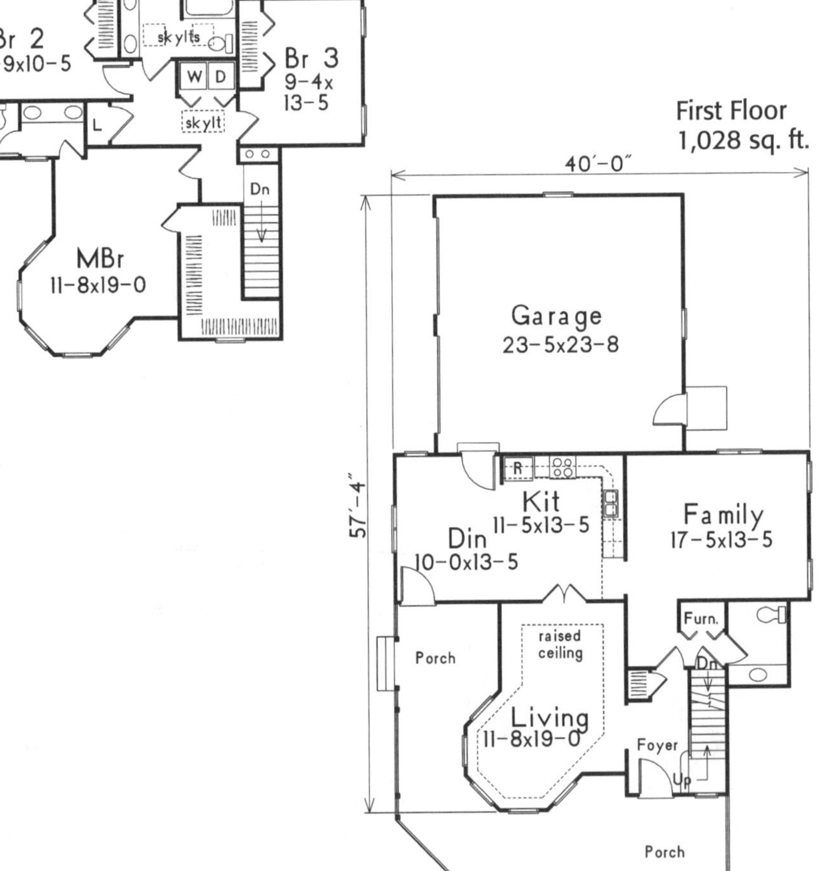
40'-0"
57'-4"
Garage
23-5x23-8
R
Kit
11-5x13-5
Din
10-0x13-5
Family
17-5x13-5
Furn.
Dn
raised
ceiling
Porch
Living
11-8x19-0
Foyer
Up
Porch

First Floor
1,028 sq. ft.

Plan #527-0521

Price Code C

Total Living Area: 2,050 Sq. Ft.

Home has 3 bedrooms, 2 1/2 baths, 2-car side entry garage and basement foundation, drawings also include crawl space and slab foundations.

Special features

- Large kitchen/dining area with access to garage and porch
- Master bedroom suite features unique turret design, private bath and large walk-in closet
- Laundry facilities conveniently located near bedrooms

LOWE'S

Signature
SERIES

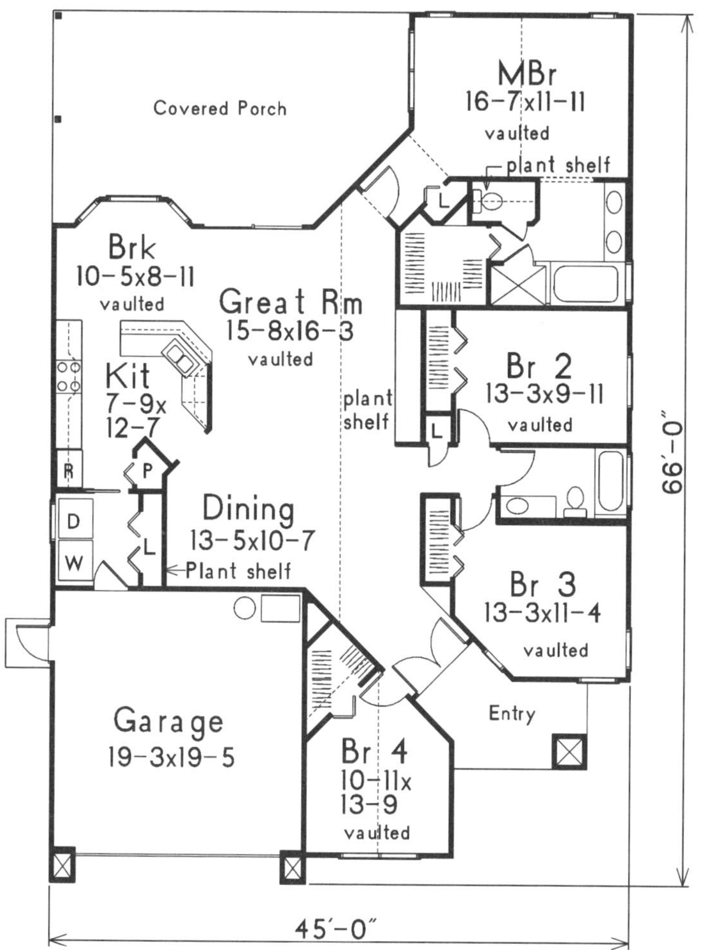
Covered Porch
MBr
16-7x11-11
vaulted
plant shelf
Brk
10-5x8-11
vaulted
Great Rm
15-8x16-3
vaulted
Kit
7-9x
12-7
plant
shelf
Br 2
13-3x9-11
vaulted
R
P
D
W
L
Dining
13-5x10-7
Plant shelf
Br 3
13-3x11-4
vaulted
Garage
19-3x19-5
Entry
Br 4
10-11x
13-9
vaulted
66'-0"
45'-0"

Plan #527-0335

Price Code D

Total Living Area: 1,865 Sq. Ft.

Home has 4 bedrooms, 2 baths, 2-car garage and slab foundation, drawings also include crawl space foundation.

Special features

- Large foyer opens into expansive dining/great room area
- Home features vaulted ceilings throughout
- Master suite features bath with double-bowl vanity, shower, tub and toilet in separate room for privacy

Plan #527-1117

Price Code A

Total Living Area: 1,440 Sq. Ft.

Home has 3 bedrooms, 2 baths, 2-car side entry garage and basement foundation, drawings also include crawl space and slab foundations.

Special features

- Foyer adjoins massive-sized space with sloping ceiling and tall masonry fireplace
- Kitchen adjoins spacious dining room and features pass-through breakfast bar
- Master suite enjoys private bath and two closets
- An oversized two-car side entry garage offers plenty of storage for bicycles, lawn equipment, etc.

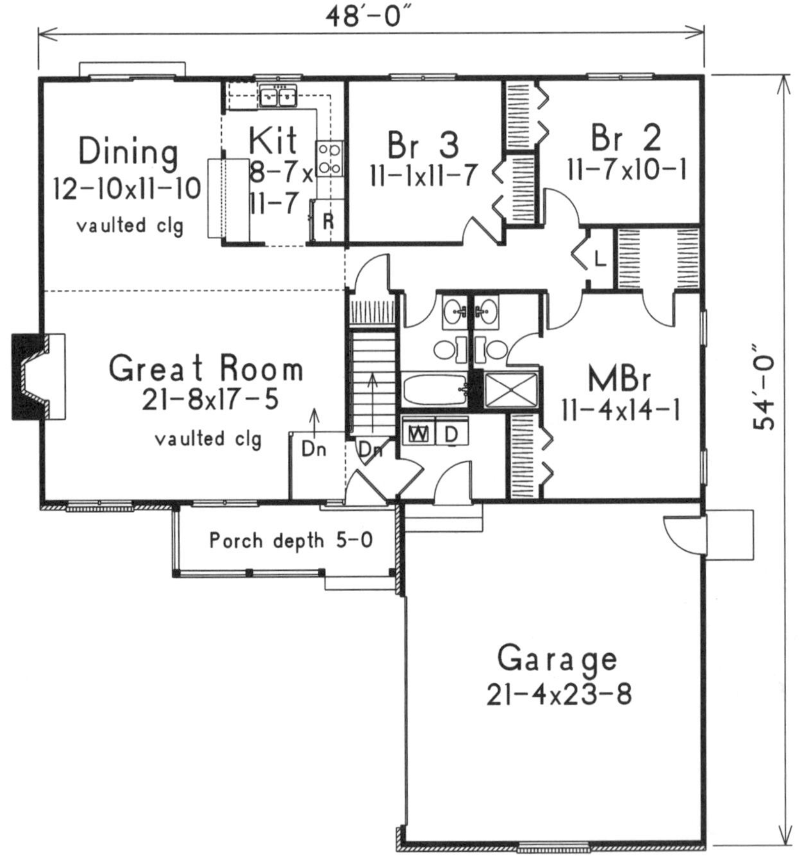

48'-0"
54'-0"
Dining
12-10x11-10
vaulted clg
Kit
8-7x
11-7
R
Br 3
11-1x11-7
Br 2
11-7x10-1
L
Great Room
21-8x17-5
vaulted clg
Dn
Dn
W D
MBr
11-4x14-1
Porch depth 5-0
Garage
21-4x23-8

Cottage With Atrium

LOWE'S

Signature
SERIES

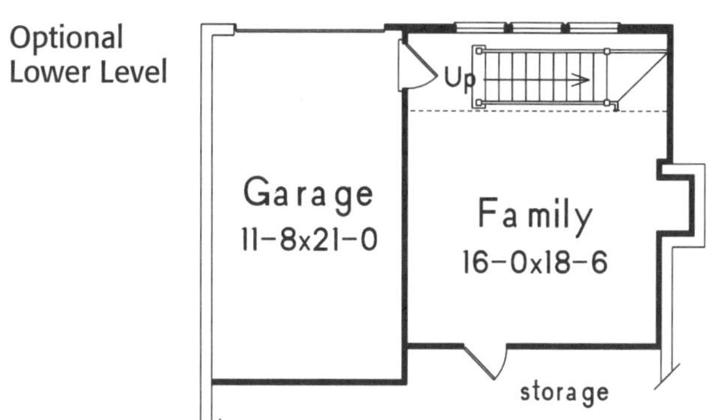
Optional
Lower Level
Up
Garage
11-8x21-0
Family
16-0x18-6
storage

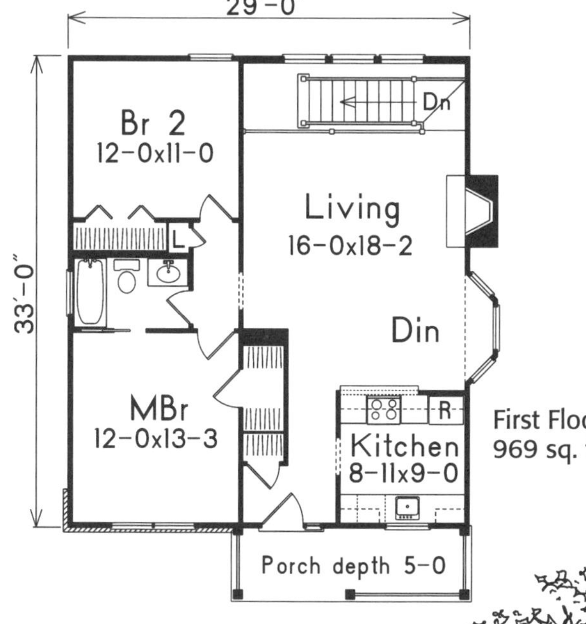
29'-0"
33'-0"
Br 2
12-0x11-0
L
Dn
Living
16-0x18-2
Din
MBr
12-0x13-3
R
Kitchen
8-11x9-0
Porch depth 5-0
First Floor
969 sq. ft.

Plan #527-0808

Price Code AA

Total Living Area: 969 Sq. Ft.

Home has 2 bedrooms, 1 bath, 1-car rear entry garage and walk-out basement foundation.

Special features

- Eye-pleasing facade enjoys stone accents with country porch for quiet evenings
- A bayed dining area, cozy fireplace and atrium with sunny two-story windows are the many features of the living room
- Step-saver kitchen includes a pass-through snack bar
- 325 square feet of optional living area on the lower level

Signature SERIES

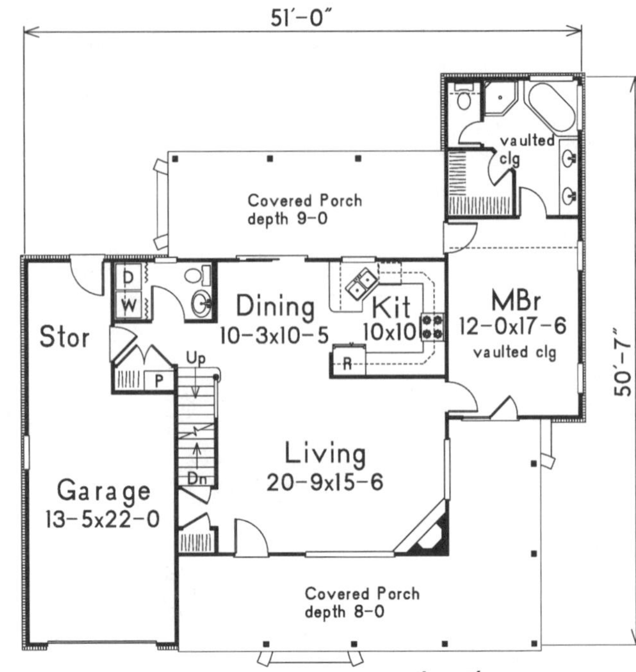
51'-0"
vaulted clg
Covered Porch
depth 9-0
D
W
Dining
10-3x10-5
Kit
10x10
MBr
12-0x17-6
vaulted clg
Stor
Up
P
R
50'-7"
Living
20-9x15-6
Garage
13-5x22-0
Dn
Covered Porch
depth 8-0

First Floor
1,112 sq. ft.

Plan #527-0723

Price Code B

Total Living Area: 1,784 Sq. Ft.

Home has 3 bedrooms, 2 1/2 baths, 1-car garage and basement foundation, drawings also include crawl space foundation.

Special features

- Secluded master suite has separate porch entrances and large master bath with walk-in closet
- Large second floor gathering area is great for kid's play area
- Spacious living area with corner fireplace offers a cheerful atmosphere with large windows

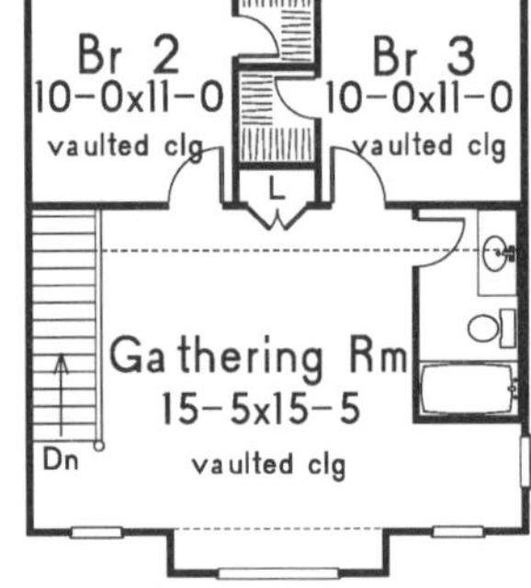
Br 2
10-0x11-0
vaulted clg
Br 3
10-0x11-0
vaulted clg
L
Gathering Rm
15-5x15-5
vaulted clg
Dn

Second Floor
672 sq. ft.

TO ORDER BLUEPRINTS USE THE FORM ON PAGE 290 OR CALL TOLL-FREE **1-800-DREAM HOME** (373-2646)

Innovative Ranch Has Cozy Corner Patio

LOWE'S

Signature SERIES

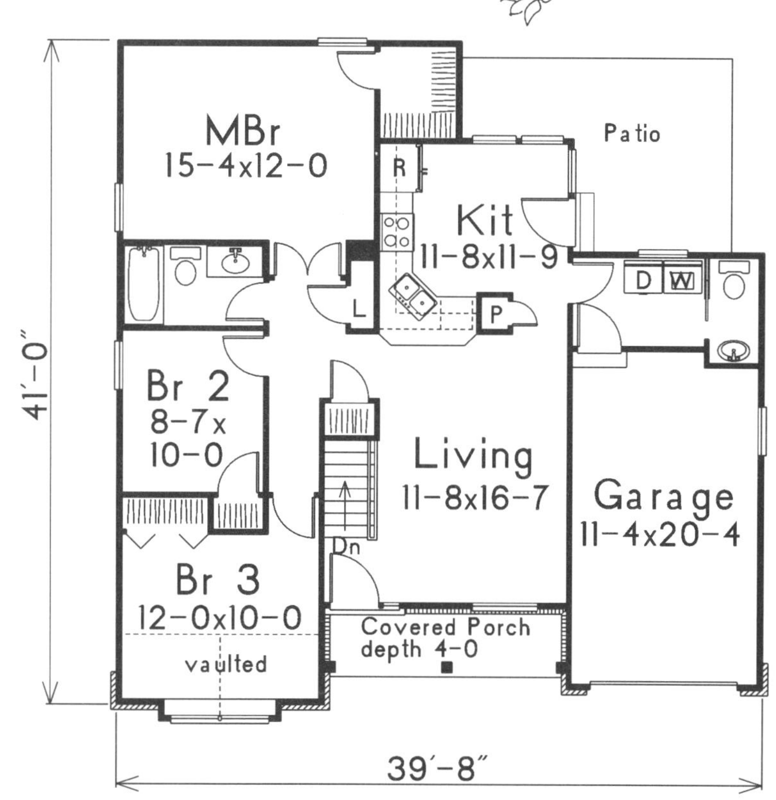
MBr
15-4x12-0
Patio
R
Kit
11-8x11-9
L
P
D
W
Br 2
8-7x
10-0
41'-0"
Living
11-8x16-7
Garage
11-4x20-4
Dn
Br 3
12-0x10-0
vaulted
Covered Porch
depth 4-0
39'-8"

Plan #527-0478

Price Code AA

Total Living Area: 1,092 Sq. Ft.

Home has 3 bedrooms, 1 1/2 baths, 1-car garage and basement foundation.

Special features

- Box window and inviting porch with dormers create a charming facade
- Eat-in kitchen offers a pass-through breakfast bar, corner window wall to patio, pantry and convenient laundry with half bath
- Master bedroom features double entry doors and walk-in closet

LOWE'S

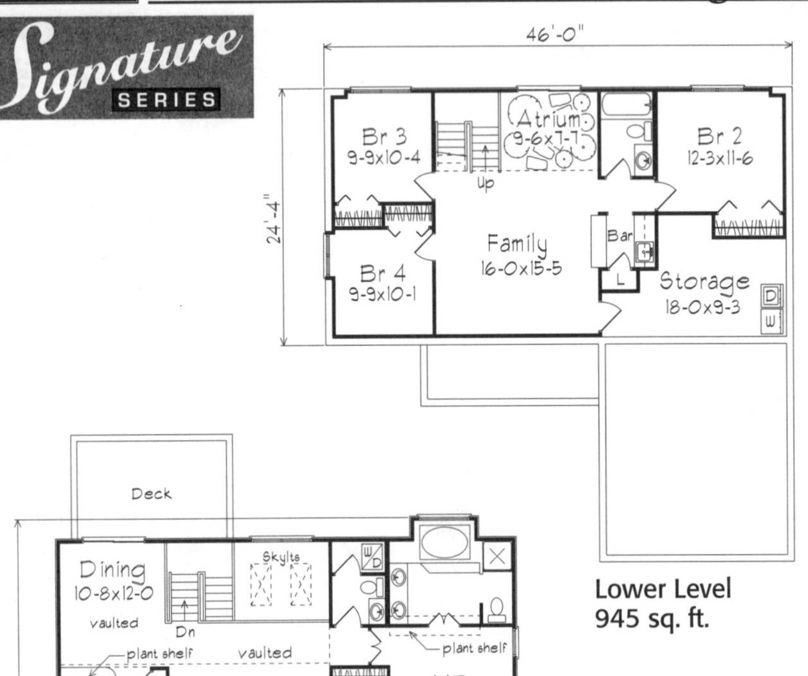
Signature
SERIES
46'-0"
24'-4"
Br 3
9-9x10-4
Atrium
9-6x7-7
Up
Br 2
12-3x11-6
Family
16-0x15-5
Bar
Br 4
9-9x10-1
L
Storage
18-0x9-3
D
W

Lower Level
945 sq. ft.

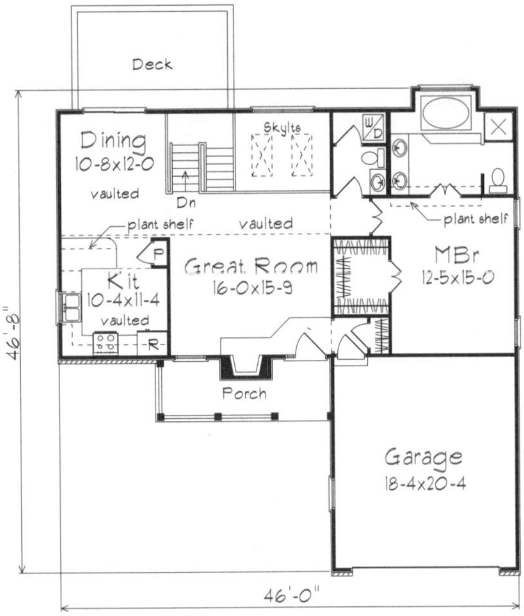

Plan #527-0420

Price Code C

Total Living Area: 1,941 Sq. Ft.

Home has 4 bedrooms, 2 1/2 baths, 2-car garage and walk-out basement foundation.

Special features

- Dramatic, exciting and spacious interior
- Vaulted great room brightened by sunken atrium window wall and skylights
- Vaulted U-shaped gourmet kitchen with plant shelf opens to dining room
- First floor half bath features space for stackable washer and dryer

First Floor
996 sq. ft.

Deck
Dining
10-8x12-0
vaulted
Skylts
Dn
W/D
plant shelf
vaulted
plant shelf
P
Great Room
16-0x15-9
MBr
12-5x15-0
Kit
10-4x11-4
vaulted
R
Porch
Garage
18-4x20-4
46'-8"
46'-0"

TO ORDER BLUEPRINTS USE THE FORM ON PAGE 290 OR CALL TOLL-FREE **1-800-DREAM HOME** (373-2646)

Garden Courtyard Lends Distinction, Privacy

LOWE'S

Signature SERIES

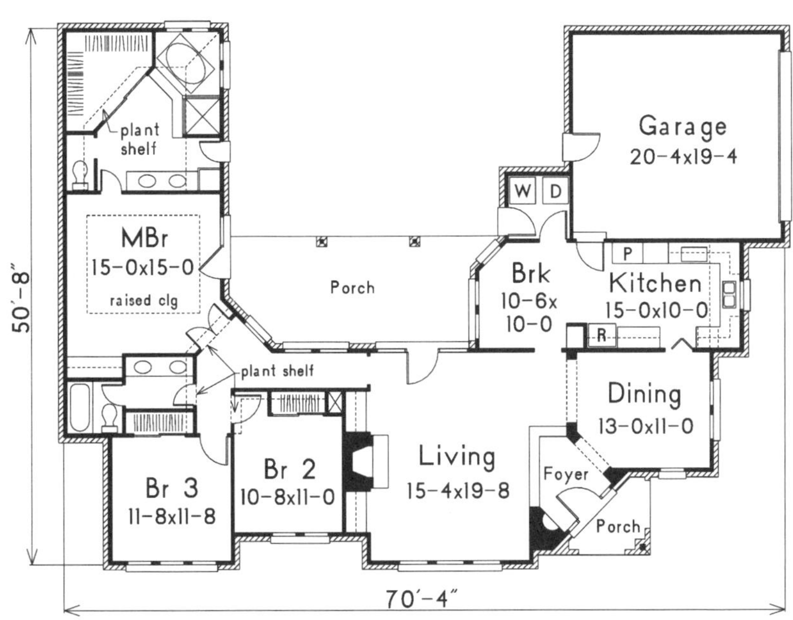
plant shelf
MBr
15-0x15-0
raised clg
Porch
W
D
Garage
20-4x19-4
P
Brk
10-6x
10-0
Kitchen
15-0x10-0
R
plant shelf
Dining
13-0x11-0
Br 3
11-8x11-8
Br 2
10-8x11-0
Living
15-4x19-8
Foyer
Porch
50'-8"
70'-4"

Plan #527-0127

Price Code D

Total Living Area: 1,996 Sq. Ft.

Home has 3 bedrooms, 2 baths, 2-car side entry garage and slab foundation, drawings also include crawl space foundation.

Special features

- Garden courtyard comes with large porch and direct access to master bedroom suite, breakfast room and garage
- Sculptured entrance with artful plant shelves and special niche in foyer
- Master bedroom boasts french doors, garden tub, desk with bookshelves and generous storage
- Plant ledges and high ceilings grace hallway

Signature SERIES

Exciting Living For A Narrow Sloping Lot

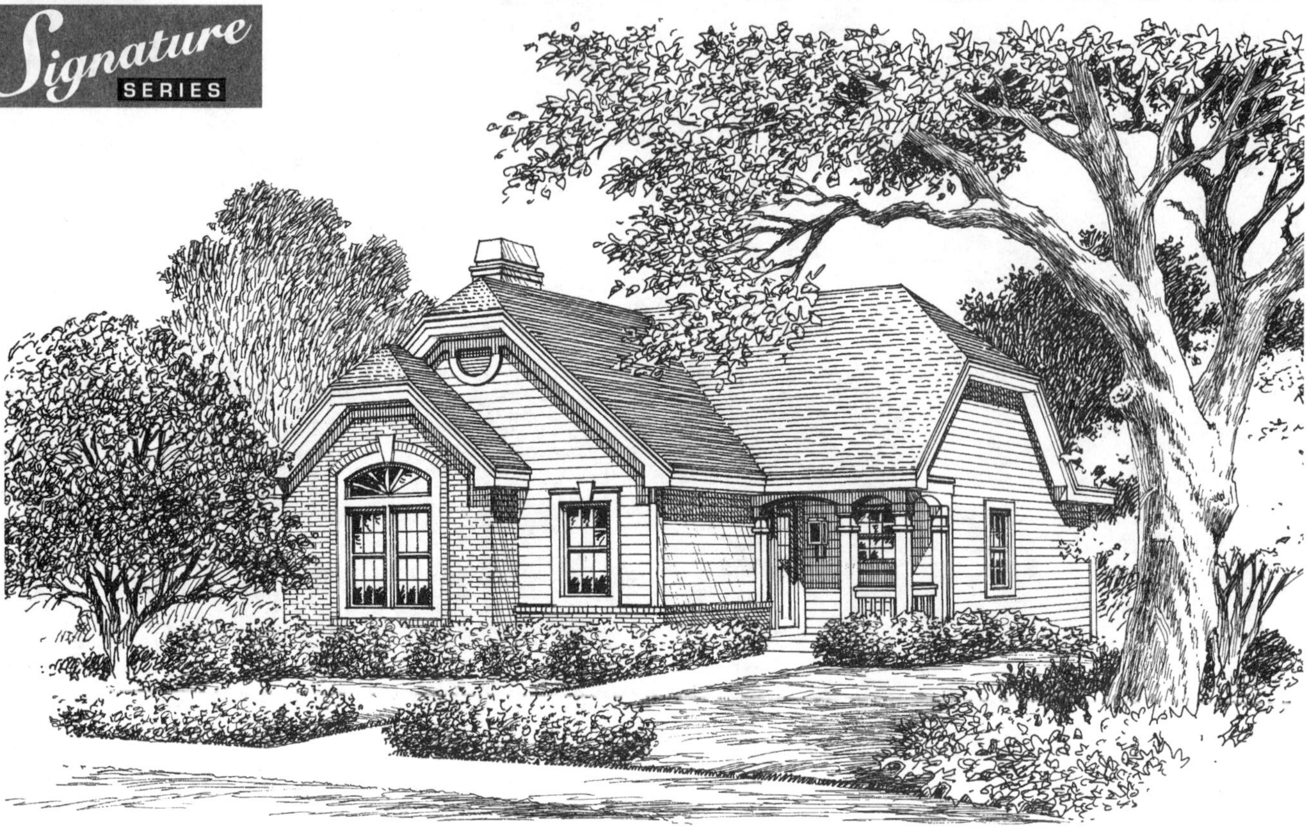

Plan #527-0810

Price Code A

Total Living Area: 1,200 Sq. Ft.

Home has 2 bedrooms, 1 bath and walk-out basement foundation.

Special features

- Entry leads to a large dining area which opens to kitchen and sun drenched living room
- An expansive window wall in the two-story atrium lends space and light to living room with fireplace
- The large kitchen features a breakfast bar, built-in pantry and storage galore
- 697 square feet of optional living area on the lower level includes a family room, bedroom #3 and a bath

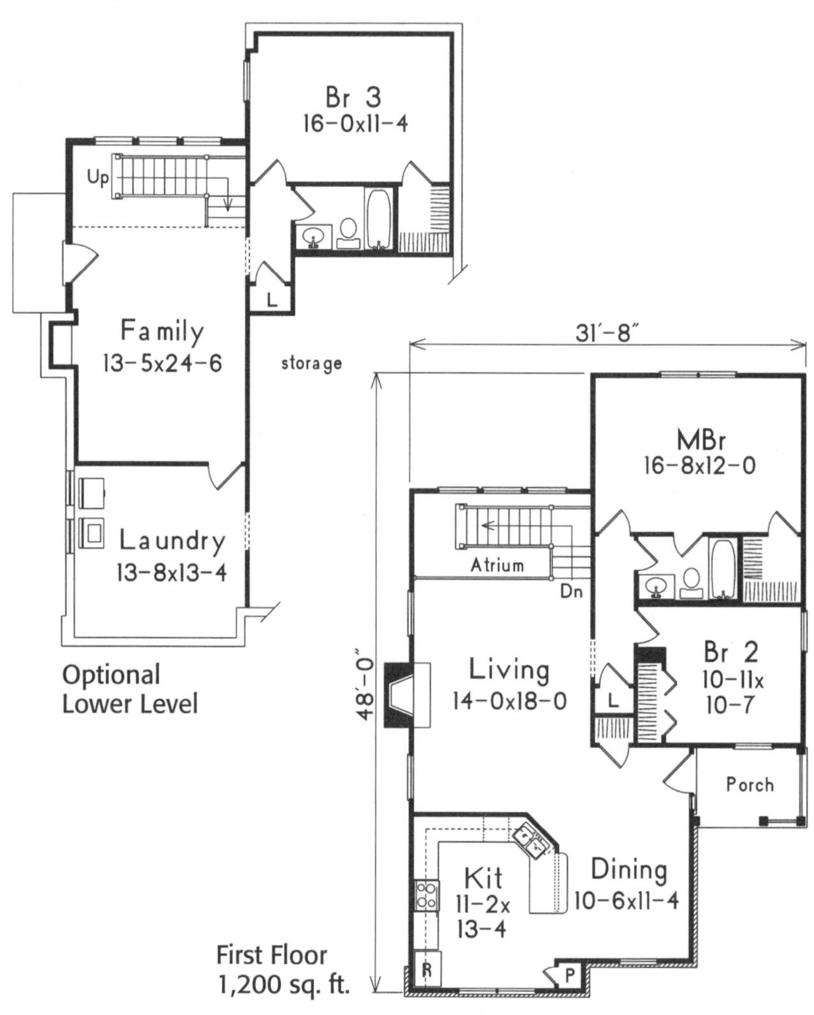

Br 3
16-0x11-4
Up
Family
13-5x24-6
storage
L
Laundry
13-8x13-4
Optional
Lower Level
31'-8"
48'-0"
MBr
16-8x12-0
Atrium
Dn
Br 2
10-11x
10-7
Living
14-0x18-0
L
Porch
Kit
11-2x
13-4
Dining
10-6x11-4
R
P
First Floor
1,200 sq. ft.

Covered Porch Surrounds Home

LOWE'S

Signature
SERIES

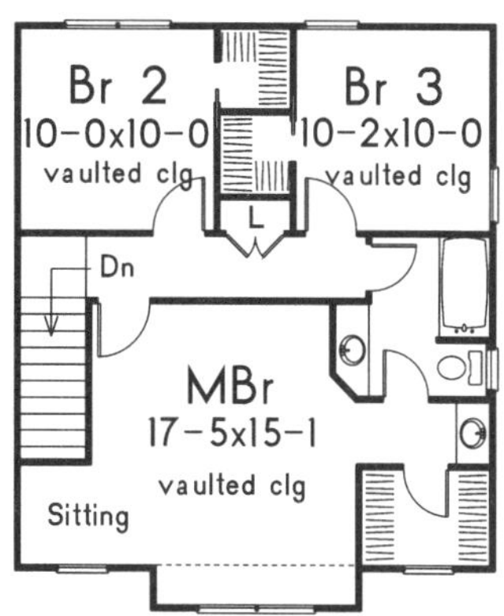
Br 2
10-0x10-0
vaulted clg
Br 3
10-2x10-0
vaulted clg
L
Dn
MBr
17-5x15-1
vaulted clg
Sitting

Second Floor
667 sq. ft.

First Floor
732 sq. ft.

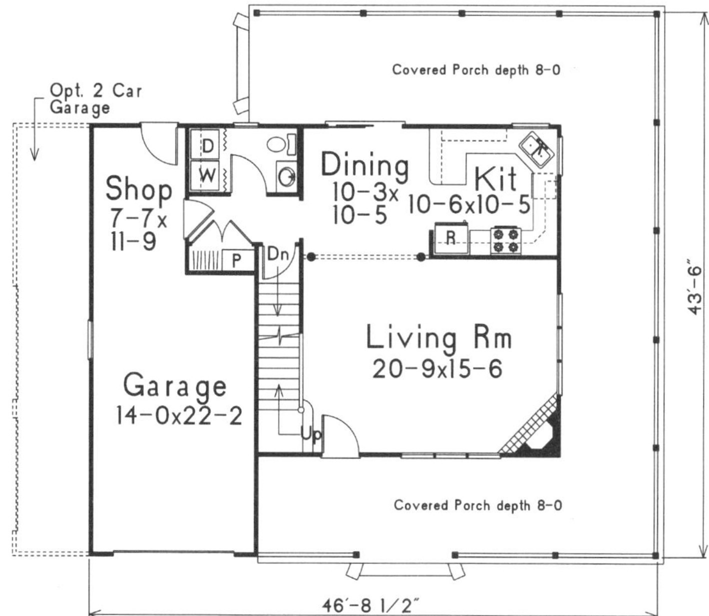
Covered Porch depth 8-0
Opt. 2 Car Garage
D
W
Shop
7-7x
11-9
P
Dn
Dining
10-3x
10-5
Kit
10-6x10-5
R
Living Rm
20-9x15-6
Garage
14-0x22-2
Up
43'-6"
Covered Porch depth 8-0
46'-8 1/2"

Plan #527-0795

Price Code A

Total Living Area: 1,399 Sq. Ft.

Home has 3 bedrooms, 1 1/2 baths, 1-car garage and basement foundation, drawings also include crawl space and slab foundations.

Special features

- Living room overlooks dining area through arched columns
- Laundry room contains handy half bath
- Spacious master bedroom includes sitting area, walk-in closet and plenty of sunlight
- Extra storage in garage

Plan #527-0794

Price Code A

Total Living Area: 1,433 Sq. Ft.

Home has 3 bedrooms, 2 baths, 2-car garage and basement foundation, drawings also include crawl space and slab foundations.

Special features

- Vaulted living room has cozy fireplace
- Separated master bedroom for privacy
- Large pantry in kitchen for efficiency

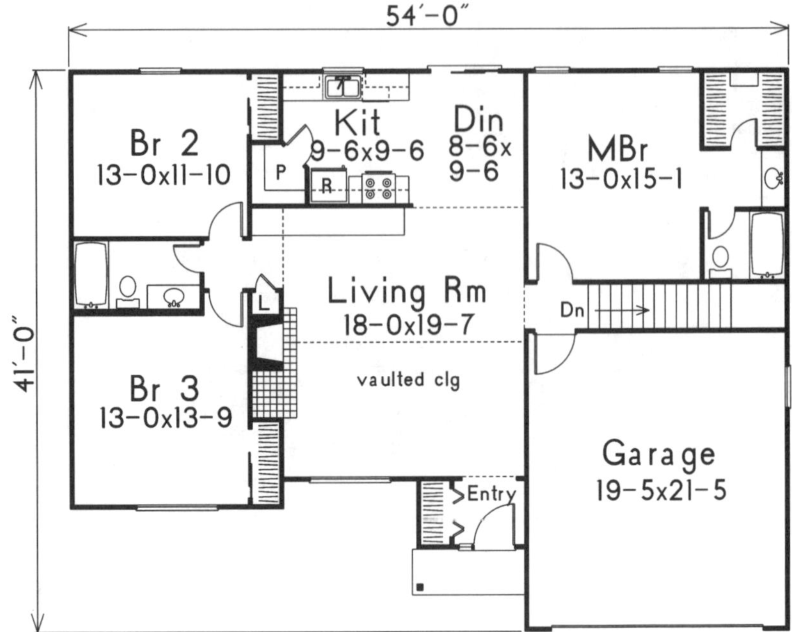
54'-0"
41'-0"
Br 2
13-0x11-10
Kit
9-6x9-6
Din
8-6x
9-6
MBr
13-0x15-1
P
R
L
Living Rm
18-0x19-7
vaulted clg
Dn
Br 3
13-0x13-9
Garage
19-5x21-5
Entry

 TO ORDER BLUEPRINTS USE THE FORM ON PAGE 290 OR CALL TOLL-FREE **1-800-DREAM HOME** (373-2646)

Smart Floor Plan Makes Efficient Design

LOWE'S

Signature
SERIES

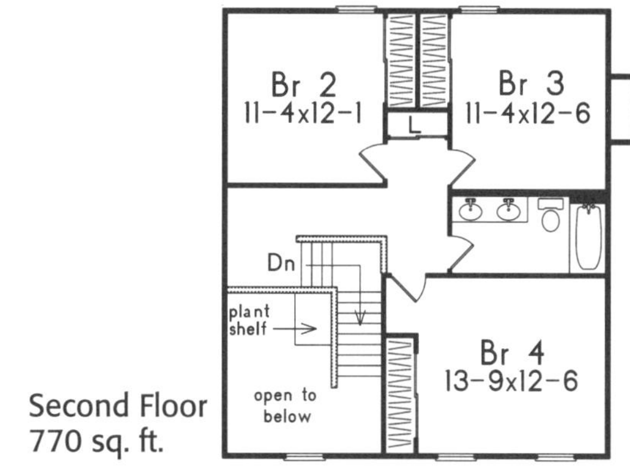
Br 2
11-4x12-1
Br 3
11-4x12-6
L
Dn
plant shelf
open to below
Br 4
13-9x12-6

Second Floor
770 sq. ft.

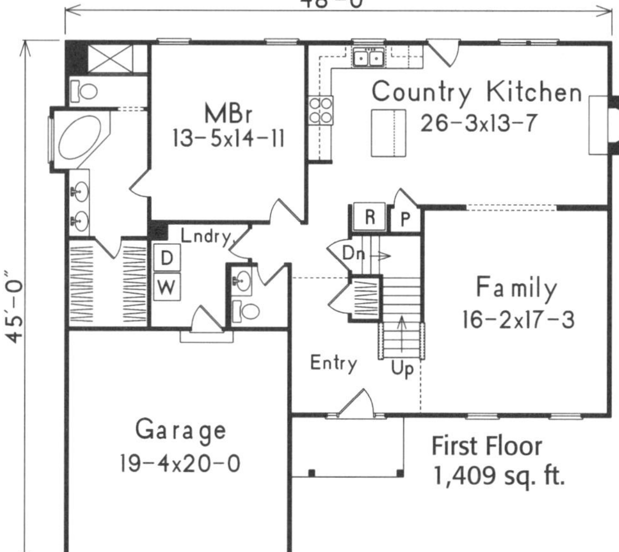
48'-0"
45'-0"
MBr
13-5x14-11
Country Kitchen
26-3x13-7
Lndry
D
W
R
P
Dn
Family
16-2x17-3
Entry
Up
Garage
19-4x20-0

First Floor
1,409 sq. ft.

Plan #527-0773

Price Code C

Total Living Area: 2,179 Sq. Ft.

Home has 4 bedrooms, 2 1/2 baths, 2-car garage and basement foundation.

Special features

- Open floor plan and minimal halls eliminate wasted space and create efficiency
- First floor master suite is conveniently located near large kitchen
- Three bedrooms on the second floor share large bath with nearby linen closet

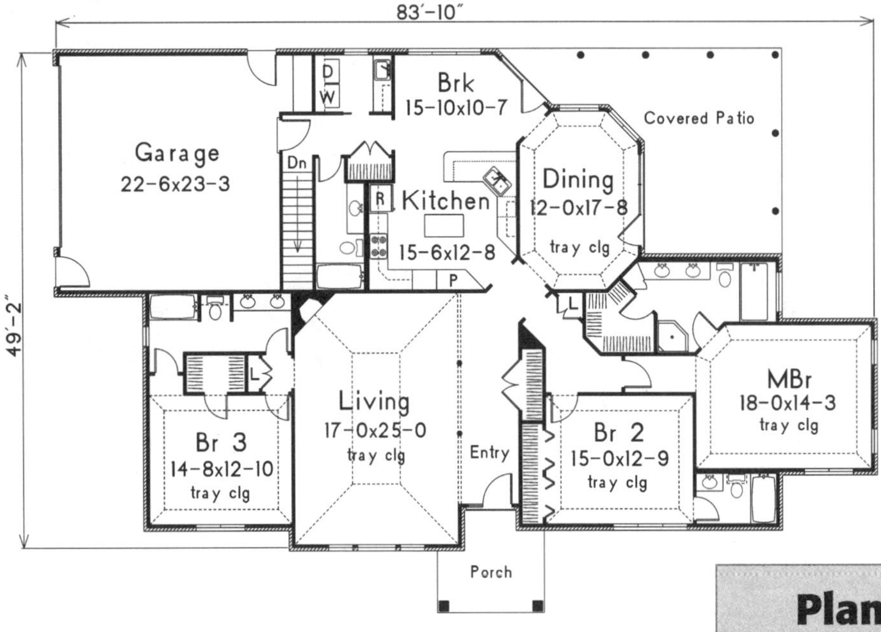

83'-10"
49'-2"
Brk
15-10x10-7
D
W
Covered Patio
Garage
22-6x23-3
Dn
Kitchen
15-6x12-8
R
P
Dining
12-0x17-8
tray clg
L
MBr
18-0x14-3
tray clg
L
Br 3
14-8x12-10
tray clg
Living
17-0x25-0
tray clg
Entry
Br 2
15-0x12-9
tray clg
Porch

Plan #527-0800

Price Code D

Total Living Area: 2,532 Sq. Ft.

Home has 3 bedrooms, 3 baths, 2-car side entry garage and crawl space foundation, drawings also include slab foundation.

Special features

- Covered patio surrounds rear of home
- Living and dining rooms feature tray ceiling
- Guest room with bath has optional entrance and lots of storage

LOWE'S

Signature SERIES

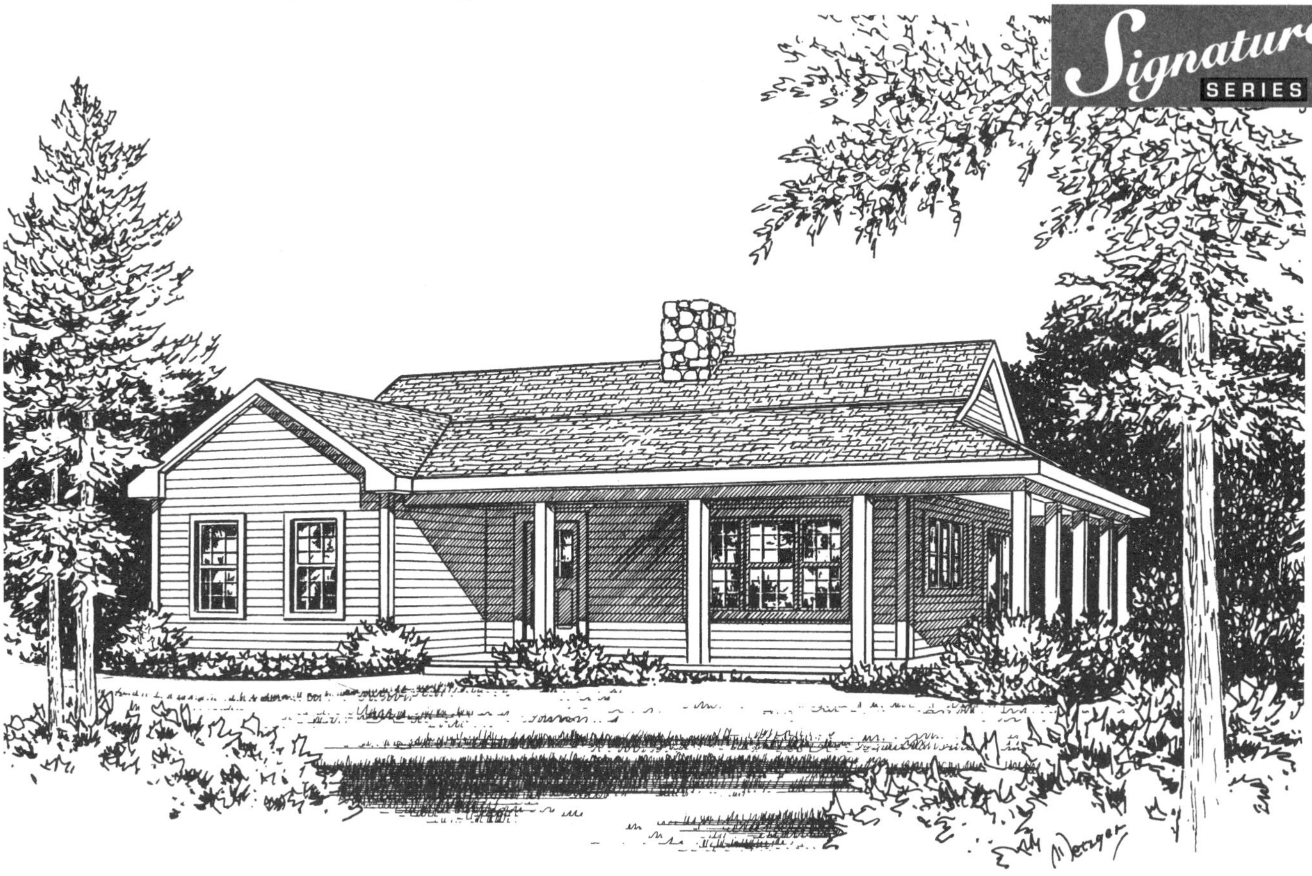

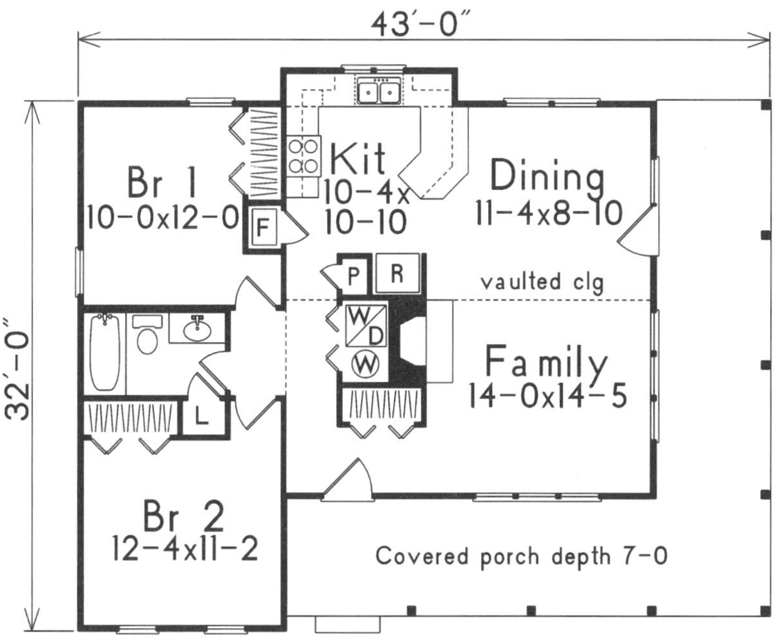
43'-0"
32'-0"
Br 1
10-0x12-0
F
Kit
10-4x
10-10
Dining
11-4x8-10
P
R
vaulted clg
W/D
W
Family
14-0x14-5
L
Br 2
12-4x11-2
Covered porch depth 7-0

Plan #527-0766

Price Code AA

Total Living Area: 990 Sq. Ft.

Home has 2 bedrooms, 1 bath and crawl space foundation.

Special features

- Wrap-around porch on two sides of this home
- Private and efficiently designed
- Space for efficiency washer and dryer unit for convenience

LOWE'S

Signature
SERIES

Open Floor Plan Makes Home Feel Larger

Plan #527-0779

Price Code A

Total Living Area: 1,277 Sq. Ft.

Home has 3 bedrooms, 2 baths, 2-car garage and basement foundation.

Special features

- Vaulted ceilings in master bedroom, great room, kitchen and dining room
- Laundry closet located near bedrooms for convenience
- Compact but efficient kitchen

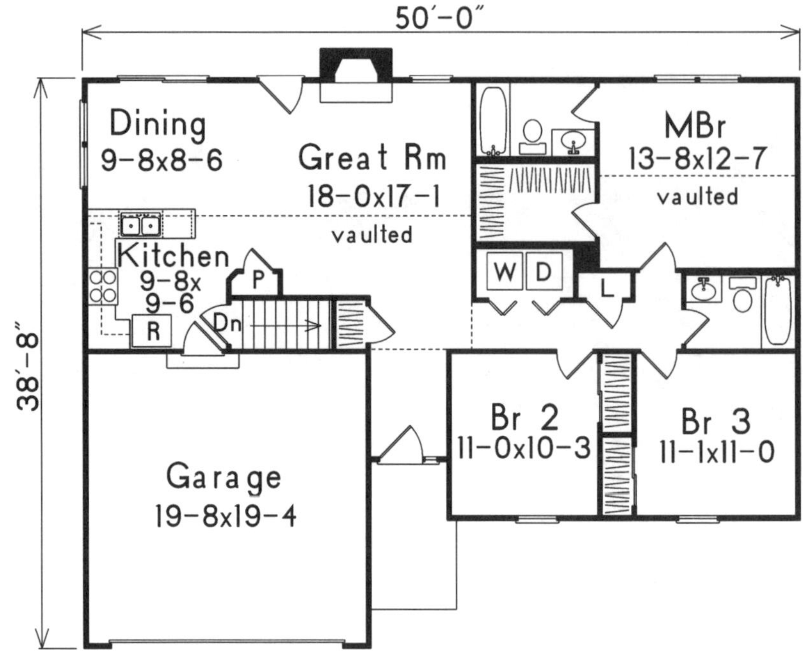
50′-0″
38′-8″
Dining
9-8x8-6
Great Rm
18-0x17-1
vaulted
MBr
13-8x12-7
vaulted
Kitchen
9-8x
9-6
P
R
Dn
W
D
L
Br 2
11-0x10-3
Br 3
11-1x11-0
Garage
19-8x19-4

Bedrooms Separate From Rest Of Home

LOWE'S

Plan #527-0799

Price Code C

Total Living Area: 1,849 Sq. Ft.

Home has 3 bedrooms, 2 1/2 baths, 2-car side entry garage and slab foundation, drawings also include crawl space foundation.

Special features

- Vaulted great room with corner fireplace
- Efficient kitchen with adjacent bay windowed breakfast room
- Large laundry/mud room
- Vaulted master suite with private bath

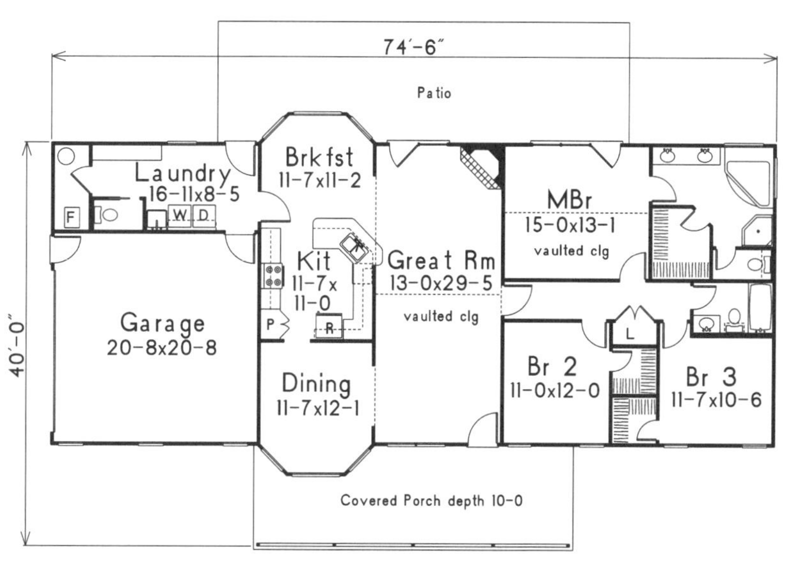
74'-6"
Patio
Brk fst
11-7x11-2
Laundry
16-11x8-5
W D
F
MBr
15-0x13-1
vaulted clg
Kit
11-7x
11-0
Great Rm
13-0x29-5
vaulted clg
P
R
L
Garage
20-8x20-8
40'-0"
Dining
11-7x12-1
Br 2
11-0x12-0
Br 3
11-7x10-6
Covered Porch depth 10-0

Open Floor Plan With Extra Amenities

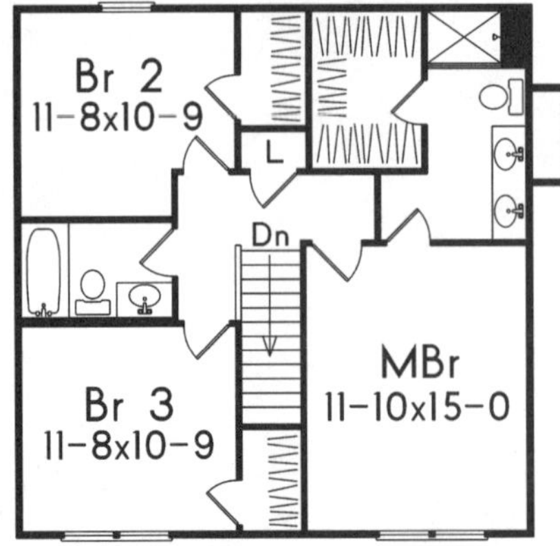

Br 2
11-8x10-9
L
Dn
Br 3
11-8x10-9
MBr
11-10x15-0

Second Floor
784 sq. ft.

Plan #527-0774

Price Code B

Total Living Area: 1,680 Sq. Ft.

Home has 3 bedrooms, 2 1/2 baths, 2-car garage and basement foundation.

Special features

- Compact and efficient layout in an affordable package
- Second floor has three bedrooms all with oversized closets
- All bedrooms on second floor for privacy

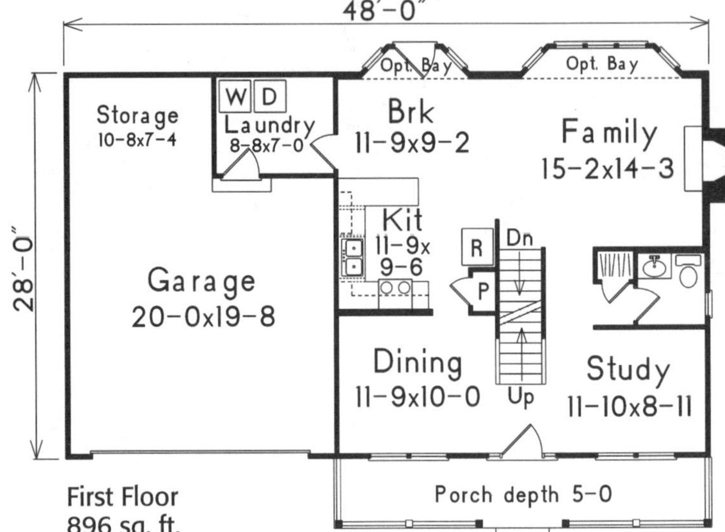

48'-0"
28'-0"
Opt. Bay
Opt. Bay
Storage
10-8x7-4
W D
Laundry
8-8x7-0
Brk
11-9x9-2
Family
15-2x14-3
Kit
11-9x
9-6
R
P
Dn
Garage
20-0x19-8
Dining
11-9x10-0
Up
Study
11-10x8-11
Porch depth 5-0

First Floor
896 sq. ft.

Home Features Generous Room Sizes

LOWE'S

Signature SERIES

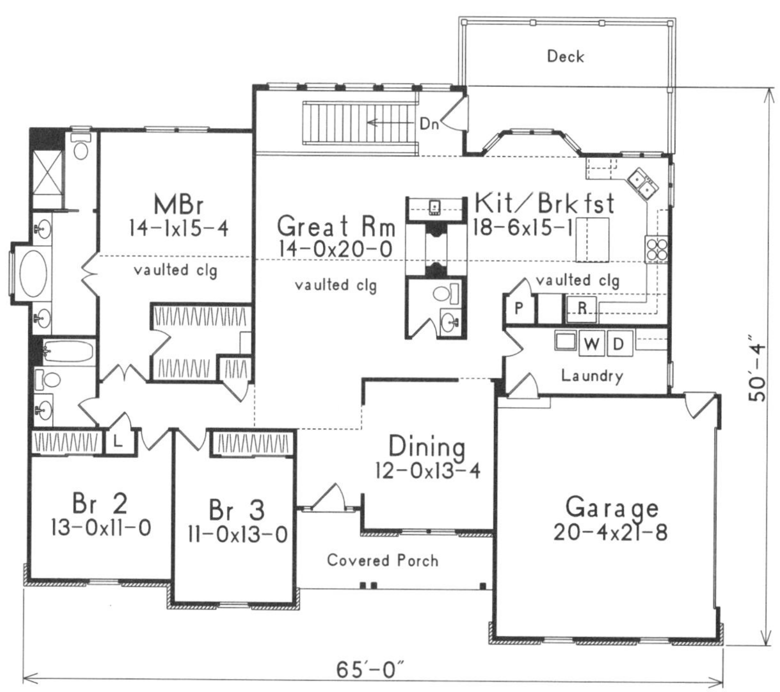
Deck
Dn
MBr
14-1x15-4
vaulted clg
Great Rm
14-0x20-0
vaulted clg
Kit/Brkfst
18-6x15-1
vaulted clg
P
R.
W
D
Laundry
L
Dining
12-0x13-4
Br 2
13-0x11-0
Br 3
11-0x13-0
Covered Porch
Garage
20-4x21-8
50'-4"
65'-0"

Plan #527-0744

Price Code C

Total Living Area: 2,164 Sq. Ft.

Home has 3 bedrooms, 2 1/2 baths, 2-car side entry garage and basement foundation.

Special features

- Great design for entertaining with wet bar and see-through fireplace in great room
- Plenty of closet space
- Vaulted ceiling enlarges the master bedroom, great room and kitchen/ breakfast area
- Great room features great view to the rear of the home

Balcony Enjoys Spectacular Views In Atrium Home

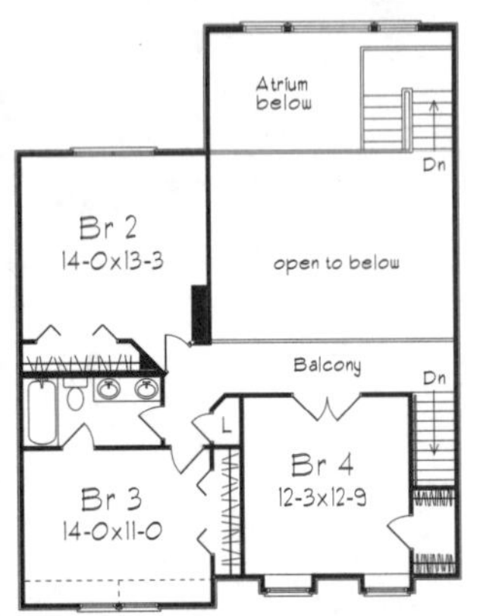
Atrium below
Dn
Br 2
14-0x13-3
open to below
Balcony
Dn
Br 3
14-0x11-0
Br 4
12-3x12-9

Second Floor
785 sq. ft.

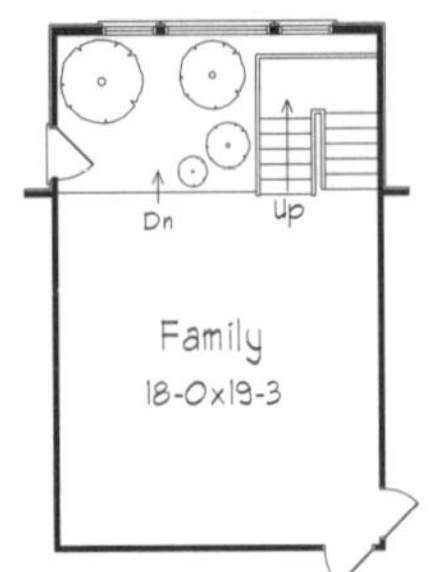
Dn
Up
Family
18-0x19-3

Lower Level
548 sq. ft.

Plan #527-0356

Price Code E

Total Living Area: 2,806 Sq. Ft.

Home has 4 bedrooms, 2 1/2 baths, 2-car garage and walk-out basement foundation.

Special features

- Harmonious charm throughout
- Sweeping balcony and vaulted ceiling soar above spacious great room and walk-in bar
- Atrium with lower level family room is a unique touch creating an open and airy feeling

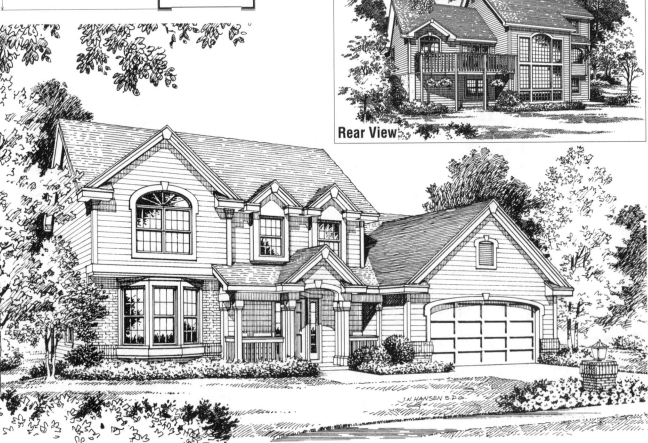

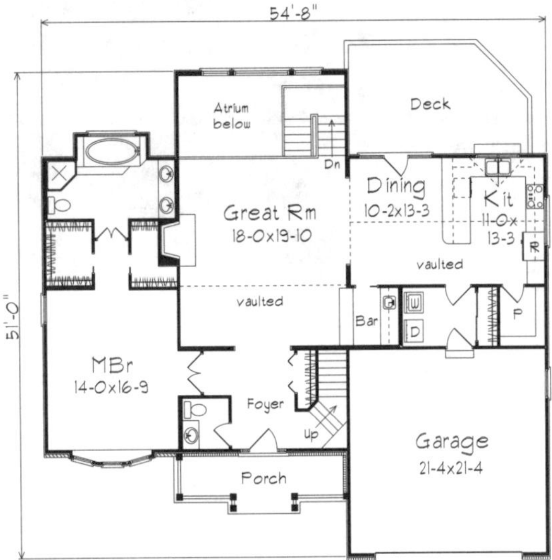
54'-8"
51'-0"
Atrium below
Deck
Dn
Dining
10-2x13-3
Kit
11-0x
13-3
Great Rm
18-0x19-10
vaulted
vaulted
Bar
MBr
14-0x16-9
Foyer
Up
Porch
Garage
21-4x21-4

First Floor
1,473 sq. ft.

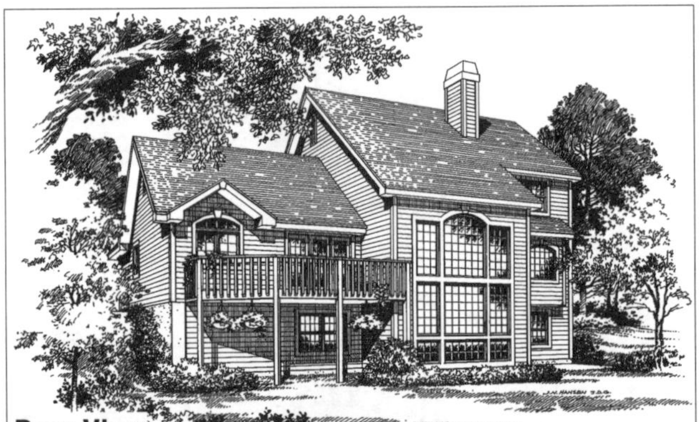

Rear View

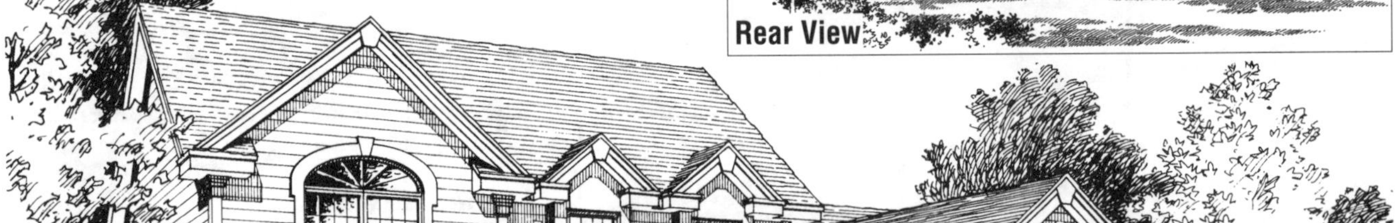

TO ORDER BLUEPRINTS USE THE FORM ON PAGE 290 OR CALL TOLL-FREE **1-800-DREAM HOME** (373-2646)

LOWE'S

Signature SERIES

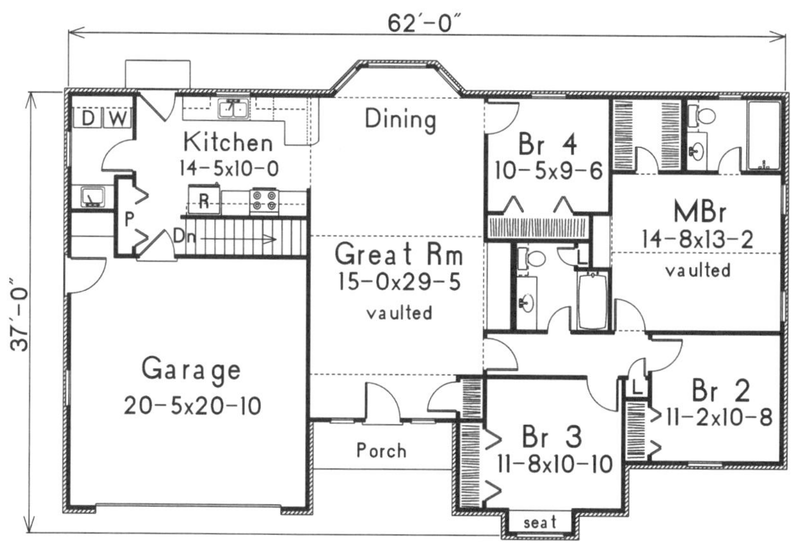

62′-0″
37′-0″
D
W
Kitchen
14-5x10-0
R
P
Dn
Dining
Great Rm
15-0x29-5
vaulted
Garage
20-5x20-10
Porch
Br 4
10-5x9-6
MBr
14-8x13-2
vaulted
Br 3
11-8x10-10
seat
Br 2
11-2x10-8

Plan #527-0796

Price Code B

Total Living Area: 1,599 Sq. Ft.

Home has 4 bedrooms, 2 baths, 2-car garage and basement foundation, drawings also include crawl space and slab foundations.

Special features

- Efficiently designed kitchen with large pantry and easy access to laundry room
- Bedroom #3 has charming window seat
- Master bedroom has a full bath and large walk-in closet

Charming Covered Porch

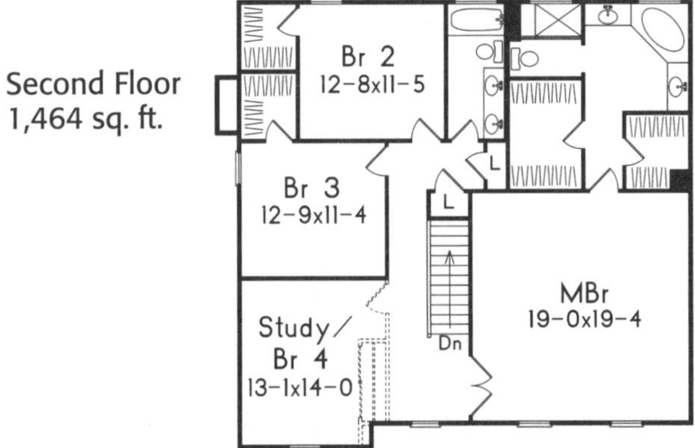
Br 2
12-8x11-5
Br 3
12-9x11-4
L
L
Study/
Br 4
13-1x14-0
Dn
MBr
19-0x19-4

Second Floor
1,464 sq. ft.

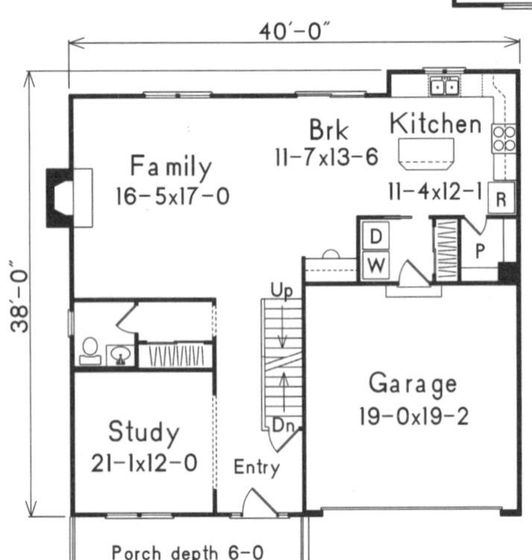
40'-0"
38'-0"
Family
16-5x17-0
Brk
11-7x13-6
Kitchen
11-4x12-1
R
D
W
P
Up
Dn
Study
21-1x12-0
Entry
Garage
19-0x19-2
Porch depth 6-0

First Floor
1,083 sq. ft.

Plan #527-0782

Price Code D

Total Living Area: 2,547 Sq. Ft.

Home has 3 bedrooms, 2 1/2 baths, 2-car garage and basement foundation.

Special features

- Second floor makes economical use of area above garage allowing for three bedrooms and a study/fourth bedroom
- First floor study ideal for home office
- Large pantry in efficient kitchen space

TO ORDER BLUEPRINTS USE THE FORM ON PAGE 290 OR CALL TOLL-FREE **1-800-DREAM HOME** (373-2646)

Generous Closets In All The Bedrooms

LOWE'S

Signature
SERIES

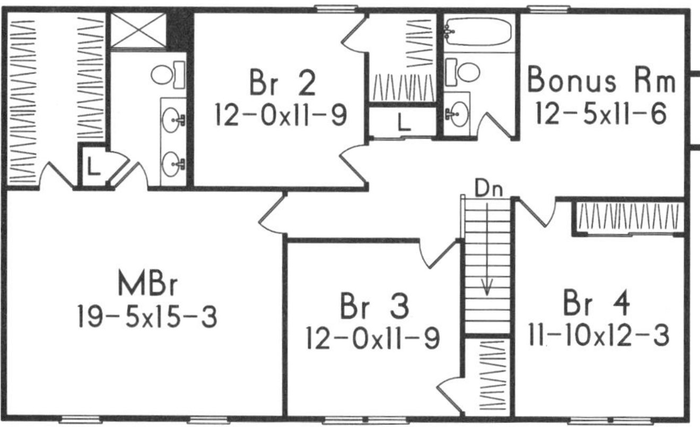
Br 2
12-0x11-9
L
Bonus Rm
12-5x11-6
L
Dn
MBr
19-5x15-3
Br 3
12-0x11-9
Br 4
11-10x12-3

Second Floor
1,344 sq. ft.

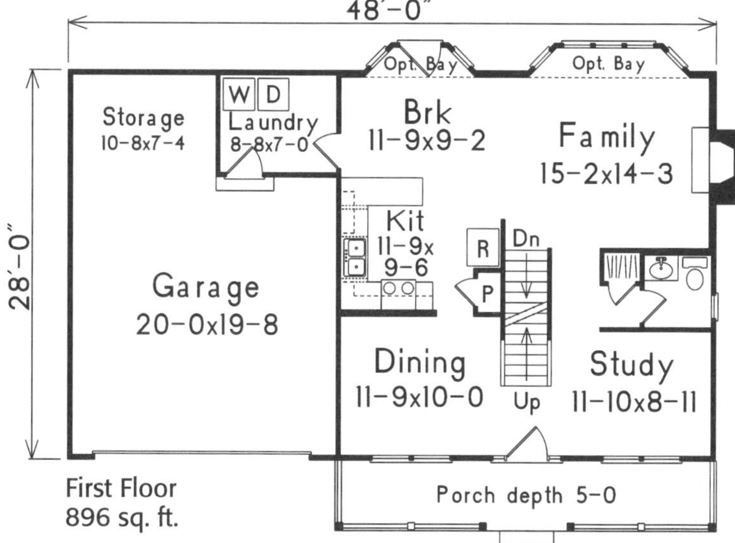
48'-0"
28'-0"
Opt. Bay
Opt. Bay
Storage
10-8x7-4
W D
Laundry
8-8x7-0
Brk
11-9x9-2
Family
15-2x14-3
Kit
11-9x
9-6
R
Dn
P
Garage
20-0x19-8
Dining
11-9x10-0
Up
Study
11-10x8-11
Porch depth 5-0

First Floor
896 sq. ft.

Plan #527-0775

Price Code D

Total Living Area: 2,240 Sq. Ft.

Home has 4 bedrooms, 2 1/2 baths, 2-car garage and basement foundation.

Special features

- Floor plan makes good use of space above garage allowing for four bedrooms and a bonus room on the second floor
- Formal dining room easily accessible to kitchen
- Cozy family room with fireplace and sunny bay window

Grandscale Great Room In A Country Ranch

Plan #527-0751

Price Code A

Total Living Area: 1,278 Sq. Ft.

Home has 3 bedrooms, 1 bath, 2-car garage and walk-out basement foundation.

Special features

- Excellent U-shaped kitchen with garden window opens to an enormous great room with vaulted ceiling, fireplace and two skylights
- Vaulted master bedroom offers double entry doors, access to a deck and bath and two walk-in closets
- The bath has a double-bowl vanity and dramatic step-up garden tub with a lean-to greenhouse window
- 805 square feet of optional living area on lower level with family room, bedroom #4 and bath

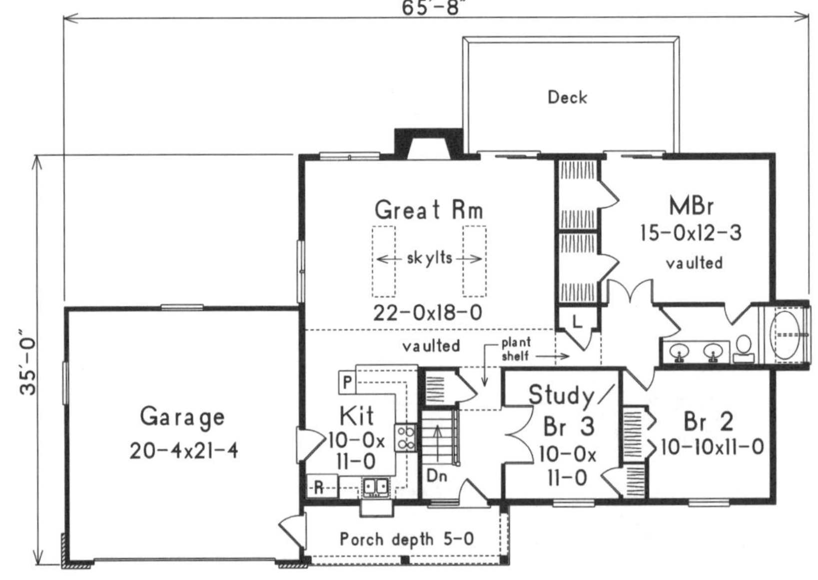
65'-8"
35'-0"
Deck
Great Rm
skylts
22-0x18-0
vaulted
plant shelf
MBr
15-0x12-3
vaulted
L
P
Kit
10-0x
11-0
R
Dn
Study/
Br 3
10-0x
11-0
Br 2
10-10x11-0
Garage
20-4x21-4
Porch depth 5-0

First Floor
1,278 sq. ft.

Family
21-6x14-4
Br 4
12-9x14-4
Up
Storage

Optional
Lower Level

TO ORDER BLUEPRINTS USE THE FORM ON PAGE 290 OR CALL TOLL-FREE **1-800-DREAM HOME** (373-2646)

Secluded Master Suite

LOWE'S

Signature
SERIES

Plan #527-0745

Price Code C

Total Living Area: 1,819 Sq. Ft.

Home has 3 bedrooms, 2 baths, 2-car side entry garage and basement foundation.

Special features

- Master suite features access to the outdoors, large walk-in closet and private bath
- 9' ceilings throughout
- Formal foyer with coat closet opens into vaulted great room with fireplace and formal dining room
- Kitchen and breakfast room create cozy casual area

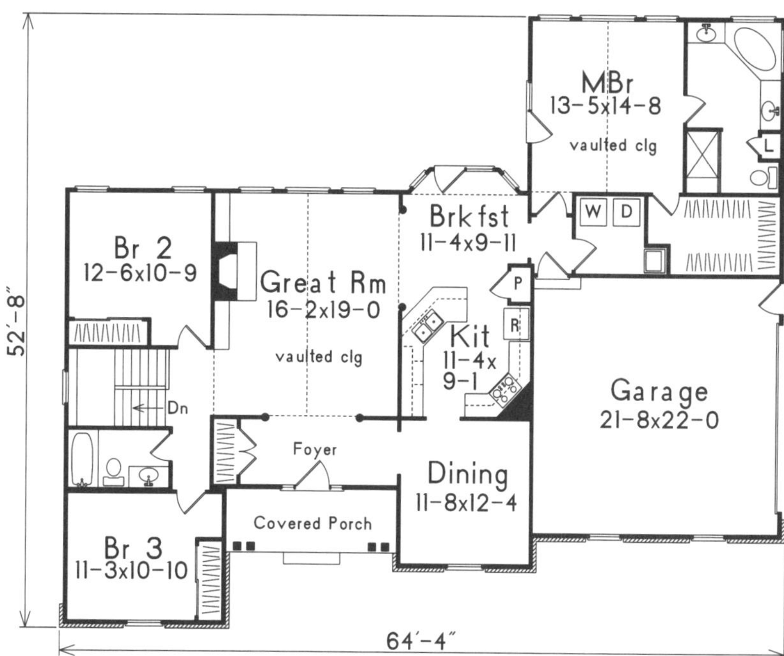
MBr
13-5x14-8
vaulted clg
L
W
D
Brk fst
11-4x9-11
P
R
Br 2
12-6x10-9
Great Rm
16-2x19-0
vaulted clg
Kit
11-4x
9-1
Dn
Garage
21-8x22-0
Foyer
Dining
11-8x12-4
Covered Porch
Br 3
11-3x10-10
52'-8"
64'-4"

LOWE'S

Signature SERIES

Inviting Gabled Entry

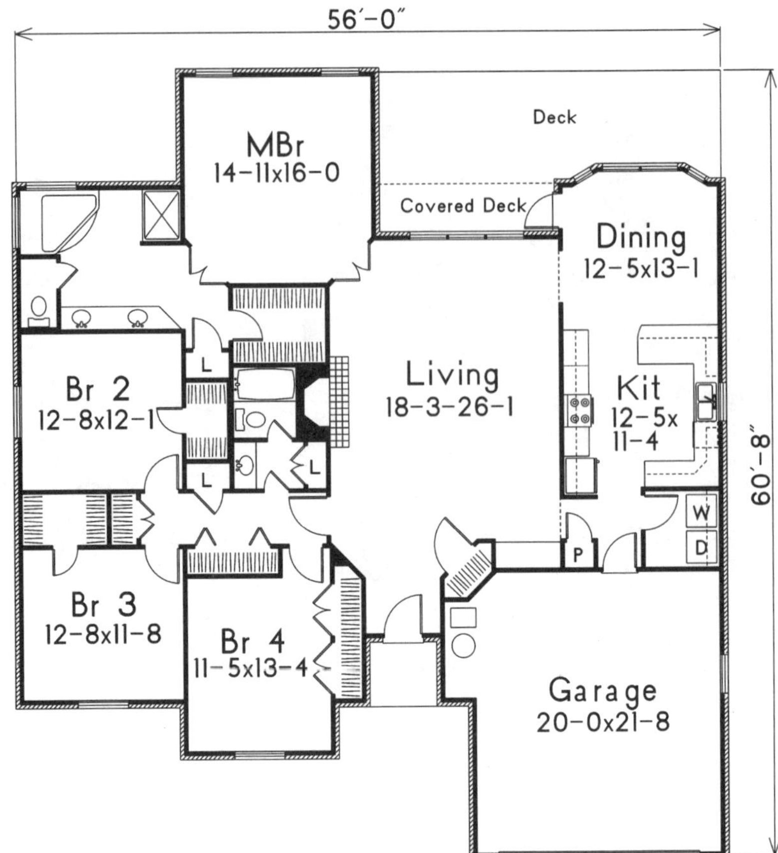
56'-0"
60'-8"
Deck
MBr
14-11x16-0
Covered Deck
Dining
12-5x13-1
Br 2
12-8x12-1
Living
18-3-26-1
Kit
12-5x
11-4
L
L
L
W
D
P
Br 3
12-8x11-8
Br 4
11-5x13-4
Garage
20-0x21-8

Plan #527-0798

Price Code C

Total Living Area: 2,128 Sq. Ft.

Home has 4 bedrooms, 2 baths, 2-car garage and slab foundation, drawings also include crawl space foundation.

Special features

- Versatile kitchen has plenty of space for entertaining with large dining area and counter seating
- Luxurious master bedroom has double-door entry and private bath with jacuzzi tub, double sinks and a large walk-in closet
- Secondary bedrooms include spacious walk-in closets
- Coat closet in front entry is a nice added feature

LOWE'S

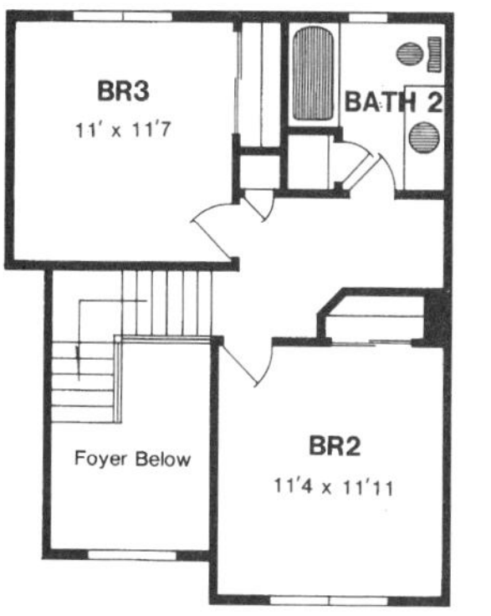
BR3
11' x 11'7
BATH 2
Foyer Below
BR2
11'4 x 11'11

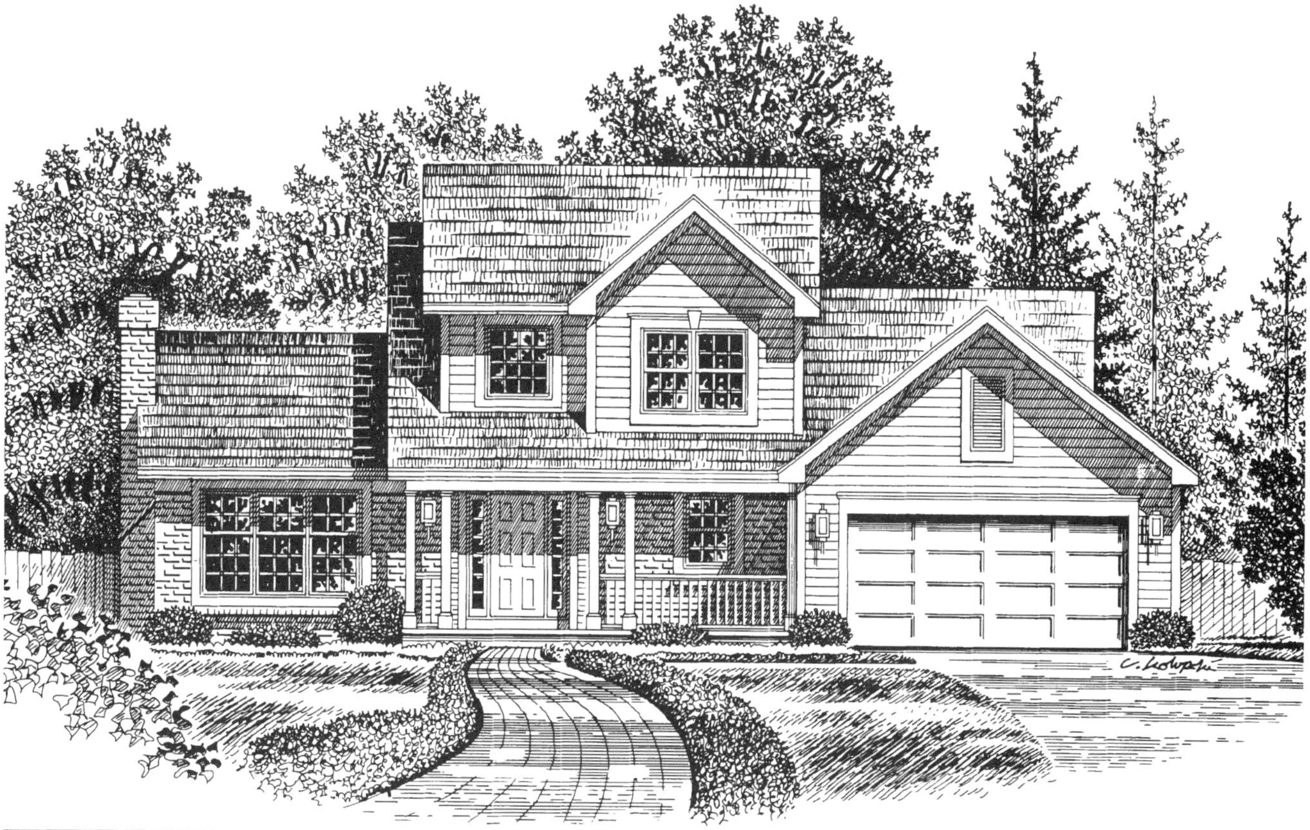

Second Floor
511 sq. ft.

Plan #527-JFD-20-17921

Price Code B

Total Living Area: 1,792 Sq. Ft.

Home has 3 bedrooms, 2 1/2 baths, 2-car garage and basement foundation.

Special features

- Traditional styling makes this a popular design
- First floor master bedroom maintains privacy
- Dining area has sliding glass doors leading to the outdoors
- Formal dining and living rooms combine for added gathering space

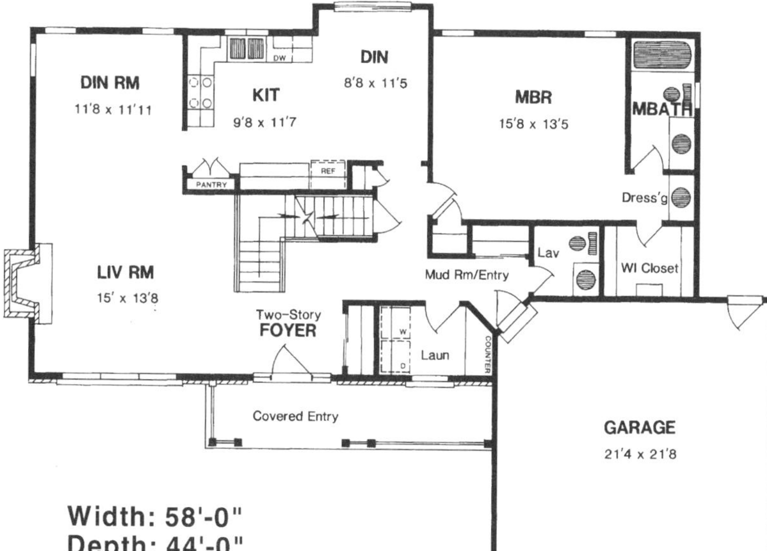
DIN RM
11'8 x 11'11
KIT
9'8 x 11'7
DW
DIN
8'8 x 11'5
MBR
15'8 x 13'5
MBATH
PANTRY
REF
Dress'g
Lav
WI Closet
LIV RM
15' x 13'8
Mud Rm/Entry
Two-Story
FOYER
Laun
COUNTER
Covered Entry
GARAGE
21'4 x 21'8

First Floor
1,281 sq. ft.

Width: 58'-0"
Depth: 44'-0"

Corner Fireplace In Grand Room

Plan #527-MG-9305

Price Code B

Total Living Area: 1,606 Sq. Ft.

Home has 3 bedrooms, 2 baths, 2-car garage and slab foundation.

Special features

- Cathedral vault in great room adds spaciousness
- Master bedroom has lots of windows with a private bath and large walk-in closet
- Kitchen has snack bar which overlooks dining area for convenience

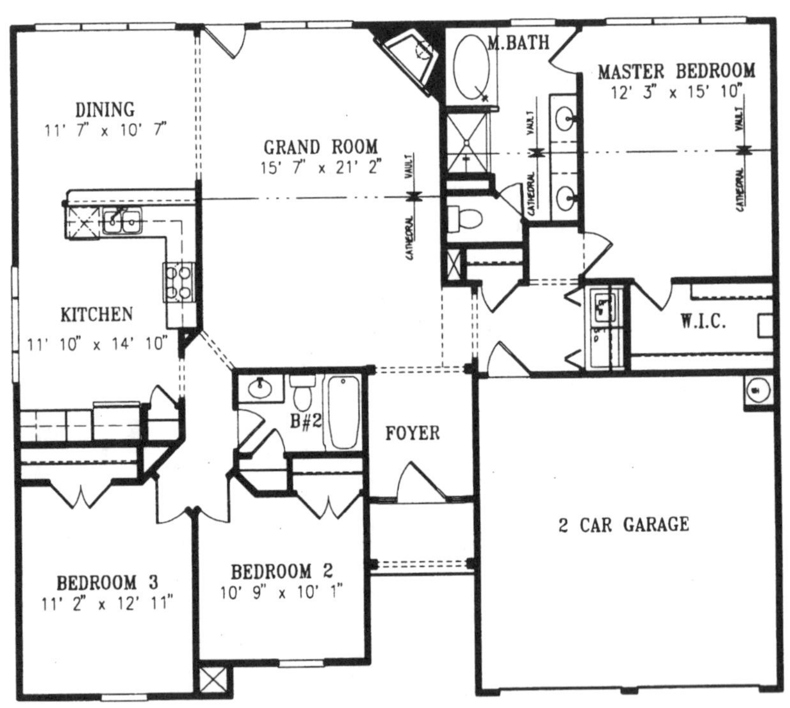
M.BATH
MASTER BEDROOM
12' 3" x 15' 10"
DINING
11' 7" x 10' 7"
GRAND ROOM
15' 7" x 21' 2"
VAULT
CATHEDRAL
KITCHEN
11' 10" x 14' 10"
W.I.C.
B#2
FOYER
2 CAR GARAGE
BEDROOM 3
11' 2" x 12' 11"
BEDROOM 2
10' 9" x 10' 1"

Width: 50'-0"
Depth: 42'-0"

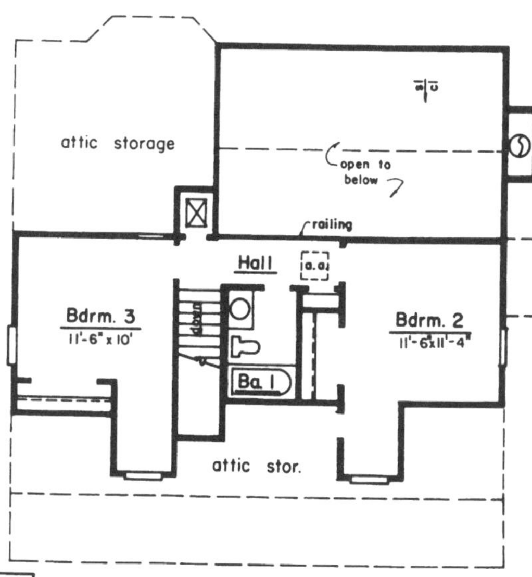
attic storage
open to below
railing
Hall
a.a.
Bdrm. 3
11'-6" x 10'
down
Ba. 1
Bdrm. 2
11'-6"x11'-4"
attic stor.

Second Floor
499 sq. ft.

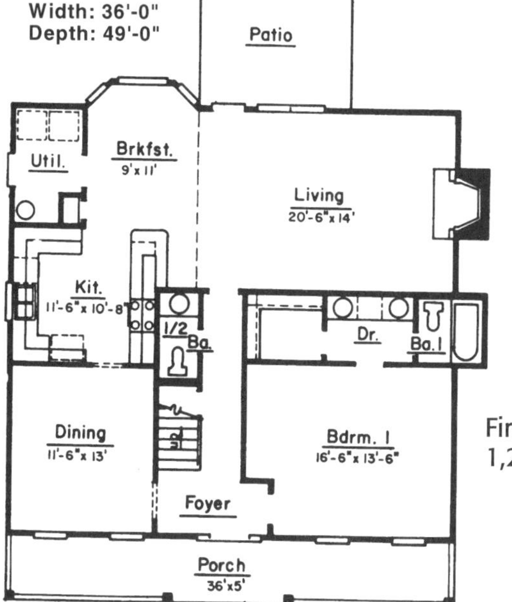
Patio
Util.
Brkfst.
9'x11'
Living
20'-6"x14'
Kit.
11'-6"x10'-8"
1/2 Ba.
Dr.
Ba. 1
Dining
11'-6"x13'
Bdrm. 1
16'-6"x13'-6"
Foyer
Porch
36'x5'

Width: 36'-0"
Depth: 49'-0"

First Floor
1,238 sq. ft.

Plan #527-CHP-1733-A-7

Price Code B

Total Living Area: 1,737 Sq. Ft.

Home has 3 bedrooms, 2 1/2 baths and slab or crawl space foundation, please specify when ordering.

Special features

- U-shaped kitchen, sunny bayed breakfast room and living area become one large gathering area
- Living area has sloped ceilings and a balcony overlook from second floor
- Second floor includes lots of storage area

Openness In A Split-Bedroom Ranch

Plan #527-1248

Price Code B

Total Living Area: 1,574 Sq. Ft.

Home has 3 bedrooms, 2 baths, 2-car garage and basement foundation, drawings also include crawl space foundation.

Special features

- Foyer enters into open great room with corner fireplace and rear dining room with adjoining kitchen
- Left wing includes two bedrooms with full bath
- Right wing includes master bedroom with full bath
- Garage accesses home through mud room/laundry

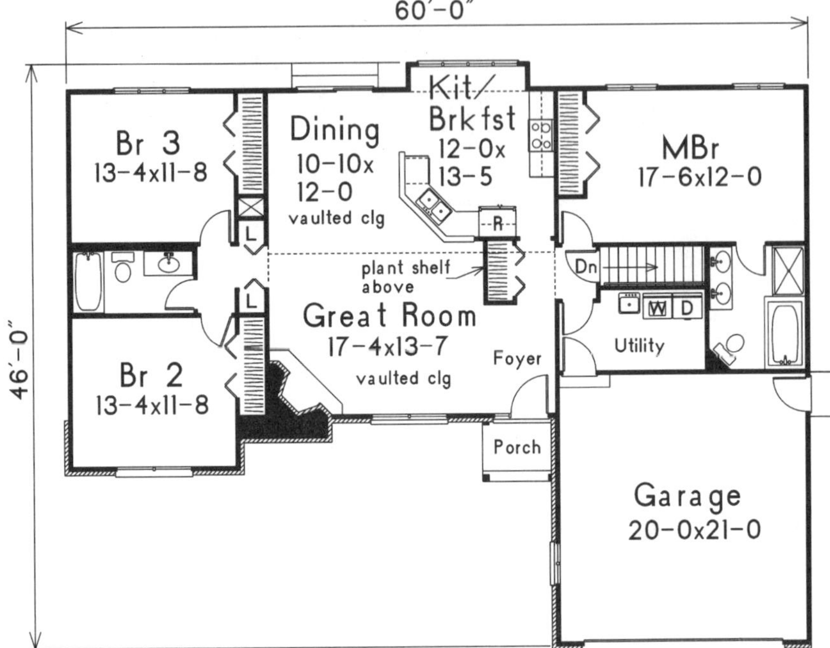
60'-0"
46'-0"
Br 3
13-4x11-8
Dining
10-10x
12-0
vaulted clg
Kit/
Brk fst
12-0x
13-5
MBr
17-6x12-0
plant shelf
above
Dn
Great Room
17-4x13-7
vaulted clg
Foyer
Utility
Br 2
13-4x11-8
Porch
Garage
20-0x21-0

Secluded Living Room

Plan #527-FB-743

Price Code C

Total Living Area: 1,978 Sq. Ft.

Home has 3 bedrooms, 2 1/2 baths, 2-car garage and basement or crawl space foundation, please specify when ordering.

Special features

- Elegant arched openings throughout interior
- Vaulted living room off foyer
- Master suite with cheerful sitting room and a private bath

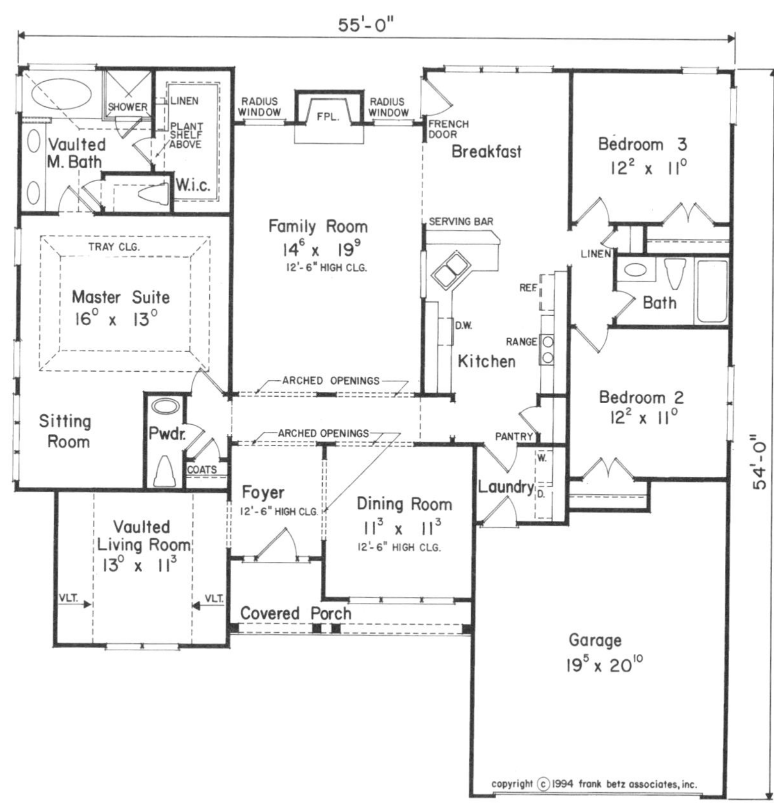
55'-0"
54'-0"
SHOWER
LINEN
PLANT SHELF ABOVE
Vaulted M. Bath
W.i.c.
RADIUS WINDOW
FPL.
RADIUS WINDOW
FRENCH DOOR
Breakfast
Bedroom 3
12^2 x 11^0
TRAY CLG.
Master Suite
16^0 x 13^0
Family Room
14^6 x 19^9
12'-6" HIGH CLG.
SERVING BAR
LINEN
REF.
Bath
D.W.
RANGE
Kitchen
ARCHED OPENINGS
Sitting Room
Pwdr.
COATS
ARCHED OPENINGS
PANTRY
Bedroom 2
12^2 x 11^0
W.
D.
Laundry
Foyer
12'-6" HIGH CLG.
Dining Room
11^3 x 11^3
12'-6" HIGH CLG.
Vaulted Living Room
13^0 x 11^3
VLT.
VLT.
Covered Porch
Garage
19^5 x 20^{10}
copyright (c) 1994 frank betz associates, inc.

MOLOU

BEDROOM 11'-9" x 13'-2"
SITTING ROOM 8'-6" x 17'-5"
BEDROOM 14'-2" x 10'-5"
DN.
L.
OPEN BELOW TO FOYER
BATH
ATTIC STORAGE SPACE

Second Floor
643 sq. ft.

Plan #527-1348

Price Code C

Total Living Area: 1,980 Sq. Ft.

Home has 3 bedrooms, 2 1/2 baths, 2-car garage and basement foundation.

Special features

- Curb appeal is captured with multi-level roof, gables and palladian windows
- Step-down into a magnificent living and activity room adorned with cozy fireplace, wet bar, pass-through to kitchen and lots of glass area
- The kitchen features plenty of storage space and an eat-in area
- A delightful sitting room accesses the second floor bedrooms and offers a view to the step-up foyer below

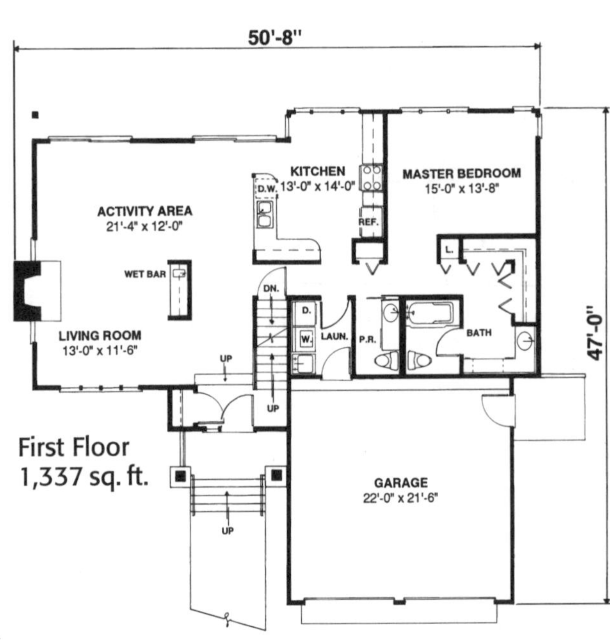
50'-8"
47'-0"
KITCHEN 13'-0" x 14'-0"
D.W.
REF.
MASTER BEDROOM 15'-0" x 13'-8"
ACTIVITY AREA 21'-4" x 12'-0"
WET BAR
DN.
L.
D.
W.
LAUN.
P.R.
BATH
LIVING ROOM 13'-0" x 11'-6"
UP
UP
GARAGE 22'-0" x 21'-6"
UP

First Floor
1,337 sq. ft.

TO ORDER BLUEPRINTS USE THE FORM ON PAGE 290 OR CALL TOLL-FREE **1-800-DREAM HOME** (373-2646)

LOWE'S

Plan #527-DBI-8016

Price Code B

Total Living Area: 1,691 Sq. Ft.

Home has 3 bedrooms, 2 baths, 2-car garage and basement foundation.

Special features

- Bay windowed breakfast room allows for plenty of sunlight
- Large inviting covered porch in the front of the home
- Great room fireplace surounded with windows

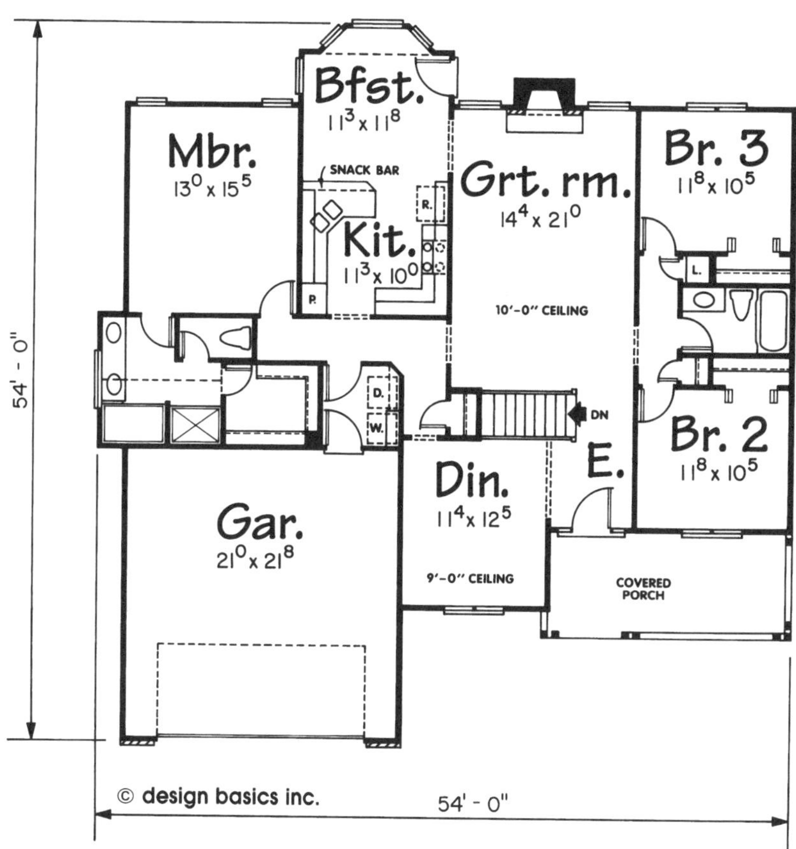
Bfst.
11³x 11⁸
Mbr.
13⁰ x 15⁵
SNACK BAR
Kit.
11³x 10⁰
Grt. rm.
14⁴x 21⁰
10'-0" CEILING
Br. 3
11⁸x 10⁵
Br. 2
11⁸x 10⁵
DN
E.
Din.
11⁴x 12⁵
9'-0" CEILING
COVERED PORCH
Gar.
21⁰x 21⁸
54' - 0"
© design basics inc.
54' - 0"

Plan #527-NDG-113-1

Price Code A

Total Living Area: 1,485 Sq. Ft.

Home has 3 bedrooms, 2 baths, 2-car garage and basement, crawl space or slab foundation, please specify when ordering.

Special features

- Corner fireplace highlighted in great room
- Unique glass block window over whirlpool tub in master bath
- Open bar overlooks both the kitchen and great room
- Breakfast room leads to outdoor grilling and covered porch

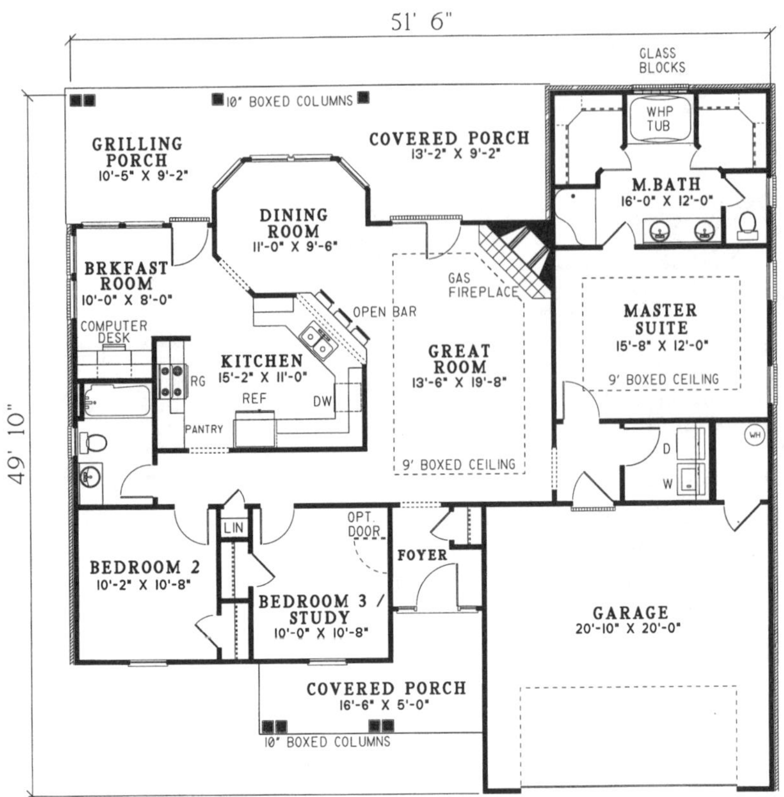
51' 6"
49' 10"
GLASS BLOCKS
10" BOXED COLUMNS
GRILLING PORCH
10'-5" X 9'-2"
COVERED PORCH
13'-2" X 9'-2"
WHP TUB
M.BATH
16'-0" X 12'-0"
DINING ROOM
11'-0" X 9'-6"
BRKFAST ROOM
10'-0" X 8'-0"
GAS FIREPLACE
OPEN BAR
MASTER SUITE
15'-8" X 12'-0"
COMPUTER DESK
KITCHEN
15'-2" X 11'-0"
RG
REF
DW
PANTRY
GREAT ROOM
13'-6" X 19'-8"
9' BOXED CEILING
9' BOXED CEILING
D
W
WH
LIN
OPT. DOOR
FOYER
BEDROOM 2
10'-2" X 10'-8"
BEDROOM 3 / STUDY
10'-0" X 10'-8"
GARAGE
20'-10" X 20'-0"
COVERED PORCH
16'-6" X 5'-0"
10" BOXED COLUMNS

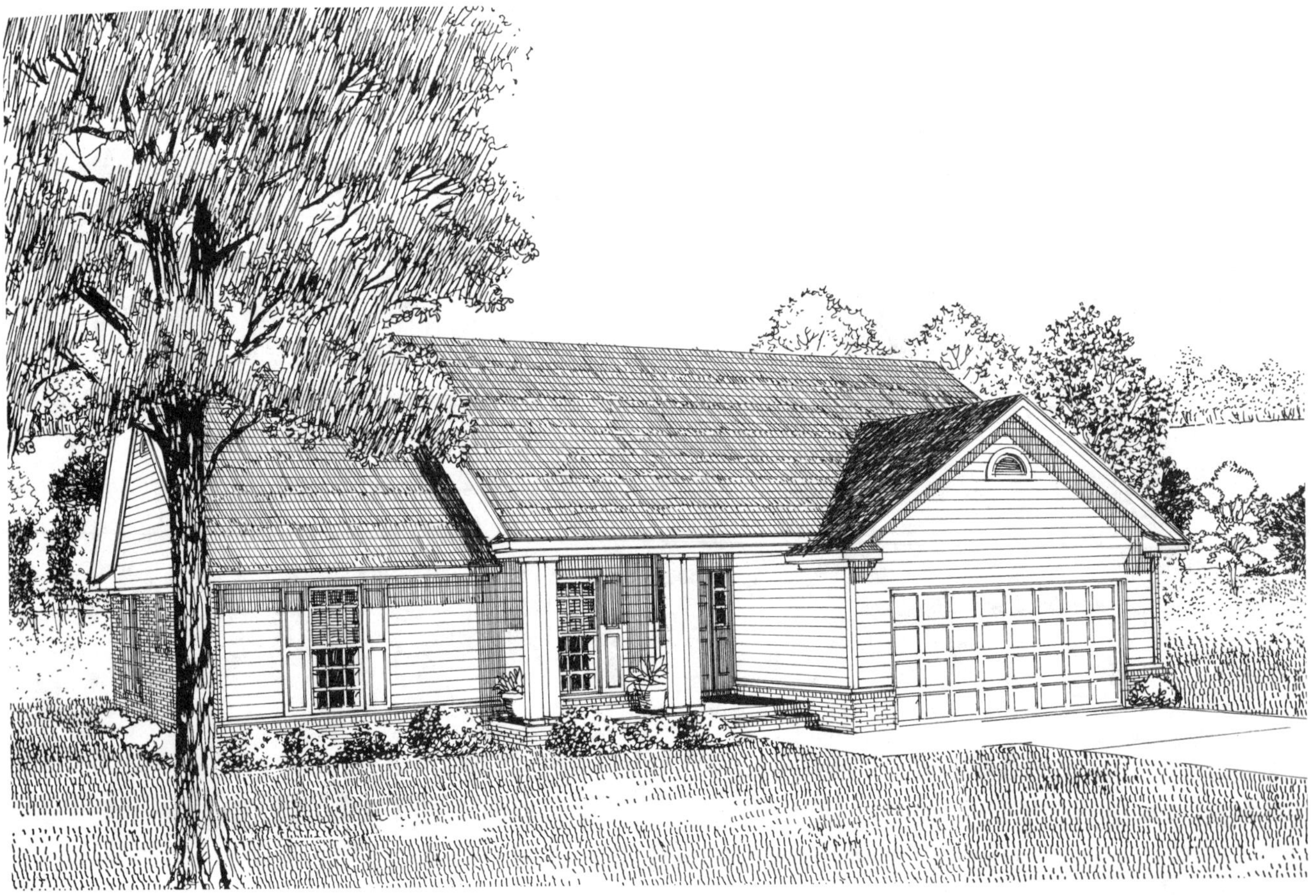

LOWE'S

Plan #527-1026-B

Price Code C

Total Living Area: 2,137 Sq. Ft.

Home has 4 bedrooms, 2 1/2 baths, 2-car garage and basement foundation.

Special features

- Foyer leads to majestic-sized living room with masonry fireplace
- Family room has beamed ceiling and adjoins a very spacious kitchen
- Oversized laundry features a full closet and convenient service sink
- Gallery-sized second floor hall leads to a roomy compartmented hall bath with a double-bowl vanity

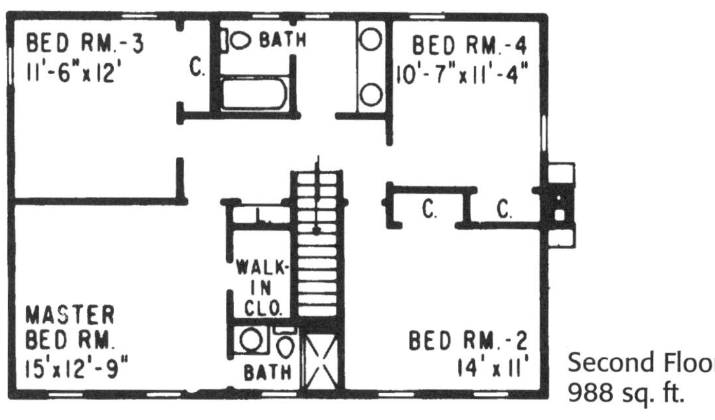
BED RM.-3
11'-6"x12'
C.
BATH
BED RM.-4
10'-7"x11'-4"
C.
C.
WALK-IN CLO.
MASTER BED RM.
15'x12'-9"
BATH
BED RM.-2
14'x11'

Second Floor
988 sq. ft.

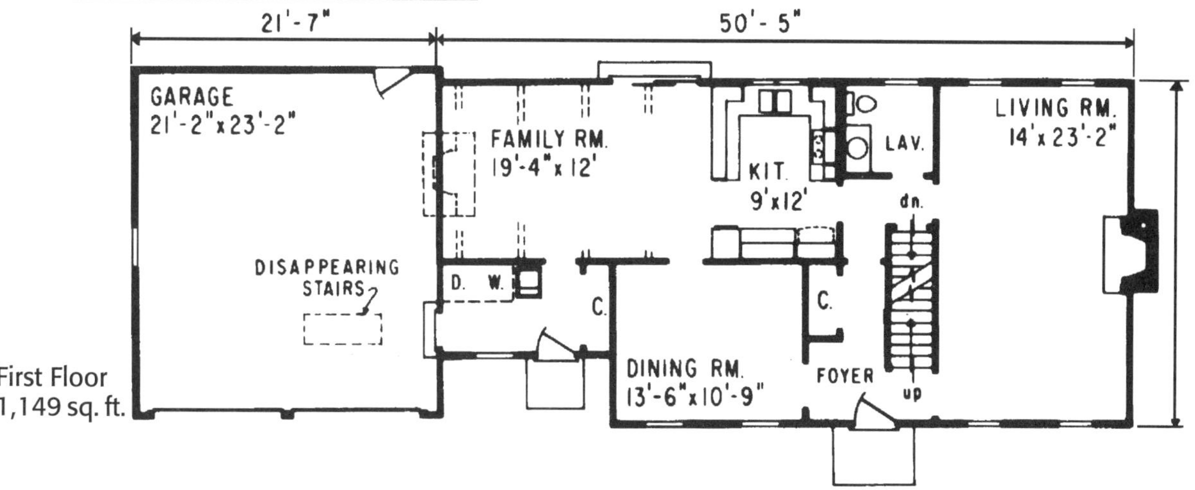
21'-7"
50'-5"
GARAGE
21'-2"x23'-2"
FAMILY RM.
19'-4"x12'
KIT.
9'x12'
LAV.
LIVING RM.
14'x23'-2"
dn.
DISAPPEARING STAIRS
D. W.
C.
C.
DINING RM.
13'-6"x10'-9"
FOYER
up

First Floor
1,149 sq. ft.

LOWE'S

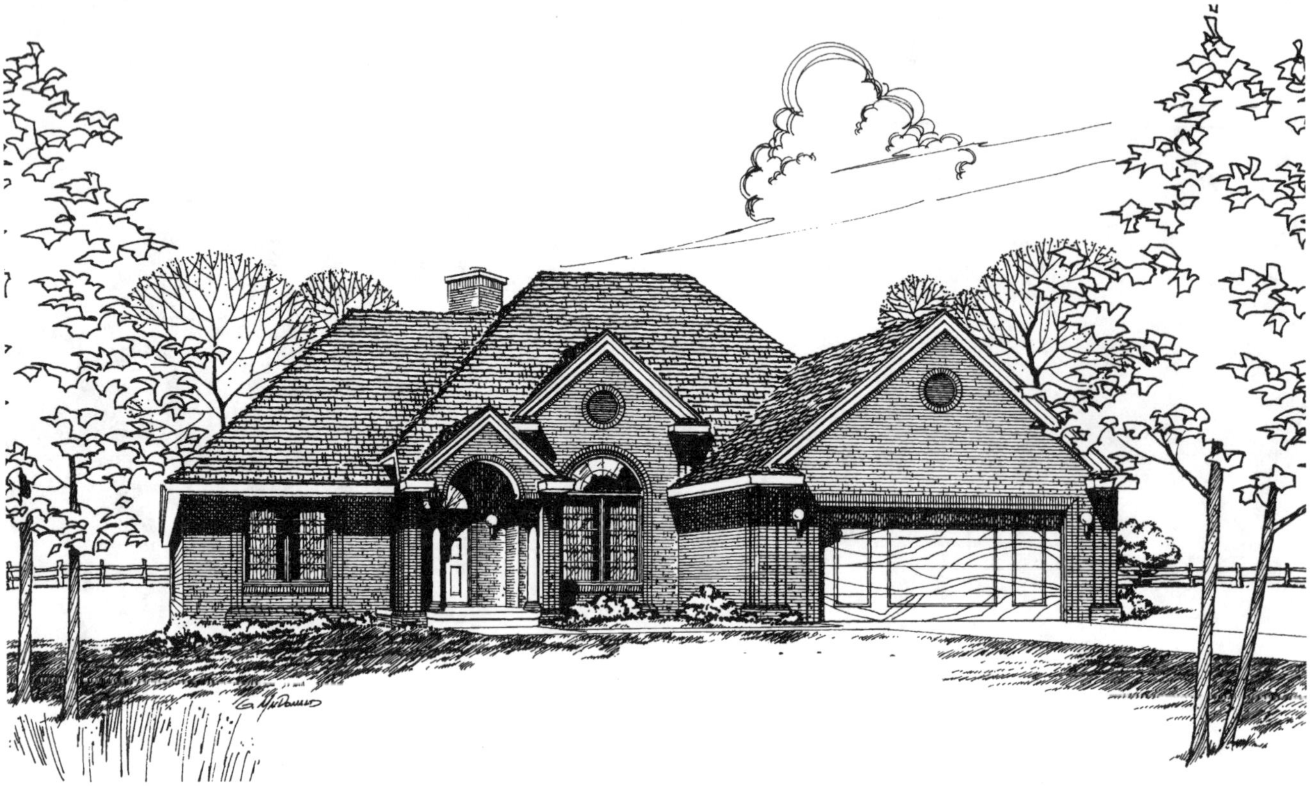

Plan #527-DBI-1748-19

Price Code C

Total Living Area: 1,911 Sq. Ft.

Home has 3 bedrooms, 2 baths, 2-car garage and basement foundation.

Special features

- Large entry opens into beautiful great room with angled see-through fireplace
- Terrific design includes kitchen/ breakfast area with adjacent sunny bayed hearth room
- Luxury master suite with privacy

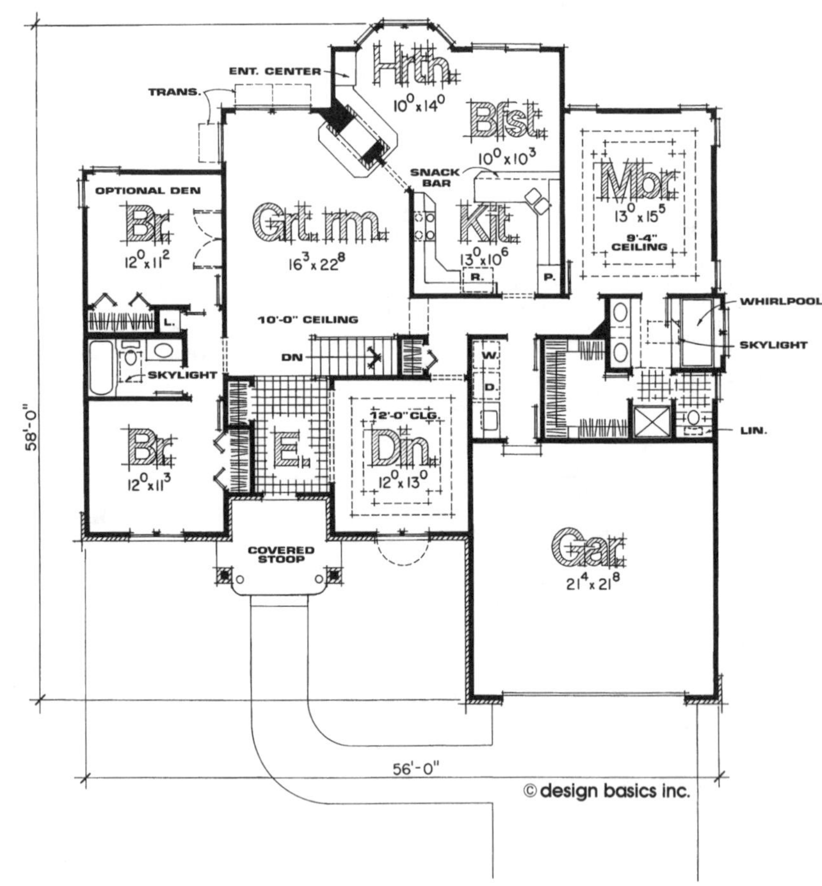
ENT. CENTER
TRANS.
Hrth.
$10^0 \times 14^0$
Bfst.
$10^0 \times 10^3$
SNACK BAR
OPTIONAL DEN
Br.
$12^0 \times 11^2$
Grt. rm.
$16^3 \times 22^8$
Kit.
$13^0 \times 10^6$
R.
P.
Mbr.
$13^0 \times 15^5$
9'-4" CEILING
WHIRLPOOL
SKYLIGHT
10'-0" CEILING
DN
L.
SKYLIGHT
W.
D.
LIN.
Br.
$12^0 \times 11^3$
E.
12'-0" CLG.
Din.
$12^0 \times 13^0$
COVERED STOOP
Gar.
$21^4 \times 21^8$
58'-0"
56'-0"
© design basics inc.

Sunny Garden Tub In Master Bath

LOWE'S

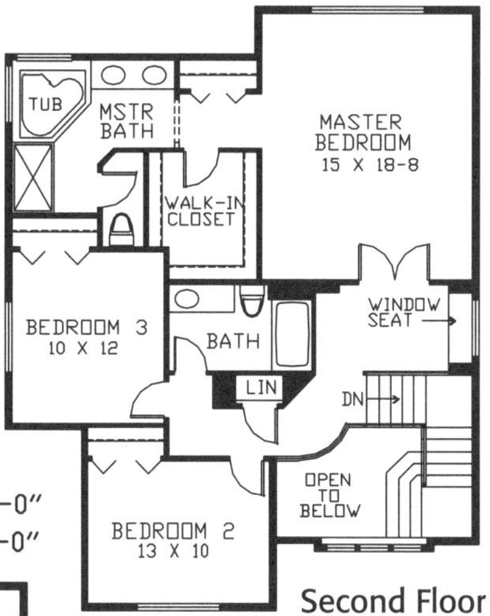

WIDTH 34'-0"
DEPTH 50'-0"

Second Floor
1,104 sq. ft.

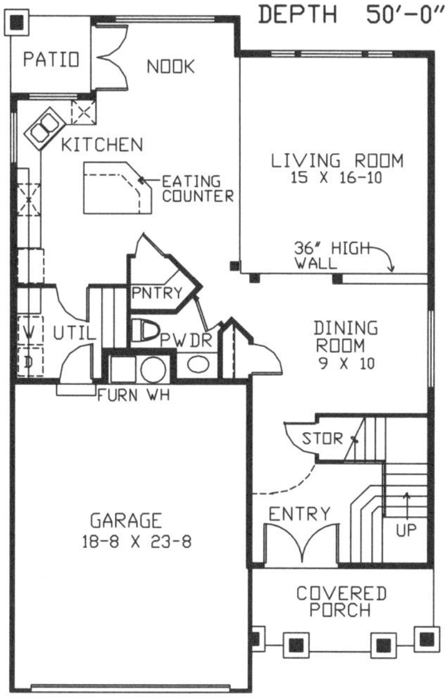

First Floor
1,058 sq. ft.

Plan #527-GSD-2073

Price Code C

Total Living Area: 2,162 Sq. Ft.

Home has 3 bedrooms, 2 1/2 baths, 2-car garage and crawl space foundation.

Special features

- Lovely covered porch
- Appealing double-door two-story entry
- Kitchen has eat-in island bar
- French doors lead to patio from nook
- Master suite has double-door entry, private bath and walk-in closet

Wrap-Around Porch Adds Warmth To Home

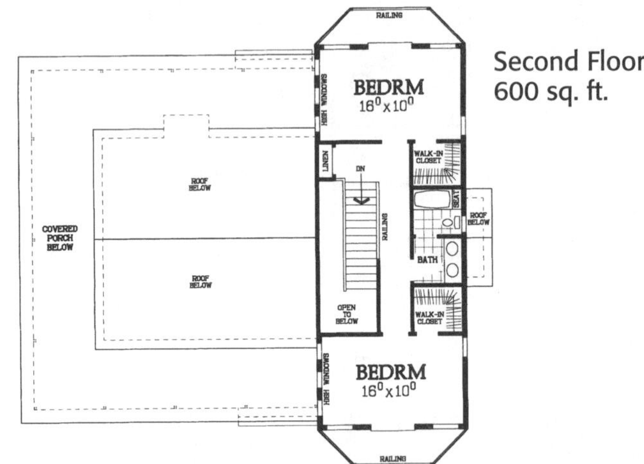
BEDRM
16⁰x10⁰
WALK-IN CLOSET
BATH
ROOF BELOW
COVERED PORCH BELOW
OPEN TO BELOW
WALK-IN CLOSET
BEDRM
16⁰x10⁰
RAILING

Second Floor
600 sq. ft.

Plan #527-HP-C687

Price Code C

Total Living Area: 1,974 Sq. Ft.

Home has 3 bedrooms, 2 1/2 baths and basement or crawl space foundation, please specify when ordering.

Special features

- Sunny bayed nook invites casual dining and shares its natural light with a snack counter and kitchen
- Spacious master bedroom occupies a bay window and offers a sumptuous bath
- Both second floor bedrooms have private balconies

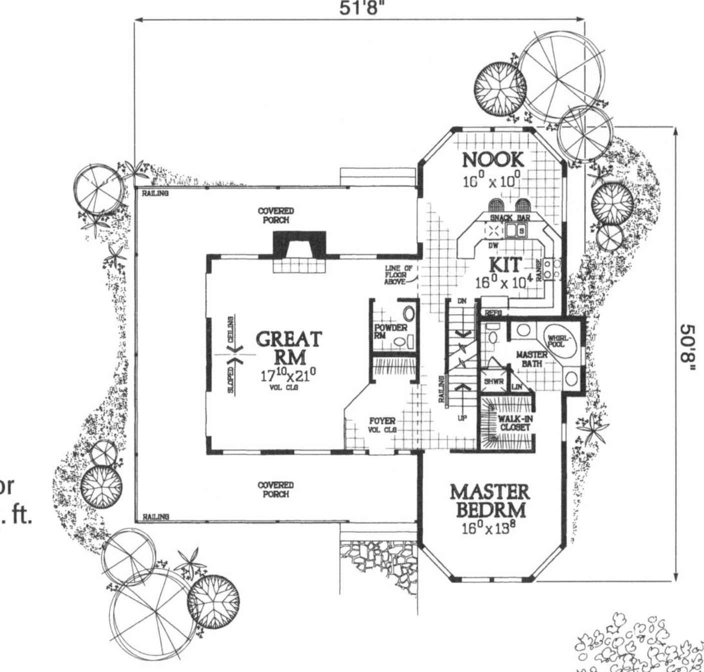
51'8"
50'8"
NOOK
10⁰ x 10⁰
SNACK BAR
KIT
16⁰ x 10⁴
COVERED PORCH
GREAT RM
17¹⁰x21⁰
POWDER RM
FOYER
MASTER BATH
WALK-IN CLOSET
MASTER BEDRM
16⁰x13⁸
COVERED PORCH
RAILING

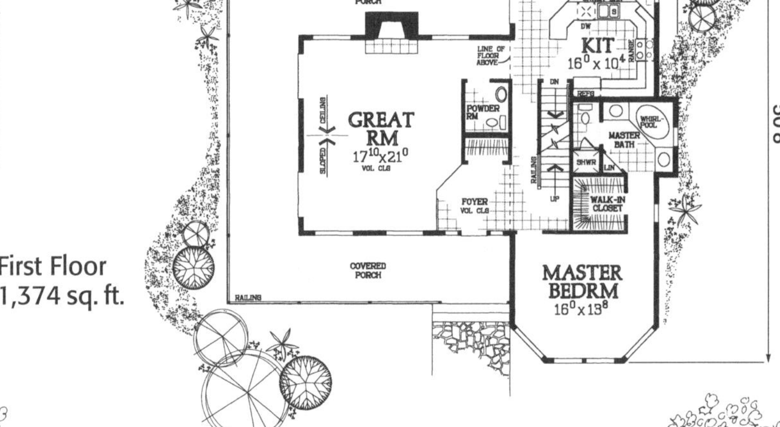

First Floor
1,374 sq. ft.

TO ORDER BLUEPRINTS USE THE FORM ON PAGE 290 OR CALL TOLL-FREE **1-800-DREAM HOME** (373-2646)

LOWE'S

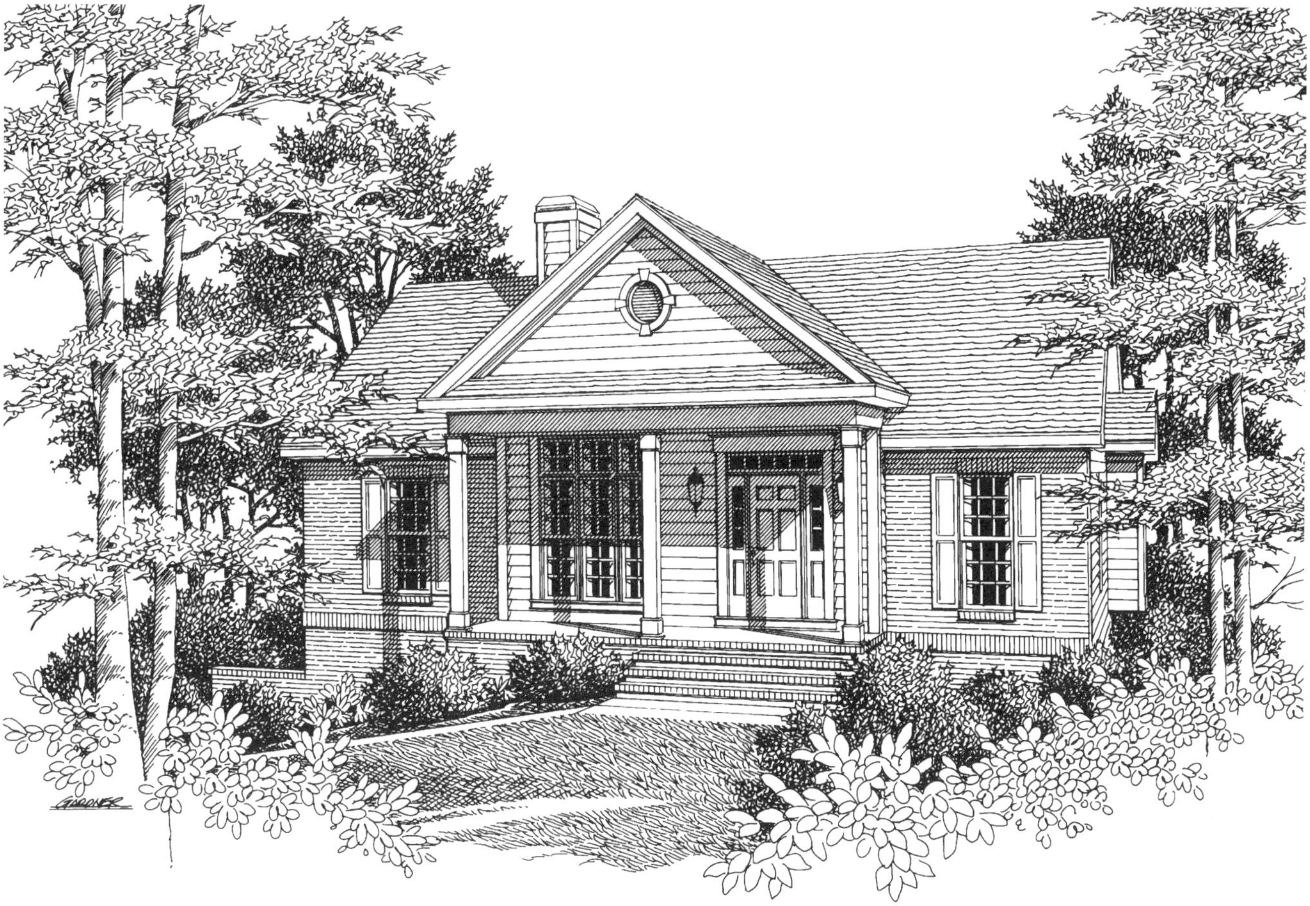

Plan #527-JV-1268A

Price Code A

Total Living Area: 1,268 Sq. Ft.

Home has 3 bedrooms, 2 baths, 2-car drive under garage and basement foundation.

Special features

- Raised gable porch is focal point creating dramatic look
- 10' ceilings throughout living/dining area
- Open kitchen is well-designed
- Master suite offers tray ceiling and private bath with both a garden tub and a 4' shower

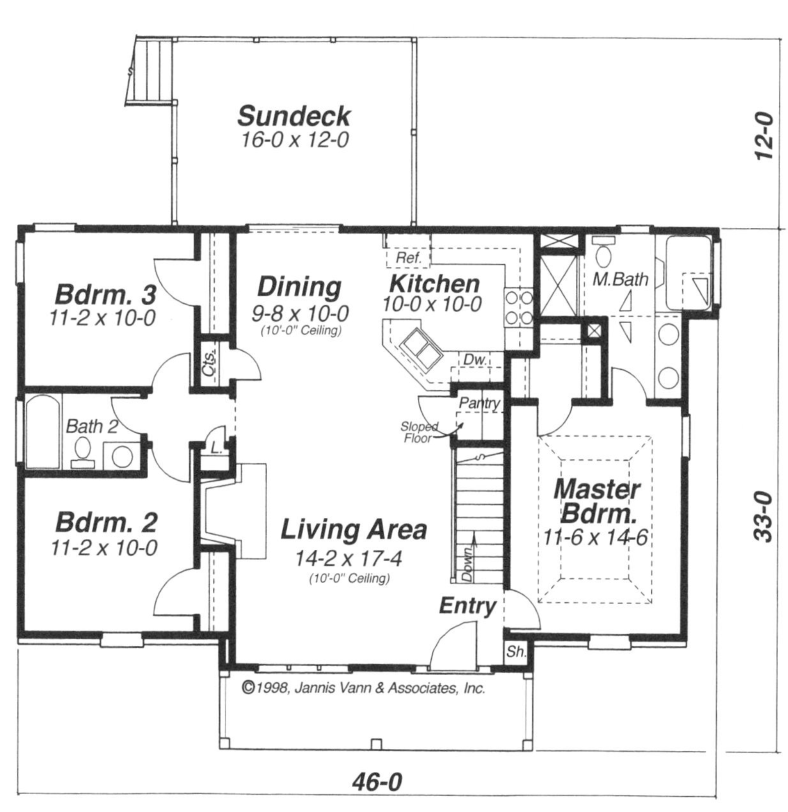
Sundeck
16-0 x 12-0
12-0
Bdrm. 3
11-2 x 10-0
Dining
9-8 x 10-0
(10'-0" Ceiling)
Ref.
Kitchen
10-0 x 10-0
Dw.
M.Bath
Cl.
Pantry
Sloped Floor
Bath 2
L.
Bdrm. 2
11-2 x 10-0
Living Area
14-2 x 17-4
(10'-0" Ceiling)
Down
Master Bdrm.
11-6 x 14-6
33-0
Entry
Sh.
©1998, Jannis Vann & Associates, Inc.
46-0

Plant Ledge Accents Foyer

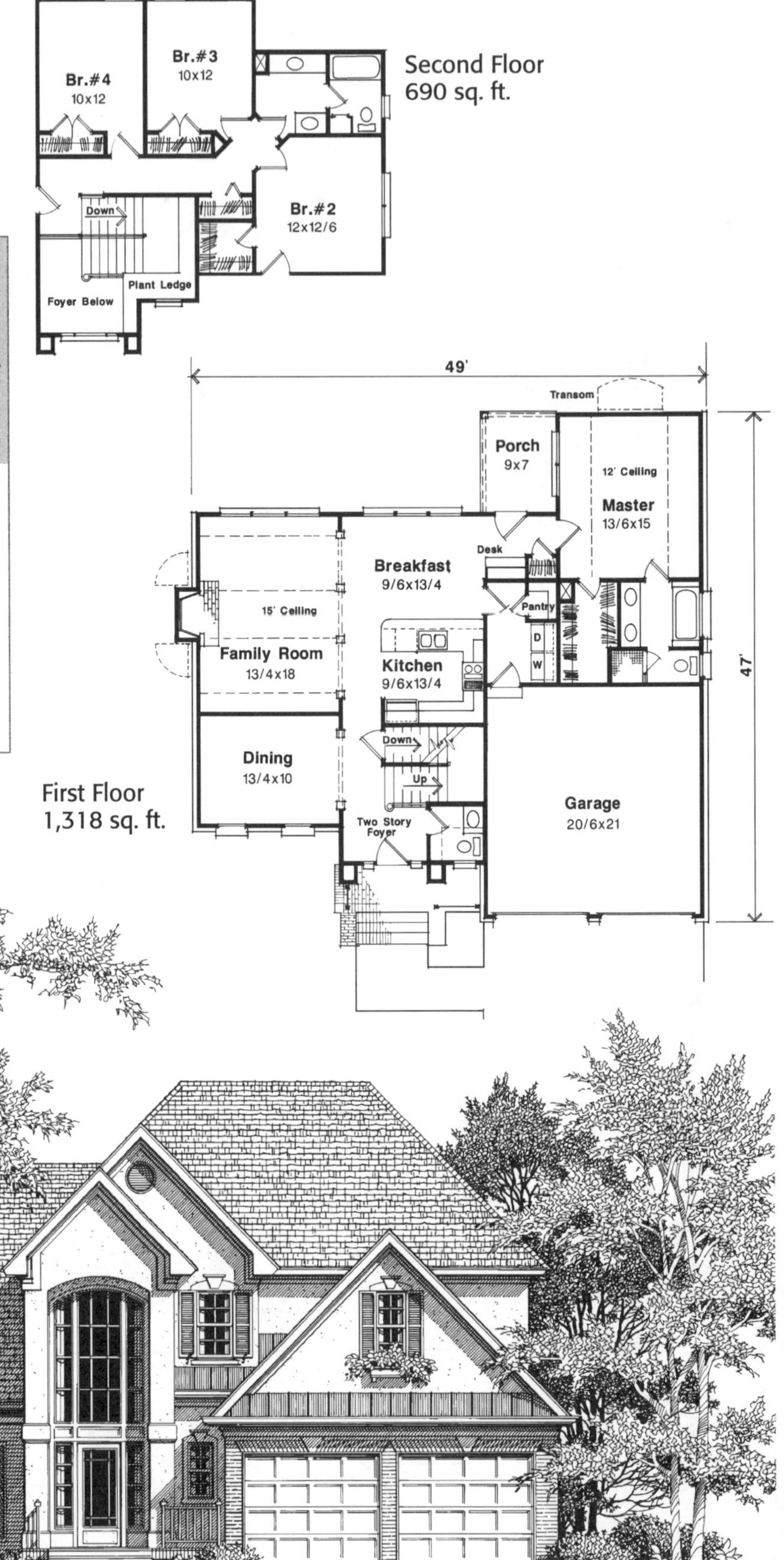

Br.#4
10x12
Br.#3
10x12
Br.#2
12x12/6
Down
Plant Ledge
Foyer Below
Second Floor
690 sq. ft.
49'
47'
Transom
Porch
9x7
12' Ceiling
Master
13/6x15
Desk
Breakfast
9/6x13/4
Pantry
D
W
15' Ceiling
Family Room
13/4x18
Kitchen
9/6x13/4
Down
Up
Dining
13/4x10
Two Story
Foyer
Garage
20/6x21
First Floor
1,318 sq. ft.

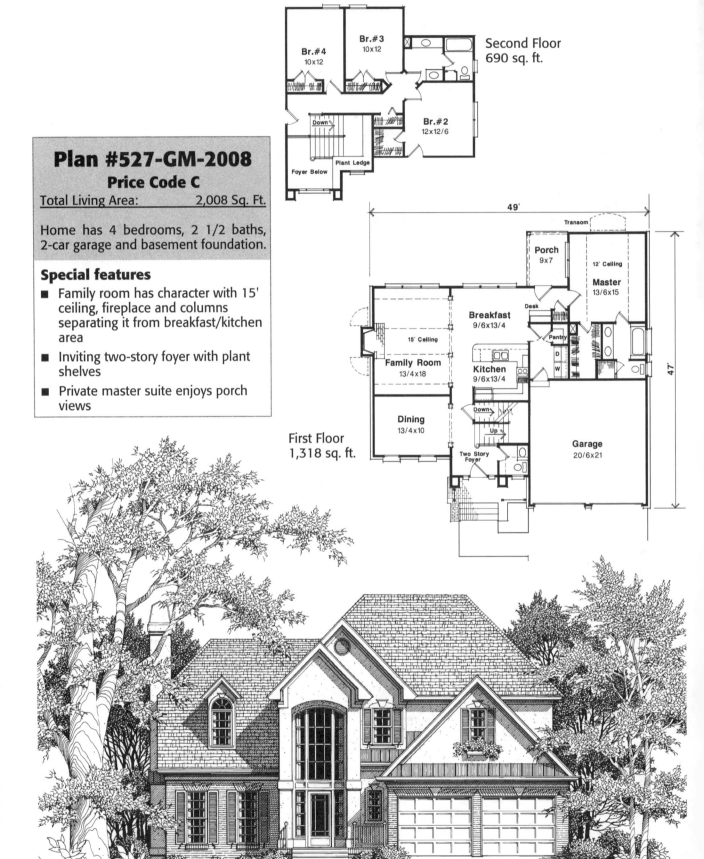

Plan #527-GM-2008

Price Code C

Total Living Area: 2,008 Sq. Ft.

Home has 4 bedrooms, 2 1/2 baths, 2-car garage and basement foundation.

Special features

- Family room has character with 15' ceiling, fireplace and columns separating it from breakfast/kitchen area
- Inviting two-story foyer with plant shelves
- Private master suite enjoys porch views

TO ORDER BLUEPRINTS USE THE FORM ON PAGE 290 OR CALL TOLL-FREE **1-800-DREAM HOME** (373-2646)

LOWE'S

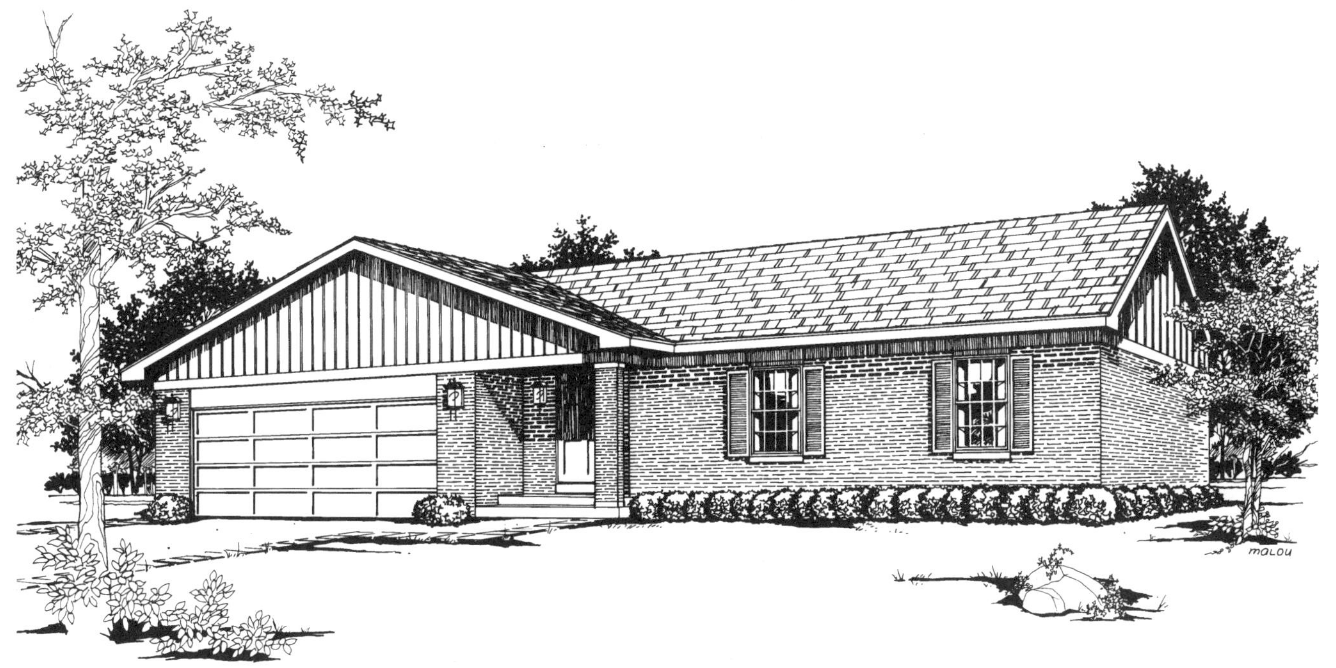

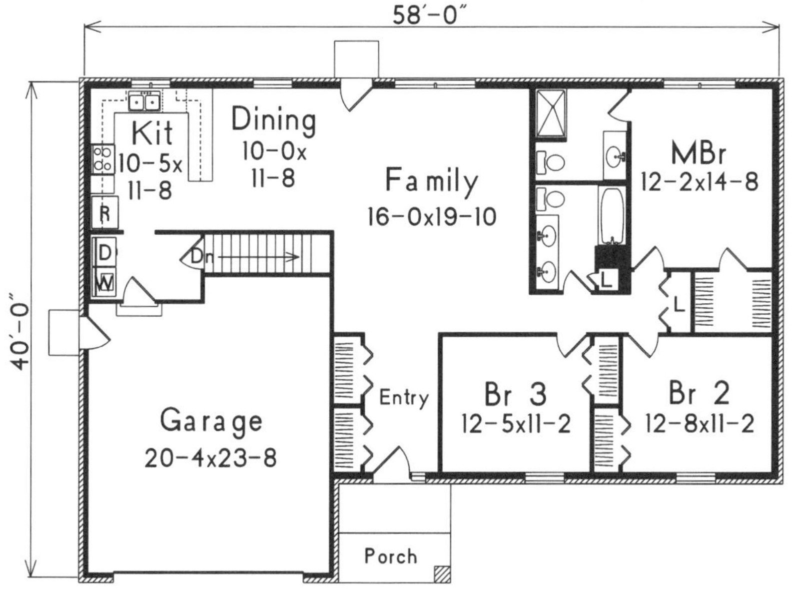
58'-0"
40'-0"
Kit
10-5x
11-8
Dining
10-0x
11-8
Family
16-0x19-10
MBr
12-2x14-8
R
D
W
Dn
L
L
Entry
Br 3
12-5x11-2
Br 2
12-8x11-2
Garage
20-4x23-8
Porch

Plan #527-ES-125-1

basement

Plan #527-ES-125-2

crawl space & slab

Price Code B

Total Living Area: 1,605 Sq. Ft.

Home has 3 bedrooms, 2 baths, 2-car garage and basement, crawl space or slab foundation, please specify when ordering.

Special features

- Detailed entry is highlighted with a stone floor and double guest closets
- Kitchen is well-designed with open view to family room
- Third bedroom can be easily utilized as a den with optional bi-fold doors off entry

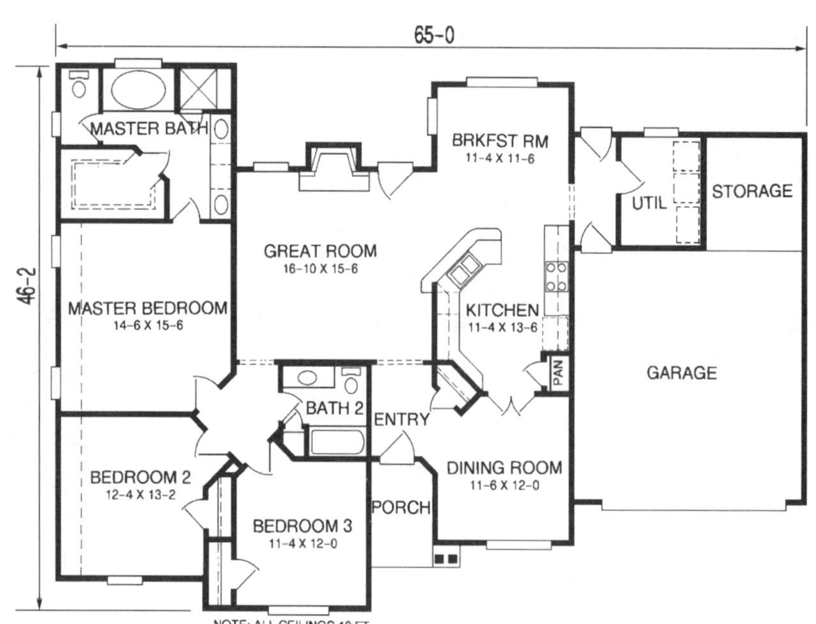
65-0
46-2
MASTER BATH
BRKFST RM
11-4 X 11-6
UTIL
STORAGE
GREAT ROOM
16-10 X 15-6
MASTER BEDROOM
14-6 X 15-6
KITCHEN
11-4 X 13-6
PAN
GARAGE
BATH 2
ENTRY
BEDROOM 2
12-4 X 13-2
DINING ROOM
11-6 X 12-0
PORCH
BEDROOM 3
11-4 X 12-0
NOTE: ALL CEILINGS 10 FT

Plan #527-LBD-18-5A

Price Code C

Total Living Area: 1,862 Sq. Ft.

Home has 3 bedrooms, 2 baths, 2-car garage and crawl space or slab foundation, please specify when ordering.

Special features

- Comfortable traditional has all the amenities of a larger plan in a compact layout
- Angled eating bar separates kitchen and great room while leaving these areas open to one another for entertaining

LOWE'S

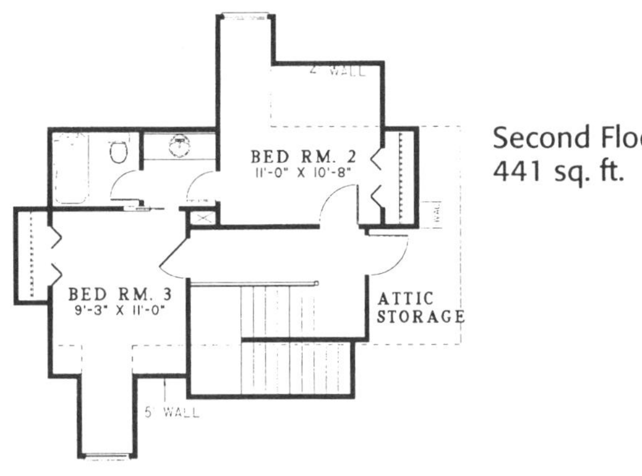
2' WALL
BED RM. 2
11'-0" X 10'-8"
BED RM. 3
9'-3" X 11'-0"
ATTIC
STORAGE
5' WALL

Second Floor
441 sq. ft.

Plan #527-NDG-303

Price Code B

Total Living Area: 1,797 Sq. Ft.

Home has 3 bedrooms, 2 1/2 baths, 2-car garage and crawl space or slab foundation, please specify when ordering.

Special features

- Formal dining area separated from other areas for entertaining
- Efficiently designed kitchen
- Great room has outdoor access, media center and a fireplace
- Attractive dormers add character to second floor bedrooms

48' 0"
43' 0"
GLASS
BLOCKS
WHP
TUB
SEAT
SHWR
M.BATH
KNEE
SPACE
LIN
MASTER
SUITE
15'-0" X 13'-3"
MEDIA
CENTER
GREAT RM.
16'-2" X 18'-0"
STRG.
6'-0" X 4'-0"
WH
LAU.
7'-2" X 6'-0"
D
W
REF.
RG
KITCHEN
9'-10" X 11'-0"
DW
GARAGE
19'-0" X 20'-0"
PAN
FOYER
10' CLNG
8" COLUMNS
BRKFAST
RM.
9'-10" X 8'-0"
DINING RM.
10' CLNG
11'-6" X 12'-6"
PRCH

First Floor
1,356 sq. ft.

malou

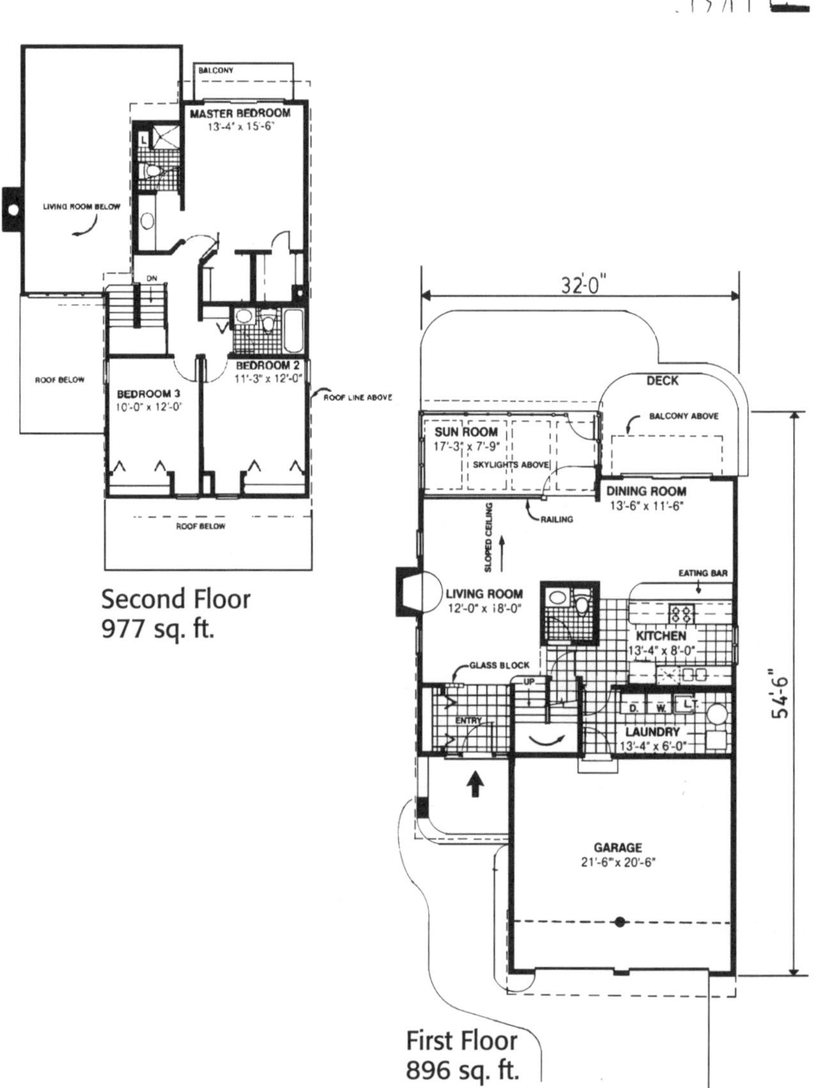
BALCONY
MASTER BEDROOM
13'-4" x 15'-6"
LIVING ROOM BELOW
DN
ROOF BELOW
BEDROOM 3
10'-0" x 12'-0"
BEDROOM 2
11'-3" x 12'-0"
ROOF LINE ABOVE
ROOF BELOW
32'-0"
DECK
BALCONY ABOVE
SUN ROOM
17'-3" x 7'-9"
SKYLIGHTS ABOVE
DINING ROOM
13'-6" x 11'-6"
RAILING
SLOPED CEILING
EATING BAR
LIVING ROOM
12'-0" x 18'-0"
KITCHEN
13'-4" x 8'-0"
GLASS BLOCK
UP
ENTRY
LAUNDRY
13'-4" x 6'-0"
GARAGE
21'-6" x 20'-6"
54'-6"

Second Floor
977 sq. ft.

First Floor
896 sq. ft.

Plan #527-1270-1
basement

Plan #527-1270-2
slab

Price Code C

Total Living Area: 1,873 Sq. Ft.

Home has 3 bedrooms, 2 1/2 baths, 2-car garage and basement or slab foundation, please specify when ordering.

Special features

- Interesting contemporary roof lines
- Vaulted living room is separated from foyer by glass block wall
- Spacious sunroom with skylights adjoins living room
- Kitchen with large window has useful breakfast bar
- Master suite has all the pleasing amenities including a balcony

Convenient Wet Bar In Living Area

LOWE'S

Second Floor
512 sq. ft.

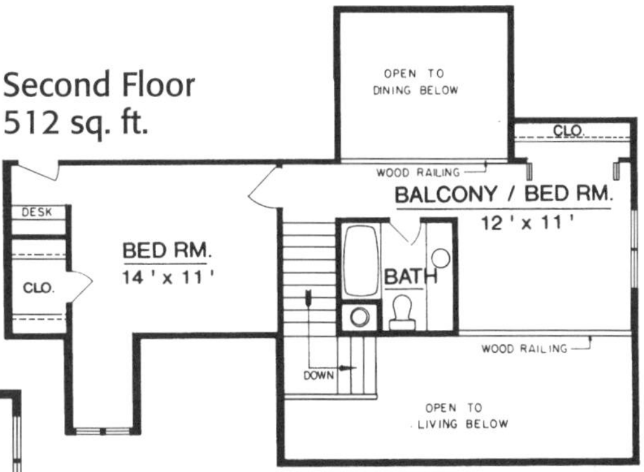

First Floor
1,546 sq. ft.

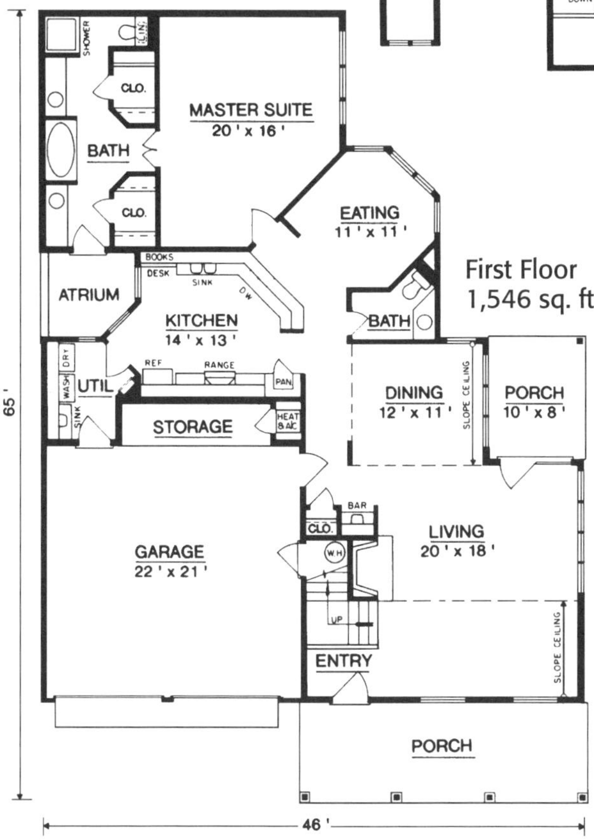

Plan #527-BF-DR2002

Price Code C

Total Living Area: 2,058 Sq. Ft.

Home has 3 bedrooms, 2 1/2 baths, 2-car garage and crawl space, slab or basement foundation, please specify when ordering.

Special features

- Energy efficient design with 2"x 6" exterior walls
- Balcony overlooks living areas below while easily converting to a bedroom
- Sunny atrium and plenty of windows in eating area brighten kitchen

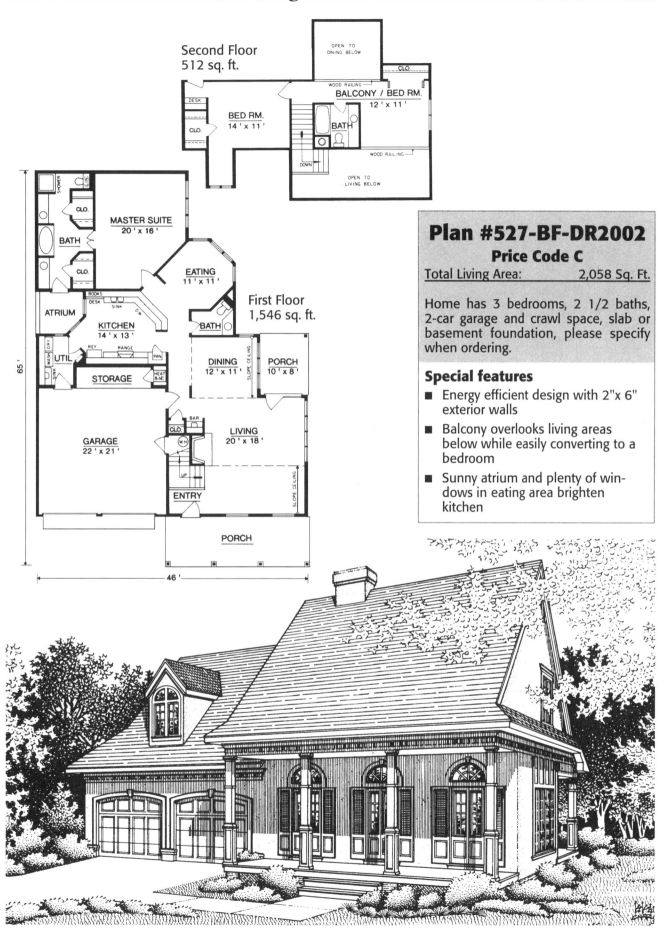

Plan #527-FB-543

Price Code C

Total Living Area: 1,945 Sq. Ft.

Home has 4 bedrooms, 2 baths, 2-car side entry garage and basement, crawl space or slab foundation, please specify when ordering.

Special features

- Master suite separated from other bedrooms for privacy
- Vaulted breakfast room is directly off great room
- Kitchen includes a built-in desk area
- Elegant dining room has an arched window

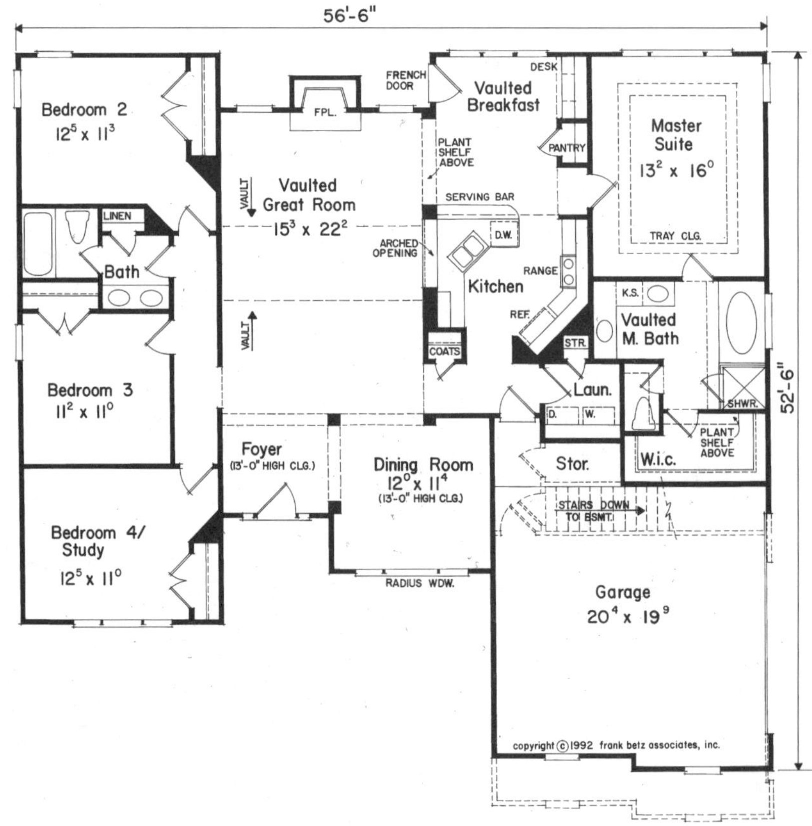
56'-6"
52'-6"
Bedroom 2
12⁵ x 11³
Linen
Bath
Bedroom 3
11² x 11⁰
Bedroom 4/ Study
12⁵ x 11⁰
FPL.
Vaulted Great Room
15³ x 22²
Foyer
(13'-0" HIGH CLG.)
Dining Room
12⁰ x 11⁴
(13'-0" HIGH CLG.)
RADIUS WDW.
FRENCH DOOR
Vaulted Breakfast
DESK
PLANT SHELF ABOVE
PANTRY
SERVING BAR
ARCHED OPENING
D.W.
RANGE
Kitchen
REF.
COATS
STR.
Laun.
D.
W.
Stor.
STAIRS DOWN TO BSMT.
Master Suite
13² x 16⁰
TRAY CLG.
K.S.
Vaulted M. Bath
SHWR.
PLANT SHELF ABOVE
W.i.c.
Garage
20⁴ x 19⁹
copyright © 1992 frank betz associates, inc.

LOWE'S

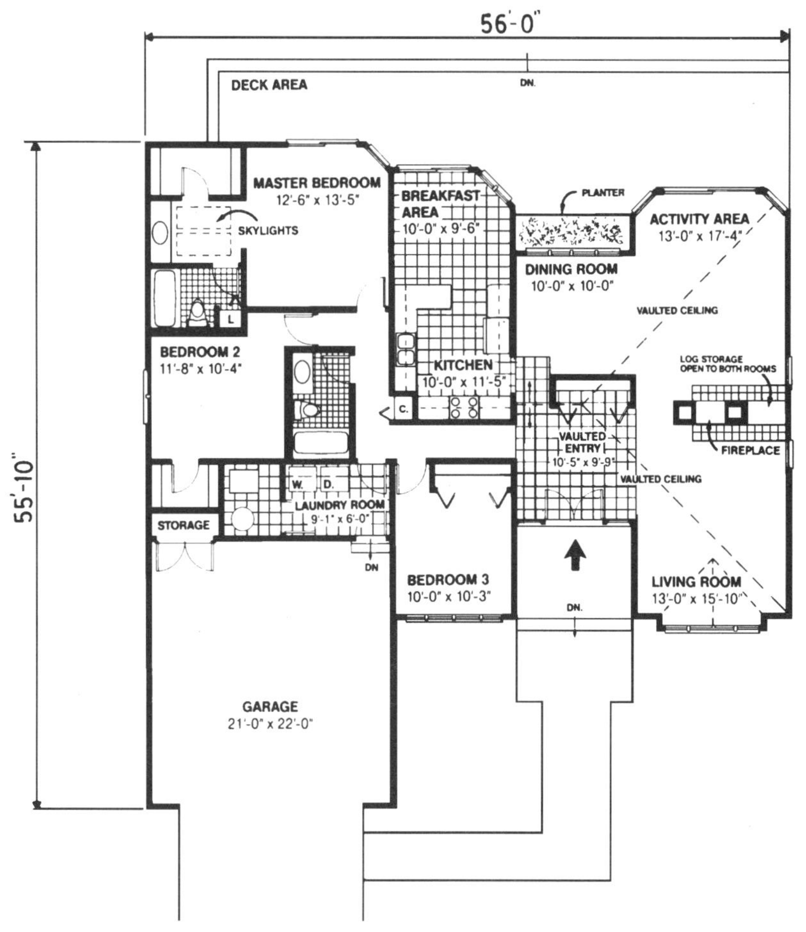
56'-0"
DECK AREA
DN.
MASTER BEDROOM
12'-6" x 13'-5"
SKYLIGHTS
BREAKFAST AREA
10'-0" x 9'-6"
PLANTER
ACTIVITY AREA
13'-0" x 17'-4"
DINING ROOM
10'-0" x 10'-0"
VAULTED CEILING
LOG STORAGE OPEN TO BOTH ROOMS
BEDROOM 2
11'-8" x 10'-4"
KITCHEN
10'-0" x 11'-5"
VAULTED ENTRY
10'-5" x 9'-9"
FIREPLACE
VAULTED CEILING
W. D.
LAUNDRY ROOM
9'-1" x 6'-0"
STORAGE
DN
BEDROOM 3
10'-0" x 10'-3"
LIVING ROOM
13'-0" x 15'-10"
DN.
GARAGE
21'-0" x 22'-0"
55'-10"

Plan #527-1255-1

partial basement/crawl

Plan #527-1255-2

slab

Price Code C

Total Living Area: 1,850 Sq. Ft.

Home has 3 bedrooms, 2 baths, 2-car garage and partial basement/crawl space or slab foundation, please specify when ordering.

Special features

- Living, dining and activity rooms have vaulted ceilings and share the warmth from an attractive see-through fireplace and log bin
- Well-equipped kitchen for mastering the culinary arts
- Master bedroom enjoys a compartmented bath with skylights and walk-in closet

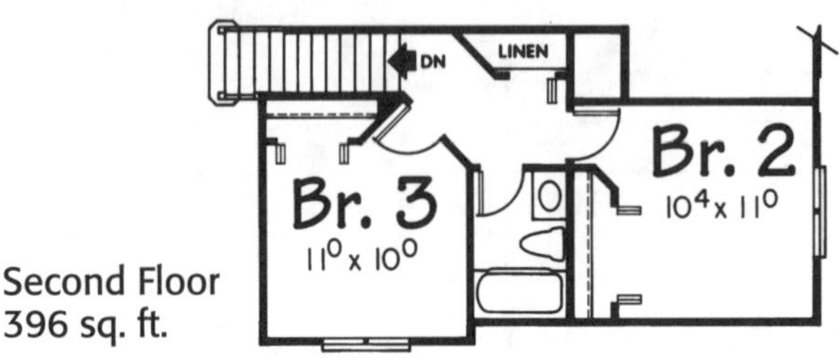
DN
LINEN
Br. 3
11^0 x 10^0
Br. 2
10^4 x 11^0
Second Floor
396 sq. ft.

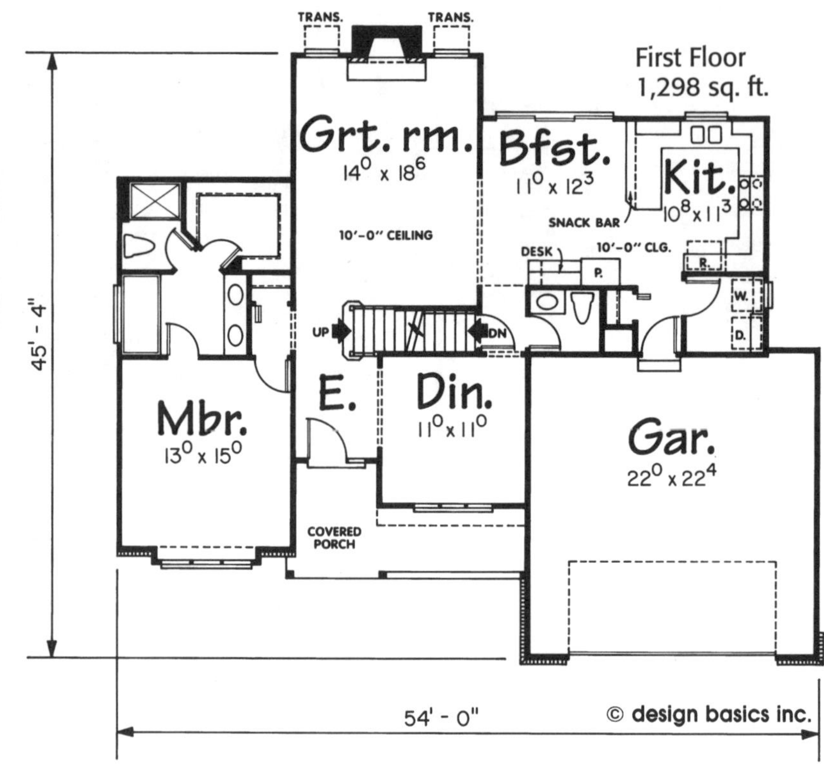
TRANS.
TRANS.
First Floor
1,298 sq. ft.
Grt. rm.
14^0 x 18^6
10'-0" CEILING
Bfst.
11^0 x 12^3
Kit.
10^8 x 11^3
SNACK BAR
DESK
10'-0" CLG.
P.
R.
W.
D.
UP
DN
45' - 4"
Mbr.
13^0 x 15^0
E.
Din.
11^0 x 11^0
Gar.
22^0 x 22^4
COVERED
PORCH
54' - 0"
© design basics inc.

Plan #527-DBI-8095

Price Code B

Total Living Area: 1,694 Sq. Ft.

Home has 3 bedrooms, 2 1/2 baths, 2-car garage and basement foundation.

Special features

- Covered front porch is charming and inviting
- Well-designed kitchen with snack bar allows for extra seating
- Large great room with 10' ceiling adds to its spaciousness

TO ORDER BLUEPRINTS USE THE FORM ON PAGE 290 OR CALL TOLL-FREE **1-800-DREAM HOME** (373-2646)

LOWE'S

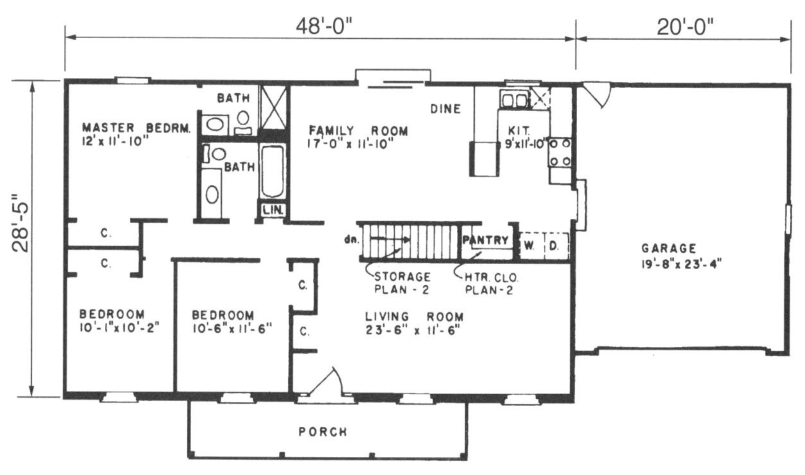
48'-0"
20'-0"
28'-5"
MASTER BEDRM.
12' x 11'-10"
BATH
BATH
LIN.
FAMILY ROOM
17'-0" x 11'-10"
DINE
KIT.
9'x11'-10"
PANTRY
W.
D.
dn.
STORAGE
PLAN - 2
HTR. CLO.
PLAN - 2
GARAGE
19'-8" x 23'-4"
C.
C.
C.
C.
BEDROOM
10'-1" x 10'-2"
BEDROOM
10'-6" x 11'-6"
LIVING ROOM
23'-6" x 11'-6"
PORCH

Plan #527-ES-103-1

basement

Plan #527-ES-103-2

crawl space & slab

Price Code A

Total Living Area: 1,364 Sq. Ft.

Home has 3 bedrooms, 2 baths, 2-car garage and basement, crawl space or slab foundation, please specify when ordering.

Special features

- A large porch and entry door with sidelights lead into a generous living room
- Well-planned U-shaped kitchen features a laundry closet, built-in pantry and open peninsula
- Master bedroom has its own bath with 4' shower
- Convenient to the kitchen is an oversized two-car garage with service door to rear

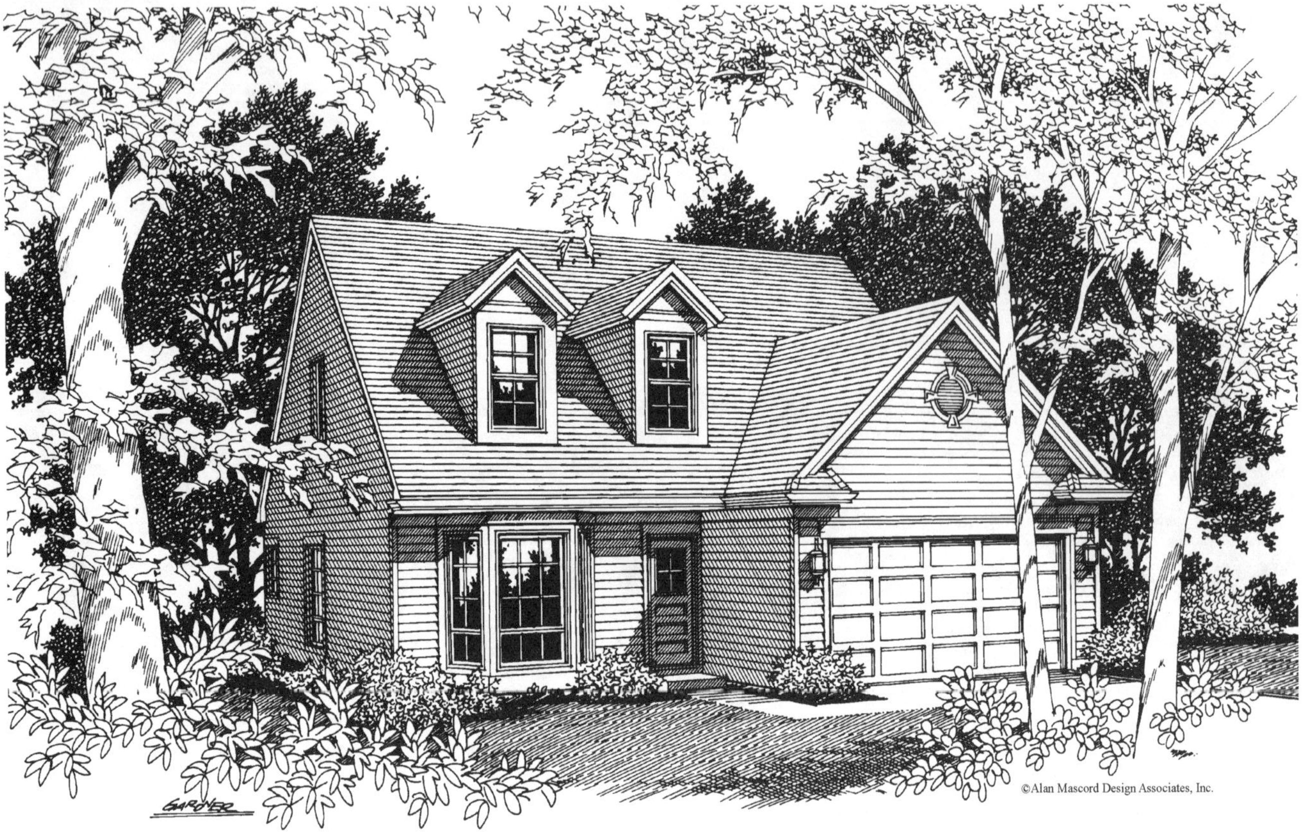

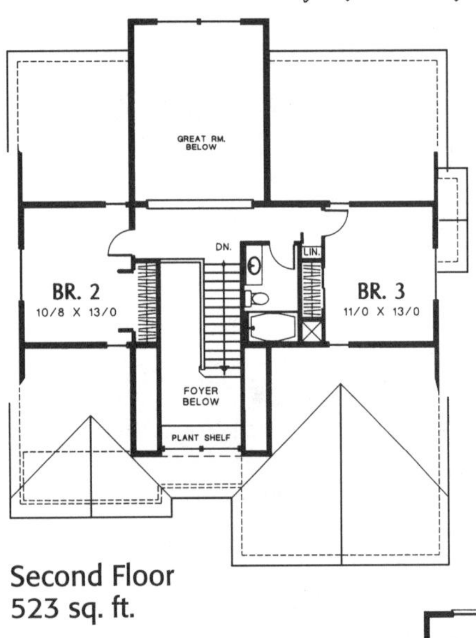
GREAT RM. BELOW
DN.
LIN.
BR. 2
10/8 X 13/0
BR. 3
11/0 X 13/0
FOYER BELOW
PLANT SHELF

Second Floor
523 sq. ft.

Plan #527-AMD-2106C

Price Code C

Total Living Area: 1,919 Sq. Ft.

Home has 4 bedrooms, 2 1/2 baths, 2-car garage and crawl space foundation.

Special features

- Great room has columns at entrance, a cozy fireplace and built-in display shelves
- A half-wall and cooktop peninsula separate the dining room and efficient L-shaped kitchen
- Vaulted master suite features a walk-in closet and spacious bath

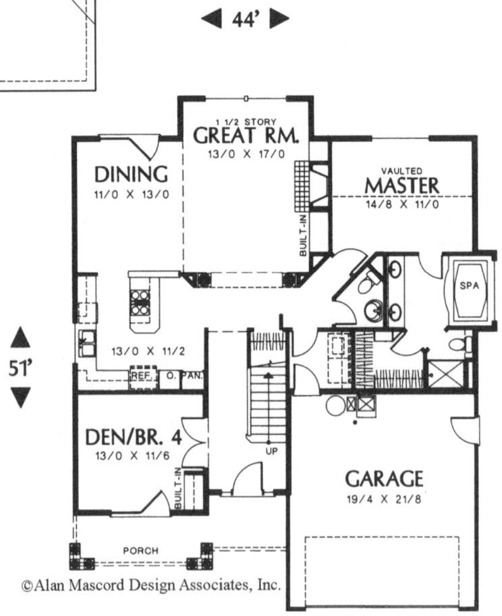

44'

51'

1 1/2 STORY
GREAT RM.
13/0 X 17/0

DINING
11/0 X 13/0

VAULTED
MASTER
14/8 X 11/0

BUILT-IN

SPA

13/0 X 11/2

REF. O. PAN.

DEN/BR. 4
13/0 X 11/6

BUILT-IN

UP

GARAGE
19/4 X 21/8

PORCH

First Floor
1,396 sq. ft.

Angles Add Interest

LOWE'S

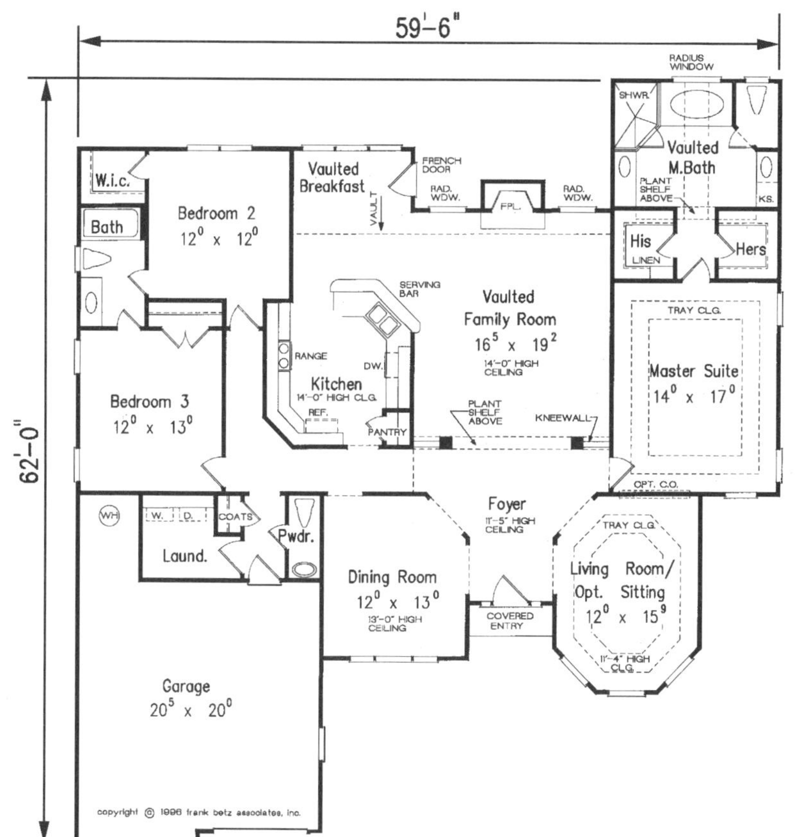
59'-6"
62'-0"
RADIUS WINDOW
SHWR.
Vaulted M.Bath
PLANT SHELF ABOVE
KS.
W.i.c.
Bath
Bedroom 2
12^0 x 12^0
Vaulted Breakfast
VAULT
FRENCH DOOR
RAD. WDW.
FPL.
RAD. WDW.
His
LINEN
Hers
SERVING BAR
Vaulted Family Room
16^5 x 19^2
14'-0" HIGH CEILING
RANGE
DW.
Kitchen
14'-0" HIGH CLG.
REF.
PANTRY
PLANT SHELF ABOVE
KNEEWALL
TRAY CLG.
Master Suite
14^0 x 17^0
OPT. C.O.
Bedroom 3
12^0 x 13^0
WH
W.
D.
COATS
Pwdr.
Laund.
Foyer
11'-5" HIGH CEILING
Dining Room
12^0 x 13^0
13'-0" HIGH CEILING
COVERED ENTRY
TRAY CLG.
Living Room/ Opt. Sitting
12^0 x 15^9
11'-4" HIGH CLG.
Garage
20^5 x 20^0
copyright © 1996 frank betz associates, inc.

Plan #527-FB-960

Price Code D

Total Living Area: 2,201 Sq. Ft.

Home has 3 bedrooms, 2 1/2 baths, 2-car garage and basement or crawl space foundation, please specify when ordering.

Special features

- Open floor plan makes home feel airy and bright
- Beautiful living room has cheerful bay window
- Master suite has his/her walk-in closets
- Family room, kitchen and breakfast combine for added space

Gabled Front Porch Gives A Country Flair

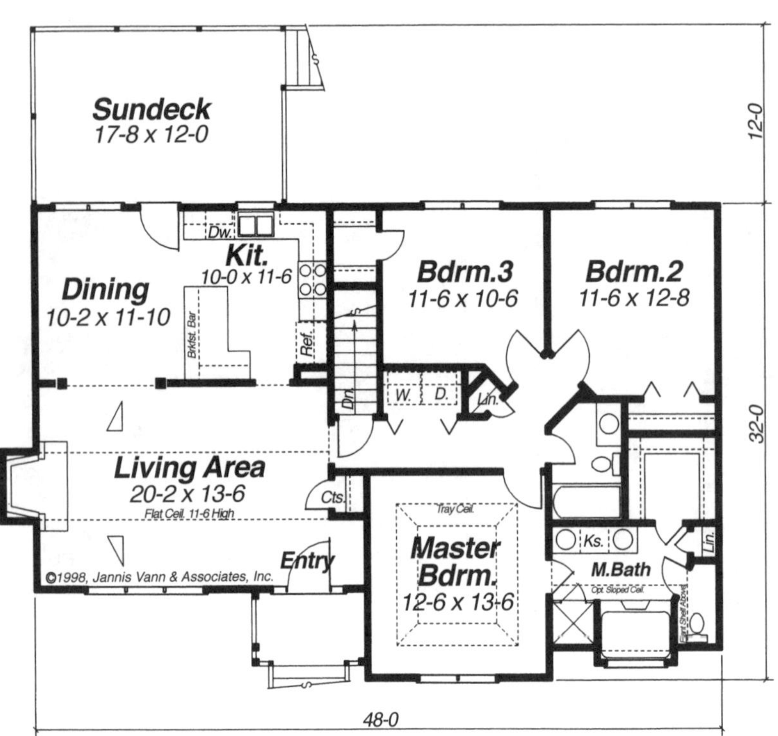
Sundeck
17-8 x 12-0
Dining
10-2 x 11-10
Kit.
10-0 x 11-6
Dw.
Brkfst. Bar
Ref.
Bdrm.3
11-6 x 10-6
Bdrm.2
11-6 x 12-8
Dn.
W.
D.
Lin.
Living Area
20-2 x 13-6
Flat Ceil. 11-6 High
Cts.
Entry
Tray Ceil.
Master
Bdrm.
12-6 x 13-6
Ks.
M.Bath
Lin.
©1998, Jannis Vann & Associates, Inc.
12-0
32-0
48-0

Plan #527-JV-1379

Price Code A

Total Living Area: 1,379 Sq. Ft.

Home has 3 bedrooms, 2 baths, 2-car drive under garage and basement foundation.

Special features

- Living area has spacious feel with 11'-6" ceiling
- Kitchen has eat-in breakfast bar open to dining area
- Laundry located near bedrooms
- Large cased opening with columns opens the living/dining areas

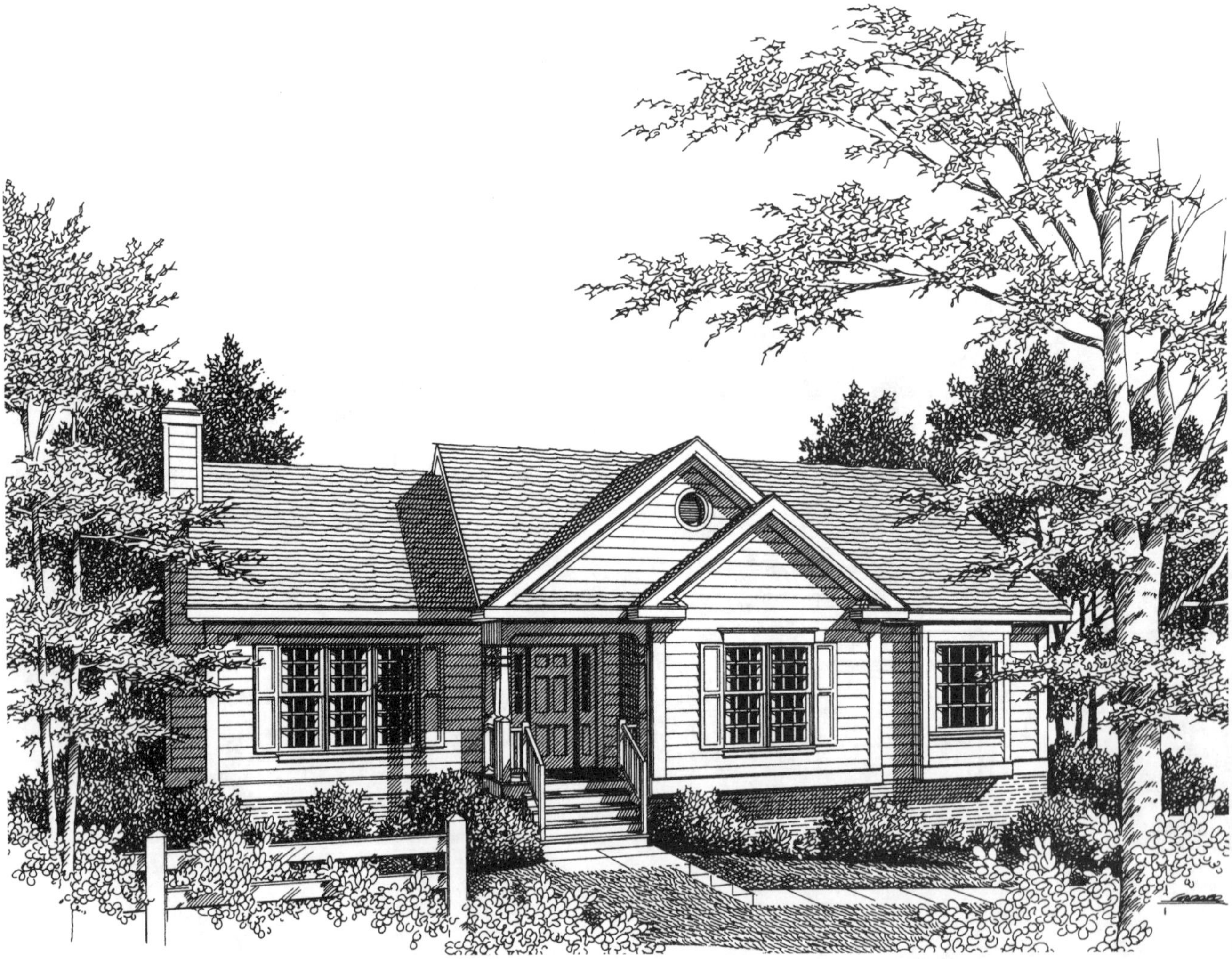

Country Styling With Splendid Floor Plan

LOWE'S

Plan #527-1112

Price Code C

Total Living Area: 2,137 Sq. Ft.

Home has 4 bedrooms, 2 1/2 baths, 2-car garage and partial basement/crawl space foundation.

Special features

- Spacious porch for plants, chairs and family gatherings
- Huge living room includes front and rear views
- U-shaped kitchen features abundant storage
- Laundry with large closet has its own porch

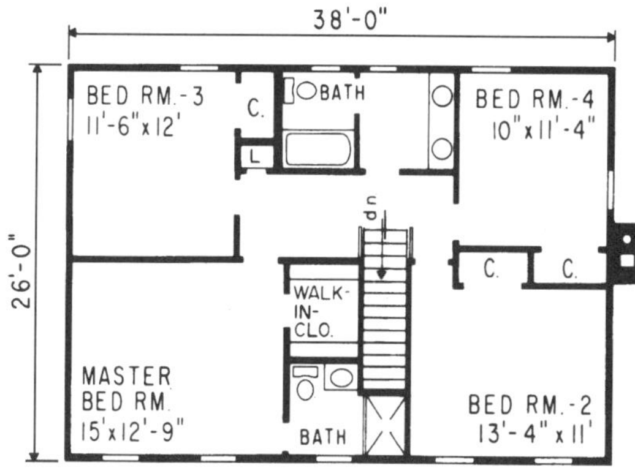
38'-0"
26'-0"
BED RM.-3
11'-6"x12'
C.
BATH
L
BED RM.-4
10"x11'-4"
dn
C.
C.
WALK-
IN-
CLO.
MASTER
BED RM.
15'x12'-9"
BATH
BED RM.-2
13'-4"x11'

Second Floor
988 sq. ft.

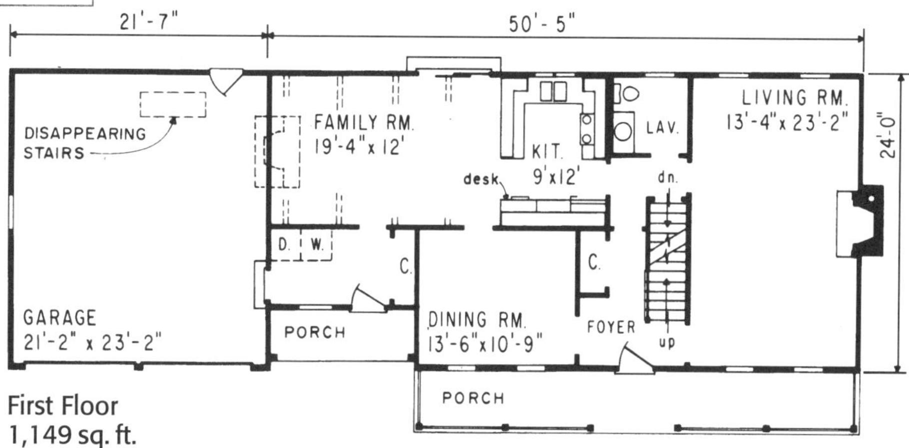
21'-7"
50'-5"
24'-0"
DISAPPEARING
STAIRS
FAMILY RM.
19'-4"x12'
KIT.
9'x12'
desk
LAV.
LIVING RM.
13'-4"x23'-2"
dn.
D.
W.
C.
C.
GARAGE
21'-2" x 23'-2"
PORCH
DINING RM.
13'-6"x10'-9"
FOYER
up
PORCH

First Floor
1,149 sq. ft.

Handsome Contemporary Design Makes Home Special

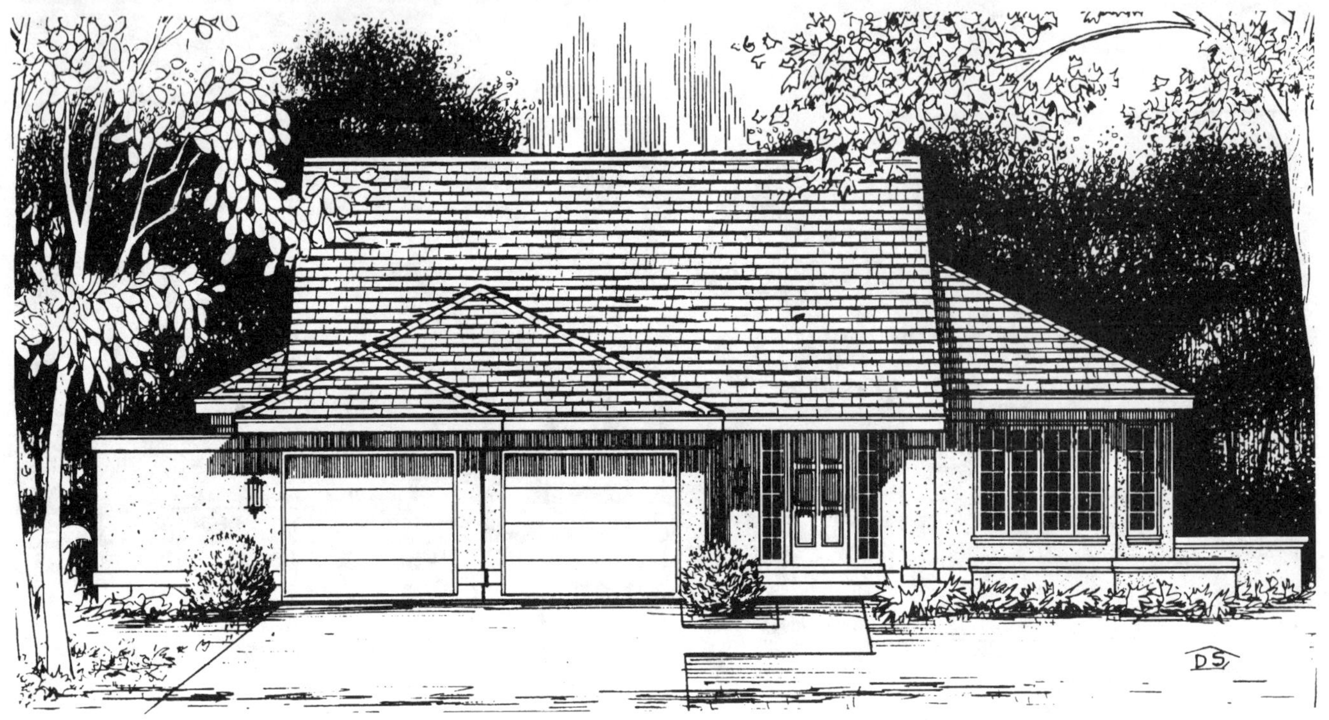

Plan #527-1324

Price Code C

Total Living Area: 1,907 Sq. Ft.

Home has 3 bedrooms, 2 baths, 2-car garage and partial basement/crawl space foundation.

Special features

- Cleverly located window in breakfast area adds charm to courtyard and view from kitchen
- Pass-through counter with bi-fold doors in kitchen provides convenience in serving to dining area
- Private bath and double closets are featured in master bedroom

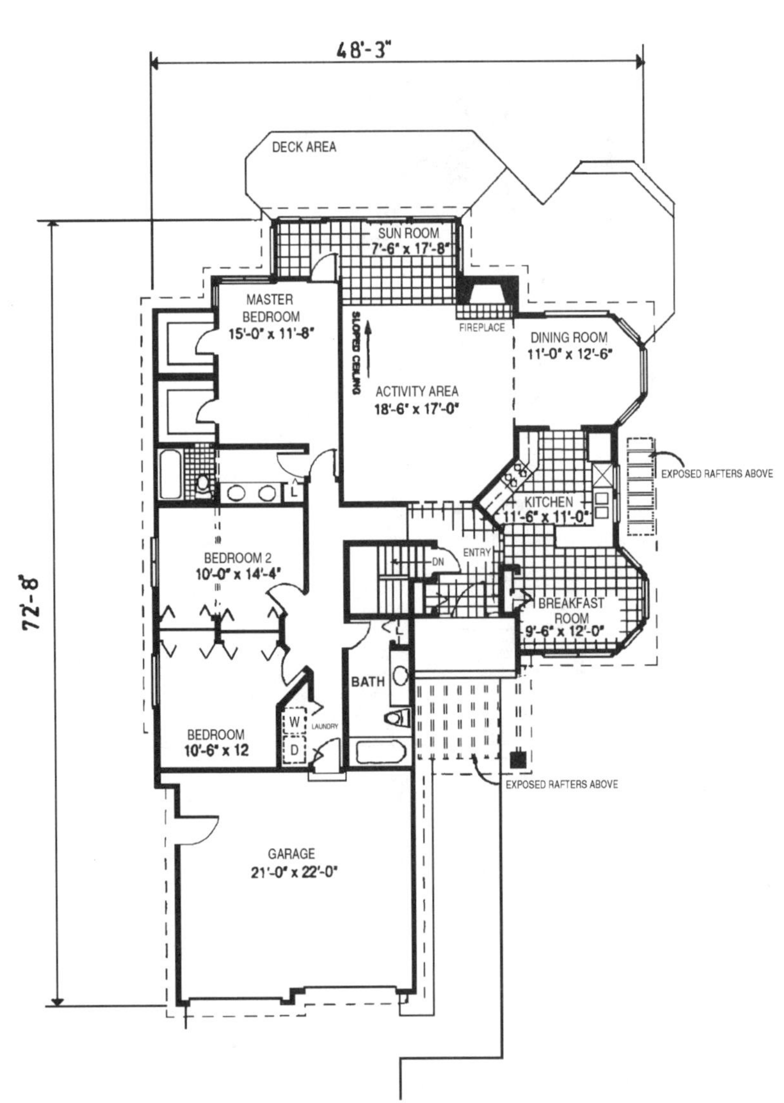
48'-3"
72'-8"
DECK AREA
SUN ROOM
7'-6" x 17'-8"
MASTER
BEDROOM
15'-0" x 11'-8"
SLOPED CEILING
FIREPLACE
DINING ROOM
11'-0" x 12'-6"
ACTIVITY AREA
18'-6" x 17'-0"
EXPOSED RAFTERS ABOVE
KITCHEN
11'-6" x 11'-0"
BEDROOM 2
10'-0" x 14'-4"
DN
ENTRY
BREAKFAST
ROOM
9'-6" x 12'-0"
BATH
W
D
LAUNDRY
BEDROOM
10'-6" x 12
EXPOSED RAFTERS ABOVE
GARAGE
21'-0" x 22'-0"

TO ORDER BLUEPRINTS USE THE FORM ON PAGE 290 OR CALL TOLL-FREE **1-800-DREAM HOME** (373-2646)

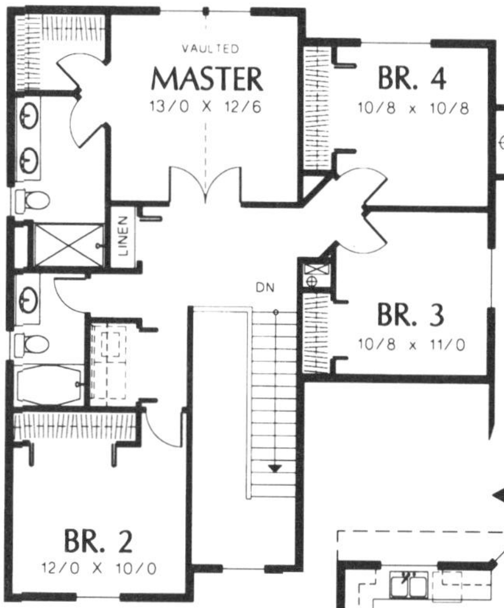

VAULTED
MASTER
13/0 X 12/6

BR. 4
10/8 x 10/8

LINEN

DN

BR. 3
10/8 x 11/0

Second Floor
982 sq. ft.

BR. 2
12/0 X 10/0

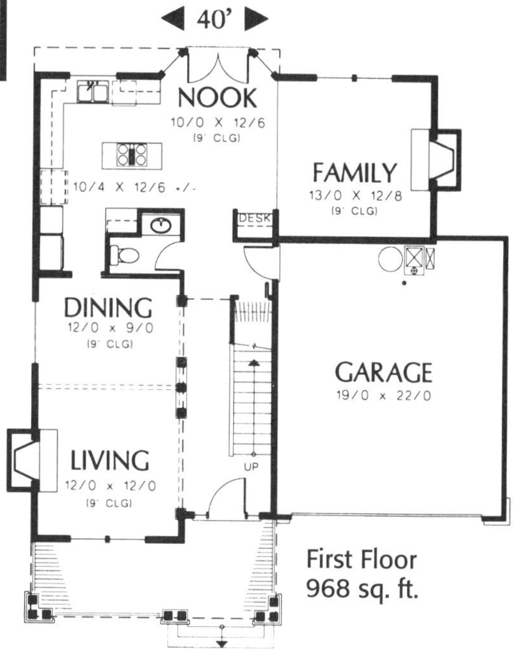

40'

NOOK
10/0 X 12/6
(9' CLG)

10/4 X 12/6 +/-

FAMILY
13/0 X 12/8
(9' CLG)

DESK

DINING
12/0 x 9/0
(9' CLG)

GARAGE
19/0 x 22/0

46'

LIVING
12/0 x 12/0
(9' CLG)

UP

First Floor
968 sq. ft.

Plan #527-AMD-2152C

Price Code C

Total Living Area: 1,950 Sq. Ft.

Home has 4 bedrooms, 2 1/2 baths, 2-car garage and crawl space foundation.

Special features

- Cooktop island, a handy desk and dining area make the kitchen highly functional
- Open floor plan with tall ceilings creates an airy atmosphere
- Family and living rooms enhanced with fireplaces

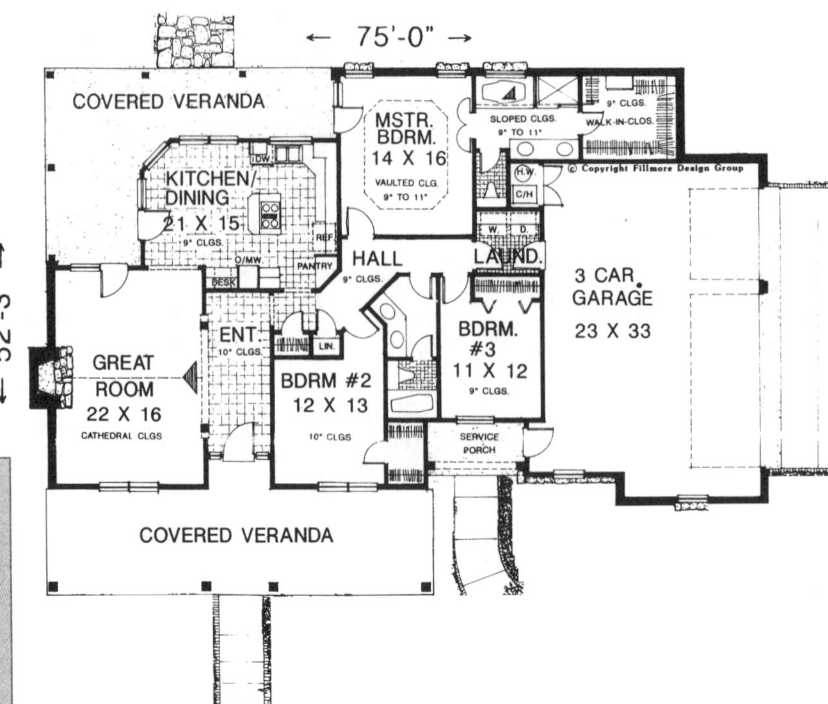
75'-0"
52'-3"
COVERED VERANDA
MSTR. BDRM. 14 X 16
VAULTED CLG. 9" TO 11"
SLOPED CLGS. 9" TO 11"
9" CLGS.
WALK-IN-CLOS.
© Copyright Fillmore Design Group
KITCHEN/ DINING 21 X 15
9" CLGS.
DW
REF.
O/MW.
PANTRY
DESK
H.W.
C/H
W.
D.
HALL
9" CLGS.
LAUND.
3 CAR GARAGE 23 X 33
ENT.
10" CLGS.
LIN.
GREAT ROOM 22 X 16
CATHEDRAL CLGS
BDRM #2 12 X 13
10" CLGS
BDRM. #3 11 X 12
9" CLGS.
SERVICE PORCH
COVERED VERANDA

Plan #527-FDG-7963-L

Price Code C

Total Living Area: 1,830 Sq. Ft.

Home has 3 bedrooms, 2 baths, 3-car side entry garage and basement, crawl space or slab foundation, please specify when ordering.

Special features

- Inviting covered verandas in the front and rear of the home
- Great room has fireplace and cathedral ceiling
- Handy service porch allows easy access
- Master suite has vaulted ceiling and private bath

TO ORDER BLUEPRINTS USE THE FORM ON PAGE 290 OR CALL TOLL-FREE **1-800-DREAM HOME** (373-2646)

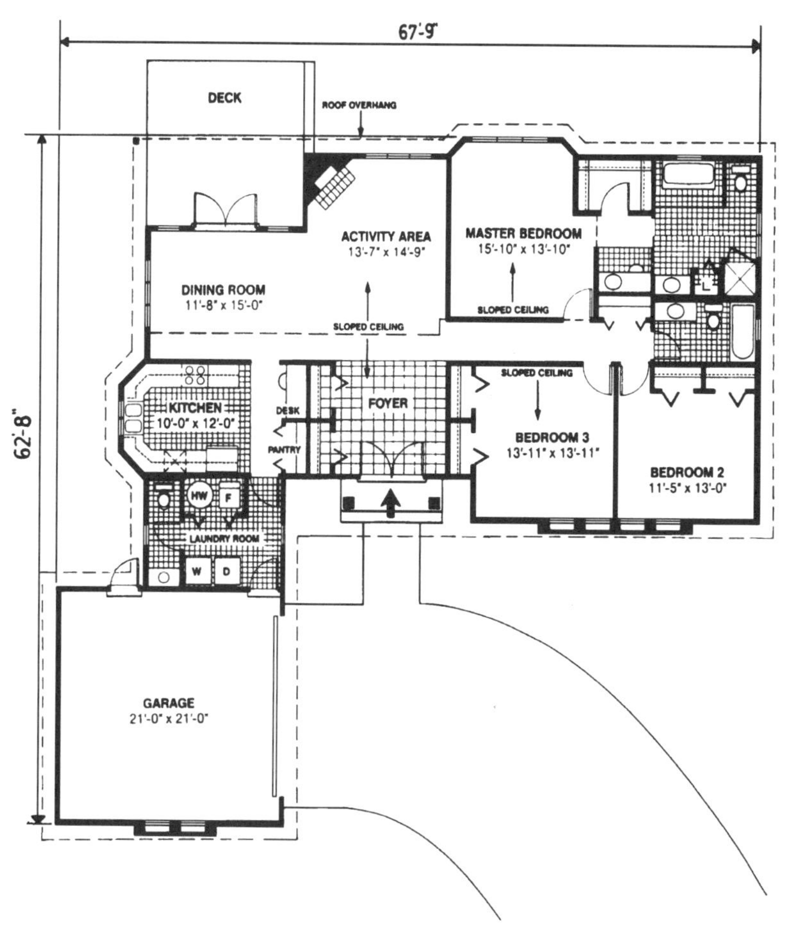
67'-9"
DECK
ROOF OVERHANG
ACTIVITY AREA
13'-7" x 14'-9"
MASTER BEDROOM
15'-10" x 13'-10"
SLOPED CEILING
DINING ROOM
11'-8" x 15'-0"
SLOPED CEILING
SLOPED CEILING
KITCHEN
10'-0" x 12'-0"
DESK
FOYER
PANTRY
BEDROOM 3
13'-11" x 13'-11"
BEDROOM 2
11'-5" x 13'-0"
62'-8"
HW
F
LAUNDRY ROOM
W
D
GARAGE
21'-0" x 21'-0"

Plan #527-1267

Price Code C

Total Living Area: 1,800 Sq. Ft.

Home has 3 bedrooms, 2 1/2 baths, 2-car side entry garage and slab foundation.

Special features

- Comforts abound in this well-designed ranch
- Sunlit entryway leads to activity area with corner fireplace at rear of home
- U-shaped kitchen with built-in pantry and desk is adjacent to dining room with optional deck
- Large laundry area/powder room conveniently located adjacent to garage, just off kitchen
- Master bedroom features large walk-in closet, dressing area with make-up vanity and compartmented master bath with shower and raised tub
- Two additional bedrooms share a full bath

Plan #527-FB-797

Price Code C

Total Living Area: 1,845 Sq. Ft.

Home has 3 bedrooms, 2 1/2 baths, 2-car side entry garage and basement or crawl space foundation, please specify when ordering.

Special features

- Vaulted living room has cozy fireplace
- Breakfast area and kitchen are lovely gathering places
- Dining room overlooks living room
- Optional second floor with bath has an additional 409 square feet of living area

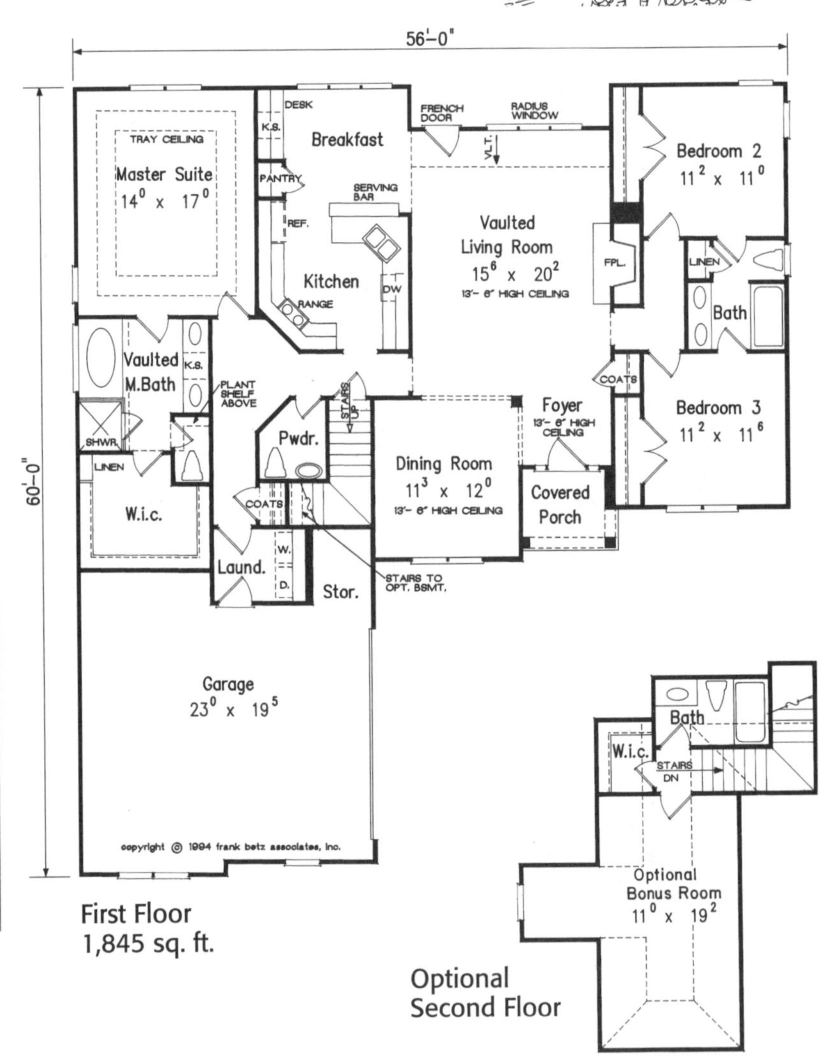
56'-0"
60'-0"
TRAY CEILING
Master Suite
14⁰ x 17⁰
DESK
K.S.
Breakfast
PANTRY
REF.
SERVING BAR
Kitchen
RANGE
DW
FRENCH DOOR
RADIUS WINDOW
V.L.T.
Vaulted
Living Room
15⁶ x 20²
13'- 6" HIGH CEILING
FPL.
Bedroom 2
11² x 11⁰
LINEN
Bath
COATS
Bedroom 3
11² x 11⁶
Vaulted
M.Bath
K.S.
PLANT SHELF ABOVE
SHWR.
LINEN
W.i.c.
Pwdr.
COATS
STAIRS UP
Foyer
13'- 6" HIGH CEILING
Dining Room
11³ x 12⁰
13'- 6" HIGH CEILING
Covered
Porch
Laund.
W.
D.
Stor.
STAIRS TO OPT. BSMT.
Garage
23⁰ x 19⁵
copyright © 1994 frank betz associates, inc.
Bath
W.i.c.
STAIRS DN
Optional
Bonus Room
11⁰ x 19²

First Floor
1,845 sq. ft.

Optional
Second Floor

Cozy Corner Fireplace

LOWE'S

Plan #527-AMD-2189

Price Code C

Total Living Area: 1,994 Sq. Ft.

Home has 3 bedrooms, 2 1/2 baths, 2-car garage and crawl space foundation.

Special features

- Breakfast nook overlooks kitchen and great room creating an airy feeling
- Enter double-doors to find a cozy den ideal as a home office
- Master suite has walk-in closet and private bath

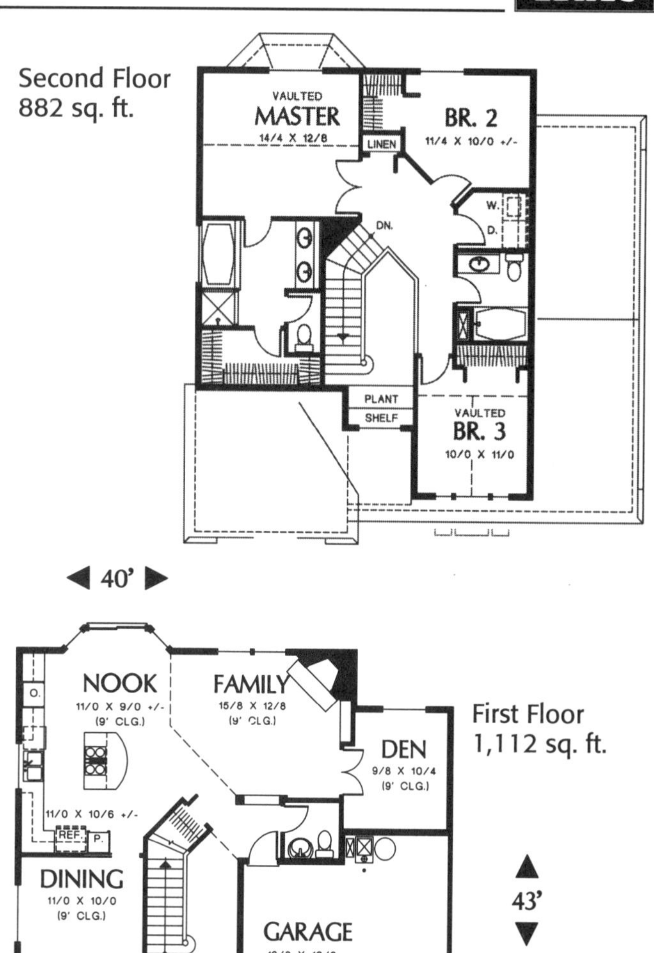
Second Floor
882 sq. ft.
VAULTED
MASTER
14/4 X 12/8
BR. 2
11/4 X 10/0 +/-
LINEN
DN.
W.
D.
PLANT
SHELF
VAULTED
BR. 3
10/0 X 11/0
40'
NOOK
11/0 X 9/0 +/-
(9' CLG.)
FAMILY
15/8 X 12/8
(9' CLG.)
DEN
9/8 X 10/4
(9' CLG.)
First Floor
1,112 sq. ft.
11/0 X 10/6 +/-
REF.
P.
DINING
11/0 X 10/0
(9' CLG.)
43'
GARAGE
19/0 X 19/6 +
UP
VAULTED
LIVING
13/0 x 12/0

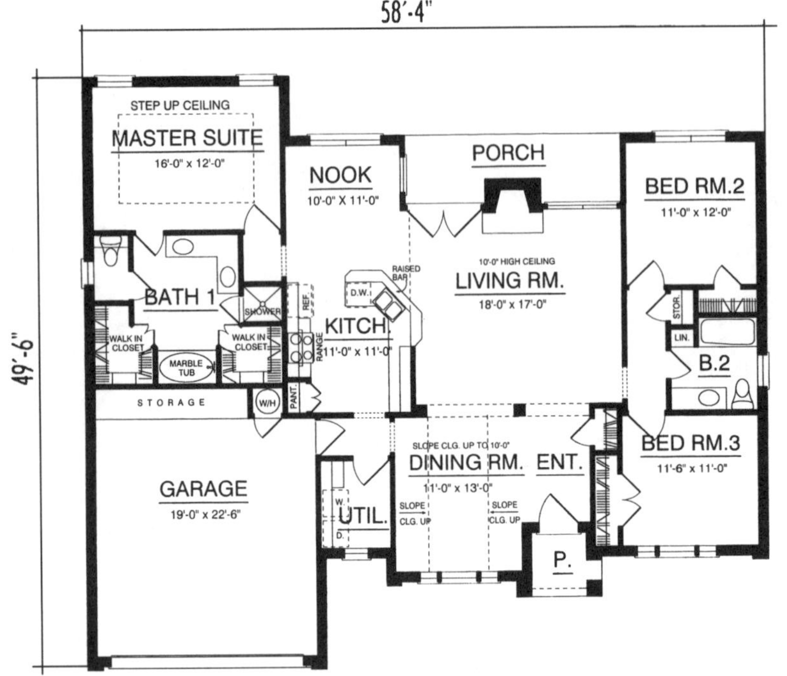
58'-4"
49'-6"
STEP UP CEILING
MASTER SUITE
16'-0" x 12'-0"
NOOK
10'-0" X 11'-0"
PORCH
BED RM.2
11'-0" x 12'-0"
10'-0" HIGH CEILING
LIVING RM.
18'-0" x 17'-0"
RAISED BAR
D.W.
BATH 1
SHOWER
REF.
KITCH.
11'-0" x 11'-0"
RANGE
WALK IN CLOSET
MARBLE TUB
WALK IN CLOSET
STOR
LIN.
B.2
STORAGE
W/H
PANT.
SLOPE CLG. UP TO 10'-0"
DINING RM.
11'-0" x 13'-0"
ENT.
BED RM.3
11'-6" x 11'-0"
GARAGE
19'-0" x 22'-6"
UTIL.
W.
D.
SLOPE CLG. UP
SLOPE CLG. UP
P.

Plan #527-RDD-1791-9

Price Code B

Total Living Area: 1,791 Sq. Ft.

Home has 3 bedrooms, 2 baths, 2-car garage and slab or crawl space foundation, please specify when ordering.

Special features

- Dining area has 10' high sloped ceiling
- Kitchen opens to large living room with fireplace and access onto a covered porch
- Master suite features private bath, double walk-in closets and whirlpool tub

TO ORDER BLUEPRINTS USE THE FORM ON PAGE 290 OR CALL TOLL-FREE **1-800-DREAM HOME** (373-2646)

WIDTH 48–10

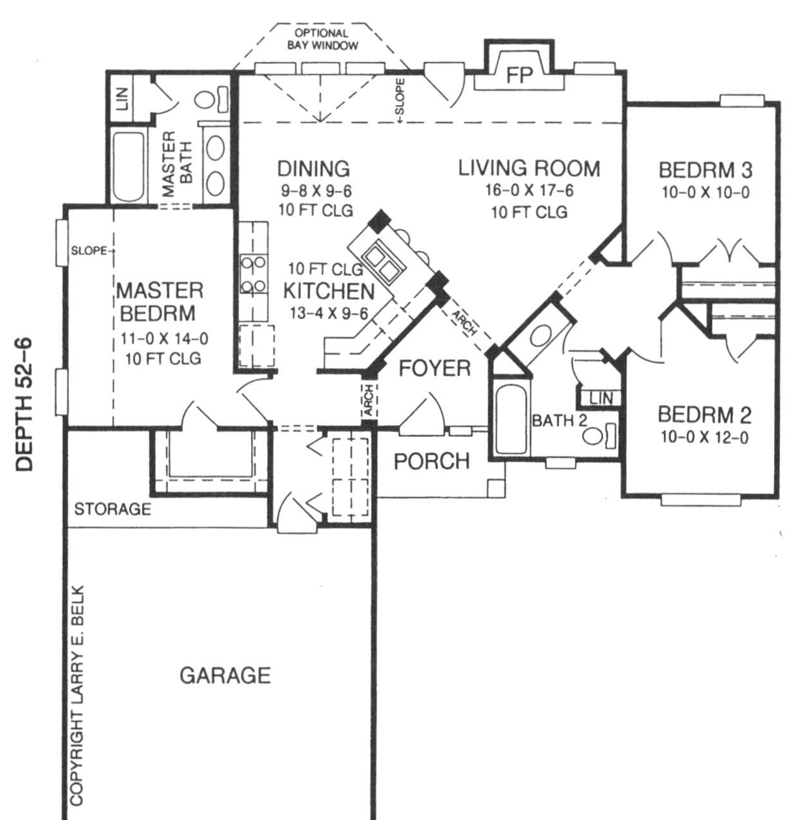
OPTIONAL BAY WINDOW
FP
SLOPE
LIN
MASTER BATH
DINING
9–8 X 9–6
10 FT CLG
LIVING ROOM
16–0 X 17–6
10 FT CLG
BEDRM 3
10–0 X 10–0
SLOPE
MASTER BEDRM
11–0 X 14–0
10 FT CLG
10 FT CLG
KITCHEN
13–4 X 9–6
ARCH
FOYER
ARCH
LIN
BATH 2
BEDRM 2
10–0 X 12–0
PORCH
STORAGE
DEPTH 52–6
GARAGE
COPYRIGHT LARRY E. BELK

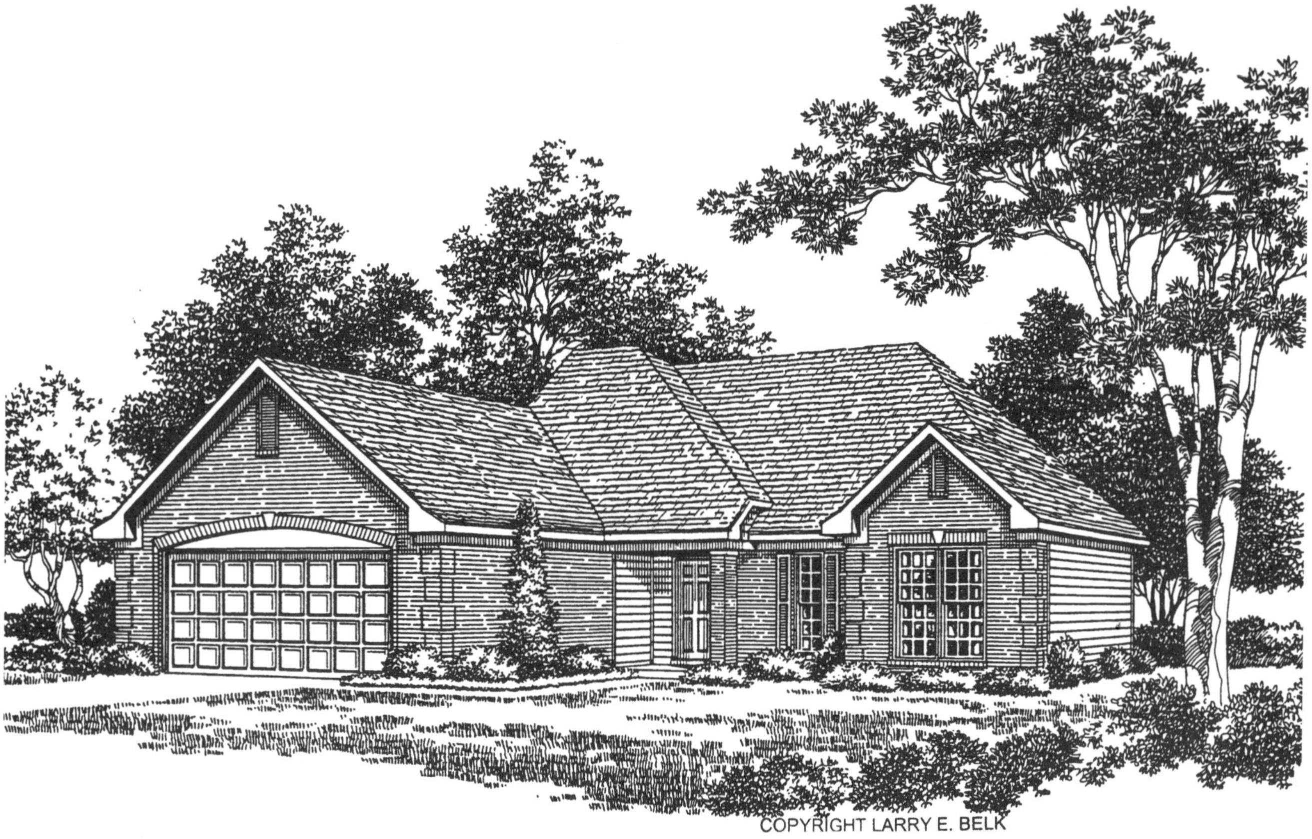

Plan #527-LBD-12-2A

Price Code A

Total Living Area: 1,282 Sq. Ft.

Home has 3 bedrooms, 2 baths, 2-car garage and crawl space or slab foundation, please specify when ordering.

Special features

- Angled entry creates the illusion of space making home appear larger
- Dining room located off kitchen serves both formal and informal occasions
- Master bedroom has walk-in closet and private bath with whirlpool/ shower combination

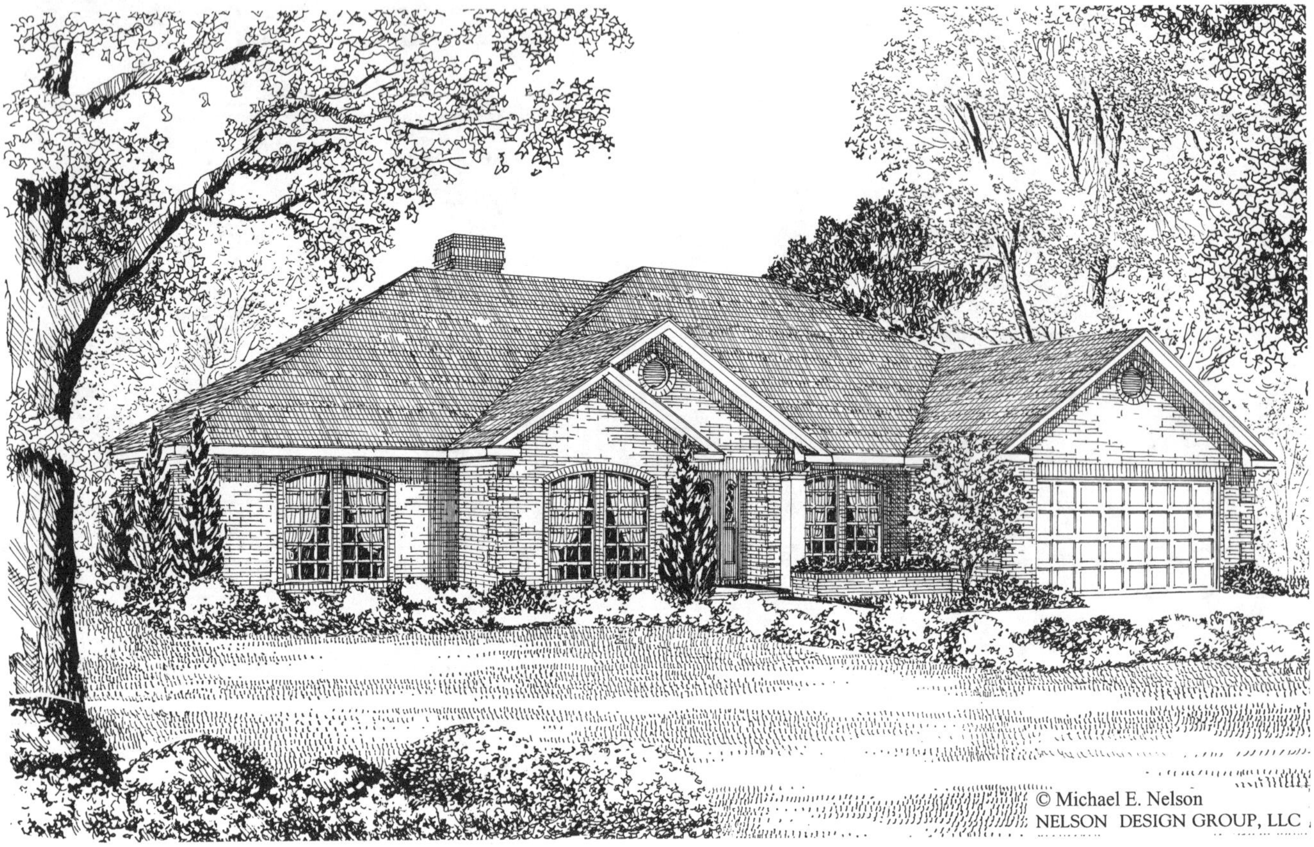

Plan #527-NDG-190

Price Code C

Total Living Area: 2,107 Sq. Ft.

Home has 4 bedrooms, 2 1/2 baths, 2-car garage and crawl space or slab foundation, please specify when ordering.

Special features

- Master suite separate from other bedrooms for privacy
- Spacious breakfast room and kitchen include center island with eating space
- Centralized great room has fireplace and easy access to any area in the home

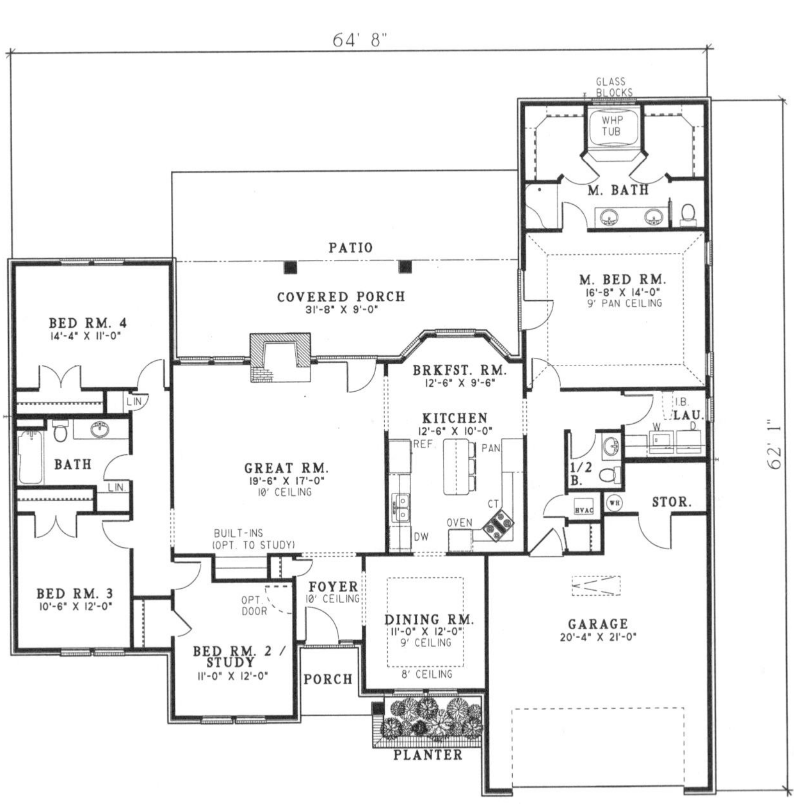
64' 8"
62' 1"
GLASS BLOCKS
WHP TUB
M. BATH
PATIO
COVERED PORCH
31'-8" X 9'-0"
M. BED RM.
16'-8" X 14'-0"
9' PAN CEILING
BED RM. 4
14'-4" X 11'-0"
BRKFST. RM.
12'-6" X 9'-6"
KITCHEN
12'-6" X 10'-0"
REF.
PAN
LIN
BATH
LIN
GREAT RM.
19'-6" X 17'-0"
10' CEILING
CT
OVEN
DW
I.B.
LAU.
W
D
1/2 B.
HVAC
WH
STOR.
BUILT-INS
(OPT. TO STUDY)
BED RM. 3
10'-6" X 12'-0"
OPT. DOOR
FOYER
10' CEILING
DINING RM.
11'-0" X 12'-0"
9' CEILING
8' CEILING
GARAGE
20'-4" X 21'-0"
BED RM. 2 / STUDY
11'-0" X 12'-0"
PORCH
PLANTER

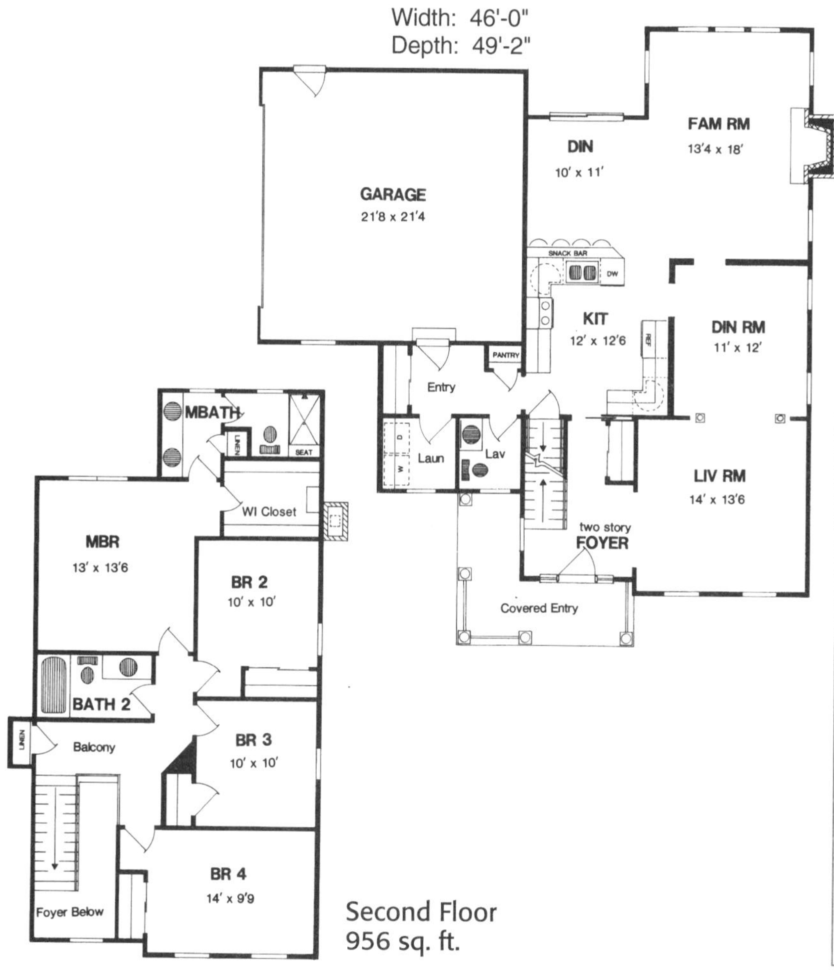
Width: 46'-0"
Depth: 49'-2"
GARAGE
21'8 x 21'4
DIN
10' x 11'
FAM RM
13'4 x 18'
SNACK BAR
DW
KIT
12' x 12'6
REF
PANTRY
DIN RM
11' x 12'
Entry
Laun
Lav
LIV RM
14' x 13'6
two story
FOYER
Covered Entry
MBATH
LINEN
SEAT
WI Closet
MBR
13' x 13'6
BR 2
10' x 10'
BATH 2
Balcony
LINEN
BR 3
10' x 10'
BR 4
14' x 9'9
Foyer Below
Second Floor
956 sq. ft.

First Floor
1,141 sq. ft.

Plan #527-JFD-20-2097-1

Price Code C

Total Living Area: 2,097 Sq. Ft.

Home has 4 bedrooms, 2 1/2 baths, 2-car side entry garage and basement foundation.

Special features

- Formal living room connects with dining room, perfect for entertaining
- Elegant two-story foyer
- Spacious entry off garage near bath and laundry area
- Family room has cozy fireplace

MAXON

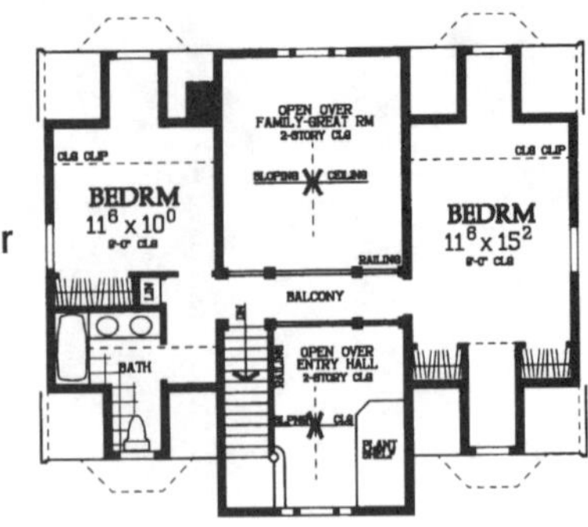
OPEN OVER FAMILY-GREAT RM
BEDRM
11⁶ x 10⁰
BEDRM
11⁸ x 15²
BALCONY
OPEN OVER ENTRY HALL
BATH

Second Floor
600 sq. ft.

Plan #527-HP-C619

Price Code B

Total Living Area: 1,771 Sq. Ft.

Home has 3 bedrooms, 2 1/2 baths, optional detached 2-car garage and basement foundation.

Special features

- Efficient country kitchen shares space with a bayed eating area
- Two-story family/great room is warmed by a fireplace in winter and open to outdoor country comfort in the summer with double French doors
- First floor master suite offers a bay window and access to the porch through French doors

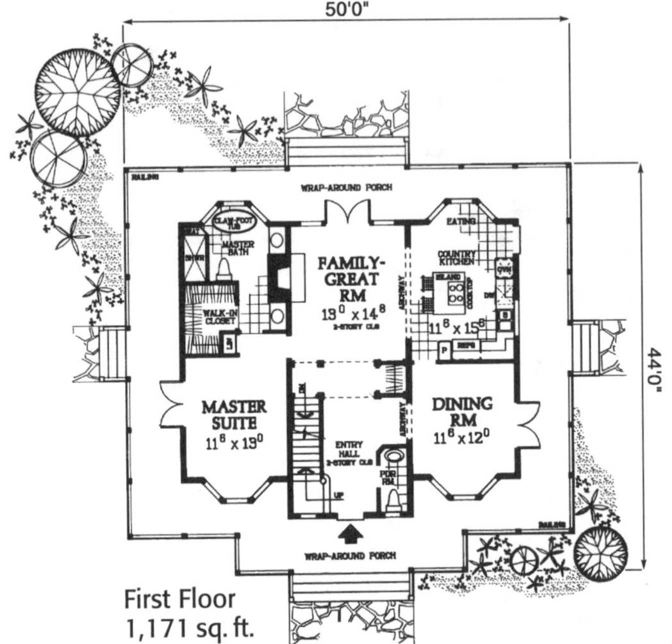
50'0"
44'0"
WRAP-AROUND PORCH
MASTER BATH
WALK-IN CLOSET
FAMILY-GREAT RM
13⁰ x 14⁸
EATING
COUNTRY KITCHEN
11⁶ x 15⁸
MASTER SUITE
11⁶ x 13⁰
ENTRY HALL
DINING RM
11⁶ x 12⁰
WRAP-AROUND PORCH

First Floor
1,171 sq. ft.

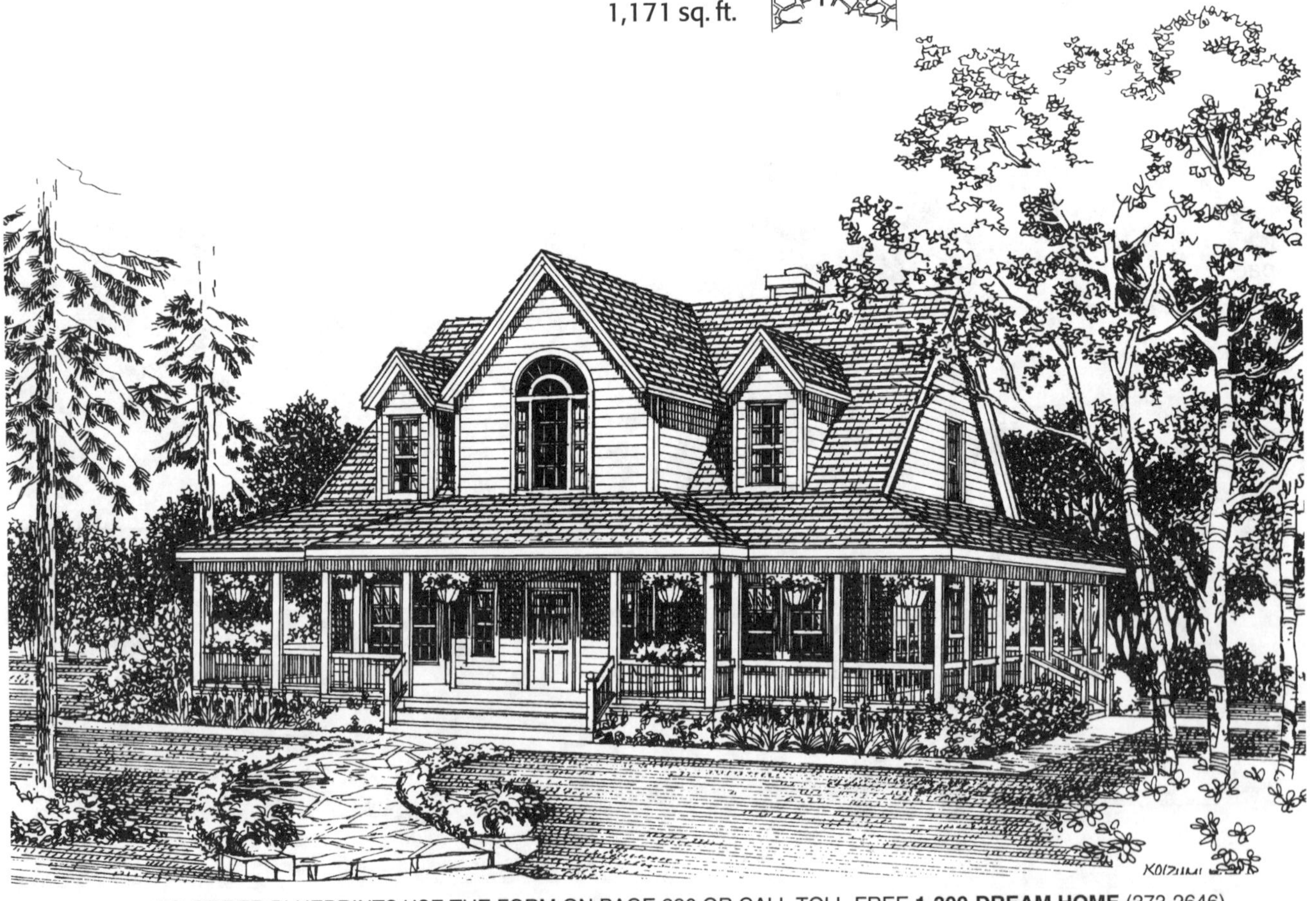

TO ORDER BLUEPRINTS USE THE FORM ON PAGE 290 OR CALL TOLL-FREE **1-800-DREAM HOME** (373-2646)

Plan #527-FB-933

Price Code C

Total Living Area: 2,193 Sq. Ft.

Home has 3 bedrooms, 3 baths, 2-car side entry garage and basement, crawl space or slab foundation, please specify when ordering.

Special features

- Master suite has sitting room
- Dining room has decorative columns and overlooks family room
- Kitchen has lots of storage
- Optional bonus room with bath on second floor has an additional 400 square feet of living area

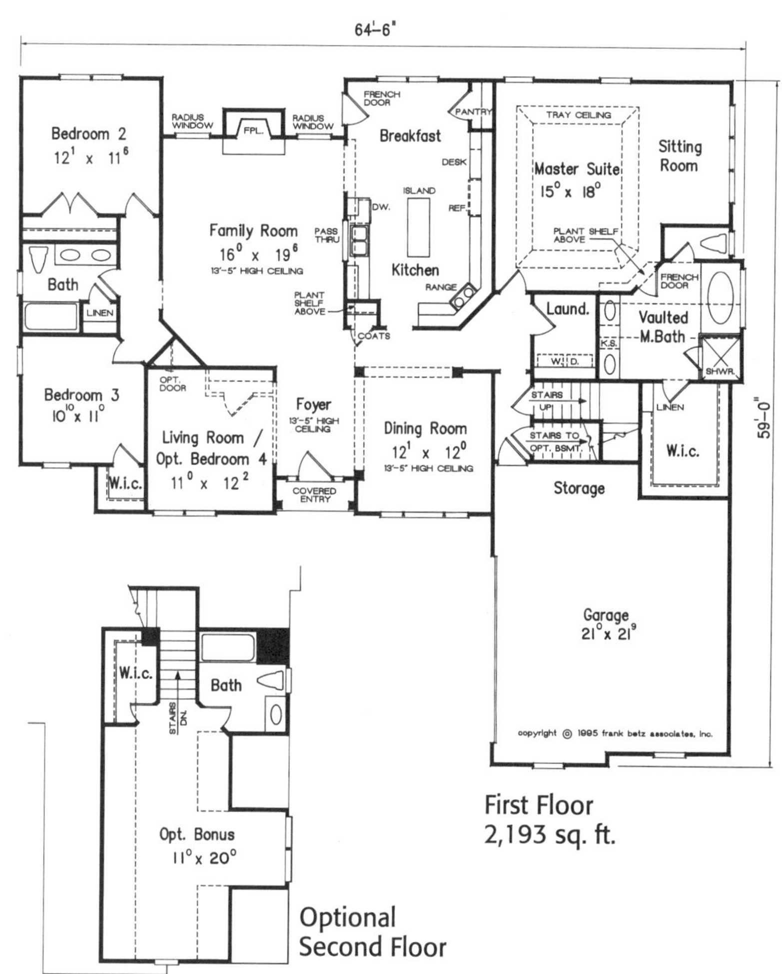
64'-6"
59'-0"
Bedroom 2
12¹ x 11⁶
Bath
LINEN
Bedroom 3
10¹⁰ x 11⁰
W.i.c.
RADIUS WINDOW
FPL.
RADIUS WINDOW
Family Room
16⁰ x 19⁶
13'-5" HIGH CEILING
PASS THRU
PLANT SHELF ABOVE
OPT. DOOR
Living Room / Opt. Bedroom 4
11⁰ x 12²
Foyer
13'-5" HIGH CEILING
COVERED ENTRY
FRENCH DOOR
PANTRY
Breakfast
DESK
ISLAND
DW.
REF.
Kitchen
RANGE
COATS
Dining Room
12¹ x 12⁰
13'-5" HIGH CEILING
TRAY CEILING
Master Suite
15⁰ x 18⁰
Sitting Room
PLANT SHELF ABOVE
FRENCH DOOR
Laund.
Vaulted M.Bath
K.S.
W D
SHWR.
STAIRS UP
STAIRS TO OPT. BSMT.
LINEN
W.i.c.
Storage
Garage
21⁰ x 21⁹
copyright © 1995 frank betz associates, inc.
First Floor
2,193 sq. ft.
W.i.c.
STAIRS DN.
Bath
Opt. Bonus
11⁰ x 20⁰
Optional Second Floor

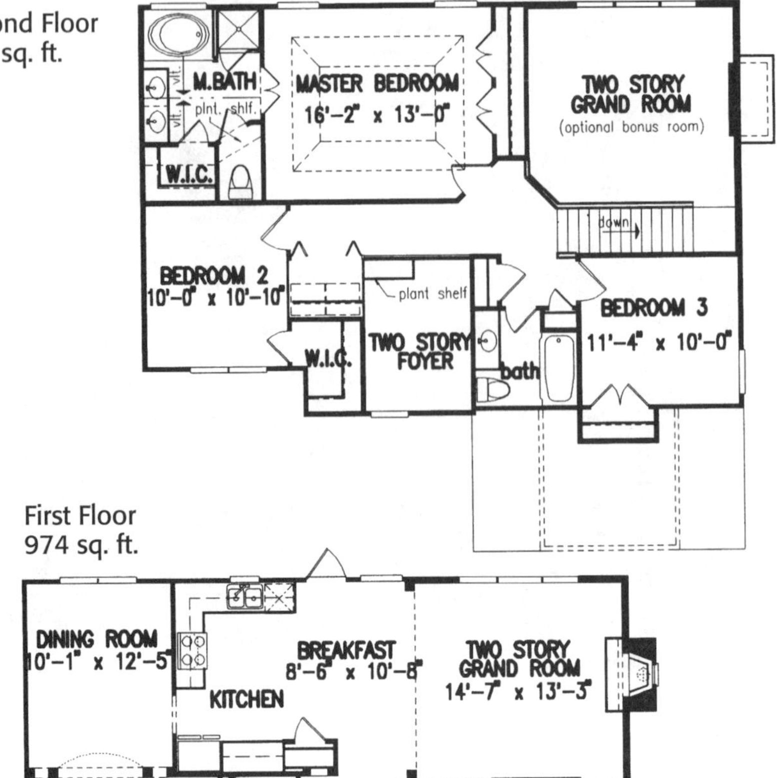
Second Floor
843 sq. ft.
M.BATH
plnt. shlf.
W.I.C.
MASTER BEDROOM
16'-2" x 13'-0"
TWO STORY
GRAND ROOM
(optional bonus room)
down
BEDROOM 2
10'-0" x 10'-10"
plant shelf
W.I.C.
TWO STORY
FOYER
bath
BEDROOM 3
11'-4" x 10'-0"
First Floor
974 sq. ft.
DINING ROOM
10'-1" x 12'-5"
BREAKFAST
8'-6" x 10'-8"
KITCHEN
TWO STORY
GRAND ROOM
14'-7" x 13'-3"
PWDR
up
LIVING ROOM
13'-4" x 11'-1"
plant shelf
above
TWO STORY
FOYER
GARAGE
Width: 45'-0"
Depth: 37'-6"
© 1998 GARRELL ASSOCIATES, INC.

Plan #527-MG-97063

Price Code C

Total Living Area: 1,817 Sq. Ft.

Home has 3 bedrooms, 2 1/2 baths, 2-car garage and basement or slab foundation, please specify when ordering.

Special features

- Two-story foyer accented with plant shelf
- Living and dining rooms separated by distinctive columns
- Laundry area located on second floor near bedrooms
- Two-story grand room has fireplace and second floor balcony

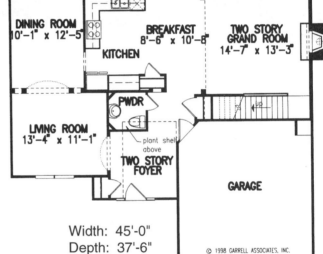

Perfect Country Haven

LOWE'S

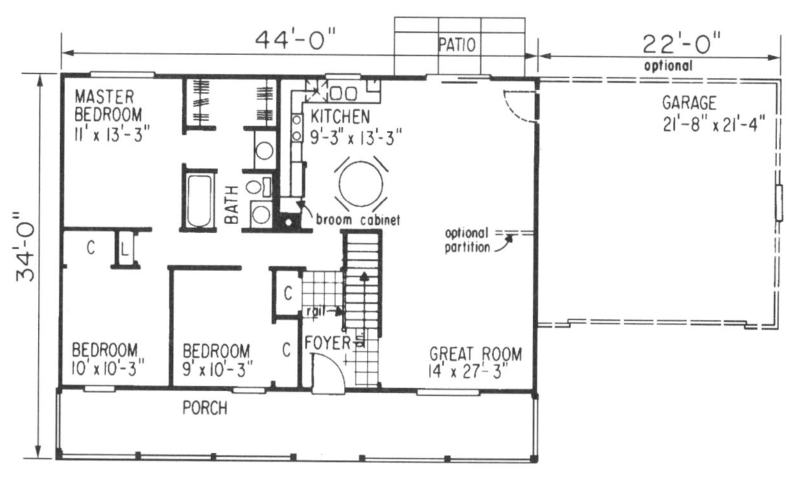
44'-0"
PATIO
22'-0"
optional
MASTER BEDROOM
11' x 13'-3"
KITCHEN
9'-3" x 13'-3"
GARAGE
21'-8" x 21'-4"
BATH
broom cabinet
optional partition
34'-0"
C
L
C
rail
BEDROOM
10' x 10'-3"
BEDROOM
9' x 10'-3"
C
FOYER
GREAT ROOM
14' x 27'-3"
PORCH

Plan #527-1120

Price Code A

Total Living Area: 1,232 Sq. Ft.

Home has 3 bedrooms, 1 bath, optional 2-car garage and basement foundation, drawings also include crawl space and slab foundations.

Special features

- Ideal porch for quiet quality evenings
- Great room opens to dining room for those large Sunday dinner gatherings
- Functional L-shaped kitchen includes broom cabinet
- Master bedroom contains large walk-in closet and compartmented bath

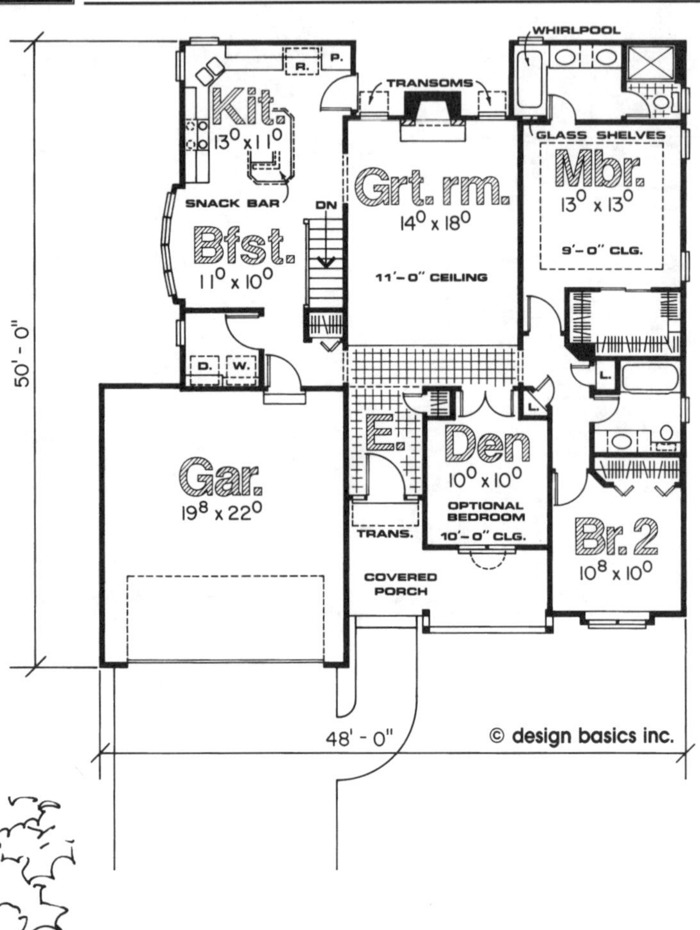
WHIRLPOOL
TRANSOMS
GLASS SHELVES
Kit.
13^0 x 11^0
R.
P.
SNACK BAR
DN
Grt. rm.
14^0 x 18^0
11'-0" CEILING
Mbr.
13^0 x 13^0
9'-0" CLG.
Bfst.
11^0 x 10^0
D.
W.
L.
E.
Den
10^0 x 10^0
OPTIONAL BEDROOM
10'-0" CLG.
TRANS.
COVERED PORCH
Gar.
19^8 x 22^0
Br. 2
10^8 x 10^0
50' - 0"
48' - 0"
© design basics inc.

Plan #527-DBI-3019

Price Code A

Total Living Area: 1,479 Sq. Ft.

Home has 2 bedrooms, 2 baths, 2-car garage and basement foundation.

Special features

- Centrally located great room enhanced with fireplace
- Den can easily convert to a third bedroom
- Master bedroom has private bath with large walk-in closet
- Sunny kitchen/breakfast room enjoys view into great room

TO ORDER BLUEPRINTS USE THE FORM ON PAGE 290 OR CALL TOLL-FREE **1-800-DREAM HOME** (373-2646)

A Great Country Farmhouse

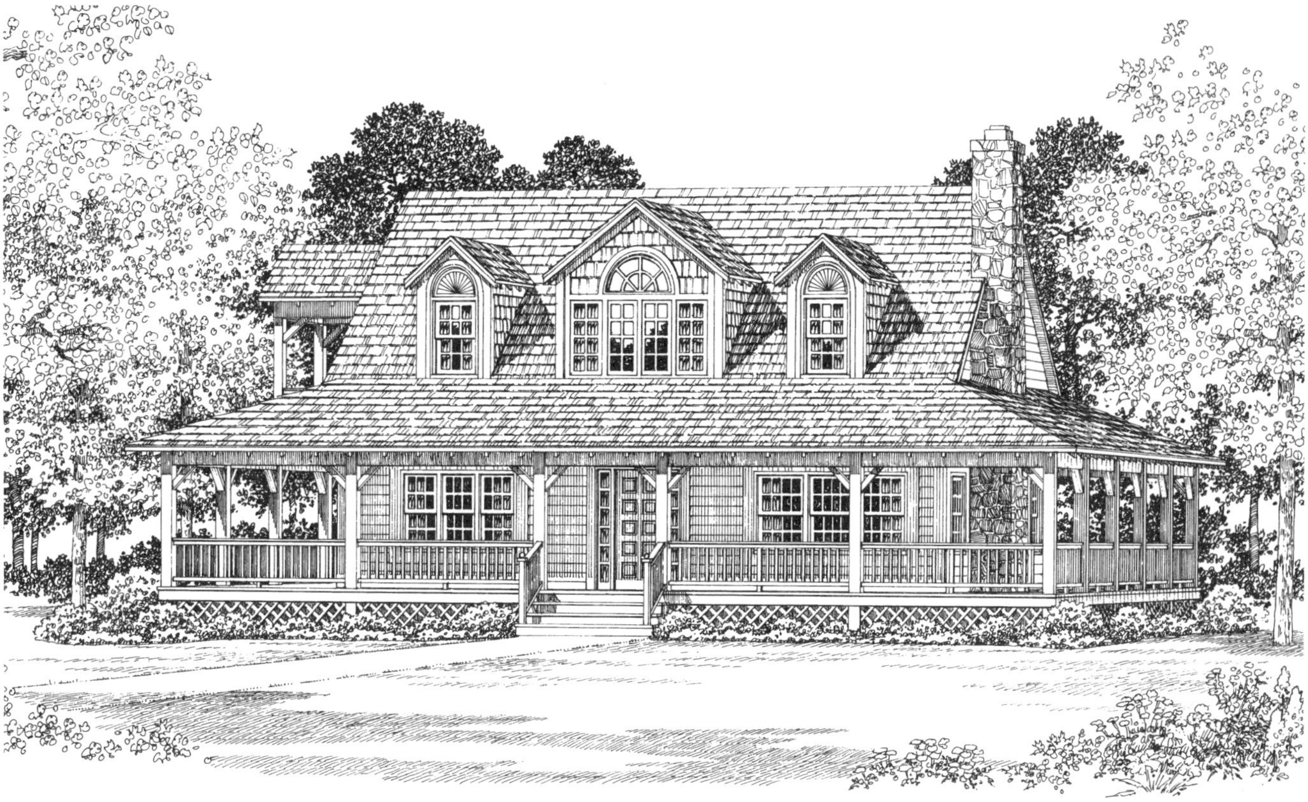

LOWE'S

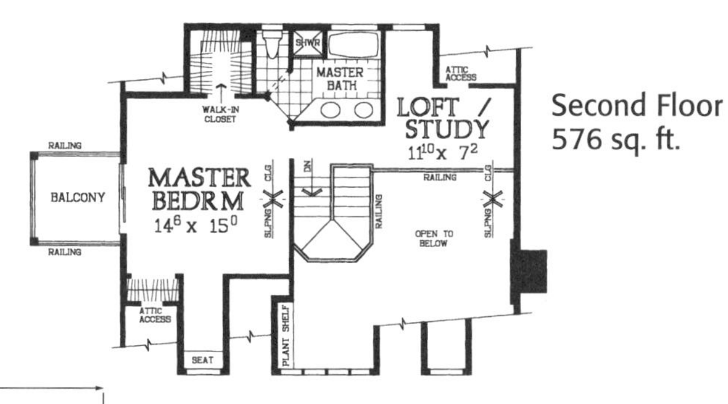

WALK-IN CLOSET
SHWR
MASTER BATH
ATTIC ACCESS
LOFT / STUDY
11¹⁰x 7²
RAILING
BALCONY
RAILING
MASTER BEDRM
14⁶ x 15⁰
SLPNG CLG
DN
RAILING
OPEN TO BELOW
SLPNG CLG
ATTIC ACCESS
SEAT
PLANT SHELF

Second Floor
576 sq. ft.

First Floor
1,093 sq. ft.

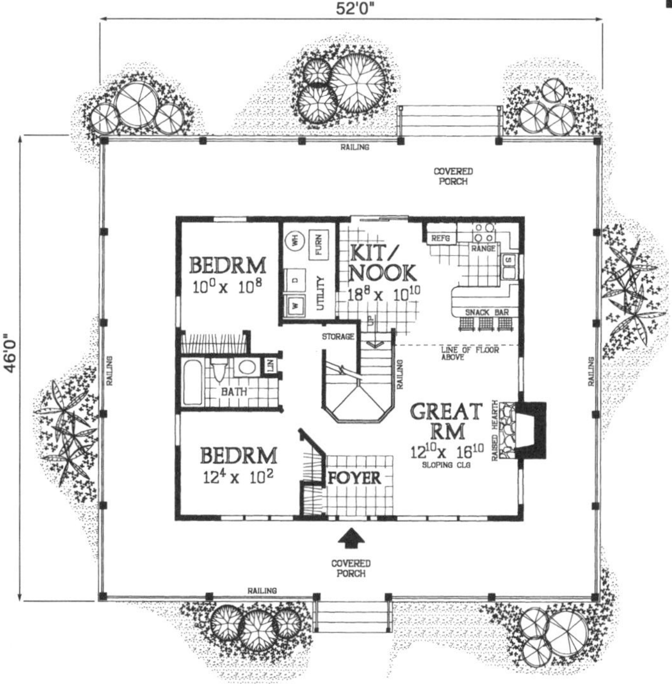

Plan #527-HP-C681

Price Code B

Total Living Area: 1,669 Sq. Ft.

Home has 3 bedrooms, 2 baths and crawl space foundation.

Special features

- Generous use of windows adds exciting visual elements to the exterior as well as plenty of natural light to the interior
- Two-story great room has a raised hearth
- Second floor loft/study would easily make a terrific home office

Open Living Spaces Create Comfortable Living

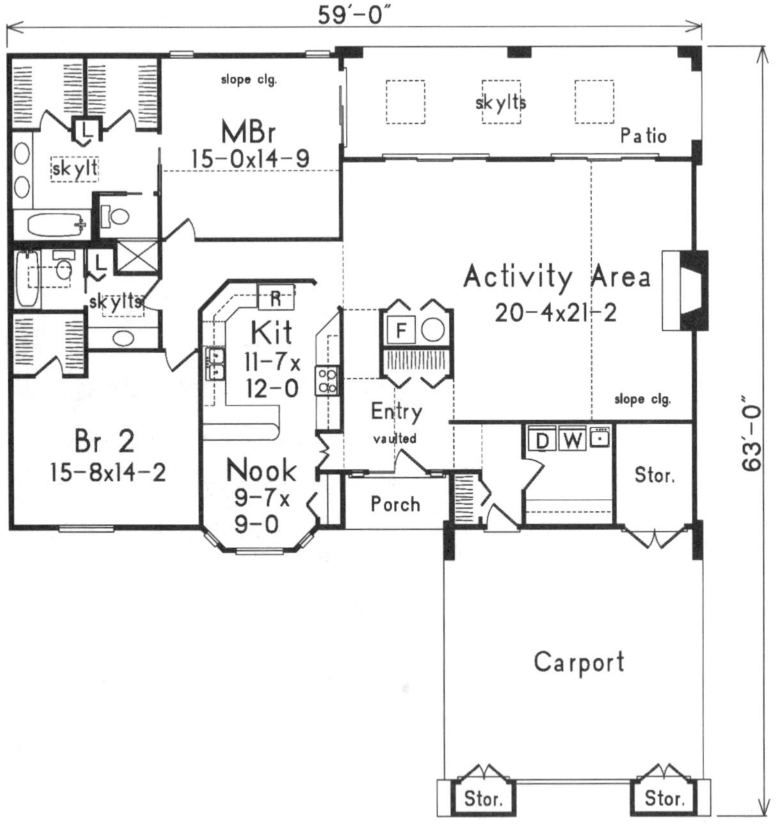
59'-0"
63'-0"
slope clg.
MBr
15-0x14-9
skylt
skylts
Patio
Activity Area
20-4x21-2
slope clg.
R
Kit
11-7x
12-0
F
skylts
Br 2
15-8x14-2
Nook
9-7x
9-0
Entry
vaulted
Porch
D
W
Stor.
Carport
Stor.
Stor.

Plan #527-1253

Price Code C

Total Living Area: 1,996 Sq. Ft.

Home has 2 bedrooms, 2 baths, 2-car carport and slab foundation.

Special features

- Centrally located activity area has fireplace and double sliding doors accessing covered patio with skylights
- Spacious master suite includes private bath with skylight and double walk-in closets
- Private nook with double-doors off entry makes an ideal office area
- Plenty of closet space throughout with walk-in closets in the bedrooms and several hall closets

LOWE'S

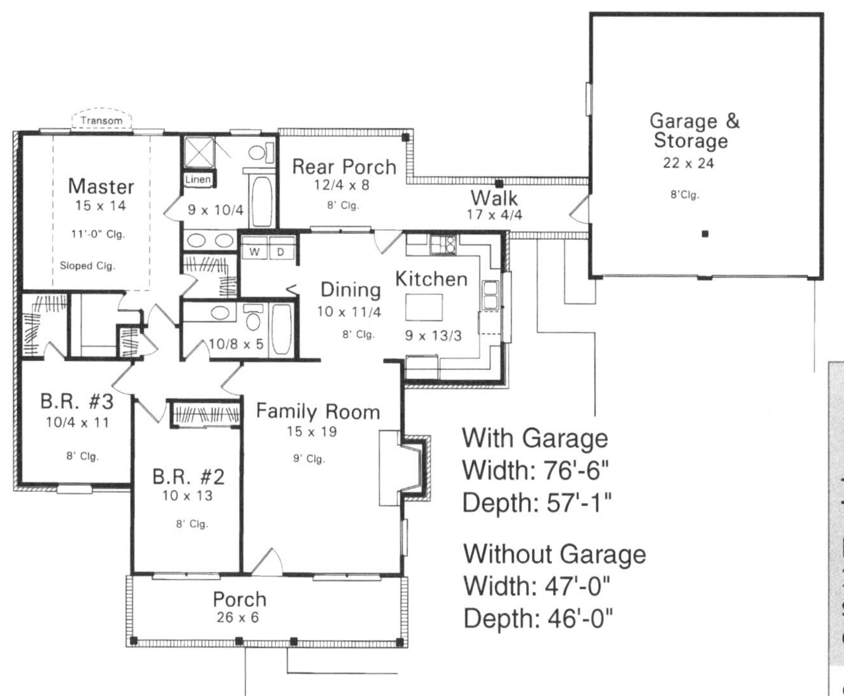
Transom
Master
15 x 14
11'-0" Clg.
Sloped Clg.
Linen
9 x 10/4
W D
Rear Porch
12/4 x 8
8' Clg.
Walk
17 x 4/4
Garage &
Storage
22 x 24
8'Clg.
Dining
10 x 11/4
8' Clg.
Kitchen
9 x 13/3
10/8 x 5
B.R. #3
10/4 x 11
8' Clg.
B.R. #2
10 x 13
8' Clg.
Family Room
15 x 19
9' Clg.
Porch
26 x 6
With Garage
Width: 76'-6"
Depth: 57'-1"
Without Garage
Width: 47'-0"
Depth: 46'-0"

Plan #527-GM-1406

Price Code A

Total Living Area: 1,406 Sq. Ft.

Home has 3 bedrooms, 2 baths, 2-car detached garage and slab or crawl space foundation, please specify when ordering.

Special features

- Enter family room from charming covered front porch and find fireplace and lots of windows
- Kitchen and dining area merge becoming a gathering place
- Master bedroom has sloped ceiling

Plan #527-GM-1253

Price Code A

Total Living Area: 1,253 Sq. Ft.

Home has 3 bedrooms, 2 baths, 2-car garage and crawl space or slab foundation, please specify when ordering.

Special features

- Sloped ceiling and fireplace in family room adds drama
- U-shaped kitchen efficiently designed
- Large walk-in closets are found in every bedroom

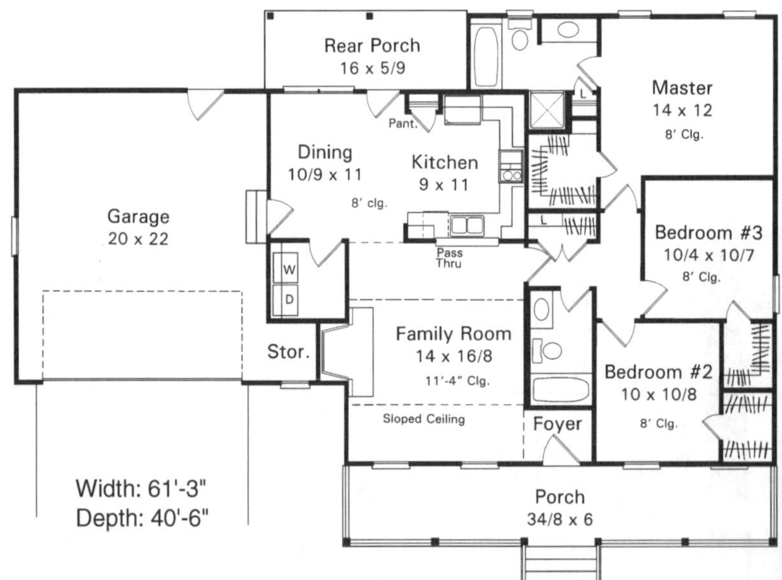
Rear Porch
16 x 5/9
Master
14 x 12
8' Clg.
Pant.
Dining
10/9 x 11
8' clg.
Kitchen
9 x 11
Garage
20 x 22
Bedroom #3
10/4 x 10/7
8' Clg.
Pass
Thru
W
D
Family Room
14 x 16/8
11'-4" Clg.
Stor.
Bedroom #2
10 x 10/8
8' Clg.
Sloped Ceiling
Foyer
Width: 61'-3"
Depth: 40'-6"
Porch
34/8 x 6

TO ORDER BLUEPRINTS USE THE FORM ON PAGE 290 OR CALL TOLL-FREE **1-800-DREAM HOME** (373-2646)

LOWE'S

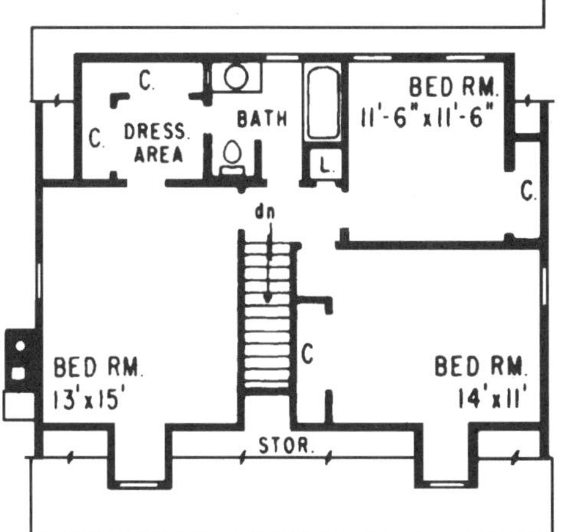
C.
C.
DRESS.
AREA
BATH
L.
BED RM.
11'-6"x11'-6"
C.
dn
C
BED RM.
13'x15'
BED RM.
14'x11'
STOR.

Second Floor
804 sq. ft.

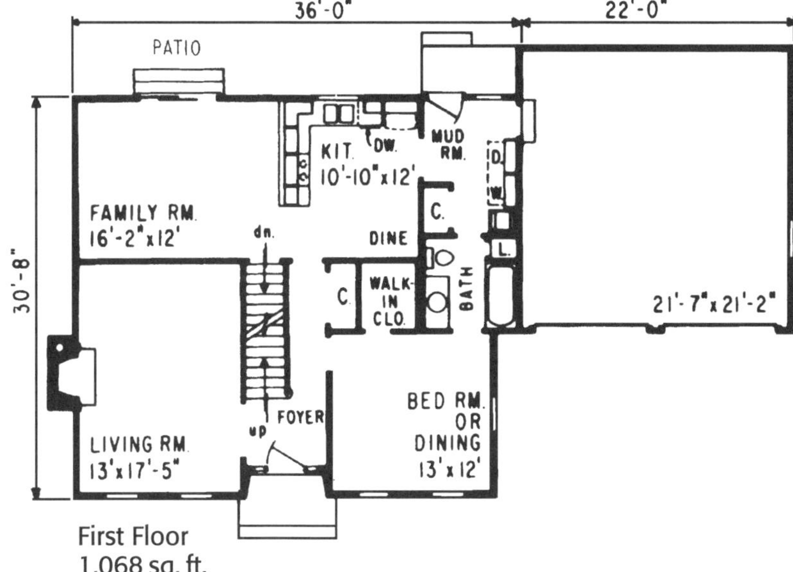
36'-0"
22'-0"
PATIO
KIT.
10'-10"x12'
DW.
MUD RM.
D
W
C.
L.
FAMILY RM.
16'-2"x12'
dn.
DINE
30'-8"
C
WALK-IN CLO.
BATH
21'-7"x21'-2"
FOYER
up
BED RM. OR DINING
13'x12'
LIVING RM.
13'x17'-5"

First Floor
1,068 sq. ft.

Plan #527-T-109-1

basement

Plan #527-T-109-2

crawl space & slab

Price Code C

Total Living Area: 1,872 Sq. Ft.

Home has 4 bedrooms, 2 baths, 2-car garage and basement, crawl space or slab foundation, please specify when ordering.

Special features

- Recessed porch has entry door with sidelights and roof dormers adding charm
- Foyer with handcrafted stair adjoins living room with fireplace
- First floor bedroom with access to bath and laundry room is perfect for master suite or live-in parent
- Largest of three second floor bedrooms enjoys his and hers closets and private access to hall bath

MASTER BATH
LAUNDRY AREA
BATH
BEDROOM
12'-0" x 12'-0"
DN.
MASTER BEDROOM
19'-0" x 14'-0"
OPEN BELOW
BEDROOM
12'-0" x 13'-0"

Second Floor
943 sq. ft.

Plan #527-1355

Price Code C

Total Living Area: 1,927 Sq. Ft.

Home has 3 bedrooms, 2 1/2 baths, 2-car garage and crawl space foundation.

Special features

- Stucco covered arches decorate a handsome covered entry porch
- Large living room features a cozy fireplace and views into dining area with wide bay window
- A smartly designed kitchen has all the amenities and opens to an expansive family room, also with fireplace
- Second floor enjoys an exquisite master suite and has convenient laundry facilities

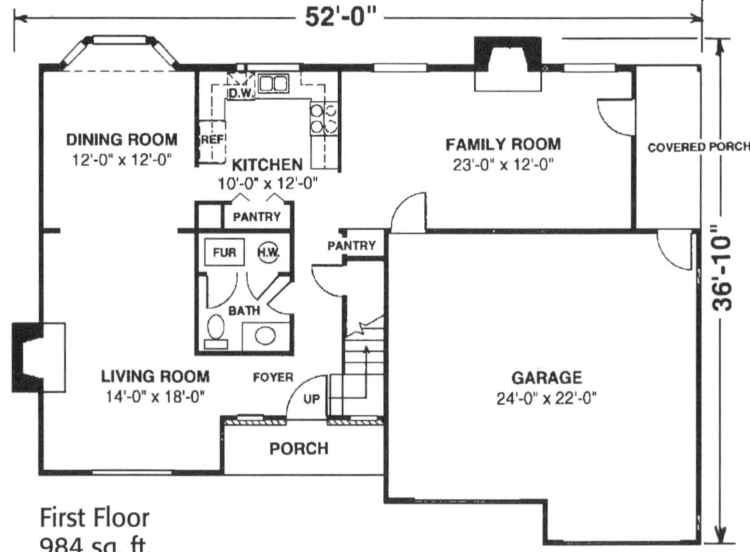
52'-0"
D.W.
REF
DINING ROOM
12'-0" x 12'-0"
KITCHEN
10'-0" x 12'-0"
FAMILY ROOM
23'-0" x 12'-0"
COVERED PORCH
PANTRY
FUR
H.W.
PANTRY
BATH
36'-10"
LIVING ROOM
14'-0" x 18'-0"
FOYER
UP
GARAGE
24'-0" x 22'-0"
PORCH

First Floor
984 sq. ft.

Rooflines Add Interest

LOWE'S

Plan #527-BF-1828

Price Code C

Total Living Area: 1,828 Sq. Ft.

Home has 4 bedrooms, 2 baths, 2-car garage and slab, crawl space or basement foundation, please specify when ordering.

Special features

- Energy efficient 2"x 6" exterior walls
- Master bath features a giant walk-in closet, built-in linen storage with convenient access to utility room
- Kitchen has a unique design that is elegant and practical

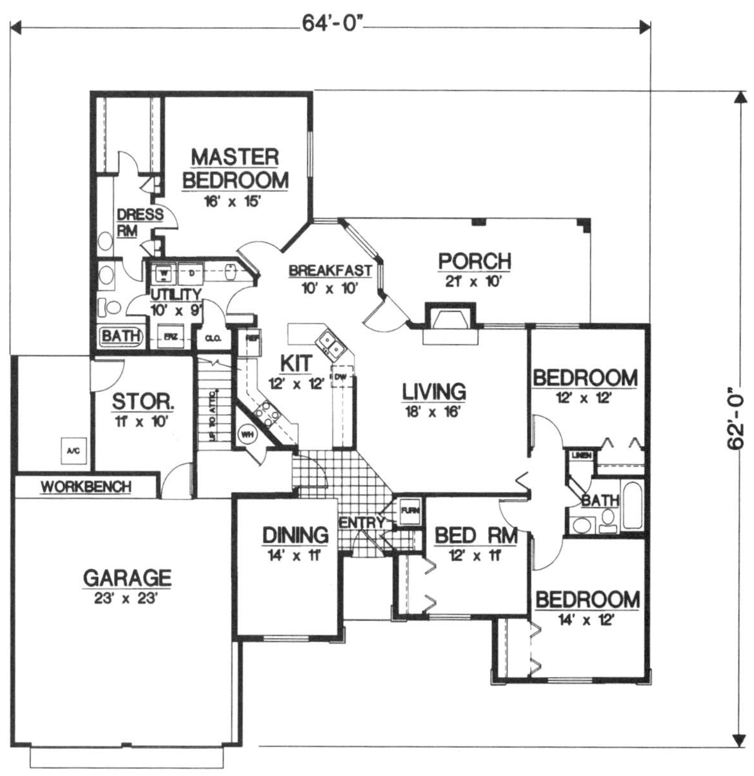
64'-0"
MASTER BEDROOM
16' x 15'
DRESS RM
BREAKFAST
10' x 10'
PORCH
21' x 10'
UTILITY
10' x 9'
BATH
KIT
12' x 12'
LIVING
18' x 16'
BEDROOM
12' x 12'
STOR.
11' x 10'
WORKBENCH
DINING
14' x 11'
ENTRY
BED RM
12' x 11'
BATH
BEDROOM
14' x 12'
GARAGE
23' x 23'
62'-0"

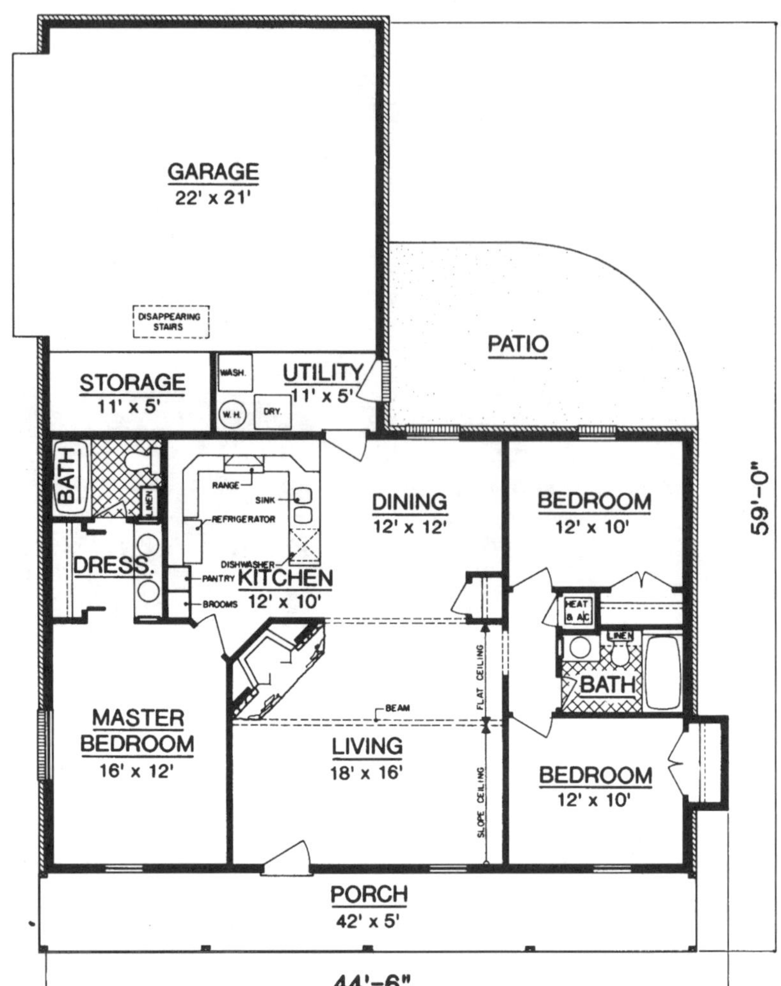
GARAGE
22' x 21'
DISAPPEARING STAIRS
STORAGE
11' x 5'
WASH.
W.H.
DRY.
UTILITY
11' x 5'
PATIO
BATH
DRESS.
RANGE
SINK
REFRIGERATOR
DISHWASHER
PANTRY
BROOMS
KITCHEN
12' x 10'
DINING
12' x 12'
BEDROOM
12' x 10'
HEAT & AC
LINEN
BATH
BEAM
FLAT CEILING
SLOPE CEILING
MASTER BEDROOM
16' x 12'
LIVING
18' x 16'
BEDROOM
12' x 10'
PORCH
42' x 5'
59'-0"
44'-6"

Plan #527-BF-DR1109

Price Code AA

Total Living Area: 1,191 Sq. Ft.

Home has 3 bedrooms, 2 baths, 2-car side entry garage and slab or crawl space foundation, please specify when ordering.

Special features

- Energy efficient 2" x 6" exterior walls
- Master bedroom located near living areas for maximum convenience
- Living room has cathedral ceiling and stone fireplace

LOWE'S

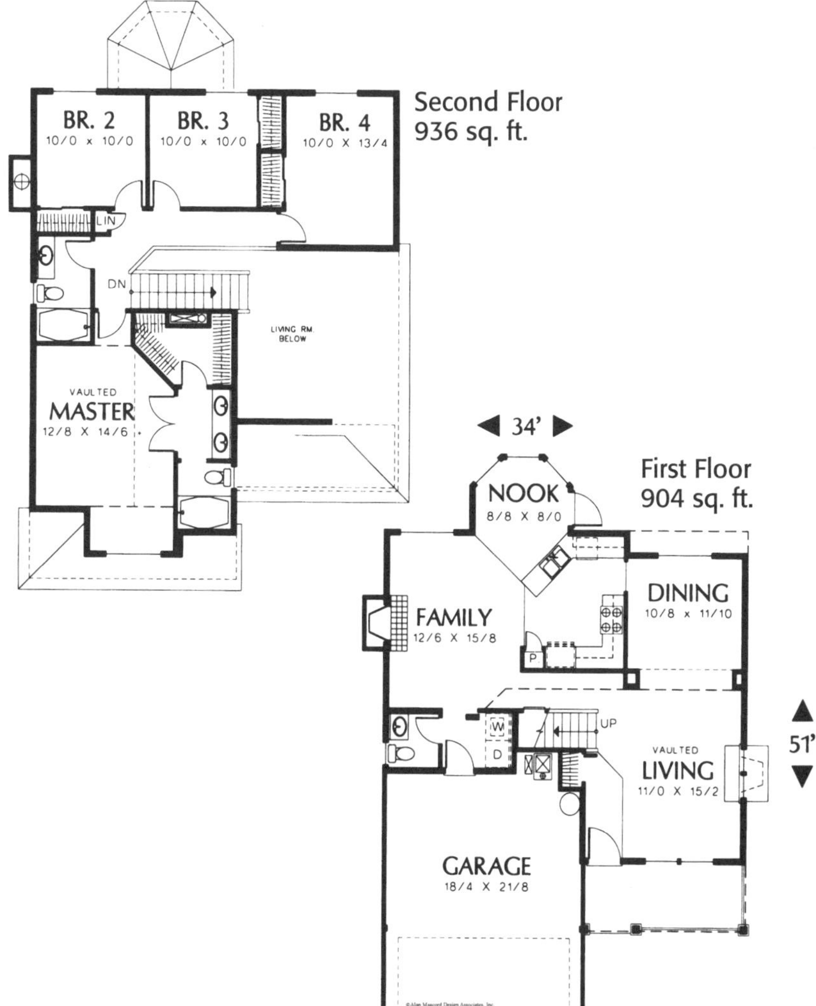

BR. 2
10/0 x 10/0
BR. 3
10/0 x 10/0
BR. 4
10/0 X 13/4
Second Floor
936 sq. ft.
LIN
DN
LIVING RM BELOW
VAULTED
MASTER
12/8 X 14/6
34'
First Floor
904 sq. ft.
NOOK
8/8 X 8/0
DINING
10/8 x 11/10
FAMILY
12/6 X 15/8
P
W
D
UP
VAULTED
LIVING
11/0 X 15/2
51'
GARAGE
18/4 X 21/8

Plan #527-AMD-2146J

Price Code C

Total Living Area: 1,840 Sq. Ft.

Home has 4 bedrooms, 2 1/2 baths, 2-car garage and crawl space foundation.

Special features

- Vaulted living and dining rooms work together when entertaining
- Sunny family room with wall of windows and fireplace
- Second floor has three bedrooms
- Vaulted master suite has private bath

Rustic Facade Features Cozy Interior

Plan #527-1118-1
basement

Plan #527-1118-2
crawl space & slab

Price Code B

Total Living Area: 1,550 Sq. Ft.

Home has 3 bedrooms, 2 baths, 2-car side entry garage and basement, crawl space or slab foundation, please specify when ordering.

Special features

- Convenient mud room between garage and kitchen
- Oversized dining area allows plenty of space for entertaining
- Master bedroom has private bath and ample closet space
- Large patio off family room brings the outdoors in

PATIO
76'-0"
FAMILY ROOM
13'-3" x 20'-10"
opt. fireplace
BATH
MASTER BEDROOM
14'-6" x 13'-5"
KITCHEN
12'-7" x 11'-6"
GARAGE
20'-4" x 21'-4"
d/w
MUD ROOM
dn.
C
china
BATH
C
40'-0"
STOR
ENTRY
C
LIVING ROOM
23'-4" x 12'
BEDROOM
10'-5" x 10'
BEDROOM
10' x 13'-6"
alternate garage door location
PORCH

Unique Angled Entry

LOWE'S

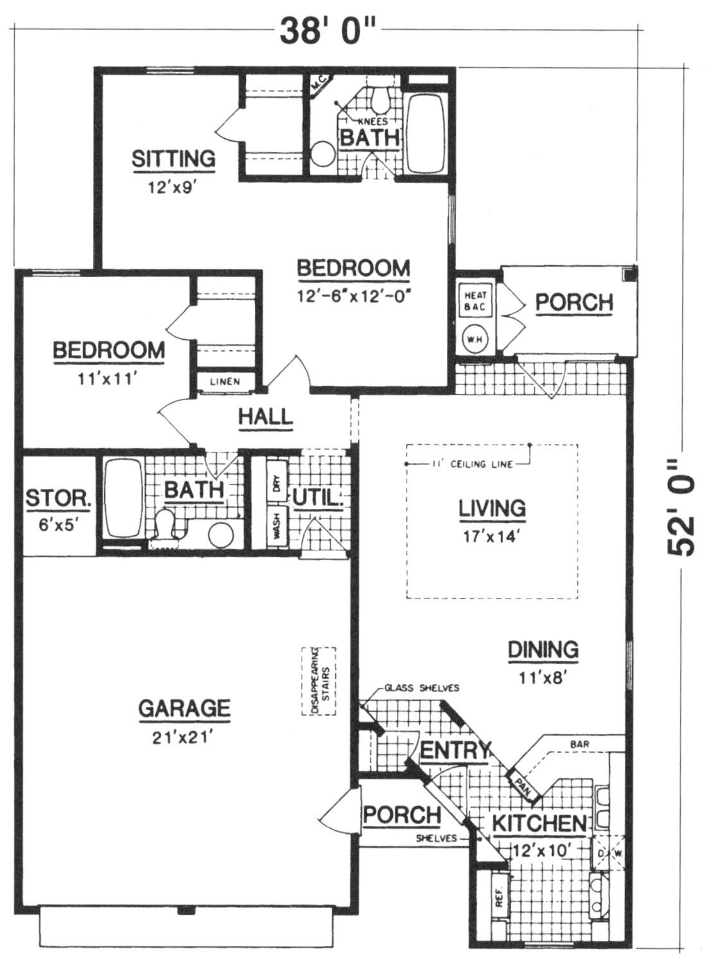

38' 0"
52' 0"
SITTING
12'x9'
M.C.
KNEES
BATH
BEDROOM
12'-6"x12'-0"
HEAT
BAC
WH
PORCH
BEDROOM
11'x11'
LINEN
HALL
11' CEILING LINE
LIVING
17'x14'
STOR.
6'x5'
BATH
DRY
WASH
UTIL.
DISAPPEARING STAIRS
DINING
11'x8'
GLASS SHELVES
GARAGE
21'x21'
ENTRY
BAR
PAN
PORCH
SHELVES
KITCHEN
12'x10'
DW
REF

Plan #527-BF-DR1108

Price Code AA

Total Living Area: 1,150 Sq. Ft.

Home has 2 bedrooms, 2 baths, 2-car garage and slab or crawl space foundation, please specify when ordering.

Special features

- Master suite has its own T.V. viewing/sitting area
- Living room/dining room has 11' high box ceiling
- Ornate trim work accents the wood sided exterior

Plan #527-BF-1426

Price Code A

Total Living Area: 1,420 Sq. Ft.

Home has 3 bedrooms, 2 baths, 2-car garage and slab or crawl space foundation, please specify when ordering.

Special features

- Energy efficient 2" x 6" exterior walls
- Living room has 12' ceiling, corner fireplace and atrium doors leading to covered porch
- Separate master suite has garden bath and walk-in closet

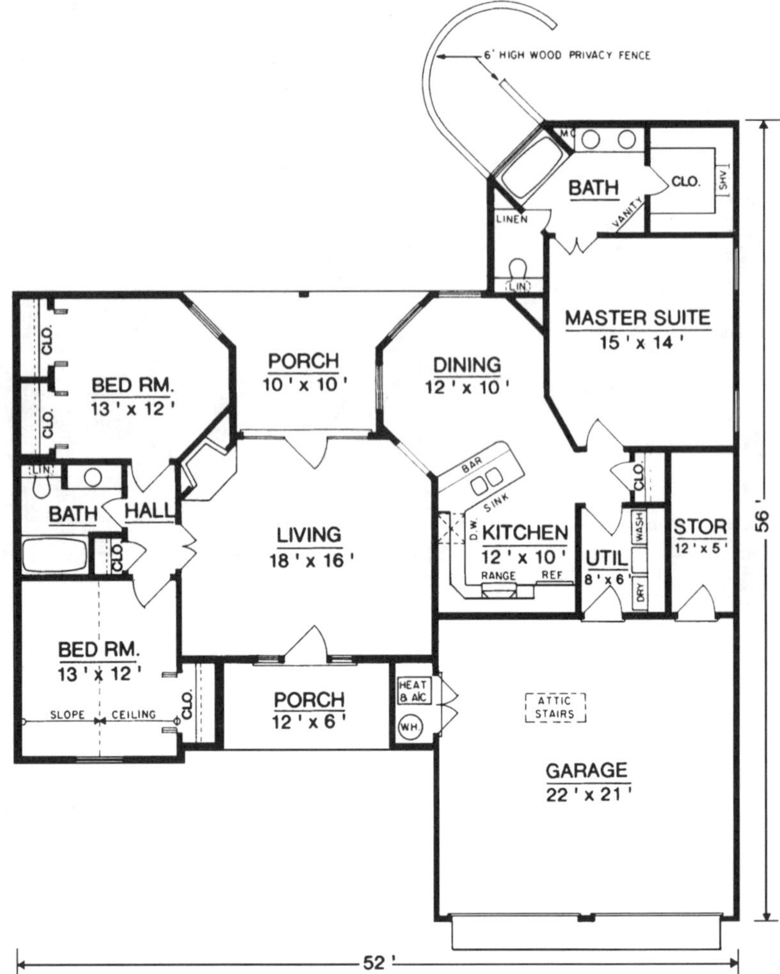
6' HIGH WOOD PRIVACY FENCE
BATH
CLO.
SHV
VANITY
LINEN
LIN
MASTER SUITE
15 ' x 14 '
PORCH
10 ' x 10 '
DINING
12 ' x 10 '
BED RM.
13 ' x 12 '
CLO.
LIN
BATH
HALL
LIVING
18 ' x 16 '
BAR
SINK
D.W.
KITCHEN
12 ' x 10 '
RANGE
REF
UTIL
8 ' x 6
WASH
DRY
STOR
12 ' x 5 '
56 '
BED RM.
13 ' x 12 '
SLOPE CEILING
PORCH
12 ' x 6 '
HEAT & A/C
WH
ATTIC STAIRS
GARAGE
22 ' x 21 '
52 '

Stately And Functional Family Room

LOWE'S

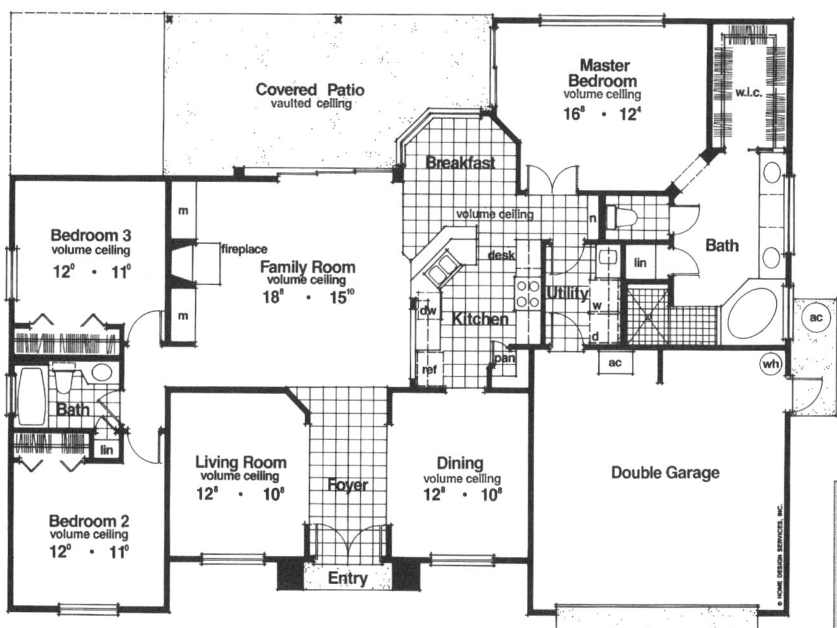
Covered Patio
vaulted ceiling
Master
Bedroom
volume ceiling
16⁸ · 12⁴
w.i.c.
Breakfast
volume ceiling
Bath
lin
n
Bedroom 3
volume ceiling
12⁰ · 11⁰
m
fireplace
Family Room
volume ceiling
18⁸ · 15¹⁰
desk
Utility
w
d
dw
Kitchen
ref
pan
ac
wh
Bath
lin
Living Room
volume ceiling
12⁸ · 10⁸
Foyer
Dining
volume ceiling
12⁸ · 10⁸
Double Garage
Bedroom 2
volume ceiling
12⁰ · 11⁰
Entry

Width: 60'-0"
Depth: 45'-0"

Plan #527-HDS-1758-2

Price Code B

Total Living Area: 1,783 Sq. Ft.

Home has 3 bedrooms, 2 baths, 2-car garage and slab foundation.

Special features

- Formal living and dining rooms in the front of the home
- Kitchen overlooks breakfast area
- Conveniently located laundry area near kitchen and master suite

© COPYRIGHTED

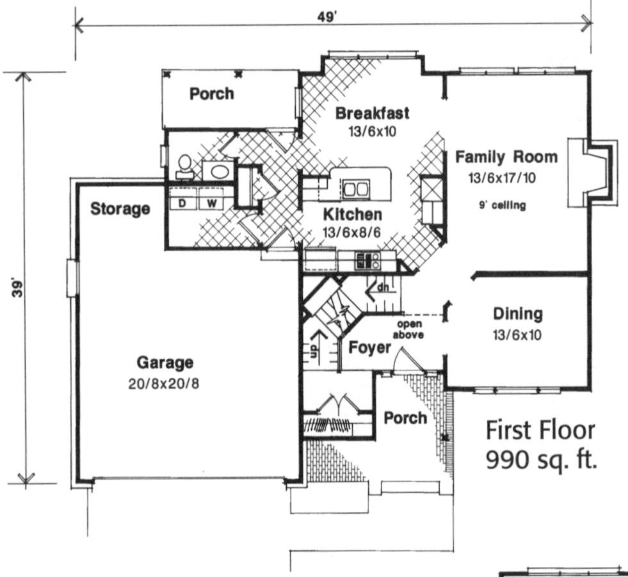

49'
39'
Porch
Breakfast
13/6x10
Family Room
13/6x17/10
9' ceiling
Storage
D W
Kitchen
13/6x8/6
dn
Dining
13/6x10
open above
Foyer
up
Garage
20/8x20/8
Porch

First Floor
990 sq. ft.

Plan #527-GM-1855

Price Code C

Total Living Area: 1,855 Sq. Ft.

Home has 3 bedrooms, 2 1/2 baths, 2-car garage and basement foundation.

Special features

- Angled stairs add character to the two-story foyer
- Secluded dining area is formal and elegant
- Sunny master bedroom has all the luxuries
- A half bath is conveniently located off the kitchen and breakfast area

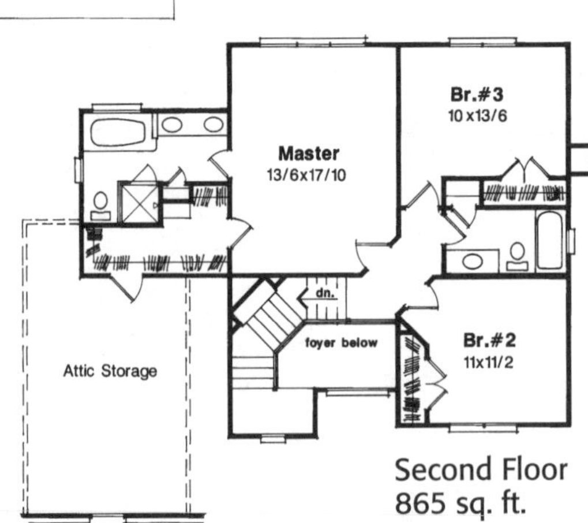
Br.#3
10x13/6
Master
13/6x17/10
Attic Storage
dn.
foyer below
Br.#2
11x11/2

Second Floor
865 sq. ft.

TO ORDER BLUEPRINTS USE THE FORM ON PAGE 290 OR CALL TOLL-FREE **1-800-DREAM HOME** (373-2646)

Breathtaking Balcony Overlook

LOWE'S

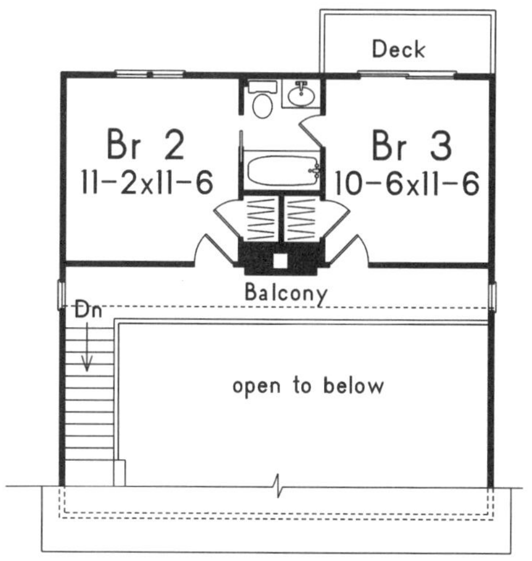
Deck
Br 2
11-2x11-6
Br 3
10-6x11-6
Balcony
Dn
open to below

Second Floor
488 sq. ft.

28′-0″

46′-0″

Deck

Stor

R

Br 1
9-11x11-6

Kit
10-7x
8-3

D

W

Din
10-10x
7-3

Living
23-10x12-3

Up

Deck

First Floor
811 sq. ft.

Plan #527-N063

Price Code A

Total Living Area: 1,299 Sq. Ft.

Home has 3 bedrooms, 2 baths and crawl space foundation, drawings also include slab foundation.

Special features

- Convenient storage for skis, etc. located outside front entrance
- Kitchen and dining room receive light from box bay window
- Large vaulted living room features cozy fireplace and overlook from second floor balcony
- Two second floor bedrooms share Jack and Jill bath
- Second floor balcony extends over entire length of living room below

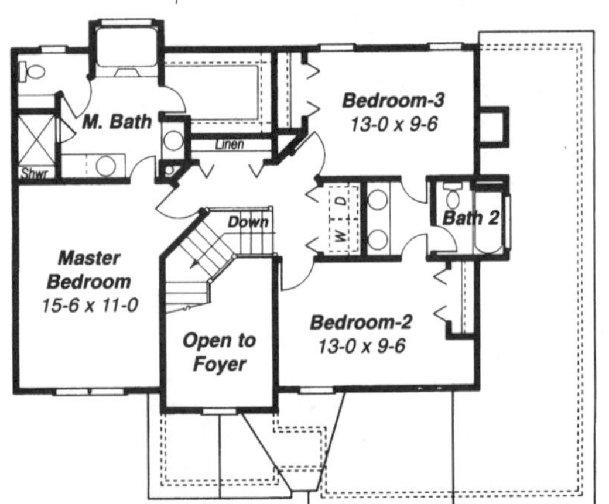
M. Bath
Linen
Shwr
Bedroom-3
13-0 x 9-6
Down
W D
Bath 2
Master
Bedroom
15-6 x 11-0
Open to
Foyer
Bedroom-2
13-0 x 9-6

Second Floor
886 sq. ft.

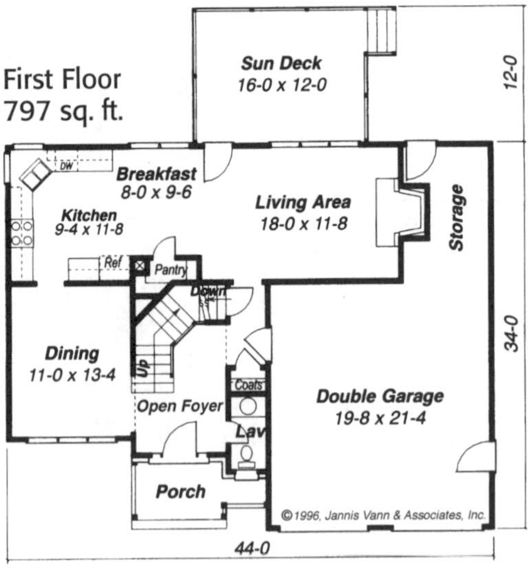

Plan #527-JV-1683-B

Price Code B

Total Living Area: 1,683 Sq. Ft.

Home has 3 bedrooms, 2 1/2 baths, 2-car garage and walk-out basement foundation.

Special features

- Open foyer and angled stairs add drama to entry
- Rear living area is open and spacious
- Master bath features garden tub, double vanities and a private toilet area

First Floor
797 sq. ft.

Sun Deck
16-0 x 12-0
12-0
DW
Breakfast
8-0 x 9-6
Kitchen
9-4 x 11-8
Living Area
18-0 x 11-8
Storage
Ref
Pantry
Down
Dining
11-0 x 13-4
Up
Coats
Open Foyer
Lav
Double Garage
19-8 x 21-4
34-0
Porch
44-0

TO ORDER BLUEPRINTS USE THE FORM ON PAGE 290 OR CALL TOLL-FREE **1-800-DREAM HOME** (373-2646)

LOWE'S

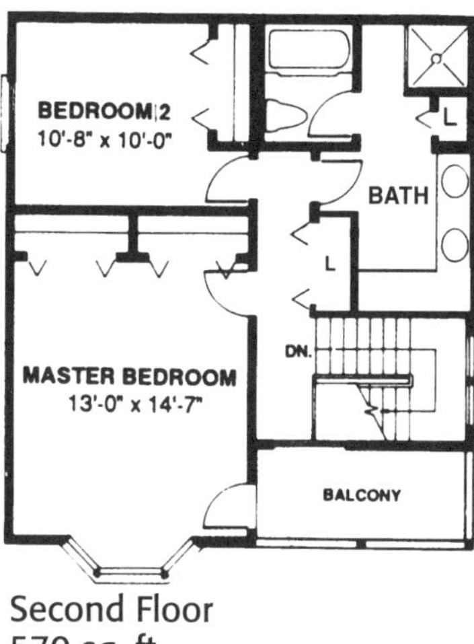
BEDROOM 2
10'-8" x 10'-0"
BATH
L
L
MASTER BEDROOM
13'-0" x 14'-7"
DN.
BALCONY

Second Floor
570 sq. ft.

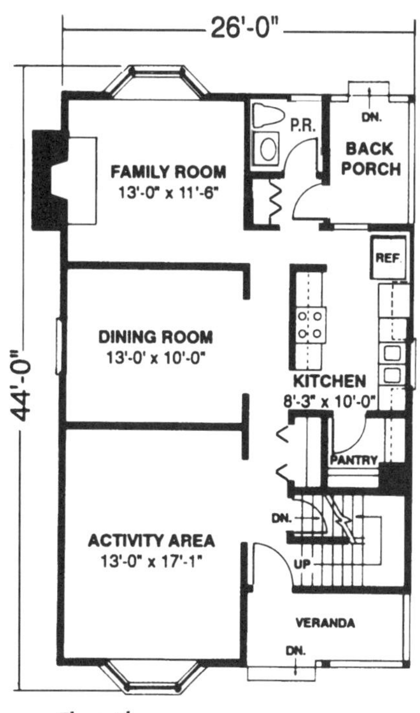
26'-0"
44'-0"
P.R.
DN.
BACK
PORCH
FAMILY ROOM
13'-0" x 11'-6"
REF
DINING ROOM
13'-0' x 10'-0"
KITCHEN
8'-3" x 10'-0"
PANTRY
DN.
ACTIVITY AREA
13'-0" x 17'-1"
UP
VERANDA
DN.

First Floor
1,092 sq. ft.

Plan #527-1295

Price Code B

Total Living Area: 1,662 Sq. Ft.

Home has 2 bedrooms, 1 1/2 baths and basement foundation.

Special features

- Activity area becomes ideal place for family gatherings
- Well-organized kitchen includes lots of storage space, walk-in pantry and plenty of cabinetry
- The rear of the home features a versatile back porch for dining or relaxing
- Master suite has a bay window and private balcony

LOWE'S

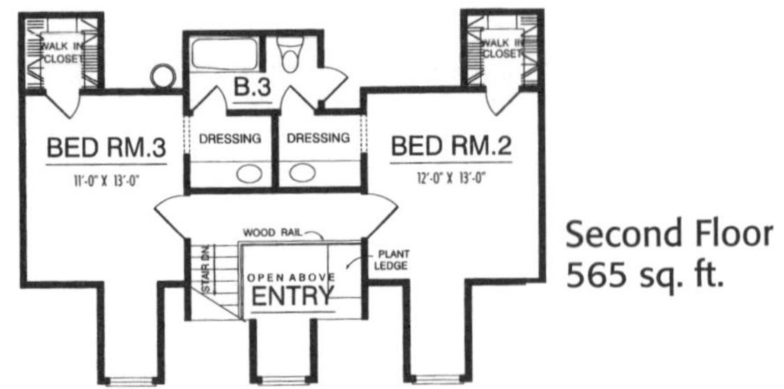
WALK IN CLOSET
B.3
BED RM.3
11'-0" X 13'-0"
DRESSING
DRESSING
BED RM.2
12'-0" X 13'-0"
WOOD RAIL
PLANT LEDGE
STAIR DN
OPEN ABOVE
ENTRY

Second Floor
565 sq. ft.

Plan #527-RDD-1895-9

Price Code C

Total Living Area: 1,895 Sq. Ft.

Home has 3 bedrooms, 2 1/2 baths, 2-car garage and basement, crawl space or slab foundation, please specify when ordering.

Special features

- Master suite has private bath and access to covered rear porch
- Living area has built-in bookshelves flanking fireplace
- Kitchen overlooks both the breakfast nook and living room for an open floor plan

70'-9"
43'-4"
PORCH
MASTER SUITE
12'-0" X 15'-0"
MEDIA CENTER
LIVING RM.
15'-0" X 17'-0"
NOOK
12'-0" X 10'-0"
B.2
GARAGE
22'-0" X 22'-0"
RAISED BAR
D.W.
KITCH.
12'-0" X 11'-6"
RANGE
REF.
UT.
W/H
BOOKS
BATH 1
SHLVS
STORAGE UNDER STAIR
ENTRY
DINING RM.
12'-0" X 12'-0"
MARBLE TUB
SHELF
GLASS SHOWER
WALK IN CLOSET
STAIR UP
PORCH

First Floor
1,330 sq. ft.

 TO ORDER BLUEPRINTS USE THE FORM ON PAGE 290 OR CALL TOLL-FREE **1-800-DREAM HOME** (373-2646)

Plan #527-1336

Price Code A

Total Living Area: 1,364 Sq. Ft.

Home has 3 bedrooms, 2 baths, optional 2-car garage and basement foundation, drawings also include crawl space foundation.

Special features

- Master suite features spacious walk-in closet and private bath
- Living room highlighted with several windows
- Kitchen with snack bar adjacent to dining area
- Plenty of storage space throughout

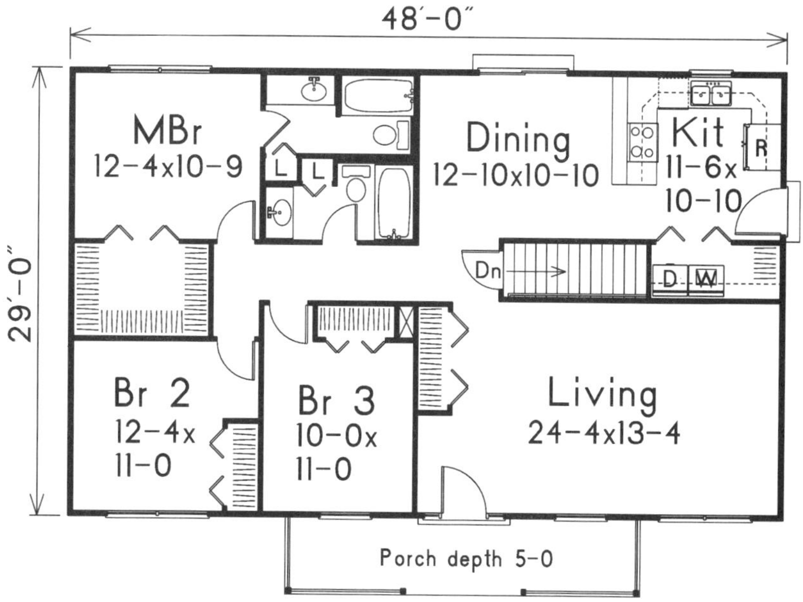
48'-0"
29'-0"
MBr
12-4x10-9
L
L
Dining
12-10x10-10
Kit
11-6x
10-10
R
Dn
D W
Br 2
12-4x
11-0
Br 3
10-0x
11-0
Living
24-4x13-4
Porch depth 5-0

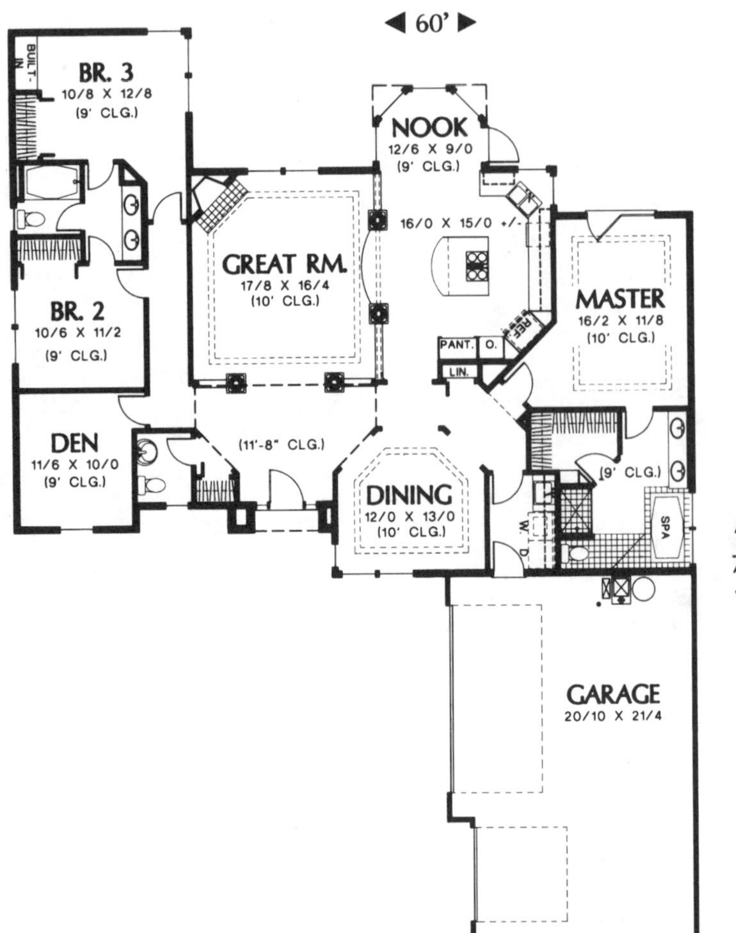
60'
BUILT-IN
BR. 3
10/8 X 12/8
(9' CLG.)
NOOK
12/6 X 9/0
(9' CLG.)
16/0 X 15/0 +/-
GREAT RM.
17/8 X 16/4
(10' CLG.)
BR. 2
10/6 X 11/2
(9' CLG.)
MASTER
16/2 X 11/8
(10' CLG.)
PANT.
O.
LIN.
REF.
DEN
11/6 X 10/0
(9' CLG.)
(11'-8" CLG.)
DINING
12/0 X 13/0
(10' CLG.)
(9' CLG.)
SPA
W
D
79'
GARAGE
20/10 X 21/4

Plan #527-AMD-1216

Price Code C

Total Living Area: 2,155 Sq. Ft.

Home has 3 bedrooms, 2 1/2 baths, 3-car side entry garage and crawl space foundation.

Special features

- Great room has 10' tray ceiling, corner fireplace and columns
- Well-appointed master suite features a 10' tray ceiling
- Two secondary bedrooms access a shared bath
- Den completes the opposite side of the home

TO ORDER BLUEPRINTS USE THE FORM ON PAGE 290 OR CALL TOLL-FREE **1-800-DREAM HOME** (373-2646)

Plan #527-1274-1
partial basement/crawl space

Plan #527-1274-2
partial slab/crawl space

Price Code C

Total Living Area: 2,180 Sq. Ft.

Home has 3 bedrooms, 2 baths, 2-car garage and partial basement/crawl space or partial slab/crawl space foundation, please specify when ordering.

Special features

- Large impressive entry for receiving guests
- Activity and dining rooms have vaulted ceilings, fireplace, wet bar, and expansive bay windows are second to none
- Master bedroom and bath have been designed on a grand scale
- All bedrooms feature vaulted ceilings and spacious closets

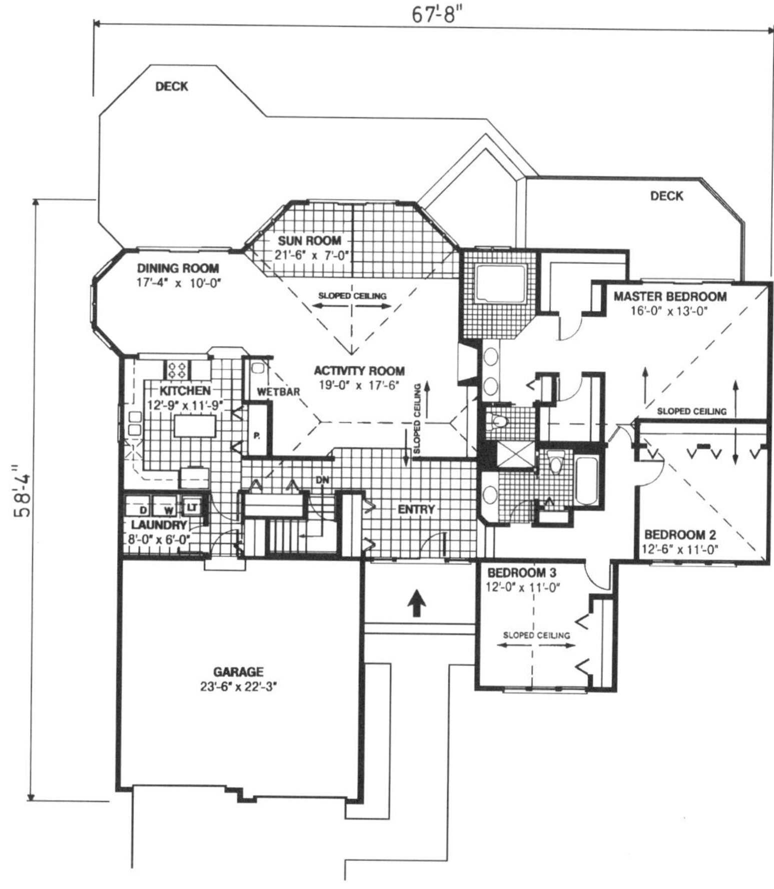
67'-8"
58'-4"
DECK
DECK
SUN ROOM
21'-6" x 7'-0"
DINING ROOM
17'-4" x 10'-0"
SLOPED CEILING
MASTER BEDROOM
16'-0" x 13'-0"
ACTIVITY ROOM
19'-0" x 17'-6"
KITCHEN
12'-9" x 11'-9"
WETBAR
SLOPED CEILING
SLOPED CEILING
DN
ENTRY
LAUNDRY
8'-0" x 6'-0"
BEDROOM 2
12'-6" x 11'-0"
BEDROOM 3
12'-0" x 11'-0"
SLOPED CEILING
GARAGE
23'-6" x 22'-3"

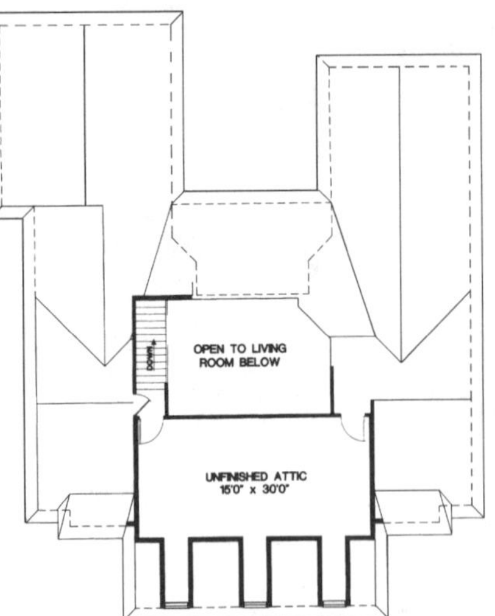
OPEN TO LIVING ROOM BELOW
UNFINISHED ATTIC 15'0" x 30'0"

Optional Second Floor

First Floor
2,123 sq. ft.

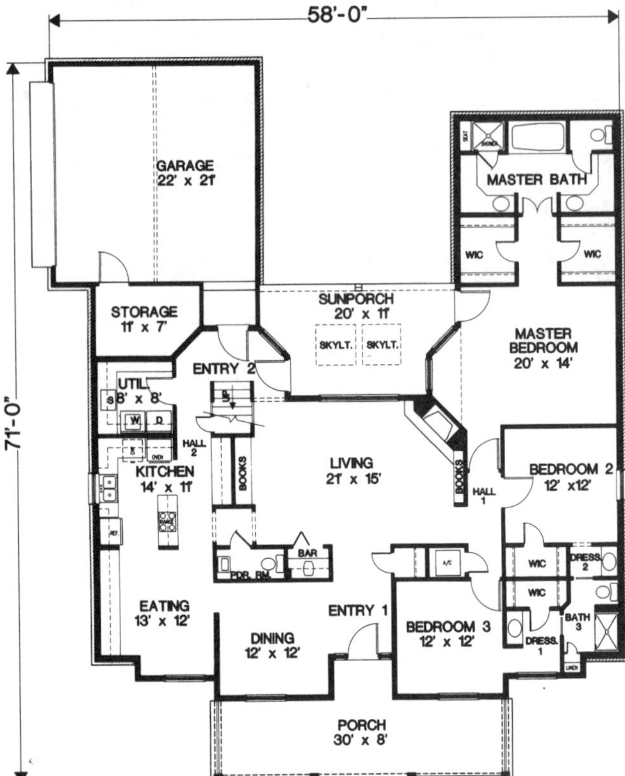
58'-0"
71'-0"
GARAGE 22' x 21'
STORAGE 11' x 7'
UTIL. 8' x 8'
ENTRY 2
SUNPORCH 20' x 11'
SKYLT.
SKYLT.
MASTER BATH
WIC
WIC
MASTER BEDROOM 20' x 14'
HALL 2
KITCHEN 14' x 11'
BOOKS
LIVING 21' x 15'
BOOKS
HALL 1
BEDROOM 2 12' x12'
PDR. RM.
BAR
WIC
DRESS. 2
WIC
EATING 13' x 12'
DINING 12' x 12'
ENTRY 1
BEDROOM 3 12' x 12'
BATH 3
DRESS. 1
PORCH 30' x 8'

Plan #527-BF-2107

Price Code E

Total Living Area: 2,123 Sq. Ft.

Home has 3 bedrooms, 2 1/2 baths, 2-car garage and crawl space, slab or basement foundation, please specify when ordering.

Special features

- Energy efficient 2"x 6" exterior walls
- Living room has wood burning fireplace, built-in bookshelves and wet bar
- Skylights make sun porch bright and comfortable
- 450 square feet of additional living area on the second floor

LOWE'S

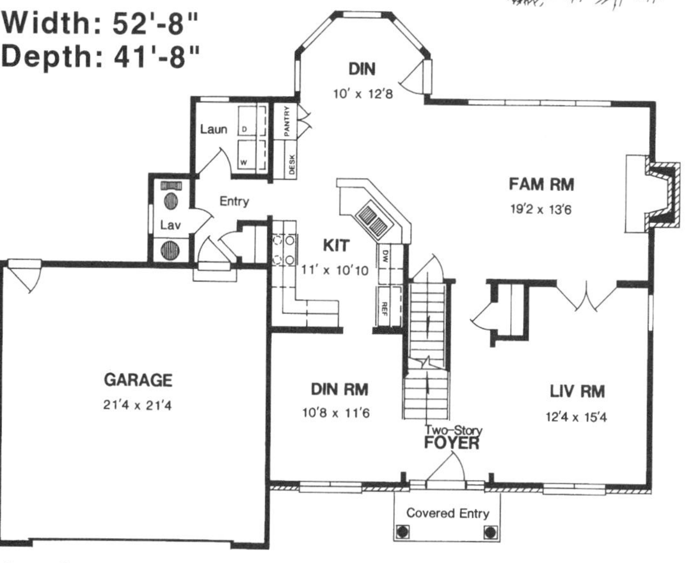
Width: 52'-8"
Depth: 41'-8"
DIN
10' x 12'8
Laun
PANTRY
DESK
FAM RM
19'2 x 13'6
Entry
Lav
KIT
11' x 10'10
DW
REF
GARAGE
21'4 x 21'4
DIN RM
10'8 x 11'6
LIV RM
12'4 x 15'4
Two-Story
FOYER
Covered Entry

First Floor
1,100 sq. ft.

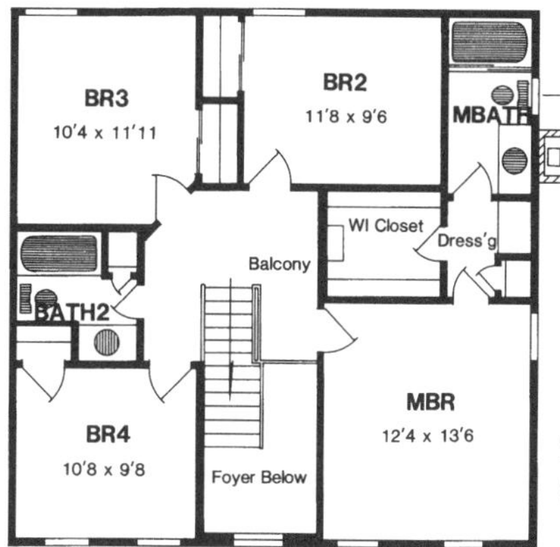
BR3
10'4 x 11'11
BR2
11'8 x 9'6
MBATH
WI Closet
Dress'g
Balcony
BATH2
MBR
12'4 x 13'6
BR4
10'8 x 9'8
Foyer Below

Second Floor
892 sq. ft.

Plan #527-JFD-20-1992-1

Price Code C

Total Living Area: 1,992 Sq. Ft.

Home has 4 bedrooms, 2 1/2 baths, 2-car garage and basement foundation.

Special features

- Sunny family room has lots of windows and a large fireplace
- Octagon-shaped dining area is adjacent to kitchen for easy access
- Formal living room is separated from family room by double-doors
- Master bedroom has private bath with dressing area and walk-in closet

Covered Porch Highlights This Home

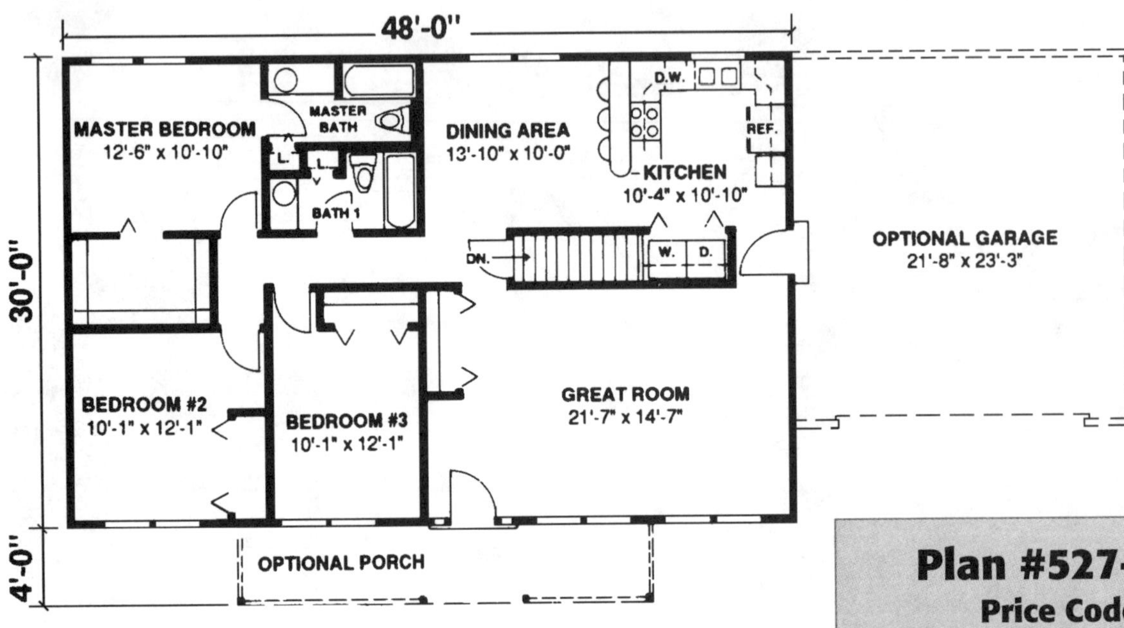
48'-0"
30'-0"
4'-0"
MASTER BEDROOM
12'-6" x 10'-10"
MASTER BATH
BATH 1
DINING AREA
13'-10" x 10'-0"
D.W.
REF.
KITCHEN
10'-4" x 10'-10"
DN.
W.
D.
OPTIONAL GARAGE
21'-8" x 23'-3"
BEDROOM #2
10'-1" x 12'-1"
BEDROOM #3
10'-1" x 12'-1"
GREAT ROOM
21'-7" x 14'-7"
OPTIONAL PORCH

Plan #527-1329

Price Code A

Total Living Area: 1,364 Sq. Ft.

Home has 3 bedrooms, 2 baths, optional 2-car garage and basement foundation.

Special features

- Bedrooms separated from living area for privacy
- Master bedroom has private bath and large walk-in closet
- Laundry area conveniently located near kitchen
- Bright and spacious great room
- Built-in pantry in kitchen

KURT KAUSS
OVIEDO · FLA

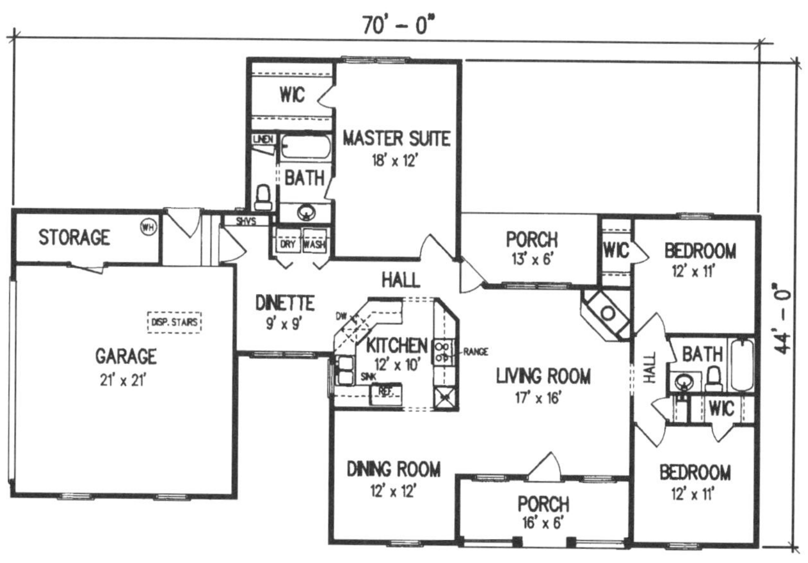
70' – 0"
44' – 0"
WIC
MASTER SUITE
18' x 12'
LINEN
BATH
STORAGE
WH
SHVS
DRY
WASH
PORCH
13' x 6'
WIC
BEDROOM
12' x 11'
HALL
DINETTE
9' x 9'
DW
DISP. STAIRS
GARAGE
21' x 21'
KITCHEN
12' x 10'
SINK
RANGE
REF.
LIVING ROOM
17' x 16'
HALL
BATH
WIC
DINING ROOM
12' x 12'
PORCH
16' x 6'
BEDROOM
12' x 11'

Plan #527-BF-1416

Price Code A

Total Living Area: 1,434 Sq. Ft.

Home has 3 bedrooms, 2 baths, 2-car side entry garage and crawl space or slab foundation, please specify when ordering.

Special features

- Isolated master suite for privacy includes walk-in closet and bath
- Elegant formal dining room
- Efficient kitchen has adjacent dinette which includes shelves and access to laundry facilities
- Extra storage in garage

Dramatic Look For Quiet Hideaway

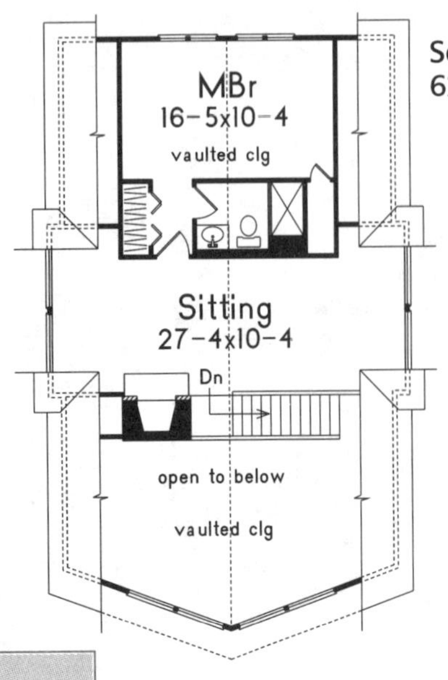
MBr
16-5x10-4
vaulted clg
Sitting
27-4x10-4
Dn
open to below
vaulted clg

Second Floor
624 sq. ft.

First Floor
1,126 sq. ft.

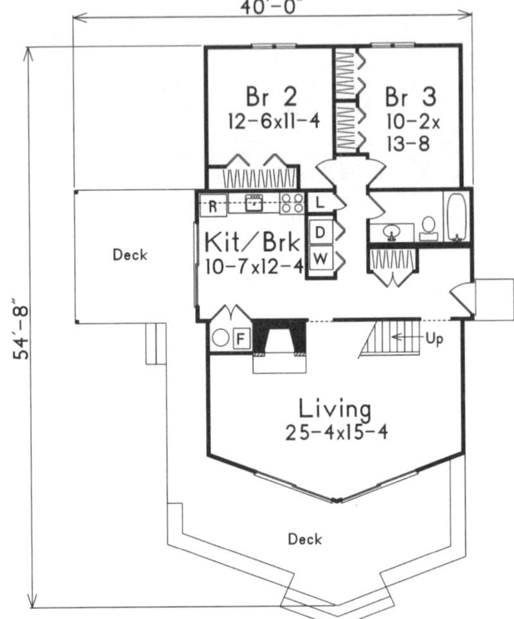
40'-0"
54'-8"
Br 2
12-6x11-4
Br 3
10-2x
13-8
Kit/Brk
10-7x12-4
Deck
Up
Living
25-4x15-4
Deck

Plan #527-N065

Price Code B

Total Living Area: 1,750 Sq. Ft.

Home has 3 bedrooms, 2 baths and basement foundation, drawings also include crawl space and slab foundations.

Special features

- Family room brightened by floor-to-ceiling windows and sliding doors providing access to large deck
- Second floor sitting area perfect for game room or entertaining
- Kitchen includes eat-in dining area plus outdoor dining patio as a bonus
- Plenty of closet and storage space throughout

TO ORDER BLUEPRINTS USE THE FORM ON PAGE 290 OR CALL TOLL-FREE **1-800-DREAM HOME** (373-2646)

Sunny Eating Area

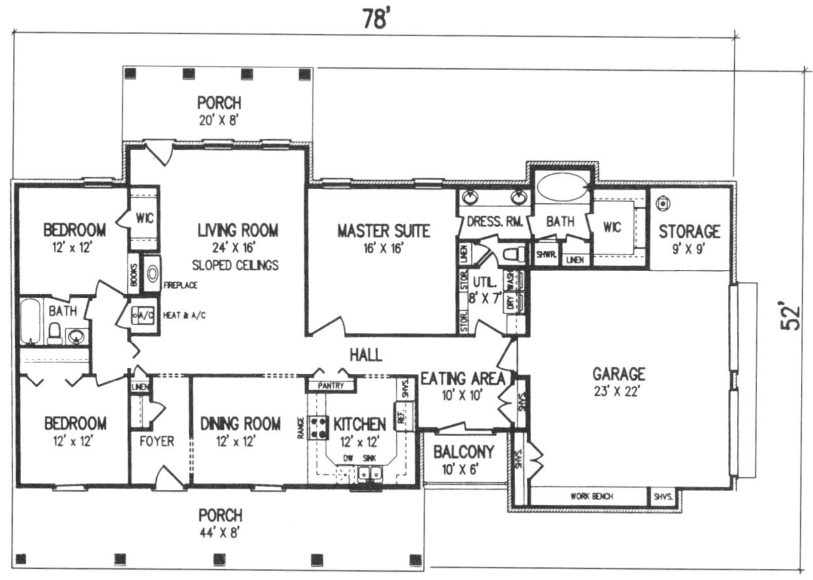
78'
PORCH
20' X 8'
BEDROOM
12' x 12'
WIC
LIVING ROOM
24' X 16'
SLOPED CEILINGS
MASTER SUITE
16' X 16'
DRESS. RM.
BATH
WIC
STORAGE
9' X 9'
BOOKS
FIREPLACE
BATH
A/C
HEAT & A/C
SHWR.
LINEN
UTIL.
8' X 7'
STOR.
DRY
WASH
52'
HALL
LINEN
PANTRY
EATING AREA
10' X 10'
GARAGE
23' X 22'
BEDROOM
12' x 12'
FOYER
DINING ROOM
12' x 12'
RANGE
KITCHEN
12' x 12'
DW
SINK
REF.
SHVS.
BALCONY
10' X 6'
WORK BENCH
PORCH
44' X 8'

Plan #527-BF-1901

Price Code C

Total Living Area: 1,925 Sq. Ft.

Home has 3 bedrooms, 2 baths, 2-car side entry garage and crawl space or slab foundation, please specify when ordering.

Special features

- Energy efficient 2"x 6" exterior walls
- Balcony off eating area adds character
- Master suite has dressing room, bath, walk-in closet and access to utility room

Plan #527-DBI-2461

Price Code C

Total Living Area: 1,850 Sq. Ft.

Home has 3 bedrooms, 2 baths, 2-car garage and basement foundation.

Special features

- Oversized rooms throughout
- Great room spotlights fireplace with sunny windows on both sides
- Master bedroom has private skylighted bath
- Interesting wet bar between kitchen and dining area is an added bonus when entertaining

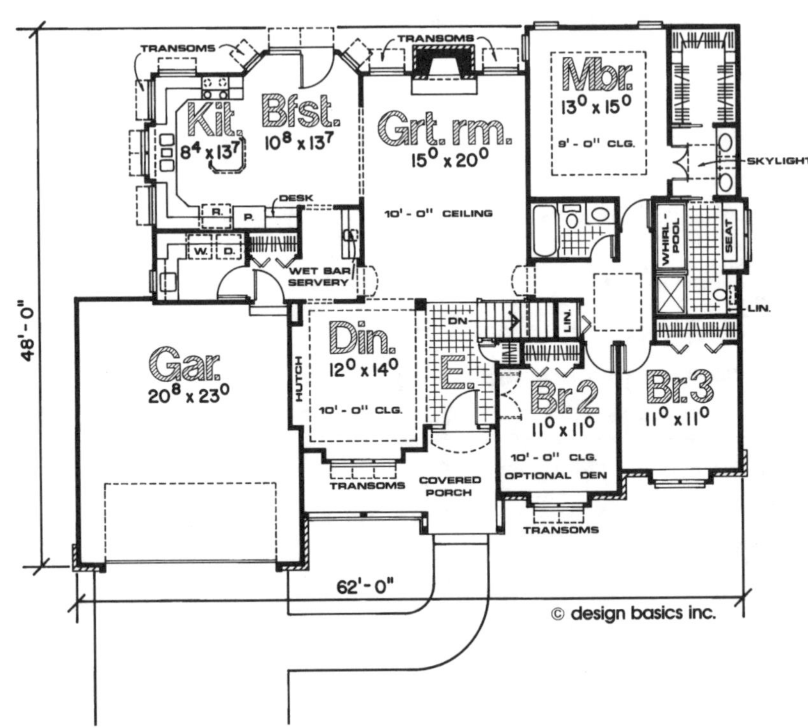
TRANSOMS
TRANSOMS
Kit.
8^{4} x 13^{7}
Bfst.
10^{8} x 13^{7}
Grt. rm.
15^{0} x 20^{0}
10'-0" CEILING
Mbr.
13^{0} x 15^{0}
9'-0" CLG.
SKYLIGHT
DESK
R.
P.
W.
D.
WET BAR SERVERY
WHIRLPOOL
SEAT
LIN.
Gar.
20^{8} x 23^{0}
Din.
12^{0} x 14^{0}
HUTCH
10'-0" CLG.
DN
LIN.
E.
Br.2
11^{0} x 11^{0}
10'-0" CLG.
OPTIONAL DEN
Br.3
11^{0} x 11^{0}
TRANSOMS
COVERED PORCH
TRANSOMS
48'-0"
62'-0"
© design basics inc.

TO ORDER BLUEPRINTS USE THE FORM ON PAGE 290 OR CALL TOLL-FREE **1-800-DREAM HOME** (373-2646)

LOWE'S

Plan #527-1271

Price Code C

Total Living Area: 1,907 Sq. Ft.

Home has 3 bedrooms, 2 baths, 2-car garage and partial basement/crawl space foundation.

Special features

- Activity area with fireplace opens to dining room
- Sunroom off activity area leads to deck
- Laundry room conveniently located in bedroom wing of home
- Two bedrooms share a full bath
- Master bedroom suite features access to the sunroom plus a deluxe master bath with clerestory window and large closets

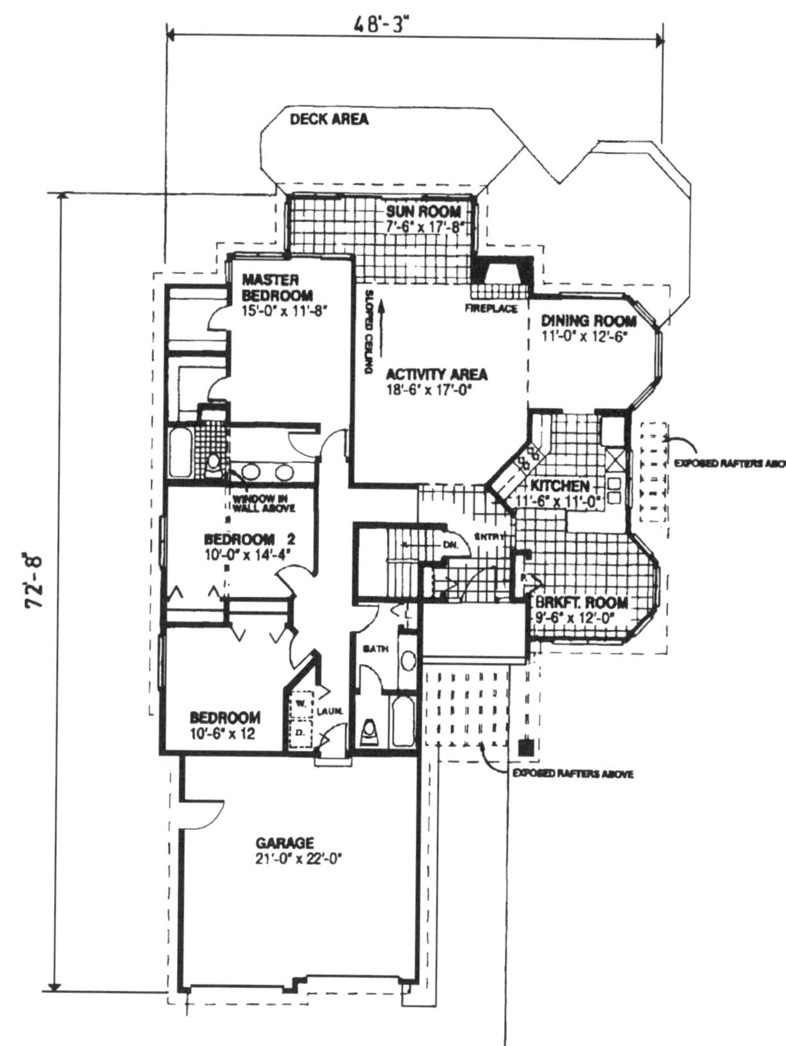
48'-3"
72'-8"
DECK AREA
SUN ROOM 7'-6" x 17'-8"
MASTER BEDROOM 15'-0" x 11'-8"
SLOPED CEILING
FIREPLACE
DINING ROOM 11'-0" x 12'-6"
ACTIVITY AREA 18'-6" x 17'-0"
EXPOSED RAFTERS ABOVE
KITCHEN 11'-6" x 11'-0"
WINDOW IN WALL ABOVE
BEDROOM 2 10'-0" x 14'-4"
DN.
ENTRY
BRKFT. ROOM 9'-6" x 12'-0"
BATH
BEDROOM 10'-6" x 12
LAUN.
EXPOSED RAFTERS ABOVE
GARAGE 21'-0" x 22'-0"

Cleverly Angled Walls Add Interest To Home

Plan #527-1413

Price Code A

Total Living Area: 1,400 Sq. Ft.

Home has 2 bedrooms, 2 baths and crawl space foundation.

Special features

- Inside and out, this home is pleasingly different
- Activity area showcases large free-standing fireplace and spacious dining room with views
- Laundry area is provided in a functional kitchen
- Master suite with double-doors leads to a grand bedroom with nice amenities

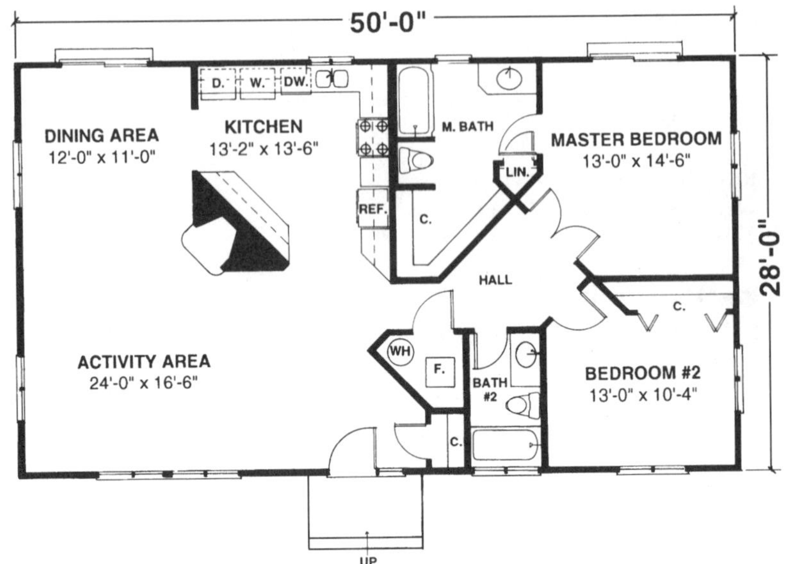
50'-0"
28'-0"
D.
W.
DW.
DINING AREA
12'-0" x 11'-0"
KITCHEN
13'-2" x 13'-6"
REF.
M. BATH
LIN.
MASTER BEDROOM
13'-0" x 14'-6"
C.
HALL
C.
WH
F.
ACTIVITY AREA
24'-0" x 16'-6"
BATH
#2
BEDROOM #2
13'-0" x 10'-4"
C.
UP

 TO ORDER BLUEPRINTS USE THE FORM ON PAGE 290 OR CALL TOLL-FREE **1-800-DREAM HOME** (373-2646)

Wonderful, Compact Home

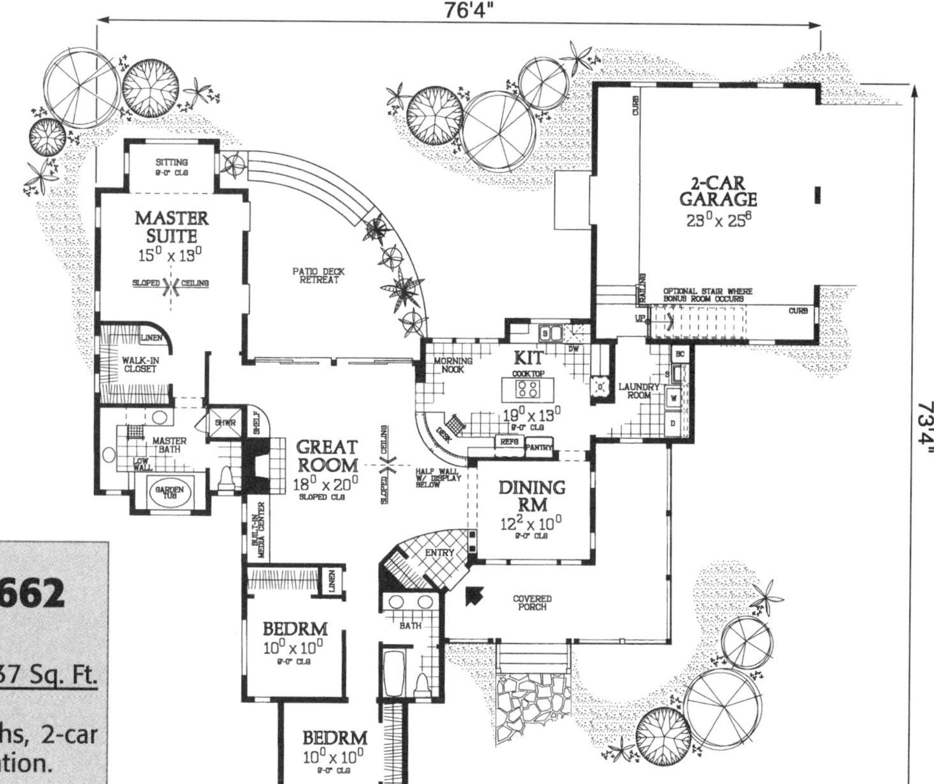
76'4"
73'4"
SITTING
MASTER SUITE
15⁰ x 13⁰
SLOPED CEILING
PATIO DECK RETREAT
2-CAR GARAGE
23⁰ x 25⁶
OPTIONAL STAIR WHERE BONUS ROOM OCCURS
MORNING NOOK
KIT
COOKTOP
19⁰ x 13⁰
LAUNDRY ROOM
WALK-IN CLOSET
LINEN
MASTER BATH
GARDEN TUB
GREAT ROOM
18⁰ x 20⁰
SLOPED CLG
HALF WALL W/ DISPLAY BELOW
PANTRY
DINING RM
12² x 10⁰
ENTRY
COVERED PORCH
BEDRM
10⁰ x 10⁰
BATH
BEDRM
10⁰ x 10⁰

Plan #527-HP-C662

Price Code C

Total Living Area: 1,937 Sq. Ft.

Home has 3 bedrooms, 2 baths, 2-car garage and crawl space foundation.

Special features

- Roomy kitchen with bright windows and convenient storage
- Octagon-shaped dining room shares a three-sided fireplace with the living room
- Covered patio in the rear of the home enhances outdoor living

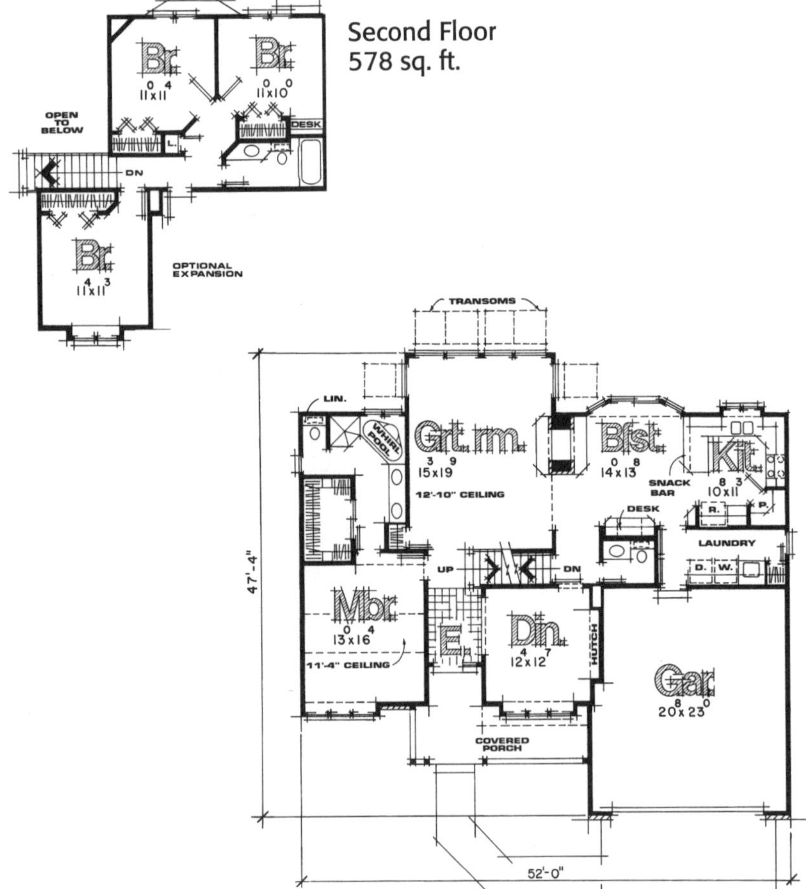
Br.
11x11
Br.
11x10
OPEN TO BELOW
DESK
DN
Br.
11x11
OPTIONAL EXPANSION
TRANSOMS
LIN.
WHIRLPOOL
Grt.rm.
15x19
12'-10" CEILING
Bfst.
14x13
SNACK BAR
DESK
Kit.
10x11
LAUNDRY
UP
DN
Mbr.
13x16
11'-4" CEILING
E.
Din.
12x12
HUTCH
Gar.
20x23
COVERED PORCH
47'-4"
52'-0"
© design basics inc.

Second Floor
578 sq. ft.

First Floor
1,421 sq. ft.

Plan #527-DBI-1380

Price Code C

Total Living Area: 1,999 Sq. Ft.

Home has 4 bedrooms, 2 1/2 baths, 2-car garage and basement foundation.

Special features

- Breakfast room and kitchen combine for a spacious gathering place including access to laundry area and a built-in desk area
- First floor master suite with private bath and a luxurious whirlpool
- Private dining area with unique built-in hutch adds interest

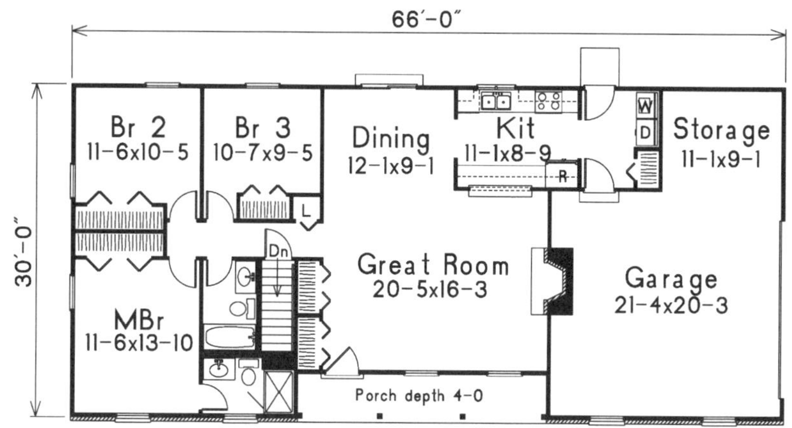
66'-0"
30'-0"
Br 2
11-6x10-5
Br 3
10-7x9-5
Dining
12-1x9-1
Kit
11-1x8-9
R
W
D
Storage
11-1x9-1
Dn
L
Great Room
20-5x16-3
Garage
21-4x20-3
MBr
11-6x13-10
Porch depth 4-0

Plan #527-1124

Price Code A

Total Living Area: 1,345 Sq. Ft.

Home has 3 bedrooms, 2 baths, 2-car side entry garage and basement foundation, drawings also include crawl space and slab foundations.

Special features

- Brick front details add a touch of elegance
- Master suite has private full bath
- Great room combined with dining area adds spaciousness
- Garage includes handy storage area which could easily convert to a workshop space

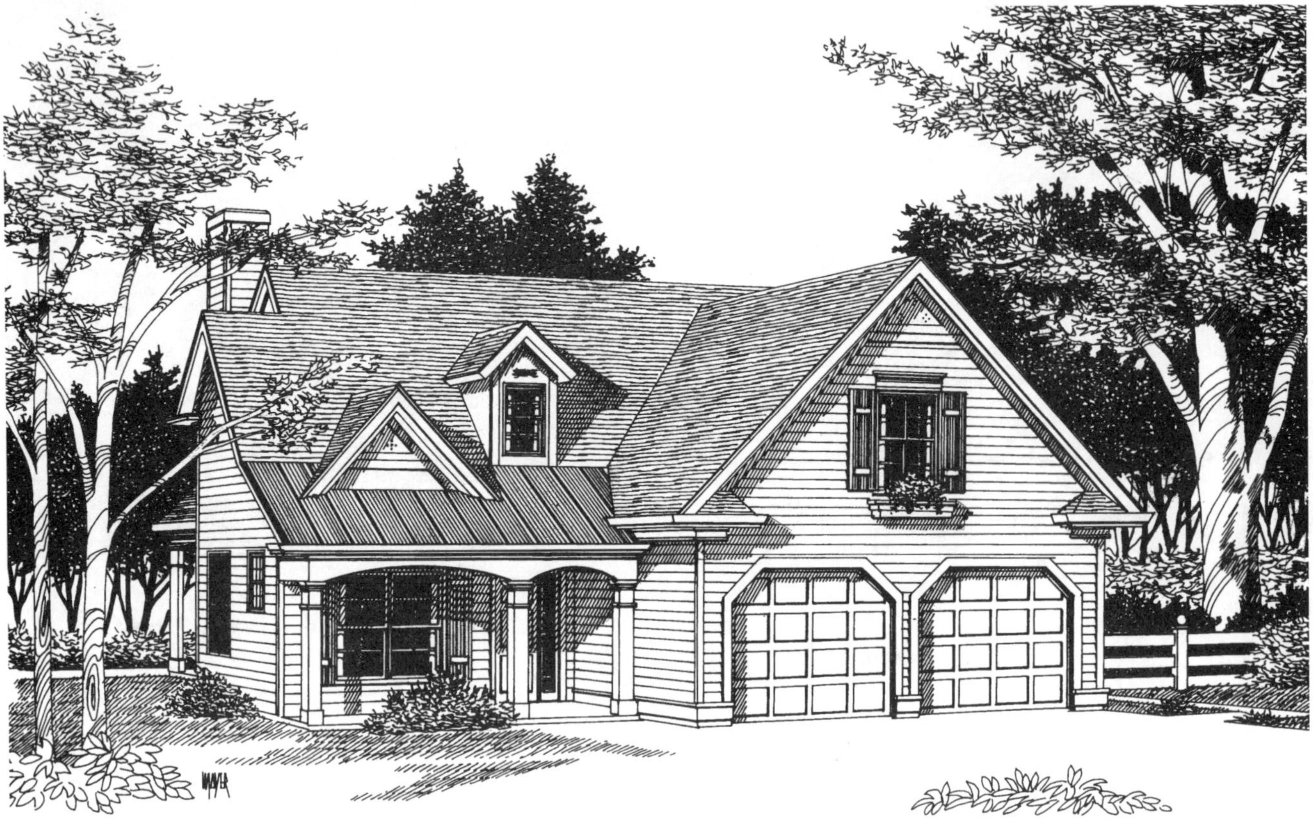

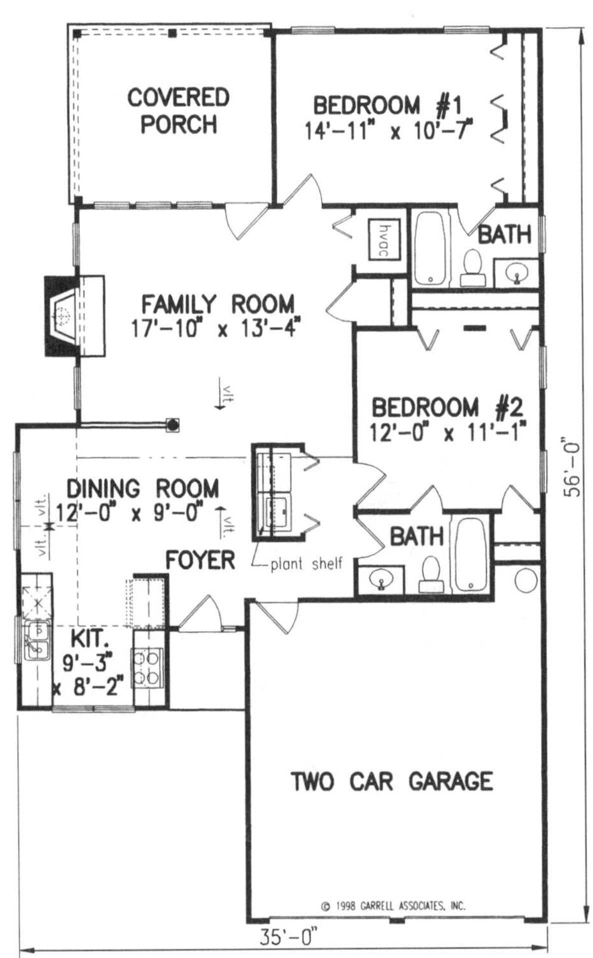
COVERED PORCH
BEDROOM #1
14'–11" x 10'–7"
hvac
BATH
FAMILY ROOM
17'–10" x 13'–4"
vlt.
BEDROOM #2
12'–0" x 11'–1"
DINING ROOM
12'–0" x 9'–0"
vlt.
vlt.
FOYER
plant shelf
BATH
KIT.
9'–3"
x 8'–2"
TWO CAR GARAGE
© 1998 GARRELL ASSOCIATES, INC.
56'–0"
35'–0"

Plan #527-MG-97099

Price Code AA

Total Living Area: 1,093 Sq. Ft.

Home has 2 bedrooms, 2 baths, 2-car garage and slab foundation.

Special features

- Family room with fireplace overlooks large covered porch
- Vaulted family and dining rooms are adjacent to kitchen
- Bedroom #2 has its own entrance into bath
- Plant shelf accents vaulted foyer
- Centrally located laundry area

Lovely Inviting Covered Porch

LOWE'S

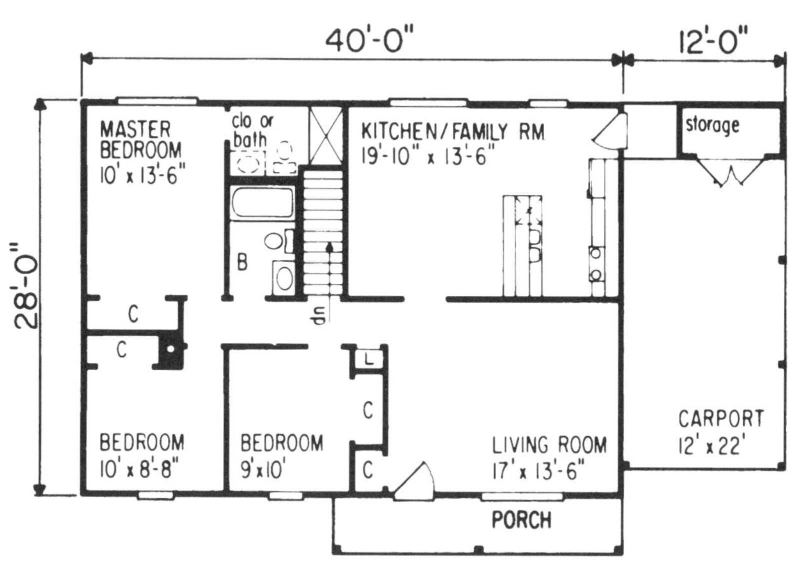
40'-0"
12'-0"
28'-0"
MASTER BEDROOM 10' x 13'-6"
clo or bath
KITCHEN/FAMILY RM 19'-10" x 13'-6"
storage
B
C
C
up
L
C
C
BEDROOM 10' x 8'-8"
BEDROOM 9'x10'
LIVING ROOM 17' x 13'-6"
CARPORT 12' x 22'
PORCH

Plan #527-1189-1

basement

Plan #527-1189-1

crawl space & slab

Price Code AA

Total Living Area: 1,120 Sq. Ft.

Home has 3 bedrooms, 2 baths, 1-car carport and basement, crawl space or slab foundation, please specify when ordering.

Special features

- Kitchen/family room creates a useful spacious area
- Rustic, colonial design perfect for many surroundings
- Oversized living room ideal for entertaining
- Carport includes functional storage area

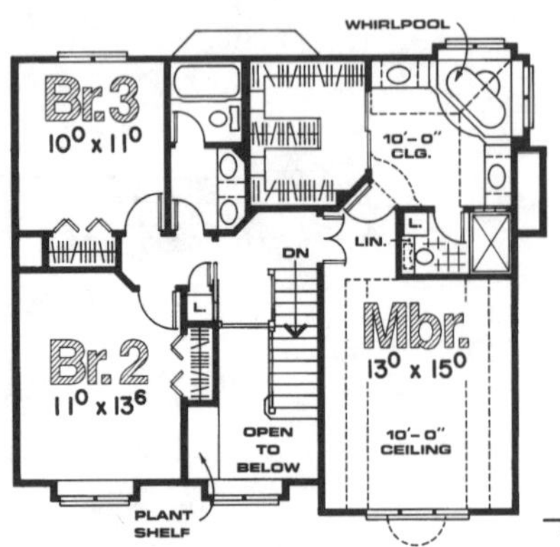
WHIRLPOOL
Br.3
10^0 x 11^0
10'-0" CLG.
LIN.
DN
Mbr.
13^0 x 15^0
Br.2
11^0 x 13^6
OPEN TO BELOW
10'-0" CEILING
PLANT SHELF

Second Floor
905 sq. ft.

First Floor
1,093 sq. ft.

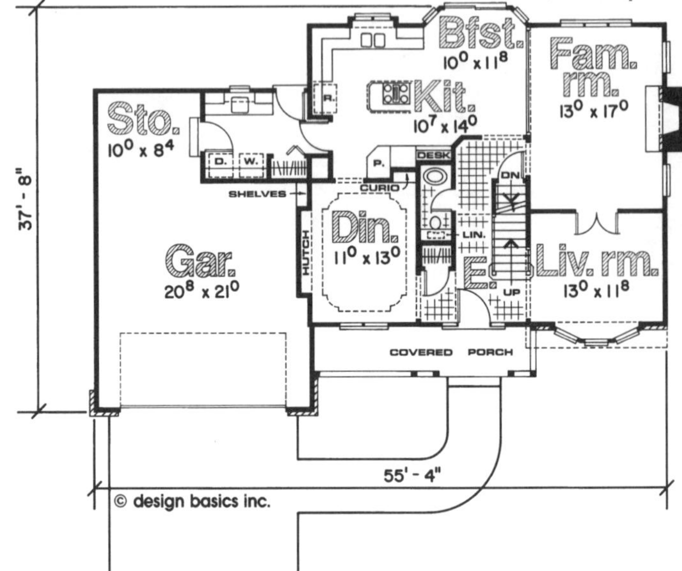
Bfst.
10^0 x 11^8
Fam. rm.
13^0 x 17^0
Kit.
10^7 x 14^0
Sto.
10^0 x 8^4
D. W.
P.
DESK
CURIO
SHELVES
37' - 8"
DN
LIN.
Din.
11^0 x 13^0
HUTCH
Gar.
20^8 x 21^0
E.
UP
Liv. rm.
13^0 x 11^8
COVERED PORCH
55' - 4"
© design basics inc.

Plan #527-DBI-2619

Price Code C

Total Living Area: 1,998 Sq. Ft.

Home has 3 bedrooms, 2 1/2 baths, 2-car garage and basement foundation.

Special features

- Lovely designed family room offers double-door entrance into living area
- Roomy kitchen with breakfast area is a natural gathering place
- 10' ceiling in master bedroom

TO ORDER BLUEPRINTS USE THE FORM ON PAGE 290 OR CALL TOLL-FREE **1-800-DREAM HOME** (373-2646)

Gables Boost Attractive Facade

LOWE'S

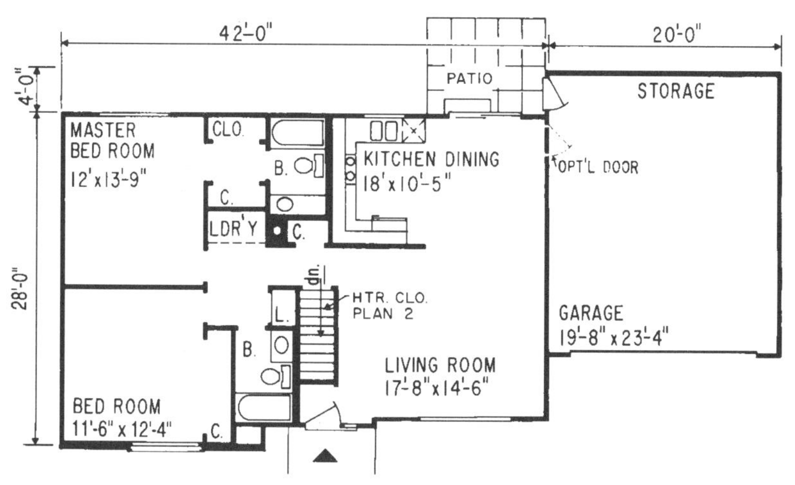
42'-0"
20'-0"
4'-0"
28'-0"
PATIO
STORAGE
MASTER BED ROOM 12'x13'-9"
CLO.
B.
C.
LDR'Y
C.
KITCHEN DINING 18'x10'-5"
OPT'L DOOR
dn.
HTR. CLO. PLAN 2
L.
B.
GARAGE 19'-8" x 23'-4"
LIVING ROOM 17'-8"x14'-6"
BED ROOM 11'-6" x 12'-4"
C.

Plan #527-1403

Price Code AA

Total Living Area: 1,128 Sq. Ft.

Home has 2 bedrooms, 2 baths, 2-car garage and basement foundation.

Special features

- Large living room borrows from dining area creating expansive space
- Well-arranged U-shaped kitchen has lots of counter and cabinet storage space
- His and hers closets and full bath accompany spacious master bedroom
- Oversized garage with ample storage area has door to rear patio that leads to dining area

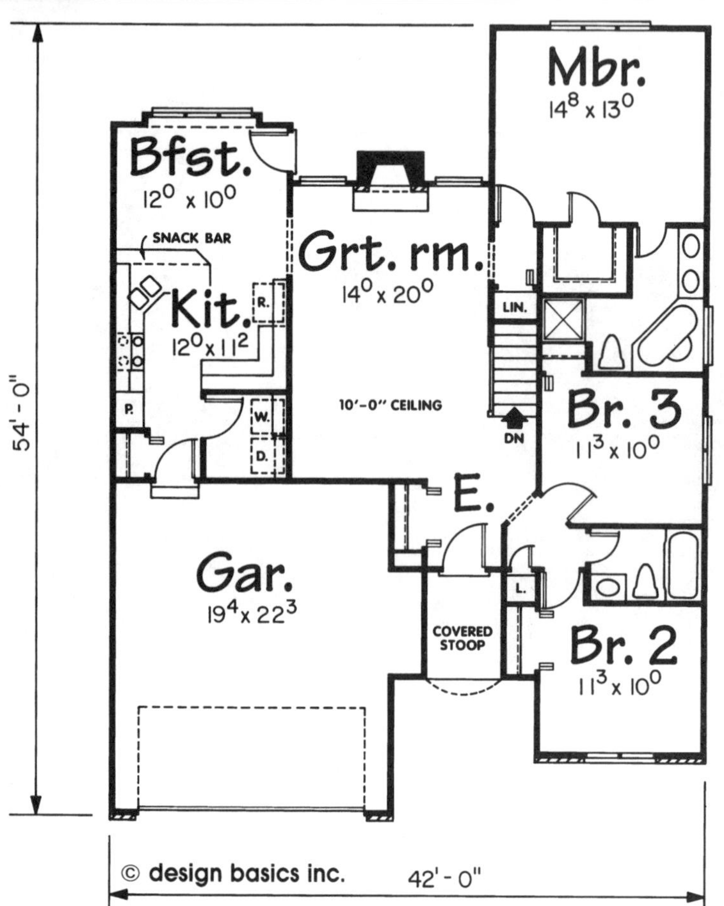
Mbr.
14^8 x 13^0
Bfst.
12^0 x 10^0
SNACK BAR
Grt. rm.
14^0 x 20^0
Kit.
12^0 x 11^2
R.
LIN.
P.
W.
D.
10'-0" CEILING
DN
Br. 3
11^3 x 10^0
E.
Gar.
19^4 x 22^3
COVERED STOOP
L.
Br. 2
11^3 x 10^0
54'-0"
© design basics inc.
42'-0"

Plan #527-DBI-8013

Price Code A

Total Living Area: 1,392 Sq. Ft.

Home has 3 bedrooms, 2 baths, 2-car garage and basement foundation.

Special features

- Centralized great room welcomes guests with a warm fireplace
- Master suite has separate entrance for added privacy
- Kitchen includes breakfast room, snack counter and laundry area

LOWE'S

Second Floor
663 sq. ft.
STORAGE
BONUS ROOM
16' x 22'
DOWN
STORAGE
STORAGE
LAUNDRY DROP
DOWN
W.I.C.
BEDROOM
16' x 12'
BALCONY
BEDROOM
16' x 12'
BATH
OPEN TO LOWER LEVEL
BATH
First Floor
1,531 sq. ft.
WORK BENCH
GARAGE
22' X 22'
RECYCLE STORAGE
STOR.
UP
BATH
STORAGE
DINETTE
16' X 10' – 8"
SLOPED CEILINGS
LAWN CHAIR STORAGE
UP
COOK TOP
BATH
10' X 10'
PORCH
11' X 8'
UTIL.
KITCHEN
11' X 12'
LAUNDRY DROP
FIREPLACE
MASTER SUITE
16' X 16'
LIVING ROOM
19' X 17'
OPEN TO 2ND FLOOR CEILING
DINING ROOM
11' X 16'
FOYER
PORCH
34' X 8'
74' – 0"
52' – 0"

Plan #527-BF-2108

Price Code C

Total Living Area: 2,194 Sq. Ft.

Home has 3 bedrooms, 3 1/2 baths, 2-car side entry garage and crawl space, slab or basement foundation, please specify when ordering.

Special features

- Energy efficient 2" x 6" exterior walls
- Utility room has laundry drop conveniently located next to kitchen
- Both second floor bedrooms have large closets and their own bath

Central Living Room Great For Gathering

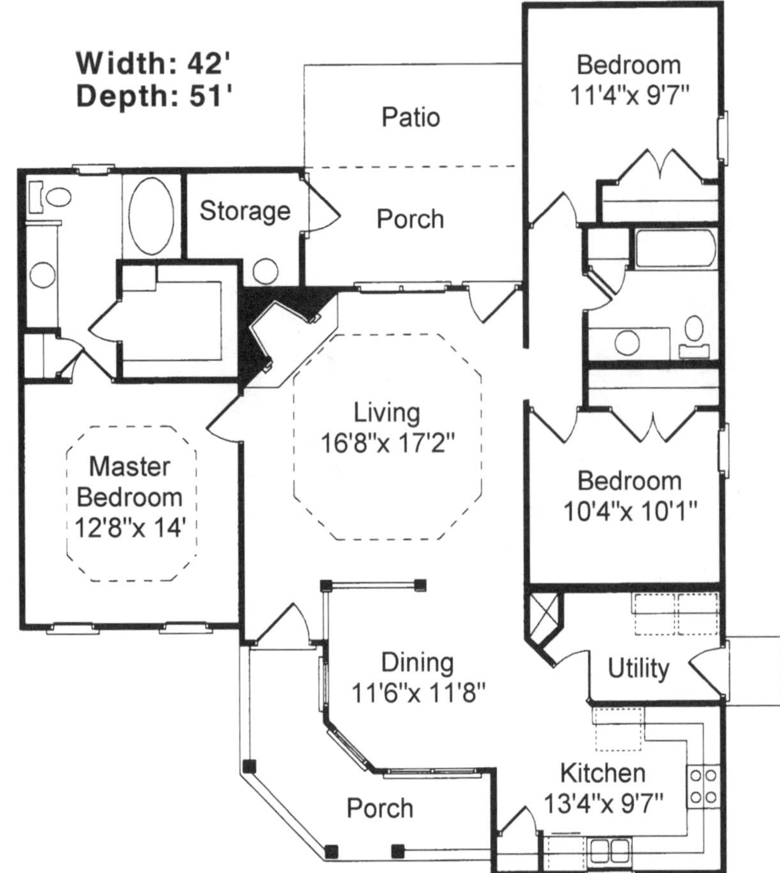
Width: 42'
Depth: 51'
Patio
Bedroom
11'4"x 9'7"
Storage
Porch
Living
16'8"x 17'2"
Master
Bedroom
12'8"x 14'
Bedroom
10'4"x 10'1"
Dining
11'6"x 11'8"
Utility
Kitchen
13'4"x 9'7"
Porch

Plan #527-CHP-1432-A-142

Price Code A

Total Living Area: 1,405 Sq. Ft.

Home has 3 bedrooms, 2 baths and slab foundation.

Special features

- Compact design has all the luxuries of a larger home
- Master bedroom has its privacy away from other bedrooms
- Living room has corner fireplace, access to the outdoors and easy access to the dining area and kitchen
- Large utility room has access outdoors

TO ORDER BLUEPRINTS USE THE FORM ON PAGE 290 OR CALL TOLL-FREE **1-800-DREAM HOME** (373-2646)

Striking Plant Shelf

LOWE'S

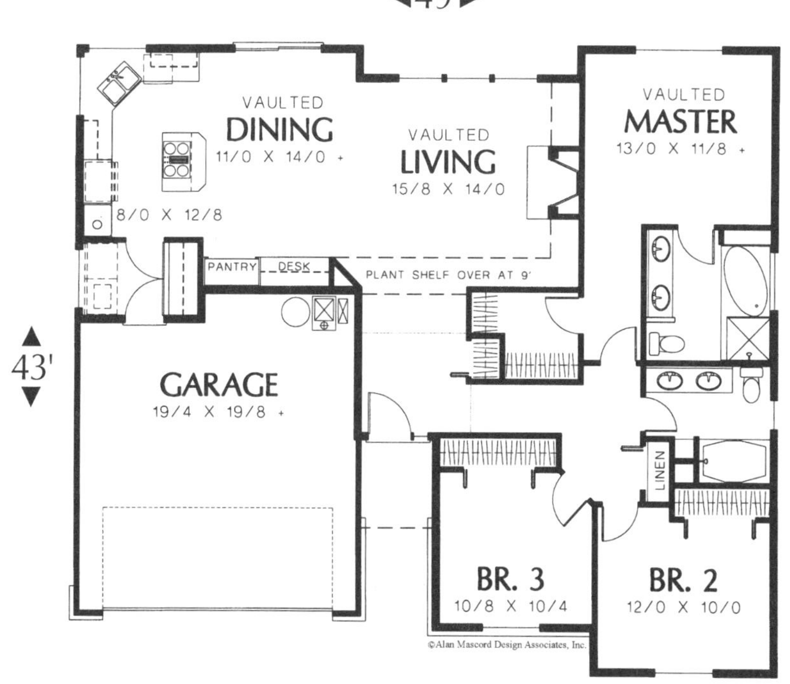
49'
43'
VAULTED
DINING
11/0 X 14/0
VAULTED
LIVING
15/8 X 14/0
VAULTED
MASTER
13/0 X 11/8
8/0 X 12/8
PANTRY
DESK
PLANT SHELF OVER AT 9'
GARAGE
19/4 X 19/8
LINEN
BR. 3
10/8 X 10/4
BR. 2
12/0 X 10/0
©Alan Mascord Design Associates, Inc.

Plan #527-AMD-1135

Price Code A

Total Living Area: 1,467 Sq. Ft.

Home has 3 bedrooms, 2 baths, 2-car garage and crawl space foundation.

Special features

- Vaulted ceilings, an open floor plan and a wealth of windows create an inviting atmosphere
- Efficiently arranged kitchen has an island with built-in cooktop and a snack counter
- Plentiful storage and closet space throughout this home

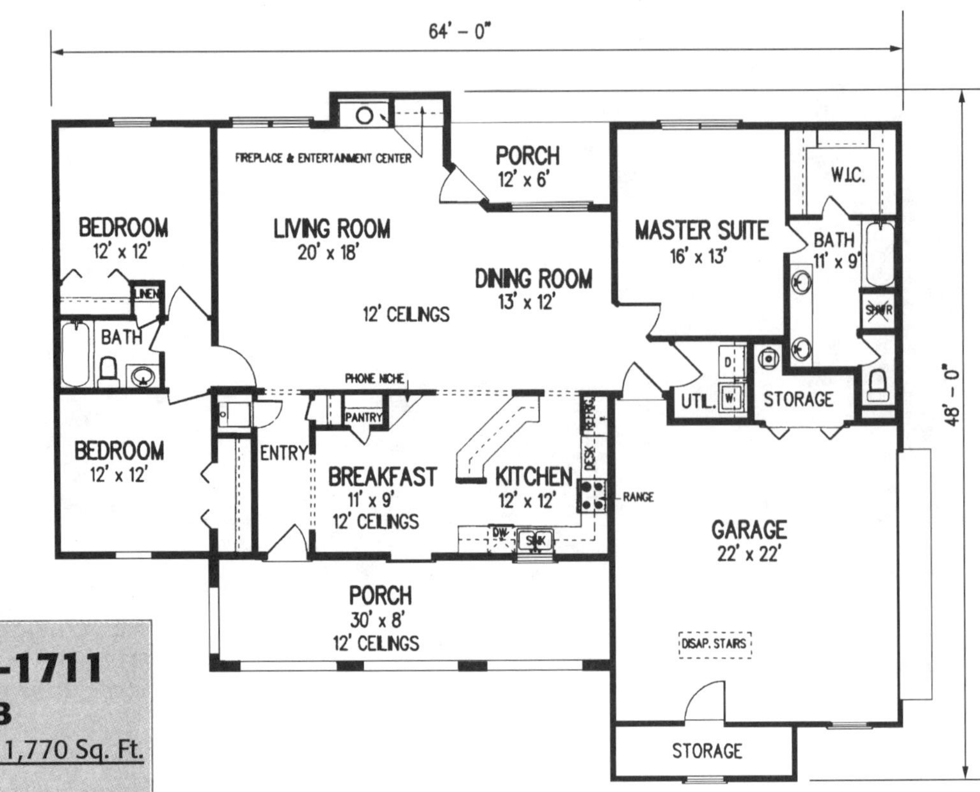
64' – 0"
48' – 0"
FIREPLACE & ENTERTAINMENT CENTER
PORCH
12' x 6'
BEDROOM
12' x 12'
LIVING ROOM
20' x 18'
MASTER SUITE
16' x 13'
W.I.C.
BATH
11' x 9'
DINING ROOM
13' x 12'
12' CEILINGS
LINEN
BATH
SHWR
PHONE NICHE
UTIL.
STORAGE
PANTRY
BEDROOM
12' x 12'
ENTRY
BREAKFAST
11' x 9'
12' CEILINGS
KITCHEN
12' x 12'
DESK
RANGE
DW
SINK
GARAGE
22' x 22'
PORCH
30' x 8'
12' CEILINGS
DISAP. STAIRS
STORAGE

Plan #527-BF-1711

Price Code B

Total Living Area: 1,770 Sq. Ft.

Home has 3 bedrooms, 2 baths, 2-car side entry garage and slab or crawl space foundation, please specify when ordering.

Special features

- Open floor plan makes this home feel spacious
- 12' ceilings in kitchen, breakfast, living and dining areas
- Kitchen is the center of activity with views into all gathering places

Plenty Of Closet Space

LOWE'S

Second Floor
848 sq. ft.

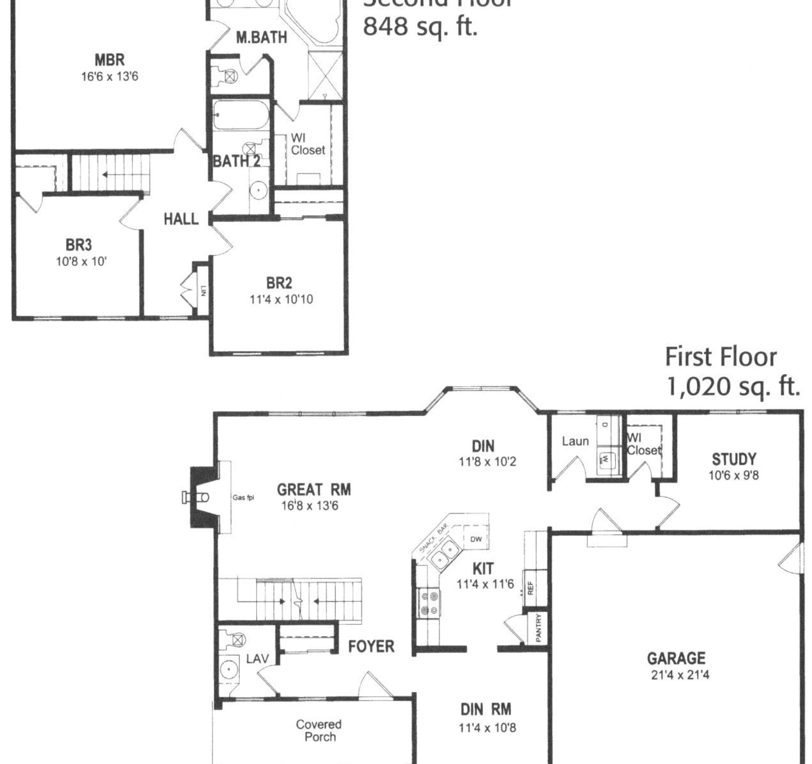

MBR
16'6 x 13'6
M.BATH
WI
Closet
BATH 2
HALL
BR3
10'8 x 10'
BR2
11'4 x 10'10
LIN
DIN
11'8 x 10'2
Laun
WI
Closet
STUDY
10'6 x 9'8
GREAT RM
16'8 x 13'6
Gas fpl
SNACK BAR
DW
KIT
11'4 x 11'6
REF
PANTRY
GARAGE
21'4 x 21'4
LAV
FOYER
DIN RM
11'4 x 10'8
Covered
Porch

First Floor
1,020 sq. ft.

Width: 52'-8"
Depth: 34'-0"

Plan #527-JFD-20-1868-1

Price Code C

Total Living Area: 1,868 Sq. Ft.

Home has 3 bedrooms, 2 1/2 baths, 2-car garage and basement foundation.

Special features

- Open floor plan creates airy feeling
- Secluded study makes an ideal home office
- Large master bedroom has luxurious private bath with a walk-in closet
- Formal dining room has convenient access to kitchen

LOWE'S

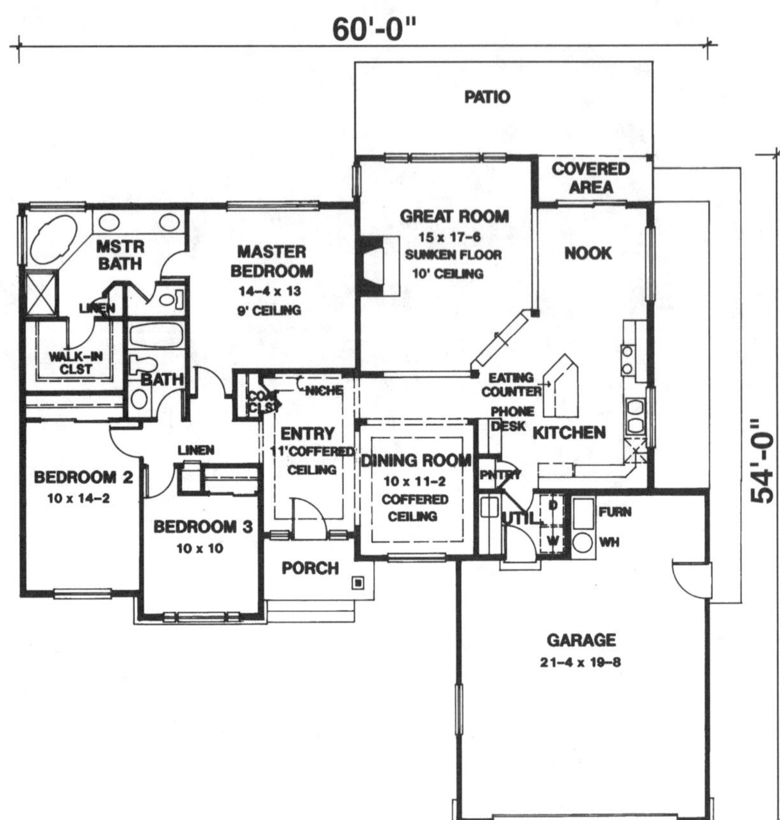
60'-0"
54'-0"
PATIO
COVERED AREA
GREAT ROOM
15 x 17-6
SUNKEN FLOOR
10' CEILING
NOOK
MSTR BATH
MASTER BEDROOM
14-4 x 13
9' CEILING
LINEN
WALK-IN CLST
BATH
COAT CLST
NICHE
EATING COUNTER
PHONE DESK
KITCHEN
ENTRY
11' COFFERED CEILING
DINING ROOM
10 x 11-2
COFFERED CEILING
PNTRY
UTIL
D
W
FURN
WH
LINEN
BEDROOM 2
10 x 14-2
BEDROOM 3
10 x 10
PORCH
GARAGE
21-4 x 19-8

Plan #527-GSD-1123

Price Code B

Total Living Area: 1,734 Sq. Ft.

Home has 3 bedrooms, 2 baths, 2-car garage and crawl space foundation.

Special features

- Large entry with coffered ceiling and display niches
- Sunken great room has 10' ceiling
- Kitchen island includes eating counter
- 9' ceiling in master bedroom
- Master bath features corner tub and dual sinks

 TO ORDER BLUEPRINTS USE THE FORM ON PAGE 290 OR CALL TOLL-FREE **1-800-DREAM HOME** (373-2646)

Inviting Home With Country Flavor

LOWE'S

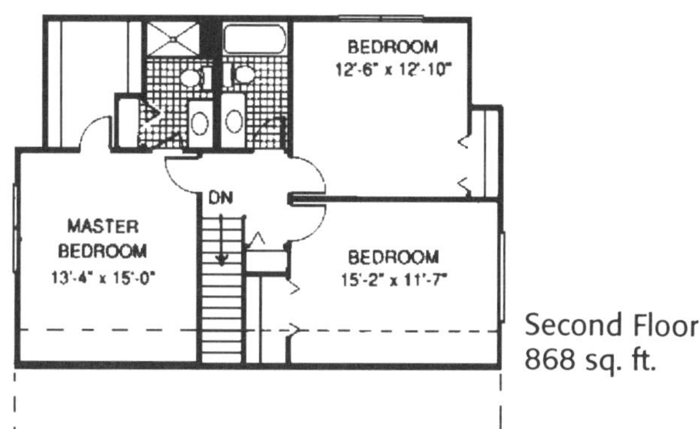
BEDROOM
12'-6" x 12'-10"
DN
MASTER
BEDROOM
13'-4" x 15'-0"
BEDROOM
15'-2" x 11'-7"

Second Floor
868 sq. ft.

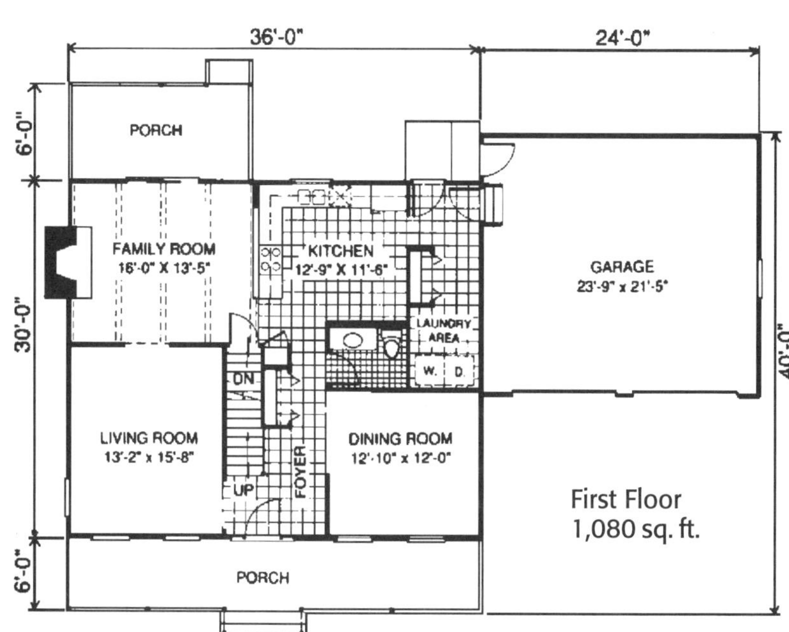
36'-0"
24'-0"
6'-0"
PORCH
FAMILY ROOM
16'-0" X 13'-5"
KITCHEN
12'-9" X 11'-6"
GARAGE
23'-9" x 21'-5"
30'-0"
LAUNDRY
AREA
W. D
40'-0"
DN
LIVING ROOM
13'-2" x 15'-8"
FOYER
DINING ROOM
12'-10" x 12'-0"
UP
6'-0"
PORCH

First Floor
1,080 sq. ft.

Plan #527-1347-1

basement

Plan #527-1347-2

crawl space

Price Code C

Total Living Area: 1,948 Sq. Ft.

Home has 3 bedrooms, 2 1/2 baths, 2-car garage and basement or crawl space foundation, please specify when ordering.

Special features

- Large elongated porch for moonlit evenings
- Stylish family room features beamed ceiling
- Skillfully designed kitchen convenient to an oversized laundry area
- Second floor bedrooms all generously sized

Plan #527-GM-2009

Price Code C

Total Living Area: 2,009 Sq. Ft.

Home has 3 bedrooms, 2 baths, 2-car side entry garage and basement foundation.

Special features

- Enter home and find large family room with fireplace flanked by double windows
- Cheerful breakfast area has access to skylighted porch
- Elegant dining area includes a built-in china cabinet

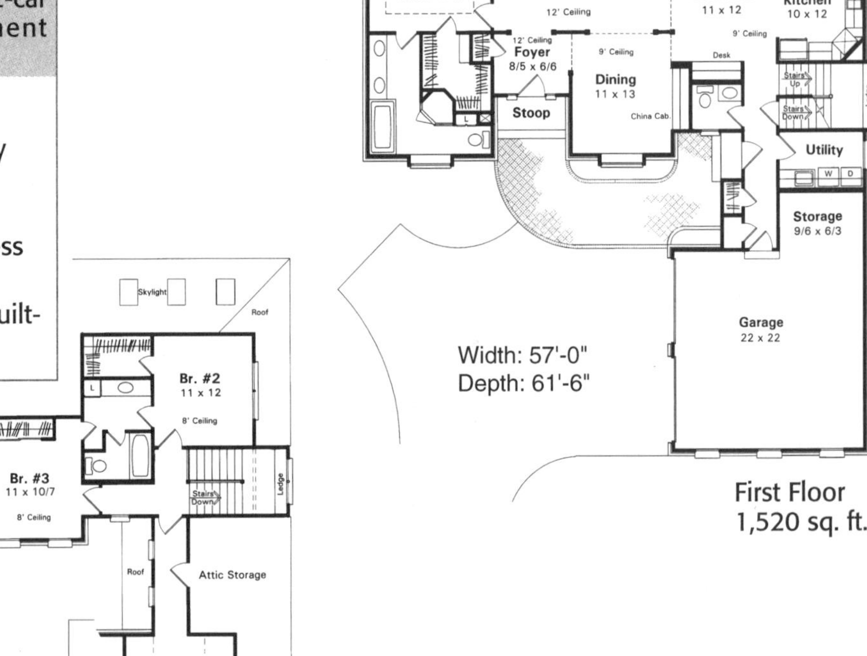
Skylight
Porch
21/8 x 6/6
Master
13/8 x 15
Recessed Ceiling
Family Room
19/8 x 15
12' Ceiling
Breakfast
11 x 12
Kitchen
10 x 12
9' Ceiling
12' Ceiling
Foyer
8/5 x 6/6
9' Ceiling
Dining
11 x 13
China Cab.
Desk
Stairs Up
Stairs Down
Ledge
Stoop
Utility
W D
Storage
9/6 x 6/3
Garage
22 x 22
Width: 57'-0"
Depth: 61'-6"
Skylight
Roof
Br. #2
11 x 12
8' Ceiling
Br. #3
11 x 10/7
8' Ceiling
Stairs Down
Ledge
Roof
Attic Storage
Opt. Bonus
12 x 21/5

First Floor
1,520 sq. ft.

Second Floor
489 sq. ft.

LOWE'S

Plan #527-N294-1

basement

Plan #527-N294-2

crawl space & slab

Price Code AA

Total Living Area: 1,092 Sq. Ft.

Home has 2 bedrooms, 2 baths, 2-car garage and basement, crawl space or slab foundation, please specify when ordering.

Special features

- Large living room is open to U-shaped kitchen/dining area which accesses rear patio through double sliding doors
- Master bedroom has two large closets which lead to private bath
- The two car garage has ample storage space and also accesses the rear patio

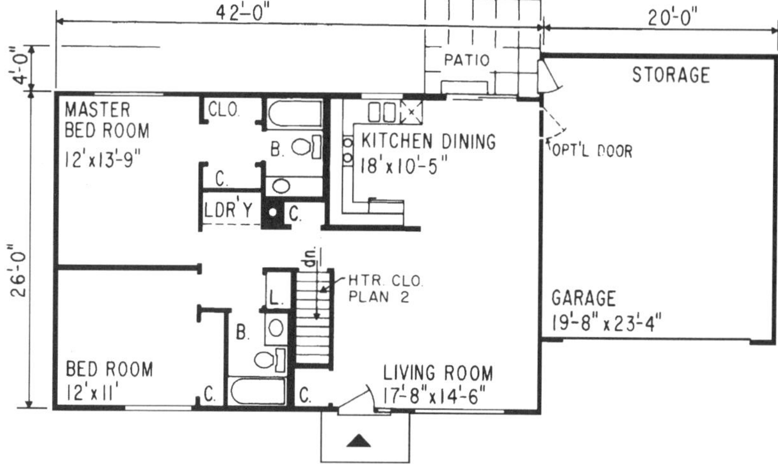
42'-0"
20'-0"
4'-0"
26'-0"
PATIO
STORAGE
MASTER BED ROOM 12'x13'-9"
CLO.
B.
C.
LDR'Y
C.
KITCHEN DINING 18'x10'-5"
OPT'L DOOR
dn.
HTR. CLO. PLAN 2
L.
B.
GARAGE 19'-8"x23'-4"
BED ROOM 12'x11'
C.
C.
LIVING ROOM 17'-8"x14'-6"

Plan #527-1349

Price Code A

Total Living Area: 1,340 Sq. Ft.

Home has 2 bedrooms, 2 baths, 2-car garage and slab foundation.

Special features

- Striking contemporary design offers complete accessibility for the handicapped
- Deep two-car garage provides ramp access into utility room
- Main entryway is via ramped front porch into foyer
- Combined kitchen, dining and living areas illuminated by three large roof windows
- Rear of home features two separated covered decks for the ultimate in relaxation and outdoor leisure

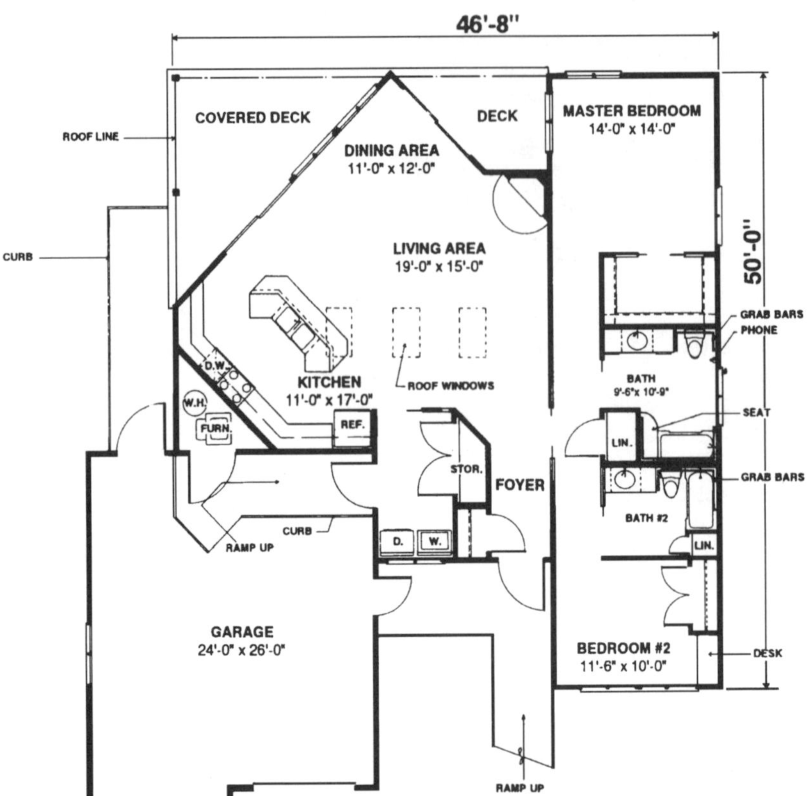
46'-8"
50'-0"
COVERED DECK
DECK
ROOF LINE
DINING AREA
11'-0" x 12'-0"
MASTER BEDROOM
14'-0" x 14'-0"
CURB
LIVING AREA
19'-0" x 15'-0"
GRAB BARS
PHONE
D.W.
W.H.
FURN.
KITCHEN
11'-0" x 17'-0"
REF.
ROOF WINDOWS
BATH
9'-6"x 10'-9"
SEAT
LIN.
STOR.
FOYER
GRAB BARS
BATH #2
CURB
RAMP UP
D.
W.
LIN.
GARAGE
24'-0" x 26'-0"
BEDROOM #2
11'-6" x 10'-0"
DESK
RAMP UP

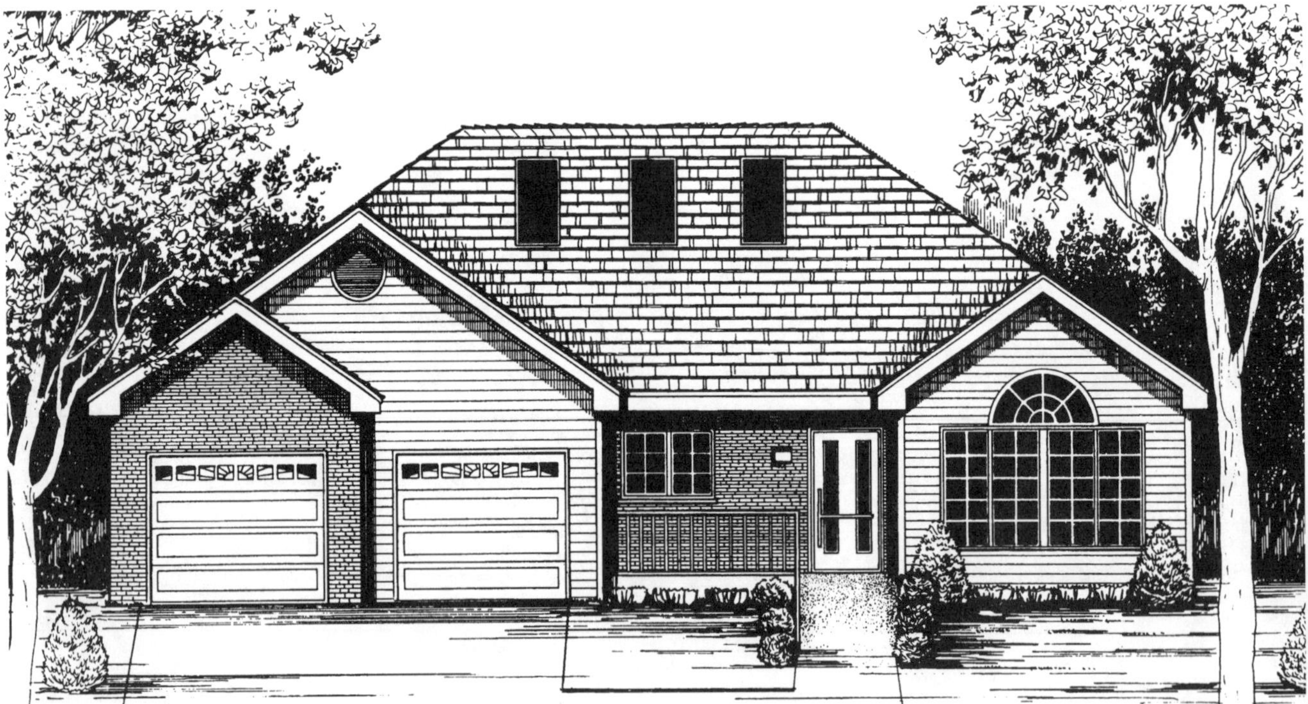

Plan #527-FB-902

Price Code C

Total Living Area: 1,856 Sq. Ft.

Home has 3 bedrooms, 2 baths, 2-car side entry garage and basement, crawl space or slab foundation, please specify when ordering.

Special features

- Beautiful covered porch creates a southern accent
- Kitchen has an organized feel with lots of cabinetry
- Large foyer has a grand entrance and leads into family room through columns and arched opening

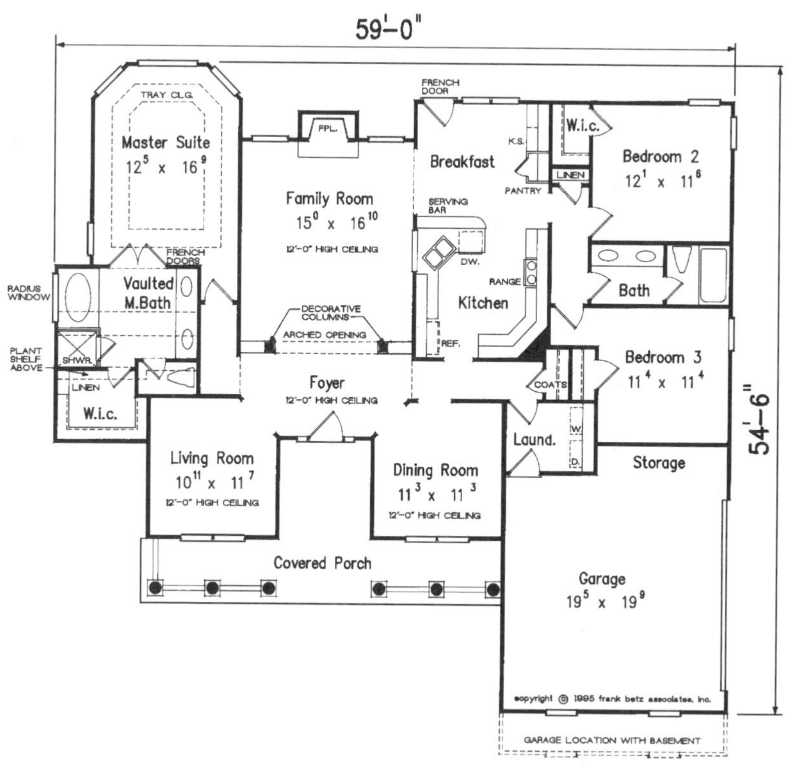
59'-0"
54'-6"
FRENCH DOOR
TRAY CLG.
Master Suite
12^{5} x 16^{9}
FPL.
Family Room
15^{0} x 16^{10}
12'-0" HIGH CEILING
Breakfast
K.S.
PANTRY
W.i.c.
LINEN
Bedroom 2
12^{1} x 11^{8}
SERVING BAR
DW.
RANGE
Kitchen
REF.
Bath
FRENCH DOORS
RADIUS WINDOW
Vaulted M.Bath
PLANT SHELF ABOVE
SHWR.
LINEN
W.i.c.
DECORATIVE COLUMNS
ARCHED OPENING
Foyer
12'-0" HIGH CEILING
COATS
Bedroom 3
11^{4} x 11^{4}
Laund.
W
D.
Storage
Living Room
10^{11} x 11^{7}
12'-0" HIGH CEILING
Dining Room
11^{3} x 11^{3}
12'-0" HIGH CEILING
Covered Porch
Garage
19^{5} x 19^{9}
copyright © 1995 frank betz associates, inc.
GARAGE LOCATION WITH BASEMENT

Second Floor
829 sq. ft.

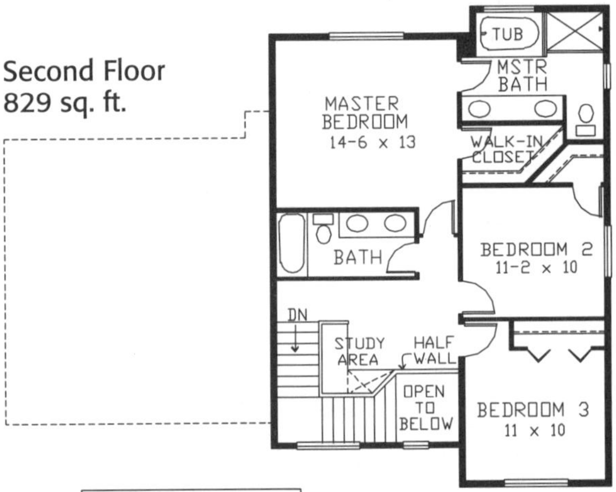

TUB
MSTR BATH
MASTER BEDROOM 14-6 x 13
WALK-IN CLOSET
BATH
BEDROOM 2 11-2 x 10
DN
STUDY AREA
HALF WALL
OPEN TO BELOW
BEDROOM 3 11 x 10

Plan #527-GSD-2004

Price Code B

Total Living Area: 1,751 Sq. Ft.

Home has 3 bedrooms, 2 1/2 baths, 2-car garage and crawl space foundation.

Special features

- Charming covered front porch
- Elegant two-story entry
- Beautifully designed great room with fireplace opens to kitchen
- Large eating counter and walk-in pantry
- Second floor study area perfect for a growing family

First Floor
922 sq. ft.

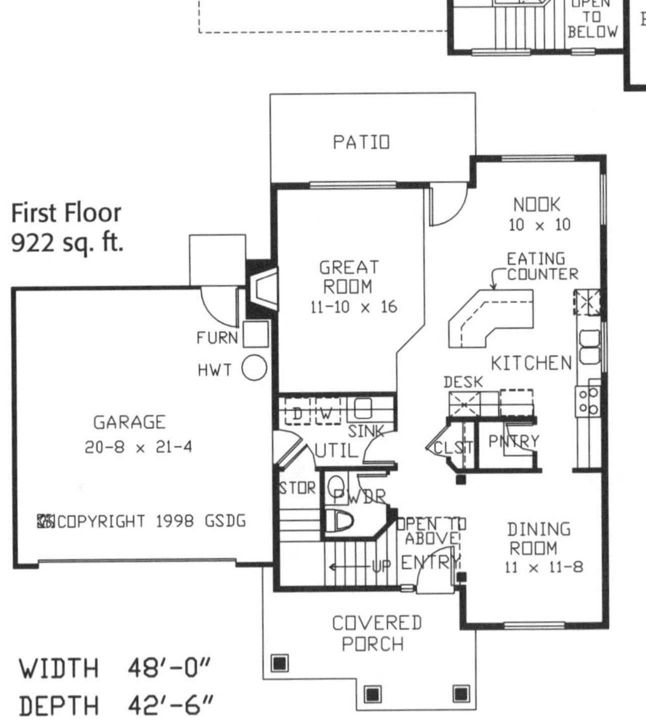
PATIO
NOOK 10 x 10
EATING COUNTER
GREAT ROOM 11-10 x 16
KITCHEN
FURN
HWT
DESK
D W
SINK
GARAGE 20-8 x 21-4
UTIL
CLST
PNTRY
STOR
PWDR
COPYRIGHT 1998 GSDG
OPEN TO ABOVE
ENTRY
UP
DINING ROOM 11 x 11-8
COVERED PORCH
WIDTH 48'-0"
DEPTH 42'-6"

TO ORDER BLUEPRINTS USE THE FORM ON PAGE 290 OR CALL TOLL-FREE **1-800-DREAM HOME** (373-2646)

LOWE'S

Plan #527-1297

Price Code C

Total Living Area: 1,992 Sq. Ft.

Home has 3 bedrooms, 2 1/2 baths and basement foundation.

Special features

- Master bedroom includes many luxuries such as an oversized private bath and large walk-in closet
- Kitchen area is spacious with a functional eat-in breakfast bar and is adjacent to nook ideal as a breakfast room
- Plenty of storage is featured in both bedrooms on the second floor and in the hall
- Enormous utility room is centrally located on the first floor

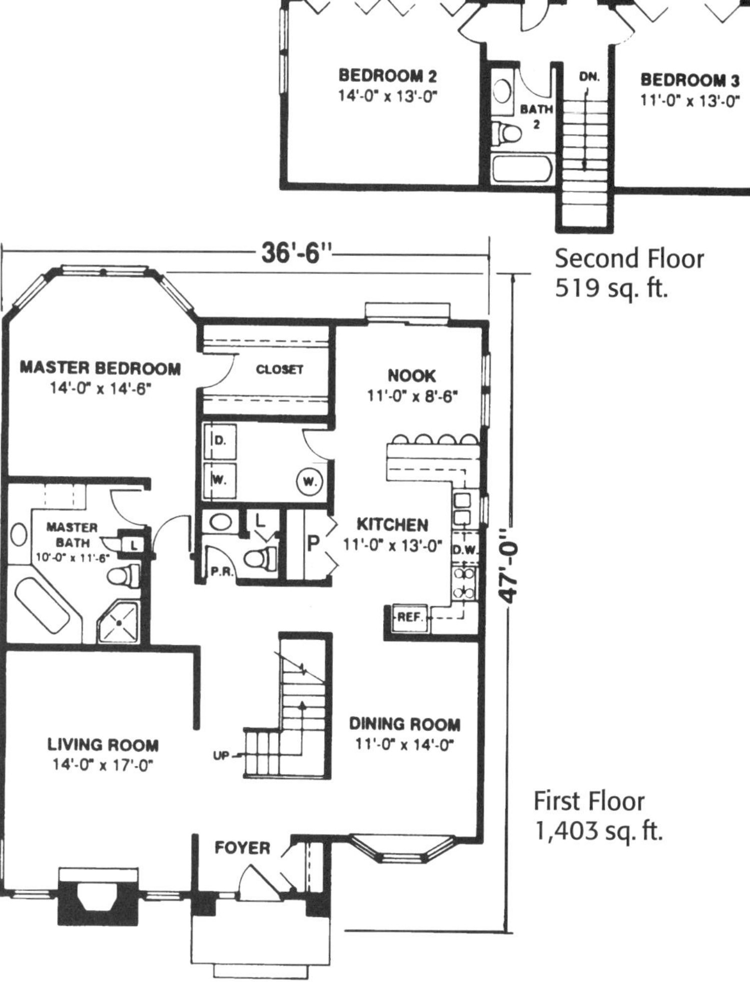
BEDROOM 2
14'-0" x 13'-0"
BATH 2
DN.
BEDROOM 3
11'-0" x 13'-0"
Second Floor
519 sq. ft.
36'-6"
MASTER BEDROOM
14'-0" x 14'-6"
CLOSET
NOOK
11'-0" x 8'-6"
D.
W.
MASTER BATH
10'-0" x 11'-6"
P.R.
P
KITCHEN
11'-0" x 13'-0"
D.W.
REF.
47'-0"
DINING ROOM
11'-0" x 14'-0"
LIVING ROOM
14'-0" x 17'-0"
UP
FOYER
First Floor
1,403 sq. ft.

Scalloped Porch Cornice Adds Flair

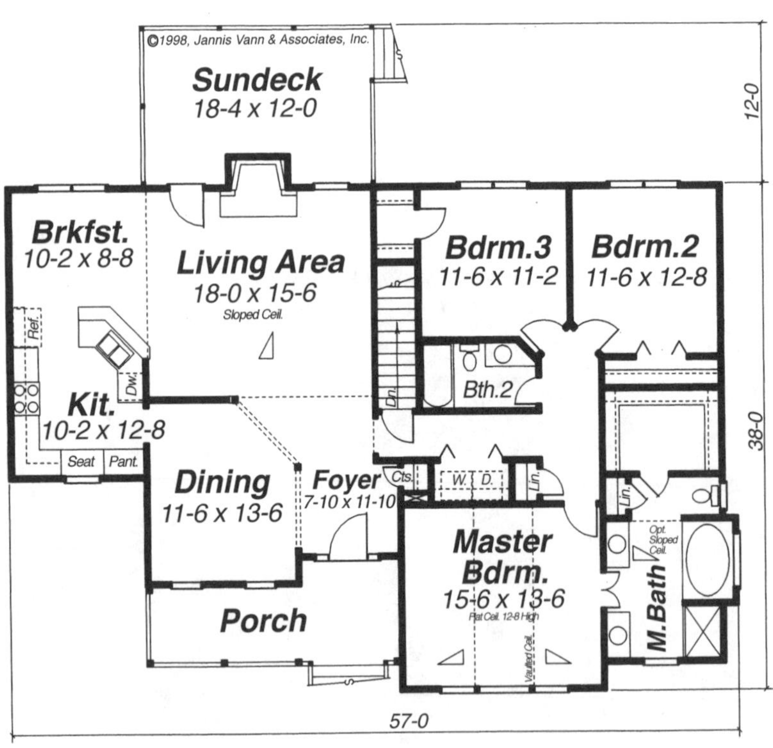
©1998, Jannis Vann & Associates, Inc.
Sundeck
18-4 x 12-0
Brkfst.
10-2 x 8-8
Living Area
18-0 x 15-6
Sloped Ceil.
Bdrm.3
11-6 x 11-2
Bdrm.2
11-6 x 12-8
Ref.
Dw.
Kit.
10-2 x 12-8
Seat
Pant.
Dn
Bth.2
Dining
11-6 x 13-6
Foyer
7-10 x 11-10
Cts.
W. D.
Lin.
Master
Bdrm.
15-6 x 13-6
Vaulted Ceil.
M.Bath
Opt. Sloped Ceil.
Porch
12-0
38-0
57-0

Plan #527-JV-1772-A-SJ

Price Code B

Total Living Area: 1,772 Sq. Ft.

Home has 3 bedrooms, 2 baths, 3-car drive under garage and basement foundation.

Special features

- Dramatic palladian window and scalloped porch are attention grabbers
- Island kitchen sink allows for easy access and views into the living/ breakfast areas
- Washer and dryer closet easily accessible from all bedrooms

TO ORDER BLUEPRINTS USE THE FORM ON PAGE 290 OR CALL TOLL-FREE **1-800-DREAM HOME** (373-2646)

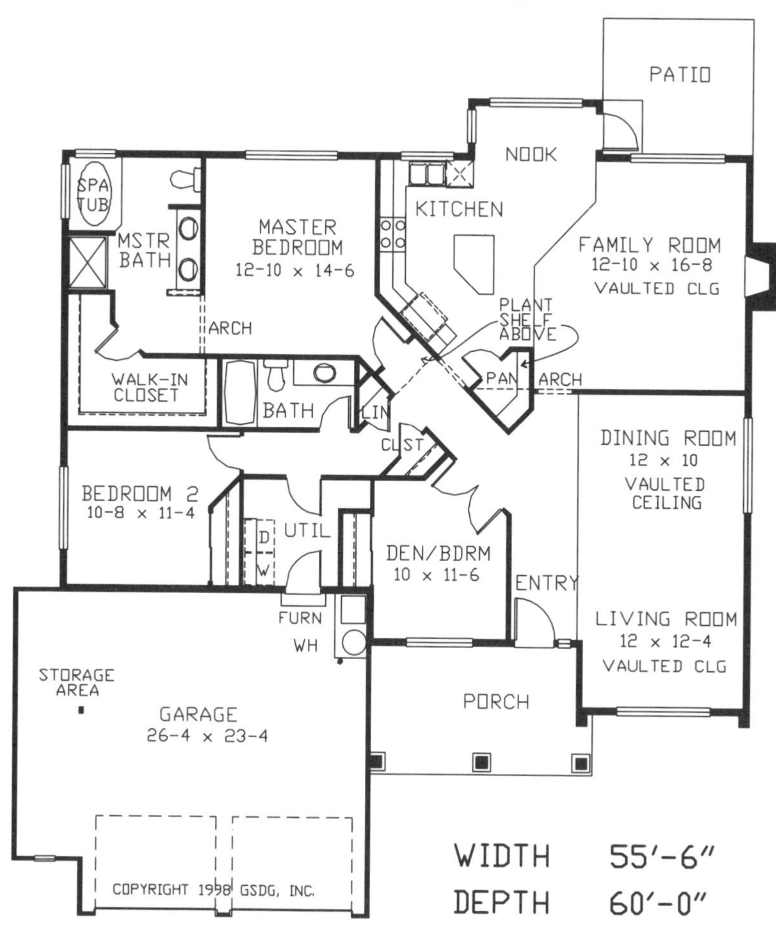
PATIO
NOOK
KITCHEN
FAMILY ROOM
12-10 x 16-8
VAULTED CLG
MASTER BEDROOM
12-10 x 14-6
SPA TUB
MSTR BATH
ARCH
PLANT SHELF ABOVE
WALK-IN CLOSET
BATH
LIN
PAN
ARCH
CLST
DINING ROOM
12 x 10
VAULTED CEILING
BEDROOM 2
10-8 x 11-4
UTIL
D
W
DEN/BDRM
10 x 11-6
ENTRY
LIVING ROOM
12 x 12-4
VAULTED CLG
FURN
WH
STORAGE AREA
GARAGE
26-4 x 23-4
PORCH
COPYRIGHT 1998 GSDG, INC.
WIDTH 55'-6"
DEPTH 60'-0"

Plan #527-GSD-1023-C

Price Code C

Total Living Area: 1,890 Sq. Ft.

Home has 3 bedrooms, 2 baths, 2-car garage and crawl space foundation.

Special features

- Inviting covered porches
- Vaulted ceilings in living, dining and family rooms
- Kitchen is open to family room and nook
- Large walk-in pantry
- Arch accented master bath has spa tub, dual sinks and walk-in closet

Ranch-Style Home With Many Extras

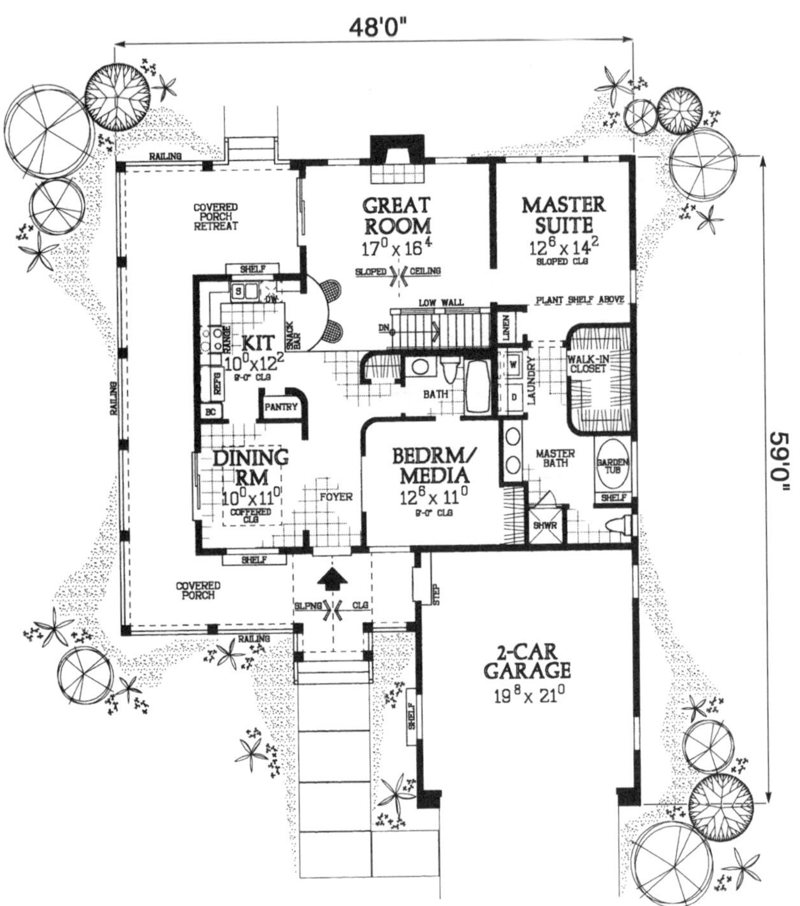
48'0"
59'0"
COVERED PORCH RETREAT
GREAT ROOM
17⁰ x 16⁴
SLOPED CEILING
MASTER SUITE
12⁶ x 14²
SLOPED CLG
KIT
10⁰x12²
DINING RM
10⁰x11⁰
COFFERED CLG
PANTRY
FOYER
BATH
BEDRM/ MEDIA
12⁶ x 11⁰
LINEN
LAUNDRY
WALK-IN CLOSET
MASTER BATH
GARDEN TUB
SHWR
COVERED PORCH
RAILING
SHELF
2-CAR GARAGE
19⁸ x 21⁰

Plan #527-HP-C689

Price Code A

Total Living Area: 1,295 Sq. Ft.

Home has 2 bedrooms, 2 baths, 2-car garage and basement foundation.

Special features

- Wrap-around porch is a lovely place for dining
- A fireplace gives a stunning focal point to the great room that is heightened with a sloped ceiling
- The master suite is full of luxurious touches such as a walk-in closet and a lush private bath

TO ORDER BLUEPRINTS USE THE FORM ON PAGE 290 OR CALL TOLL-FREE **1-800-DREAM HOME** (373-2646)

LOWE'S

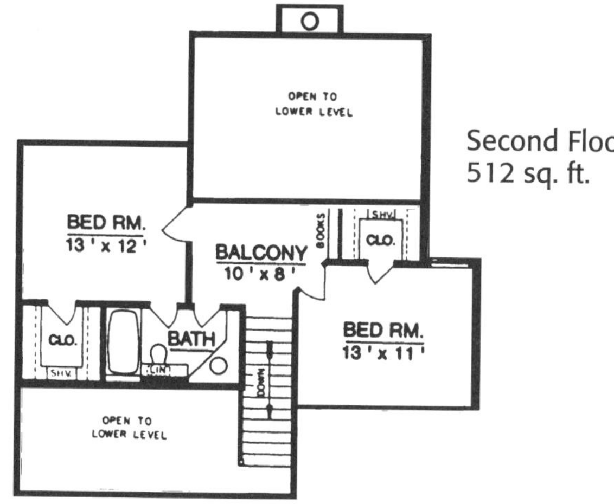
OPEN TO LOWER LEVEL
BED RM.
13' x 12'
BALCONY
10' x 8'
BOOKS
SHV
CLO.
CLO.
BATH
LIN
SHV.
BED RM.
13' x 11'
DOWN
OPEN TO LOWER LEVEL

Second Floor
512 sq. ft.

Plan #527-BF-1708

Price Code B

Total Living Area: 1,717 Sq. Ft.

Home has 3 bedrooms, 2 baths, 2-car garage and slab or crawl space foundation, please specify when ordering.

Special features

- Energy efficient 2" x 6" exterior walls
- Kitchen has eat-in bar which overlooks gallery and living areas
- Master suite has sloped ceiling and two walk-in closets
- Covered porch connects living room to the outdoors

First Floor
1,205 sq. ft.

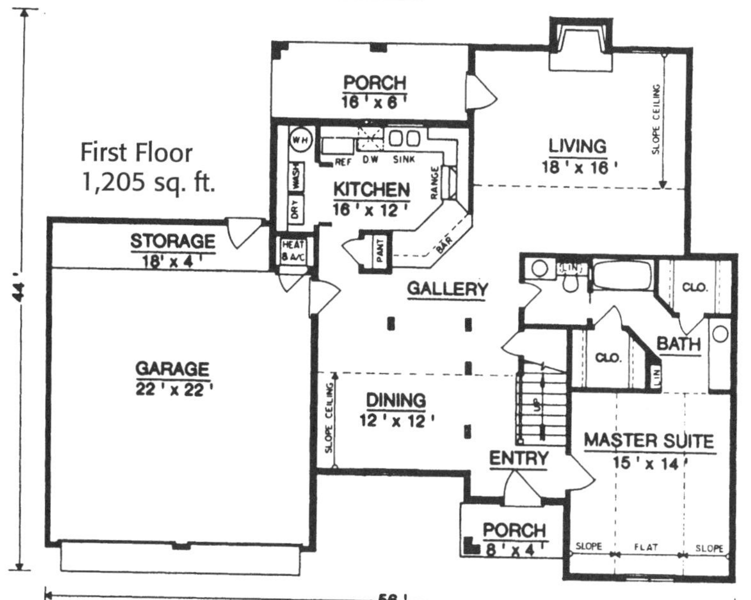
PORCH
16' x 6'
WH
REF
DW
SINK
WASH
DRY
KITCHEN
16' x 12'
RANGE
PANT
BAR
HEAT & A/C
STORAGE
18' x 4'
LIVING
18' x 16'
SLOPE CEILING
GALLERY
CLO.
LIN
BATH
CLO.
GARAGE
22' x 22'
DINING
12' x 12'
SLOPE CEILING
UP
MASTER SUITE
15' x 14'
ENTRY
PORCH
8' x 4'
SLOPE
FLAT
SLOPE
44'
56'

Bayed Breakfast Room

Plan #527-FB1119

Price Code C

Total Living Area: 1,915 Sq. Ft.

Home has 4 bedrooms, 3 baths, 2-car garage and basement or crawl space foundation, please specify when ordering.

Special features

- Plan features unique in-law suite with private bath and walk-in closet
- Master suite has cheerful sitting room and a private bath
- Spacious laundry area conveniently located near kitchen

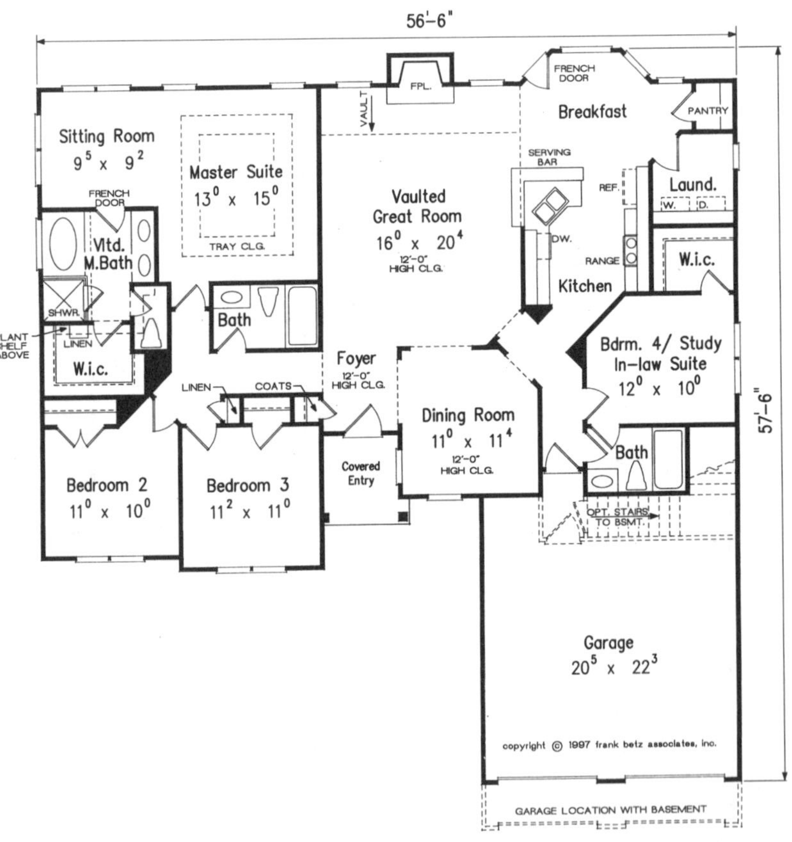
56'-6"
57'-6"
FRENCH DOOR
Breakfast
PANTRY
FPL.
VAULT
Sitting Room
9⁵ x 9²
Master Suite
13⁰ x 15⁰
TRAY CLG.
FRENCH DOOR
Vltd. M.Bath
SHWR.
LINEN
W.i.c.
PLANT SHELF ABOVE
Vaulted Great Room
16⁰ x 20⁴
12'-0" HIGH CLG.
SERVING BAR
REF.
DW.
RANGE
Kitchen
Laund.
W. D.
W.i.c.
Bath
Foyer
12'-0" HIGH CLG.
LINEN
COATS
Dining Room
11⁰ x 11⁴
12'-0" HIGH CLG.
Bdrm. 4/ Study
In-law Suite
12⁰ x 10⁰
Bath
OPT. STAIRS TO BSMT.
Covered Entry
Bedroom 2
11⁰ x 10⁰
Bedroom 3
11² x 11⁰
Garage
20⁵ x 22³
copyright © 1997 frank betz associates, inc.
GARAGE LOCATION WITH BASEMENT

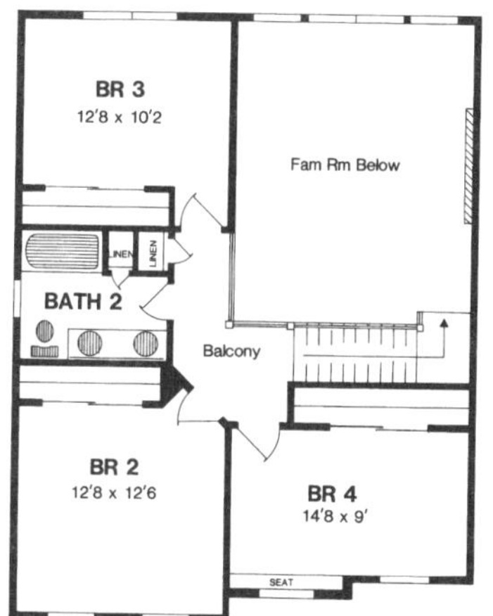
BR 3
12'8 x 10'2
Fam Rm Below
LINEN
LINEN
BATH 2
Balcony
BR 2
12'8 x 12'6
BR 4
14'8 x 9'
SEAT

Second Floor
570 sq. ft.

Plan #527-JFD-20-2018-1

Price Code C

Total Living Area: 2,018 Sq. Ft.

Home has 4 bedrooms, 2 1/2 baths, 2-car garage and basement foundation.

Special features

- Family room situated near dining area and kitchen create a convenient layout
- First floor master suite features private bath with step-up tub and bay window
- Laundry area located on the first floor

First Floor
1,448 sq. ft.

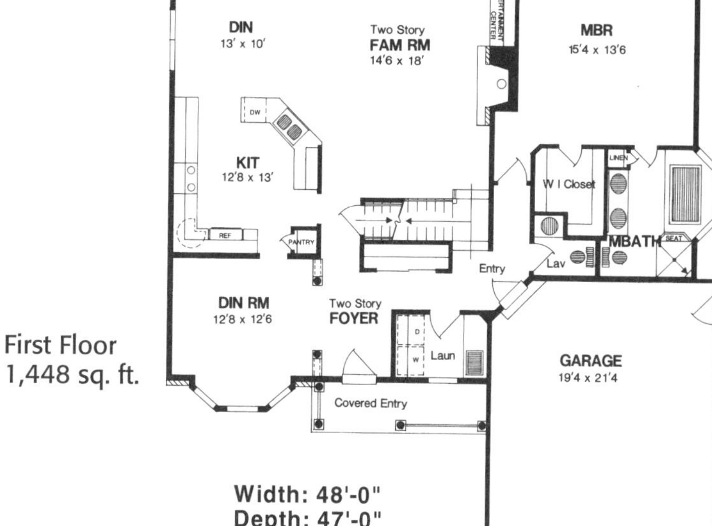
DIN
13' x 10'
Two Story
FAM RM
14'6 x 18'
ENTERTAINMENT CENTER
MBR
15'4 x 13'6
KIT
12'8 x 13'
DW
REF
PANTRY
W I Closet
LINEN
MBATH
SEAT
Lav
Entry
DIN RM
12'8 x 12'6
Two Story
FOYER
Laun
GARAGE
19'4 x 21'4
Covered Entry

Width: 48'-0"
Depth: 47'-0"

MARIBEL MAXON

Plan #527-LBD-19-15A

Price Code C

Total Living Area: 1,955 Sq. Ft.

Home has 3 bedrooms, 2 baths, 2-car side entry garage and crawl space or slab foundation, please specify when ordering.

Special features

- Porch adds outdoor area to this design
- Dining and great rooms visible from foyer through a series of elegant archways
- Kitchen overlooks great room and breakfast room

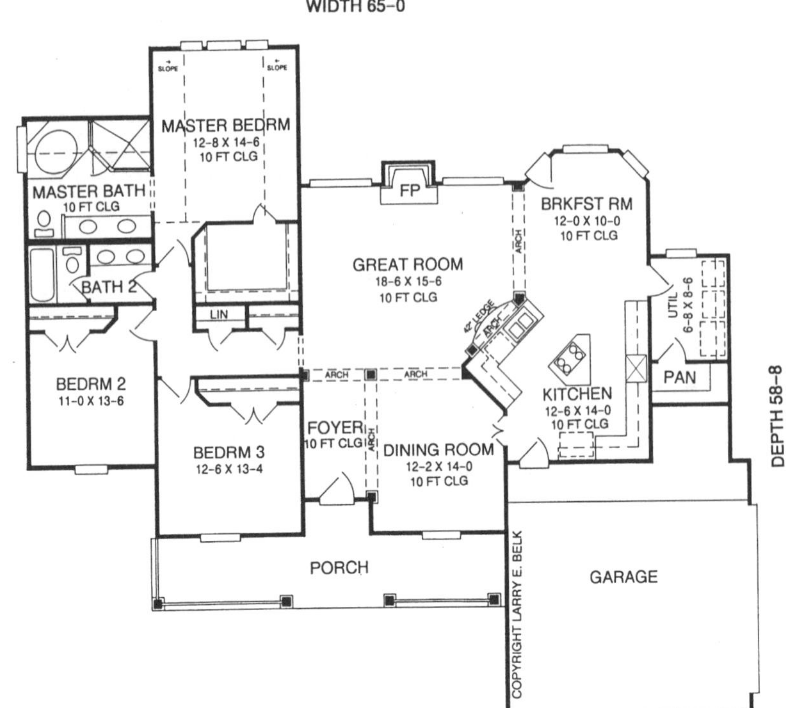
WIDTH 65–0
DEPTH 58–8
SLOPE
SLOPE
MASTER BEDRM
12–8 X 14–6
10 FT CLG
MASTER BATH
10 FT CLG
BATH 2
LIN
FP
GREAT ROOM
18–6 X 15–6
10 FT CLG
BRKFST RM
12–0 X 10–0
10 FT CLG
ARCH
UTIL
6–8 X 8–6
PAN
KITCHEN
12–6 X 14–0
10 FT CLG
BEDRM 2
11–0 X 13–6
BEDRM 3
12–6 X 13–4
FOYER
10 FT CLG
DINING ROOM
12–2 X 14–0
10 FT CLG
PORCH
GARAGE
COPYRIGHT LARRY E. BELK

Appealing Touches Abound

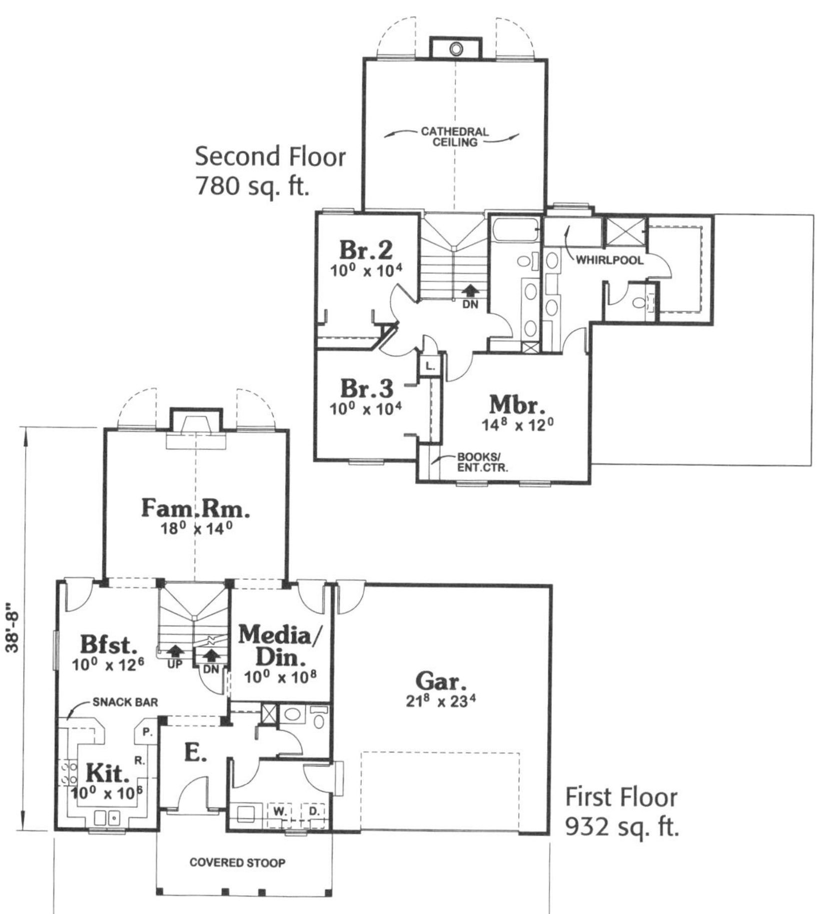
Second Floor
780 sq. ft.
CATHEDRAL CEILING
Br.2
10⁰ x 10⁴
DN
WHIRLPOOL
Br.3
10⁰ x 10⁴
L.
Mbr.
14⁸ x 12⁰
BOOKS/ ENT.CTR.
Fam.Rm.
18⁰ x 14⁰
38'-8"
Bfst.
10⁰ x 12⁶
UP
DN
Media/ Din.
10⁰ x 10⁸
SNACK BAR
Gar.
21⁸ x 23⁴
P.
R.
Kit.
10⁰ x 10⁶
E.
W.
D.
COVERED STOOP
First Floor
932 sq. ft.
50'-0"
© design basics inc.

Plan #527-DBI-4642

Price Code B

Total Living Area: 1,712 Sq. Ft.

Home has 3 bedrooms, 2 1/2 baths, 2-car garage and basement foundation.

Special features

- Cathedral ceiling in family room adds drama and spaciousness
- Roomy utility area
- Master bedroom has a private bath, walk-in closet and a whirlpool tub
- Efficient kitchen with snack bar

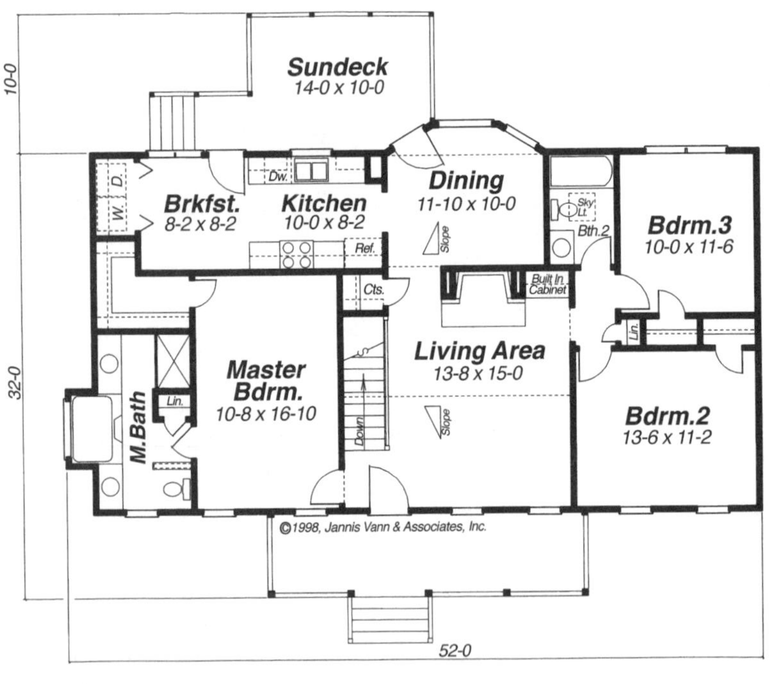
Sundeck
14-0 x 10-0
10-0
Dining
11-10 x 10-0
Brkfst.
8-2 x 8-2
Kitchen
10-0 x 8-2
Dw.
Ref.
W. D.
Sky Lt.
Bth.2
Bdrm.3
10-0 x 11-6
Cts.
Built In Cabinet
Living Area
13-8 x 15-0
Slope
Lin.
Master
Bdrm.
10-8 x 16-10
M.Bath
Lin.
Down
Bdrm.2
13-6 x 11-2
32-0
©1998, Jannis Vann & Associates, Inc.
52-0

Plan #527-JV-1325-B

Price Code A

Total Living Area: 1,325 Sq. Ft.

Home has 3 bedrooms, 2 baths, 2-car drive under garage and basement foundation.

Special features

- Sloped ceilings and a fireplace in living/dining area creates a cozy feeling
- Formal dining and breakfast areas have an efficiently designed kitchen between them
- Master bedroom has walk-in closet with luxurious private bath

TO ORDER BLUEPRINTS USE THE FORM ON PAGE 290 OR CALL TOLL-FREE **1-800-DREAM HOME** (373-2646)

Arched Accents Enhance Facade

LOWE'S

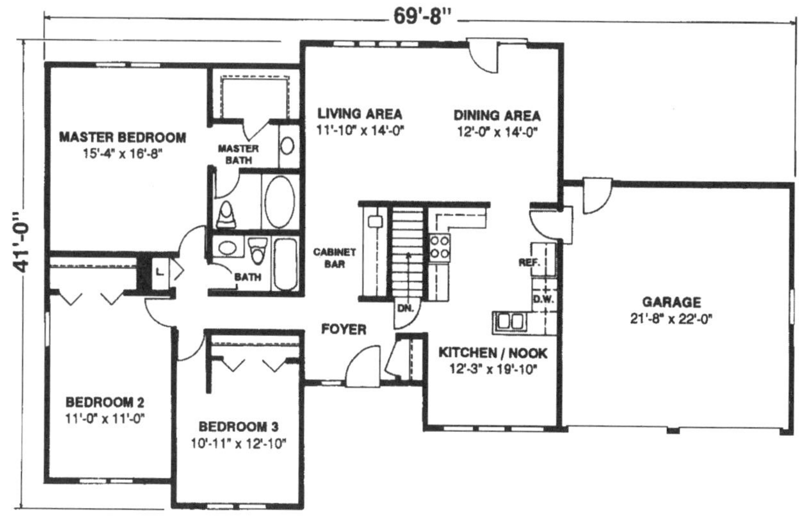

69'-8"
41'-0"
MASTER BEDROOM
15'-4" x 16'-8"
MASTER BATH
LIVING AREA
11'-10" x 14'-0"
DINING AREA
12'-0" x 14'-0"
CABINET BAR
REF.
D.W.
DN.
BATH
L
FOYER
KITCHEN / NOOK
12'-3" x 19'-10"
GARAGE
21'-8" x 22'-0"
BEDROOM 2
11'-0" x 11'-0"
BEDROOM 3
10'-11" x 12'-10"

Plan #527-1310

Price Code B

Total Living Area: 1,704 Sq. Ft.

Home has 3 bedrooms, 2 baths, 2-car garage and basement foundation.

Special features

- Open living and dining areas combine for added spaciousness
- Master bedroom with private bath and walk-in closet
- Sunny kitchen with nook
- Cheerful breakfast room extends onto covered private porch

Appealing Master Suite

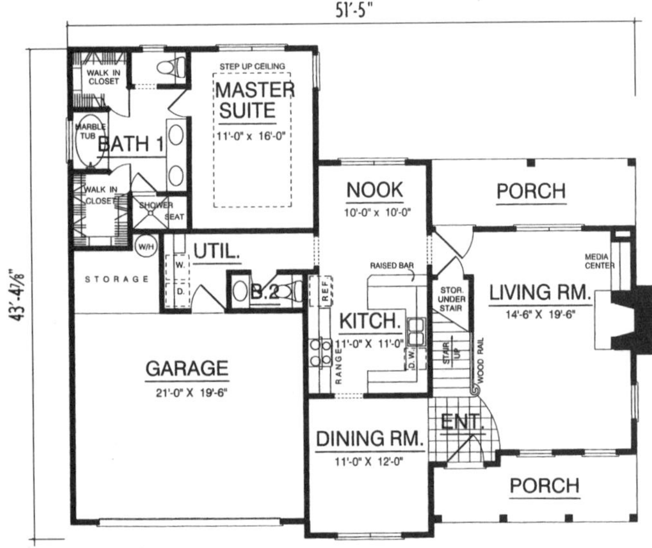
51'-5"
43'-4 1/8"
WALK IN CLOSET
STEP UP CEILING
MASTER SUITE
11'-0" x 16'-0"
MARBLE TUB
BATH 1
WALK IN CLOSET
SHOWER
SEAT
W/H
UTIL.
W.
D.
STORAGE
B.2
REF.
NOOK
10'-0" x 10'-0"
RAISED BAR
KITCH.
11'-0" X 11'-0"
RANGE
D.W.
PORCH
STOR. UNDER STAIR
STAIR UP
WOOD RAIL
MEDIA CENTER
LIVING RM.
14'-6" X 19'-6"
GARAGE
21'-0" X 19'-6"
DINING RM.
11'-0" X 12'-0"
ENT.
PORCH

First Floor
1,235 sq. ft.

Plan #527-RDD-1896-9

Price Code C

Total Living Area: 1,896 Sq. Ft.

Home has 4 bedrooms, 2 1/2 baths, 2-car garage and basement, crawl space or slab foundation, please specify when ordering.

Special features

- Living room has lots of windows, a media center and a fireplace
- Centrally located kitchen with breakfast nook
- Extra storage in garage
- Covered porched in front and rear of home
- Optional balcony on second floor

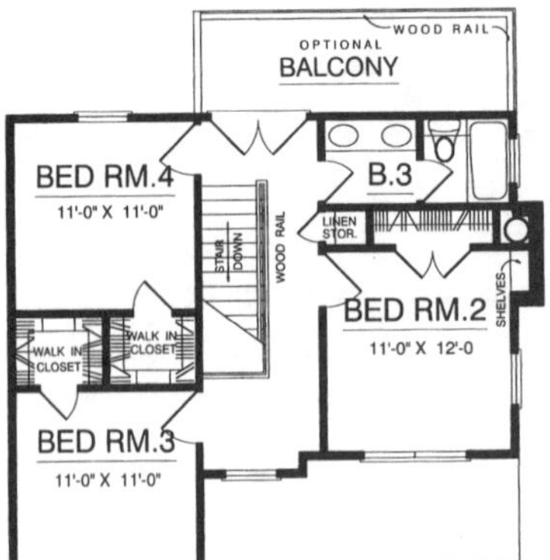

WOOD RAIL
OPTIONAL BALCONY
BED RM.4
11'-0" X 11'-0"
B.3
LINEN STOR.
STAIR DOWN
WOOD RAIL
BED RM.2
11'-0" X 12-0
SHELVES
WALK IN CLOSET
WALK IN CLOSET
BED RM.3
11'-0" X 11'-0"

Second Floor
661 sq. ft.

TO ORDER BLUEPRINTS USE THE FORM ON PAGE 290 OR CALL TOLL-FREE **1-800-DREAM HOME** (373-2646)

LOWE'S

Plan #527-AMD-2175

Price Code A

Total Living Area: 1,464 Sq. Ft.

Home has 3 bedrooms, 2 1/2 baths, 2-car garage and crawl space foundation.

Special features

- Contemporary styled home has breathtaking two-story foyer and lovely open staircase
- Efficiently designed U-shaped kitchen
- Elegant great room has a cozy fireplace

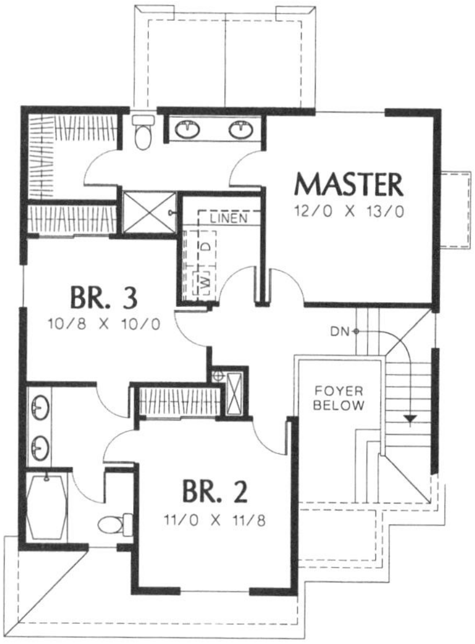

Second Floor
809 sq. ft.

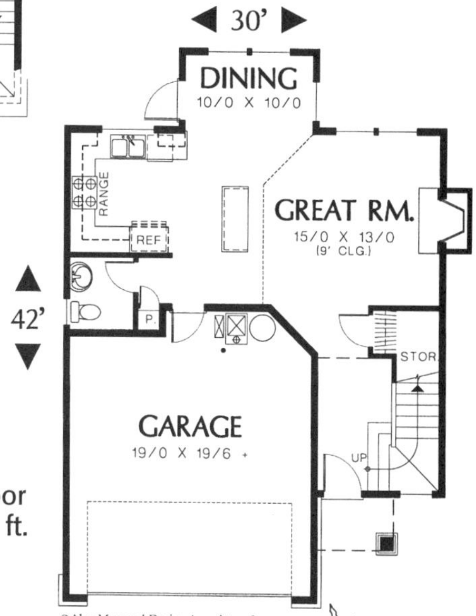

MASTER 12/0 X 13/0

LINEN

W D

BR. 3 10/8 X 10/0

DN

FOYER BELOW

BR. 2 11/0 X 11/8

30'

DINING 10/0 X 10/0

RANGE

REF

GREAT RM. 15/0 X 13/0 (9' CLG.)

42'

P

STOR.

GARAGE 19/0 X 19/6 +

UP

First Floor
655 sq. ft.

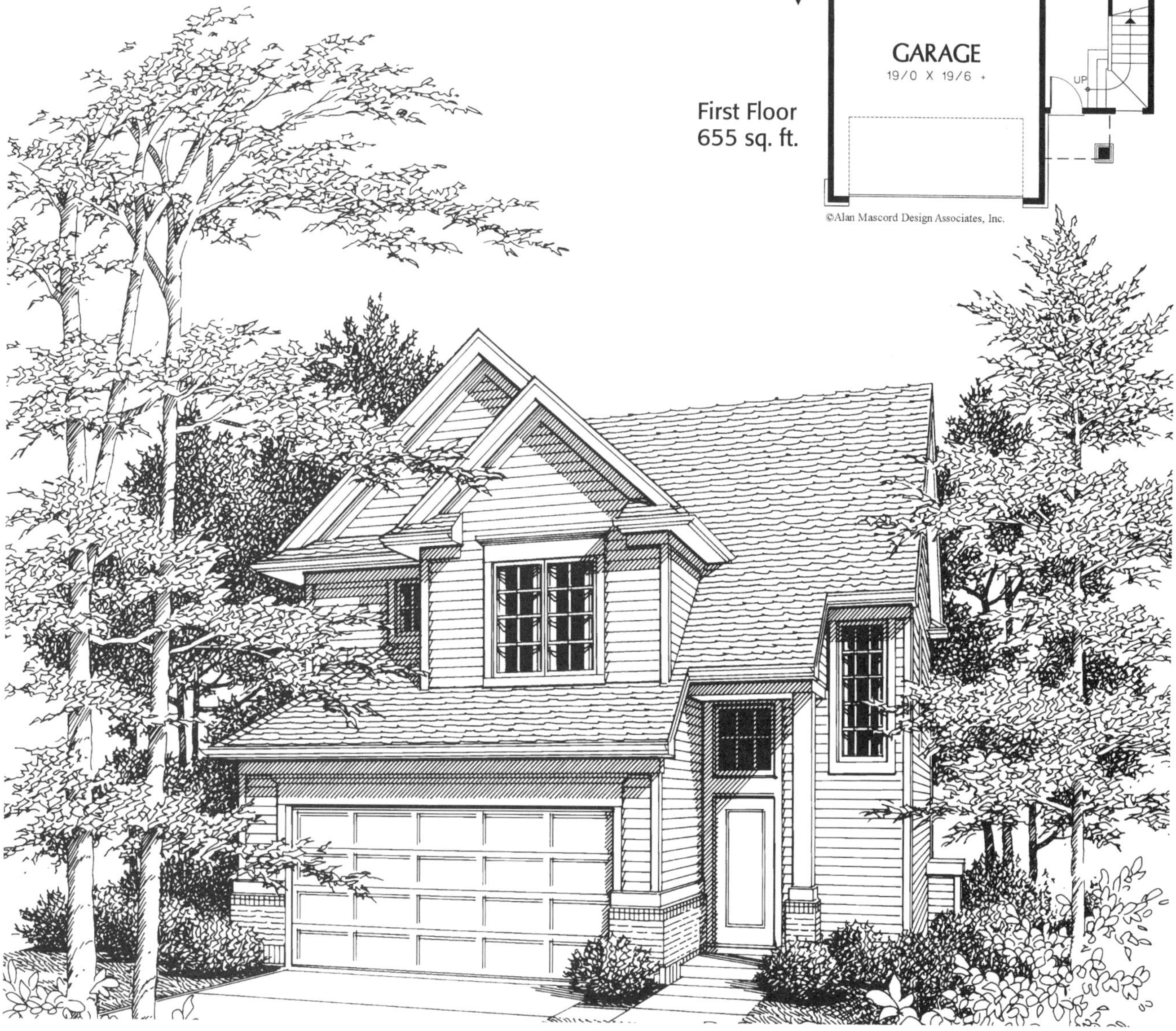

Simple Rooflines And Inviting Porch

44'8"
54'6"
FAMILY RM
VAULTED CLG
12^4 x 12^0
BAY WINDOW
MASTER BEDRM
VAULTED CLG
13^0 x 12^0
MASTER BATH
PLANT SHELF ABOVE
BEDRM
VAULTED CLG
10^0 x 10^8
SNACK BAR
DW
PANTRY
D
W
LAUNDRY
COVERED PORCH
KIT
12^4 x 10^0
SINK
R
REFG
LINEN
BEDRM
VAULTED CLG
10^0 x 10^8
BATH
DINING
BAY WINDOW
LIVING RM
VAULTED CLG
13^{10} x 19^0
PLANT SHELF ABOVE
F.A.U.
W.H.
CURB
ENTRY
HALF WALL
COVERED PORCH
GARAGE
21^4 x 23^8

Plan #527-HP-C460

Price Code A

Total Living Area: 1,389 Sq. Ft.

Home has 3 bedrooms, 2 baths, 2-car garage and slab foundation.

Special features

- Formal living room has warming fireplace and a delightful bay window
- U-shaped kitchen shares a snack bar with the bayed family room
- Lovely master suite has its own private bath

TO ORDER BLUEPRINTS USE THE FORM ON PAGE 290 OR CALL TOLL-FREE **1-800-DREAM HOME** (373-2646)

LOWE'S

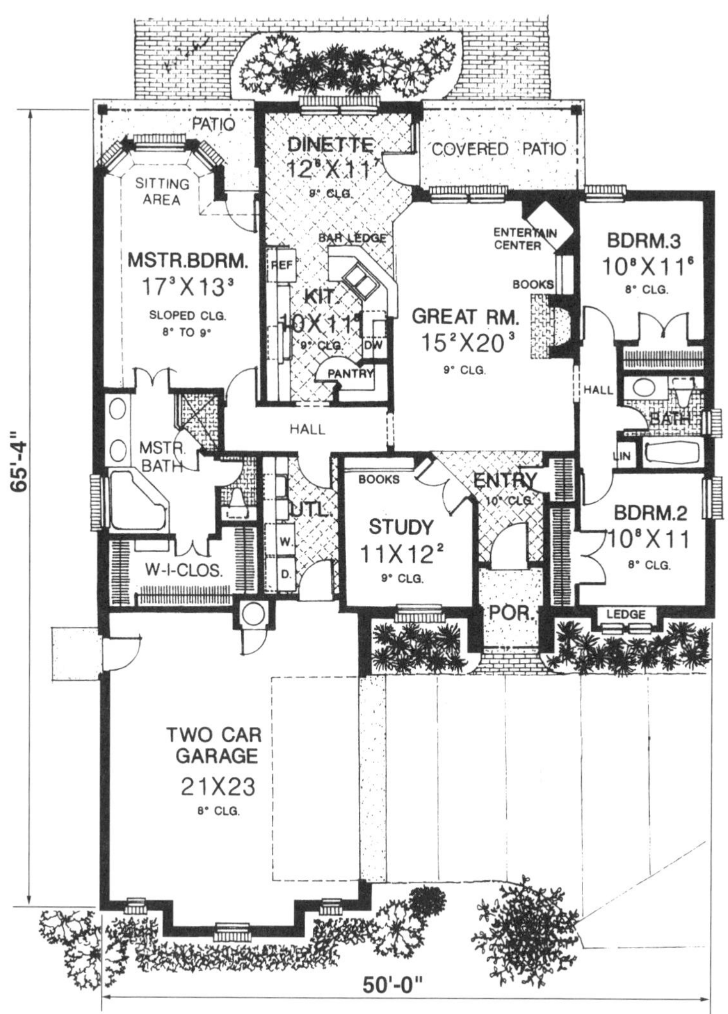
PATIO
DINETTE
12^8X11^7
9' CLG.
COVERED PATIO
SITTING AREA
MSTR.BDRM.
17^3X13^3
SLOPED CLG.
8' TO 9'
BAR LEDGE
REF
KIT.
10X11^9
9' CLG.
DW
PANTRY
ENTERTAIN CENTER
BOOKS
GREAT RM.
15^2X20^3
9' CLG.
BDRM.3
10^8X11^6
8' CLG.
HALL
BATH
LIN
MSTR. BATH
UTL.
W.
D.
W-I-CLOS.
BOOKS
STUDY
11X12^2
9' CLG.
ENTRY
10' CLG.
POR.
BDRM.2
10^8X11
8' CLG.
LEDGE
TWO CAR GARAGE
21X23
8' CLG.
65'-4"
50'-0"

Plan #527-FDG-9035

Price Code B

Total Living Area: 1,760 Sq. Ft.

Home has 3 bedrooms, 2 baths, 2-car side entry garage and slab foundation.

Special features

- Stone and brick exterior has old world charm
- Master suite includes a sitting area and is situated away from other bedrooms for privacy
- Kitchen and dinette access the outdoors
- Great room includes fireplace, built-in bookshelves and entertainment center

49'-9"
48'-6"
PORCH
W.I.C.
W.I.C.
B.1
SHR.
NOOK
9'-0" x 10'-0"
KIT.
9' x 10'
LIVING RM.
12'-0" x 15'-0"
BED RM.2
11'-0" X 9'-6"
MASTER SUITE
16'-0" x 11'-0"
LIN.
B.2
W/H
SHLVS.
UTIL.
STORAGE
PANT.
DINING
10'-0" x 12'-0"
ENT.
BED RM.3
11'-0" X 9'-6"
PORCH
GARAGE
20'-0" x 20'-0"

Plan #527-RDD-1374-9

Price Code A

Total Living Area: 1,374 Sq. Ft.

Home has 3 bedrooms, 2 baths, 2-car garage and slab or crawl space foundation, please specify when ordering.

Special features

- Separated master suite maintains privacy
- Well-designed kitchen with adjacent breakfast nook
- Spacious living room has fireplace
- Garage has extra storage space

TO ORDER BLUEPRINTS USE THE FORM ON PAGE 290 OR CALL TOLL-FREE **1-800-DREAM HOME** (373-2646)

Dormers Add Charm

LOWE'S

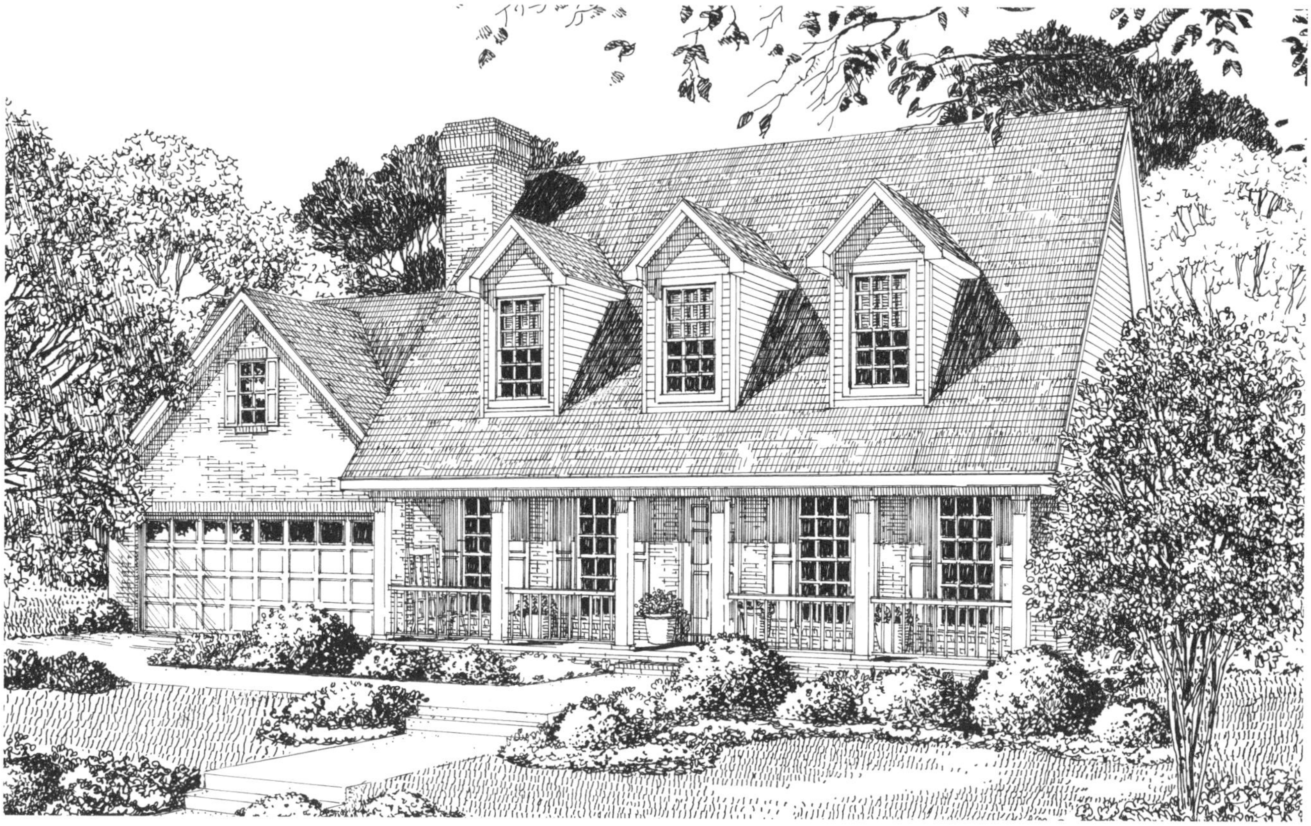

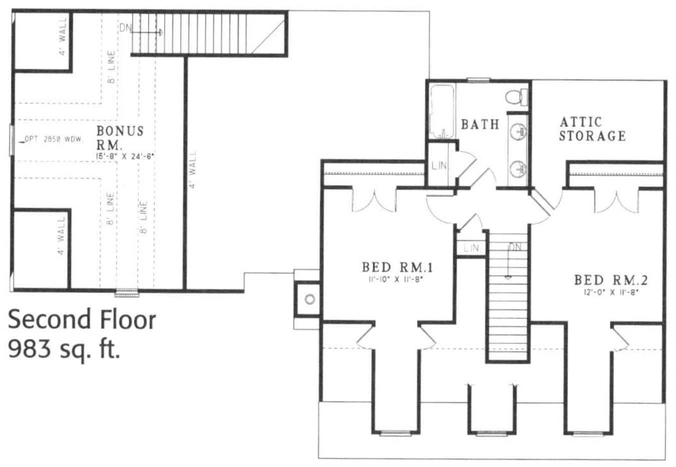
DN
4' WALL
8' LINE
OPT. 2858 WDW
BONUS RM.
15'-8" X 24'-6"
4' WALL
BATH
LIN
ATTIC STORAGE
BED RM.1
11'-10" X 11'-8"
LIN
DN
BED RM.2
12'-0" X 11'-8"

Second Floor
983 sq. ft.

60' 2"
STORAGE
TO BONUS ABOVE
UP
1/2 BATH
DINING
9'-2" X 13'-2"
DW
KITCHEN
10'-4" X 10'-2"
REF
WHP TUB
M.B.
GARAGE
21'-0" X 24'-6"
HVAC
PAN
W
D
HOBBY/LAU.
GREAT RM.
14'-10" X 17'-8"
ZERO CLR FIREPLACE
UP
MASTER SUITE
12'-0" X 13'-10"
COVERED PORCH
31'-8" X 5'-0"
39' 10"

First Floor
1,124 sq. ft.

Plan #527-NDG-142

Price Code C

Total Living Area: 2,107 Sq. Ft.

Home has 3 bedrooms, 2 1/2 baths, 2-car garage and basement, crawl space or slab foundation, please specify when ordering.

Special features

- Kitchen has pantry and adjacent dining area
- Master bedroom with bath and large walk-in closet
- Second floor bedrooms have attic storage
- Rear stairs open into bonus room above garage

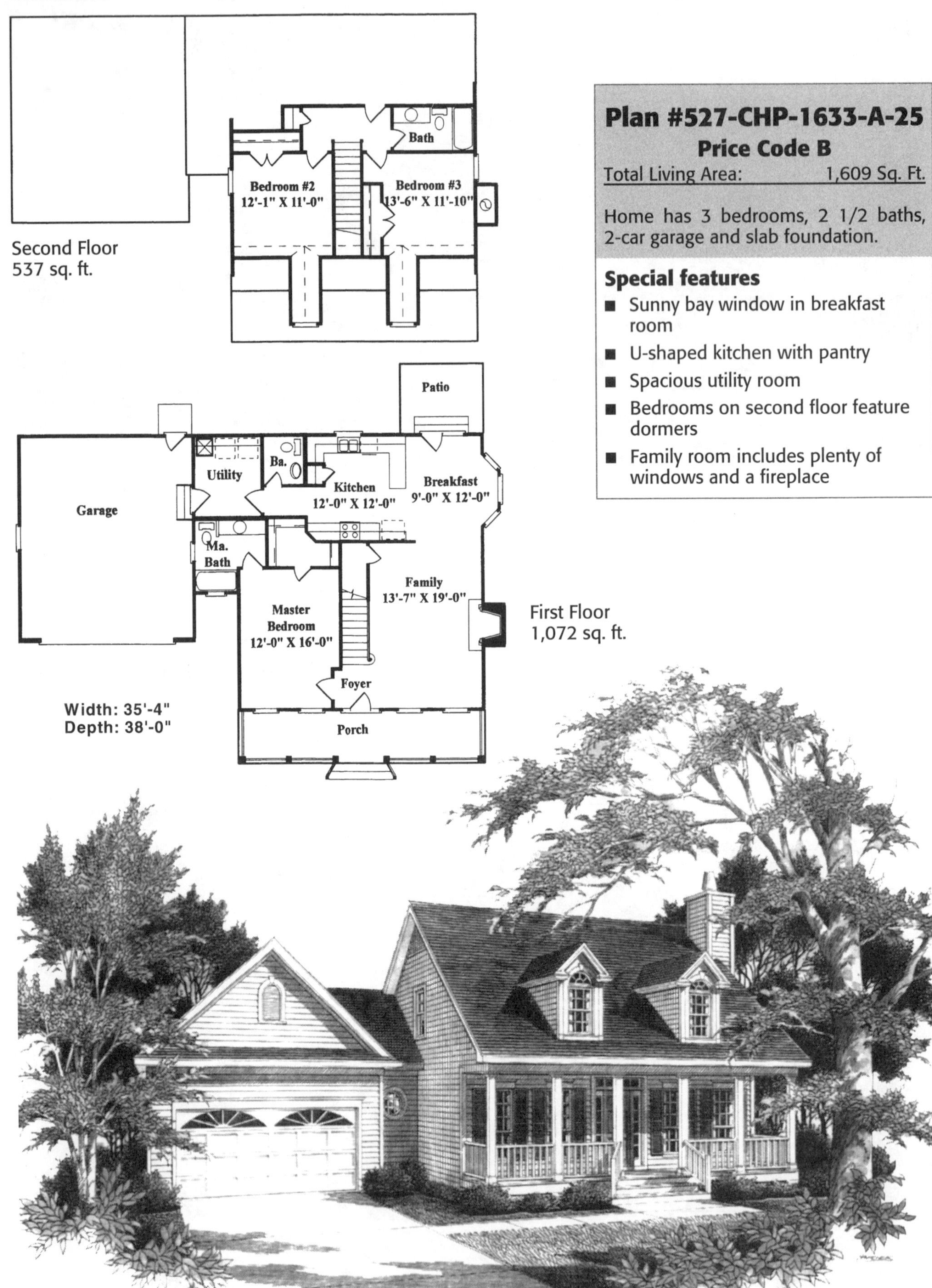
Bath
Bedroom #2
12'-1" X 11'-0"
Bedroom #3
13'-6" X 11'-10"
Second Floor
537 sq. ft.
Patio
Utility
Ba.
Kitchen
12'-0" X 12'-0"
Breakfast
9'-0" X 12'-0"
Garage
Ma. Bath
Family
13'-7" X 19'-0"
Master Bedroom
12'-0" X 16'-0"
First Floor
1,072 sq. ft.
Foyer
Porch
Width: 35'-4"
Depth: 38'-0"

Plan #527-CHP-1633-A-25

Price Code B

Total Living Area: 1,609 Sq. Ft.

Home has 3 bedrooms, 2 1/2 baths, 2-car garage and slab foundation.

Special features

- Sunny bay window in breakfast room
- U-shaped kitchen with pantry
- Spacious utility room
- Bedrooms on second floor feature dormers
- Family room includes plenty of windows and a fireplace

TO ORDER BLUEPRINTS USE THE FORM ON PAGE 290 OR CALL TOLL-FREE **1-800-DREAM HOME** (373-2646)

Cozy Cottage Feeling

LOWE'S

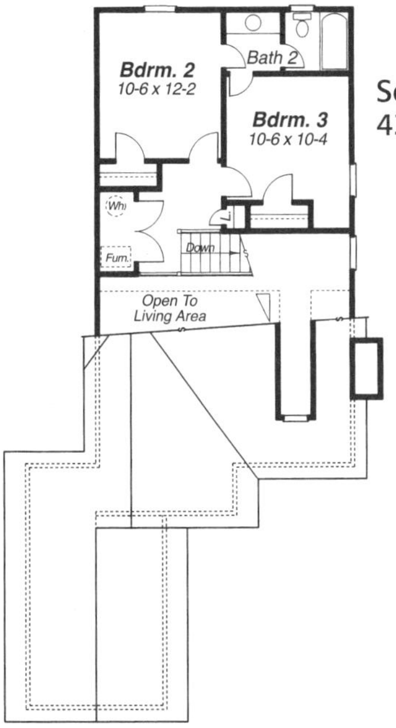

Second Floor
436 sq. ft.

First Floor
861 sq. ft.

Plan #527-JV-1297-A

Price Code A

Total Living Area: 1,297 Sq. Ft.

Home has 3 bedrooms, 2 1/2 baths, 1-car garage and slab foundation.

Special features

- Dramatic raised ceiling with dormers adds spacious feeling
- Master bedroom has large storage closet
- Two secondary bedrooms share compartmentalized bath and balcony

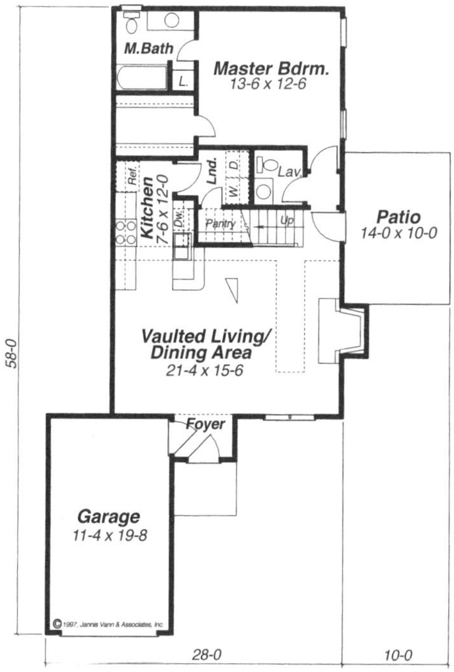

LOWE'S

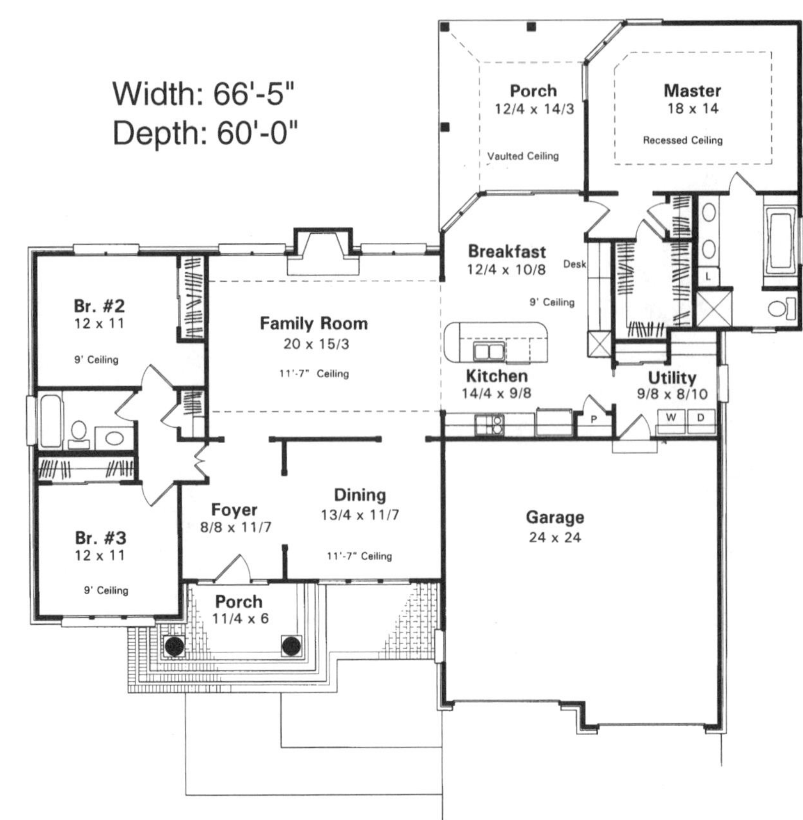
Width: 66'-5"
Depth: 60'-0"
Porch
12/4 x 14/3
Vaulted Ceiling
Master
18 x 14
Recessed Ceiling
Breakfast
12/4 x 10/8
Desk
9' Ceiling
Br. #2
12 x 11
9' Ceiling
Family Room
20 x 15/3
11'-7" Ceiling
Kitchen
14/4 x 9/8
Utility
9/8 x 8/10
W
D
P
L
Foyer
8/8 x 11/7
Dining
13/4 x 11/7
11'-7" Ceiling
Garage
24 x 24
Br. #3
12 x 11
9' Ceiling
Porch
11/4 x 6

Plan #527-GM-1849

Price Code C

Total Living Area: 1,849 Sq. Ft.

Home has 3 bedrooms, 2 baths, 2-car garage and crawl space or slab foundation, please specify when ordering.

Special features

- Open floor plan creates airy feeling
- Kitchen/breakfast area has center island, pantry and built-in desk
- Master bedroom has private entrance off breakfast area and view of vaulted porch

 TO ORDER BLUEPRINTS USE THE FORM ON PAGE 290 OR CALL TOLL-FREE **1-800-DREAM HOME** (373-2646)

LOWE'S

COPYRIGHT LARRY E. BELK

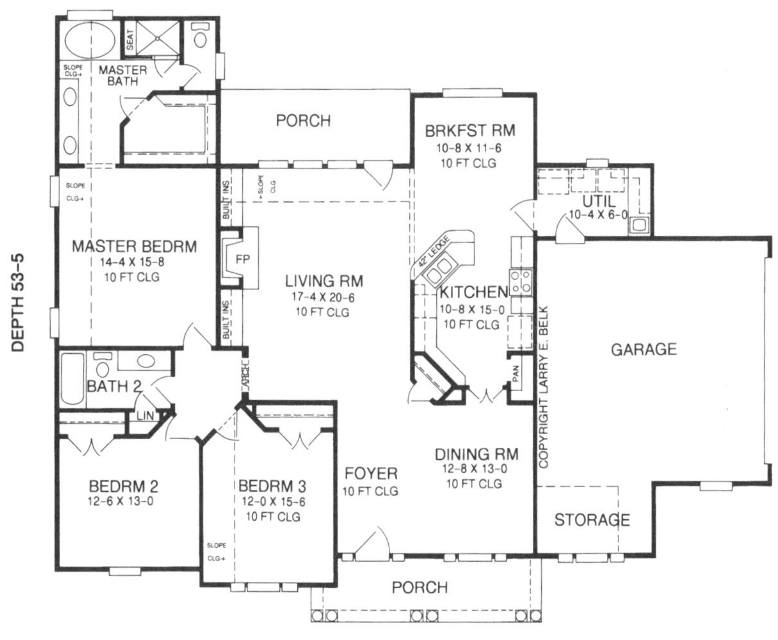
MASTER BATH
SEAT
SLOPE CLG
PORCH
BRKFST RM
10-8 X 11-6
10 FT CLG
UTIL
10-4 X 6-0
MASTER BEDRM
14-4 X 15-8
10 FT CLG
BUILT INS
FP
LIVING RM
17-4 X 20-6
10 FT CLG
KITCHEN
10-8 X 15-0
10 FT CLG
PAN
GARAGE
COPYRIGHT LARRY E. BELK
DEPTH 53-5
BATH 2
LIN
BEDRM 2
12-6 X 13-0
BEDRM 3
12-0 X 15-6
10 FT CLG
FOYER
10 FT CLG
DINING RM
12-8 X 13-0
10 FT CLG
STORAGE
PORCH
WIDTH 65-10

Plan #527-LBD-19-23A

Price Code C

Total Living Area: 1,932 Sq. Ft.

Home has 3 bedrooms, 2 baths, 2-car side entry garage and crawl space or slab foundation, please specify when ordering.

Special features

- Double arches form entrance to this elegantly styled home
- Two palladian windows add distinction to facade
- Kitchen has angled eating bar opening to the breakfast and living rooms

LOWE'S

Gabled Facade For A Lasting Impression

Plan #527-1266

Price Code C

Total Living Area: 2,086 Sq. Ft.

Home has 3 bedrooms, 2 baths, 2-car garage and partial basement/crawl space foundation.

Special features

- An angled foyer leads to vaulted living room with sunken floor
- Dining room, activity room, nook and kitchen all have vaulted ceilings
- Skillfully designed kitchen features an angled island with breakfast bar
- Master bedroom is state-of-the-art with luxury bath, giant walk-in closet and deck area for hot tub

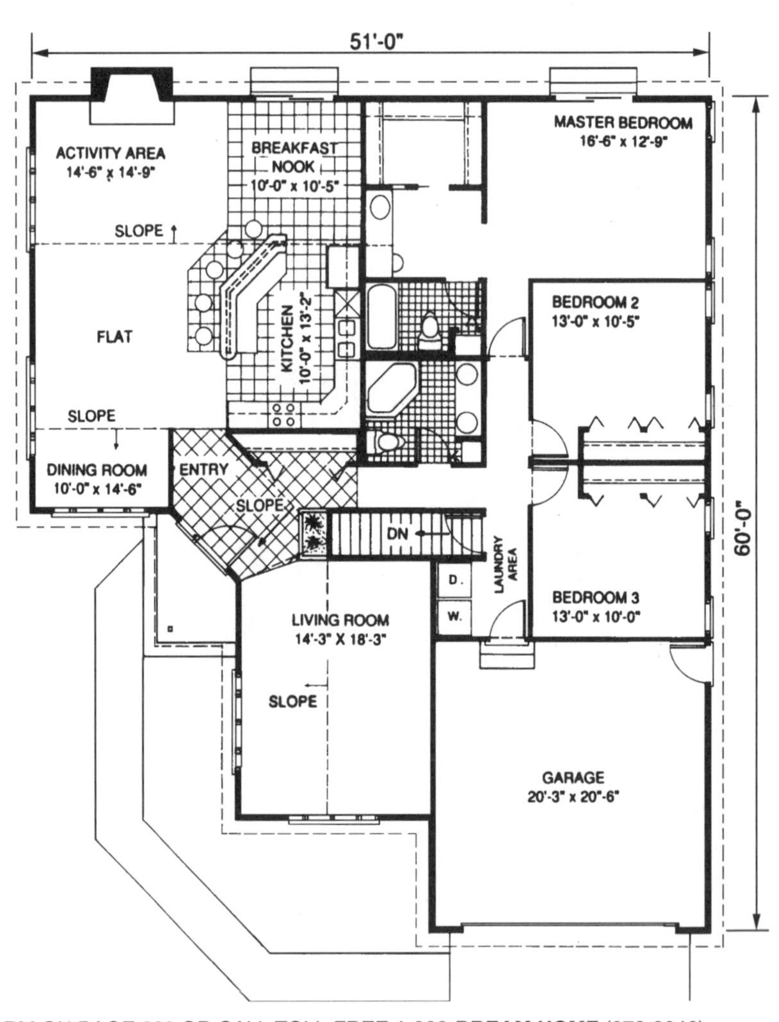
51'-0"
60'-0"
ACTIVITY AREA
14'-6" x 14'-9"
BREAKFAST NOOK
10'-0" x 10'-5"
MASTER BEDROOM
16'-6" x 12'-9"
SLOPE
FLAT
KITCHEN
10'-0" x 13'-2"
BEDROOM 2
13'-0" x 10'-5"
SLOPE
DINING ROOM
10'-0" x 14'-6"
ENTRY
SLOPE
DN
LAUNDRY AREA
D.
W.
BEDROOM 3
13'-0" x 10'-0"
LIVING ROOM
14'-3" X 18'-3"
SLOPE
GARAGE
20'-3" x 20'-6"

 TO ORDER BLUEPRINTS USE THE FORM ON PAGE 290 OR CALL TOLL-FREE **1-800-DREAM HOME** (373-2646)

Br. 2
12⁷ x 11⁴
OPEN TO GREAT ROOM
DN
UNFINISHED
Bonus
15⁰ x 23⁰
Br. 3
11⁴ x 11⁴
10'-0" CEILING
Second Floor
453 sq. ft.
TRANSOMS
Grt. rm.
15⁴ x 19⁸
13'-0" CEILING
Kit.
13⁴ x 11³
SNACK BAR
Bfst.
11⁰ x 11³
DN
UP
Din.
11⁴ x 11⁸
E.
Gar.
20⁸ x 23⁰
Mbr.
13⁰ x 16⁰
10'-0" CLG.
COVERED PORCH
47' - 4"
52' - 0"
First Floor
1,405 sq. ft.
© design basics inc.

Plan #527-DBI-8077

Price Code C

Total Living Area: 1,858 Sq. Ft.

Home has 3 bedrooms, 2 1/2 baths, 2-car garage and basement foundation.

Special features

- Transom windows in great room add a light and airy feeling
- U-shaped kitchen has lots of counter space
- Second floor includes large unfinished bonus room ideal for playroom or home office

LOWE'S

Plan #527-T-110

Price Code C

Total Living Area: 1,973 Sq. Ft.

Home has 3 bedrooms, 2 1/2 baths, 2-car garage and partial basement/crawl space foundation.

Special features

- This country colonial offers grand-sized living room with views to front and rear of home
- Living room features cozy fireplace and accesses master suite complete with walk-in closet and compartmented bath
- Laundry room with half bath and coat closet convenient to garage
- Second floor comprised of two large bedrooms and a full bath

Second Floor
636 sq. ft.

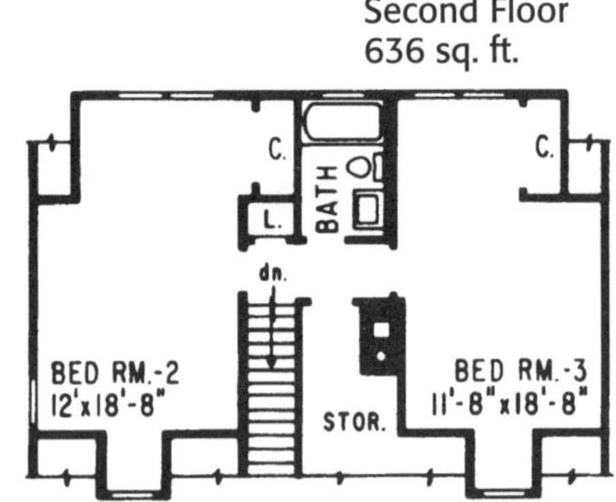
C.
BATH
L.
C.
dn.
BED RM.-2
12'x18'-8"
STOR.
BED RM.-3
11'-8"x18'-8"

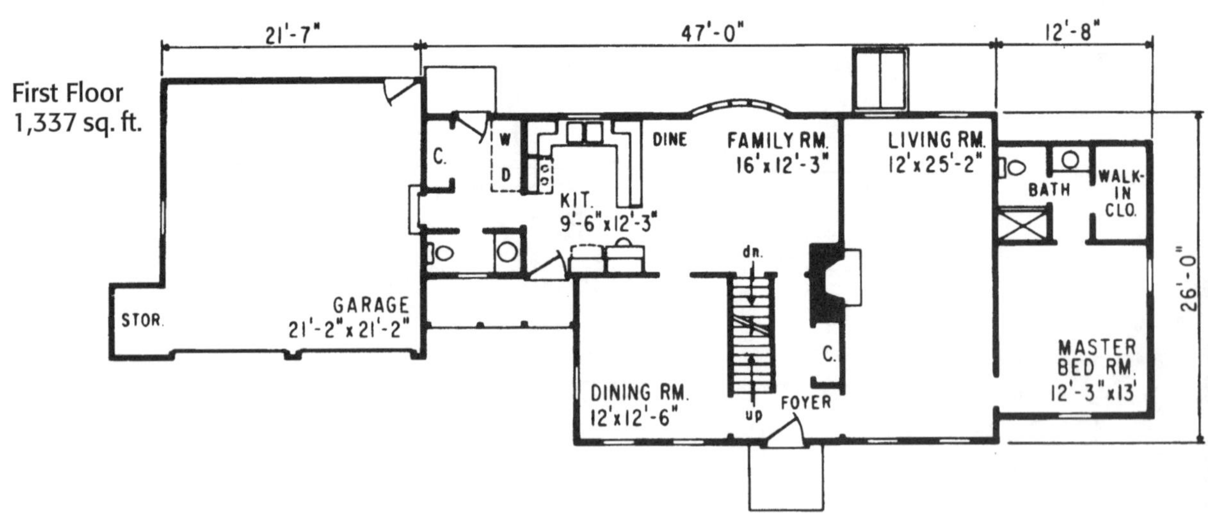
First Floor
1,337 sq. ft.
21'-7"
47'-0"
12'-8"
C.
W
D
DINE
FAMILY RM.
16'x12'-3"
LIVING RM.
12'x25'-2"
BATH
WALK-IN CLO.
KIT.
9'-6"x12'-3"
dn.
26'-0"
STOR.
GARAGE
21'-2"x21'-2"
C.
MASTER BED RM.
12'-3"x13'
DINING RM.
12'x12'-6"
up
FOYER

TO ORDER BLUEPRINTS USE THE FORM ON PAGE 290 OR CALL TOLL-FREE **1-800-DREAM HOME** (373-2646)

Bonus Room Above Garage

LOWE'S

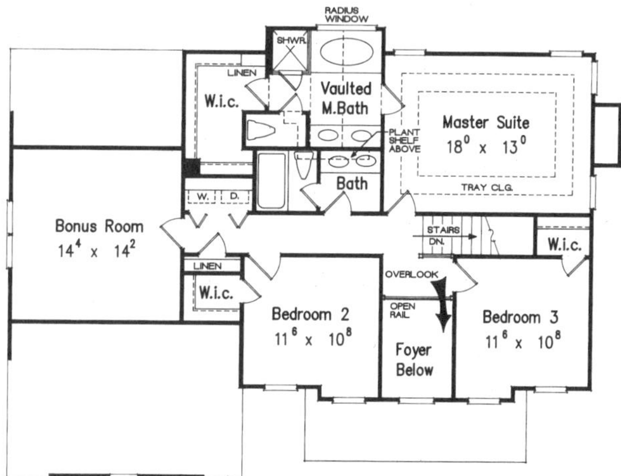
RADIUS WINDOW
SHWR.
LINEN
W.i.c.
Vaulted M.Bath
PLANT SHELF ABOVE
Master Suite
18^0 x 13^0
TRAY CLG.
Bath
W. D.
Bonus Room
14^4 x 14^2
STAIRS DN.
W.i.c.
LINEN
W.i.c.
OVERLOOK
Bedroom 2
11^6 x 10^8
OPEN RAIL
Foyer Below
Bedroom 3
11^6 x 10^8

Second Floor
917 sq. ft.

Plan #527-FB-895

Price Code C

Total Living Area: 2,052 Sq. Ft.

Home has 4 bedrooms, 3 baths, 2-car garage and basement, crawl space or slab foundation, please specify when ordering.

Special features

- Terrific family room has a fireplace and several windows adding sunlight
- Bedroom #4/Study has private bath making it an ideal in-law suite
- Bonus room on second floor has an additional 216 square feet of living area

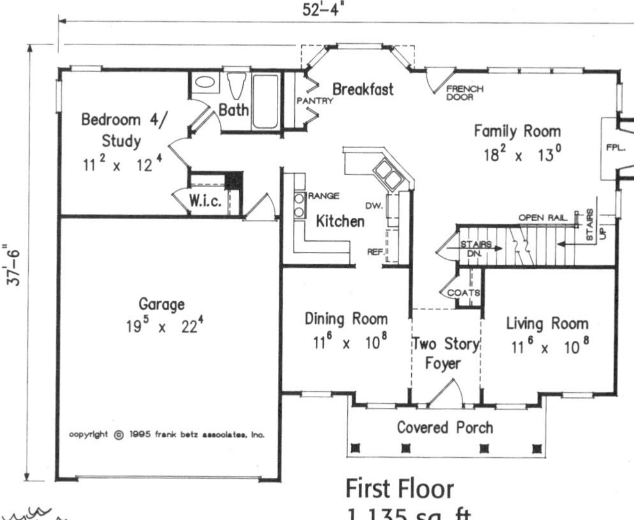
52'-4"
37'-6"
Bedroom 4/ Study
11^2 x 12^4
Bath
PANTRY
Breakfast
FRENCH DOOR
Family Room
18^2 x 13^0
FPL.
W.i.c.
RANGE
DW.
Kitchen
REF.
OPEN RAIL
STAIRS UP
STAIRS DN.
COATS
Garage
19^5 x 22^4
Dining Room
11^6 x 10^8
Two Story Foyer
Living Room
11^6 x 10^8
Covered Porch
copyright © 1995 frank betz associates, Inc.

First Floor
1,135 sq. ft.

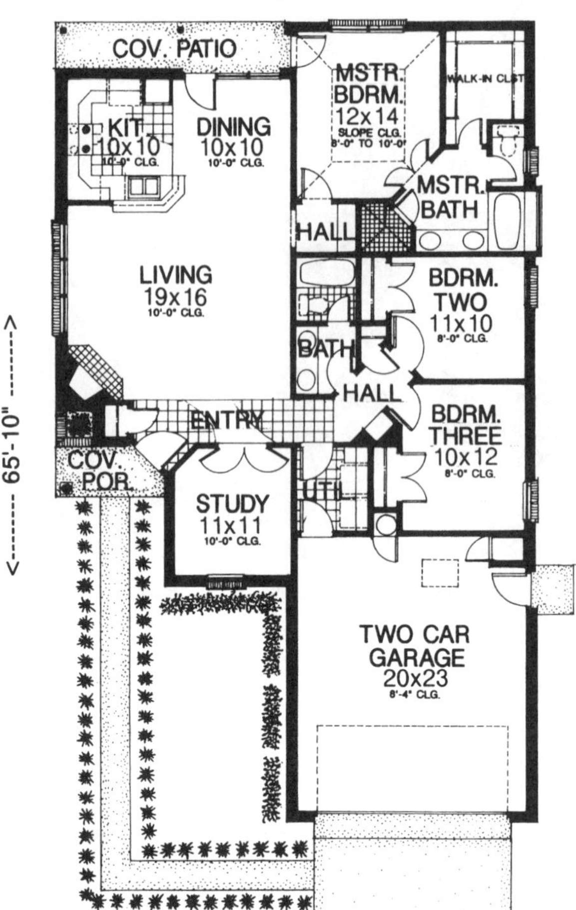
40'-0"
65'-10"
COV. PATIO
MSTR. BDRM. 12x14 SLOPE CLG. 8'-0" TO 10'-0"
WALK-IN CLST
KIT. 10x10 10'-0" CLG.
DINING 10x10 10'-0" CLG.
MSTR. BATH
HALL
LIVING 19x16 10'-0" CLG.
BDRM. TWO 11x10 8'-0" CLG.
BATH
HALL
ENTRY
BDRM. THREE 10x12 8'-0" CLG.
COV. POR.
STUDY 11x11 10'-0" CLG.
UTIL
TWO CAR GARAGE 20x23 8'-4" CLG.

Plan #527-FDG-8673

Price Code B

Total Living Area: 1,604 Sq. Ft.

Home has 3 bedrooms, 2 baths, 2-car garage and slab foundation.

Special features

- Ideal design for a narrow lot
- Living and dining areas combine for a spacious feel
- Secluded study has double-doors for privacy
- Master bedroom has a spacious private bath

TO ORDER BLUEPRINTS USE THE FORM ON PAGE 290 OR CALL TOLL-FREE **1-800-DREAM HOME** (373-2646)

Cozy Nook

LOWE'S

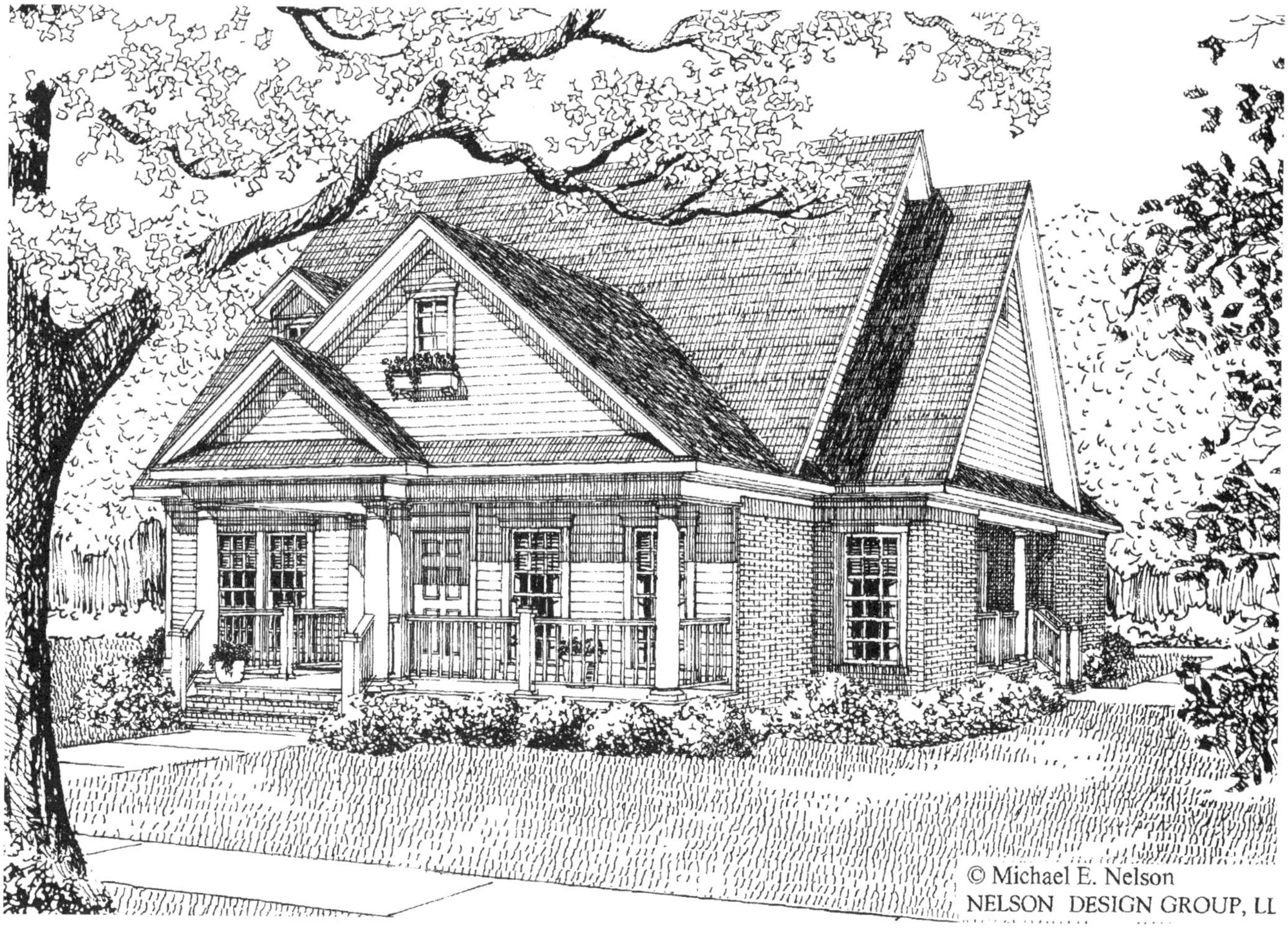

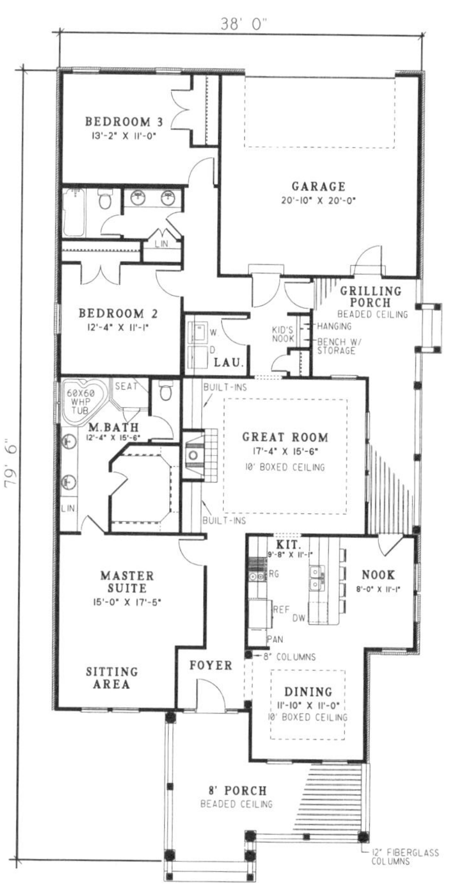
38' 0"
79' 6"
BEDROOM 3
13'-2" X 11'-0"
GARAGE
20'-10" X 20'-0"
LIN
BEDROOM 2
12'-4" X 11'-1"
GRILLING PORCH
BEADED CEILING
KID'S NOOK
HANGING
BENCH W/ STORAGE
LAU.
60X60 WHP TUB
SEAT
M.BATH
12'-4" X 15'-6"
BUILT-INS
GREAT ROOM
17'-4" X 15'-6"
10' BOXED CEILING
LIN
KIT.
9'-8" X 11'-1"
RG
REF
DW
PAN
NOOK
8'-0" X 11'-1"
MASTER SUITE
15'-0" X 17'-5"
SITTING AREA
FOYER
8" COLUMNS
DINING
11'-10" X 11'-0"
10' BOXED CEILING
8' PORCH
BEADED CEILING
12" FIBERGLASS COLUMNS

Plan #527-NDG-338

Price Code C

Total Living Area: 1,848 Sq. Ft.

Home has 3 bedrooms, 2 baths, 2-car rear entry garage and crawl space or slab foundation, please specify when ordering.

Special features

- Kitchen conveniently located near dining area
- Great room has fireplace and built-in bookshelves
- Kid's nook near laundry includes bench with storage and hanging clothes space
- Master suite has a sitting area

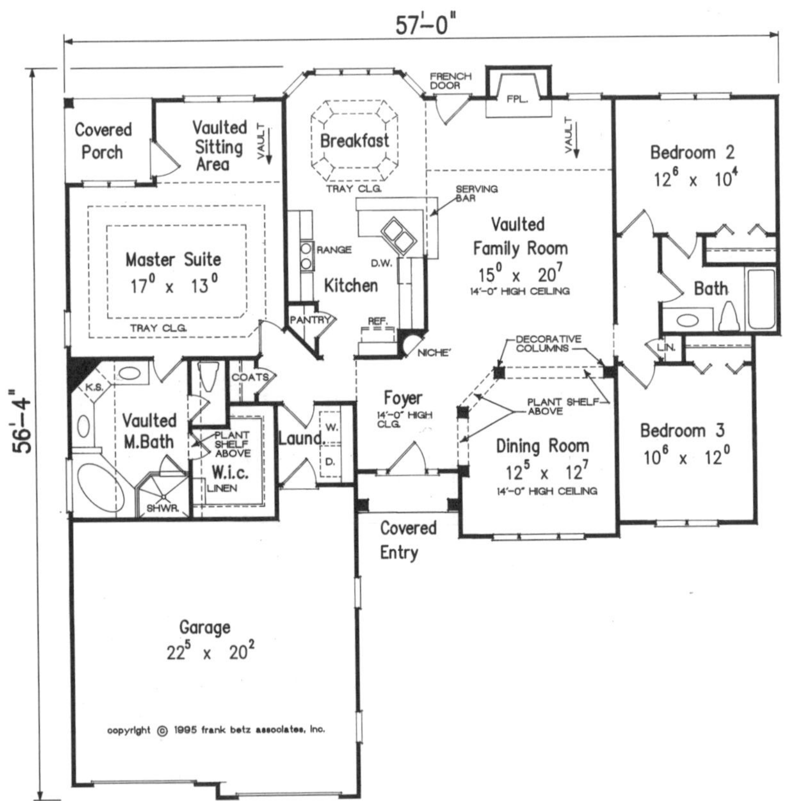
57'-0"
56'-4"
Covered Porch
Vaulted Sitting Area
VAULT
Breakfast
TRAY CLG.
FRENCH DOOR
FPL.
VAULT
Bedroom 2
12^6 x 10^4
SERVING BAR
Vaulted Family Room
15^0 x 20^7
14'-0" HIGH CEILING
Master Suite
17^0 x 13^0
TRAY CLG.
RANGE
D.W.
Kitchen
PANTRY
REF.
NICHE
Bath
LIN.
DECORATIVE COLUMNS
K.S.
COATS
Vaulted M.Bath
PLANT SHELF ABOVE
W.i.c.
LINEN
SHWR.
Laund.
W.
D.
Foyer
14'-0" HIGH CLG.
PLANT SHELF ABOVE
Dining Room
12^5 x 12^7
14'-0" HIGH CEILING
Bedroom 3
10^6 x 12^0
Covered Entry
Garage
22^5 x 20^2
copyright © 1995 frank betz associates, inc.

Plan #527-FB-845

Price Code B

Total Living Area: 1,779 Sq. Ft.

Home has 3 bedrooms, 2 baths, 2-car garage and basement or crawl space foundation, please specify when ordering.

Special features

- Well-designed floor plan has vaulted family room with fireplace and access to the outdoors
- Decorative columns separate dining area from foyer
- Master suite includes private bath and a spacious vaulted sitting area with access to covered porch

TO ORDER BLUEPRINTS USE THE FORM ON PAGE 290 OR CALL TOLL-FREE **1-800-DREAM HOME** (373-2646)

LOWE'S

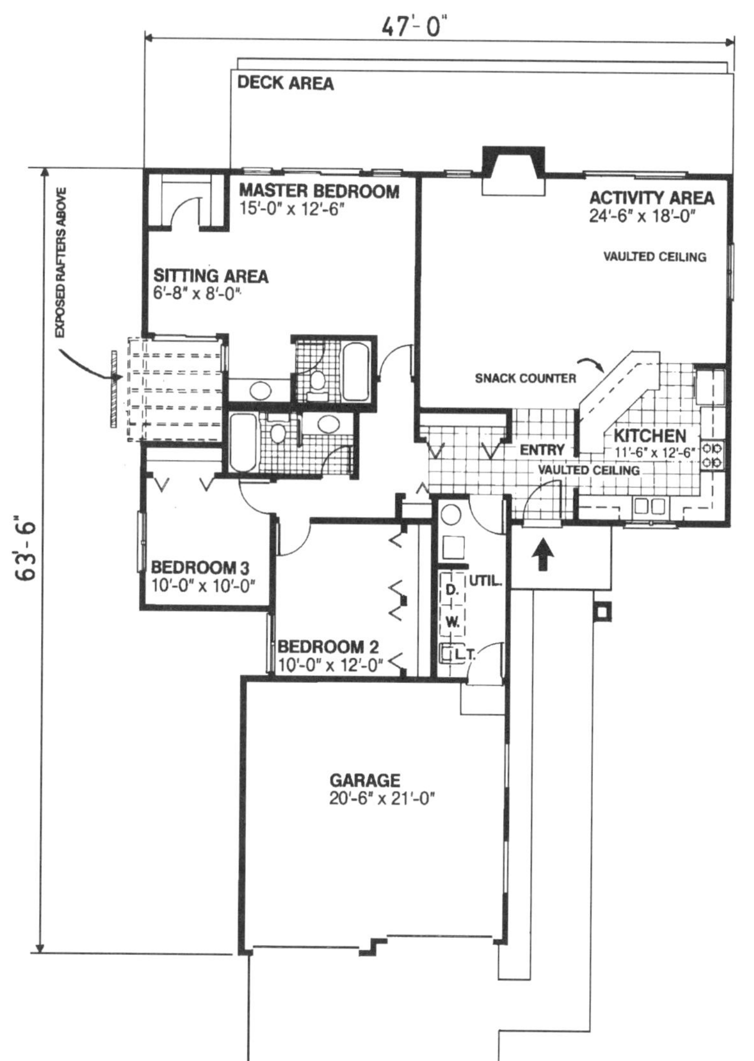
47'-0"
DECK AREA
MASTER BEDROOM
15'-0" x 12'-6"
ACTIVITY AREA
24'-6" x 18'-0"
VAULTED CEILING
EXPOSED RAFTERS ABOVE
SITTING AREA
6'-8" x 8'-0"
SNACK COUNTER
KITCHEN
11'-6" x 12'-6"
ENTRY
VAULTED CEILING
63'-6"
BEDROOM 3
10'-0" x 10'-0"
UTIL.
D.
W.
L.T.
BEDROOM 2
10'-0" x 12'-0"
GARAGE
20'-6" x 21'-0"

Plan #527-1276

Price Code B

Total Living Area: 1,533 Sq. Ft.

Home has 3 bedrooms, 2 baths, 2-car garage and partial basement/crawl space foundation, drawings also include slab foundation.

Special features

- Private deck outside the master bedroom sitting area
- Sloped ceilings add volume to the large activity area
- Activity room has fireplace, snack bar and shares access to the outdoors with the master bedroom
- Convenient utility room located near the garage

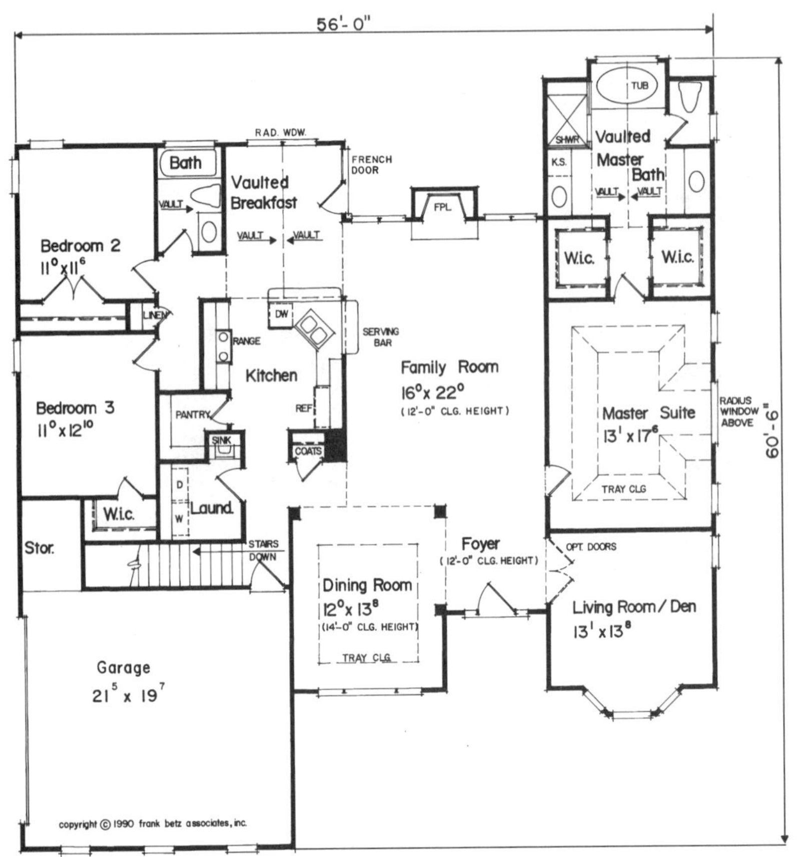
56'-0"
60'-6"
RAD. WDW.
FRENCH DOOR
Bath
Vaulted Breakfast
VAULT
Bedroom 2
11⁰x11⁶
LINEN
DW
RANGE
SERVING BAR
Kitchen
Family Room
16⁰x 22⁰
(12'-0" CLG. HEIGHT)
FPL
Bedroom 3
11⁰x12¹⁰
PANTRY
REF
SINK
COATS
Laund.
W.i.c.
Stor.
STAIRS DOWN
Dining Room
12⁰x 13⁸
(14'-0" CLG. HEIGHT)
TRAY CLG.
Foyer
(12'-0" CLG. HEIGHT)
OPT. DOORS
Living Room / Den
13¹ x13⁸
Garage
21⁵ x 19⁷
copyright © 1990 frank betz associates, inc.
TUB
SHWR
K.S.
Vaulted Master Bath
W.i.c.
W.i.c.
Master Suite
13¹ x17⁶
TRAY CLG
RADIUS WINDOW ABOVE

Plan #527-FB-174

Price Code C

Total Living Area: 2,115 Sq. Ft.

Home has 3 bedrooms, 2 baths, 2-car side entry garage and basement, crawl space or slab foundation, please specify when ordering.

Special features

- Cozy den/living room has a double-door entry and makes an ideal office space
- Kitchen has serving bar which overlooks vaulted breakfast and family room
- Master suite has all the amenities

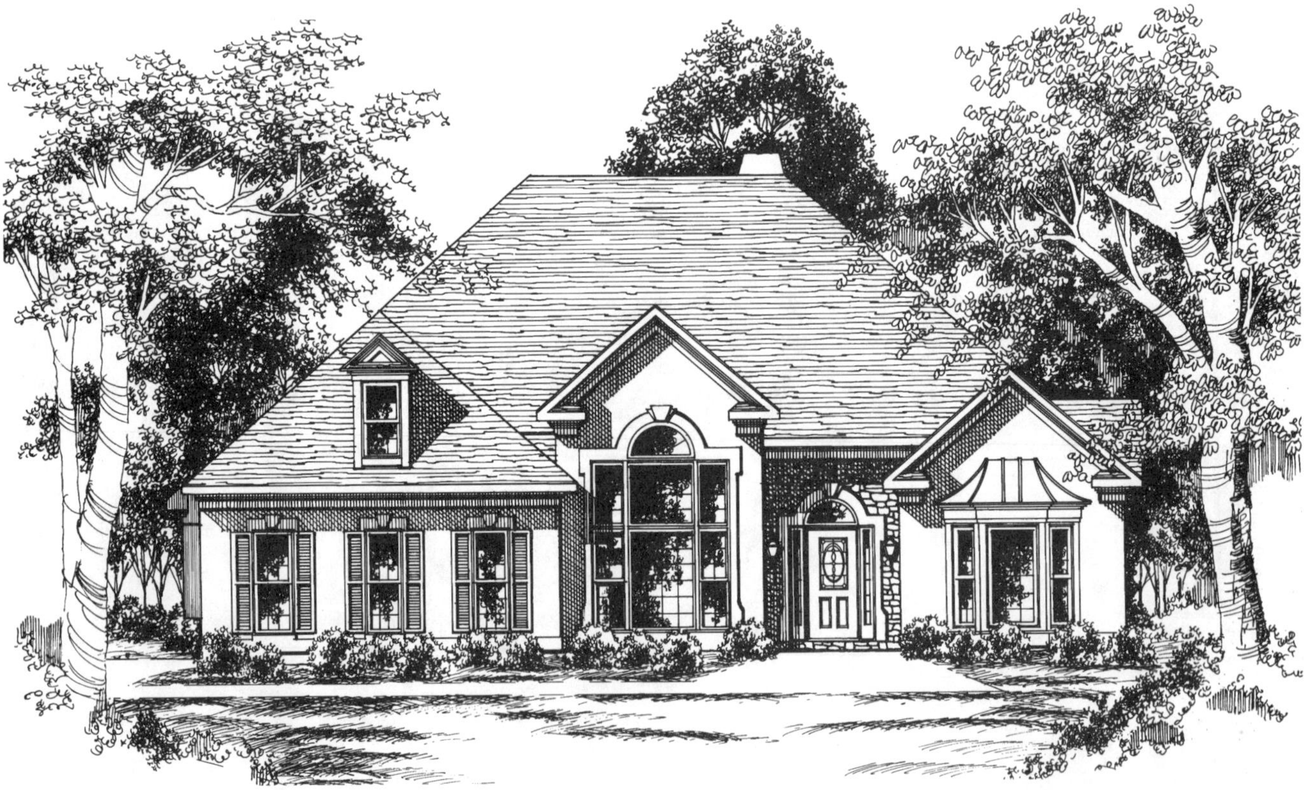

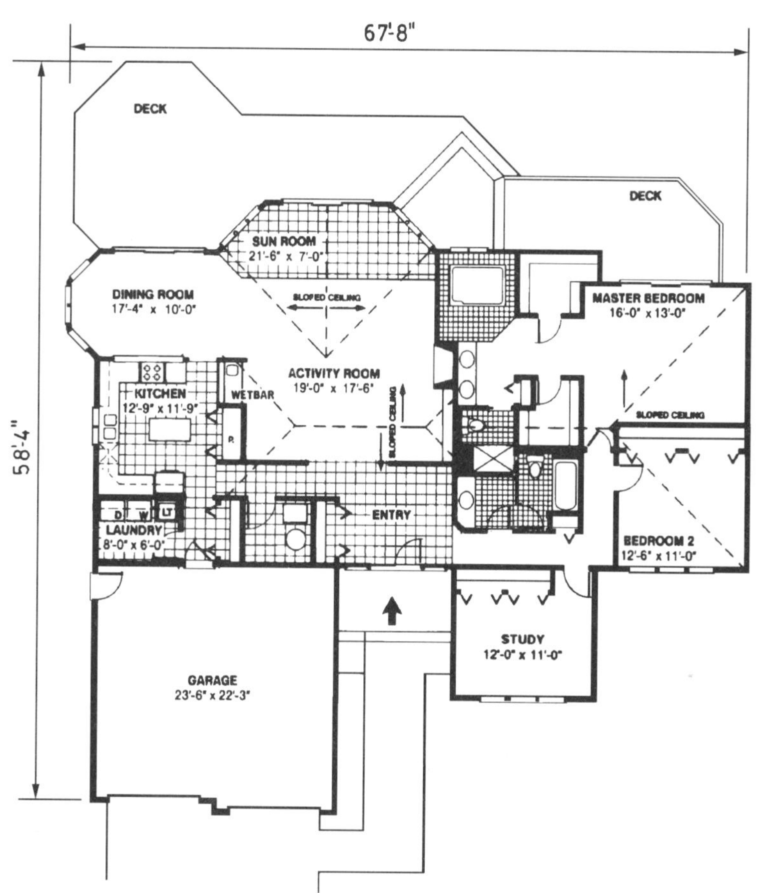
67'-8"
58'-4"
DECK
DECK
SUN ROOM
21'-6" x 7'-0"
DINING ROOM
17'-4" x 10'-0"
SLOPED CEILING
MASTER BEDROOM
16'-0" x 13'-0"
ACTIVITY ROOM
19'-0" x 17'-6"
KITCHEN
12'-9" x 11'-9"
WETBAR
SLOPED CEILING
SLOPED CEILING
ENTRY
LAUNDRY
8'-0" x 6'-0"
BEDROOM 2
12'-6" x 11'-0"
STUDY
12'-0" x 11'-0"
GARAGE
23'-6" x 22'-3"

Plan #527-1418

Price Code C

Total Living Area: 2,180 Sq. Ft.

Home has 2 bedrooms, 2 baths, 2-car garage and crawl space foundation.

Special features

- Exterior provides eye-catching roof lines
- Entry has cathedral ceiling and leads to activity room which features vaulted ceilings, sunken sunroom and wet bar
- Master bedroom has dual walk-in closets, raised tub and compartmented shower
- Front-facing study with closet would make a perfect office or third bedroom
- Study could easily be converted to a third bedroom

Plan #527-FB-1085

Price Code C

Total Living Area: 1,818 Sq. Ft.

Home has 3 bedrooms, 2 1/2 baths, 2-car garage and basement or crawl space foundation, please specify when ordering.

Special features

- Spacious breakfast area extends into family room and kitchen
- Master suite has tray ceiling, vaulted bath with walk-in closet
- Optional bonus room has an additional 298 square feet of living area

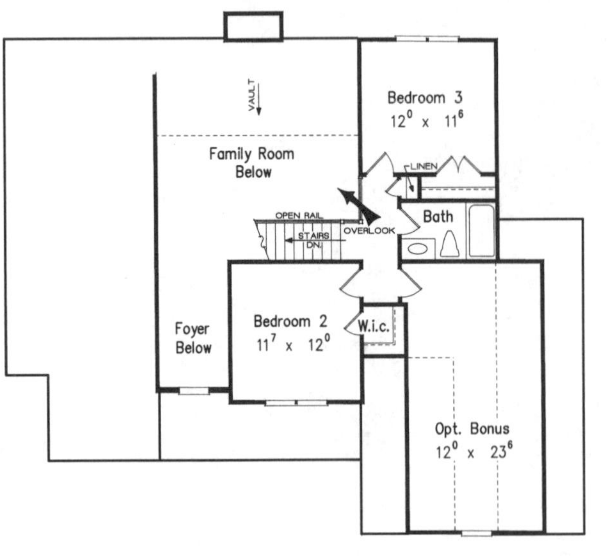
VAULT
Bedroom 3
12° x 11⁶
Family Room Below
LINEN
Bath
OPEN RAIL
STAIRS DN.
OVERLOOK
Foyer Below
Bedroom 2
11⁷ x 12⁰
W.i.c.
Opt. Bonus
12⁰ x 23⁶

Second Floor
436 sq. ft.

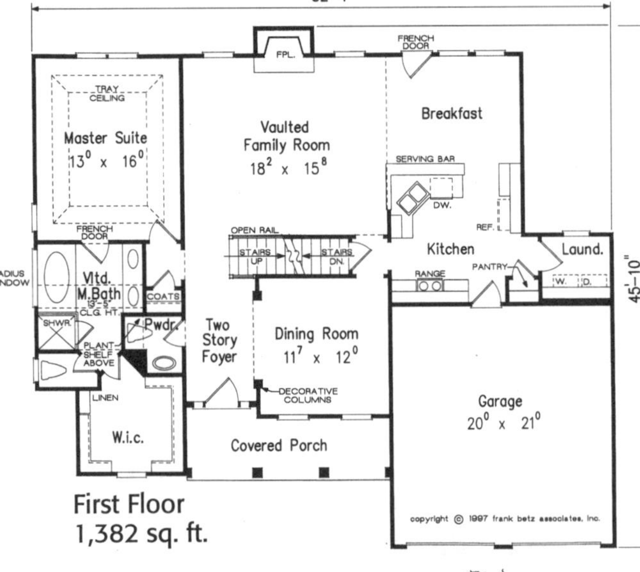
52'-4"
FRENCH DOOR
FPL.
TRAY CEILING
Master Suite
13⁰ x 16⁰
Vaulted Family Room
18² x 15⁸
Breakfast
SERVING BAR
DW.
REF.
FRENCH DOOR
OPEN RAIL
STAIRS UP
STAIRS DN.
Kitchen
Laund.
PANTRY
RANGE
W. D.
RADIUS WINDOW
Vltd. M.Bath
COATS
SHWR.
Pwdr.
PLANT SHELF ABOVE
Two Story Foyer
Dining Room
11⁷ x 12⁰
DECORATIVE COLUMNS
LINEN
W.i.c.
Covered Porch
Garage
20⁰ x 21⁰
45'-10"
copyright © 1997 frank betz associates, inc.

First Floor
1,382 sq. ft.

TO ORDER BLUEPRINTS USE THE FORM ON PAGE 290 OR CALL TOLL-FREE **1-800-DREAM HOME** (373-2646)

Inviting Covered Corner Entry

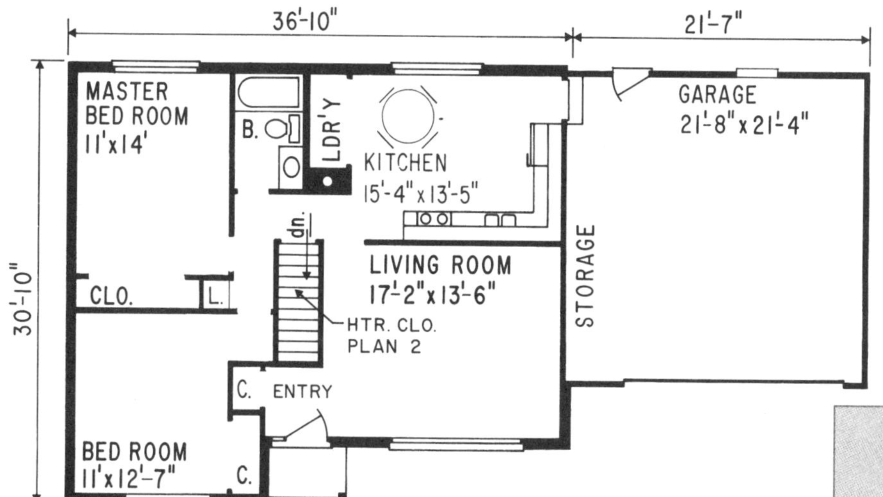
36'-10"
21'-7"
30'-10"
MASTER BED ROOM 11'x14'
B.
LDR'Y
KITCHEN 15'-4"x13'-5"
GARAGE 21'-8"x21'-4"
dn.
LIVING ROOM 17'-2"x13'-6"
STORAGE
CLO.
L.
HTR. CLO. PLAN 2
C. ENTRY
BED ROOM 11'x12'-7"
C.

Plan #527-N297-1
basement

Plan #527-N297-2
crawl space & slab

Price Code AA

Total Living Area: 1,042 Sq. Ft.

Home has 2 bedrooms, 1 bath, 2-car garage and basement, crawl space or slab foundation, please specify when ordering.

Special features

- Living room brightened by several windows
- Spacious kitchen area includes laundry closet for washer and dryer and space for dining area
- Front entry has handy coat closet
- Plenty of extra storage space in the garage

Plan #527-RDD-1429-9

Price Code A

Total Living Area: 1,429 Sq. Ft.

Home has 3 bedrooms, 2 baths, 2-car garage and crawl space or slab foundation, please specify when ordering.

Special features

- Master suite with sitting area and private bath includes double walk-in closets
- Kitchen and dining area overlooks living room
- Living room has fireplace, media center and access to covered porch

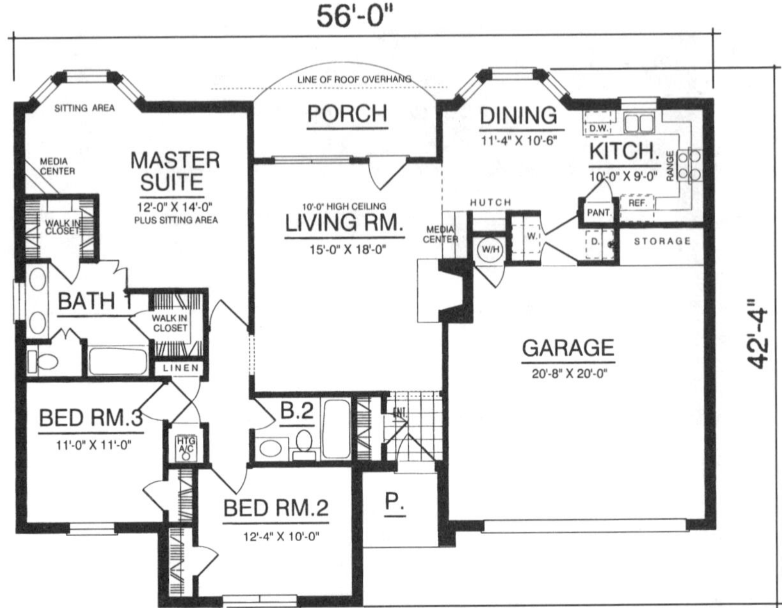
56'-0"
42'-4"
LINE OF ROOF OVERHANG
SITTING AREA
MEDIA CENTER
MASTER SUITE
12'-0" X 14'-0"
PLUS SITTING AREA
WALK IN CLOSET
BATH 1
WALK IN CLOSET
LINEN
PORCH
10'-0" HIGH CEILING
LIVING RM.
15'-0" X 18'-0"
MEDIA CENTER
DINING
11'-4" X 10'-6"
D.W.
KITCH.
10'-0" X 9'-0"
RANGE
REF.
PANT.
HUTCH
W/H
W.
D.
STORAGE
GARAGE
20'-8" X 20'-0"
BED RM.3
11'-0" X 11'-0"
HTG A/C
B.2
BED RM.2
12'-4" X 10'-0"
P.

TO ORDER BLUEPRINTS USE THE FORM ON PAGE 290 OR CALL TOLL-FREE **1-800-DREAM HOME** (373-2646)

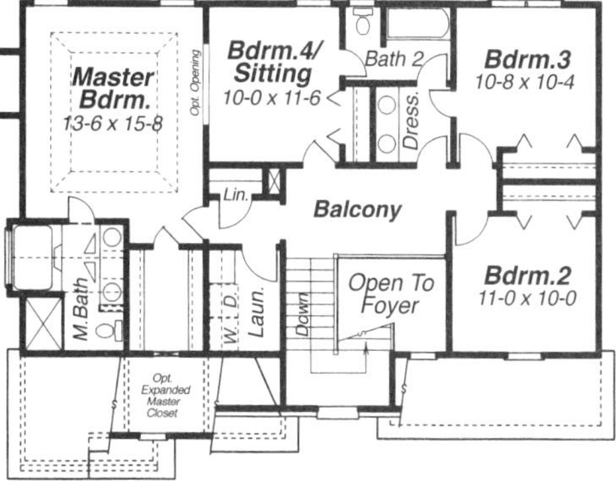
Master Bdrm.
13-6 x 15-8
Opt. Opening
Bdrm.4/ Sitting
10-0 x 11-6
Bath 2
Dress.
Bdrm.3
10-8 x 10-4
Lin.
Balcony
M.Bath
W. D.
Laun.
Down
Open To Foyer
Bdrm.2
11-0 x 10-0
Opt. Expanded Master Closet

Second Floor
1,129 sq. ft.

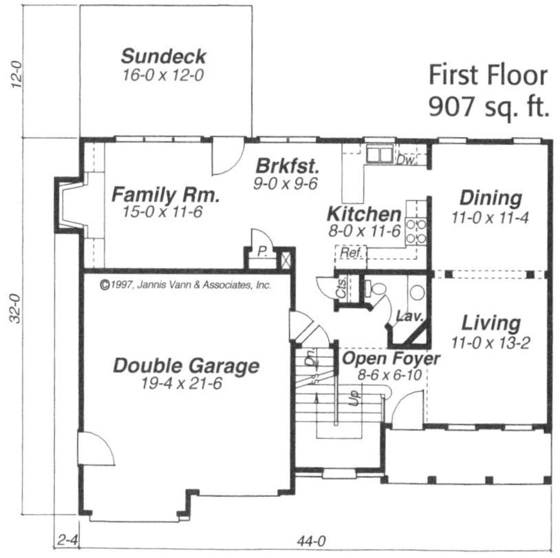
Sundeck
16-0 x 12-0
12-0
Brkfst.
9-0 x 9-6
Dw.
Family Rm.
15-0 x 11-6
Kitchen
8-0 x 11-6
Dining
11-0 x 11-4
P
Ref.
©1997, Jannis Vann & Associates, Inc.
Clo.
Lav.
32-0
Living
11-0 x 13-2
Double Garage
19-4 x 21-6
Dn
Open Foyer
8-6 x 6-10
Up
2-4
44-0

First Floor
907 sq. ft.

Plan #527-JV-2036-D

Price Code C

Total Living Area: 2,036 Sq. Ft.

Home has 4 bedrooms, 2 1/2 baths, 2-car garage and basement, crawl space or slab foundation, please specify when ordering.

Special features

- Stonework accents the facade giving it a European flair
- U-shaped staircase has a window lighting the foyer
- Family room and kitchen area combine for added space
- Vaulted living and dining areas create a formal feel

Perfect Home For Escaping To The Outdoors

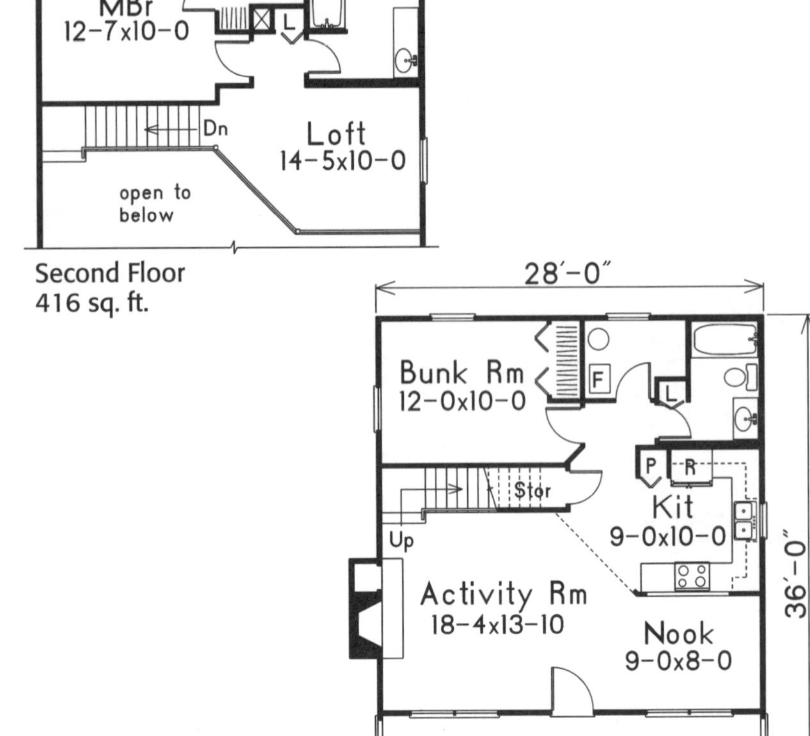
MBr
12-7x10-0
L
Dn
Loft
14-5x10-0
open to below
28'-0"
Bunk Rm
12-0x10-0
F
L
P
R
Stor
Kit
9-0x10-0
Up
Activity Rm
18-4x13-10
Nook
9-0x8-0
Covered Porch depth 8-0
36'-0"

Second Floor
416 sq. ft.

First Floor
784 sq. ft.

Plan #527-1293

Price Code A

Total Living Area: 1,200 Sq. Ft.

Home has 2 bedrooms, 2 baths and crawl space foundation.

Special features

- Enjoy lazy summer evenings on this magnificent porch
- Activity area has fireplace and ascending stair from cozy loft
- Kitchen features built-in pantry
- Master suite enjoys large bath, walk-in closet and cozy loft overlooking room below

TO ORDER BLUEPRINTS USE THE FORM ON PAGE 290 OR CALL TOLL-FREE **1-800-DREAM HOME** (373-2646)

Plan #527-FB-992

Price Code C

Total Living Area: 2,155 Sq. Ft.

Home has 3 bedrooms, 2 1/2 baths, 2-car garage and basement or crawl space foundation, please specify when ordering.

Special features

- Vaulted breakfast and keeping rooms create informal area off kitchen
- All bedrooms have walk-in closets
- Optional bonus room on second floor has an additional 207 square feet of living area

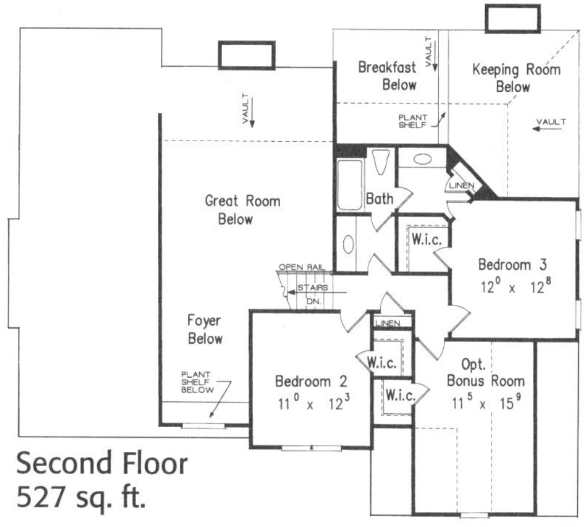
Breakfast Below
VAULT
Keeping Room Below
PLANT SHELF
VAULT
Great Room Below
Bath
LINEN
W.i.c.
Bedroom 3
12⁰ x 12⁸
OPEN RAIL
STAIRS
DN.
Foyer Below
LINEN
PLANT SHELF BELOW
Bedroom 2
11⁰ x 12³
W.i.c.
W.i.c.
Opt. Bonus Room
11⁵ x 15⁹

Second Floor
527 sq. ft.

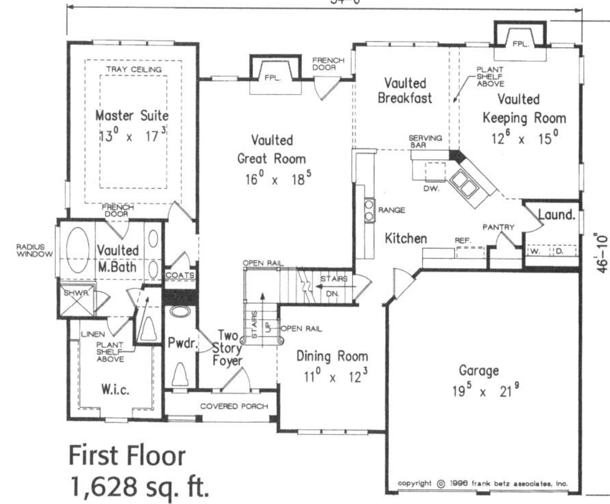
54'-0"
46'-10"
TRAY CEILING
Master Suite
13⁰ x 17³
FPL.
FRENCH DOOR
Vaulted Breakfast
PLANT SHELF ABOVE
FPL.
Vaulted Keeping Room
12⁶ x 15⁰
Vaulted Great Room
16⁰ x 18⁵
SERVING BAR
DW.
FRENCH DOOR
RANGE
Laund.
RADIUS WINDOW
Vaulted M.Bath
Kitchen
REF.
PANTRY
W.
D.
COATS
OPEN RAIL
STAIRS
DN.
SHWR.
LINEN
PLANT SHELF ABOVE
Pwdr.
Two Story Foyer
STAIRS
UP
OPEN RAIL
Dining Room
11⁰ x 12³
Garage
19⁵ x 21⁹
W.i.c.
COVERED PORCH
copyright © 1996 frank betz associates, inc.

First Floor
1,628 sq. ft.

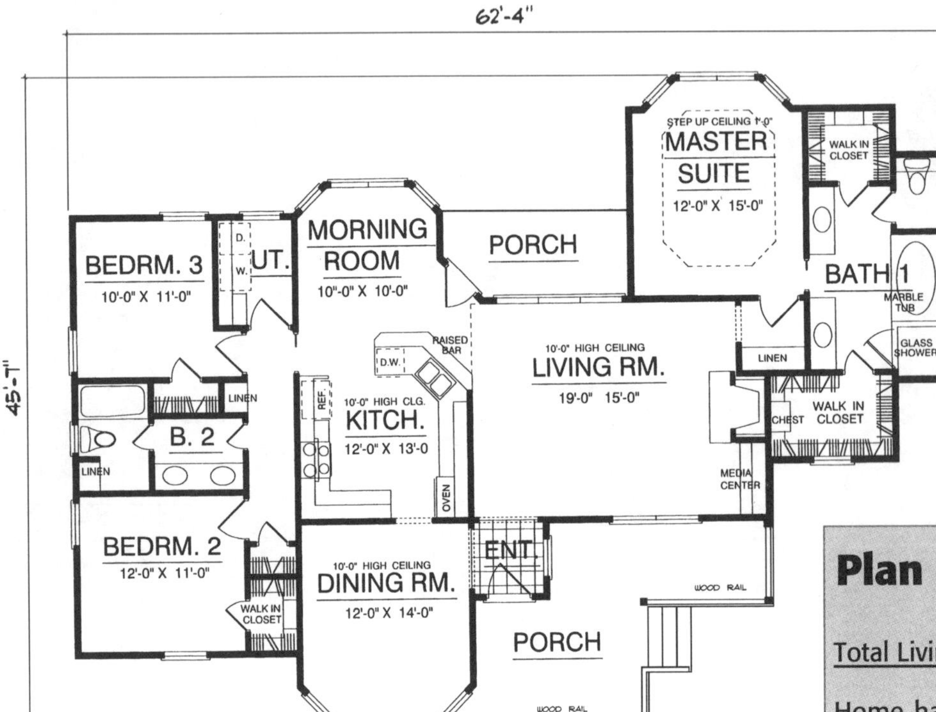
62'-4"
45'-7"
STEP UP CEILING 1'-0"
MASTER SUITE
12'-0" X 15'-0"
WALK IN CLOSET
BATH 1
MARBLE TUB
GLASS SHOWER
LINEN
WALK IN CLOSET
CHEST
MORNING ROOM
10'-0" X 10'-0"
PORCH
BEDRM. 3
10'-0" X 11'-0"
UT.
D.
W.
RAISED BAR
D.W.
10'-0" HIGH CEILING
LIVING RM.
19'-0" 15'-0"
LINEN
B. 2
LINEN
REF.
10'-0" HIGH CLG.
KITCH.
12'-0" X 13'-0
OVEN
MEDIA CENTER
BEDRM. 2
12'-0" X 11'-0"
10'-0" HIGH CEILING
DINING RM.
12'-0" X 14'-0"
ENT.
WOOD RAIL
WALK IN CLOSET
PORCH
WOOD RAIL

Plan #527-RDD-1753-9

Price Code B

Total Living Area: 1,753 Sq. Ft.

Home has 3 bedrooms, 2 baths and a slab or crawl space foundation, please specify when ordering.

Special features

- Large front porch has charming appeal
- Kitchen with breakfast bar overlooks morning room and accesses covered porch
- Master suite with amenities like private bath, spacious closets and sunny bay window

LOWE'S

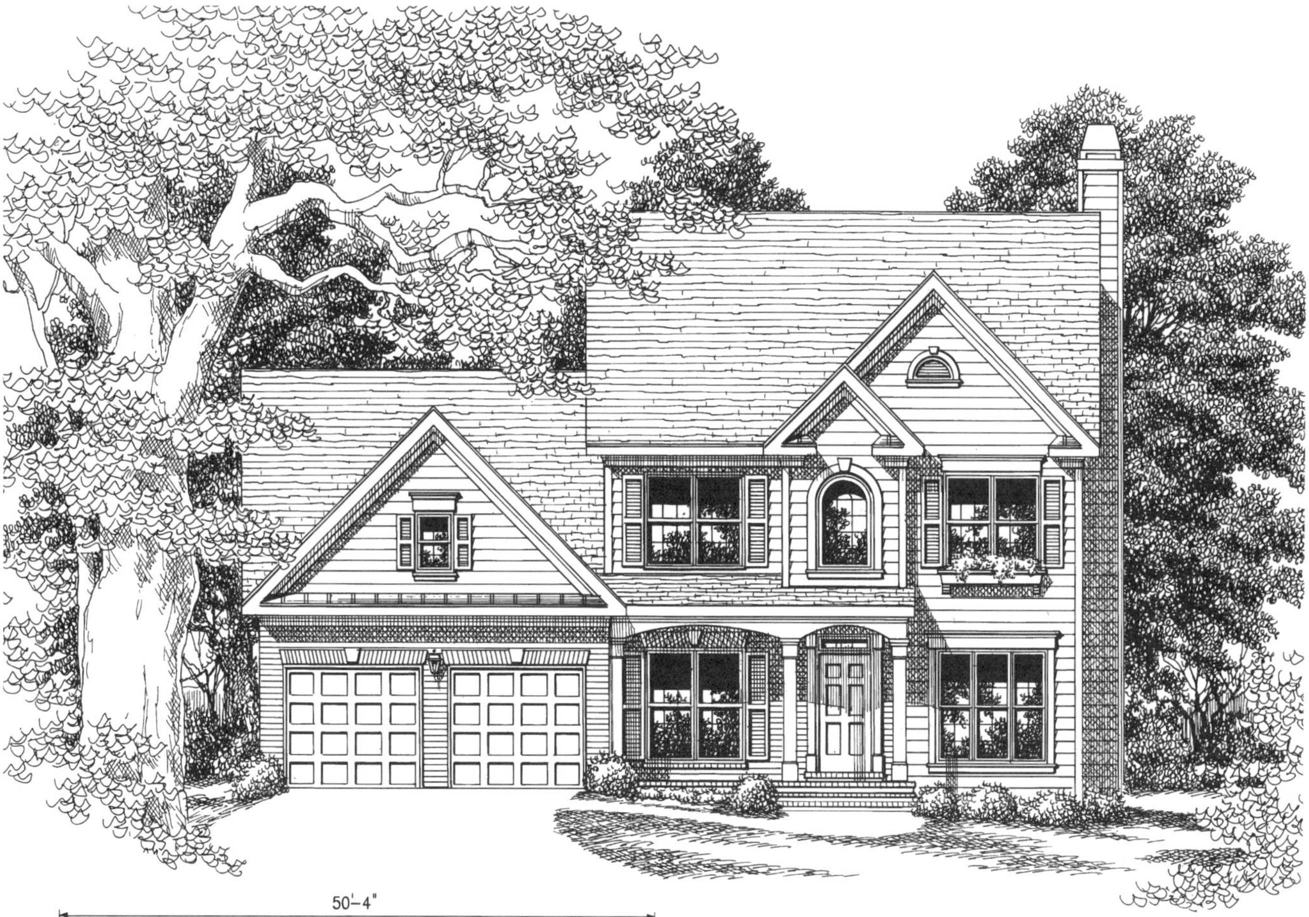

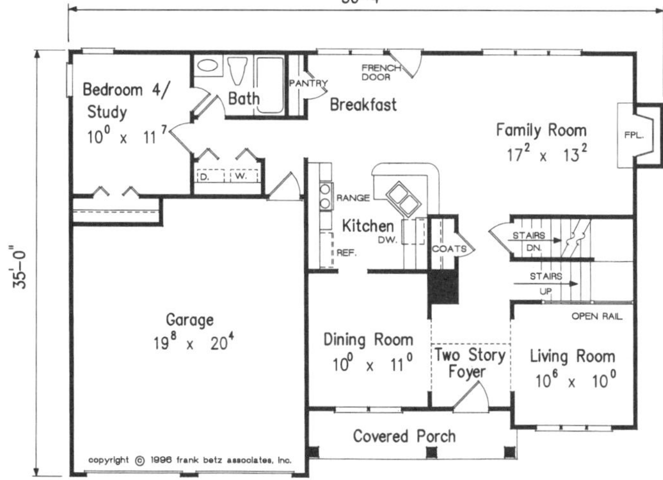
50'-4"
35'-0"
Bedroom 4/
Study
10⁰ x 11⁷
Bath
PANTRY
FRENCH DOOR
Breakfast
Family Room
17² x 13²
FPL.
D.
W.
RANGE
Kitchen
DW.
REF.
COATS
STAIRS DN.
STAIRS UP
OPEN RAIL
Garage
19⁸ x 20⁴
Dining Room
10⁰ x 11⁰
Two Story
Foyer
Living Room
10⁶ x 10⁰
Covered Porch
copyright © 1996 frank betz associates, inc.

First Floor
1,103 sq. ft.

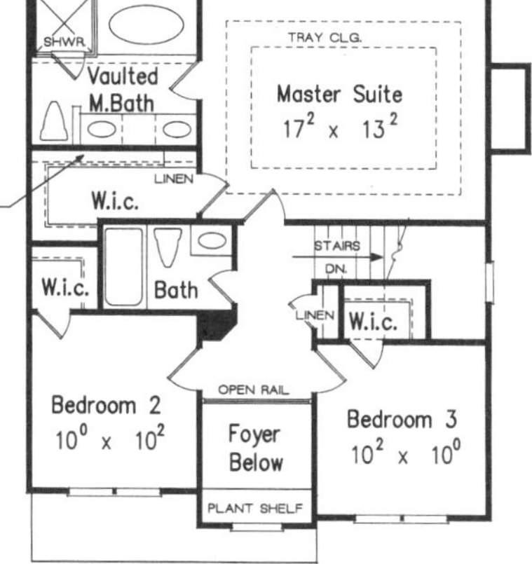
SHWR.
Vaulted
M.Bath
TRAY CLG.
Master Suite
17² x 13²
PLANT SHELF ABOVE
LINEN
W.i.c.
STAIRS DN.
W.i.c.
Bath
LINEN
W.i.c.
OPEN RAIL
Bedroom 2
10⁰ x 10²
Foyer
Below
Bedroom 3
10² x 10⁰
PLANT SHELF

Second Floor
759 sq. ft.

Plan #527-FB-959

Price Code C

Total Living Area: 1,862 Sq. Ft.

Home has 4 bedrooms, 3 baths, 2-car garage and basement or crawl space foundation, please specify when ordering.

Special features

- Dining and living rooms flank grand two-story foyer
- Open floor plan combines kitchen, breakfast and family rooms
- Study is tucked away on first floor for privacy
- Second floor bedrooms have walk-in closets

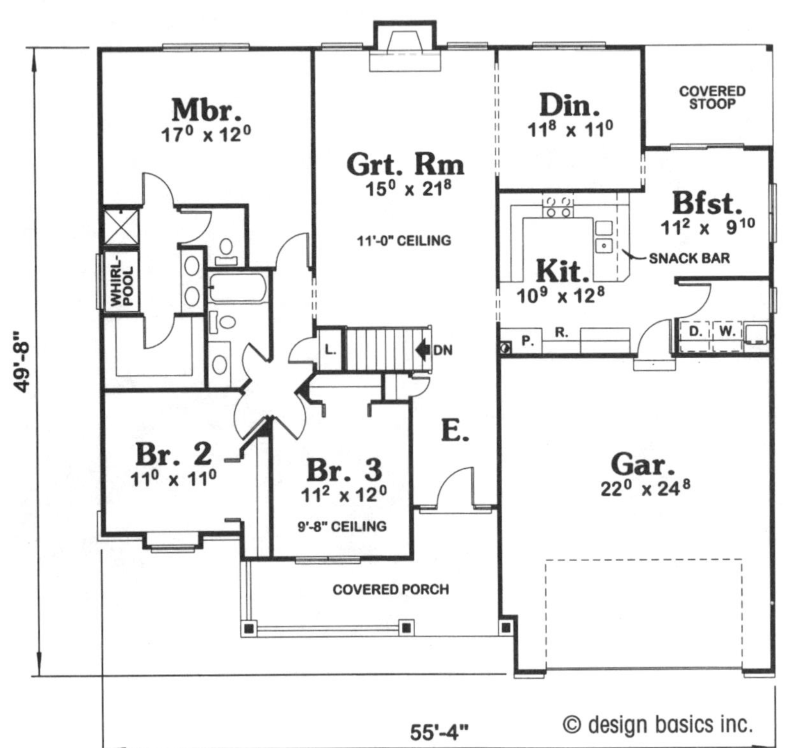
Mbr.
17⁰ x 12⁰
WHIRL-POOL
Grt. Rm
15⁰ x 21⁸
11'-0" CEILING
Din.
11⁸ x 11⁰
COVERED STOOP
Bfst.
11² x 9¹⁰
SNACK BAR
Kit.
10⁹ x 12⁸
P.
R.
D.
W.
L.
DN
E.
Br. 2
11⁰ x 11⁰
Br. 3
11² x 12⁰
9'-8" CEILING
Gar.
22⁰ x 24⁸
COVERED PORCH
49'-8"
55'-4"
© design basics inc.

Plan #527-DBI-4948

Price Code B

Total Living Area: 1,758 Sq. Ft.

Home has 3 bedrooms, 2 baths, 2-car garage and basement foundation.

Special features

- Secluded covered porch off breakfast area is a charming touch
- Great room and dining room combine for terrific entertaining possibilities
- Master bedroom with all the amenities
- Spacious foyer area opens into large great room with 11' ceiling

TO ORDER BLUEPRINTS USE THE FORM ON PAGE 290 OR CALL TOLL-FREE **1-800-DREAM HOME** (373-2646)

LOWE'S

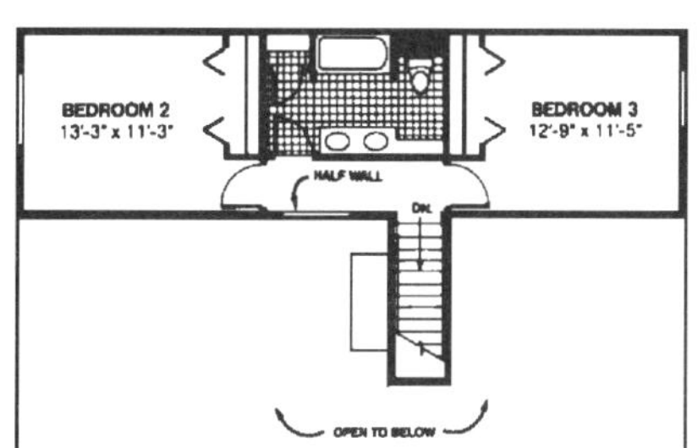
BEDROOM 2
13'-3" x 11'-3"
BEDROOM 3
12'-9" x 11'-5"
HALF WALL
DN.
OPEN TO BELOW

Second Floor
480 sq. ft.

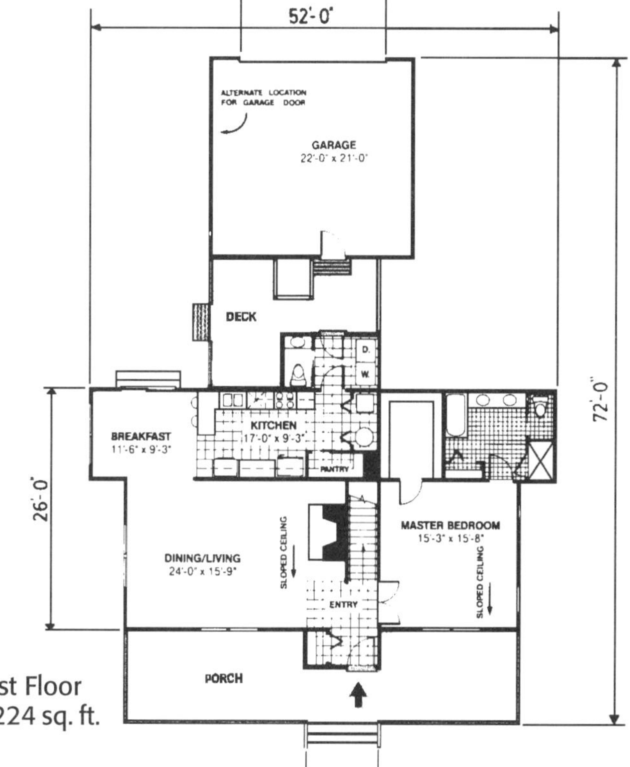
52'-0"
ALTERNATE LOCATION FOR GARAGE DOOR
GARAGE
22'-0" x 21'-0"
DECK
D.
W.
BREAKFAST
11'-6" x 9'-3"
KITCHEN
17'-0" x 9'-3"
PANTRY
DINING/LIVING
24'-0" x 15'-9"
SLOPED CEILING
ENTRY
MASTER BEDROOM
15'-3" x 15'-8"
SLOPED CEILING
PORCH
26'-0"
72'-0"

First Floor
1,224 sq. ft.

Plan #527-1254-1

basement

Plan #527-1254-2

slab

Price Code B

Total Living Area: 1,704 Sq. Ft.

Home has 3 bedrooms, 2 1/2 baths, 2-car rear entry garage and basement or slab foundation, please specify when ordering.

Special features

- Sensational large front porch for summer evenings and rear breezeway for enjoying outdoors
- Entry leads to living/dining area featuring sloped ceilings and second floor balcony overlook
- Sophisticated master suite complemented by luxury bath with separate shower and toilet area
- Two good-sized bedrooms with centrally located bath

Plan #527-CHP-1532-A-141

Price Code B

Total Living Area: 1,500 Sq. Ft.

Home has 3 bedrooms, 2 baths, 2-car garage and slab foundation.

Special features

- Living room features corner fireplace adding warmth
- Master suite has all the amenities like walk-in closet, private bath and porch access
- Sunny bayed breakfast room is cheerful and bright

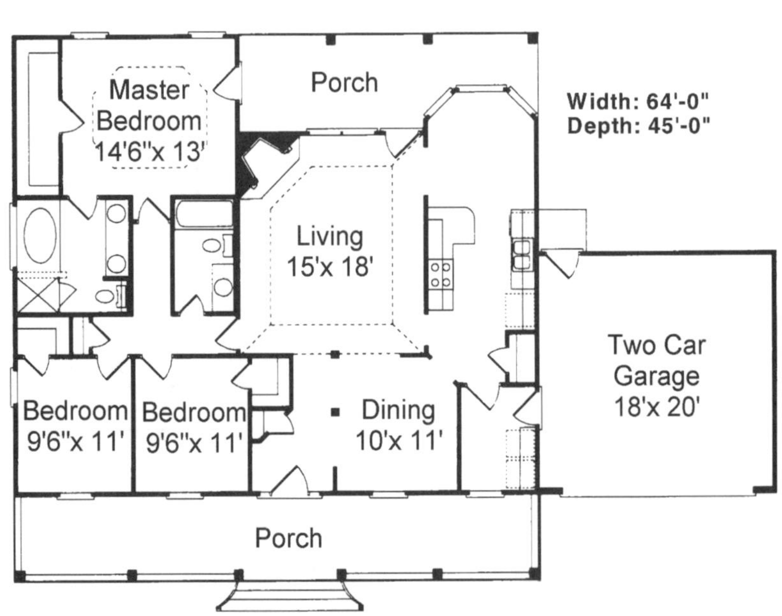
Master Bedroom 14'6"x 13'
Porch
Width: 64'-0"
Depth: 45'-0"
Living 15'x 18'
Two Car Garage 18'x 20'
Bedroom 9'6"x 11'
Bedroom 9'6"x 11'
Dining 10'x 11'
Porch

LOWE'S

Plan #527-GM-1815

Price Code C

Total Living Area: 1,815 Sq. Ft.

Home has 3 bedrooms, 2 1/2 baths, 2-car side entry garage and basement foundation.

Special features

- Inviting covered porch
- Lots of counterspace and cabinetry in kitchen
- Two doors into laundry area make it handy from master bedroom and the rest of the home
- Second floor has built-in desk in hall ideal as a computer work station or mini office area

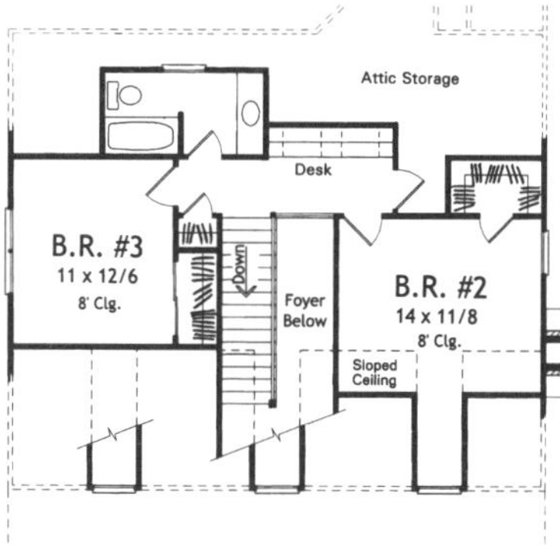

Attic Storage
Desk
B.R. #3 11 x 12/6 8' Clg.
B.R. #2 14 x 11/8 8' Clg.
Foyer Below
Sloped Ceiling

Second Floor 559 sq. ft.

Width: 43'-0"
Depth: 74'-0"

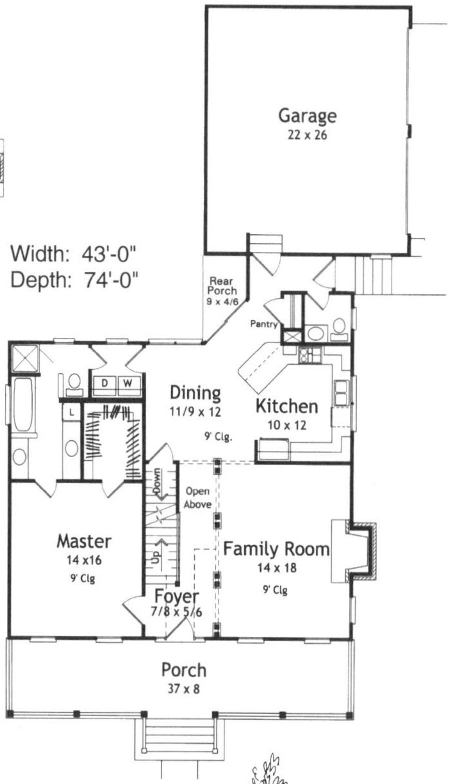

Garage 22 x 26
Rear Porch 9 x 4/6
Pantry
Dining 11/9 x 12 9' Clg.
Kitchen 10 x 12
Open Above
Master 14 x16 9' Clg
Family Room 14 x 18 9' Clg
Foyer 7/8 x 5/6
Porch 37 x 8

First Floor 1,256 sq. ft.

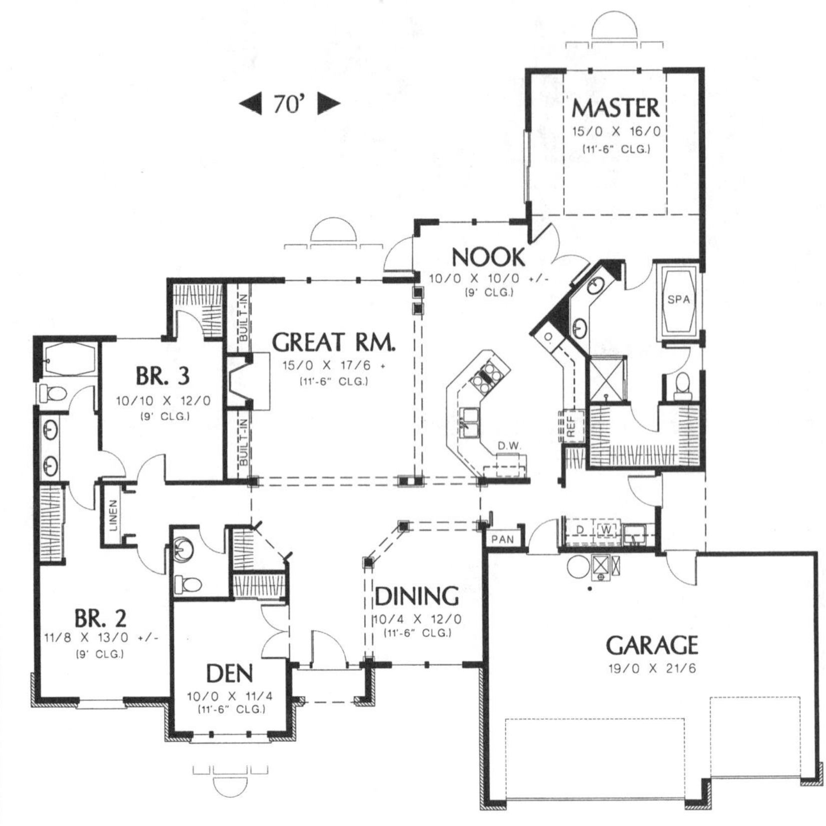
70'
64'
MASTER
15/0 X 16/0
(11'-6" CLG.)
NOOK
10/0 X 10/0 +/-
(9' CLG.)
SPA
GREAT RM.
15/0 X 17/6 +
(11'-6" CLG.)
BUILT-IN
BUILT-IN
BR. 3
10/10 X 12/0
(9' CLG.)
REF
D.W.
LINEN
PAN
D
W
BR. 2
11/8 X 13/0 +/-
(9' CLG.)
DINING
10/4 X 12/0
(11'-6" CLG.)
GARAGE
19/0 X 21/6
DEN
10/0 X 11/4
(11'-6" CLG.)

Plan #527-AMD-1213

Price Code C

Total Living Area: 2,197 Sq. Ft.

Home has 4 bedrooms, 2 1/2 baths, 3-car garage and crawl space foundation.

Special features

- Centrally located great room opens to kitchen, breakfast nook and private backyard
- Den located off entry ideal for home office
- Vaulted master bath has spa tub, shower and double vanity

TO ORDER BLUEPRINTS USE THE FORM ON PAGE 290 OR CALL TOLL-FREE **1-800-DREAM HOME** (373-2646)

Bay Creates Bright Sunroom

LOWE'S

Plan #527-GM-2148

Price Code C

Total Living Area: 2,148 Sq. Ft.

Home has 3 bedrooms, 2 1/2 baths, 2-car side entry garage and basement foundation.

Special features

- Cheerful bayed sunroom has attached porch and overlooks kitchen and breakfast area
- Varied ceiling heights throughout entire plan
- All bedrooms have walk-in closets
- Laundry area includes handy sink

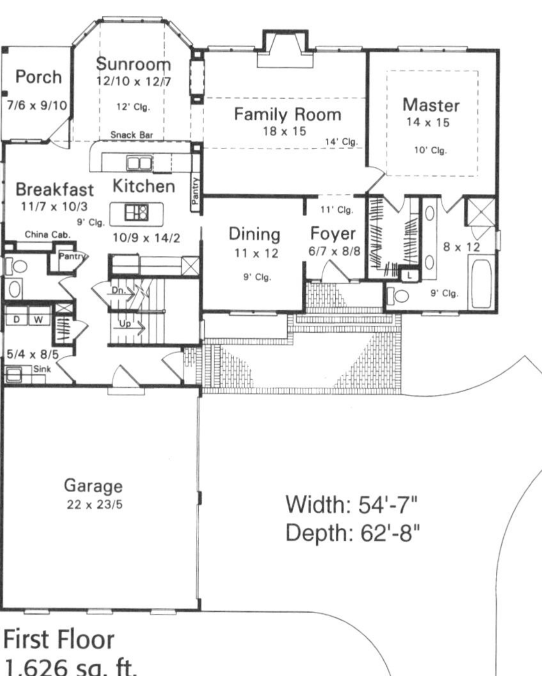
Porch
7/6 x 9/10
Sunroom
12/10 x 12/7
12' Clg.
Snack Bar
Family Room
18 x 15
14' Clg.
Master
14 x 15
10' Clg.
Breakfast
11/7 x 10/3
9' Clg.
Kitchen
10/9 x 14/2
Pantry
China Cab.
Pantry
Dining
11 x 12
9' Clg.
Foyer
6/7 x 8/8
11' Clg.
8 x 12
9' Clg.
L
Dn.
Up
D W
5/4 x 8/5
Sink
Garage
22 x 23/5
Width: 54'-7"
Depth: 62'-8"

First Floor
1,626 sq. ft.

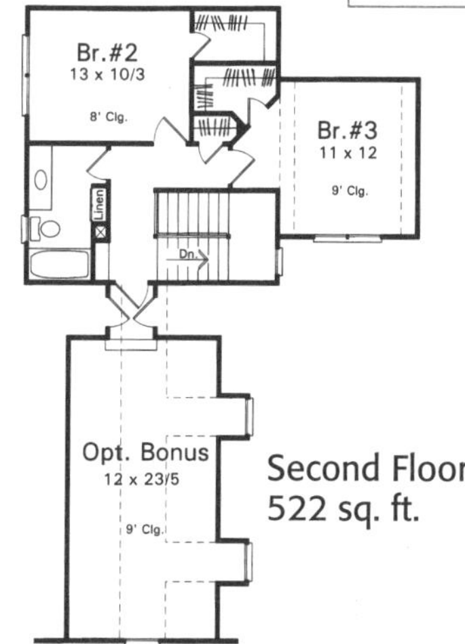
Br.#2
13 x 10/3
8' Clg.
Br.#3
11 x 12
9' Clg.
Linen
Dn.
Opt. Bonus
12 x 23/5
9' Clg.

Second Floor
522 sq. ft.

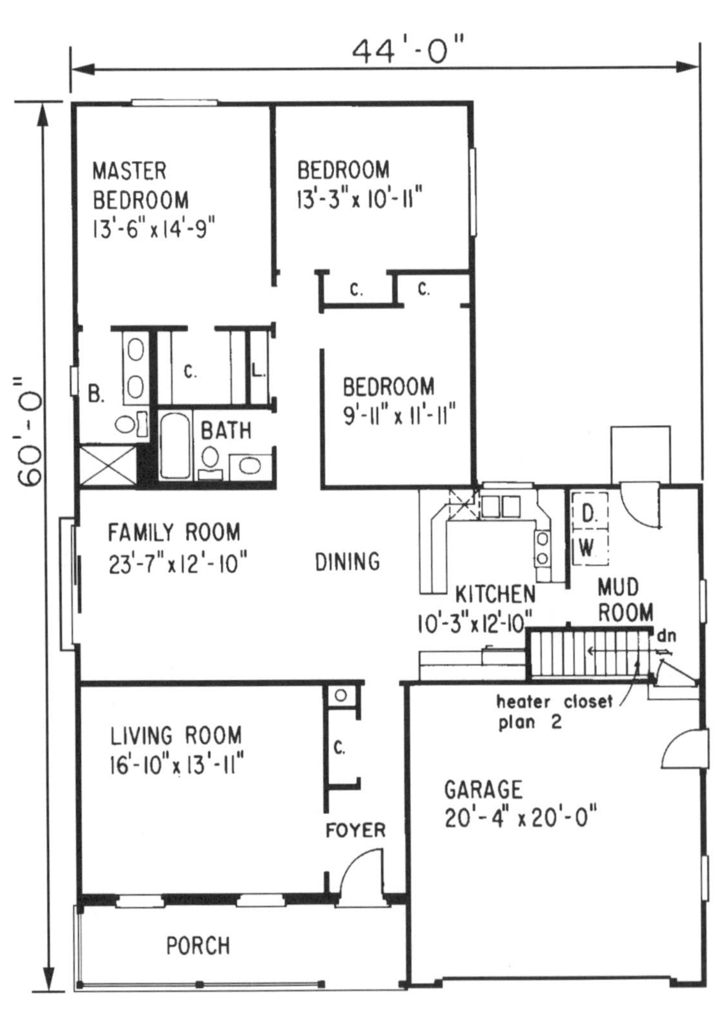
44'-0"
60'-0"
MASTER BEDROOM 13'-6"x14'-9"
BEDROOM 13'-3"x10'-11"
C.
C.
B.
C.
L.
BATH
BEDROOM 9'-11"x11'-11"
FAMILY ROOM 23'-7"x12'-10"
DINING
KITCHEN 10'-3"x12'-10"
D
W
MUD ROOM
dn
heater closet plan 2
LIVING ROOM 16'-10"x13'-11"
C.
FOYER
GARAGE 20'-4"x20'-0"
PORCH

Plan #527-1216-1

partial basement/crawl space

Plan #527-1216-2

crawl space & slab

Price Code B

Total Living Area: 1,668 Sq. Ft.

Home has 3 bedrooms, 2 baths, 2-car garage and partial basement/crawl space or crawl space and slab foundation, please specify when ordering.

Special features

- Attractive styled ranch home is perfect for a narrow lot
- Front entry porch with entrance foyer with closet opens to living room
- Garage entrance to home leads to kitchen through mud room/laundry
- U-shaped kitchen opens to dining area and family room
- Three bedrooms are situated at the rear of the home with two full baths
- Master bedroom has walk-in closet

LOWE'S

Plan #527-LBD-18-11A

Price Code C

Total Living Area: 1,890 Sq. Ft.

Home has 3 bedrooms, 2 baths, 2-car side entry garage and crawl space or slab foundation, please specify when ordering.

Special features

- 10' ceilings give the home a spacious feel
- Efficient kitchen has breakfast bar which overlooks living room
- Master bedroom has private bath with walk-in closet

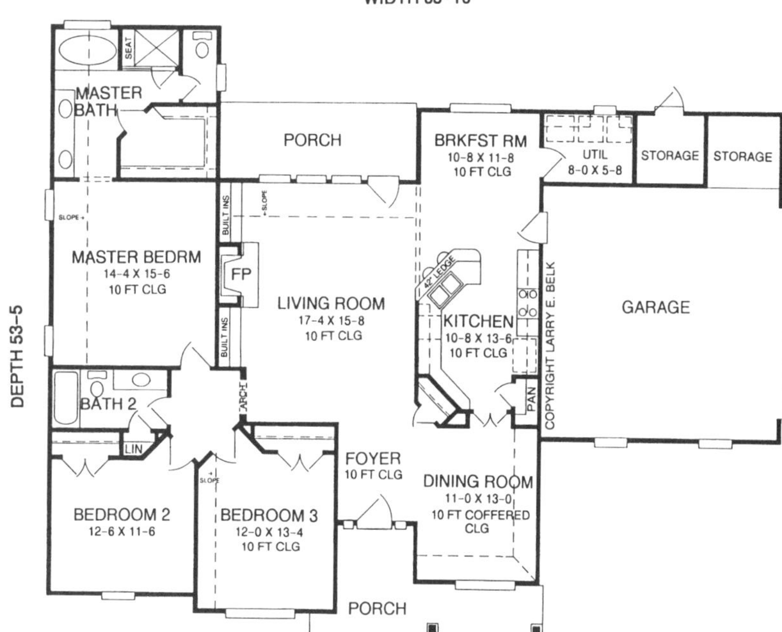
WIDTH 65-10
DEPTH 53-5
MASTER BATH
SEAT
PORCH
BRKFST RM
10-8 X 11-8
10 FT CLG
UTIL
8-0 X 5-8
STORAGE
STORAGE
MASTER BEDRM
14-4 X 15-6
10 FT CLG
BUILT INS
FP
LIVING ROOM
17-4 X 15-8
10 FT CLG
42" LEDGE
KITCHEN
10-8 X 13-6
10 FT CLG
GARAGE
COPYRIGHT LARRY E. BELK
PAN
BATH 2
LIN
ARCH
FOYER
10 FT CLG
DINING ROOM
11-0 X 13-0
10 FT COFFERED CLG
BEDROOM 2
12-6 X 11-6
BEDROOM 3
12-0 X 13-4
10 FT CLG
PORCH

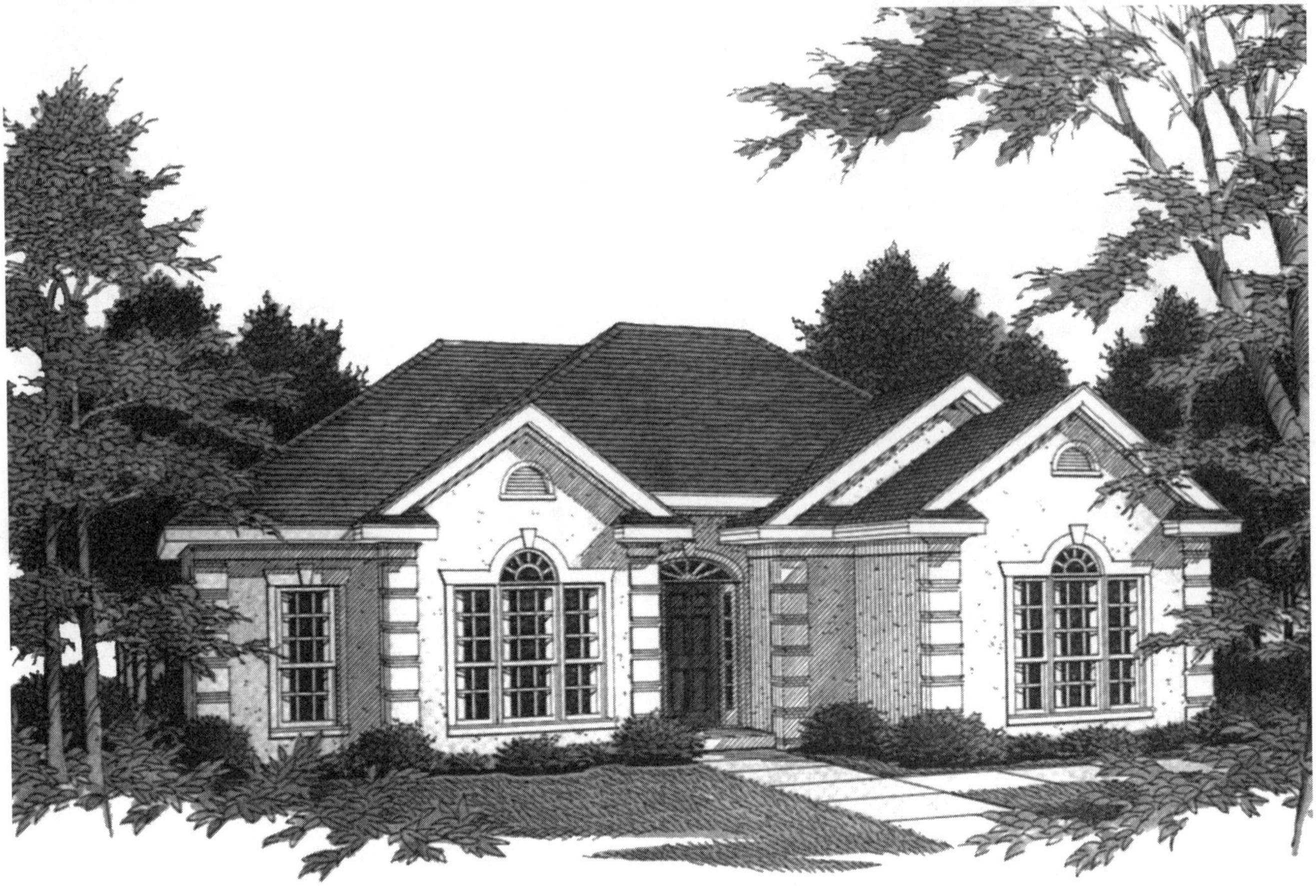

Plan #527-CHP-1732-A-101

Price Code B

Total Living Area: 1,704 Sq. Ft.

Home has 3 bedrooms, 2 baths and slab foundation.

Special features

- Open floor plan combines foyer, dining and living rooms together for an open airy feeling
- Kitchen has island that adds workspace and storage
- Bedrooms are situated together and secluded from the rest of the home

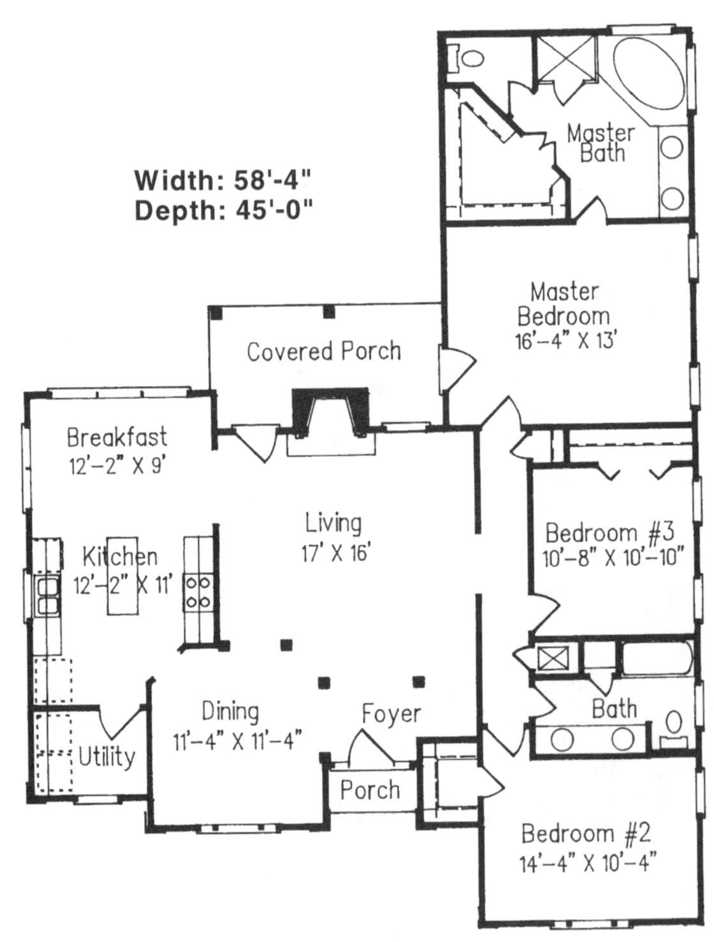
Width: 58'-4"
Depth: 45'-0"
Master Bath
Master Bedroom 16'-4" X 13'
Covered Porch
Breakfast 12'-2" X 9'
Living 17' X 16'
Kitchen 12'-2" X 11'
Bedroom #3 10'-8" X 10'-10"
Bath
Dining 11'-4" X 11'-4"
Foyer
Utility
Porch
Bedroom #2 14'-4" X 10'-4"

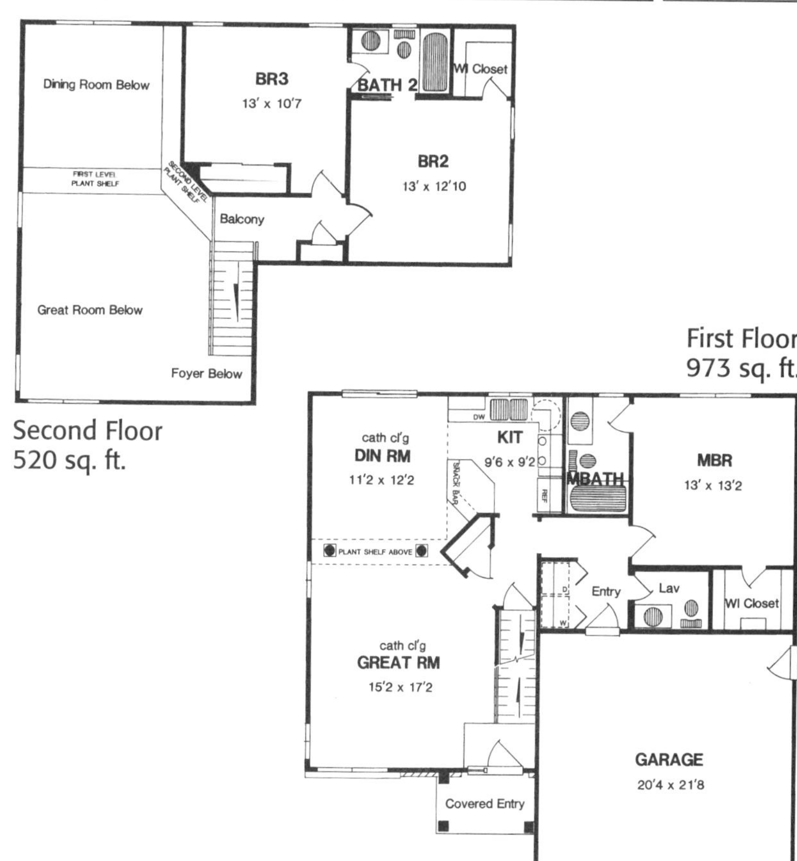
Dining Room Below
BR3
13' x 10'7
BATH 2
WI Closet
BR2
13' x 12'10
FIRST LEVEL PLANT SHELF
SECOND LEVEL PLANT SHELF
Balcony
Great Room Below
Foyer Below
Second Floor
520 sq. ft.
First Floor
973 sq. ft.
cath cl'g
DIN RM
11'2 x 12'2
DW
KIT
9'6 x 9'2
SNACK BAR
REF
MBATH
MBR
13' x 13'2
PLANT SHELF ABOVE
Entry
Lav
WI Closet
cath cl'g
GREAT RM
15'2 x 17'2
GARAGE
20'4 x 21'8
Covered Entry
Width: 40'-0"
Depth: 41'-0"

Plan #527-JFD-15-14931

Price Code A

Total Living Area: 1,493 Sq. Ft.

Home has 3 bedrooms, 2 1/2 baths, 2-car garage and basement foundation.

Special features

- First floor master bedroom maintains privacy
- Dining room and great room have a feeling of spaciousness with two-story high ceilings
- Utilities are conveniently located near garage entrance

Sunken Family Room

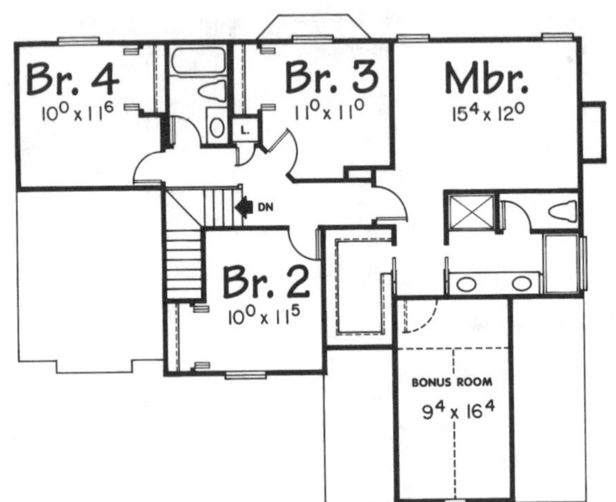
Br. 4
10⁰ x 11⁶
Br. 3
11⁰ x 11⁰
Mbr.
15⁴ x 12⁰
DN
Br. 2
10⁰ x 11⁵
BONUS ROOM
9⁴ x 16⁴

Second Floor
983 sq. ft.

First Floor
1,046 sq. ft.

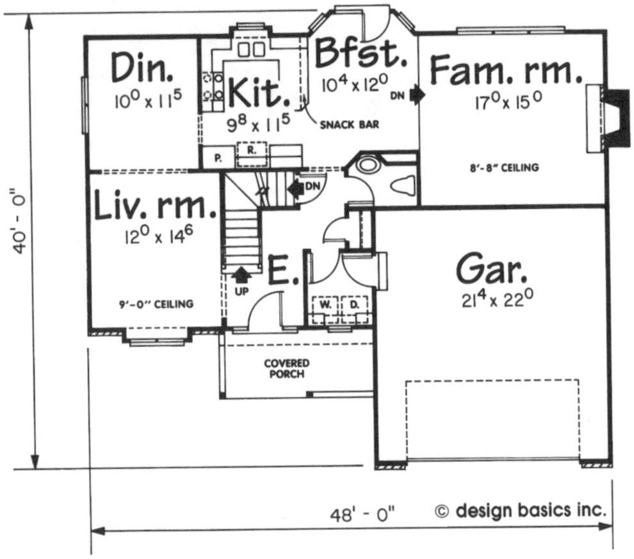

Din. 10⁰ x 11⁵
Kit. 9⁸ x 11⁵
Bfst. 10⁴ x 12⁰
SNACK BAR
Fam. rm. 17⁰ x 15⁰
8'-8" CEILING
Liv. rm. 12⁰ x 14⁶
9'-0" CEILING
E.
Gar. 21⁴ x 22⁰
COVERED PORCH
40' - 0"
48' - 0"
© design basics inc.

Plan #527-DBI-8031

Price Code C

Total Living Area: 2,029 Sq. Ft.

Home has 4 bedrooms, 2 1/2 baths, 2-car garage and basement foundation.

Special features

- Oversized rooms throughout
- Breakfast room has access to the outdoors
- Dining and living rooms combine to create ideal gathering place
- Master suite has all the amenities
- Bonus room for added space in the future

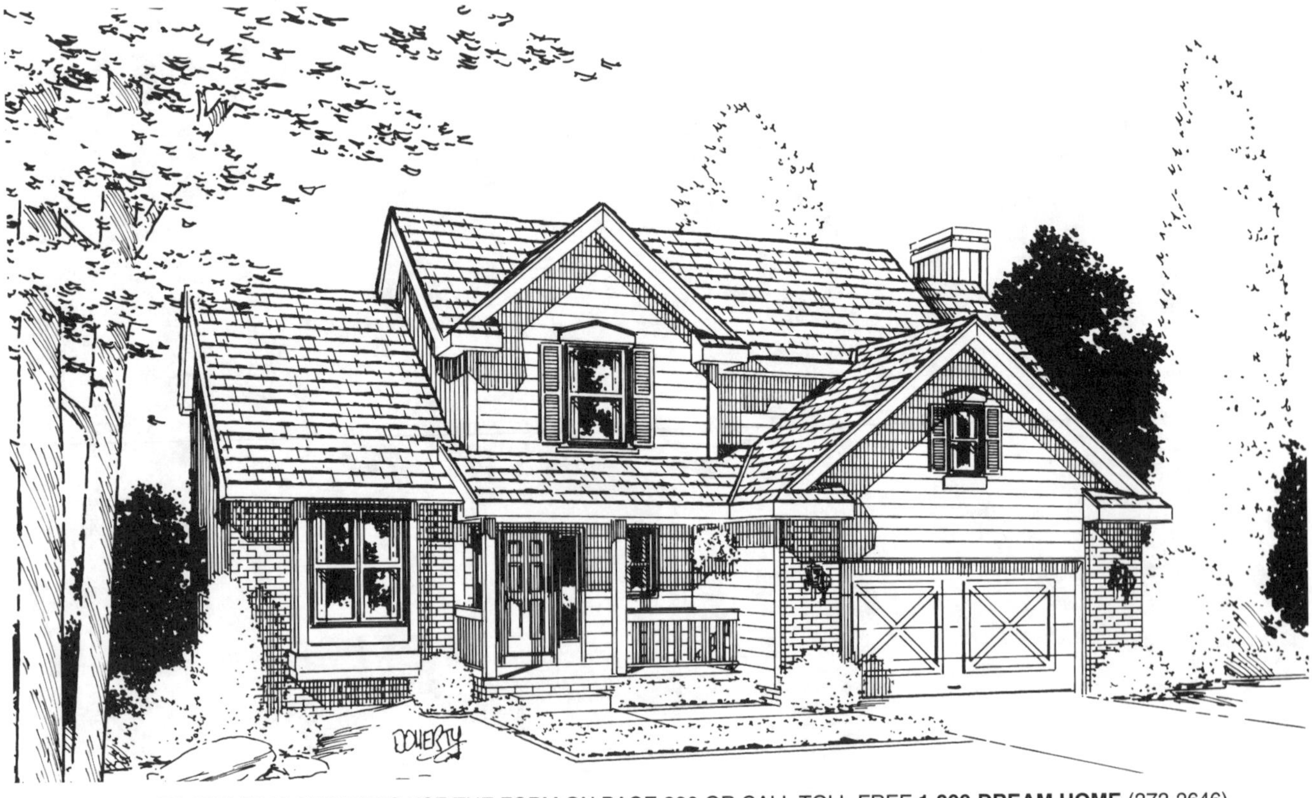

Kitchen Overlooks Living Area

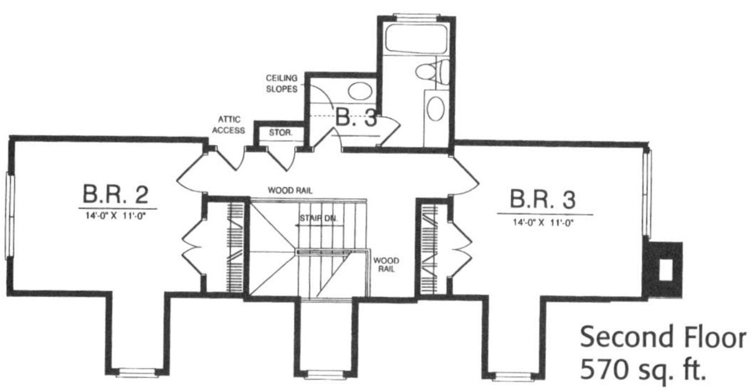
CEILING SLOPES
ATTIC ACCESS
STOR.
B. 3
B.R. 2
14'-0" X 11'-0"
WOOD RAIL
STAIR DN.
WOOD RAIL
B.R. 3
14'-0" X 11'-0"

Second Floor
570 sq. ft.

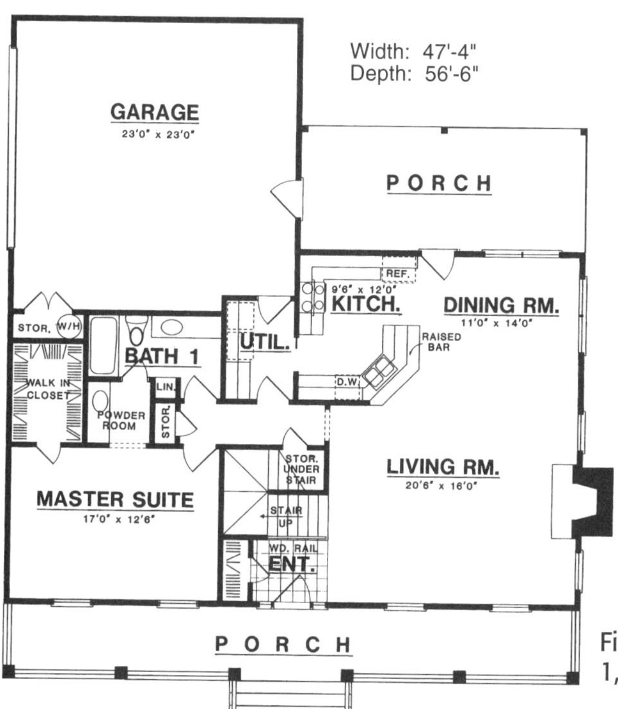
Width: 47'-4"
Depth: 56'-6"
GARAGE
23'0" x 23'0"
PORCH
REF.
9'6" x 12'0"
KITCH.
DINING RM.
11'0" x 14'0"
STOR.
W/H
UTIL.
RAISED BAR
BATH 1
D.W.
WALK IN CLOSET
LIN.
POWDER ROOM
STOR.
STOR. UNDER STAIR
LIVING RM.
20'6" x 16'0"
MASTER SUITE
17'0" x 12'6"
STAIR UP
WD. RAIL
ENT.
PORCH

First Floor
1,245 sq. ft.

Plan #527-RDD-1815-8

Price Code C

Total Living Area: 1,815 Sq. Ft.

Home has 3 bedrooms, 2 baths, 2-car side entry garage and basement, crawl space or slab foundation, please specify when ordering.

Special features

- Front and back porches unite home with the outdoors
- First floor master suite with walk-in closet
- Well-designed kitchen opens to dining room and features raised breakfast bar

Plan #527-RDD-2050-7A

Price Code C

Total Living Area: 2,050 Sq. Ft.

Home has 3 bedrooms, 2 baths, 2-car side entry garage and crawl space or slab foundation, please specify when ordering.

Special features

- Cozy family room with built-in shelves and fireplace
- Master suite with amenities like double walk-in closets, private bath and view onto covered porch
- Living room immersed in sunlight from wall of windows

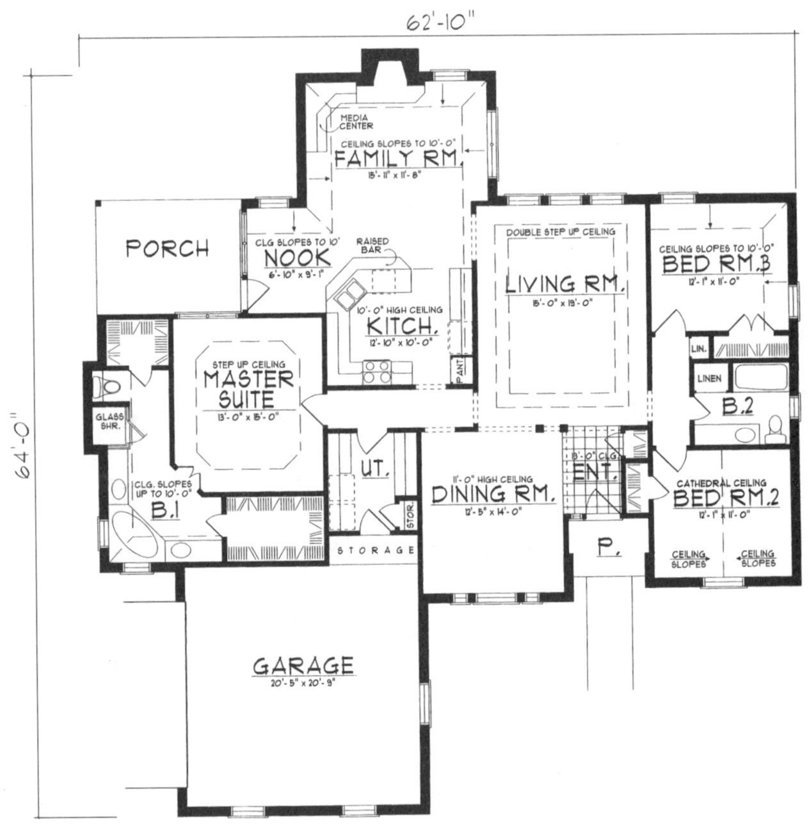
62'-10"
64'-0"
MEDIA CENTER
CEILING SLOPES TO 10'-0"
FAMILY RM.
15'-11" x 11'-8"
PORCH
CLG SLOPES TO 10'
NOOK
6'-10" x 9'-1"
RAISED BAR
10'-0" HIGH CEILING
KITCH.
12'-10" x 10'-0"
PANT.
DOUBLE STEP UP CEILING
LIVING RM.
15'-0" x 19'-0"
CEILING SLOPES TO 10'-0"
BED RM.3
12'-1" x 11'-0"
LIN.
LINEN
B.2
STEP UP CEILING
MASTER SUITE
13'-0" x 15'-0"
GLASS SHR.
CLG. SLOPES UP TO 10'-0"
B.1
UT.
STOR.
STORAGE
11'-0" HIGH CEILING
DINING RM.
12'-5" x 14'-0"
ENT.
CATHEDRAL CEILING
BED RM.2
12'-1" x 11'-0"
CEILING SLOPES
CEILING SLOPES
P.
GARAGE
20'-5" x 20'-9"

TO ORDER BLUEPRINTS USE THE FORM ON PAGE 290 OR CALL TOLL-FREE **1-800-DREAM HOME** (373-2646)

LOWE'S

Plan #527-LBD-13-1A

Price Code A

Total Living Area: 1,310 Sq. Ft.

Home has 3 bedrooms, 2 baths, 2-car garage and crawl space or slab foundation, please specify when ordering.

Special features

- Family room features corner fireplace adding warmth
- Efficiently designed kitchen has a corner sink with windows
- Master bedroom includes large walk-in closet and private bath

WIDTH 49–10

DEPTH 40–6

BRKFST RM 9-4 X 11-0 10 FT CLG
42" LEDGE
SLOPE
KITCHEN 9-6 X 11-0 10 FT CLG
ARCH
FP
STORAGE
LIVING RM 14-6 X 17-8 10 FT CLG
MASTER BEDRM 14-8 X 12-6 10 FT CLG
SLOPE
SHLV
MASTER BATH
GARAGE
FOYER
BATH 2
PORCH
BEDRM 2 10-0 X 11-0
LIN
BEDRM 3 11-0 X 10-0
OPTIONAL BAY WINDOW
COPYRIGHT LARRY E. BELK

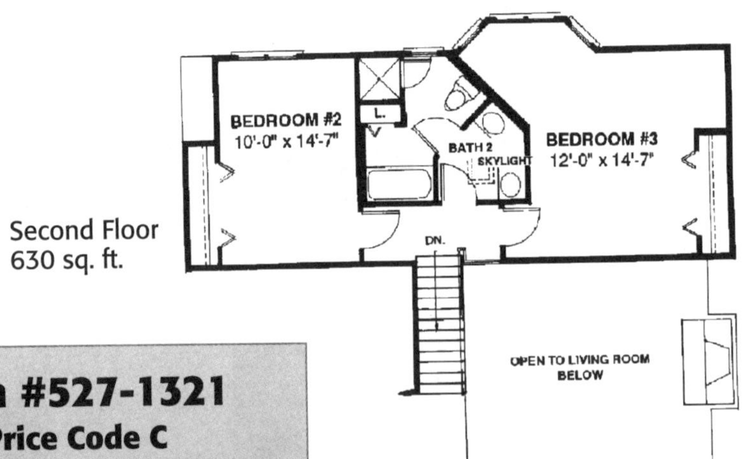
BEDROOM #2
10'-0" x 14'-7"
BATH 2
SKYLIGHT
BEDROOM #3
12'-0" x 14'-7"
DN.
OPEN TO LIVING ROOM BELOW

Second Floor
630 sq. ft.

Plan #527-1321

Price Code C

Total Living Area: 1,850 Sq. Ft.

Home has 3 bedrooms, 2 1/2 baths, 2-car garage and basement foundation.

Special features

- Large living room with fireplace is illuminated by three second story skylights
- Living room and dining area are separated by a low wall while the dining area and kitchen are separated by a snack bar creating a spacious atmosphere
- Master bedroom has a huge bath with double vanity and large walk-in closet
- Two second floor bedrooms share a uniquely designed bath with skylight

First Floor
1,220 sq. ft.

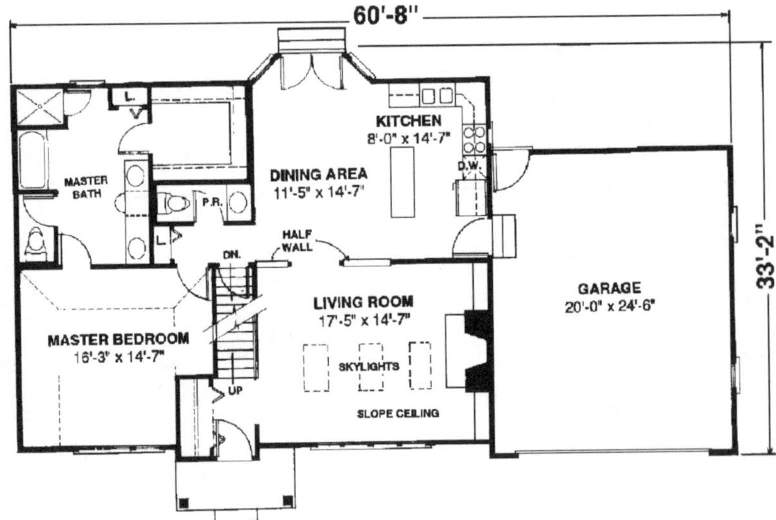
60'-8"
33'-2"
KITCHEN
8'-0" x 14'-7"
D.W.
DINING AREA
11'-5" x 14'-7"
MASTER BATH
P.R.
HALF WALL
DN.
LIVING ROOM
17'-5" x 14'-7"
SKYLIGHTS
SLOPE CEILING
UP
MASTER BEDROOM
16'-3" x 14'-7"
GARAGE
20'-0" x 24'-6"

LOWE'S

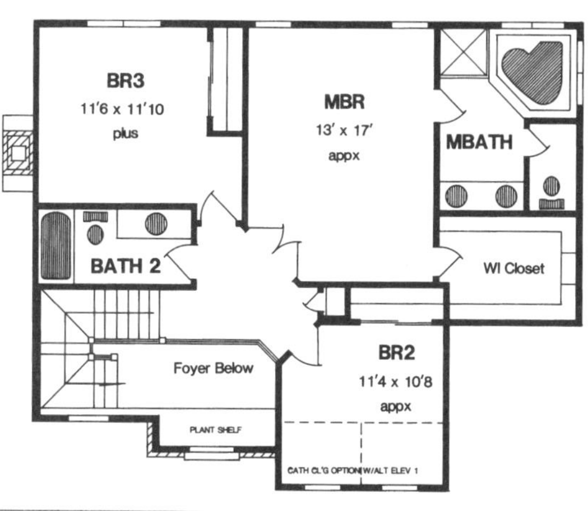
BR3
11'6 x 11'10
plus
MBR
13' x 17'
appx
MBATH
BATH 2
WI Closet
Foyer Below
PLANT SHELF
BR2
11'4 x 10'8
appx
CATH CL'G OPTION W/ALT ELEV 1

Second Floor
942 sq. ft.

Plan #527-JFD-20-1873-1

Price Code C

Total Living Area: 1,873 Sq. Ft.

Home has 3 bedrooms, 2 1/2 baths, 2-car garage and basement foundation.

Special features

- Formal dining area in the front of the house is conveniently located near kitchen
- Large great room with fireplace and lots of windows
- Master bedroom has double-door entry with a private bath

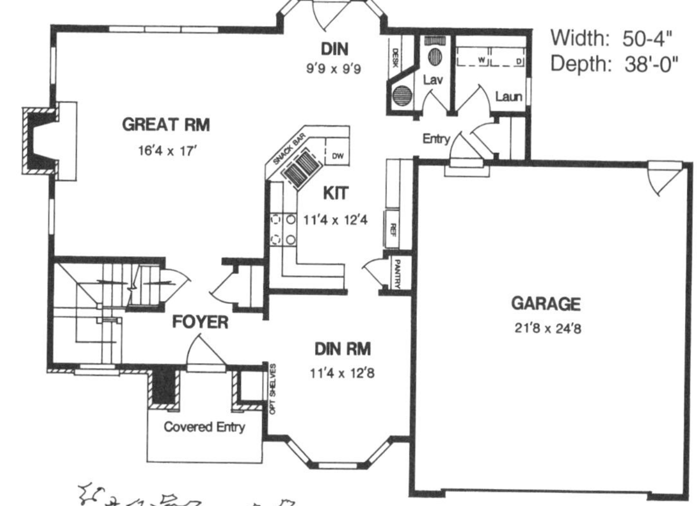
DIN
9'9 x 9'9
DESK
Lav
Laun
W
D
GREAT RM
16'4 x 17'
SNACK BAR
DW
Entry
KIT
11'4 x 12'4
REF
PANTRY
GARAGE
21'8 x 24'8
FOYER
DIN RM
11'4 x 12'8
OPT SHELVES
Covered Entry

Width: 50-4"
Depth: 38'-0"

First Floor
931 sq. ft.

Plan #527-1429

Price Code B

Total Living Area: 1,500 Sq. Ft.

Home has 3 bedrooms, 2 baths, 2-car garage and basement foundation.

Special features

- Living room features a cathedral ceiling and opens to breakfast room
- Breakfast room has a spectacular bay window and adjoins a well-appointed kitchen with generous storage
- Laundry is convenient to kitchen and includes a large closet
- Large walk-in closet gives the master bedroom abundant storage

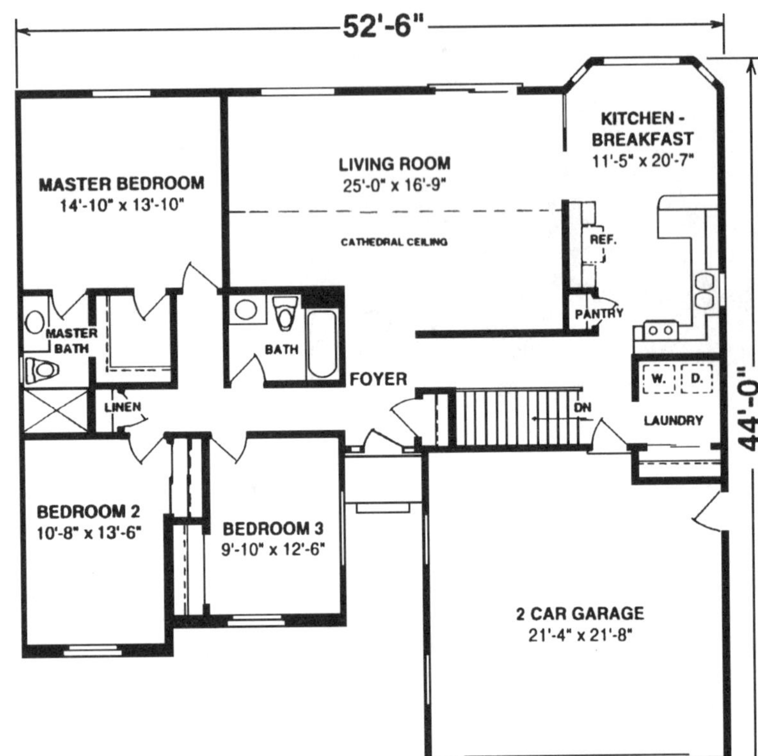
52'-6"
44'-0"
KITCHEN - BREAKFAST
11'-5" x 20'-7"
LIVING ROOM
25'-0" x 16'-9"
CATHEDRAL CEILING
MASTER BEDROOM
14'-10" x 13'-10"
REF.
PANTRY
MASTER BATH
BATH
FOYER
W.
D.
LINEN
DN
LAUNDRY
BEDROOM 2
10'-8" x 13'-6"
BEDROOM 3
9'-10" x 12'-6"
2 CAR GARAGE
21'-4" x 21'-8"

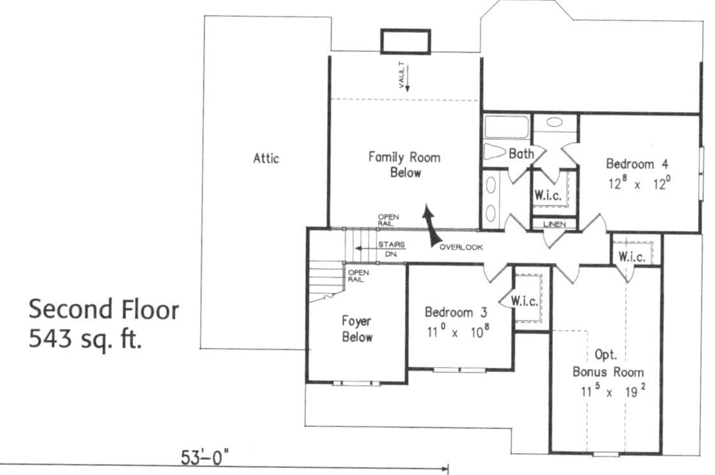
Attic
VAULT
Family Room Below
Bath
W.i.c.
Bedroom 4 12⁸ x 12⁰
LINEN
OPEN RAIL
STAIRS DN.
OVERLOOK
W.i.c.
OPEN RAIL
Foyer Below
Bedroom 3 11⁰ x 10⁸
W.i.c.
Opt. Bonus Room 11⁵ x 19²

Second Floor
543 sq. ft.

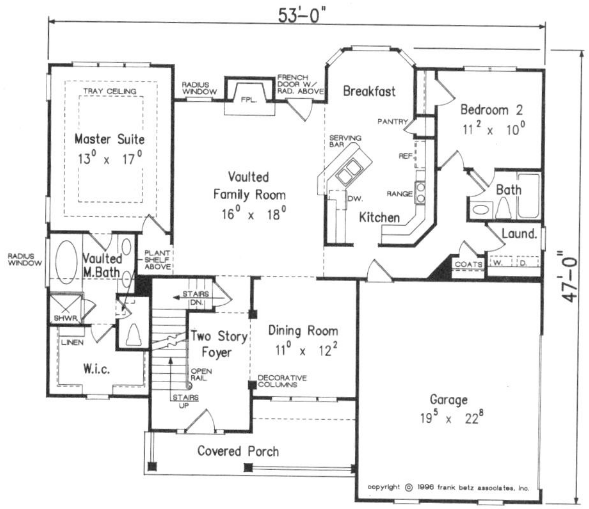
53'-0"
TRAY CEILING
RADIUS WINDOW
FPL.
FRENCH DOOR W/ RAD. ABOVE
Breakfast
Master Suite 13⁰ x 17⁰
PANTRY
Bedroom 2 11² x 10⁰
SERVING BAR
REF.
Vaulted Family Room 16⁰ x 18⁰
RANGE
DW.
Kitchen
Bath
Laund.
RADIUS WINDOW
Vaulted M.Bath
PLANT SHELF ABOVE
COATS
W.
D.
47'-0"
SHWR.
STAIRS DN.
LINEN
Two Story Foyer
Dining Room 11⁰ x 12²
W.i.c.
OPEN RAIL
DECORATIVE COLUMNS
STAIRS UP
Garage 19⁵ x 22⁸
Covered Porch
copyright © 1996 frank betz associates, inc.

First Floor
1,583 sq. ft.

Plan #527-FB-963

Price Code C

Total Living Area: 2,126 Sq. Ft.

Home has 4 bedrooms, 3 baths, 2-car side entry garage and basement, crawl space or slab foundation, please specify when ordering.

Special features

- Two-story foyer creates airy feeling
- Kitchen overlooks vaulted family room with a handy serving bar
- Second floor includes an optional bonus room with an additional 251 square feet of living area

Efficiently Designed Kitchen

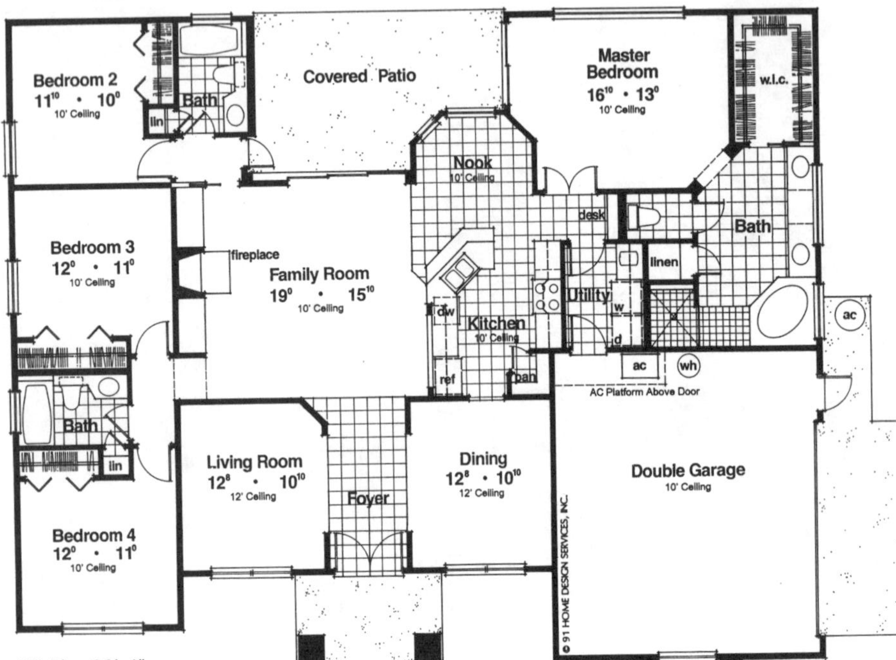

Bedroom 2
11¹⁰ · 10⁰
10' Ceiling
Bath
lin
Covered Patio
Master Bedroom
16¹⁰ · 13⁰
10' Ceiling
w.i.c.
Nook
10' Ceiling
desk
Bath
linen
Bedroom 3
12⁰ · 11⁰
10' Ceiling
fireplace
Family Room
19⁰ · 15¹⁰
10' Ceiling
dw
Kitchen
10' Ceiling
Utility
w
d
ac
ref
pan
wh
AC Platform Above Door
Bath
lin
Living Room
12⁸ · 10¹⁰
12' Ceiling
Foyer
Dining
12⁸ · 10¹⁰
12' Ceiling
Double Garage
10' Ceiling
Bedroom 4
12⁰ · 11⁰
10' Ceiling
© 91 HOME DESIGN SERVICES, INC.

Width: 62'-4"
Depth: 51'-0"

Plan #527-HDS-2140

Price Code C

Total Living Area: 2,140 Sq. Ft.

Home has 4 bedrooms, 3 baths, 2-car side entry garage and slab foundation.

Special features

- Living and dining area traditionally separated by foyer
- Media wall and fireplace in cozy family room
- Generous master suite with sliding glass doors onto patio, walk-in closet and a private bath

TO ORDER BLUEPRINTS USE THE FORM ON PAGE 290 OR CALL TOLL-FREE **1-800-DREAM HOME** (373-2646)

Attractive Dormers Enhance Facade

LOWE'S

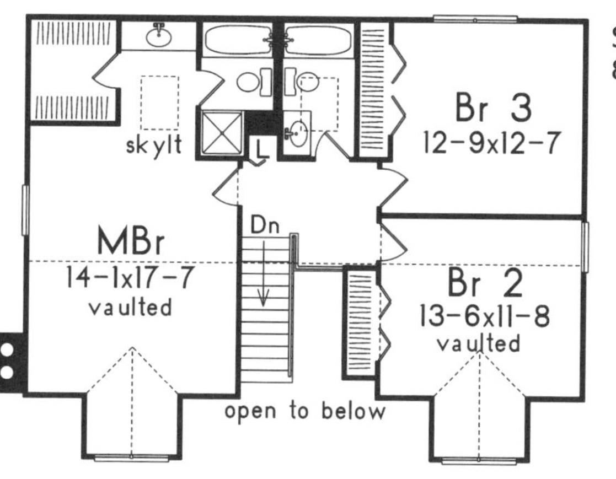
skylt
MBr
14-1x17-7
vaulted
Dn
Br 3
12-9x12-7
Br 2
13-6x11-8
vaulted
open to below

Second Floor
896 sq. ft.

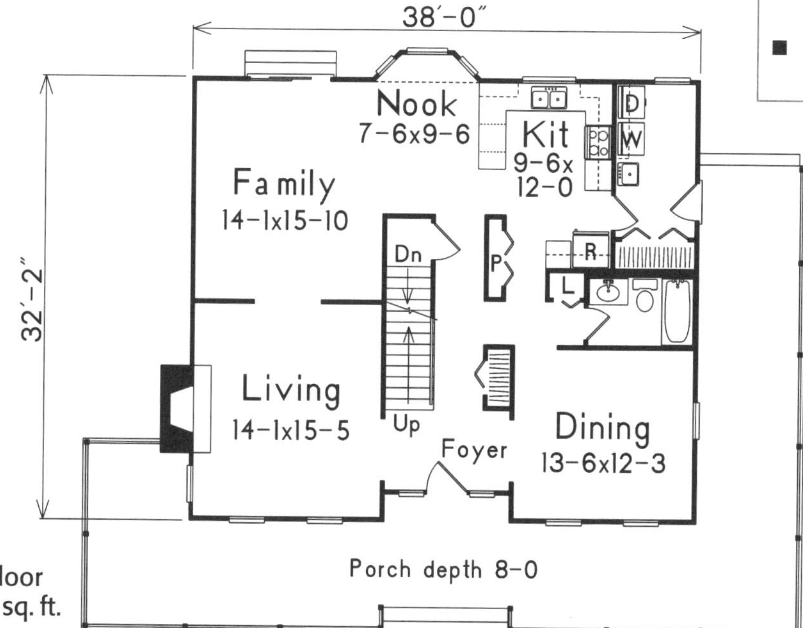
38'-0"
32'-2"
Nook
7-6x9-6
Kit
9-6x
12-0
D
W
Family
14-1x15-10
Dn
P
R
L
Living
14-1x15-5
Up
Foyer
Dining
13-6x12-3
Porch depth 8-0

First Floor
1,216 sq. ft.

Plan #527-1311

Price Code C

Total Living Area: 2,112 Sq. Ft.

Home has 3 bedrooms, 2 1/2 baths and basement foundation, drawings also include crawl space foundation.

Special features

- Double-door entrance from kitchen to dining area
- Family room with adjacent nook makes ideal breakfast area
- Both bathrooms on second floor feature skylights

Well-Designed Ranch With Plenty Of Space

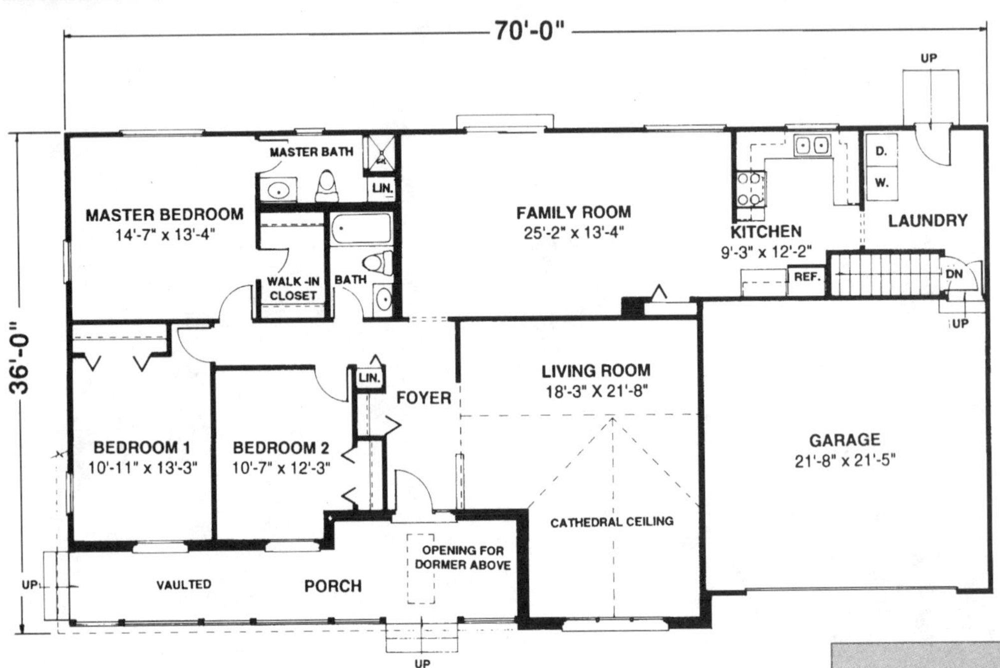

70'-0"
36'-0"
UP
MASTER BATH
LIN.
MASTER BEDROOM
14'-7" x 13'-4"
FAMILY ROOM
25'-2" x 13'-4"
KITCHEN
9'-3" x 12'-2"
REF.
D.
W.
LAUNDRY
DN
WALK-IN CLOSET
BATH
BEDROOM 1
10'-11" x 13'-3"
BEDROOM 2
10'-7" x 12'-3"
LIN.
FOYER
LIVING ROOM
18'-3" X 21'-8"
GARAGE
21'-8" x 21'-5"
CATHEDRAL CEILING
OPENING FOR DORMER ABOVE
VAULTED
PORCH

Plan #527-1396

Price Code C

Total Living Area: 1,820 Sq. Ft.

Home has 3 bedrooms, 2 baths, 2-car garage and basement foundation.

Special features

- Living room has stunning cathedral ceiling
- Spacious laundry room with easy access to kitchen, outdoors and garage
- Plenty of closet space throughout
- Covered front porch enhances outdoor living

TO ORDER BLUEPRINTS USE THE FORM ON PAGE 290 OR CALL TOLL-FREE **1-800-DREAM HOME** (373-2646)

LOWE'S

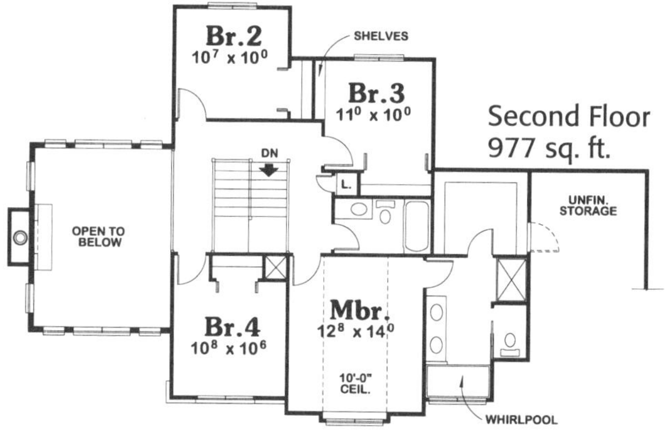
Br.2
10⁷ x 10⁰
SHELVES
Br.3
11⁰ x 10⁰
DN
L.
OPEN TO BELOW
UNFIN. STORAGE
Br.4
10⁸ x 10⁶
Mbr.
12⁸ x 14⁰
10'-0" CEIL.
WHIRLPOOL

Second Floor
977 sq. ft.

Plan #527-DBI-5458

Price Code C

Total Living Area: 1,814 Sq. Ft.

Home has 4 bedrooms, 2 1/2 baths, 3-car garage and basement foundation.

Special features

- Handy bench located outside laundry area for changing
- Charming garden room located off great room brings the outdoors in
- Kitchen features lots of cabinetry and counterspace

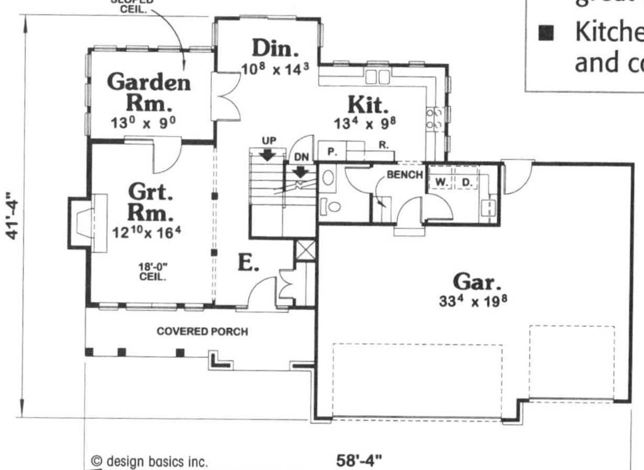
SLOPED CEIL.
Din.
10⁸ x 14³
Garden Rm.
13⁰ x 9⁰
Kit.
13⁴ x 9⁸
UP
DN
P.
R.
BENCH
W.
D.
Grt. Rm.
12¹⁰ x 16⁴
18'-0" CEIL.
E.
Gar.
33⁴ x 19⁸
COVERED PORCH
41'-4"
58'-4"
© design basics inc.

First Floor
837 sq. ft.

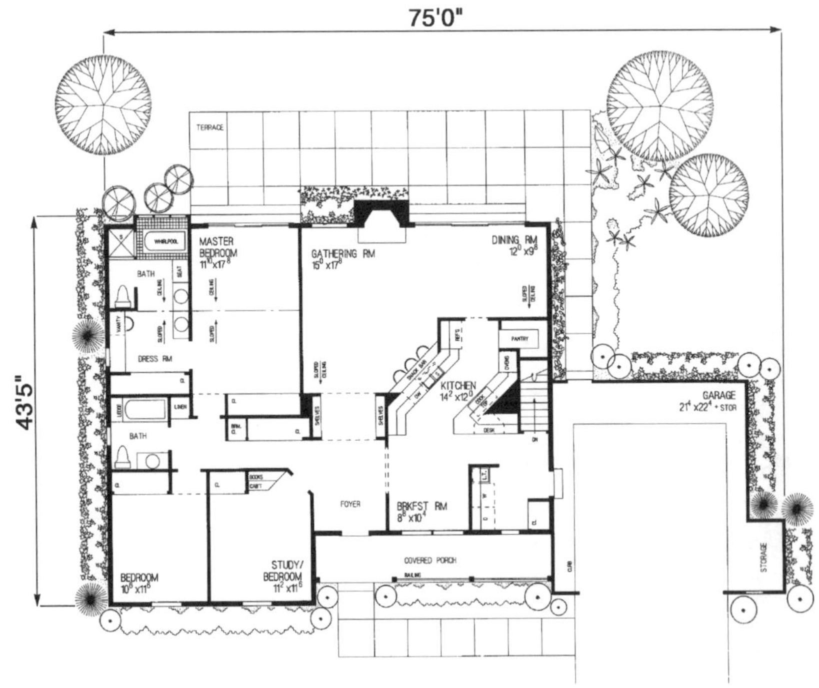
75'0"
43'5"
TERRACE
WHIRLPOOL
MASTER BEDROOM
BATH
GATHERING RM
DINING RM
PANTRY
DRESS RM
KITCHEN
GARAGE
LINEN
BATH
DESK
FOYER
BRKFST RM
COVERED PORCH
BEDROOM
STUDY/ BEDROOM
STORAGE

Plan #527-HP-B947

Price Code C

Total Living Area: 1,830 Sq. Ft.

Home has 3 bedrooms, 2 baths, 2-car garage and basement foundation.

Special features

- A uniquely shaped galley-style kitchen shares a snack bar with the spacious gathering room with fireplace
- Dining room has sliding glass doors to the rear terrace as well as the master bedroom
- Master suite includes a luxury bath with a whirlpool tub and separate dressing room

 TO ORDER BLUEPRINTS USE THE FORM ON PAGE 290 OR CALL TOLL-FREE **1-800-DREAM HOME** (373-2646)

Plan #527-DBI-5498

Price Code C

Total Living Area: 2,188 Sq. Ft.

Home has 3 bedrooms, 2 baths, 3-car side entry garage and basement foundation.

Special features

- Corner fireplace accentuates great room
- Master suite includes private covered porch
- Spacious kitchen has center island, snack bar and laundry access

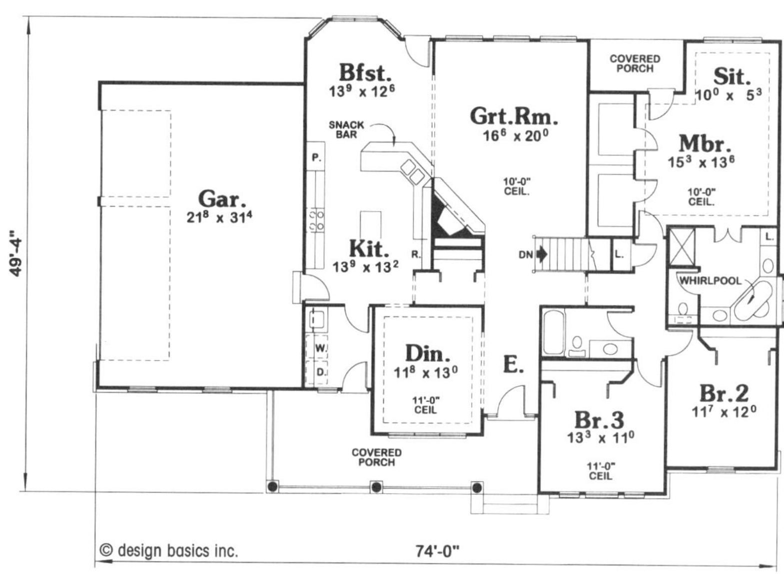
Bfst.
13⁹ x 12⁶
SNACK BAR
P.
Gar.
21⁸ x 31⁴
Kit.
13⁹ x 13²
R.
Grt.Rm.
16⁶ x 20⁰
10'-0" CEIL.
DN
COVERED PORCH
Sit.
10⁰ x 5³
Mbr.
15³ x 13⁶
10'-0" CEIL.
L.
WHIRLPOOL
W.
D.
Din.
11⁸ x 13⁰
11'-0" CEIL
E.
Br.3
13³ x 11⁰
11'-0" CEIL
Br.2
11⁷ x 12⁰
COVERED PORCH
49'-4"
74'-0"
© design basics inc.

Our Blueprint Packages Offer...

Quality plans for building your future, with extras that provide unsurpassed value, ensure good construction and long-term enjoyment.

A quality home - one that looks good, functions well, and provides years of enjoyment - is a product of many things - design, materials, craftsmanship. But it's also the result of outstanding blueprints - the actual plans and specifications that tell the builder exactly how to build your home.

And with our BLUEPRINT PACKAGES you get the absolute best. A complete set of blueprints is available for every design in this book. These "working drawings," are highly detailed, resulting in two key benefits:

- *Better understanding by the contractor of how to build your home, and...*
- *More accurate construction estimates.*

When you purchase one of our designs, you'll receive all of the BLUEPRINT components shown here - elevations, foundation plan, floor plans, sections, and details. Other helpful building aids are also available to help make your dream home a reality.

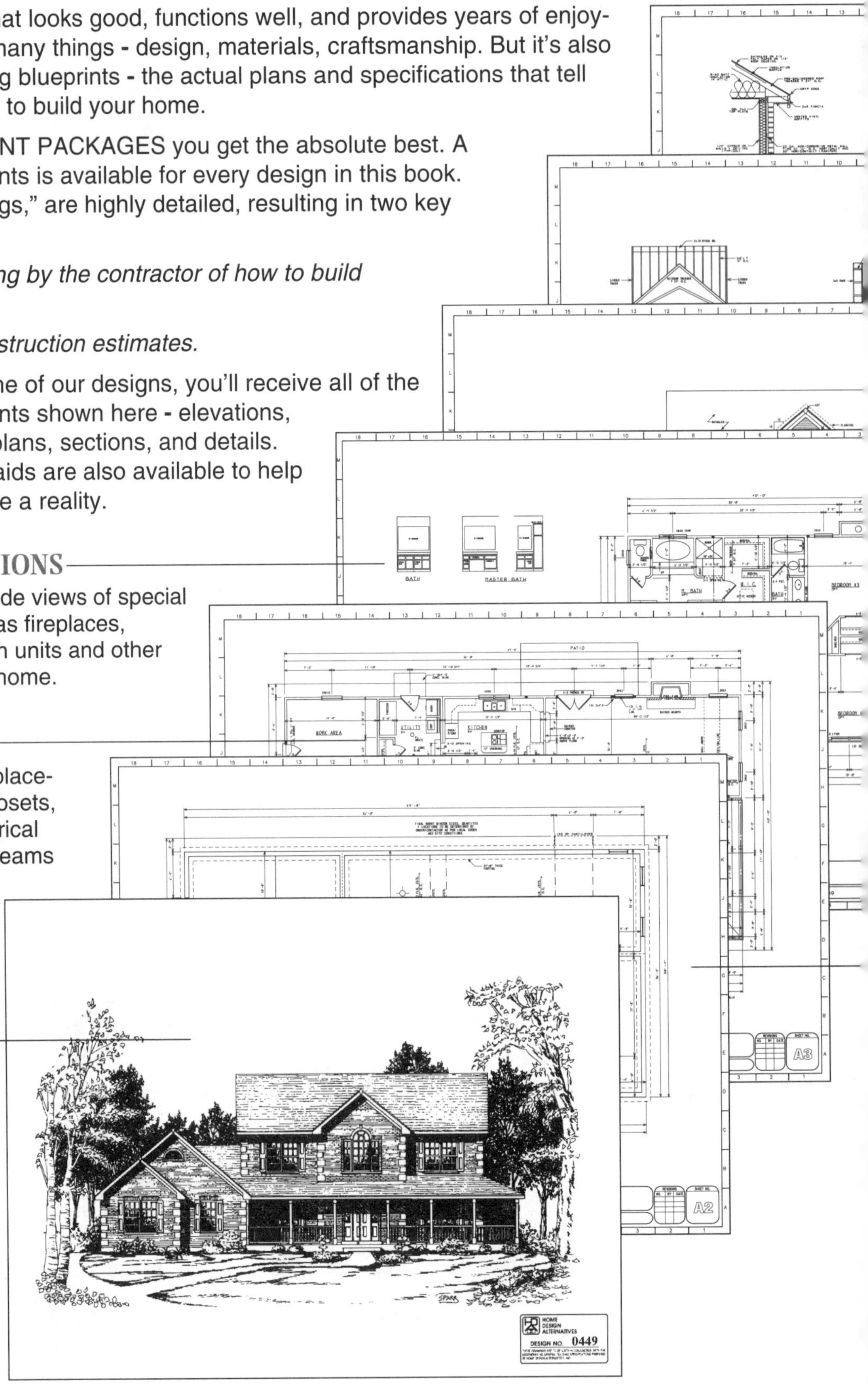

INTERIOR ELEVATIONS

Interior elevations provide views of special interior elements such as fireplaces, kitchen cabinets, built-in units and other special features of the home.

FLOOR PLANS

These plans show the placement of walls, doors, closets, plumbing fixtures, electrical outlets, columns, and beams for each level of the home.

COVER SHEET

This sheet is the artist's rendering of the exterior of the home. It will give you an idea of how your home will look when completed and landscaped.

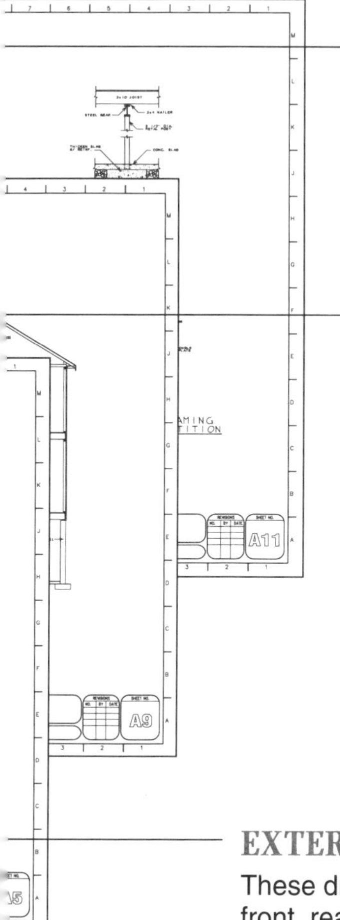

DETAILS

Details show how to construct certain components of your home, such as the roof system, stairs, deck, etc.

SECTIONS

Sections show detail views of the home or portions of the home as if it were sliced from the roof to the foundation. This sheet shows important areas such as load-bearing walls, stairs, joists, trusses and other structural elements, which are critical for proper construction.

EXTERIOR ELEVATIONS

These drawings illustrate the front, rear and both sides of the house, with all details of exterior materials and the required dimensions.

FOUNDATION PLAN

The foundation plan shows the layout of the basement, crawl space, slab, or pier foundation. All necessary notations and dimensions are included. See plan page for the foundation types included. If the home plan you choose does not have your desired foundation type, our Customer Service Representatives can advise you on how to customize your foundation to suit your specific needs or site conditions.

Other Helpful Building Aids...

Your Blueprint Package will contain all the necessary construction information to build your home. We also offer the following products and services to save you time and money in the building process.

Rush Delivery

Most orders are processed within 24 hours of receipt. Please allow 7 working days for delivery. If you need to place a rush order, please call us by 11:00 a.m. CST and ask for overnight or second day service.

Technical Assistance

If you have questions, call our technical support line at 1-314-770-2228 between 8:00 a.m. and 5:00 p.m. CST. Whether it involves design modifications or field assistance, our designers are extremely familiar with all of our designs and will be happy to help you. We want your home to be everything you expect it to be.

Material List

Material lists are available for many of our plans. Each list gives you the quantity, dimensions and description of the building materials necessary to construct your home. You'll get faster and more accurate bids from your contractor and material suppliers, and you'll save money by paying for only the materials you need. Look for the Lowe's Signature Series Logo on the plan pages.

Customizer Kit™

Many of the designs in this book can be customized using our exclusive Customizer Kit. It's your guide to custom designing your home. It leads you through all the essential design decisions and provides the necessary tools for you to clearly show the changes you want made. Customizer Kits are available on all designs that display the Lowe's Signature Series Logo on the plan pages. For more information about this exclusive product see page 5.

HOME PLANS INDEX

Shaded Plans Denote Lowe's Signature Series Plans - Material List and Customizer Kit Available

Plan Number	Sq. Ft.	Price Code	Page	Plan Number	Sq. Ft.	Price Code	Page	Plan Number	Sq. Ft.	Price Code	Page
527-AMD-1135	1,467	A	213	527-GSD-2004	1,751	B	222	527-0209	1,556	B	68
527-AMD-1213	2,197	C	266	527-GSD-2073	2,162	C	141	527-0213	2,059	C	73
527-AMD-1216	2,155	C	192	527-HDS-1758-2	1,783	B	185	527-0217	1,360	A	48
527-AMD-2106C	1,919	C	154	527-HDS-2140	2,140	C	280	527-0218	1,998	D	86
527-AMD-2146J	1,840	C	181	527-HP-B947	1,830	C	284	527-0221	1,619	B	93
527-AMD-2152C	1,950	C	159	527-HP-C460	1,389	A	236	527-0227	1,674	B	55
527-AMD-2175	1,464	A	235	527-HP-C619	1,771	B	168	527-0229	1,676	B	37
527-AMD-2189	1,994	C	163	527-HP-C662	1,937	C	203	527-0230	2,073	D	8
527-BF-DR1108	1,150	AA	183	527-HP-C681	1,669	B	173	527-0234	2,066	C	44
527-BF-DR1109	1,191	AA	180	527-HP-C687	1,974	C	142	527-0244	1,994	D	13
527-BF-1416	1,434	A	197	527-HP-C689	1,295	A	226	527-0249	1,501	B	79
527-BF-1426	1,420	A	184	527-JFD-15-14931	1,493	A	271	527-0252	1,364	A	23
527-BF-1708	1,717	B	227	527-JFD-20-17921	1,792	B	131	527-0283	1,800	D	14
527-BF-1711	1,770	B	214	527-JFD-20-1868-1	1,868	C	215	527-0284	1,672	C	101
527-BF-1828	1,828	C	179	527-JFD-20-1873-1	1,873	C	277	527-0291	1,600	B	58
527-BF-1901	1,925	C	199	527-JFD-20-1992-1	1,992	C	195	527-0294	1,655	B	90
527-BF-DR2002	2,058	C	149	527-JFD-20-2018-1	2,018	C	229	527-0296	1,396	A	83
527-BF-2107	2,123	E	194	527-JFD-20-2097-1	2,097	C	167	527-0335	1,865	D	107
527-BF-2108	2,194	C	211	527-JV-1268A	1,268	A	143	527-0348	2,003	D	60
527-CHP-1432-A-142	1,405	A	212	527-JV-1297-A	1,297	A	241	527-0356	2,806	E	124
527-CHP-1532-A-141	1,500	B	264	527-JV-1325-B	1,325	A	232	527-0357	1,550	B	31
527-CHP-1633-A-25	1,609	B	240	527-JV-1379	1,379	A	156	527-0370	1,721	C	25
527-CHP-1732-A-101	1,704	B	270	527-JV-1683-B	1,683	B	188	527-0382	1,546	B	42
527-CHP-1733-A-7	1,737	B	133	527-JV-1772-A-SJ	1,772	B	224	527-0410	1,742	B	56
527-DBI-1380	1,999	C	204	527-JV-2036-D	2,036	C	257	527-0412	2,109	C	29
527-DBI-1748-19	1,911	C	140	527-LBD-12-2A	1,282	A	165	527-0415	1,492	A	45
527-DBI-2461	1,850	C	200	527-LBD-13-1A	1,310	A	275	527-0416	1,985	C	65
527-DBI-2619	1,998	C	208	527-LBD-18-5A	1,862	C	146	527-0419	1,882	C	12
527-DBI-3019	1,479	A	172	527-LBD-18-11A	1,890	C	269	527-0420	1,941	C	112
527-DBI-4642	1,712	B	231	527-LBD-19-15A	1,955	C	230	527-0447	1,393	B	84
527-DBI-4948	1,758	B	262	527-LBD-19-23A	1,932	C	243	527-0448	1,597	C	100
527-DBI-5458	1,814	C	283	527-MG-9305	1,606	B	132	527-0450	1,708	B	11
527-DBI-5498	2,188	C	285	527-MG-97063	1,817	C	170	527-0477	1,140	AA	18
527-DBI-8013	1,392	A	210	527-MG-97099	1,093	AA	206	527-0478	1,092	AA	111
527-DBI-8016	1,691	B	137	527-N063	1,299	A	187	527-0481	2,012	C	104
527-DBI-8031	2,029	C	272	527-N065	1,750	B	198	527-0482	1,619	B	87
527-DBI-8077	1,858	C	245	527-N294-1 & 2	1,092	AA	219	527-0484	1,403	A	7
527-DBI-8095	1,694	B	152	527-N297-1 & 2	1,042	AA	255	527-0485	1,195	AA	71
527-ES-103-1 & 2	1,364	A	153	527-NDG-113-1	1,485	A	138	527-0487	1,189	AA	46
527-ES-125-1 & 2	1,605	B	145	527-NDG-142	2,107	C	239	527-0488	2,059	C	76
527-FB-174	2,115	C	252	527-NDG-190	2,107	C	166	527-0498	954	AA	22
527-FB-543	1,945	C	150	527-NDG-303	1,797	B	147	527-0502	864	AAA	27
527-FB-743	1,978	C	135	527-NDG-338	1,848	C	249	527-0503	1,000	AA	47
527-FB-797	1,845	C	162	527-RDD-1374-9	1,374	A	238	527-0505	1,104	AA	51
527-FB-845	1,779	B	250	527-RDD-1429-9	1,429	A	256	527-0507	1,197	AA	61
527-FB-895	2,052	C	247	527-RDD-1753-9	1,753	B	260	527-0510	1,400	A	21
527-FB-902	1,856	C	221	527-RDD-1791-9	1,791	B	164	527-0512	1,827	C	36
527-FB-933	2,193	C	169	527-RDD-1815-8	1,815	C	273	527-0515	1,344	A	34
527-FB-959	1,862	C	261	527-RDD-1895-9	1,895	C	190	527-0518	1,705	B	92
527-FB-960	2,201	D	155	527-RDD-1896-9	1,896	C	234	527-0520	1,720	B	88
527-FB-963	2,126	C	279	527-RDD-2050-7A	2,050	C	274	527-0521	2,050	C	106
527-FB-992	2,155	C	259	527-T-109-1 & 2	1,872	C	177	527-0523	1,875	C	35
527-FB-1085	1,818	C	254	527-T-110	1,973	C	246	527-0526	2,262	D	30
527-FB1119	1,915	C	228	527-0102	1,246	A	28	527-0529	1,285	B	63
527-FDG-7963-L	1,830	C	160	527-0112	1,668	C	9	527-0533	1,440	A	49
527-FDG-8673	1,604	B	248	527-0118	1,816	C	97	527-0534	1,288	A	33
527-FDG-9035	1,760	B	237	527-0127	1,996	D	113	527-0536	1,664	B	59
527-GM-1253	1,253	A	176	527-0162	1,882	D	82	527-0543	1,160	AA	69
527-GM-1406	1,406	A	175	527-0163	1,772	C	40	527-0548	1,154	AA	24
527-GM-1815	1,815	C	265	527-0171	2,058	C	62	527-0549	1,230	A	74
527-GM-1849	1,849	C	242	527-0173	1,220	A	95	527-0587	1,120	AA	19
527-GM-1855	1,855	C	186	527-0174	1,657	B	10	527-0598	1,818	C	67
527-GM-2008	2,008	C	144	527-0176	1,404	A	75	527-0652	1,524	B	20
527-GM-2009	2,009	C	218	527-0190	1,600	C	16	527-0656	1,700	B	17
527-GM-2148	2,148	C	267	527-0191	1,868	D	103	527-0659	1,516	B	38
527-GSD-1023-C	1,890	C	225	527-0201	1,814	D	32	527-0660	1,321	A	105
527-GSD-1123	1,734	B	216	527-0203	1,475	B	6	527-0670	1,170	AA	78

HOME PLANS INDEX - *continued*

Plan Number	Sq. Ft.	Price Code	Page
527-0676	1,367	A	77
527-0678	1,567	B	81
527-0682	1,941	C	57
527-0686	1,609	B	72
527-0688	1,556	B	85
527-0690	1,400	A	52
527-0692	1,339	A	99
527-0698	1,143	AA	94
527-0699	1,073	AA	70
527-0702	1,558	B	89
527-0706	1,791	B	39
527-0707	2,723	E	54
527-0711	1,575	B	41
527-0712	2,029	C	15
527-0717	1,268	A	80
527-0718	1,340	A	91
527-0723	1,784	B	110
527-0724	1,969	C	96
527-0726	1,428	A	66
527-0727	1,477	A	102
527-0744	2,164	C	123
527-0745	1,819	C	129
527-0751	1,278	A	128
527-0766	990	AA	119
527-0773	2,179	C	117
527-0774	1,680	B	122
527-0775	2,240	D	127
527-0779	1,277	A	120
527-0782	2,547	D	126
527-0794	1,433	A	116
527-0795	1,399	A	115
527-0796	1,599	B	125
527-0798	2,128	C	130
527-0799	1,849	C	121
527-0800	2,532	D	118
527-0806	1,452	A	50
527-0807	1,231	A	26
527-0808	969	AA	109
527-0809	1,084	AA	64
527-0810	1,200	A	114
527-0814	1,169	AA	53
527-1026-B	2,137	C	139
527-1101	1,643	B	43
527-1112	2,137	C	157
527-1117	1,440	A	108
527-1118-1 & 2	1,550	B	182
527-1120	1,232	A	171
527-1124	1,345	A	205
527-1189-1 & 2	1,120	AA	207
527-1216-1 & 2	1,668	B	268
527-1220	1,540	B	98
527-1248	1,574	B	134
527-1253	1,996	C	174
527-1254-1 & 2	1,704	B	263
527-1255-1 & 2	1,850	C	151
527-1266	2,086	C	244
527-1267	1,800	C	161
527-1270-1 & 2	1,873	C	148
527-1271	1,907	C	201
527-1274-1 & 2	2,180	C	193
527-1276	1,533	B	251
527-1293	1,200	A	258
527-1295	1,662	B	189
527-1297	1,992	C	223
527-1310	1,704	B	233
527-1311	2,112	C	281
527-1321	1,850	C	276
527-1324	1,907	C	158
527-1329	1,364	A	196
527-1336	1,364	A	191
527-1347-1 & 2	1,948	C	217
527-1348	1,980	C	136
527-1349	1,340	A	220
527-1355	1,927	C	178
527-1396	1,820	C	282
527-1403	1,128	AA	209
527-1413	1,400	A	202
527-1418	2,180	C	253
527-1429	1,500	B	278

OTHER GREAT PRODUCTS TO HELP YOU BUILD YOUR DREAM HOME

FRAMING, PLUMBING AND ELECTRICAL DETAIL PLAN PACKAGES

Three separate packages offer homebuilders details for constructing various foundations; numerous floor, wall and roof framing techniques; simple to complex residential wiring; sump and water softener hookups; plumbing connection methods;installation of septic systems, and more. Each package includes three-dimensional illustrations and a glossary of terms. Purchase one or all three. *Cost: $20.00 each or all three for $40.00*

Note: Plan packages are not specific to any certain plan.

THE LEGAL KIT

Avoid many legal pitfalls and build your home with confidence using the forms and contracts featured in this kit. Included are request for proposal documents, various fixed price and cost plus contracts, instructions on how and when to use each form, warranty statements and more. Save time and money before you break ground on your new home or start a remodeling project. All forms are reproducible. The kit is ideal for homebuilders and contractors. *Cost: $35.00*

WHAT KIND OF PLAN PACKAGE DO YOU NEED?

Now that you've found the plan you've been looking for, here are some suggestions on how to make your Dream Home a reality. To get started, order the type of plans that fit your particular situation.

Your Choices:

The One-set package - This single set of blueprints is offered so you can study or review a home in greater detail. These study sets are marked "not for construction." A single set is is never enough for construction and it's a copyright violation to reproduce blueprints.

The Minimum 5-set package - If you're ready to start the construction process, this 5-set package is the minimum number of blueprint sets you will need. It will require keeping close track of each set so they can be used by multiple subcontractors and tradespeople.

The Standard 8-set package - For best results in terms of cost, schedule and quality of construction, we recommend you order eight (or more) sets of blueprints. Besides one set for yourself, additional sets of blueprints will be required by your mortgage lender, local building department, general contractor and all subcontractors working on foundation, electrical, plumbing, heating/ air conditioning, carpentry work, etc.

Reproducible Masters - If you wish to make some minor design changes, you'll want to order reproducible masters. These drawings contain the same information as the blueprints but are printed on erasable and reproducible paper. This will allow your builder or a local design professional to make the necessary drawing changes without the major expense of redrawing the plans. This package also allows you to print as many copies of the modified plans as you need.

Mirror Reverse Sets - Plans can be printed in mirror reverse. These plans are useful when the house would fit your site better if all the rooms were on the opposite side than shown. They are simply a mirror image of the original drawings causing the lettering and dimensions to read backwards. Therefore, when ordering mirror reverse drawings, you must purchase at least one set of right reading plans.

ORDER FORM

IMPORTANT INFORMATION TO KNOW BEFORE YOU ORDER YOUR HOME PLANS

❑ **Building Codes & Requirements -** Our plans conform to most national building codes. However, they may not comply completely with your local building regulations. Some counties and municipalities have their own building codes, regulations and requirements. The assistance of a local builder, architect or other building professional may be necessary to modify the drawings to comply with your area's specific requirements. We recommend you consult with your local building officials prior to beginning construction.

❑ **Exchange Policies -** Since blueprints are printed in response to your order, we cannot honor requests for refunds. However, if for some reason you find that the plan you have purchased does not meet your requirements, you may exchange that plan for another plan in our collection. At the time of the exchange, you will be charged a processing fee of 25% of your original plan package price, plus the difference in price between the plan packages (if applicable) and the cost to ship the new plans to you. ***Please note: Reproducible drawings can only be exchanged if the package is unopened, and exchanges are allowed only within 90 days of purchase.***

❑ **Material List -** Remember to order your material list. You'll get faster and more accurate bids while saving money.

Plan prices guaranteed through December 31, 2002

CALL TOLL-FREE 1-800-DREAM HOME (1-800-373-2646) DAY OR NIGHT

THREE EASY WAYS TO ORDER

1. CALL toll free 1-800-373-2646 for credit card orders. Lowe's, Master Card, Visa, Discover and American Express are accepted.

   ——— *or* ———

2. FAX your order to 1-314-770-2226.

   ——— *or* ———

3. MAIL the Order Form to the address below. For proper delivery, make sure to use your street address and not a P.O. Box.

Rush Delivery —if you need to place a rush order, please call us by 11:00 a.m. CST and ask for overnight or second day service.

Questions? Call Our Customer Service Number 314-770-2228

BLUEPRINT PRICE SCHEDULE

Price Code	One-Set	*SAVE $75.00* Five-Sets	*SAVE $150.00* Eight-Sets	Material List*	BEST VALUE Reproducible Masters
AAA	$195	$260	$290	$50	$390
AA	245	310	340	55	440
A	295	360	390	60	490
B	345	410	440	60	540
C	395	460	490	65	590
D	445	510	540	65	640
E	495	560	590	70	690
F	545	610	640	70	740
G	650	715	745	75	845
H	755	820	850	80	950

OTHER OPTIONS...

Customizer Kit™* .... $ 45.00
Additional Plan Sets* .... $ 35.00
Print In Mirror Reverse* .. add $ 5.00 per set
Legal Kit .... $ 35.00

Detail Plan Packages: *(Buy 2, get 3rd FREE)*
Framing, Electrical & Plumbing $20.00 ea.
Rush Charges ...... Next Day Air $38.00
Second Day Air $25.00

****Available only within 90 days after purchase of plan package or reproducible masters of same plan.***

ORDER FORM

Please send me Plan Number 527 - ____________
Price Code ____________
(See Home Plans Index)

Specify Foundation Type - see plan page for availability
❑ Basement ❑ Slab ❑ Crawl space ❑ Walk-out basement

❑ Reproducible Masters $________
❑ Eight-Set Plan Package $________
❑ Five-Set Plan Package $________
❑ One-Set Plan Package (no mirror reverse) $________
❑ ___ (Qty.) Additional Plan Sets ($35.00 each) $________
❑ Print ___(Qty.) sets in Mirror Reverse (add $5.00/set) $________
❑ Material List (see index for availability) $________
❑ Customizer Kit (see index for availability) $________
❑ Legal Kit (see page 289) $________
Detail Plan Packages: (see page 289)
❑ Framing ❑ Electrical ❑ Plumbing $________
SUBTOTAL $________
SALES TAX (MO residents add 7%) $________
❑ Rush Charges $________
SHIPPING & HANDLING $ 12.50
TOTAL ENCLOSED (US funds only) $________

❑ Enclosed is my check or money order payable to HDA, Inc.
(Sorry, no COD's)

Please note that plans are not returnable.

Mail to: HDA, Inc.
4390 Green Ash Drive
St. Louis, MO 63045-1219

I hereby authorize HDA, Inc. to charge this purchase to my credit card account (check one):

❑ Lowe's ❑ MasterCard ❑ VISA ❑ Discover Novus ❑ American Express

My card number is ____________________
The expiration date is ____________________
Signature ____________________
Name ____________________
(Please print or type)
Street Address ____________________
(Please **do not** use P.O. Box)
City, State, Zip ____________________
My daytime phone number (______) - ______ - ______
I am a ❑ Builder/Contractor ❑ Homeowner ❑ Renter
I ❑ have ❑ have not selected my general contractor.

Thank you for your order!